Introduction to Film Studies

'This fourth edition is even more comprehensive and accessible than previous editions. It addresses new generations of students, asks new questions of film studies and rises to the radical challenge of answering those questions superbly well.'
Pat Brereton, *Dublin City University*

Introduction to Film Studies is a comprehensive leading textbook for students of cinema. This completely revised and updated fourth edition guides students through the key issues and concepts in film studies, traces the historical development of film and introduces some of the world's key national cinemas. A range of theories and theorists is presented, from formalism to feminism, from Eisenstein to Deleuze. Each chapter is written by a subject specialist, including four new authors, and a wide range of films is analysed and discussed. It is lavishly illustrated with over 123 film stills and production shots, many of them in colour. Reviewed widely by teachers in the field and with a foreword by Bill Nichols, it will be essential reading for any introductory student of film, media studies or the visual arts worldwide.

Key features of the fourth edition are:

- full coverage of all important topics for introductory level
- updated coverage of a wide range of concepts, theories and issues in film studies
- in-depth discussion of the contemporary film industry
- new chapters on rediscovering film; ethnicity, race and cinema; documentary; film form and narrative; British cinema; approaches to cinematic authorship
- new case studies on films such as *Bamboozled*, *Wild Strawberries*, *Run Lola Run*, *Grey Gardens*, *Grizzly Man*, *Boys Don't Cry*, *Love Actually*, among many others
- marginal key terms, notes, cross-referencing
- suggestions for further reading, further viewing and a comprehensive glossary and bibliography
- website resources including updated popular case studies from previous editions, a chapter on German cinema and links to supporting sites.

Contributors:
Chris Darke, Terri Francis, Lalitha Gopalan, Chris Jones, Mark Joyce, Searle Kochberg, Lawrence Napper, Jill Nelmes, Patrick Phillips, Suzanne Speidel, Paul Ward, Paul Watson, Paul Wells

Editor: **Jill Nelmes** is Senior Lecturer in film studies at the University of East London. Her research interests include gender and film, and screenwriting. She recently spent two years studying screenwriting at UCLA and working in the film industry in Los Angeles.

Praise for the third edition:

'I know of no other introductory film text that covers so much ground, nor that so readily connects up film theory and discourse with work in mass and popular culture. The revised edition keeps up with changes in technology ... the discussions of Hollywood are particularly illuminating ... I highly recommend *An Introduction to Film Studies.*'
Denise Albanese, *George Mason University, Fairfax, Virginia, USA*

'I highly recommend this text to any student embarking on a study of film ... An admirable synthesis of historical, social and theoretical considerations of cinema, presented in an engaging and accessible manner.'
Alan Burton, *De Montfort University, Leicester, UK*

What readers said about the second edition:

'The first edition went a long way to meeting the need for an introductory text accessible to A level, further education and beginning higher education students of film. The second edition builds on the success of the first, reflecting some of the newer emphases in the subject in revised or rewritten chapters, and incorporating more cross-referencing, useful "think points" and new material on areas such as spectatorship. Overall, *An Introduction to Film Studies* is now an even more valuable resource.'
Jim Hillier, *ex-Chief Examiner, Film Studies A Level, Senior Lecturer in Film Studies at the University of Reading, UK*

'Probably the clearest, most comprehensive and accessible introduction to film studies available. A book which is appropriate for both A Level and undergraduate students and, for those working in further education, the book we have been waiting for.'
Martin Price, *Stratford-upon-Avon College, UK*

Comments on the first edition:

'To me, it is simply the best introductory volume in the field so far.'
Jesus B. Sanchez, *Castilla La Mongha University, Ciudad Real, Spain*

Introduction to Film Studies

Fourth Edition

Edited by Jill Nelmes

Foreword by Bill Nichols

Routledge
Taylor & Francis Group

LONDON AND NEW YORK

First published 1996 by Routledge

Second edition first published 1999 by Routledge

Third edition first published 2003 by Routledge

Fourth edition first published 2007
by Routledge
2 Park Square, Milton Park, Abingdon, Oxon OX14 4RN

Simultaneously published in the USA and Canada
by Routledge
270 Madison Ave, New York, NY 10016

Routledge is an imprint of the Taylor & Francis Group, an informa business

Editorial Selection and Material © 1996, 1999, 2003, 2007 Jill Nelmes
Individual chapters © 1996, 1999, 2003, 2007 individual contributors

Typeset in Helvetica 55 by Fakenham Photosetting Ltd, Fakenham Norfolk
Printed and bound in Great Britain by CPI Bath Press, Bath

British Library Cataloguing in Publication Data
A catalogue record for this book is available from the British Library

Library of Congress Cataloging-in-Publication Data
Introduction to film studies/foreword by Bill Nichols; edited by Jill Nelmes.
-- 4th ed.
p. cm.
Includes bibliographical references and index.
1. Motion pictures. I. Nelmes, Jill, 1954–
PN1994.I537 2007
791.43--dc22
2006026119

ISBN10: 0–415–40929–2 (hbk)
ISBN10: 0–415–40928–4 (pbk)

ISBN13: 978–0–415–40929–2 (hbk)
ISBN13: 978–0–415–40928–5 (pbk)

Contents

Illustrations

Contributors

Chris Darke has written on film and the arts for a variety of publications. A collection of his essays, *Light Readings: Film Criticism and Screen Arts*, was published in 2000 by Wallflower Press. His monograph on Godard's *Alphaville* was published in 2005 by I.B. Tauris. He is co-author (with Kieron Corless) of a book on the Cannes Film Festival (Faber & Faber, forthcoming). He has lectured at the universities of Warwick, Middlesex and Kent and at the Art Academy in Malmo, Sweden.

Terri Francis is Assistant Professor of film studies and African American Studies at Yale University. Her current research interests focus on Josephine Baker's stardom. Her work on Baker, 'Embodied Fictions, Melancholy Migrations: Josephine Baker's Cinematic Celebrity', has been published in *Modern Fiction Studies*. Her next project will concern Jamaican film history.

Lalitha Gopalan is an Associate Professor and teaches film studies at Georgetown University in Washington, DC. She is the author of *Cinema of Interruptions: Action Genres in Contemporary Indian Cinema* (BFI, 2002) and *Bombay* (BFI, 1995).

Chris Jones has taught literature, theatre and film studies for a number of years. He has participated in gay-related theatre and video work. He wrote about Derek Jarman for his film MA. He has taught film theory and creative writing at the University of Greenwich.

Mark Joyce is Senior Lecturer in Communication and Cultural Studies at Southampton Solent University. He is also course leader of the recently validated BA degree programme in media communication. He has co-authored *Advanced Level Media* (Hodder & Stoughton, 2001) and is currently writing a chapter on 'Consumer Identities for Key Themes in Interpersonal Communication' (OUP, 2007).

Searle Kochberg is Senior Lecturer in film studies and Video Production at the University of Portsmouth. He also works as a film critic and as a consultant to various media/arts organisations.

Lawrence Napper gained his Ph.D. from the University of East Anglia in 2001. He taught at UEA for a number of years, and has also taught at the University of Warwick and at Kings College, London. He has written variously on British cinema, including articles on Quota Quickies in Robert Murphy (ed.), *The British Cinema Book* (BFI Publishing, 1999) and 'British Cinema and the Middlebrow' in Justine Ashby and Andrew Higson (eds), *British Cinema: Past and Present* (Routledge, 2000). His book on *British Cinema and Middlebrow Culture* is due to be published by the University of Exeter Press in 2007. He currently lives and works in London.

Jill Nelmes is Senior Lecturer in film studies at the University of East London and has taught a range of courses from A level to postgraduate. She has been an examiner for WJEC Media Studies. She is also a scriptwriter and has a variety of projects in development. Over the past three years she has spent much time in LA where she worked as a script reader as well as studying screenwriting at UCLA.

Bill Nichols is Professor of Cinema and Director of the Graduate Program in Cinema Studies at San Francisco State University and a historian and theoretician of documentary film. He edited the two-volume anthology *Movies and Methods* which helped to define film studies. He is the author of *Newsreel: Documentary Filmmaking on the American Left* (Arno Press, 1980), *Ideology and the Image* (Indiana University Press, 1981), *Maya Deren and the American Avant-Garde* (University of California Press, 2001) and *Introduction to Documentary* (Indiana University Press, 2001).

Patrick Phillips is Principal Lecturer in film studies at Middlesex University and heads up its Media Studies Department. He wrote the national syllabus for A level film studies initiated in the year 2000 and is Chief Examiner in A level film studies. He is the author of *Understanding Film Texts* (British Film Institute, 2000).

Suzanne Speidel is Senior Lecturer in film studies and Course Leader for the BA in Film and Literature at Sheffield Hallam University. She is currently working on a book of film adaptations of the works of E.M. Forster (forthcoming, 2008), and has published articles in books and journals on Joseph Conrad and cinema, and TV drama and narrative theory.

Paul Ward is Senior Lecturer in Animation Theory and History at the Arts Institute at Bournemouth. He is the author of *Documentary: The Margins of Reality* (Wallflower Press, 2005), and numerous journal and anthology articles on documentary and animation. His work has appeared in *Animation: An Interdisciplinary Journal*, *Scope: An Online Journal of Film Studies* and the *Historical Journal of Film, Radio and Television*. He is Reviews Editor for *Animation: An Interdisciplinary Journal* and a Board member of the Society for Animation Studies.

Paul Watson is a Senior Lecturer in Film and Media Studies at the University of Teesside, UK. He is the co-author of *Three-Minute Wonders: Music Video and the Politics of Representation* (forthcoming) and has written numerous other articles on aspects of film, media and the politics of representation.

Paul Wells is Director of Animation in the Animation Academy at Loughborough University. He has published widely in the field, including *Understanding Animation* (Routledge, 1998), *Animation and America* (Rutgers University Press, 2002), and *Animation: Genre and Authorship* (Wallflower Press, 2002). He has also made a Channel 4 documentary called *Cartoons Kick Ass*, three BBC programmes on British animation and an educational video on special effects for the British Film Institute.

Foreword

Bill Nichols

How to tell the story of a discipline and a medium? This question stands as the challenge that *Introduction to Film Studies* confronts and solves through a series of individually authored but conceptually integrated essays. Each essay reminds us of the power and fascination of the movies as a medium through detailed analyses that are offered of a wide range of film, old and new, local and global, widely popular and sometimes unknown. Each essay also introduces us to the conceptual tools and critical questions that film scholars have asked and are now asking about the nature, function and value of film. Both film studies as a discipline and filmmaking as a practice possess a history that represents diverse attempts to create and understand a range of imaginative worlds that could not exist in any other form in quite the same way as they do in film. Attention to form is necessary so that the distinctiveness of cinematic expression may be fully appreciated, but attention to content is also needed if this distinctiveness is to be understood in the wider historical context to which it contributes. *Introduction to Film Studies* marries the two in a seamless blend of astute critical essays that survey the breadth and depth of film as an object of study today.

Apart from a common object, what do the essays in this volume have in common? A commonsensical answer to this question might be that the book provides a map to the most important theoretical tools and critical methodologies currently in use within film studies, and that it surveys the films and types of films, old and new, that loom as works of seminal importance. *Introduction to Film Studies* does offer this sort of answer, but it does so obliquely. Rather than explaining a standardised critical methodology, this book introduces a range of critical approaches and conceptual tools that become more or less valuable as the specific topic of inquiry shifts, and rather than simply pointing out what some of the greatest films have been, this book also introduces a much wider range of films that challenge, complicate and broaden our understanding of what film is and can be. There is a refreshingly broad, complementary array of approaches and commentaries offered here, facilitating for the reader an engagement with the cinema that is distinctive and rewarding in its particularities.

This diversity of critical approaches and rich range of cinematic examples does not prevent a certain sense of commonality from emerge in the essays all the same. Rather than a dominant theory, method or canon of films, this commonality, it would seem, resides in the ways in which each essay undercuts a commonsensical understanding of the cinema. Common-sense ideas are the most typical and unreflective ideas. Not necessarily wrong, they are, most often, limited to the knowledge needed to handle the most common situations. Common sense tells us that most movies are entertaining and disposable but the form of judgement brought to bear in this book tells us that this may well be true in many cases but that memorable works also exist that may support or confound our customary ideas of entertainment and disposability.

These essays go beyond common-sense understandings of movies to help readers see film with an expanded sense of the possible. They help us to see cinema anew, with fresh eyes and refreshing questions that move beyond the impressions and judgements that common sense would have us believe mark the limits of subjective, affective or critical engagement. Common sense tells us that 'Hollywood' is a monolith of immense power that sets the terms and conditions for filmmaking and reception worldwide. True, to an extent, several essays here complicate this truism by examining how British cinema, or documentary film, for example, not only exist but sometimes thrive in the context of a dominant Hollywood model. Other essays question the monolithic quality of Hollywood cinema itself. Film critics have long appreciated the subtle distinctions different directors bring to similar subject matter, especially in genre films. Hollywood films can be understood within the context of individual creativity as well as within an historical frame that must account for massive changes in how dominant, mainstream films have been produced and marketed for well over half a century.

Similarly, common sense tells us that important films for film history must have also been important films for their original audiences. This is not necessarily so, as the essay on 'The Soviet montage cinema of the 1920s' makes clear: the most popular films were the least innovative films and the most innovative films, such as those by Sergei Eisenstein, Dziga Vertov or Alexander Dovzhenko, were seldom popular. This disparity has also been true of the vast majority of documentary and avant-garde films despite their enormous significance to an understanding of the formal and social importance of film. It is also true of the Italian neo-realist films that did not win popular acceptance despite the global impact of the neo-realist style, and also true of the French New Wave, despite its enormous influence on other filmmakers and the continuing productivity of many of its most important figures.

Common sense tells us that movement and waves have their moment; they come and go. The essays assembled here suggest otherwise: important works may or may not find popular acceptance, at first or later, but their impact ripples outward in discernible patterns that can be traced and understood. So, too, the 'settled', common-sense idea that 'of course' a national cinema is a separate and distinct entity can be complicated to understand; how a national cinema often begs the question of a national identity and displays, in its complex weave of stories and styles, influences that are anything but purely national in origin. The monolithic idea of the audience that responds in a uniform way to a film, measured by box office receipts, for example, is also shown to be a commonsensical understanding that neglects to account for the divergent responses of different subcultures, ethnicities and, more obviously still, men and women. Hollywood cinema has historically presented itself as a cinema for all, but as the essay on 'Ethnicity, race, and cinema – African American film' argues, this commonsense impression has excluded recognition of a long history of filmmaking by and for African-American audiences. Not only did African American performers provide a, usually, stereotypical form of 'entertainment' in front of the Hollywood camera, they also contributed to a parallel stream of largely lost, forgotten or suppressed alternative films whose re-examination broadens our sense of the cinematically possible and of the actual history of film itself.

These are significant achievements, and the *Introduction to Film Studies* deftly guides the reader through the advances in understanding that characterise film studies today. What questions will vex the discipline in the future? These essays suggest some of the directions in which this question might lead, but it will also be the readers of this book who will give the most comprehensive and decisive answer to this question through the patient pursuit of their own desire to know more and understand better.

Acknowledgements

I would like to thank all the contributors who have given their time so willingly and put so much work into the fourth edition. My thanks especially to Moira Taylor at Routledge for nurturing the new edition through the development and production process with such skill and patience. Finally I would like to thank readers, students and academics for their constructive suggestions when planning the new edition.

Jill Nelmes

Introduction to the fourth edition

Jill Nelmes

Introduction to Film Studies is more than a guide to studying film, it is a celebration of the medium of film and our desire to understand this complex medium. How film is interpreted and perceived, how film affects an audience and, indeed, how films are constructed are aspects which many of us find fascinating.

This completely updated and renewed fourth edition is testament to the continued interest in the study of film. *Introduction to Film Studies* was first published in 1996 and it was apparent to many lecturers and students at the time that there was a shortage of film studies texts which explained the subject in a straightforward and entertaining way while still offering a degree of complex analysis. We were not especially surprised when the first edition was immediately popular with students at FE and HE level and became recommended reading on a number of courses in the UK; perhaps most surprising, though, was the burgeoning sales in various parts of the globe, from the US, where the book has proven particularly popular, to countries with very different types of film industries and cultures, such as Taiwan and Hong Kong.

Each edition of *Introduction to Film* Studies has reflected changing theoretical viewpoints and new concerns in the study of film while continuing to engage with the key concepts that have emerged in the last century. Each edition has included new chapters and new authors, where it was felt the reader would benefit from a differing perspective, and original chapters have been updated with new information, usually with new case studies of recent films.

Introduction to Film Studies' appeal emphasises the worldwide reach of cinema and our desire to understand and find out more about film; an interest that has no national boundaries as long as there is a place to show a film or to read a book.

Cinema has now spanned three centuries and, despite new and competing media technologies, the cinema experience is still an extremely popular one. Cinema audiences are at their highest since the 1960s, though DVD sales soar and access to the internet is widespread. These new media, as was the case with video, have instead become aids in allowing the promotion of film and an extra means of viewing and enjoying the medium. Yet surrendering oneself to the pleasures of the big screen and the excitement of watching a film narrative unfold on a giant screen is still an unmatchable experience. Many films are now watched at home. The DVD market has expanded astronomically, video is almost extinct, and the rise of the internet and more powerful computers will again change the way we access and view film, perhaps also the way we perceive film. The film short, for instance, is likely to become a more popular form as it is easily made with the technology available and quick to download from the net.

The number of colleges and universities offering film studies is still growing. What is it about this medium which was invented over a century ago that so fascinates us? Why do we enjoy film so much? Why indeed should we study film? Film is not just an integral part of Western society and culture but of many other cultures such as India and China.

It is not only fascinating to look at how films are constructed and how they affect us but also what they tell us about a society, how film can affect or challenge our understanding of the world around us and how this differs from nation to nation.

Film theory has been influenced by many differing philosophies, political theorists, cultural theorists and indeed film theorists. For film studies to remain 'alive' it must respond to new ways of thinking, and be affected by films that are produced not just in Hollywood but in other cultures as well. Film theory has to some extent been moving away from the 'grand theory' that so influenced psychology, literature and philosophy in the 1970s; the overarching psychoanalytic theories of Freud and Lacan, the political theories of Marx and Althussar, and the semiotic theories of Saussurre. That is not to say that these theories are not valuable or, on later reflection, may not be fashionable once more. Neither should they be discarded but, rather, reassessed. Postmodernism, for instance, has encouraged a critiquing of the grand narrative approach; affect theory discussed by Patrick Phillips in Chapter 8 is a less political and more reactive way of analysing our response to film.

Film is no longer a new medium, and new media such as the internet, mobile phones and DVDs will no doubt affect and change how films are made, how we receive them and how we understand and interpret film. The classical model of Hollywood no longer exists, new technology has affected our understanding of film and the boundaries as to what film is are less clearly defined. As society changes we look at the world in differing ways and thus our perception of film changes. Film studies both records and is a fascinating part of these changes which may open up the potential for creative collaborations. New ways of making films and telling stories using new media will undoubtedly emerge and these changes should be embraced rather than be seen as a threat. We look forward with excitement and interest to the next century of film.

HOW TO USE THIS BOOK

Introduction to Film Studies is designed as a resource which readers can use either as part of a course or for general interest. It is hoped they will be inspired and encouraged to read further, and extensive cross-referencing to other chapters suggests where to look for related topics and concepts.

Useful features
- Coverage of a wide range of concepts, theories and opinions about film studies. The authors, from both the US and the UK, are subject specialists in their field of film.
- In-depth discussion of the film industry in Hollywood and Britain, with reference to other cinemas and their conditions of production.
- Reference to a wide range of films from different periods and different countries.
- Case studies which include discussion of classical and contemporary film.
- Generous use of film stills.
- Self-contained chapters which introduce the subject area.

New features of the fourth edition
- All chapters have been revised and updated while some have been substantially modified or extended. Most chapters include new case studies.
- Two new chapters, 'Rediscovering film studies' and 'African American cinema'.
- Three new authors of chapters on film form and narrative, British cinema and documentary film.
- A foreword by Bill Nicholls, one of the most prominent and respected film theorists in the US.

- Full colour stills where available.
- A support website which features additional material and case studies from earlier editions.

PART ONE: APPROACHES TO STUDYING CINEMA

In Chapter 1, 'Rediscovering film studies', Patrick Phillips suggests we need to look at film with fresh eyes and in doing so will gain a renewed understanding and appreciation of the form. The chapter discusses the crisis in film history, how we understand and respond to film and how the emphasis on narrative in film theory has resulted in the neglect of the study of film as a performance.

PART TWO: CINEMA AS INSTITUTION – INDUSTRIES, TECHNOLOGIES AND AUDIENCES

This section explores the relationship between cinema as a cultural product and as a complex and ever-changing industry with its own rules and methods of working. In Chapter 2 Searle Kochberg explains how the film industry has had to respond to competition from, initially television, then video and now the internet, and the rise of the multi-media empires and conglomerates. The focus is on the Hollywood film industry which has so dominated film style and production in the twentieth century, although there is some discussion of the film industry in the UK, an industry which has often been dominated by Hollywood.

PART THREE: APPROACHES TO STUDYING FILM TEXTS

This section addresses methods of interpreting and analysing film, examining differing ways a film text may be understood. Suzanne Speidel, the new author of Chapter 3, 'Film form and narrative', discusses not only how film is constructed, shaped and formed but also how films tell stories. Chapters 4, 5 and 6, by Paul Watson, focus on Hollywood cinema. 'Approaches to cinematic authorship' discusses the role of the director, who has historically often been viewed as sole creator and artist, though more recently used as a commodity and marketing tool for promoting a film. 'Genre theory and Hollywood cinema' discusses the legacy left by the studio system, suggesting that genre works by difference in repetition. The author argues that genre can still be challenging and surprising, citing *Moulin Rouge* (2001) as an example. 'Stardom and Hollywood cinema' examines the notion of the star and how our understanding of the term has changed since the fall of the studio system. Chapter 7, 'Spectator, audience and response', written by Patrick Phillips, explores how the audience makes sense of film and the relationship between the film and the audience. The chapter discusses the role of the spectator and a new section on affect theory asks why the cinematic experience is so pleasurable.

PART FOUR: OTHER GENRE FORMS

This section examines two very different genres, documentary and animation, both of which have enjoyed something of a resurgence in popularity over the past ten years. A number of documentaries such as *Fahrenheit 9/11* have gained cinema release and surprisingly good box office takings. New author Paul Ward's chapter, 'The documentary form', traces the history of the documentary, asking what we mean by the term and how the form can be defined. Chapter 9, 'The language of animation', also gives an historical perspective, examining experimental as well as mainstream animation which has been somewhat revived by the use of computer software that has allowed the making of films such as *The Incredibles*.

PART FIVE: CINEMA, IDENTITIES AND THE POLITICS OF REPRESENTATION

This section discusses how different groups with different identities of sexuality, gender and ethnic origin are represented in film. Chapter 10, 'Gender and film', by Jill Nelmes, discusses how concepts of masculinity and femininity are represented in film and understood by an audience. In Chapter 11, 'Lesbian and gay cinema', Chris Jones argues for a separate theory to account for the way lesbians and gays are represented on screen and also how they, as an audience, interpret film. The new Chapter 12, by Terri Francis, 'Ethnicity, race, and cinema – African American film', explores the history of the African American in film, discussing what makes a film racist and the stereotypes that have been used when depicting black characters in film. Francis argues for an interdisciplinary approach to the subject which examines the visual nature of these films rather than focusing on the social conditions of the time.

PART SIX: CINEMA, NATIONHOOD AND NATIONAL IDENTITIES

In Western society we tend to think of Hollywood as the dominant form of cinema, yet other national cinemas past and present have made their presence felt for a variety of reasons, ranging from their productivity and popularity, as in the case of Bollywood cinema, to their aesthetic or political and social value. This section focuses on four very different types of national cinema: the chapters on British cinema and Indian cinema offer an overview from an historical perspective, and Soviet montage cinema of the 1920s and the French New Wave are examined at particular moments in time. The new Chapter 13 on British cinema, written by Lawrence Napper, asks: how can we define a British film? The author discusses how the film industry developed ties with Hollywood in its early years and yet films made in Britain are a product of British culture. Chapter 14, Lalitha Gopalan's chapter on Indian cinema, compares Bollywood to the Hollywood film industry. Film form, narrative and genre in Indian popular cinema are also discussed, as well as the increasing interest in Indian cinema in the West and its influence on films such as *Moulin Rouge* (2001). Soviet montage cinema emerged out of the Russian Revolution of 1917. In Chapter 15, Mark Joyce argues, this cinema has had a lasting effect and theories developed in that period are still influential today. The French New Wave (Chapter 16) really only existed for a relatively brief period from the late 1950s to the mid-1960s. Chris Darke points out that its influence, though, was profound: many of the directors were also film theorists who argued that Hollywood filmmakers such as Hitchcock and Ford should be considered artists and film an important art form.

Chapter 1

Rediscovering film studies: some fresh starting points

Patrick Phillips

■ Rediscovering film studies: some fresh starting points

INTRODUCTION: *FILM IS*

Film is a beautiful and amazing medium that has become too familiar. Although we continue to be surprised by particular sequences in films, by surprising turns in a plot, we are in increasing danger of taking the medium itself, whether in its celluloid or digital form, for granted. We expect slickly produced images, a rich and complex soundtrack and we want films to feed our insatiable appetite for story and sensation. Yet we are in danger of becoming complacent in our attitudes. Constantly we need to rediscover film – and recognise this as a primary purpose of film studies.

How can film studies help us to approach film with the surprise and delight and wonder that the first audiences experienced over a hundred years ago? We have to start looking with fresh eyes and listening with sharpened hearing. We need to start asking different questions that give different kinds of explanations.

In the 1970s when film studies was established as an academic discipline, much was borrowed from the field of linguistics. The language-like qualities of a film were considered central in defining some of the core interests of the subject. Important work was done in identifying the structural principles of film narrative, the recurring patterns that allowed us to name genres and the 'signatures' of particular directors who we were able thereby to be named auteurs. The language-like qualities of a film were also considered central to an understanding of how a film works in communicating meaning and ideas. The film was a 'text'[1] with the implication that the methods of criticism developed for literary work could more or less be carried over to this audio-visual medium. Studies in representation using the principles of semiotics have been very productive in peeling away layers of signification contained in images (though applied much less often and with greater difficulty to sound). At the macro level we have narrative, genre and auteur studies as core elements and at the micro level studies in representation through close analysis. These and other approaches, many of which are covered in this book, help to construct the subject called film studies.

The proliferation of courses on screenwriting has tended to reinforce the sense that film can be successfully approached in terms of formula, patterns, structures, and even if a smart film idea is judged as one that breaks with a formula, that surprises by its twist, it gains its surprise in relation to a set of normative ideas. A well-plotted story, based on cause-and-effect logic, characters with clearly defined functions, and a sequence of episodes that provide contrasting moods can be taught without picking up a camera or a microphone. Courses in the practice of filmmaking often refer to the 'grammar' or the 'syntax' of a shot. For sure, certain ways of framing a shot and moving the camera are likely to be more successful than others. Certain combinations of shots are likely to make more sense to a spectator than others. However, we need to be careful in differentiating between practices that work and 'rules'.[2] In fact most of the 'rules' are practices that became part of a professional practice as far back as 1915. As with the work of the screenwriter, so the work of director, cinematographer and editor is understood (and usually judged) in relation to normative assumptions. A striking shot is often one which transgresses the deeply established conventions.

See Chapter 7, p. 149.

While film studies does scrutinise the conventional practices and effects of film–making, we need to be aware that at its more introductory levels any subject is in danger of reinforcing dominant ways of thinking and understandestioning ting rather than quhem. Yet the productive relationship between an academic subject (here film studies) and its object of study (here film/cinema) is one in which the academic subject makes its object 'strange'. This is even more important now when there is such a 'knowingness' about film and where one of the pleasures of contemporary cinema is to play on this 'knowingness', identifying references to other films or looking for patterns of resemblance between different films. Film studies must do more than feed this comfortable 'knowingness'. Indeed, a subject that simply reflects its object, that is complicit with it, lacks ambition, reinforcing methods and procedures which it could be radically engaged in interrogating. How, in film studies, can we make film 'strange', how can we de-familiarise ourselves to its practices and its products?.

Perhaps we need to rediscover some naivety in film studies – look again with astonishment at workers leaving a factory in the Lumiere Brothers' film of 1895. Delight in the recently discovered Mitchell and Kenyon archive of films[3] found a hundred years after they were made, perfectly preserved in a milk churn in Blackburn. And perhaps we need to look at the abstract colour films Len Lye made to promote the Post Office in the 1930s with delight and amazement. And perhaps we need to look at 'boring' old home movie footage with a sense of wonder. Jonathan Caouette's *Tarnation* (2004) is celebrated as a documentary that achieved an international release, having been made for $218.32 and edited on an iMac home computer.[4] It is also celebrated for the bravery with which the filmmaker deals with an awful and very personal story. But already *Tarnation* is being delimited in these statements. They invite us to remove ourselves from the direct experience, even protect us from the footage shot on a variety of cameras Caouette has owned since the age of 8, ranging from Super 8 to mini-DVD. Instant labelling and categorising of a film, placing it within the 'machinery' of film studies, can remove us from the direct impact of the family photos, the clips from feature films, the snatches of audio tapes, which along with the home movie material make up the film.

The Austrian filmmaker Gustav Deutsch has been working since 1996 on a project called *Film ist*.[5] He uses found footage, mainly very old material shot for scientific purposes which he has found in film archives, apparently to illustrate certain propositions: *Film ist*/film is:

1. movement and time
2. light and darkness
3. an instrument
4. material
5. a blink of an eye
6. a mirror

7. comic
8. magic
9. conquest
10. writing and language
11. emotions and passions
12. memory and document

However, the work does something far more, or far other than contribute some kind of audio-visual lexicon, a kind of 'writing' in film theory. First of all, '*Film ist*' has a full stop. Film is. Film is. Film is. Each apparent attempt to complete the sentence leaves us with an increasing sense that film evades any particular definition. Deutsch writes:

Film cannot be defined, because its limitations are those of existence itself. The phrases which follow [film is], I realised, are not intended as even possible definitions, nor even as sub-categories of film's existence. Rather, each articulates a perception, a facet, of film's continuous metamorphosis, its display of the secret life of existence itself. Thus the succession of film's affinities becomes multiple and transitory. No single term can occupy this space for long.[6]

Deutsch appears to offer a language-like set of propositions, but each image, each combination of images outruns any verbal equivalent. The first six films relate to the physical phenomenon of film and depend more on scientific material than the second

For further discussion of Mitchell and Kenyon see pp. 306–7.

• **Plate 1.1**
Film ist ... ein Spiegel
– Film is a mirror. This
still from the sixth film
in Deutsch's series
creates the impression
through editing of
spectators looking
at gruesome images
of eye surgery. The
play here is on eye/
looking/mirror/cinema/
spectatorship

six films. But to describe them as 'scientific' loses the playfulness with which they are presented, and the simultaneous ways in which they mean so many different things; documentary material presented as ways into all kinds of simultaneous thoughts, experiences, associations. In 4, *Film is Material*, the audience is presented with single frames from reels of chemically decaying film. Each image is a beautiful object, figurative in part where we can still make out a face, abstract in part where colours have changed, disintegration set in. In 9, *Film is Conquest*, archive material taken by colonial documentary makers in Asia and Africa is edited for devastating effect – indicting film as a medium that participates in conquest and yet also as a medium that may be used to turn the tables, expose colonialism, through playful use of montage. *Material* and *Conquest* could not be more different at first glance – but both draw us through a portal into the virtuality of visual images. Walter Benjamin, the German theorist writing in the 1930s, talked about all those things which the human senses are somehow aware of but which only a camera can visualise as the 'optical unconscious'.[7] Deutsch captures both the materiality of film, its basis in optics and its ability to record material that escapes our senses but which somehow is part of our conscious/unconscious experience of the world.

Sean Cubitt in his demanding but important book *The Cinema Effect* (2004) talks about the relationship between sensation, cognition and comprehension.

Think for example, of a football game. In the first instance there is only grass, air, milling figures. In the second there are the structures defining the action: the goals, the touchlines – and the apperception that identifies all this as "the game". Third is the appreciation of the running – the strategic pass, the lightning dart, the feint, the skill and grace of a game well played.[8]

Gustav Deutsch makes his work somewhere around the interface between sensation and cognition – where, to extend Cubitt's metaphor, the possibilities of grass, sky, human figures becoming a football game is left open to the possibility of something else shaping out of this – instead of, additional too, simultaneous with. But Deutsch's work also, to extend the metaphor still further, depends on the game already played. We live in a postmodern age where irony can liberate us or cynicism sink us. The ironic joy in Deutsch's s work is that the accumulated knowledge of over a century of filmmaking is used to produce a rich array of internal dialogues within the work, none of which is contained or containable. Not only does film become a less familiar medium, it also offers us the chance to reflect again on what film is, what film does. *Film ist* is just a particular example of a film that calls into question our relationship to our material world, our sense of space, of time, of consciousness.

Tom Gunning writes:

I believe that in the twenty first century we will finally learn how to understand the moving image, rediscovering the wonder of first audiences, but also gaining a broad field of reference in which all these diverse gestures, movements, actions, expressions, enigmatic objects and wavering illuminations will form, not a true lexicon, but a range of possibilities, a table of combinations, the stuff of a new art form of collage and montage.[9]

Using digital media, and raiding the (virtual) archive, we have the opportunity in film studies to explore these possibilities – and to link them to a range of relatively new developments in film history and film theory. In this short chapter it is impossible to do more than suggest possible lines of investigation. These will be based on the re-emergence in film studies of interest in aspects of the image[10] which are not motivated primarily by interests in narrative or representation.

In reflecting on the image we do something artificial, we suspend the movie. However, this can be justified not just because it is a routine aspect of the way we consume films today on DVD, but also because it offers us a different kind of relationship to those films and a much greater opportunity to use the medium in a reflective way.[11] We know that images were recorded in the past and that their 'presence' is an illusion but this tends to be suppressed when we watch a film by our need to place any particular image in a narrative context – of what went before and what comes after. The suggestion here is that a reflection on images coming out of the past to be experienced so vividly in the present provides a simple basis for exploring areas of cinematic fascination that have not been at the centre of introductory film studies. And tied up closely with this interest in the image are explorations in that most profound of cinematic subjects: time.

There follow four short sections. The second of these (p. 9) is central and opens up some ideas about the image as a document in time, in ways that make problematical both our understanding of what is the nature of the image as document and how film can invite us to reflect on our experience of time. This is preceded by a section considering new approaches to the composing of film history based on the digital co-presence of all images from the past of cinema. This is followed by a section on performance and, finally and most briefly, some thoughts on the reintegration of narrative into our studies of the image. The route may appear something of a zigzag, that just falls short of being fashionably rhizomatic,[12] but it is hoped that some new discoveries occur along the way. In each case the provocation is in what Gustav Deutsch has claimed for film, its 'continuous metamorphosis, its display of the secret life of existence itself'.

NON-LINEAR FILM HISTORY

We can only engage with the past in the present. We draw out information about the past gathered from all kinds of sources of evidence in order to construct narrative accounts, stories of the past, interpretations of the past, for the needs of the present. Sometimes histories change because new documents are found which require that the writing on that subject be updated, but just as often it is because the same documents from the past are being given a different interpretation due to some need in the present to give the past a particular meaning. This is as true in the writing of film history as it is in the writing of the history of any other subject.[13] History is never a once and for all 'given' but rather its writing is an endless process of re-engagement with sources, documents, earlier histories in an intellectual and creative process of working with the past in the present.

The history of cinema extends from 1895 – and much earlier if we take account of the long prehistory of the moving image. To immerse ourselves in this history is a principal pleasure of film studies. There is a range of excellent chronological histories of cinema.[14] Some tell their story in terms of technological innovations and aesthetic developments associated with particular national cinemas or film movements. Others tell their story more by references to changes in the economic and professional organisation of the film industry and the changing patterns of audience consumption. Indeed, a history of film studies could now be written which charts the shifts in fortunes of the academic subject itself and the various turns it has taken.

This linear, often teleological[15] approach can be contrasted with the way that filmmakers and audiences have become familiar with a very different approach to film history. In significant ways since the 1960s filmmakers have actively referred to other films, sometimes to simply pay homage to them, but in the process inviting links to be made that may be thematic or stylistic. Sometimes references to other films are many and complex, conscious borrowings that add density to the film through the associations these references bring. This intertextuality demonstrates how aware a filmmaker is of aspects of film history – creating an interchange of images, ideas between past and present. The audience has responded, taking a particular pleasure in picking up these references which are both playful and satisfying – a happy meeting point for cinephiliac filmmaker and spectator.[16]

Over the past few years there has been a huge increase in the availability of films on DVD. When a film fan goes to a specialist store or shops online, he or she is presented with a reasonable sample of the history of cinema. Film fans have the opportunity to build their own collection of films, be it through specialising in films of a particular genre or national cinema or the work of a favourite star. In the process they are creating their own personal historical collection with links and connections distinctive to it. These same fans will also be familiar with the intertextual pleasures offered by certain filmmakers as outlined in the previous paragraph.

The whole of the past of cinema is virtually co-present. A good cross-section of films may actually be co-present as part of the collection of a cinephile. The connections made between these films are many and various – some reflecting narrative histories of cinema written by respected experts, but most often improvised and idiosyncratic. A diagram of this history would not be neatly linear with clear causal connections. It would be better represented as a hypertext model with multiple connections going off in different directions and with little to help us privilege one line over many others.[17]

Without being aware of it, filmmakers and film fans, in the ways in which they move through the past of cinema, weaving together images from disparate films, contribute to an undermining of confidence in traditional linear narrative history now shared by many contemporary professional historians.[18] Until the impact of critical theory in the 1970s and 1980s, with its emphasis on the never innocent or 'neutral' selection of material and the construction of a 'story' of the past, historians could feel confident about their traditional ways of working. Indeed, the classic historical account is not dissimilar to a film screenplay in its emphasis on a cause–effect logic, its general plausibility and its confidence in working within a linear time frame. In addition, and more ideologically significant, a traditional history like a well-made Hollywood film disguises its own construction, appearing seamless and fully formed rather than the result of calculation.

This similarity between the construction of 'seamless' narratives in history and in film draws attention to the uncomfortable similarity between the production of what we call the factual and what we call fictional. In French, *histoire* can mean history or simply story. To use the phrase *c'est des histoires*! is to dismiss something along the lines of 'that's all fiction!' Now you could say that we have happily avoided this ambiguity in English by using the word 'history' to distinguish something based on facts, on documents, on research. But perhaps it is more accurate to say the opposite, that we have used the word 'history' to sustain the illusion that it is possible to distinguish stories about the past written by learned experts called historians from other kinds of stories that circulate in culture.

The impact of these insights, the contribution which critical theory has made to **historiography** (the study of how history is written, constructed) has had a number of

historiography
The study of how history is written – or constructed. This has become acutely important as we become more aware of how narratives are the result of processes of selection and construction. Film history, like other kinds of history, needs to be reflected upon, not just in relation to its content, but also in relation to the processes by which it has been written.

metanarrative
Refers to an overarching
account of some area
of human experience
which attempts to make
complete sense of that
area. Meta-theory is,
similarly, an overarching,
all-embracing system
for explaining some area
of human experience.
In film studies there
has been a move away
from metanarratives in
historical studies and
from meta-theory in
theoretical studies.

interesting consequences over the past twenty years or so. One is that historians often have much less confidence in producing a **metanarrative** – that is one that attempts to make sense of everything, by weaving a grand, overarching narrative in which everything neatly 'fits' in its place. Rather historians are more likely to dwell on the contradictions, the things that 'rupture' the otherwise smooth skin of the story. This shift towards an appreciation of the necessary plurality of accounts of the past, together with an embracing of contradiction, encourage smaller scale 'thicker' histories.[19]

At a further extreme the postmodern historian accepts that critical theory radically undermines what we have conventionally thought of as history. The postmodern historian 'plays among the ruins' of history, mixing more reliable and less reliable material from the past, and mixing both with the present in ways that sometimes collapse the distinction between fact and fiction, objective and subjective, public and personal, acknowledging the single space occupied by the past and the present.

We can see this turn from traditional narrative accounts towards the postmodern over the past few years reflected in films themselves. While a conventional feature film works to make perfect sense through its cause–effect logic, producing a metanarrative that seems to tell itself rather than be constructed by a narrator and closing down contradiction in a well-constructed plot that brings everything to resolution and closure, in some contemporary cinema there is a greater openness of form. Filmmakers exploit the ways in which memory collapses the distinction between past and present – so that recalled events are as 'present' as the present moment. This in turn makes problematic the relationship between the past as history and the past as memory. Films dwell on the uncertainty of knowledge from the past, if only to increase suspense. Some films go further in their construction, blurring the distinction between past and present to the point where not just history as a retrieved 'factual' past seems difficult, but where our common-sense understanding of time is undermined. Contemporary film, and indeed contemporary film theory, are particularly interested in questions of memory and time, not least because cinema seems particularly adept at asking these questions.[20]

Robert Rosenstone asks a very direct question of postmodern film history – Where are the examples?[21] It is one thing to theorise about a history which collapses the difference between fact and fiction, which gives legitimacy to very subjective responses to things from the past in the present, and which plays with documentary material without any ambition to produce a conclusive and closed narrative. It is another to produce this. Rosenstone answers his own question by referring to a variety of recent film documentaries that begin to show postmodern tendencies in the ways they construct their historical accounts of their different subjects. Certainly it is easier to 'write' this kind of history using digital audio-visual media. While a book imposes a linearity and a logical progression, digital media can superimpose, dissolve and in various other ways create relationships of co-presence between sounds and images. Interactive media allow for further relationships, indeed further and different kinds of authoring.

*For further discussion of
Godard and his influence
on the French New Wave
see Chapter 16, pp.
399–406, 413–420.*

We can compare two personal film histories made for the screen by great auteur film directors. *A Personal Journey with Martin Scorsese Through American Movies* is structured around the great genres of the Hollywood studio system – the western, the musical and the gangster movie. Jean-Luc Godard's *Histoire(s) du cinéma* plays on the double meaning in French of 'histoire' that has already been referred to. Both works demonstrate the presence of the past of history. However, while Scorsese organises his work more or less around a conventional chronological structure and is faithful to the integrity of the sequences he chooses, Godard's work is much more experimental. Indeed, his self-awareness of the range of critical and theoretical issues that have so far been outlined in this chapter can lead to the impression that *Histoire(s) du cinéma* was made with the express purpose of demonstrating what a postmodern history might look like.

Scorsese offers us a traditional account of Hollywood genre cinema through well-chosen extracts. He acknowledges the 'personal' in his choice and communicates

• **Plate 1.2**
Marilyn collage from essay
by Jean-Luc Godard,
Histoire(s) du cinéma (1998)

his well-known cinephilia in the warmth and enthusiasm of his commentary. Godard, using digital technology, draws images out from their origin in particular films made at particular historical moments and uses them as ghostly presences from the domain of the virtual. Sometimes superimposition and overlap link images – forcing new kinds of expressive connection. These images, and fragments of images are often dissociated from their soundtrack, 'called back into existence' against the soundtrack from an entirely different film. In summoning up the image as ghostly, Godard exploits both the uncanny and the fetishistic qualities of the cinematic image. For the single, indivisible nature of past and present in the life of the image is both a haunting and a kind of magic. The commentary, together with other verbal material, does not close down or limit the significance of these images but rather seems to do the opposite, to expand them further.

Godard's work seems to be based on the centrality in film of images – separated from any narrative. As Jacques Ranciere writes: 'Godard turns these images into units caught up in a double relationship – with all the things that have left their impression on them, and with all the other images with which they compose a specific sensorium, a world of inter-expressivity.'[22]

Film appears to encourage a different kind of historical 'writing', offering the possibility of retrieving the past in the present and then setting out that which is retrieved in a whole variety of different ways, ways that reflect personal memory and forms of personal desire. History becomes subsumed by the subjectivity of the producer of the work. There is a sense in which film appears to exist in a continuous present tense and may be experienced as such, with the historian weaving patterns of association. The historical time of the production of these images and the present time of their reworking encourages what Tom Gunning in an earlier quotation described as 'a range of possibilities, a table of combinations, the stuff of a new art form of collage and montage'.[23]

THE IMAGE AS DOCUMENT IN TIME

When we pull an old photograph out of a box, we are aware of a number of things. In front of us is an image from the past. The people in it may well have long since passed away. There is something amazing about the 'presence' of an image which makes it more than a representation. There is a ghostly quality – maybe a hint of the uncanny – as we see in Godard's *Histoire(s) du cinéma*. There is also a sense of thing-in-itself which can stimulate levels of imaginative and poetic engagement in the viewer. As often as not, the image from the past provokes nostalgia, melancholy, making the present a time and space of loss.

A moving image has to deal with something a still photograph is untroubled by – the before and after of time. A moving image can distract us from this sense of presence, if our viewing is being driven by narrative time, by the desire for narrative knowledge. In such a situation the movement of the object – its 'life' – is likely to be lost in its narrative function, the story knowledge it contains. And rather than existing in its own time, it exists within the time of the narrative. Popular mainstream film narratives are most often based on running with measurable time, with drawing the peculiar and particular back into a clock-based understanding of before and after. But it is not the only way to deal with the temporal dimension of a moving image. For example, the moving image need not be presented within the before and after of narrative. The object/person filmed can be presented in a way in which it occupies a moment out of time, or rather its movement occupies its own time. The 'presence' of the moving image can offer us different ways of thinking about time.

Jacques Rancière in his *Film Fables* identifies two poetics, One is a poetics of action and representation which he sees as deriving from Aristotle. The other is a **poetics of presence** which he sees as emerging in the Romantic period. This poetics of presence includes the possibility of the whole of some phenomenon or experience being contained in a single 'statement' such as an image. It has the capacity to suggest infinite relationships with other things.

Cinema, the predominantly modern art, experiences more than any other art the conflict of these two poetics, though it is, by the same token, the art that most attempts to combine them. Cinema is the combination of the gaze of the artist who decides and the mechanical gaze that records, of constructed images and chance images.[24]

The American filmmaker Ken Burns has produced several highly successful documentaries on historical subjects, including *The American Civil War* (1991) and *The West* (1996). Central to his work is the simple and common technique of zooming in, out and panning across still images, thus giving them a sense of movement. These 'animated' photographs cut loose from the structures of narrative, even though they are heavily burdened by a voice-over commentary. They speak directly about history – which is to say they speak directly about time. And in this quite literal example of still images that 'move' through the application of movie camera techniques, we see the point of contrast between the time of the image and the narrative time that they are being drawn into. They create connections that are both intellectual, in that we process the information contained in the photographs, and affective, in that we feel the melancholy of the pastness of the past, the haunting by the presentness of the past.

While a narrative realist feature film using actors may produce spectacular cinema and an engaging narrative in, say, the western genre, it is most likely to address the imaginary that exists in the mind of the audience, the already seen, already imagined, tying the world of the film back into a closed system, defined by the expectations which both filmmakers and audiences bring to the viewing situation. Sometimes when we watch a typical mainstream film with its narrative priorities and its heavy investment in creating the realist illusion through its sets, locations and so on, we are stopped short by a moment, a single shot perhaps, which steps outside both narrative and illusionist priorities, whether by accident or design, and which we remember for ever – long after we have forgotten the detail of the plot and maybe even how the film ends.

These moments become the nodes of a hypertextual system. Existing in their own independent time, they can go any which way, forming relationships across the time

poetics of presence
Refers to the way in which an image can contain a whole world of significance and meaning, as, for example, a painting or a still photograph. Normally in watching 'movies' we are concerned with narrative progression and are often startled when the film offers us the opportunity to engage with the stillness or near stillness of an image.

of a narrative history of the movies. It is a basis for what Jean-Luc Godard does in his *Histoire(s) du cinéma*. It is what we all do when we talk passionately about the movies.

In 1940 John Ford made a film version of John Steinbeck's novel *The Grapes of Wrath*. This film of the Oakies migrating from the Oklahoma Dust Bowl to California in search of the promised land is fairly faithfully adapted from a novel which itself was written in response to contemporary events in the America of the 1930s. Many things give the film distinction: its direction, its cinematography, its acting, its screenplay adaptation. But the film visualises the prose world of the novel by making moving images that are inspired by the now famous still photographs taken as part of the Farm Security Administration (FSA) Project begun in 1935, documenting the lives of the rural poor.[25] *The Grapes of Wrath* constantly invokes these images in order to give the film a high degree of verisimilitude (see Plate 1.3(a)). At the same time these still photographs re-created as moving images allow the film to resonate with a particular quality. This can partly be explored in terms of the interface between documentary and fiction and partly in terms of the way these images exceed their narrative function, each in their singularity makes a complete statement about the world of the film – exemplifying the poetics of presence.

In 2003 Lars von Trier made a film set in the same time period as *The Grapes of Wrath* about a poor white rural community. Von Trier's three-hour *Dogville* is filmed entirely on a single sound stage in which there is no attempt to create a realistic set.[26] Indeed, there is no conventional scenery – walls of buildings are indicated by masking tape as in a rehearsal studio. There is little attempt, by the standards of 'realist' filmmaking, to produce verisimilitude. Yet *Dogville*, despite its unusual staging as a fictional film, is both narrative and realist in fairly conventional ways.

The brilliant move on Von Trier's part is to show the audience how much they contribute to the realism of a film by projecting their own imagination. (It is strange that theatre has only at certain periods in its history felt the burden of having to work with anything approaching the illusion of verisimilitude that film assumes!) Cinematic realism as a product of the imagination does not require excessive amounts of money to be spent in creating the fake real of stage sets and location shots. A blank backdrop may be used for more than the projection of CGI illusions.

After the challenge presented to the audience by the minimalism of the staging of the film, there is a final confrontation in the closing credit sequence of *Dogville*: a series of photographs documenting the poor, mainly from the 1930s of the kind on which John Ford modelled the **mise-en-scène** of *The Grapes of Wrath*.[27] The shock of these still images (and towards the end of the sequence a few of the images are subject to panning close-ups similar to the technique found in Ken Burns' work referred to earlier) is their deliberate contrast with the theatrically false world of the film. The sudden presence of the past, as the film moves beyond dramatic representation, offers a more direct experience of the world the film has imaginatively suggested (it is accompanied by David Bowie's song 'Young Americans'). Now, of course, these photographs are themselves representations – but they are not used as such. After a three-hour film that despite its radical staging has offered a fairly conventional narrative film of action and representation, and just as the audience are preparing to leave the cinema, they are offered a different kind of dramatic experience, one based on the poetics of presence. Each of the images may be said to contain a whole world in a way that contrasts with the action and representation of the narrative film.

Of course, a film is made up of images. A film, as was made clear in the earlier Ranciere observation, combines the poetics of action and representation and the poetics of presence. New technologies for private viewing and the capturing of images allows us to recognise and make use of this 'presence' for the first time in the history of cinema.

Among the questions we may wish to ask are ones to do with the nature of the way we experience the still image over the moving image, the relationship between fictional and factual images from the past as 'documents' and what it is that might constitute what is here being called a poetics of presence.

From what has been said thus far, it is clear that some filmmaking practices offer a

mise-en-scène
Refers to both what is filmed (setting, props, costumes, etc.) and to how it is filmed (cinematographic properties of the shot, such as depth of field, focus, lighting, and camera movement). In an attempt to counter the imprecision of the term, this latter aspect is sometimes called mise-en-shot. Mise-en-scène is one way of producing meaning in films which can be both straightforward and extremely complex, depending upon the intentions and skill of the director (the metteur-en-scène: see **auteur**).

• **Plate 1.3**

(a) *The Grapes of Wrath* (John Ford, 1940)   (b) 'Ditched, Stalled, and Stranded. San Joaquin Valley, 1936' (Dorothea Lange)

movement image
The term coined by Gilles Deleuze to refer to a cinema in which the image is at the service of narrative, and in which the audience experience is of the 'movement' of the film toward the closure of narrative resolution.

time image
A development from the movement image. It suggests a cinema in which the narrative priorities of mainstream commercial cinema are replaced by ones which are more reflective. In particular, our understanding and experience of time becomes central.

sensory motor mechanism (SMM)
Refers to the mental processing of audio-visual information in ways that allow us to 'place' and 'manage' the film experience. There is an implication that the automatic nature of this processing is part of the relatively passive pleasure of mainstream commercial cinema. Other kinds of cinema may disrupt the sensory motor mechanism.

more direct engagement with what is here being called 'presence', and call into question different experiences of cinematic time. The French philosopher Gilles Deleuze, in his two very influential books on cinema,[28] described the mainstream narrative film as belonging to the cinema of the '**movement image**' and various kinds of film that differ from this as belonging to the cinema of the '**time image**'. Deleuze highlights the end of the Second World War and the development of Italian neo-realism as the key moment in the emergence of the time image after cinema had been dominated by the demands of narrative and genre.

Deleuze proposes that the movement image of narrative cinema addresses a particular capacity within the film spectator which he calls the **sensory motor mechanism**. This 'mechanism' is a means by which we recognise familiar patterns, or fit things into the familiar structures of thought. A conventional narrative with a story that conforms to generic expectations will be processed with ease. In the processing of such material, certain ways of understanding the world, ways that are already deeply embedded in what was earlier referred to as the social imaginary (p. 10), are further confirmed. We are asked to imagine within the terms of this sensory motor mechanism. It is not surprising that there should have been an instinctive desire on the part of some filmmakers to look towards some other kind of cinema experience at the end of the Second World War – a desire to break with previous methods of representing social reality, and to give audiences the possibility of different experiences of the 'real' through cinematic sound and image.

Deleuze argues that it was the movement called neo-realism in Italy around 1945 which gave impetus to this very different kind of cinema. Roberto Rosselini, the key figure of the movement with his films *Paisa*, *Rome Open City* and *Germany Year Zero*, had begun his career working in the mainstream fascist cinema – precisely the kind of cinema that exploited the 'sensory motor mechanism' in, for example, those films referred to as 'white telephone' movies. The Rossellini films, together with others made between 1944 and 1950, perhaps most notably Visconti's *La Terra Trema*, put an emphasis on the iconic – the moving image as capable of breaking with its narrative function, achieving a greater autonomy.[29] Rossellini's *Journey to Italy* of 1952 has recently been described as the first modern film[30] as it lets go of narrative priorities, creating cinematic drama around a series of encounters with objects and places that exemplify cinema's particular ability to communicate the sense of the past in the present.

Some modernist films add to this neo-realist technique of drawing out the iconic quality of the image, a fluid kind of montage that re-creates the experience of memory or dream – where past and present become interwoven. For example, Alain Resnais's 1959 film *Hiroshima mon amour* works between the present of Hiroshima, fourteen years after the dropping of an atomic bomb on the city, and a town in France, Nevers, where in the war a young French woman had a relationship with a German soldier. A Japanese man who lost his family in 1945 and this French woman, now an actress, working on a film in the city, have a brief affair in which the present of the past is collapsed in a beautiful cinematic exploration of history, memory and subjective experience.

Some postmodernist films take this montage further, scrambling the chronological order of events, creating an obsessive relationship to time as that which is continuously running away or slowing down or speeding up, or where time seems to fold into or emerge out of other time zones. (Digital technologies allow an apparently limitless set of possibilities which we are only just beginning to explore.) In films which capture something of the flow of time, there is sometimes a compulsive need to register 'clock time' – if only to demonstrate its hopelessness in measuring how time is actually experienced, how time slows down, speeds up, days drag, years fly. The time of consciousness is set against the mechanical time we take for granted and apparently conform our lives to. This is particularly well illustrated in most of Wong Kar Wai's films from *Days of Being Wild* to *2046*. Fixing time is a way of trying to hold on to an experience – so Yuddy near the beginning of *Days of Being Wild* meets Su Lizhen and the following dialogue takes place:

Yuddy: What day's today?
Su Lizhen: 16th.
Yuddy: 16th ... April the 16th. At one minute before 3pm on April the 16th, 1960, you're together with me. Because of you, I'll remember that one minute. From now on, we're friends for one minute. This is a fact, you can't deny. It's done.

By isolating moments, extracting them from the flow of time, we try to create memorials to them – memories need fixing, or they flow, merge, overlap, disintegrate one into another. In a sense we try to maintain a belief in the workings of a sensory motor mechanism which allows us not just the illusion of fixing points in time but thereby the possibility to create narratives which structure and make sense of these flows of time. Wong Kar Wai's films are often about the impossibility of two people being able to 'connect', suggesting that love is impossible. But perhaps it is time which is impossible. These films are indeterminate in so many ways – life has moved, apparently according to the clockwork of daily routines – and while characters can measure the difference between time past and time present, if only by the levels of nostalgia or melancholy they experience, we are aware also of negotiations with time itself, particularly in objects that join past to present as a single flow. These objects become fetishised – 'invested with magic' – just as they do in Godard's *Histoire(s)* because they capture the single, indivisible nature of past and present, even as the characters measure change in their material and physical lives.

The cinematic image is inherently of this kind – always in the past, always in the present. A filmmaker can choose to adopt a functional approach to images, make them subservient to narrative, motivated by plot. The result is a standard film that offers structure, clear causal connections and closure. A filmmaker can choose to use images quite differently, privileging the time of consciousness over a mechanical structuring of time.[31] Both kinds of cinema in their different ways draw attention to time itself as a central preoccupation of the medium.

PERFORMANCE: IMAGE AND INTENSITY

Both of the previous sections have considered how the organisation of the past as narrative is complex and problematic, whether in constructing history or story. The image as past/present compounds our uncertainty by putting into doubt time – upon which narrative depends. This section begins by raising a further question about narrative, especially in relation to its centrality in film studies.

Referring again to Aristotle, we find an enormously useful distinction between a tale that is told – such as a tale told by a great storyteller sitting with an audience at night around an open fire – as narrative, and set this against a tale that is acted out – as drama. Even though it may be blindingly obvious that film is dramatic, that there are actors who perform roles in situations of conflict, film studies has tended to approach film as a narrative rather than a dramatic medium. The obvious reason is that there is no live enactment; indeed, actors within a single scene may have been filmed separately and never performed face to face. Less obvious is the sense that the tale is being 'told', maybe controlled by the work of the director/screenwriter. Even less obvious is the idea that a film story may be told by cinema itself as some kind of impersonal 'story machine', a communication system that is language-like in its structuring of audio-visual material. We might consider a number of offscreen tellers of the narrative tale. If we take a popular blockbuster such as *Independence Day* (1996), then we could say that the tale is told by the director, in collaboration with a screenwriter and other key members of the filmmaking team – cinematographer, designer, editor. We could also say that the tale is told by the conventions of the genre to which it conforms. And we could, at a further level of abstraction, say the film is somehow told by 'Hollywood' as a particular kind of cinematic 'machine'. Debates over the 'authorship' of a film do nothing but reinforce the assumption that a film is a tale told – the question is by whom, or by what – which leaves alone the ways in which the film is an enactment.

Certainly film theory in its turn towards linguistics in the 1970s focused on the language-like aspects of film. Structuralist approaches gave a privileged role to narrative in order to show how film material is organised and with what effects on an audience. This was reinforced by interests in the politics of film, in which structuralist approaches could reveal how certain ideological assumptions and values were embedded within the organisation of the film, in the way the story of the film was told. The adoption of Lacanian psychoanalysis with ideas that even the unconscious was language-like in the way it was structured further located film as a narrative medium – that was told, not least by political and psychic forces which extended far beyond any idea of a human teller, even one as quirky and distinctive as Hitchcock.[32]

This has already been alluded to in the introductory remarks to this chapter – p. 3.

Film is not 'live' drama – in that the actors are absent. Indeed the ghostly qualities of the image referred to earlier seem even more striking if we think about the illusion of presence that we experience when we see Tom Cruise or Julia Roberts projected by light on to a screen. In fact a documentary of actual people presents us with exactly the same problem of presence/absence – raising further the problem that distinctions between a story and a history are not so easy to make. Both are after all illusions of presence, and central to that presence is acting. Dramatic conflict in film can be represented by purely cinematic means – such as the montage collision between two shots or through a turbulent soundtrack to a simple and possibly static image. However, drama is usually enacted through actors, either professionals paid to take on roles or real social actors participating in a documentary. In everyday language we talk about how dramatic or how lacking in drama was a particular film and we most vividly recall moments of conflict between actors which generated emotional intensity and carried forward the narrative.

So it may be said that film is possibly a hybrid – it has characteristics of a tale that is told – and characteristics of a tale that is enacted. Gilberto Perez argues this and asks a further question which arises from this: What tense is a film? A told tale is one that happened in the past, an enacted tale is one happening in the present time of its enactment. He writes:

A photograph is past; a painting is present; a play is present, a novel is past. The tense of the film image is dual, one might say: sometimes it acts like the present, sometimes like the past. Is light a wave or a stream of particles? Sometimes it acts like a wave, sometimes like particles, as modern physics has discovered; particle and wave, matter and energy, are not two different things but two different aspects of the same thing, two different ways in which the thing behaves. Present and past, icon and index, fiction and documentary, drama and narrative, these are different aspects of the film medium, different ways in which it can behave.[33]

As more film studies are conducted in a theory–practice mode, in which philosophical questions about the medium are explored through film/video-making, it is possible to play with the multiple dimensions of film as Perez outlines above – 'present and past', 'fiction and documentary', 'drama and narrative'. Working with actors on a 'staged' 'dramatic' sequence, a filmmaker can begin to theorise about some of the complex relationships between, for example, the present of the film becoming the past of representation and how the documenting of actors in performance becomes the fiction of a narrative being told. The rest of this section will focus specifically on the 'presence' of performers and the 'presence' of the drama they enact.

As spectators, we enter into the world of the drama through a variety of technical procedures such as the use by filmmakers of point-of-view shots and shot–reverse shot–dialogue conventions. Particularly interesting is the process by which we find ourselves, as it were, positioned within the illusory space of the film on screen, a process called interpellation.

In addition, as spectators we enter into a very distinctive kind of relationship to the actor – because while he or she is not physically present in front of us as in live theatre, by contrast the proximity we are offered is far more vivid. The most obvious cinematic practice in this regard is the close-up. The human face is lit and otherwise made up to look glamorous, dramatic, horrific, depending on the priorities of the film sequence. Roland Barthes wrote famously about Greta Garbo's face in his ground-breaking book in semiotic analysis, *Mythologies* (1957):

For more information see p. 151.

Garbo still belongs to that moment in cinema when capturing the human face still plunged audiences into the deepest ecstasy, when one literally lost oneself in a human image as one would a philtre, when the face represented a kind of absolute state of the flesh, which could be neither reached nor renounced.[34]

Writers on film aesthetics, such as Bela Balazs writing in the 1930s, saw the **close-up** as a key defining characteristic of cinema.[35] As a photographic image it is often highly stylised. In a Hollywood studio film, and in other popular cinemas, the close-up seems to offer the experience of a different order of time from narrative time. It is closer to what was described earlier as the moving image occupying a moment out of time, or rather its movement occupies its own time. Again, it can be said that the close-up represents that kind of cinematic intensity that we remember long after we have forgotten the narrative – or possibly even the name of the film.[36] Here we are again in that area of experience which has been called the poetics of presence.

close-up
Normally defined as a shot of the head from the neck up.

In 2000 Bill Viola began to produce moving image work studying the depth of emotion that can be captured on the human face. He uses actors who are presented in silence and in extreme slow motion. He shoots on high-speed 35mm film at 210 frames per second, almost seven times normal speed. This produces the extreme slow motion. The material is then transferred on to high-definition digital video for post-production enhancement of colour and texture. Indeed, the slow motion is so extreme that spectators may be forgiven for thinking that they are looking at still images brilliantly illuminated, replicating the effect of renaissance portrait paintings. (For example, *The Quintet of the Astonished* is based on Bosch's *Christ Crowned with Thorns*.) But there is movement – and the relation between movement and time becomes as fascinating as the images themselves. Or rather it is more accurate to say that the emotional shaping of these faces cannot be separated from the time of these emotions. In *Dolorosa 2000*, a man and a woman are shown in separate frames as a diptych. Both appear to be grieving, tears run down their faces – each is independent of the other and yet a relationship between them is unavoidable, as though they have separate but shared sorrows. We are aware of the emotions outside of any narrative context – rather we confront the pure singularity[37] of 'grief' as performed in the faces of this man and this woman actor. Again it may be observed that just as images can be locked into conventional time and into a sequence of events, so images can be extracted from this kind of time and take on a different kind of 'presence'.

• **Plate 1.4**
Man of Sorrows (Bill Viola, 2001). Colour video on freestanding LCD flat panel. Unlike in *Dolorosa*, here a single figure is used by Viola in a work that is part of a collection called *The Sorrows*. Photo: Mike Bruce, courtesy Anthony d'Offay, London

If the close-up was an early discovery of cinema (it may be found in films made at the beginning of the twentieth century[38]), a different kind of intense relationship with the actor came with the introduction of lightweight cameras which allowed for handheld filming. John Cassavetes' *Shadows* and Jean-Luc Godard's *A bout de souffle* were made within a year of each other in New York and Paris respectively at the end of the 1950s. They announce a different kind of film practice and with it a different kind of cinematic experience, one which appears more spontaneous, unpredictable, imperfect, exciting. It feels more like a live 'event' than previous attempts to replicate the drama of performance. This revolution in camera technology also encouraged new kinds of documentary practice: *cinéma vérité* in France, *direct cinema* in the States. In both approaches (and they not strictly speaking interchangeable with one another), the subject of the documentary appears for the first time to be entirely 'alive', apparently capable of exceeding whatever narrative functions may be imposed by the filmmaker.

A recent revival of interest in the work of John Cassavetes is timely.[39] As a filmmaker he was interested in the knowledge that would be discovered in the process of making his films, especially through his close working relationships with his actors, most notably Peter Falk, Ben Gazzarra and his wife, Gena Rowlands. Cassavetes was the opposite of the kind of filmmaker who has an 'answer' before they start their film, and whose film is conceived primarily in order to illustrate a thesis to the audience. He used to say what was the point in asking questions to which you already knew the answers.

All my life I've fought against clarity – all those stupid definitive answers. Phooey on a formula life, on slick solutions. It's never easy. I think it's only in the movies that it's easy .... I won't call [my work] entertainment. It's exploring. It's asking questions of people .... A good movie will ask you questions you haven't been asked before.[40]

Making films becomes a risk – and arguably watching them becomes a risk too. Cassavetes did not improvise, but rehearsal with his ensemble of carefully chosen actors was about collectively searching for forms of human drama and human expression that escaped conventional cinematic expression through narrative and generic conventions. (This is one reason why Cassavetes's films appear 'difficult' to many audiences.) With the emphasis on performance, the knowledge that Cassavetes seeks, and which the audience share in, is not necessarily the kind that can be verbalised – caught in speech – and which we refer to as 'ideas'. Rather there is a respect for the power of the medium to both excite and capture levels of emotion and understanding that may be expressed purely in body language, in gesture. It is knowledge as affect – knowledge as feeling. However, to repeat, these are not the feelings that are highly predictable within the structures of generic narratives, but rather the feelings that come from the electric flows of energy that we associate with the 'live' encounter. The real is never fixed, never precisely 'there' to be pinned down. Things appear provisional, transitional – and the role of the spectator is maybe less to reduce the complexities of human behaviour to a neat formula – but rather to bear witness to whatever is revealed.[41] While the performance-as-image may be most purely represented by the close-up referred to earlier, the kind of performance being described here is still one based on the sense of presence, of enactment in which the moment of performance has an intensity independent of the before and after of narrative.

Cassavetes often worked as his own camera operator – directing as he filmed. The handheld camera produces an effect of intimacy, but one very different from the composed close-up of narrative realist cinema (of what Deleuze called the cinema of the movement image). Just as interesting is the illusion of realism that comes from our associating the handheld camera with the 'aesthetic' of home moviemaking or a location news report. This is an example of the 'imperfect' appearing more authentic than the 'perfect'. The Dogme95 movement, with films such as *Festen*, *Idiots* and *Julien Donkey Boy*, is a more recent example of this 'imperfect' realism. We experience the dramatic world of the film through the handheld camera. (Dogme95 Rule 3: 'The camera must be handheld. Any movement or immobility attainable in the hand is permitted.')

Lars Von Trier's *Dogville* creates the heightened realism of the handheld camera effect while locating the actors within a studio set as described earlier. This contrast is important, as it suggests that a convincing 'as-if' live drama can be created using a certain kind of cinematography and staging. The 'presence' of the performances, enhanced by the style of shooting, persuades the spectator to grant the suspension of disbelief to a film that refuses many of the assumed requirements for producing cinematic realism.

Von Trier is, like most filmmakers, committed to narrative – and to the tale as told. There is a clear set of ideas that have been fully thought through in advance and the film sets out to illustrate them. (Though to be fair, Von Trier has a sense of humour – and is remarkably self-reflexive about cinema as a medium on to which any amount of random rules may be applied – like the rules of the Dogme95 manifesto.) The most telling feature of *Dogville* in the context of this discussion is that Von Trier has recourse throughout to a voice-over narrator. The tale is enacted – but it is also told.

The difference between Von Trier's *The Idiots* or *Dogville* and Cassavetes's films such as *A Woman Under the Influence* is that, whereas both filmmakers use handheld cameras to enhance the illusion that we are watching something from the past in the present that feels more like 'live' drama than conventional film representation, Von Trier uses drama in the service of narrative, the tale told – while for Cassavetes it is the opposite: there is just sufficient narrative framework to provide a context for enacted drama. Viola, in his portraits of human emotion, goes a stage further, placing the 'performance' outside of any narrative context to produce a kind of pure presence for the moving image of a type that we normally associate with painting. What we find here are different levels of commitment by filmmakers to the potential intensity of the image and to a willingness to dwell on the singularity of an emotion, brought from the past of its enactment into the present.

NARRATIVE, REALISM AND THE IMAGE

This chapter began by arguing that there is the need in film studies to begin to ask different kinds of questions, particularly ones that help us to better understand and appreciate some of the very special qualities of film that can so easily be bypassed if we concentrate on narrative and representational systems. Here the theme of the past in the present has opened up explorations into relationships between film and history, film and time and film and performance. In some ways they offer approaches to the old philosophical questions that do not go away – what is film and what kinds of knowledge can film provide?[42]

Michael Haneke's *Hidden* (2005) is a suspense film with a strong investment in narrative. Why things happen and who did what and what were their motives are central to the pleasure of the film – and exemplify our normal desire for narrative knowledge. But *Hidden* is one of those films that leave us in doubt about a question that precedes the others listed above. That question is: what happens? Here the mystery is in the image itself, in the inexplicable videotapes that keep arriving at the house of a married couple, the film's two central characters. In asking questions simply for narrative knowledge we find ourselves repeating the big fundamental questions about film mentioned above: precisely what is it – and what knowledge does it provide? We are not sure of the answer to either of these questions, as *Hidden* offers us a suspense film dependent on the uncomfortable ambiguity and indeterminacy of moving images.[43]

There is something deeply unsettling about what we are seeing if only because we cannot grasp a point of view from which what we see can be located and thus anchored. The sense of time created by the reinsertion of the past into the present through the videotapes unnerves our sense of the order of things – the past inhabits the present. The integrity of the performances is thrown into doubt by the inexplicable nature of what happens, so we are left wondering how composite and false are each of the central characters. Much of the normal stability that underlies a film – the sense of a story told – seems to have been removed. At the same time the sense of a story enacted leaves open the possibility that much of what we see is false. Although it is possible to rest content with a straightforward 'solution' (after two viewings!), there remains a lingering sense that as spectators we may have imposed coherence on moving images that actually may be impossible to make sense of.[44]

Sensitivity to the power and effect of the image also raises a whole set of complex issues about cinematic realism. It was suggested earlier that the close-up often creates the sense of 'time out' from the forward progression of the film, and similar claims can be made for the kind of cinematic performances referred to in the previous section. *Hidden* offers an example of the disturbance that is caused to the spectator when images with a different status are inscribed into a film. Vivian Sobchack writes of the particularly disturbing effect documentary footage can have when used in a fiction film, and refers particularly to a Bill Clinton press conference about the possible discovery of life on Mars used in *Contact* (1997).[45] She makes a useful distinction not just between the 'true' and the 'false', but between both of these and the 'irreal'. The irreal is a separate category, an area of experience where our normal judgements about what is real are suspended; it is precisely the space where we watch fictional films and the space we are only made conscious of when it is disturbed. Now it could be reasonably argued that the video material in *Hidden* is just part of the 'irreal' of the fiction film, like the video 'haunting' in the *Ring* horror series. However, in drawing attention to the production of images, to their indeterminate status, to their uncanny presence, they demonstrate how the foregrounding of the image may not only disrupt the sense of narrative continuity, but may throw into disarray our normal comfortable sense of what constitutes film realism.

CONCLUSION

This chapter has offered a variety of examples of film/video material that draw attention to the power of the image. In their different ways each makes film appear less familiar to us, more strange. This, it is suggested, is a basis for rediscovering film and for setting out some exploratory questions we may wish to engage within film studies.

NOTES

1 This sense of the film as a text has, in truth, marked the work of the present author – see *Understanding Film Texts* (London, BFI, 2000). However, there is an emphasis there on the experience of the spectator as someone who does more than 'read' the film 'text'.

2 Dogme95, the manifesto put forward by Lars Von Trier and colleagues in Denmark, demonstrated simultaneously that cinematic rules are entirely arbitrary and yet creatively useful.

3 See the BFI DVD *Electrical Edwardians – The Films of Mitchell and Kenyon*.

4 *Tarnation* was made for the suspiciously exact sum of $218.32, though infinitely more than this was spent on enhancing the soundtrack at George Lucas's Skywalker Studio and blowing the picture up to 35mm for a wide distribution following its success at the Sundance Festival.

5 *Film ist* is available on DVD – Index/DVD 012.

6 From Tom Gunning, *Film Ist: A Primer for a Visual World*, contained in the booklet accompanying the DVD. And available at:
http://www.sixpackfilm.com/archive/texte/01_filmvideo/filmiest_gunningE.html.

7 Benjamin's idea of the 'optical unconscious' is referred to in the Gunning essay. See Walter Benjamin, *The Work of Art in the Age of its Mechanical Reproduction*. This long quote is very rich:

Our bars and city streets, our offices and furnished rooms, our railroad stations and our factories seemed to close relentlessly about us. Then came film and exploded this prison-world with the dynamite of the split second, so that now we can set off calmly on journeys of adventure among its far-flung debris. With the close-up, space expands; with slow motion, movement is extended. And just as enlargement not merely clarifies what we see indistinctly 'in any case', but brings to light entirely new structures of matter, slow motion not only reveals familiar aspects of movements, but discloses quite unknown aspects within them – aspects 'which do not appear as the retarding of natural movements but have a curious gliding, floating character of their own'. Clearly it is another nature which speaks to the camera compared to the eye. 'Other' above all in the sense that a space informed by human consciousness gives way to a space informed by the unconscious. Whereas it is a commonplace that, for example, we have some idea what is involved in the act of walking (if only in general terms), we have no idea at all what actually happens during the split second when a person actually takes a step. We are familiar with the movement of picking up a cigarette lighter or a spoon, but know almost nothing of what really goes on between hand and metal, and still less how this varies with different moods. This is where the camera comes into play, with all its resources for swooping and rising, disrupting and isolating, stretching or compressing a sequence, enlarging or reducing an object. It is through the camera that we first discover the optical unconscious, just as we discover the instinctual unconscious through psychoanalysis. (*Walter Benjamin Selected Writings Volume 3: 1935–1938*, Cambridge, MA: Harvard University Press, 2002, p. 117).

8 Cubitt (2004) is referring to the American semiotician C.S. Pierce's distinction between three levels at which we make meaning: firstness, secondnesss and thirdness – which Cubitt goes on to reconfigure in terms of what he calls, in digital terms, the pixal, the cut and the vector.

9 Gunning (op. cit.).

10 Laura Mulvey's *Death 24x a Second*, London, Reaktion, 2006 is essential reading for an extension of many of the ideas raised here.

11 Laura Mulvey talks about the 'pensive spectator': 'The new technologies work on the body of film as mechanisms of delay, delaying the forward movement of narrative and taking the spectator into the past. Whatever its drive or desire, this look transforms perception of cinema just as the camera had transformed the human eye's perception of the world (op. cit, p.181).

12 The rhizomatic is associated with the work of Gilles Deleuze and Felix Guattari. They oppose the tree-like conventional shaping of thought and argument (the arborescent) to that of roots, tubors which go every which way. The rhizome is literally an underground stem that produces roots and shoots and is used by them to signify a more free association of thought than is normally associated with academic presentation. It is an overstatement to describe this chapter as rhizomatic, but the underpinning argument about the different ways we now associate images, drawing on hypertext models as part of our free play within the virtual justifies the introduction of the term.

The rhizome has no beginning or end; it is always in the middles, between things, interbeing, intermezzo. The tree is filiation, but the rhizome is alliance, uniquely alliance.

The tree imposes the verb "to be" but the fabric of the rhizome is the conjunction, "and ... and ... and ..." This conjunction carries enough force to shake and uproot the verb "to be". Where are you going? Where are you coming from? What are you heading for? These are totally useless questions (Deleuze and Guattari, *A Thousand Plateaus*, London: Athlone, 1988, p. 25).

13 See, for example, three different interpretations of German (Weimar) cinema in the 1920s. Siegfried Krakauer in his famous *From Caligari to Hitler* (1947) attempted to show that a body of films produced in the 1920s in Germany was symptomatic of an unconscious desire for totalitarian order – a desire for the coming Nazism. Lotte Eisner by contrast in *The Haunted Screen* (1952) saw many of the same films as illustrating a continuity out of the past of German folk culture and romanticism. Thomas Elsaesser in *Weimar Cinema and After* (2000) has no truck with either of these and argues that what was distinctive about films from this period may be explained by a conscious 'branding' by the German film industry in order to distinguish their product from that of other countries, particularly the United States.

14 For example, David Cook's *A History of Narrative Film* (4th edition), New York: Norton, 2004 and Kristin Thompson and David Bordwell's *Film History* (2nd edition), New York: McGraw-Hill, 2002.

15 Many historical accounts are based on a notion of development towards some better or even final state of completion. These are most likely to conform to story-narratives with their clear sense of arriving at an end-point in which all that went before was working towards that end.

16 Quentin Tarantino probably remains the archetypal cinephile director wishing to share with his cinephile audience a knowledge of popular cinema.

17 See n. 12 above.

18 The impact of critical theory on history has been profound. Gertrude Himmelfarb, a traditionally trained historian, is typical in struggling to find a way to maintain her working practices in relation to fundamental doubts about the very possibility of achieving an adequate representation of the past. (see 'Telling it as you like it: postmodernist history and the flight from fact' in Jenkins, 1997).

Reflective, cautious, but passionate about her subject, she identifies three 'fallibilities' in history – and each of these can certainly be mapped onto film history.

Fallibility of the historical record:

We are never able to retrieve or 'salvage' more than a proportion of what existed in the past – and what we are able to retrieve is often less reliable than we would like it to be for the purposes of the factual story we want to tell. For example, the majority of films made before 1930 are 'lost' –

that is, they no longer exist. We are left to construct a history of cinema based on the films that have survived or which archives have allowed to survive.

Fallibility of the historian:

Each of us writes with a particular intention to demonstrate some idea and communicate it persuasively. We tend to leave out examples that do not support our argument and put excessive emphasis on those examples that do. To produce a contradictory story (because the source material is endlessly contradictory!) or an incomplete story (because source material we need is missing) flies in the face of a commonsense notion of what it is to make sense of the past in narrative form. That historians produce competing

histories of the same bit of the past is a good thing – but it confirms the fallible nature of any particular historian's work. *Fallibility in the writing of history:*

The history we write is determined by conventions, by the discourse of history. A written history will need to be written according to the 'rules' that give respectability to it as a form of knowledge production. In the process the historian, aware of contemporary critical theory, will be acutely aware that in profound ways language does our thinking for us – we are limited in our thinking about a subject, in our conceptualising the issues and in our articulation of the 'story' by the communication structures and conventions that are available to us.

19 See, for example, Adrienne L. McLean's excellent *Being Rita Hayworth: Labour, Identity and Hollywood Stardom,* New Brunswick, NJ: Rutgers University Press, 2005. In looking at one particular star, McLean produces a 'thick' history of aspects of Hollywood in the 1940s and 1950s.

20 There are many possible examples of films that play on ideas of memory and time, some more successful and interesting than others from *Memento* (2000) through *Eternal Sunshine of the Spotless Mind* (2004) to *The Lake House* (2006); the two versions of *Solaris* are particularly to be recommended: directed by Tarkovsky (1972) and Soderbergh (2002).

21 Robert Rosenstone, 'The future of the past: film and the beginnings of postmodern history' in Vivian Sobchack (ed.), *The Persistence of History – Cinema, Television and the Modern Event*, London: Routledge, 1996.

22 Jacques Rancière (2006, p. 74).

23 At this point the objections of tradition historians should be voiced. To freely associate disparate material in such a subjective way is to fly in the face of the 'discipline' of history. See ns 12 and 17 above.

24 Op. cit., p. 161.

25 See James Agee and Walker Evans's *Let Us Now Praise Famous Men* (London: Penguin, 2006) – the book that made famous these images. In 1933, the new President, Franklin D. Roosevelt, passed legislation to deal with unemployment in the wake of the Depression. It was the foundation for Roosevelt's 'New Deal'. Among the measures taken was the setting up of the Farm Security Administration (FSA) in 1935 to support small farmers. Roy Stryker was appointed to organise a photographic collection of the FSA work. To carry this out he employed a small group of photographers that included among others Russell Lee, Dorothea Lange, Arthur Rothstein, Walker Evans, Russell Lee, John Vachon, Carl Mydans and Ben Shahn (see later references to Lars Von Trier's *Dogville*).

26 The sound stage used was in Sweden. There is a particular point to Von Trier making a film about the United States using well-known American actors in Europe. A documentary about the making of the film, *Dogville Confessions*, is in some respects as disturbing as *Dogville* itself.

27 The photographs used are credited to Russell Lee, Dorothea Lange, Jack Collier, A Siegel, Ben Shahn, Carl Mydans, John Vachon and Arthur Rothstein.

28 Gilles Deleuze: *Cinema 1 – The Movement Image* and *Cinema 2 – The Time Image*.

29 As we have already made claims for something similar happening in Ford's pre-1945 film *The Grapes of Wrath*, perhaps we should emphasise that Deleuze's time line should be seen as indicative rather than a strict periodising of film history. Of course, many films representing the 'movement image' continued to be made after 1945 – indeed, they still represent the dominant form of popular cinema. But it also

has to be said that many beautiful examples of the 'time image' are to be found in films from the very earliest days of cinema. In addition, it should be said that many films which are primarily examples of the 'movement image' contain individual sequences in which the film seems to escape the narrative and genre requirements, even if only in celebrating the star's presence.

30 Mulvey (op. cit., Ch. 6): 'it was dismissed on release, with only a few critics understanding that it was carefully constructed to undermine conventions of narrative and open out space and time for thought' (p.105).

31 Rancière (2006) claims that 'In *Histoire(s) du cinéma*, Godard announces a poetics – of pure presence'. He argues that Godard accuses the cinema of having betrayed its specific role as a medium of poetic presence through its preoccupation with narrative, with the 'movement image' of mainstream cinema (p.179).

32 See, for example, *Everything You Always Wanted to Know About Lacan: (But Were Afraid to Ask Hitchcock)*, edited by Slavoj Zizek, London: Verso, 1992.

33 Gilberto Perez (1998, p. 37).

34 Roland Barthes, *Mythologies* (London: Vintage, 1993).

35 'Bela Balasz, from *Theory of the Film; The Close-up; The Face of Man*' in Gerald Mast, Leo Braudy and Marshall Cohen (eds) *Film Theory and Criticism: Introductory Readings.*

36 Close-ups can have powerful and disruptive effects on a narrative realist film. Good examples of this may be found in Rita Hayworth film noirs from the 1940s – *Gilda* and *Lady from Shanghai*. In the latter we are presented with a close-up of the Rita Hayworth character lying horizontally, motionless on the deck of a yacht at night, singing. This close-up was a contractual obligation, a necessary part of Hayworth's function as 'star', but the director Orson Welles exploits the inherent strangeness of the glamour close-up to further disturb the audience's already uncomfortable relationship to the fictional world of this film.

37 Singularity is another Deleuzian term. It communicates the idea of that which is left unnoticed or deliberately ignored because it does not fit into some pre-given structure of thought or category of being. The singular is the unaccountable anomaly. As part of a liberationist philosophy, Deleuze uses the singular as a nodal point for what may simply happen, an occurrence full of chance possibilities. Not just Viola's highly formalist moving image work but even more so, Cassavetes' feature films seem full of these singularities.

38 See the BFI DVD compilation *Early Cinema – Primitives and Pioneers.*

39 See the documentary *The Constant Forge* (Kiselyak, US, 2004) – included in the Criterion five-DVD box set of Cassavetes' films.

40 Quoted in Tom Charity, *John Cassavetes – Lifeworks*, London: Omnibus, 2001.

41 George Kouvaros asks the question in the title of his book – *Where Does It Happen?: John Cassavetes and Cinema at the Breaking Point* (University of Minnesota Press, 2004).

42 These are ontological questions (what is film?) and epistemological questions (what kind of knowledge can film provide?).

43 In relation to Hidden, it is perhaps productive to return to Benjamin's idea of an 'optical unconscious' (see n. 5 above).

44 Another view is that Haneke is simply playing 'funny games' (to use the title of another of his films) with the audience.

45 See Vivian Sobchack, *Carnal Thoughts: Embodiment and Moving Image Culture*, Berkeley: University of California Press, 2004, ch. 10. This disturbance of the 'irreal' draws attention to the imaginary world we enter as spectators. This can be taken further through what Deleuze called 'the power of the false' (*Cinema 2 – the Time Image*, p.131).

FURTHER READING

The following are the books that have most directly informed this chapter. None of them give up their ideas easily and you may well find that thinking through the ideas raised in this chapter by reference to films that you know and are fascinated by is the best way of developing your understanding, before turning to these books at a later stage.

Cubitt, Sean, *The Cinema Effect*, MIT Press, Cambridge, MA, 2004.

Deleuze, Gilles, *Cinema 2: The Time-Image*, Athlone Press, London, 1989.

Mulvey, Laura, *Death 24x a Second*, Reaktion, London, 2006.

Perez, Gilberto, *The Material Ghost*, MD, Johns Hopkins University Press, Baltimore, 1998.

Rancière, Jacques, *Film Fables*, Berg, Oxford, 2006.

More advanced even than these are:

Sobchack, Vivian, *Carnal Thoughts: Embodiment and Moving Image Culture*, University of California Press, Berkeley, 2004.

Stewart, Garrett, *Between Film and Screen: Modernism's Photo Synthesis* University of Chicago Press, Chicago, IL, 1999.

Two useful books informing the study of film history, both in the text and in the notes, are:

Allen, Robert and Gomery, Douglas, *Film History: Theory and Practice*, McGraw-Hill, New York, 1985.

Jenkins, Keith (ed.), *The Postmodern History Reader*, Routledge, London, 1997.

Reading on case studies referred to in this chapter include:

Sellars, Peter and Walsh, John (eds), *Bill Viola:*

The Passions, Getty Trust Publications, Los Angeles, CA, 2003.

Mora, Gilles and Brannan, Beverly, *FSA: The American Vision*, Harry N. Abrams, New York, 2006.

Other titles are referred to in the notes.

FURTHER VIEWING

It is important to move away from the idea that there are films and then there are books of film theory. The films listed below are all in their different ways forms of theoretical work in film. Films themselves are the best 'essays' in film theory that we have.

Introduction: film is

Film ist (Deutsch, Austria, 2005)
Tarnation (Coulette, US, 2005)

Non-linear film history

A Personal Journey with Martin Scorsese Through American Movies (Scorsese, UK/US, 1995)
Histoire(s) du Cinema (Godard, France, 1998) released on DVD by Gaumont, France, in 2006

The image as document in time

The American Civil War (Burns, US, 1990)

The West (Burns, US, 1996)
Dogville (Von Trier, US, 2003)
Hiroshima mon amour (Resnais, France, 1959)
Days of Being Wild (Wong Kar Wai, Hong Kong, 1991)

Performance: image and intensity

A bout de souffle/Breathless (Godard, France, 1959)
Shadows (Cassavetes, US, 1959)
A Woman Under the Influence (Cassavetes, US, 1974)
Bill Viola: The Eye of the Heart (Kidel, UK, 2004)
(This is a documentary – Viola's *The Sorrows* is not available on DVD – also see 'Further reading' above).

Narrative, realism and the image

Caché/Hidden (Haneke, France, 2005)

RESOURCE CENTRES

Websites that you may find useful include:
http://www.film-philosophy.com
   Film philosophy.
http://www.sensesofcinema.com
   Senses of cinema.

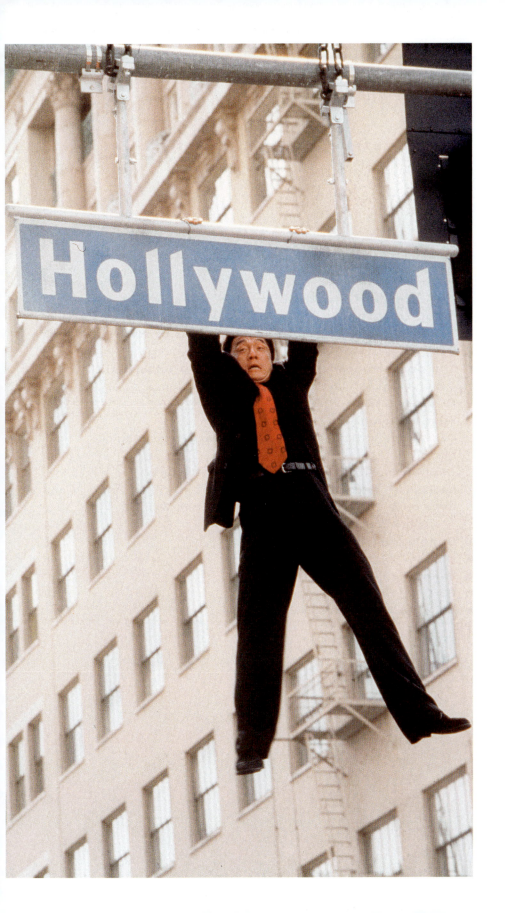

Part two

Cinema as institution – industries, technologies and audiences

Chapter 2

The industrial contexts of film production

Searle Kochberg

■ The industrial contexts of film production

INTRODUCTION

Films do not exist in a vacuum: they are conceived, produced, distributed and consumed within specific economic and social contexts.

The chapter that follows is a journey through the mainstream institutional frameworks of US and UK film. The American film industry has dominated all others for the past 100 years and for this reason the section largely centres around it. I do not claim the itinerary to be definitive, but I have sought to cite some key issues in the socio-economic infrastructure of American and British film.

The origins and consolidation of the American industry are traced from 1895 to 1930, a period which saw a fledgling industry harness new industrial practices and quickly grow into an important popular medium, organised into highly defined exhibition, production and distribution components.

The Hollywood studio era (1930 to 1949) is the next stop on the tour. Monopolistic practice and the finely tuned industrial organisation of the Hollywood 'factories' are discussed at some length. This section looks specifically at Warner Brothers as an example of a vertically integrated film company during the studio era.

There follows an exploration of the contemporary institutional framework of US (global) and UK commercial film, starting with a review of the position of the 'Majors' in the light of multi-media empires, new media technologies and (mainstream) independent production. In the chapter, the production/distribution history of *Gladiator* (2000) is taken as a case study.

For discussion of Gladiator and classical cinema see pp. 82–4.

The chapter ends with a review of audiences for film, and the context of viewing, from the 1940s onwards. The case studies are taken from the recent past, and are *The Blair Witch Project* (1999) and *Trainspotting* (1996).

THE ORIGINS OF THE AMERICAN FILM INDUSTRY (1900 TO 1915)

The American film industry has been in existence as long as there has been American film. This section looks at how the film industry organised itself into three main divisions in the early years of this century, divisions that exist to this day – **exhibition, distribution and production**.

Exhibition until 1907

By 1894, the exhibition of moving pictures had been established in New York City with the introduction of the box-like kinetoscope. This allowed an individual customer to watch a 50-foot strip of film through a slit at the top of the machine. In 1895, a projector called the Pantopticon was demonstrated, again in NYC, and for the first time more than one person could watch the same moving images simultaneously.

Once projectors were available, single-reel films started to be shown in vaudeville theatres as novelties. Exhibition outlets began to multiply and by the first years of the last century small high street stores and restaurants were being converted into small-scale cinemas or nickelodeons. As the name suggests, the cost of entry to these cinemas was 5 cents – an amount affordable to the (predominantly) working-class audiences of nickelodeons. By the end of 1905 there were an estimated 1,000 of these theatres in America and by 1908 there were 6,000.

exhibition
Division of the film industry concentrating on the public screening of film.

distribution
Division concentrating on the marketing of film, connecting the producer with the exhibitor by leasing films from the former and renting them to the latter.

production
Division concentrating on the making of film.

• **Plate 2.1**
A nickolodeon (5 cents
entry fee) in New
York City in the first
decade of the twentieth
century. Converted high
street stores like this
one were typical of the
first cinemas

Distribution until 1907

As the film industry expanded, exhibitors had a growing commercial need for an
unbroken supply of films to show. To meet this need, the first film exchange was in
operation by 1902 and acted as a go-between for the producers and exhibitors (Balio
1976: 14). The exchanges purchased (later leased) films from producers and distributed
films to exhibitors by renting to them. By 1907 there were between 125 and 150 film
exchanges covering the whole of the USA.

Production until 1907

Until 1900 the average length of films was around 50 feet. Three major companies
dominated production in the US: Edison, Biograph and Vitagraph. Although filming on
location was very common at this stage, as early as 1893 the world's first 'kinetographic
theatre' or film studio was in operation. This was built by the Edison Company and called
the 'Black Maria'.

After 1900, films started to get longer, and by 1903, films of 300 to 600 feet were fairly
common. The Edison Company's *The Great Train Robbery* (1903) was over 1,000 feet
long (ibid.: 7–9) and is an example of early cinema utilising increased running time and
primitive continuity editing to tell, for then, a fairly ambitious story. By this time there were
several major film producers in the USA, including (as well as the companies mentioned
above) Selig, Kalem, Essanay and Lubin. These companies ensured their dominant
position in the industry by holding patents in camera and projection equipment.

The industrial organisation of film production until 1907 has been referred to as the
'cameraman' system of production (Bordwell *et al.* 1985: 116–17). As the name suggests,
films were largely the creation of one individual, the cameraman, who would be responsible for planning, writing, filming and editing. Edwin Porter, working for the Edison
Company, is a good example of such a craftsman.

Thus, by 1907, the American film industry was already organised into three main
divisions: exhibition, distribution and production. The creation of these separate

kinetograph
Edison's first movie
camera

commercial divisions demonstrates pragmatic, commercial streamlining by a very young industry, which was designed to maximise profits in an expanding market.

The Motion Picture Patents Company and industry monopolies (1908 to 1915)

In 1908, the Edison and Biograph companies attempted to control the fledgling film industry through the key patents they held in camera and projection technology. They set up the Motion Picture Patents Company, a **patent pool**, which issued licences for a fee to companies on a discretionary basis. Only licensed firms could legally utilise technology patented by or contracted to the MPPC without fear of litigation. The MPPC was soon collecting royalties from all sectors of the industry, including manufacturers of equipment, film producers and exhibitors. The MPPC's ultimate ambition was to monopolise the film industry in the US Its goal was a situation in which films would be shot on patented cameras, distributed through its General Film Company and screened on its patented projectors.

patent pool
An association of companies, operating collectively in the marketplace by pooling the patents held by each individual company.

Exhibition and audience during the MPPC era

An important contribution to the profits of the MPPC was from the licensing of projection equipment to exhibitors. In 1908 the most important exhibition outlet was the nickelodeon.

The year 1910 marked the peak of the nickelodeon theatre, with an estimated 26,000,000 people attending the 10,000 'nickels' in the continental US every week (Balio 1976: 63). The meteoric rise of the nickel theatres was remarkable and reflected the general expansion of popular entertainment during America's prosperous start to the twentieth century. Enormous expansion in film exhibition occurred throughout the USA and inner-city locations were particularly important due to their concentrated populations. The growth of the nickelodeon in large American cities has been well documented and may in part be attributable to mass working-class immigration to the US at the time (Allen and Gomery 1995: 202–5).

The exhibition industry understood that its successful future lay in securing a wide audience-base. It appears to have accomplished this even in its nickelodeon years, by successfully positioning nickels in middle-class as well as working-class districts. Exhibitors realised, however, that even greater profit lay in larger theatres and more ambitious narratives. As early as 1909, large movie theatres were being constructed. Film producers were also being encouraged by exhibitors to provide films that would appeal to middle- as well as working-class audiences, including 'women's' stories and one-reel adaptations of literary classics. This process continued to gather momentum in the final years of the MPPC era, when large luxurious theatres began to supplant the nickels in movie exhibition, and audiences reached 49,000,000 per week (Balio 1976: 75). Feature-length films at an average length of four to six reels also became established.

Distribution in the MPPC era

Soon after its inception, the MPPC turned its attention to film distribution and licensed 70 per cent of the film exchanges operating in the US By 1910, the MPPC had set up its own distribution company – the General Film Company – which soon had nationwide cover through the purchase of forty-eight key exchanges in the US (Elsaesser 1990: 192–3). By 1911, the MPPC had constructed the first effective example of **vertical integration** in the film industry through a combination of takeovers and patent rights.

Changing conditions were soon to challenge the MPPC's supreme position in the industry. First, independent distributors, exhibitors and producers quickly and successfully organised themselves in response to the MPPC's attempted monopoly.[1] Then, a

vertical integration
Where a company is organised so that it oversees a product from the planning/ development stage, through production, through market distribution, through to the end-user – the retail consumer. In the case of the film industry, this translates to a company controlling production, marketing and exhibition of its films.

trust
A group of companies operating together to control the market for a commodity. This is illegal practice in the USA.

charge of anti-**trust** violation was filed against the MPPC by the Department of Justice in 1912. The outcome of the case (announced in 1915) was that the MPPC was ordered to break up. Ironically, by this time, other vertically integrated companies were being organised within the industry (see next section).

Production during the MPPC era

The years 1908 to 1915 were not only marked by the rise and fall of the industrial giant – the Motion Picture Patents Company – but also by the rise of the multi-reel feature film and the relative demise of the single-reel film. Greater length and greater narrative complexity coincided with the application of scientific management principles to the industrial organisation of film production.

By 1908, the 'cameraman' system of production had already been discarded and replaced by the 'director system' (1907–1909) (Bordwell et al 1985: 113–20). For the first time a director was responsible for overseeing a group of operative workers, including the cameraman. The director was central to the planning, filming and editing stages of film-making. Production was centralised in a studio/factory, permitting greater control of production, thus keeping costs down. Around 1909, this system was in turn discarded in favour of the 'director–unit' system (ibid.: 121–7). Directors were now in charge of autonomous production units within companies, each with a separate group of workers. Companies were subdivided into various departments, for ever greater productivity and efficiency, informed no doubt by the then current 'scientific management' model of labour and workshop organisation popularised by F.W. Taylor.

By the end of the MPPC era, the 'central producer' system (ibid.: 128–41) had been introduced, which was to dominate as a model in production management until the start of the studio era around 1930. This was a fully structured hierarchical system, with a strict 'scientific' division of labour. Production-line filmmaking was now the order of the day, all under the central control of a producer who used very detailed shooting scripts to plan budgets before giving the go-ahead to studio projects.

Summary

During the first twenty years of its life, the film industry increased in scale from a cottage-scale enterprise to an established mass popular medium. Its rapid and enormous growth was largely driven by the explosion in exhibition, which in turn triggered a streamlining in distribution methods and the industrialisation of production. The predominant position of exhibition within the industry was also to be a hallmark of the studio era of American film.

THE STUDIO ERA OF AMERICAN FILM (1930 TO 1949)

This section looks at the studio era of film production. By 1930 the film industry in America was dominated by five companies – all vertically integrated – known as the 'Majors' or the 'Big Five': Warner Brothers, Loew's–MGM, Fox, Paramount and Radio-Keith-Orpheum (RKO). Three smaller companies, the 'Little Three', were also part of the **oligopoly**: Columbia, Universal (both with production and distribution facilities) and United Artists (a distribution company for independent producers).

oligopoly
Where a state of limited competition exists between a small group of producers or sellers.

The origins of the studio-era oligopoly

Vertical integration made sense to the power brokers of the film industry: companies with the financial resources to organise themselves in this way stood to dominate the market-place through their all-pervasive influence and their ability to block out competition.

Despite the alarm bells of the MPPC anti-trust case in 1915, film companies continued to seek out legal ways to construct vertically integrated companies through mergers and acquisitions. In December 1916 an industry merger occurred which became the corner-stone of the future Hollywood studio era. This involved the Famous Players and Jesse L. Lasky production companies and Paramount, a distribution company. By 1920 Famous Players–Lasky (as the new company was called) had established a pre-eminent position in the American film industry with the purchase of theatre chains throughout the US and Canada (Gomery 1986: 26–8).

The trend set by Famous Players–Lasky was soon copied elsewhere in the industry. In 1922 the distribution–exhibition giant First National became vertically integrated with the construction of a large production facility in Burbank, California (Balio 1976: 114).[2] By 1924 Loew's Incorporated, the major exhibition firm, had acquired both Metro Pictures (producer–distributor) and Goldwyn Pictures (producer–exhibitor). Henceforth, Loew's production subsidiary would be known as Metro–Goldwyn–Mayer (MGM) (Gomery 1986: 54–5).

Exhibition during the studio era

Exhibition continued to be the most powerful and influential branch of the American film industry during the studio era. The reason for this was simple: it was where the money was made. Reflecting this, the Majors channelled most of their investment into exhibition, which accounted for 90 per cent of the Majors' total asset value during the years 1930 to 1949 (ibid.: 14).

In spite of the fact that the Majors owned only 15 per cent of the movie theatres in the US, they collected approximately 75 per cent of exhibition revenues in the US during the studio era (ibid.: 12, 18). This was possible because the Big Five film companies owned 70 per cent of the **first-run** movie houses in the US during this period. Their numbers were relatively small, but the first-run theatres accounted for most of the exhibition revenue due to their very large seating capacity (on average over 1,200 seats), prime locations (in key urban sites) and higher price of admission. The Majors further strengthened their grip on exhibition by 'encouraging' the (30 per cent) independent first-run theatres to book their films, sight unseen, to the exclusion of competitors (see below). By bowing to the wishes of the Majors, the independents safeguarded their access to the Majors' popular films. All in all, it was the Majors' control of cinemas during the years of vertical integration that ensured their profits.

first-run
Important cinemas would show films immediately upon their theatrical release (or their 'first-run'). Smaller, local theatres would show films on subsequent runs, hence the terms second-run, third-run.

The successful theatre chains

By the 1920s, American innovations in national wholesaling and chain-store retailing had been absorbed into cinema exhibition methods. The introduction of scientific management methods and economies of scale led to the building up of chains of theatres, lower per-unit costs and faster, more efficient operations.

By far the most financially successful and innovative of the exhibition companies in the lead-up to the studio era was Balaban and Katz, with corporate headquarters in Chicago (until taken over by Paramount in 1925). Its success influenced the whole exhibition industry, especially at the top end of the market. Key innovations of Balaban and Katz included locating cinemas in outlying business and residential areas as well as downtown, building large, ornate, air-conditioned movie palaces (trips to which were 'events' in themselves for movie-goers), and accompanying screen presentations with quality vaudeville acts (Gomery 1992:40–56).

The 1930s and 1940s saw a continuation of the scientific management practices inaugurated by innovators like Balaban and Katz. Changes were made in exhibition during the studio era, some a direct result of the fall in attendance brought about by the Great Depression which followed the Wall Street Crash of 1929. Vaudeville acts were eliminated in all but the grandest of movie houses and replaced by talkie shorts, new movie theatres were less elaborate, double bills were introduced, air-conditioning was more universally adopted, and food and drink stands – in the form of popcorn (pre-Second World War onwards) and Coke/Pepsi (post-Second World War) – were introduced into foyers. These concession stands became, and were to remain, major profit earners for exhibitors right up until the present day.

The war years (1941 to 1945) and the immediate postwar period were to mark the heyday of studio-era exhibition in the US, with 1946 bringing in the greatest profits for the Big Five.

Distribution during the studio era

The distribution of films in America was effectively controlled by the Big Five during the studio era, even though the Little Three were also heavily engaged in the distribution business. The reason for this lay in the Majors' complete domination of exhibition. To ensure access for their films to the nationwide cinema network controlled by the Majors, the Little Three went along with the distribution system of the Big Five. Areas were zoned by the Majors, and theatres designated first-run, second-run and so on. The average period between runs, or clearance, was thirty days or more.

When booking films into their own theatres, each of the Majors ensured that precedence was given to their own product, followed by films of the other Majors. Any exhibition slots still available would be allocated to the Little Three. Finally, in distributing films to independent theatres, the Big Five and Little Three utilised a system of advance block-booking (films booked en masse and in advance).[3] Under this system, independent exhibitors were forced to book a full year's feature-film output of an individual film company, sight unseen, in order to secure likely box-office hits (Gomery 1992: 67–9).

For further discussion of stars and marketing, see Chapter 6, pp. 129–30.

It is worth noting that genre films and star vehicles of the studio era owed their popularity with distributors and exhibitors to the fact that they were useful marketing tools for distributors – providing marketing 'hooks' on which to hang a campaign – and at the same time helped provide box-office insurance for exhibitors, providing product recognition and differentiation for audiences.

Production during the studio era

By the onset of the studio era, the major movie factories were each producing an average of fifty features per year to satisfy the voracious demands of the highly profitable exhibition end of the business. As in other areas of the film industry, production management was 'scientific': film studios were organised as assembly-line plants with strict divisions of labour and hierarchies of authority.

As early as 1931, Hollywood Majors had begun to move away from the central-producer system which had dominated production since 1915. Columbia Pictures was the first company to announce the adoption of a producer–unit system in October 1931. Under the new organisational framework, the company appointed a head of production to oversee the running of the studio. Several producers were then appointed under the head, and each had the job of supervising the production of a group of films and of delivering the films on completion to the head of production (Bordwell et al 1985: 321).

Those firms that adopted the new system (not all did)[4] were convinced that it was an advance in scientific management for several reasons. First, it was felt that the system saved money, since it allowed each producer to keep a closer control of individual budgets (overseeing far fewer films than a central producer). Second, the system was felt to foster 'better quality' films, and encourage specialisms in individual units, by investing in the creativity of the delegated producers.

Certain production units were associated with particular genres: Jerry Wald's unit at Warner Brothers specialised in noir-melodrama, e.g. *Mildred Pierce* (1945); Arthur Freed's unit at Metro–Goldwyn–Mayer specialised in the integrated musical, e.g. *Meet Me in St. Louis* (1944).

Contracts and unions

It was standard studio practice during the 1930s and 1940s to employ personnel on long-term or permanent contracts. Workers' unions had firmly established themselves in American film production by the early years of the Roosevelt administration (in the mid-1930s) under the auspices of the **National Recovery Administration (NRA)** and the Wagner Act (Gomery 1986: 10). Ironically, by defining and enforcing rigidly delineated areas of responsibility for specific jobs to protect their members' jobs, the unions were directly instrumental in reinforcing the hierarchical structure of film production practice.

Stars

Long before the 1930s, a whole subsidiary industry of fan magazines and gossip columns in popular newspapers had grown up, promoting the Hollywood 'dream factory', its films and its stars. This continued throughout the studio era, fuelled by the publicity machines of the film companies themselves.

Long-term contracts (normally seven years in duration) secured the ongoing services of stars for the film companies. This was key to the financial security of the corporations since the acting ability and personality of the stars provided added value to the films in which they appeared. Why? Because stars helped differentiate films that were otherwise very standard in content and format. Their popularity reinforced consumer brand loyalty for the films of individual film companies, and provided the Majors with the necessary 'carrot' with which to entice independent exhibitors into booking blocks of films sight unseen (or 'blind').

NRA
National Recovery Administration) programme – 1930s' government programme designed to rescue the American economy from the Great Depression (commonly known as the 'New Deal').

For further discussion of the star see chapter 6.

• **Plate 2.2**
An aerial view of Paramount's production facility in Hollywood in the 1930s. This studio was one of the most modern talking-picture production plants in the world. It covered an area of 26 acres, had fourteen sound stages on the grounds, and had a working population of 2,000 people

Summary

During the Hollywood studio era, a small group of manufacturers-cum-distributors-cum-retailers controlled the film market between them. Smaller US producers were forced to make do with subsequent-run cinemas in which to show their films or to arrange distribution deals with the Big Five and Little Three. Likewise, foreign films could not get a foothold in the US unless they too had arrangements with one of the eight US film companies comprising the oligopoly. Examples of UK production companies that had US distribution through the studio era were London Films (distributing through UA), Imperator Films (distributing through RKO) and the Rank Organisation (distributing through Universal).

It wasn't until after 1948 that the Majors were forced to divest themselves of their cinema chains, as a result of the Supreme Court's decision in the Paramount anti-trust case (see next section).

☐ CASE STUDY 1: WARNER BROTHERS

From its origins as a small production company in the mid-1920s, Warner Brothers rose to become one of the five major vertically integrated film companies by the end of the decade. This was largely achieved through debt-financing – expansion financed through loans. Key to Warner's exponential growth were the following financial deals: its takeover of Vitagraph Corporation (with distribution and production facilities) in 1925, its exclusive licensing of Western Electric sound equipment for 'talking pictures' in 1926, and its purchase of the Stanley Company cinema chain with its associated film company First National in 1928.

Warner Brothers was the first of the Majors to establish the commercial viability of sound in film, and until the onset of the Depression (late 1929) its huge corporate debt (due to corporate expansion) was more than held in check by the enormous profits generated by its first 'talkies'. Starting in 1926, its corporate subsidiary for sound productions, Vitaphone Corporation, premiered Vitaphone 'shorts' and the first Hollywood 'feature' with recorded musical accompaniment, *Don Juan*. This was followed in 1927 by the release of Warner's first feature-length part-talkie, *The Jazz Singer*, and in 1928 by the release of its first all-talkie feature, *The Lights of New York*.

The Great Depression seriously weakened Warner's financial base. While big profits were being generated at the box office, the company could carry its enormous debt-load. However, after 1930 box-office takings fell off so sharply that the company began to lose money and had difficulty meeting its loan commitments. Warner was not to show a profit again until 1935.[5]

Its response to the financial crisis was to sell off assets (e.g. cinemas), introduce production units (to help control film budgets) and make feature films as cheaply as possible.[6] Its series of studio-bound, fast-paced, topical films in the early 1930s were the direct result of this corporate policy.

By 1935, the fortunes of the company had improved sufficiently for it to return to profit again. As profits increased, so did film budgets. Studio genres changed too, with the entrenchment of the melodrama, biopic, Merrie England and film noir genres in the late 1930s and early 1940s. As with the other Majors, profits reached record levels for Warner during and immediately after the Second World War.

Warner as auteur during the studio era (its authorial style)

For further discussion of auteur theory read Chapter 4.

As discussed already, film production during the studio era was all about standardised assembly-line manufacturing practice. This is why there is such impressive consistency in the physical make-up of the classic Hollywood film of the period. However, individual film companies also needed to differentiate their products if they were to develop brand loyalty in their customers. Differentiation was partly a reflection of financial profiles of individual companies and partly a reflection of corporate worldview/ideology.

Throughout the studio era, Warner established and consolidated a house style based on casting, subject, treatment and technical standards: all evident across the work of different (contract) directors and across genres. Senior management control was very strong. Staff workers were assigned projects by management, they did not choose them. Indeed, management retained ultimate authority on all matters concerning productions, including control over the final cut, much to the chagrin of directors and stars.

Yet despite the authoritarian management style, ironically Warner's films of the studio era articulate a populist, liberal ethos. Several productions of the early 1930s were hard-hitting social critiques of the then Republican administration. The tone changes, however, from 1933 onwards, as Warner discards its anti-government position in favour of support for the new Roosevelt (Democratic) administration and its NRA programme (popularly known as the 'New Deal'). The ultimate endorsement of the NRA and Roosevelt must be *Footlight Parade* (1933), with its 'Shanghai Lil' dance routine incorporating images of the NRA eagle and Roosevelt, and its leading protagonist (played by James Cagney) apparently inspired by Roosevelt himself![7]

From the mid-1930s onwards, the radical streak in Warner's films is somewhat muted, no doubt reflective of the ideological change in America, changing from a climate of confrontation in the early to mid-1930s, to one of conciliation by the end of the decade. And profits were up again: the company was back 'in the black' by 1935, leading perhaps to greater conservatism in the boardroom, less risk-taking, and a desire for middle-brow respectability. Certainly the shift to costume drama (in the mid- to late 1930s) would suggest this. Whatever, Warner's liberal voice did continue throughout the 1930s and into the War Years (1941 to 1945), its support of the Roosevelt administration unabated. Seen today, the company's films of the studio era retain an 'edge' not really apparent in the films of any of the other Majors, except perhaps RKO in the 1940s.

• **Plate 2.3**
Still from *Footlight Parade* (Lloyd Bacon, 1933). James Cagney's character at the helm in this NRA-inspired musical

• **Plate 2.4**
Still from *Mildred Pierce* (Michael Curtiz, 1945). This shot typifies the studio-bound cinematographic style and art direction of Warner during the studio era. The scene, photographed by Ernest Haller, is shot with low-key lighting; the art direction by Anton Grot conveys an impression of a quayside through its use of space, shadow, silhouette and perspective.

Warner Brothers (like most of the major film companies of the studio era) specialised in particular genres. Up till the mid-1930s, the company concentrated on low-budget contemporary urban genres such as the gangster cycle, the social conscience film and the fast-talking comedy/drama. The one costly genre that Warner specialised in during this period was the musical. Later, from the mid-1930s onwards, new genres began to dominate: the Merrie England cycle, the biopic, the melodrama and the film noir.

As one might expect, Warner's roster of players during the studio era reflected to a large extent the studio's reputation for straightforwardness and toughness. It is worth noting that Warner's stars tended to be very genre-specific; e.g. Bette Davis = melodrama, James Cagney = gangster film/musical, Humphrey Bogart = gangster film/film noir.

Costume design at Warner was to a large degree in keeping with the contemporary stories of many of its films. The studio's principal designers, Orry-Kelly for instance, designed modern clothes for ordinary people, in keeping with Warner's edgy urban image.

The factory-like regimentation of Warner's production methods meant that its studio style inevitably overwhelmed the individual creative talents of its contract directors. Pressure of work and division of labour meant that there was little active collaboration on projects between director and editor, or director and writer (Campbell 1971: 2). Directors were assigned projects and as soon as their task was done they were moved on to others, leaving editors to complete the post-production work. It is thus particularly problematic to assign to Warner's contract directors such as Michael Curtiz, William Keighley, Mervyn Le Roy and Raoul Walsh[8] individual authorship of their films. Warner's films too had a 'fast' editing style, particularly evident in the early to mid-1930s. Narratives were developed in a rapid succession of scenes, with extensive use of classic Hollywood montage sequences. The overall effect was one of dynamism and compression of time.

Warner's art direction again reflected a low-cost policy: location work was avoided, films were designed around a studio-bound look and sets were regularly reused. The work of Anton Grot, a major art director at Warner during the studio era, typifies the studio style. His sets were designed to convey a mood. To this end his storyboards suggested camera and lighting strategies. The sets were not literal reproductions of life, but instead used shadow, silhouette and angular perspective.[9] He is quoted as saying,

'I for one do not like extremely realistic sets. I am for simplicity and beauty and you can achieve that only by creating an impression' (Deschner 1975: 22). The end result was art direction that was both economic and atmospheric, and in total sympathy with the studio's cinematography. Here, studio cameramen such as Tony Gaudio (see e.g. *The Adventures of Robin Hood* (1938)), Sol Polito (see e.g. *Now Voyager* (1942)), and Ernest Haller (see e.g. *Mildred Pierce* (1945)) reinforced the art direction of people like Grot, utilising a visual style based on low-key lighting, with a propensity for night scenes. Necessity is the mother of invention, and this corporate strategy for economic but effective mise-en-scène soon set the standard for generic conventions across the industry (particularly in film noir, the gangster film and in the swashbuckler).

Finally, most people could recognise Warner's films even with their eyes shut! If in other areas of production the byword was economy, here grandeur was the order of the day. Warner's composers of incidental music were among the most celebrated of the studio era. From the mid-1930s to the end of the studio era, studio composers Max Steiner (*Now Voyager* (1942) and *Mildred Pierce* (1945)) and Erich Wolfgang Korngold (*The Adventures of Robin Hood* (1938) and *King's Row* (1942)) created many scores in the Middle-European tradition of romantic composition, using Wagner-like leitmotifs (recurring melodic phrases to suggest characters or ideas) throughout.

In summary, Warner's style of the 1930s and 1940s can thus be identified as a composite one, the product of its creative personnel working under the control and direction of corporate management. The various signifying elements that made up this style were reinforced film after film, year after year, producing what one now identifies as the studio-era Warner Brothers film.

THE CONTEMPORARY FILM INDUSTRY (1949 ONWARDS)

The early twenty-first-century film industry is a very different affair from the system in operation during the studio era. This section looks at the contemporary institutional framework of film, first by examining the specifics within the film industry itself, and then by looking at the wider media context within which film exists today.

1949 to the present: a brief review

The Majors were finally forced to divest themselves of their theatres at the end of the 1940s as a result of the 'Paramount' anti-trust suit filed against them by the Justice Department of the US government.

The suit had been in the pipeline since the late 1930s, only the War had intervened. Paramount and RKO were the first of the Majors to agree with the US government as to the terms of their **consent decrees** in 1949 (Balio 1976: 317), putting to rest the government's charge against them of monopolistic practice in exhibition. The terms agreed were the divorcement of cinemas from the parent corporations. This effectively marked the end of the studio era.

The next few years saw a retrenchment of the Majors. Shorn of their cinemas, they no longer had a guaranteed market for their films and had to compete with independent producers for exhibition slots. Under the circumstances, they found their old studio infrastructure too expensive in the face of new market competition from the independents.

Meanwhile, for independents, things had never been better, with the Majors only too willing to rent them studio space and distribute their (better) films, and exhibitors eager to show them. The 1950s was to see an enormous explosion in independent production in the US. By 1957, 58 per cent of the films distributed by the erstwhile Big Five and Little Three were independent productions that they financed and/or distributed (ibid.: 353). United Artists led the industry in the distribution of independent films. With no studios to restructure and no long-term contract players, UA was able to respond very quickly

consent decree
A court order made with the consent of both parties – the defendant and the plaintiff – which puts to rest the lawsuit brought against the former by the latter.

OLD STANDARD SCREEN

- C I N E M A S C O P E -

to the post-1949 reality. In the year 1957, only Columbia Pictures distributed more films than UA.[10]

Another shock to the film industry around the early 1950s was the postwar focus on the home and on consumer durables, evidenced in the exponential growth of television. People simply didn't go to the cinema in the same numbers any more (see next section). Between 1947 and 1950, the number of TV sets in the US rose from 14,000 to 4 million (see section below on film audiences). The film industry's response was twofold: differentiation from and collaboration with TV.

In the 1950s, various film presentation strategies were introduced to emphasise the difference between the film-going experience and TV viewing in a bid to stave off the harmful competition from film's 'at home' rival. Widescreen, colour, 3-D and stereophonic sound were all introduced in the period 1952 to 1954. However, at the end of the day it proved expedient for the industry to collaborate with 'the enemy'. Film companies began to sell (and later lease) their films to TV,[11] to make films for TV,[12] and to merge with TV companies.[13] By the late 1960s, the futures of the two media industries were inextricably linked. The situation by the mid-1980s was more complicated. The two industries had become integrated into multi-media conglomerates where they represented just two of the many associated interests of their parent corporations.

Cinema exhibition today

Throughout the studio era and before, the most powerful sector of the film industry was exhibition. In today's film economy, however, distribution is the dominant sector (see below). If the shift was originally a pragmatic response to anti-trust legislation, today it is a reflection of where the Majors make their money. It is simply not necessary for them to own cinemas to make big money. This is because the growth of home entertainment and a shift to digitisation have led to very large 'downstream' profits (see below). But the profits of Majors *also* depend on product recognition and visibility, and here cinemas continue to be fundamental to the financial well-being of the Industry as a whole. Simply put, cinema runs are the primary means of promoting films, and hence for generating downstream profits.

Theatrical presentation is no longer dominated by large, select, first-run movie theatres as in the studio era. Individual theatres are now usually small mini-theatres (average seating capacity 200 to 300 seats), and mainstream commercial films distributed by the Majors generally open simultaneously at a large number of these 'screens'.[14] Several screens are commonly housed under one roof – in multiplex theatres – where economies of scale (several screens sharing overheads) allow for low per-unit costs. These cinemas are often purpose-built, located on key artery roads outside of town centres (where land is cheaper and more readily available), and associated with shopping-mall develop-ments. Since the mid-1990s there has been a large investment in new screens in the US (and elsewhere): in 1996 there were 26,500 screens in the US sector, and by 2000 the figure was 38,000 screens.[15] As a consequence, cinema attendance has increased, but the construction boom has also led to over-capacity in the marketplace, to bankruptcies and mergers (by 2002 over two-thirds of the US sector screens were owned by only five national chains).

A history of multiplex theatres

The company to first realise the potential of the purpose-built, multi-screen theatre was American Multi-Cinema (AMC) in the 1960s. Its success with the multi-screen formula was so great that by the 1980s AMC was one of the five largest cinema chains in the US. Based on the statements of AMC's senior management in 1983, exhibitor aspira-tions appear to be the same as those way back in the days of the nickelodeon theatres: 'we prefer to locate theatres in middle-class areas inhabited by college-educated families .... These groups are the backbone of the existing motion picture audience and of our future audience' (Squire 1986: 329–30).

Another company notable for its development of the multi-screen concept is the Canadian company Cineplex. It opened its eighteen-screen Cineplex in Toronto's Eaton Centre in 1979, followed by a complex in the Beverly Centre, Los Angeles in 1982. After its purchase of the Odeon chain in Canada in the mid-1980s, it began its US acquisi-tions in earnest, so that by 1988 it was the largest theatre-chain in North America (Jowett and Linton 1989: 47). Cineplex–Odeon's UK acquisitions began in May 1988 with the purchase of the ten-screen Maybox Theatre in Slough. Within a year its Gallery Cinema chain in the UK consisted of eleven multiplexes.[16]

From the mid-1980s, Cineplex–Odeon led the exhibition industry in its construction of several mini-picture palaces and the introduction of cafés and kiosks selling film-related materials. The company did find itself in a fragile financial position in 1989: its debt-financing left it over-extended in a major recession (much like Warner in 1931). But by then the company's style and innovation had set the tone for contemporary mainstream exhibition practice.

In June 2005, Loew's Cineplex Entertainment (as it was called by now) merged with AMC Entertainment, making it the second largest cinema chain in the US with 5,900 screens.

E-cinema and implications for exhibition

By 2020 media analysts generally agree that the transition from 35mm to digital files in movie exhibition will be complete. The changeover offers many advantages to the Industry: no more expensive prints to manufacture (currently 35mm prints for a feature are approximately US$1,500); relative ease and flexibility of delivery to theatres (by DVD, IP networks, cable or satellite); and the chance to expand into theatrical pay-per-view non-film content (eg football, pop concerts). And for independent distributors and producers in particular, the move to digital should prove a boon in bringing down their costs. However, there are disadvantages as well, the leading one being the cost and shelf life of the digital projector ($150,000 each, and lasting on average five years) as opposed to an analogue film projector ($70,000, and lasting thirty to forty years). Exhibitors are keen to know who is going to pick up the tab for the conversion, and given the huge financial savings for financiers-cum-distributors, exhibitors are naturally seeking financial support from them. As I write, cinema owners and major distributors are in dialogue about this.

Other challenges to overcome include the assurance that movies will arrive at theatres without being degraded, altered or stolen.

Runs

It is worth noting that there are a variety of different types of cinema-run in operation today. A run can be **exclusive**, **multiple** or **saturation**. Combinations of runs are selected (largely at the discretion of distributors) on the basis of a film's likely performance. For instance, the exhibition of a word-of-mouth 'sleeper' – a small-budget film that does unexpectedly well at the box office – will usually begin with a semi-exclusive run, until it has built up enough of a reputation to warrant a wider run.

A typical example of a saturation run is to be found in the release of *Harry Potter and the Sorcerer's Stone* in 2001 (UK title *Harry Potter and the Philosopher's Stone*). This film set a record in US exhibition history on Friday 16 November, 2001, by opening 'superwide' in a record number of cinemas – 3,672 – and on around 8,000 screens (approximately 21 per cent of the nation's total). In the UK the number was around 500 cinemas and 1,140 screens (approximately 38 per cent of the nation's total). In both cases, openings were accompanied by huge marketing campaigns around the time of release (see the end of this section on Time Warner synergy and marketing).

The UK scenario

Britain is the third largest cinema market in the developed world, with 3,400 screens. As is the case elsewhere, digitalisation has 'coincided' with the international Majors divesting themselves of cinema chains. Why? Because they control exhibition/distribution money deals anyway (see below), and the big profits are to be made elsewhere, in the digital home-entertainment sector. Hence witness the fact that since the last edition of this book, Universal and Warner Brothers have got out of exhibition in the UK completely. Paramount remains the only Hollywood major that is still represented here (in the form of National Amusements, a shareholder of Viacom – owner of Paramount).

According to industry estimates, the UK's five largest exhibition companies account for 75 per cent of the UK screens and 80 per cent of the box-office returns. These companies are Odeon, Cineworld, Vue, National Amusements Showcase and Empire. Odeon is the biggest of the exhibitors with approximately 800 'screens', followed by Cineworld (700 screens), Vue (500 screens), National Amusements (250 screens) and Empire (150 to 200 screens).

Independent cinemas account for only 20 per cent of the box-office revenue in the UK. Under the label 'independent' there are many different types of cinema organisation. Some independents are simply smaller chains showing mainstream fare. Others show a mixture of blockbuster, 'off-centre' (mainstream but not blockbuster) and 'art' films. Other cinemas specialise in the screening of minority interest/alternative films.

Schemes to offset the dominance of the blockbuster in UK cinemas include the Europa Cinemas scheme (administered by EU Media Programme) which makes available to UK exhibitors public monies to assist in the showing of European film. However, cinemas must meet a minimum target of 15 to 25 per cent non-national EU/Norway/Iceland/Liechtenstein/Switzerland/Bulgaria film to qualify.

Power and control are two hotly disputed areas in the film industry in the UK today. Some parties argue that despite the renaissance in cinema-going in the UK, structural

---

exclusive run
Where a film is only screened in one cinema.

multiple run
Where a film is shown simultaneously at a number of cinemas. 'Platforming' a movie in a few cities, in up to 200 screens, can help build up word-of-mouth enthusiasm for 'off-centre' (mainstream but not blockbuster) films.

saturation run
Where a film opens 'wide' and is shown simultaneously at an enormous number of cinemas, accompanied by heavy media promotion. Increasingly, 'superwide' openings are becoming an entrenched strategy for 'event' films such as the big summer releases where a film can open in 3,000-plus US and Canadian screens simultaneously. 'Superwide' openings help ensure that big films reap big returns at the box office, particularly on the opening weekend, before the reviews come out.

For further discussion of British cinema see Chapter 13, pp. 303–33.

domination by the Majors in distribution means that non-Hollywood product (including UK film) does not get a fair crack of the whip in UK cinemas. This is due to the Majors' influence over exhibitors, who will not endanger the main source of their revenue. Others dismiss the conspiracy theories and point out the obvious – that the Hollywood product has the advantage of high production costs, high marketing budgets and film stars, and that these are the films that the public want to see and exhibitors want to show.

Whatever lies behind exhibition practice in the UK today, the publicly funded UK Film Council is mindful of the concerns of European producers, and is nudging big cinema chains to widen their exhibition base and show a greater variety of fare. One of the ways it is doing so is through the UK Film Council 'Digital Circuit', which was set up at the end of 2005. Exhibitors that qualify for the scheme have their projectors paid for by the Film Council. The bidding process requires that cinemas identify which screens will be given over to cultural/minority interest film. By 2007, it is expected that 240 screens and 220 sites will be fitted out digitally under this scheme.

Whether considering large chains or small, most UK cinemas are multiplexes today. The turning point in UK exhibition is usually taken as November 1985 when the purpose-built multiplex, the Point, first opened its doors in Milton Keynes. However, it should be noted that the company Screen 4 had been building four-screens in the north since the mid-1960s, and ones that were effectively purpose-built. Nevertheless, the success of the Point and other early multiplexes, such as the Maybox in Slough, triggered a new investment in British exhibition and a resurgence in the cinema-going habit in the UK. A year prior to the opening of the Point, cinema attendance was down to 52 million admissions per year. By 1996, that figure had risen to 123.5 million admissions, and in 2005 to 166 million. The multiplex has played a crucial role in this renaissance of cinema-going by offering the punter a choice of viewing in a modern, comfortable environment. (See section on 'Film audiences' below for more information on contemporary UK cinema-going.)

Distribution today

The role of the Majors today embraces film production, distribution, and (since the mid-1980s) exhibition. In the area of exhibition, the Majors' participation is very significant but not completely dominant. In the fields of production finance and distribution, however, the Majors rule supreme. Their names are all very familiar from the studio era: Paramount, Warner Brothers, Columbia, Universal, Disney and Twentieth Century Fox.

Since the late 1940s' consent decrees, the power base in the industry has shifted from exhibition to production finance and distribution, i.e. from the power base of the pre-1949 Majors to the power base of the post-1949 Majors (Balio 1976: 458–67). This shift reflects the fact that film revenue is no longer purely a function of cinema receipts. With the financial dominance of other distribution 'windows' (especially DVD) and merchandising spin-offs, access to a major's worldwide distribution/marketing network has become the determining factor in a film's financial success. Through their domination of marketing and promotion, the Majors ensure that it is their films that the public wants to see and that cinema owners want to secure for their cinemas. Witness the reaction of the public and the exhibitors to the beat of the distributors' tom-tom with blockbuster releases such as *Jurassic Park* (summer 1993) and *Harry Potter and the Sorcerer's Stone* (autumn 2001).

Today, a major financier–distributor stands between the producer (if not directly producing the film itself) and the exhibitor. It will largely dictate the business terms which shape a film's finance and exploitation.

As noted by the ex-chairman of Cineplex-Odeon Garth Drabinsky in 1976:

If, but only if, a distributor . . . decides that the picture merits release and the kind of expenditures necessary to get it off the ground, the distributor will enter into a distribution agreement with the producer to govern their relationship.[18]

For the most part, the distributor dictates the terms of its deal with the exhibitor as well: the nature of the run, the length of the engagement, the advertising to be employed and the financial split of box-office receipts between the various parties. It has also been reported that it is common practice for distributors to exploit their upper hand with exhibitors and to insist on blind-bidding and block-booking (Jowett and Linton 1989: 43–4).

Distribution windows

Up until the mid-1970s, apart from the theatrical release, the only distribution windows were network and syndicated TV. The new age of film distribution began in 1975 with the introduction of Time Inc.'s Home Box Office cable pay-TV (HBO) and Sony's domestic Betamax videocassette recorder (VCR). The following year, Matsushita introduced the VHS format for domestic VCRs. This soon became the industry standard.

Roll on two decades, and the first commercial Digital Versatile Disc (DVD) players appeared in Japan in 1996. Early manufacturers were Toshiba, Pioneer and Matsushita. DVDs were designed to compete with VHS, which they have completely superseded. As early as 2001 the DVD market was growing at ten times the VHS market, with Blockbuster Video estimating that 30 per cent of its US rental business was DVD.[19]

The phenomenal success of DVD lay in the high quality of the image and sound, the increased storage capacity compared to video (up to eight hours of high-quality video, up to eight tracks of digital audio and interactive features) and DVD as a cross-platform. As I write, manufacturers are vying with each other for control of the marketplace. Will it be HD DVD (Toshiba) or the 'Blu-ray' format (Sony)? The money seems to be on Sony, as five out of six Majors appear to be backing it.[20] This shouldn't come as any surprise, given Sony's pre-eminence in the film business (see 'Multi-media empires', below).

Today, DVD is an important window in determining film profits. In terms of marketing, however, the *theatrical window* is still the most important window, because DVDs, TV windows and so on all rely on the publicity generated by a theatrical release to make money. Without one, the film is a far less valuable commodity. That said, actual revenues for the Majors are far greater from DVDs than from cinemas. In 2004, for instance, box-office revenue in the US was $9.5 billion whereas DVD/video sales and rentals were in the order of $24.5 billion.[21]

The economic importance of DVD has led to a closing of the gap between the cinema release and the DVD release dates. Thus a typical distribution sequence for a studio film in the US will now be an initial theatrical release of around four months (down from six months ten years ago), followed by a DVD window (which remains open for an indefinite period). This is followed by pay-per-view telecasts anywhere from two to three weeks after a film goes on DVD release, and a premium cable movie channel window (for approximately one year), a network TV window, and finally, a syndicated TV window.

For a discussion on DVDs and audiences, see Case study on Gladiator (pp. 44–7), and section on 'Film audiences', pp. 49–55.

And what of the future? Industry pundits predict that soon we will be back to two windows: the theatrical window and an online, domestic, video-on-demand window, replacing the DVD completely. The home entertainment market will be transformed by a system of 'time-critical' downloads whereby customers are charged different prices depending on how long the video-on-demand (VOD) download is good for on their computers – whether it is permanent or for just a few days.

The importance of new media distribution is indicated by the success of web companies such as ifilm and atomfilms, who more than five years ago revolutionised the distribution of short films by releasing them on their websites. A notable early 'short' to be distributed this way was *405* (2000), put out on ifilm.com. Flash forward a few years, to 2006, and another multi-media company, 2929 Entertainment, announced a 'universal release' (simultaneously on VOD and in cinemas) of their new film *Bubble*, directed by Steven Soderbergh. So will the gap between theatrical and VOD eventually disappear altogether, as in this particular case? Unlikely, given the industry's reliance on a theatrical window for building a market for its product.

Marketing

One of the key roles of a financier–distributor is to successfully orchestrate the marketing of a film. The three main types of advertising used in film marketing are: **free publicity**, **paid advertising** and **tie-ins/merchandising** (see next section on 'Film audiences').

How this manifests in reality may be seen in Universal's UK marketing campaign for *Jurassic Park* at the time of its cinema release in 1993.[22]

Free media publicity included reports on:

- Spielberg
- the making of the film and the special effects
- the premiere
- genetic engineering
- dinomania

Paid advertising included:

- TV, radio, billboards, newspapers, magazines (today this would include the internet)
- A TV blitz the week before and the week of the film's opening

Tie-ins included:

- multi-million-dollar tie-ins with McDonald's and selected hotels

Merchandising included:

- JP holographic watches
- JP vinyl model dinosaur kits
- JP pinball machines
- JP socks
- JP briefs
- JP Christmas cards!

free publicity
Free coverage of subjects the media feel are newsworthy.

paid advertising
Promotion on TV, radio, billboards, printed media and the internet (see 'Multi-media empires' below).

tie-ins
Mutually beneficial promotional liaisons between films and other consumer products and/ or personalities.

merchandising
Where manufacturers pay a film company to use a film title or image on their products.

The UK scenario

The international majors dominate UK distribution, and each of them has a UK subsidiary to handle its distribution (namely UIP, Buena Vista International, Columbia/Tristar, Fox International and Warner Brothers International). However, there are also public mechanisms available to assist smaller, independent European distributors with the marketing and distribution of their films. The Media Programme, for instance, is an EU initiative whereby European distributors of films and DVD receive loans to help with distribution and promotion costs within European markets (70 per cent of the Programme's main budget is devoted to the distribution of new films).[23] As welcome as the Programme is, inevitably it is a 'drop in the ocean' when set against the power of the Majors. It is not surprising, then, that the future trends in UK distribution patterns are expected to mirror those in the US.

I have mentioned already the predicted shift to two distribution windows: cinema and VOD. This is because many in the industry see DVD as old technology. The UK market moved a little closer to this in March 2006 when Universal announced a deal with lovefilm.com – an online DVD rental firm – whereby costumers would be able to download the latest Universal releases on to their laptops, either for a few days or for keeps.

Production today

Before examining those key players that dominate mainstream film production today – the Majors, independent producers, agents/management groups and stars (see below) – it is useful to review the current industrial organisation of film production.

The industrial system in operation today is called the 'package-unit' system (Bordwell et al 1985: 330–7). Under this system, the self-contained studio and long-term contract studio employee of the studio era have been replaced by rented studio space and short-term contract employment.

The shift to the package-unit system from the mid-1950s onwards was a direct response to the combined effects of the 1949 consent decrees: in other words, the rise of independent production, cost-cutting and rationalisation at the Majors' studios, and the Majors leasing studio space to independent producers.

Today, individual producers are responsible for bringing together all the components of a film's production – finance, personnel, the 'property', equipment, studio space – on a short-term, film-by-film basis.

Budget has always been the principal preoccupation of the producer, but today, under the package-unit system, this is true more than ever. So called 'above-the-line' budget costs are those that are up-front (such as book rights, fees for producers, directors, stars), whereas 'below-the-line' costs refer to the day-to-day expenses incurred on a production (such as crew fees, post-production costs).

independent
A highly problematic term, meaning different things in different situations. Here, the term simply implies a production realised outside one of the Majors. Here, the term does not imply a production context outside the mainstream institutional framework altogether, nor does it imply a film produced in an alternative aesthetic format to 'Classic Hollywood'.

Majors v. independents

Despite the growth of **independent** production after the consent decrees, the Majors had reclaimed their dominance in production by the early 1970s. Between the years 1970 and 1987, films directly produced by the Majors collected on average 84 per cent of the total US/Canadian box-office returns (Jowett and Linton 1989: 38).

Recently, however, there is clear evidence that independent production is once again making inroads, at the expense of the Majors' directly produced features. In 1991, for instance, films produced independently accounted for one-third of the summer box-office grosses in the US and Canada.[24] And with the success of the independents comes the increased value of their film libraries; libraries that the Majors are very keen to exploit in the lucrative home-entertainment market. This goes a long way to explain the recent spate of high-profile acquisitions, such as Paramount's purchase of the (independent) studio Dreamworks SKG Inc.[25]

New media and production

Launched by Artisan Films at the 1999 Sundance Film Festival (a showcase for independent film), *The Blair Witch Project* (1999) was perhaps the first big box-office film (albeit a 'sleeper' hit) to use extensive digital camera footage. Since then, the industry interest in digital video-making has skyrocketed, due partly to the flexibility of the technology, and to the lower costs of production. So much so that by 2001, more than 40 per cent of the projects submitted to the Sundance Festival were shot on digital formats.[26] In the intervening years Hollywood has also jumped on the digital bandwagon, so that hi-definition cameras on blockbuster productions are now the order of the day in films such as *Superman Returns* (2006), with a reported budget of $225 million.[27]

Agents

The ending of long-term studio contracts for creative personnel in the early 1950s (a consequence of the rationalisation of studios by the Majors after the consent decrees) meant that important stars, directors, writers and other talent could now negotiate very lucrative freelance deals with film companies.[28] Their increased negotiating power also strengthened the hand of their agents who negotiated their deals with the film companies. The most powerful agency at the time was MCA, controlled by Jules Stein and Lew Wasserman.

So successful was MCA during the 1950s that it purchased Universal in 1959. The agency's dominance in the industry ended in 1962, when it closed down that part of the business to concentrate on film production. Today there are several big talent agencies in Hollywood: Creative Artists Agency (CAA), William Morris, International Creative Management (ICM), United Talent Agency (UTA) and Endeavor. Apart from these five, there are many smaller 'boutique' agencies who handle a select number of important clients.

Agencies do occasionally get more directly involved in the production of film projects, as evidenced by the agency 'package', where big agents offer groups of creative personnel (with possibly a literary property as well) as a joint package to a production company for a single film or TV production. The most famous example of this in recent decades has been the agency packages put together by CAA for films such as *Ghostbusters II* (1989) (Kent 1991: 210–45).

Stars

A star's association with a film project affects the ease with which it can be financed and marketed. A star's presence in a film is also held to be an important factor in a film's box-office performance. These three factors explain stars' huge salaries today. However, some statistics suggest that stars are less a factor in a film's box-office success than was once the case.[29] Certainly, stars cannot ensure box office success for films in which they appear (if they ever could), but their position within the current Hollywood economic structure is central.

For further discussion of the star in film, see Chapter 6.

The 1980s–90s star Arnold Schwarzenegger is a good case in point. Such was his popularity in the early 1990s that for *Total Recall* he was able to command a $10 million fee, plus 15 per cent of the gross takings of the picture. However, even Arnie could not guarantee massive profits at the box office all the time, and his 1993 summer release, *Last Action Hero*, was a huge commercial flop in cinemas.

The UK scenario

British feature films today are generally made on low to medium budgets, and are usually co-productions where film finance comes from a range of sources. Dominant players are UK and foreign terrestrial TV companies, film companies, and cable/satellite companies. In addition, funding assistance in the form of a loan is available from the UK Film Council.

For further discussion of the funding and finance of British film see Chapter 13, pp. 305–27.

By nature the UK industry is fiscally conservative, and therefore its producers are, by experience, usually short of money. 'Pack-of-cards' financing is generally the order of the day, where each source of funding is dependent on the participation of the other co-producers.

For most low- to medium-budget productions, a typical sequence of events for developing and producing a feature film is as follows. Applications are first made by the creative team[30] for development money to produce a preliminary script and project budget. Funding sources include the commissioning groups themselves, the Film Council and the European Media Programme (19 per cent of whose main budget is allocated for development money).[31]

Having produced its preliminary script and budget, the creative team then seeks sources to fund the production proper. As each source of finance comes on board, the script is changed to fit in with the requirements of the specific investor. The backers are inevitably financiers-cum-distributors, and monies from the distribution deals made for each 'territory' – i.e. US, UK and the rest of the world – are used to fund the production. Once the budget is fixed, pre-production begins in earnest with the preparation of the final script and budget.

TV money for UK film production

For twenty years Channel 4 was the British channel most actively engaged in film production. From its launch in 1982, it participated in well over 300 films including *My Beautiful Launderette* (1986), *The Crying Game* (1992), *Four Weddings and a Funeral* (1994), *Trainspotting* (1996) and *Secrets and Lies* (1996). And, like the BBC – its terrestrial rival in film production – it favoured co-productions. But in 2002 Channel 4 announced a huge cutback in film finance, partly as a consequence of the failure of its big-budget films at the box office: films such as *Charlotte Gray* (co-produced with Warner, 2001). In the past few years its old rival, BBC Films, has enjoyed a moderate success with films such as *Match Point* (2006), directed by Woody Allen. And the Corporation looks like 'upping the anti' with the announcement, in 2006, of a minimum investment of £150 million in domestic film production over ten years (up from £10 million a year). Many in the UK industry are banking on this, and on the words of BBC creative director Alan Yentob, when he says, 'the relationship between TV and film [in the UK] is a very potent one'.[32]

The UK Film Council

This agency, which was set up in May 2000, has replaced the Arts Council as the coordinator of National Lottery funds earmarked for British film. The Film Council puts money into development (£4 million per year), the production of small-budget innovative film (funded at £5 million per year), and the production of big-budget film (funded at £8 million per year). It has also set itself the challenge of overseeing structural changes in the UK industry, by facilitating the exhibition of a broader range of films in UK multiplexes than is normally the case (see 'Exhibition' above).

Wherever the money comes from, many commentators on the British film scene would suggest that what is needed is popular film that is also distinctive and personal. British filmmaking needs to break away from its own somewhat entrenched position of pigeon-holing film as either 'cultural' or 'genre' (as per the Richard Curtis romantic comedies, *Four Weddings and a Funeral* (1994), *Notting Hill* (1999) and *Bridget Jones's Diary* (2001), produced by Working Title Films).[33]

☐ CASE STUDY 2: A US 'BLOCKBUSTER' PRODUCTION, *GLADIATOR* (2000)

Script development and pre-production

In 1996 David Franzoni (producer–writer) approached Dreamworks SKG with a story about gladiators in ancient Rome. The story was then developed by him in collaboration with head of Dreamworks Pictures Walter Parkes and producer Douglas Wick. In the process they revived the 'ancient epic' genre, one that hadn't really seen the light of day since the mid-1960s, with such films as *The Fall of the Roman Empire* (1964). This older film, in fact, was to share many of the same protagonists as the future production *Gladiator*.

For further discussion of Gladiator see Chapter 3, pp. 82–4 and Chapter 10, p. 241.

The producers felt that their planned film needed a director who could manage the cinematic spectacle that would feature in it. Hence, they approached Ridley Scott who relished the prospect of re-creating a detailed historical environment that would be realistic. The creation of detailed worlds that were believable on their own terms, irrespective of genre, had been a hallmark of earlier Scott productions such as *Alien* (1979), *Blade Runner* (1982) and *Someone to Watch Over Me* (1987). Once the great metteur-en-scène agreed to direct, script development began in earnest.

Franzoni produced the first draft of the screenplay, with John Logan and William Nicholson working as collaborators later on. In the process, the games in the Roman arena came to occupy the central focus of the narrative. And for many months before production began, Scott worked on sketches of the key scenes and on storyboards with Sylvain Despretz. This production was to reflect Scott's long-held notion that direction

● **Plate 2.6**
Still from *Gladiator* (Ridley Scott, 2000). Maximus (Russell Crowe) and his fellow gladiators – tensile, hard-muscled and armoured – salute the roaring crowds in the Colosseum as they and their Dreamworks/Universal picture enjoy the sweet smell of success

is akin to orchestration, with incident, sound, movement, colour, sets and computer graphics all knitted together under his watchful eye.[34]

The film would be jointly produced, financed and distributed by Dreamworks and Universal – the former having had a long-standing distribution arrangement with the latter.[35]

It was decided that location shooting would bring down the cost of the production, rather than trying to construct everything in Hollywood. However, filming on the site of historical monuments was impossible because of the likely damage incurred during filming, and because of the often poor condition of the sites to begin with. Therefore scouting commenced in Europe and North Africa for locations that could accommodate new sets. Such was the scale of the production that individual design departments were assigned to each of the major locations (UK, Morocco and Malta) by Arthur Max, the film's overall production designer. In each location, 'sets, props and costumes were custom-made for the film', or sets were added to existing buildings (Landau 2000: 66).

The biggest set, that of 'ancient Rome', was built at Port Mifisalfi, Malta, over nineteen weeks in the winter of 1998–99, immediately prior to filming. The set included a full-scale section of the Roman Colosseum (the rest would be filled in using computer graphics), as well as sets for the emperor's palace, the Forum and the Roman marketplace. This huge complex of sets was built on to disused nineteenth-century barracks on the site to add an air of authenticity to the look of the production. This is a favoured technique of Scott's to add verisimilitude to the world he is creating, as per the sets of *Blade Runner* which were built on to old Warner Brothers' city sets to legitimise the film's noir mise-en-scène.

Production and post-production

From the beginning, the shoot was a very complex affair. The scale of the production –
with a mammoth budget of over US$100 million, scenes involving thousands of extras
and a four-month shoot in four countries – necessitated the use of four different crews.

Principal photography commenced at the beginning of February 1999 in Bourne
Woods, Farnham, Surrey, after the construction of a Roman encampment, a stake
barricade and a forest dwelling. The opening battle scene – set in Germania in the film –
was a hugely involved affair incorporating replicas of Roman war machines and an army
of 1,000 extras. Shooting was finally wrapped up in the UK on 24 February 1999[36] from
where the production moved to Morocco.

Morocco was the setting in the movie for the gladiator school. In preparation for
filming, the local production crew had been busy for nine weeks, since December,
1998.[37] In all, the shoot took three weeks here, after which the production moved to
Malta for the 'Rome' scenes.

Again, preparation of the sets had begun long before shooting: because of the scale
of the set, construction had begun nineteen weeks earlier. And despite bad storms
damaging the set,[38] filming commenced around mid-March and was completed by the
end of May 1999.[39] This part of the shoot involved the large-scale Colosseum scenes
incorporating 2,000 extras.

Finally, there followed a two-day shoot in Tuscany, which was the chosen location
for the home of Maximus in the film. This work – involving Ridley Scott, the main crew
(which travelled from location to location), doubles and stunt doubles – marked the end
of the long location schedule.[40]

The film was then completed at Shepperton studios, but not before the extraordinary
computer visual effects work of Mill Film (London) was incorporated into the film to
create the composite shots of the Colosseum. Computer-graphic imaging (CGI) was
used to complete the circumference of the first tier of the stadium and to create the
second and third tiers. CGI was also used to increase the number of spectators in the
Colosseum from 2,000 to 35,000, and to extend other vistas on the Rome set.[41]

The film was edited by Ridley Scott and Pietro Scalia, and scored by Hans Zimmer
(head of Dreamworks' film music division) and Lisa Gerrard. With the completion of post-
production, Scott delivered the picture to Dreamworks on time and on budget (US$106
million).[42]

Distribution and exhibition

For the film's marketing poster, Dreamworks SKG (responsible for marketing the film in
the US–Canada territory) and United International Pictures (Universal's marketing arm
and responsible for international distribution) promoted a low-angled, medium-long shot
of the film's star, Russell Crowe, in costume as Maximus. Here for all to see was the
towering presence of a rectilinear, hard, tough male action star with classical adornments
of armour and phallic sword. At his feet, literally, lay the Colosseum, across the base of
the poster. The powerhouse epic, *Gladiator*, had been launched!

The movie's marketing campaign was the standard one for a blockbuster: saturation
booking technique with simultaneous media promotion on a massive scale. The film
opened superwide in the US–Canada market on 5 May 2000 in approximately 3,000
screens. With such a big opening, the film caught the imagination of the punters even
before the reviews came out – which is of course the purpose of a big opening. But the
makers needn't have worried, since the reviews were very favourable. In its opening
weekend the film grossed around US$35 million and went straight to number one at the
box office. This success was repeated the following weekend in the UK, where the film
opened in around 400 screens and grossed approximately £3.5 million.[43]

Merchandising was kept to a minimum so as not to undermine the 'quality' message
of the marketing campaign. Available to buy were the soundtrack, books on the film's

production and the movie poster – which was soon becoming an iconic image. Tie-ins included Sega games and offers of holidays to Rome.

By the end of the film's box-office run, *Gladiator* had grossed around US$452 million worldwide, with takings of $188 million in the US market alone.[44] But the story didn't end there. On 21 November 2000, the DVD and video were released in the US/Canada market. The DVD two-disc set included the following extras: audio commentary by Ridley Scott, eleven deleted scenes from the movie, a behind-the-scenes documentary, a history of gladiatorial games and a theatre trailer, among others.

Evidently, large sales of the DVD were anticipated for the forthcoming holiday season because prior to the release date 2.6 million copies of the DVD were shipped to retail outlets. *Gladiator* sales more than met expectations, since it went on to become the biggest selling DVD in the US. Sales everywhere were remarkable: in the UK too it became the biggest selling DVD. Eventually, worldwide sales clocked in at around 4.5 million units – the biggest selling DVD up until that time.

And so, with the financial and critical momentum afforded the film, nothing could prevent it from being nominated for twelve Oscars or from winning five in March 2001: for best film, best actor (Russell Crowe), best costume design (Janty Yates), best sound and best visual effects.

The film was, of course, distributed to pay-per-view channels, and subsequently to premium cable/satellite movie channels. In the UK, the film debuted on Sky Premier movie channel in October 2001, and announcements were made in 2001 of a deal having been struck for its terrestrial TV debut in 2003. The keenly contested battle among UK broadcasters for the first-run terrestrial rights was further evidence – if indeed further evidence was necessary – of the global distribution phenomenon that *Gladiator* had become.

In summary, the UK distribution windows for *Gladiator* are to date as follows:

1st commercial theatrical release
12 May 2000

|

DVD/video release date
20 November 2000

|

Premium satellite movie channel premiere
Sky Premier
27 October 2001

Multi-media empires

Today, it is not adequate to consider the film industry in isolation, for it is only one part of a network of media, entertainment and communications industries controlled by vertically and laterally integrated multi-media conglomerates,

[e]ach company controlling a vast empire of media and entertainment properties that amounts to a global distribution system.[45]

Examples of such organisations are Time Warner, Viacom (owner of Paramount), Sony Corporation of Japan (owner of Columbia Pictures) and News Corporation (owner of Twentieth Century Fox).

Time Warner merged with AOL (America Online) in January 2001. The new global media giant is the largest in the world, and has interests in the internet, film and TV,

synergy strategy
Combined or related action by a group of individuals or corporations towards a common goal, the combined effect of which exceeds the sum of the individual efforts.

Still from *Harry Potter and the Sorcerer's Stone* (Chris Columbus, 2001). Madam Hooch looks on as Neville Longbottom awkwardly takes to the skies. Box-office and merchandising, on the other hand, had no problem soaring due to the synergy strategy adopted by AOL Time Warner for the film's promotion

publishing, cable and satellite systems and the music industry. The underlying philosophy behind the merger is to work across the corporation's holdings to create new business opportunities/associations; in other words a **synergy strategy**. A good example of this is the Time Warner 'marketing council' set up in 2001.

AOL Time Warner synergy and marketing

After the merger with AOL, Time Warner set up a 'marketing council' to optimise marketing opportunities across the whole corporation. *Harry Potter and the Sorcerer's Stone* (US title, 2001) was the first substantive evidence of this new synergy strategy in operation. Marketing was planned carefully across all media to take into account the fact that a series of films was planned for 'Harry Potter' (anywhere from three to seven films in the series),[46] and the Corporation didn't want the series to suffer from overkill in the early stages.

As was noted in the *Financial Times* on the film's opening weekend (16–18 November, 2001),[47] the film was being promoted on the HBO and Warner networks in the USA, the music was being issued on Warner Music's Atlantic Records label, and a series of articles was appearing across the Corporation's print media empire. Of particular note, however, was the promotional activity of AOL itself. The online service was offering merchandising (with ninety licensing partners and 700 products), ticket promotions and giveaways tied in with subscriptions to AOL services.

The coordinated activities of the marketing council paid off, for on the opening weekend the film took approximately $90 million in the US territory and approximately £16 million in the UK.[48] (For more examples of building audiences, see 'Film audiences' section below.)

A synergy strategy also lay behind the purchase by Sony Corporation of Japan of Columbia Pictures entertainment in 1989 for $5 billion.[49] Sony bought Columbia to boost sales of its home electronics hardware and to achieve synergy between its software and hardware enterprises. Since it acquired Columbia, Sony has used the studio to showcase its electronic high-definition technology such as high-definition TV, 'Blu-ray' DVDs and interactive multi-media video games.

The UK scenario

Rupert Murdoch's News Corporation is the media conglomerate with the highest visibility in the UK. As an example of its synergy strategy we need only look at its UK Sky (satellite) digital service comprising hundreds of TV, CD quality radio and pay-per-view channels, interactive services, e-mail and so on. This service uses press media and film and TV production companies owned by News Corporation across Europe, Asia and America (such as the film company, Twentieth Century Fox and the US terrestrial TV Fox Network) to help promote it and provide programmes for it.

For further discussion of new technology see Chapter 9.

Summary

The communications revolution is being orchestrated by only a handful of global players. Although in the recent past some of these multi-media conglomerates, such as Viacom, have decided to break themselves up (in an attempt to unlock value in some of their divisions), the fact remains that most of them have not. Unless these firms are properly regulated by the international community – an unlikely event given the powers behind global market liberalisation – they stand to enjoy an oligopolistic power not dreamed of in the far-off days of the MPPC and the studio era.

FILM AUDIENCES

Fundamental to the study of cinema as institution is a study of cinema audiences. This section reviews the changes in cinema audience patterns/profiles from the end of the Second World War to the present day, and considers their likely causes.

The section ends with a review of how film companies attempt to build audiences for their films.

From the late 1940s onwards

Before the 1950s, cinema-going was a very major recreational activity. According to one official report,[50] it was the number one recreational activity for most people in wartime US The year 1946 marked the peak in cinema-going in the USA, unsurpassed to this day. In that year, the average weekly attendance in the US was 95 million.[51]

Studies of the composition of audiences in the 1940s identify certain key trends. Although men and women registered the same average monthly picture attendance,[52] a greater percentage of men were very high-frequency cinema-goers.[53]

Age was the major determinant in the frequency of attendance. All surveys of the 1940s point to the fact that young people attended much more frequently than older persons.[54]

Statistics from the 1940s also indicate that expenditure on motion pictures increased with annual income and that those with higher levels of education (i.e. high school and/or college) were more frequent cinema-goers than those with only a grade school education.[55]

By the 1950s, cinema attendance was in rapid decline. Average weekly attendance figures had dropped in 1950 to 60 million (from their 95 million peak four years earlier), and by 1956 the number had slipped to 46.5 million.[56] What happened to bring about this sudden decline? Two reasons are most often cited: the first is the change in living patterns of Americans following the Second World War, and the second is the estab-lishment of TV.

'Being at home' explains the drop in cinema attendance after the peak of the mid- to late 1940s. There was a radical change in social trends in the US after the war:

home ownership, suburbanization of metropolitan areas, traffic difficulties, large families, family-centred leisure time activities, and the do-it-yourself movement.

(Bernstein 1957: 74)

• **Plate 2.8**
Still from *No Down Payment* (Martin Ritt, 1957). The film industry in the 1950s would certainly have wished this fate on all domestic TV sets!

These new trends put the focus firmly on domestic lifestyle, to the detriment of 'outside-the-home' film entertainment. In this climate, TV was born as a social phenomenon: the number of TV sets in America grew from 250,000 in 1947, to 8,000,000 by 1950 and to 42.2 million by 1956. TV's rise was directly proportional to falls in cinema attendance, particularly in residential neighbourhoods. It is thus logical to assume that the audiences who previously frequented local theatres were now (in part at least) at home watching TV instead (Bernstein 1957: 73).

A branch of cinema-going that bucked the trend of 'being at home' in the early 1950s was the outdoor drive-in cinema, its rise in popularity clearly a consequence of postwar suburbanisation. Now parents could choose to have a night out at the movies in the comfort of their own car, with the kids in the back of the vehicle. By 1954, there were 3,800 drive-ins in America, whose box-office grosses accounted for 16 per cent of the total US box-office receipts.[57]

The 1960s and 1970s saw an enormous growth in the leisure industry in the US. Yet, despite this, film-going continued to decline: in 1960, the weekly attendance figure had been 40 million; by 1980, the average weekly attendance was down to 19.7 million (Austin 1989: 36, 40–1). A Gallup poll taken in 1977 underlined the dominance of home-based leisure pursuits as a 'favourite way to spend an evening'.[58] The survey also confirmed the long-standing trends of movie-going being more popular with younger persons,[59] those with higher incomes and those who were college educated.

The 1970s and 1980s saw the expansion of home-based, 'TV-related' media entertainment in the form of VCRs, subscription cable and satellite services and video games, all of which weakened cinema-going as a commercial leisure activity.

The UK scenario

The history of cinema attendance in the UK since the Second World War mirrors US statistics to a large degree. As in the US, 1946 marked the peak in UK cinema-going. That year, the average weekly cinema attendance was 31.5 million (Docherty et al 1987:

14–15), and as in the US, high-frequency cinema-going in the 1940s was predominantly the habit of the young.[60] However, unlike statistics in the US, working-class people went to the cinema significantly more often than others.[61]

Attendance figures fell dramatically in the 1950s: by 1956 weekly attendance was down to 21.1 million and by 1960 to 9.6 million (ibid.: 14–15). As in the US, the precipitous drop correlated with the dramatic rise in the number of TV sets in circulation.[62] This phenomenon was symptomatic of a much larger social change of the 1950s: the growth of outlying residential areas[63] and the subsequent establishment of a home-based consumer culture. The decline in attendance among the frequent cinema-going age group (16–24 years) might also be attributable to the sudden appearance of a distinct youth culture in the 1950s, which led to new forms of recreation for teenagers (ibid.: 26–7).

By the early 1970s, cinema-going was just one of many options in the expanding leisure industry. The long decline continued through the 1970s, so that by the mid-1980s weekly attendance had plummeted to just over one million (ibid.: 29). Other changes were apparent too: by the early 1980s the percentage of working-class people attending cinemas had declined significantly for the first time.[64]

Recent and future trends

Attendance figures have markedly improved in recent decades. By 2005,[65] the figure in the US sector stood at around twenty-seven million tickets sold per week. This increase in attendance (though levelled off since 2000) is partly a product of the growth in multiplexes and the number of 'screens' since the 1990s. Between 1996 and 2000, the number of screens rose from 26,500 to 38,000 – a figure still applicable in 2005.[66]

Two factors that continue to be a focus of interest for film industry analysts are age and education level of audiences. In the past, it was the 16- to 24-year-old demographic group that predominated among customers, but today frequent cinema-goers are a more diverse bunch. For starters, there is a *new*, enlarged (and male-dominated) frequent cinema-goer group, the 12- to 24-year-olds: an expansion of the original 16- to 24-year-old group. This group is, at once, the most likely group to attend the opening weekends of blockbusters, and (conveniently for the Majors!), the important target consumer group for the synergetic computer games distributed by the Majors to accompany their blockbusters.[67]

However, if the under thirties still account for the largest number of yearly admissions at cinemas, in recent years the percentage of the movie audience over the age of 30 has climbed significantly. Now the 30+ individual without kids, and indeed the older 'empty nester', are identified as important demographic groups in movie attendance statistics.

There has also long been evidence to support the claim that increased education levels translate to increased frequency of cinema-going. If, and it is a big if, the number of college-educated individuals continues to rise, as it has in recent years, we can suppose that movie attendance may also go up.

DVDs, PCs and audiences as 'viewers'

The number of DVD players in the US grew from around 350,000 in 1997 to approximately 1.4 million in 1998, 5.5 million in 1999, 14 million in 2000 and to an estimated 30 million by the end of 2001.[68] This exponential growth mirrored the growth in numbers of TV sets in the late 1940s, with DVD now replacing video as the latest home-based entertainment phenomenon. Thus by the turn of the new century DVDs' interactive features – multiple story-lines, games, instant search controls, different camera angles for the same action[69] – heralded the new digital home viewer, the viewer-cum-user or **'viewer'**. But this viewer – most likely the 12- to 24-year-old, frequent cinema-goer – had bigger fish to fry, in the form of PC downloads. The industry got the message, and

For discussion of contemporary British film see Chapter 13, pp. 322–34.

now the Majors, such as Universal, offer blockbuster movies as temporary or permanent downloads. Some industry pundits feel that the move to online distribution 'windows' signals the beginning of the end of DVDs. (See p. 40 on Distribution, in 'The contemporary film industry'.)

The UK Scenario

In recent years, multiplexes have also been at the centre of a renaissance in cinema-going in the UK. Attendance rose from a derisory 1 million per week in 1984 to 2.7 million per week by 1997 (Buncombe 1998: 9), and levelling off somewhat after that at 2.8 million in 2000[70] and 3.2 million per week in 2005.[71] Similar trends in audience profiles to the US have also been noticed, since if the 30+ individual without kids and the 'empty nester' are both making impacts as 'frequent audience' categories, it is the 12- to 24-year-old group that is, without doubt, the most important demographic group in the UK. Statistics show that among this newly expanded frequent cinema-goer group, A, B and C1 class/education categories are over-represented (in relation to their percentage in the general population), whereas C2 and D groups are under-represented.

The shift towards better-off and better educated young audiences is, in part at least, a consequence of the growth of purpose-built, suburban or out-of-town multiplexes which invariably need to be reached by car. However, new planning guidelines will see cinemas built in city centres and on 'brown-field' sites in a policy of urban revitalisation. This may reverse the demographic trend somewhat.

Equally important, and rarely commented upon in relation to audience demographics, is the price of admission. There is no doubt that the relative rise of A, B and C1s has also been exacerbated by cost, where the price of admission to a multiplex cinema in London now stands at a level 30 per cent higher than in New York.

Building an audience

Since the earliest days of the film industry, there have been attempts by makers, distributors and exhibitors to build audiences for their films. In today's film industry, building an audience is a sophisticated business: audience profiling, advertising (see section on contemporary film industry) and psychological testing are all incorporated to help 'deliver' an audience for a film.

Audience profiling

Audience-profile data – age, sex, income level, education – is influential in determining the kinds of films that receive finance and the shape the projects take.

Demographic trends – such as the recent rise in the 30+ audience – really do feed back into the films financed and those distributed by the industry. Recently, this was evident in the support the Majors gave to 'adult' fare during the 2005–6 winter cinema season. They put their weight behind some of the season's top critical and financial hits: films such as *Walk the Line* (Twentieth Century Fox), *Capote* (Sony Pictures Classics), *Syriana* (Warner Brothers) and *Munich* (Dreamworks SKG–Universal Pictures). Having said all that, the *big* money that season was still on what Edward Jay Epstein has called the 'Midas formula' films. These are films that are (generally) based on children's stories, feature a child or adolescent protagonist, have a fairy-tale (Proppian) plot, use 3D animation, and have ratings no more restrictive than PG–13 (Epstein 2005: 236–8). Why? The reason is simple enough: because blockbuster films target the most frequent film-goer – the 12- to 24-year-old. The specific films that season were *The Chronicles of Narnia: The Lion, the Witch and the Wardrobe* (Buena Vista Pictures Distribution), *Harry Potter and the Goblet of Fire* (Warner Brothers) and *King Kong* (Universal Pictures Distribution), but the titles are mere detail, because each year the story is the same. The Majors' 'Midas formula' blockbuster films dominate in the multiplex cinemas because these films, and their associated merchandising and tie-ins, reflect the huge consumer power of their adolescent audiences.

TV and other advertising

This topic has already been covered in the previous section on the contemporary film industry. However, it is important to restate that TV advertising is an essential tool in building audience interest for big-budget films. And because it is expensive, advertising budgets tend to be very high for such films: in recent years it has been noted that the total marketing costs of a US mainstream film can 'devour' up to 25 per cent of a film's total revenue.

Since the release of *Jaws* (1975), concentrated national TV promotion – allied with saturation booking strategies – has proven to be a most effective way to exploit big-budget films. To that we can add the recent successes of online, new media advertising (see the case study of 'AOL Time Warner synergy and marketing' in the previous section), and to a lesser extent the efficacy of the print media.

Blockbusters need to show big returns at the box office in the first week of release, before potentially bad reviews and word-of-mouth reduce the returns. *Jurassic Park* (1993) is a case in point: 'after taking $50 million in its first American weekend in June, [it] took half of that in weekend three.'[72] Thus, to maximise early box-office takings, TV advertising is at saturation level in the immediate weeks preceding and following a theatrical release.

Building audiences is obviously of crucial importance in the exploitation of low-budget films as well and, given the lack of resources, the techniques involved can be different and highly innovative, as evidenced below.

□ **CASE STUDY 3: SUNN CLASSIC PICTURES AND PSYCHOLOGICAL TESTING**

Elaborate psychological test-systems have long been used in market research to help producers determine what audiences care to see or not to see in films. An early (and extreme) example of this was Sunn Classic Pictures who, in the 1970s, identified a huge 'untapped audience for movies – working class families which attended films only once or twice a year' (Jowett and Linton 1989: 106). By carrying out extensive market research on the narrative and formal elements that would appeal to this target audience, and by then submitting the data to computer analysis, the company was successful in creating a substantial audience for its low-budget heritage/nature movies, for example, *The Life and Times of Grizzly Adams* (1974).[73]

□ **CASE STUDY 4: THE YOUTH MARKET AND BUILDING AN AUDIENCE FOR *TRAINSPOTTING* (1996)**

For the UK release of the £1.5 million budget *Trainspotting*, Polygram (the Dutch entertainment group which was largely sold off to Universal in 1999) invested the dispro-portionately high marketing sum of £800,000 in an attempt to widen the appeal of the film beyond cult status.

The film was marketed aggressively like an album in the popular charts to appeal to young consumers. A design firm was brought in to create the distinctive posters, made up of black and white portraits of the cast mixed with bright orange graphics. The film also benefited from a Britpop music track (Iggy Pop, Primal Scream, Elastica, Blur).

Publicity stories appeared in youth-style magazines and later on in magazines of a more general appeal,[74] and prior to the film's release a promotional trailer was chosen to emphasise the film's humour rather than its social realism.

The strategic emphasis on a young, cocky 'Brit' style paid off handsomely, with the film becoming a major domestic and international hit of its year: the UK box-office alone was £11 million.

☐ CASE STUDY 5: BUILDING AN AUDIENCE ON THE WEB FOR *THE BLAIR WITCH PROJECT* (1999)

This film earns its place in film history as the first internet-driven theatrical release, although the marketing potential of the web for film had begun to be exploited from the mid-1990s onwards, particularly in the independent sector.

This low-budget video–16mm work cost only $35,000 to make, and was shot and edited by Eduardo Sanchez and Daniel Myrick from late 1997 through 1998. A screening at the Sundance Film Festival in early 1999 resulted in a distribution deal with Artisan Entertainment, who decided to build on the air of 'authenticity' of the handheld footage in the film as a promotional tool.

A pre-existing website for the film had been set up by the makers in June 1998, but Artisan added fake documentary evidence – police records, histories of the Blair Witch, journals – all to create the film's official site. Www.blairwitch.com posed an enigma around the events depicted in the film: 'Did they happen or is the whole thing invented?'

By April 1999, a trailer for the film had appeared on the aint-it-cool-news.com website, and unofficial sites were debating the authenticity of the story's events. By the time of the film's US release on 16 July 1999, a marketing phenomenon had occurred with the official website having been visited 22 million times.[75] This promotion went a long way to explain the film's eventual box-office take of over $240 million worldwide.[76]

This cross-media phenomenon of film and web has, since its first appearance, reinvented film marketing. 'Word-of-internet' is now an integral strategy of film promotion. Fortunately for the industry, the predominant online users correspond conveniently to the frequent film-goers, the 16- to 24-age group. Hence, a marketing strategy such as this makes especially good sense since it is cheap to run and targets the 'lean-forward' young PC viewer/film-goer, rather than the stay-at-home 'lean-back' TV viewer.

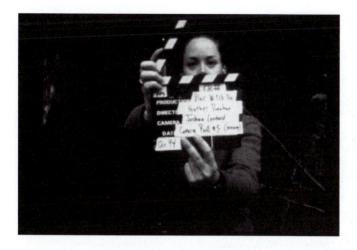

• **Plate 2.10**
Production still from
The Blair Witch Project
(Daniel Myrick and
Eduardo Sanchez,
1999). How to build
an audience: pose an
enigma around the
authenticity of your
footage and mount a
very clever campaign
on the internet to entice
punters to see the film

More recently, the cross-media campaign for the blockbuster *Harry Potter and the Sorcerer's Stone* (2001) bears witness to the lessons learned by the industry from *The Blair Witch Project*. The campaign used to great effect the web, TV and the press to promote and publicise the movie.

Summary

Film as communication is not unidirectional, with the producer presenting the consumer with a fixed diet of consumables. Quite the contrary. Increasingly, ICT allows market analysts to access accurate information from and about movie-goers – information which is then used to determine production decisions.

CONCLUSION

This chapter has centred on the institutional framework of mainstream film, and the historical relationship between text and context. Any change in production, exhibition or distribution practice, in communication technology (both hardware and software), or in audience demographics, will have repercussions for the films we see and how we see them.

Films and their socio-economic contexts are part of a much broader history, that of the cultural history of the past 100 years. The purpose of this overview has been to go some way towards illuminating that point.

NOTES

1 Immediately after the formation of the General Film Company, independents began operating their own distribution company – the Motion Picture Distributing and Sales Company (May 1910). This was superseded by the Film Supply Company of America, the Universal Film Manufacturing Company and Mutual Films in 1912. Later, the introduction of feature-length films further weakened the MPPC, when many of its own members began dissociating themselves from the GFC and distributed their features through alternative distribution organisations (Elsaesser 1990: 194–6, 201).

2 In 1928, First National was purchased by Warner Brothers Film Company.

3 An early form of block-booking had existed during the days of the MPPC called standing-orders (Elsaesser 1990: 193).

4 This system was not universally adopted nor did companies refrain from changing production systems periodically. Taking 1941 as an example, it is interesting to note that the three most financially successful companies, in terms of box-office receipts, were all operating different production systems:

- United Artists had a system of director units and producer units
- MGM operated a producer–unit system
- Twentieth Century Fox used a central-producer system. (Bordwell et al. 1985: 320–9)

5 See Warner Brothers' balance sheet for the studio era (Gomery 1986: 102).

6 In 1932, the average production cost per feature was US $200,000.00, whereas at MGM it was $450,000.00. See R. Campbell, 'Warner Bros in the 1930s' (1971: 2).

7 See M. Roth's essay, 'Some Warners Musicals and the Spirit of the New Deal', in Altman (1981: 41–56).

8 For a discussion on the relationship of this director to Warner's studio style see E. Buscombe's essay, 'Walsh and Warner Brothers', in Hardy (1974).

9 See drawings for Mildred Pierce sets in Deschner (1975, p. 20).

10 And 30 per cent of Columbia's releases were also produced by them (balio 1976: 353).

11 The first major film company to sell its film library to TV was RKO, in December 1955 (Balio 1976: 322).

12 From the late 1940s onwards, film companies began producing programmes for TV (e.g. Warner's weekly series for ABC-TV, Warner Bros. Presents (1955). By the early 1960s, producing TV shows was standard film industry practice and a major source of its revenue. Shortly after-wards (from the mid-1960s onwards), TV networks began commissioning made-for-TV films from major studios and independent producers (Balio 1976: 322–4).

13 For example, in 1956, United Paramount Theatres (ex-exhibition arm of Paramount) merged with ABC-TV (Balio 1976: 324).

14 The pattern of exclusive first-run releases having been broken with The Godfather in 1972 (Jowett and Linton 1989: 59).

15 C. Parkes, 'Everyone Goes to Hollywood', Financial Times, 13 March 2001, p. 10.

16 Screen International, No. 750, 31 March 1990.

17 Many thanks to John Wilkinson, of the UK-based Cinema Exhibitors' Association, whose interviews with me assisted in the compilation of the following information.

18 G. Drabinsky, Motion Pictures and the Arts in Canada: The Business and the Law (McGraw-Hill Ryerson, Toronto, 1976), quoted in Jowett and Linton (1989: 56).

19 'DVD Rising', Chicago Tribune, 14 October 2001.

20 The Times, 22 March 2006, p. 56.

21 'Film Giants May Shrink DVD Gap', The Times, 22 April 2005.

22 'The Sunday Review', Independent on Sunday, 11 July 1993, p.15.

23 See www.ukfilmcouncil.org.uk.

24 US $600 million of the summer's $1.8 billion gross. The independent productions that were major box-office winners were Terminator 2 (Carolco Productions), Robin Hood (Morgan Creek Productions), City Slickers (Castle Rock Productions), Backdraft (Imagine Productions), Point Break (Largo Productions). Reported in Biskind (1991: 6).

25 See www.businessweek.com (12 December 2005).

26 See Scott Smith's online article, 'Byte Me ...', dated 24 January 2001, at www.atomfilms.com.

27 Reported in N. Christie, 'A Defining Moment', in 'FT Magazine', Financial Times, 16 October 2005, p. 52.

28 In 1950 James Stewart's agent MCA (Music Corp. of America), arranged for him to be paid 50 per cent of the net profits of the Universal film Winchester '73, in lieu of his normal salary of $250,000. This arrangement would not have been possible under the terms of his MGM contract during the studio era (Kent 1991: 86).

29 A 1989 audience survey reported that the presence of stars was not an important factor in movie attendance decisions, but only important as a means of publicising a film (Jowett and Linton 1989: 39).

30 In the form of writer–producer teams, writer–producer–director teams, and unattached writers.

31 See www.ukfilmcouncil.org.uk.

32 See Guardian, 23 February 2006, p. 7.

33 See Chris Collins's comments in his essay 'British Film: The Next Generation', in the Guardian, 16 November 2001, and available online at http://film.guardian.co.uk/features/featurepages.

34 See S. Bukatman's BFI modern classic on Blade Runner (BFI, London, 1997).

35 See www.hollywoodreporter.com/hollywoodreporter/.wrap/wrap00/dreamworks.jsp dated 24 October 2001.

36 See www.upcomingmovies.com/gladiator.html.

37 Source: Ali Cherkaoui, Second Assistant Director.

38 Reported in an interview with Ridley Scott in the 'Magazine' section of The Times, Saturday 25 November 2000, p. 39.

39 See www.upcomingmovies.com/gladiator.html.

40 Source: Enrico Ballarin, Mestiere Cinema Productions.

41 See Gladiator UK press release produced by Media Enterprises, 2000, pp.15–16.

42 See the 'Magazine' section of The Times, 11 November 2000, p.39.

43 See http://us.imdb.com/charts.

44 See http://www.the-movie-times.com/thrsdir/top100world.html.

45 'Plenty of Fish in Pond Time-Warner Wants to Swim In', Wall Street Journal, 7 March 1989, P.B1, cited in Balio (1990: 315).

46 Warner owns the film rights to J.K. Rowling's first three books and has options on the next four. Reported in an article by T. Reid and L. Peek entitled, 'Potter Playtime ...', The Times, 6 November 2001, p. 11.

47 See C. Grimes's article, 'Harry Potter and the Sales Team', Financial Times, 16 November 2001, p. 17.

48 See Guardian, 23 November 2001, p. 27.

49 See 'Will Sony Make it in Hollywood?', Fortune, 9 September, 1991.

50 Report by the US Department of Labour entitled Family Spending and Saving in Wartime, Bulletin No. 822. Quoted in Handel (1950: 104).

51 Film Daily Year Book, and quoted in Handel (1950: 96). As a comparison, attendance figures for 1940 (pre-Second World War) were 80 million/week, and around 85 million/week for 1945 (end of the Second World War) (Austin 1989: 36).

52 Women: 3.75 times per month; Men: 3.7 times per month. See: L. Handel, Studies of the Motion Picture Audience (New York), December 1941. Cited in Handel (1950: 100).

53 Defined as attending ten times a month or more: figures for men were 11.8 per cent, as opposed to only 7.5 per cent for women; see Handel (1950: 100).

54 For example, in a state-wide survey conducted in Iowa in 1942, 31 per cent of men and 24.9 per cent of women aged 15 to 20 attended cinemas over five times a month, as opposed to only 11.4 per cent and 7.6 per cent respectively of those aged 21 to 35 years; see F. Whan and H. Summers, The 1942 Iowa Radio Audience Survey (Des Moines, 1942) cited in Handel (1950: 103).

55 In actual numbers, persons with higher levels of education

were a minority among cinema-goers in the 1940s (Handel 1950: 104–8).

56 See *Film Daily Year Book*, quoted in Bernstein (1957: 2).

57 Department of Commerce's census of business for 1954. Cited in Bernstein (1957: 5).

58 Thirty per cent of those surveyed cited watching TV as their favourite way to spend an evening. Only 6 per cent of those surveyed cited going to the movies (*The Gallup Opinion Index*, Report 146, pp. 14–15, September 1977, quoted in Austin (1989: 40)).

59 Defined in this survey as persons under the age of 30.

60 In a 1948 Gallup poll, 79 per cent of people surveyed between the ages of 18 and 20, and 76 per cent of those between the ages of 21 and 29 had been to the cinema within the past three weeks; this declined to 57 per cent for those aged 30–49 (Gallup, cited in Docherty et al. (1987: 17)).

61 In a survey in 1949, 19 per cent of the working-class people surveyed (i.e. those with low levels of income and education) went to the cinema (at least) twice a week, as opposed to 13 per cent of middle-class people interviewed, and 8 per cent of upper-class people surveyed (Hulton research, Cited in Docherty et al. (1987: 16).

62 'There was an increase in TV licences from 343k in 1950 to 10 million in 1960' (Docherty et al. 1987: 23).

63 Partly a product of 1950s prosperity and a move towards greater owner-occupation, and partly the result of the Town and Country Planning Act of 1947 which 'led to the clearing of slums, the growth of new towns . . . and, crucially, the resiting of large sections of the working class . . . around the edges of cities' (Docherty et al. 1987: 25–6).

64 Dropping from half the total audience to one-third between 1977 and 1983 (Docherty et al. 1987: 30–1).

65 See the MPAA (Motion Picture Association of America) report, *Annual Theatrical Market Statistics* (2005).

66 Source: the National Association of Theatre Owners.

67 Males of this age are the most likely audience for a block-buster movie in its opening two weekends. See D. Denby, 'Aiming Low', *New Yorker*, 13 and 20 June 2005, p. 187.

68 'DVD Shipments Seen Reaching Lofty Heights', Reuters, 24 October 2001.

69 See www.dvddemistified.com.

70 British Film Institute.

71 Cinema Exhibitors' Association, UK.

72 Quoted from 'The Sunday Review', *Independent on Sunday*, 11 July 1993.

73 'Every element of this heart-warming drama (*Grizzly Adams*), from the hair and eye colouring of the actors to the type of animals they frolic with, was pre-tested . . . your family's every 'ooh' and 'ahh' was anticipated in tests taken by other families demographically identical to yours', from P. Morrisroe, 'Making Movies the Computer Way', *Parade*, vol. 16, 3 February 1980, quoted in Jowett and Linton (1989: 106).

74 See A. Rawsthorn, 'Small Budget Movie with Big Ambitions', 'Weekend' section, *Financial Times*, 27 January 1996.

75 See B. Farrow's article dated 8 October 1999, 'Hollywood Runs Scared', on *The Times* website.

76 See http://us.imdb.com/charts/worldtopmovies.

FURTHER READING

Austin, B., *Immediate Seating: A Look at Movie Audiences*, Wadsworth Publishing Company, Belmont, CA, 1989.

Balio, T. (ed.), *The American Film Industry*, University of Wisconsin Press, Madison, 1976.

Balio, T. (ed.), *Hollywood in the Age of Television*, Unwin Hyman, Boston, MA, 1990.

Bernstein, I. *Hollywood at the Crossroads: An Economic Study of the Motion Picture Industry*, Hollywood Film Council, LA, 1957.

Bordwell, D. Staiger, J. and Thompson, K., *The Classical Hollywood Cinema*, Routledge & Kegan Paul, London, 1985.

Docherty, D., Morrison, D. and Tracey, M., *The Last Picture Show?*, British Film Institute, London, 1987.

Epstein, E.J., *The Big Picture*, Random House, New York, 2005.

Finney, A., *The Egos Have Landed*, Mandarin, London, 1997.

Giles, J., *The Crying Game*, BFI Publishing, London, 1997.

Gomery, D., *The Hollywood Studio System*, Macmillan, London, 1986.

Gomery, D., *Shared Pleasures*, British Film Institute, London, 1992.

Handel, L., *Hollywood Looks at its Audience*, University of Illinois Press, Urbana, 1950.

Jowett, G. and Linton, J., *Movies as Mass Communication*, Sage, Newbury Park, CA, 1989.

Kent, N., *Naked Hollywood*, BBC Books, London, 1991.

Landau, D. (ed.), *Gladiator: The Making of the Ridley Scott Epic*, Boxtree, London, 2000.

Leff, L. and Simmons, J., *The Dame in the Kimono*, Grove Weidenfeld, NY, 1990.

Merritt, G., *Celluloid Mavericks*, Thunder's Mouth Press, NY, 2000.

Roddick, N., *A New Deal in Entertainment*, British Film Institute, London, 1983.

FURTHER VIEWING

Key Warner Brothers (genre) films
The gangster film
Little Caesar (1930)
The Public Enemy (1931)
Bullets or Ballots (1935)
Marked Woman (1937)
The Roaring 'Twenties (1939)

The social conscience film
I Am A Fugitive From A Chain Gang (1932)
Wild Boys of The Road (1933)

The fast-talking comedy/drama
Five-star Final (1931)
Lady Killer (1933)
Hard To Handle (1933)

The musical
42nd Street (1933)
Gold Diggers of 1933 (1933)
Dames (1934)

The biopic
The Story of Louis Pasteur (1936)
The Life of Emile Zola (1937)
Juarez (1939)

The Merrie-England cycle
Captain Blood (1935)
The Adventures of Robin Hood (1938)
The Sea Hawk (1940)

The melodrama
Jezebel (1938)
The Letter (1940)
Now Voyager (1942)
Mildred Pierce (1945)

The film noir
The Maltese Falcon (1941)
The Big Sleep (1946)
Dark Passage (1947)

UK resource addresses
British Film Institute Library
21 Stephen Street
London W1P 1PL
tel 020 7255 1444

The Cinema Exhibitors' Association
22 Golden Square
London W1R 3PA
tel 020 7734 9551

Dodona Research
12 The Crescent, King Street
Leicester LE2 2YE
tel 0116 285 4550

The Film Council
10 Little Portland Street
London W1W 7JG
tel 020 7861 7861

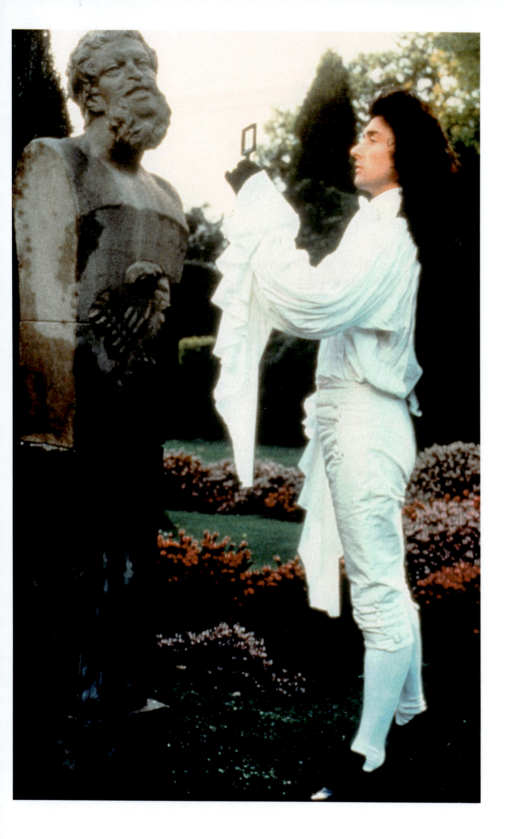

Part three

Approaches to studying film texts

Chapter 3

Film form and narrative

Suzanne Speidel

■ Film form and narrative

INTRODUCING FORM AND NARRATIVE

Films tell stories. Of course, this is not true of all films: documentaries, abstract animations, and early film genres such as 'cinema of attractions' (see Tom Gunning in Elsaesser 1990: 57) are all types of film which exploit other properties of cinema besides its narrative capabilities. Yet for most of us, our principal experience of cinema is the experience of narrative film. This chapter seeks to analyse how films tell stories, and what kinds of stories films tell.

For a film to be a 'narrative' it must present us with a series of events in ways that imply connections between one event and the next. Narratives must, therefore, have constituent parts, which are also discernibly related (though the type of relationship may vary greatly). Most commonly we expect a 'cause-and-effect' relationship: one event has the effect of causing another event, which causes another, and so on. Narratives also require 'narration', or communication. Cinematic narration is arguably the most sophisticated of all narrative media, because it is 'multi-track', both visual and audio. This enables films to co-opt the communicative capabilities of a whole host of other media and forms. For example, films have linguistic communication through the presence of dialogue or voice-over on the soundtrack, or the inclusion of printed text within the image (such as intertitles, shots of newspapers, books, letters).

Since moving images also record the three-dimensional physical world, film can incorporate other visual arts, such as painting, still photography, theatre and architecture. Thus the tomb of 'El Khasne' in Petra, Jordan, features in *Indiana Jones and the Last Crusade* (Steven Spielberg, 1989), Richard Neutra's modernist Lovell House is used as a location for *LA Confidential* (Curtis Hanson, 1997), while Alberto Libera's Casa Malaparte is the Capri setting of *Le Mépris* (Jean-Luc Godard, 1963). In Grigori Kozintsev's *Hamlet* (1964), meanwhile, pictures and tapestries that resemble the film itself decorate the walls within the castle of Elsinore. Films not only have the potential to photograph the other visual arts, they may also copy their techniques. The techniques developed in theatre, painting and photography in staging, framing and image composition have been highly influential in shaping cinema. We may understand filmic expression, therefore, as combining a mixture of practices which are unique to narrative cinema with those it has borrowed and developed from other media. In its narration and its narrative structures cinema has also been heavily influenced by the novel.

This chapter will examine both the techniques which make up cinematic narration and the structures which combine to make a narrative. It is concerned with rules (or 'codes') which shape the production of images and sounds on the small scale and with rules (or 'conventions') which shape the depiction of scenes, events and characters on a large scale. The visual codes of cinema may be broadly divided into **mise-en-scène** and **editing**. The audio codes may be divided into speech, music and noise.

CONVENTIONS, HOLLYWOOD, ART AND AVANT-GARDE CINEMA

The notion of 'rules', albeit ones that are fluid and adaptable, is crucial to the study of form and narrative. As with other narrative media, such as novels, theatre, comic books and epic poems, films organize stories according to sets of conventions, which are understood by filmmakers and recognized by film viewers. Thus we respond to films based on not only our experience of the 'real world', but also the expectations we have formed through watching other films. Film narratives only gain meaning through these expectations, which may be met, or else thwarted in ways that reference and influence such expectations.

For discussion of early cinema and the evolution of film form see pp. 149–50.

mise-en-scène
Meaning, literally, 'putting into the scene', this term originated in the theatre. Precise critical definitions differ, but it is most simply understood as everything which appears within the frame, including setting, props, costume and make-up, lighting, the behaviour of performers, cinematography and special effects.

editing
Sometimes also referred to as 'montage' (from the French 'monter', meaning 'to assemble'), this refers to the joining together of different pieces of film stock in post-production.

classical Hollywood
This term refers both to an historical period within Hollywood cinema (which ended with the decline of the vertically integrated studio system in the 1950s), and to the narrative and formal conventions established and promoted during this time; the terms 'classical narrative' and 'Hollywood narrative' are frequently used interchangeably with the term 'mainstream narrative,' since this constitutes cinema's dominant mode of story-telling.

avant-garde
Meaning literally 'advanced guard' (those who 'march ahead' of the troops in a military campaign), 'avant-garde' has been taken up as an aesthetic term for art (and artists) seeking to challenge, subvert or reinvent artistic tenets and conventions.

Modernism
This refers to a dramatically experimental trend within the arts (painting, sculpture, architecture, literature, music and film) which grew up at the start of the twentieth century, encompassing a wide array of movements (Expressionism, Vorticism, Symbolism, Imagism, Surrealism) along with the innovations of individual artists not directly affiliated with a particular movement. Modernism involved a rejection of nineteenth-century styles, traditions and ideas, and a self-conscious (or 'self-reflexive') approach to aesthetic forms, in which artistic expression was itself explored, questioned and reinvented.

For further discussion of Indian cinema see Chapter 13, pp. 336–62.

Russian formalism
A literary theory which developed in Russia in the early 1920s, which sought to establish a scientific basis for the study of literature and literary effects.

The history and evolution of cinematic narrative conventions allows us to distinguish between, on one hand, '**classical Hollywood**' or mainstream cinema, and on the other, art cinema, which has traditionally been the province of Europe. In other words, it is possible to identify a series of narrative conventions which emerged out of the imperatives of commercial cinema, in which the project of entertainment for the purpose of profit is paramount, and a series of narrative conventions which emerged in industries where state subsidies, and a tendency towards small-scale independent production, facilitated an emphasis on aesthetic innovation and personal expression.

Obviously such generalizations require qualification. For example, in contemporary Hollywood horizontal integration and increasing conglomeration have brought about the emergence of large independent producers and specialized production and distribution wings within the major companies. This environment has resulted in films such as *The Usual Suspects* (Bryan Singer, 1995), *Memento* (Christopher Nolan, 2000) and *Crash* (Paul Haggis, 2004) which arguably use a number of art cinema characteristics. Conversely European film industries have consistently produced films, such as comedies and musicals, belonging to genres popularized by Hollywood, while the European propensity for art cinema may also be understood in commercial terms, with aesthetic and national specificity proving a profitable means of product differentiation in a global market. As narrative categories, classical and art cinema are linked, each responding to the methods, creativity and competitive presence of the other. Thus French New Wave cinema pays homage to and parodies film noir (itself indebted to German Expressionism). Hollywood cinema, always particularly adept at cinematic 'borrowing', has tended to adopt art cinema aesthetics and conventions as a means of refreshing its own genres, and the inventiveness of the films listed above may be understood in these terms.

Art cinema is also closely related to a further category, the **avant-garde**. The avant-garde is most readily distinguishable from art cinema in economic and institutional, rather than aesthetic, terms, in that avant-garde films are distributed outside the structures of the film industry (in film clubs, galleries or academic institutions). Art films, though frequently subsidized, are exhibited in commercially run cinemas and their larger production scales demand greater financial success than do avant-garde films. In terms of content and form the two categories are overlapping, and both may be related to the rise of **Modernism**.

Both art cinema and avant-garde cinema may be understood in terms of responses to – and *reactions against* – mainstream cinema. Indeed many critical accounts of art cinema define its conventions as being opposite to Hollywood's, describing it explicitly in terms of what Hollywood is not. As a means of getting to grips with art cinema's conventions this is a useful approach, but it is important to bear in mind that art cinema is not only this. In its relation to Modernism, and in its existence within different national cinemas, art cinema is varied, and has conventions of its own that are not simply 'other' than what Hollywood does.

The above definitions of both 'mainstream' and 'art' in cinema are admittedly Western and 'first-world centric', since the former is conceived in terms of Hollywood and the latter in terms of Europe. This reflects Hollywood's global domination of the film industry, and the powerful influence American and European cinematic traditions have had worldwide. However, there are a number of other powerfully influential national and transcontinental cinemas which offer their own art and commercially orientated conventions (the cinemas of India and Japan most obviously come to mind).

Story and plot

In order to understand the fundamental components of any narrative it is first necessary to make a distinction between a narrative's 'story' and its 'plot'. 'Story' (labelled 'fabula' by **Russian formalist** literary theorists) refers to the events of the narrative, and the actions and responses of characters. 'Plot' (or 'syuzhet') refers to the ways in which the story is presented to us in terms of its order, emphases and logic. A succinct distinction between these two ideas has been provided by Seymour Chatman, who suggests that 'the story is the *what* in a narrative that is depicted', and plot 'the *how*' (Chatman 1980: 19).

The most conspicuous way that the plot shapes how the story is told is in terms of its chronology. One way in which a plot may present a story is the order in which we presume events take place and the characters experience them. Thus the film *Bambi* (David Hand, 1942), which is essentially the story of the central character's life from birth to parenthood, has a narrative in which the story and plot order are the same. By contrast, Marcel Carné's *Le Jour se lève* (1939) has a plot which begins close to the end of the story (and the hero's life), with François (Jean Gabin) committing a murder. There then follow three separate flashbacks, which show us the events that led to the murder. This plot structure clearly has the effect of creating intrigue by raising the question of how François could have descended to such desperate measures. It also imbues the film with a pervasive air of pessimism, since even as flashbacks show us a burgeoning romance, we know that the liaison must be ill-fated.

Thus our responses to the story are shaped by the manipulations of the plot. Plot strategies which play with the story's chronology demand that we piece together the order in which we presume the events take place. The ease with which this can be done depends on the method and degree of connection between one story-moment and the next. *Le Jour se lève*, for example, employs cinematic codes (such as the **ripple-dissolve**) to make such links clear. (Of course, these only work because there is a shared understanding between filmmakers and viewers that ripple-dissolves introduce characters' memories.) The plot can also emphasize or de-emphasize moments of the story through other types of temporal manipulation. The least important moments of story are liable to be missed out of the plot altogether (as when, for example, a character travels from one story-location to another). The omission (or ellipsis) of a portion of the story from the plot may have a number of other effects, such as the evocation of mystery. In *Bambi* the plot does not dramatize the period of Bambi's life immediately after the death of his mother, a gap which eases our shock and allows us to assume, without having to witness it, that Bambi has recovered from his grief. The film's tone is immediately lifted with the lively, comical 'Let's Sing a Gay Little Spring Song' number; thus the plot manipulates our emotional responses to the story, providing a musical interlude as recovery-time and as a means of cheering us up.

Film plots also operate in conjunction with film running times; where an ellipsis occurs the portion of the film's running time assigned to the incident in question is none; however, a story-incident can be emphasized if a large portion of the film's running time is devoted to it. Thus, Robert Mulligan's *To Kill a Mockingbird* (1962) devotes thirty-five minutes of its 129-minute running time to the trial of Tom Robinson. The plot's uneven distribution of the story across the running time of the film gives us time to appreciate Atticus's (Gregory Peck) defence tactics, the injustice of the racially motivated conviction, and the profound effect the trial has on Atticus's children. The relationship between the three temporal categories of story, plot and running time can be further manipulated by such cinematic codes as editing and fast- or slow-motion photography.

The plot also stages the story across space as well as across time. In *Bambi* the story takes place in the two distinct spaces of the forest and the meadow, and we are guided as to the type of story-incident liable to occur in the meadow on Bambi's first visit there, when his mother warns him that 'Out there we are unprotected'. When the plot next dramatizes a scene in the meadow Bambi is stranded while gunfire sounds off-screen, and in the third meadow scene Bambi's mother is shot. The plot therefore uses the spaces of the story to alternate between periods of safety (represented by the forest) and danger (represented by the meadow). The climax of the narrative is signalled by a breaking of this pattern, and we are alarmed by the threat of the hunt and the fire precisely because they invade the safe spaces of the forest.

ripple-dissolve
A dissolve is an editing technique using superimposition, which produces a gradual transition between one image and the next, during which the two shots for a time occupy the frame simultaneously, appearing merged together; a ripple-dissolve emphasizes this transition through the introduction of ripples, or waves, within the image.

The plot's staging of the action in space is also crucial to our grasp of narrative point of view. The presentation of point of view takes place at the level of cinematic codes, where editing and camera movement may be used to posit certain shots as representing (or approximating) what it is a particular character sees. However, a broader notion of point of view – or what Gerard Genette (Genette 1980: 189) has termed 'focalization' – also exists at the level of narrative conventions, in that we often infer that a particular story 'belongs to' someone. Where the plot remains always, or for the most part, in the same space as a particular character, then the film will seem entirely, or principally, 'focalized' through that character (as in *The Big Sleep* (Howard Hawks, 1946) where Philip Marlowe (Humphrey Bogart) is shown in almost every scene, so that we know and understand as much as he does). Curtis Hanson's *LA Confidential* (1997) uses multiple focalization, with the three opening scenes introducing our three police-officer, central characters in turn. Our understanding of the ensuing narrative is dictated by the way the plot switches between the investigative activities of the three men so that we know more than any one of them.

The operations of focalization are crucial to the emotional investment most Hollywood films ask us to make in the fate of central characters. Often focalization through a particular character invites us to like that character, since we understand what causes them to act as they do. *LA Confidential* engages our interest by guiding us to understand why two focalizing characters, Bud (Russell Crowe) and Ed (Guy Pearce), conceive a violent dislike for each other. We like and understand both men, though they do not like or understand each other, and this heightens our expectations of the moment when they realize that they are in fact on the same side. However, focalization through a particular character need not necessarily result in our feeling empathy for them: Thompson is the 'focalizer' of *Citizen Kane* (Orson Welles, 1941) but remains little more than a narrative device, since he only sees the story rather than acts in it. A number of Hollywood films in recent years, such as *The Shawshank Redemption* (Frank Darabont, 1994), *The Sixth Sense* (M. Night Shyamalan, 1999), *Fight Club* (David Fincher, 1999) and *Memento*, have played with the conventions of focalization, providing focalizers whose understanding is partial or deluded. Such strategies influence our response to characters, either through provoking distrust of the characters' unreliability or pleasure at the plot's ingenuity.

Hollywood and mainstream narratives

Many of the examples given above shed light on the key characteristics of classical film narratives. Because entertainment is the principal priority, the operations and conventions of mainstream films are dictated by the need to arouse and sustain our interest. This has led to a particular stress on character – on active characters, whose exploits reveal motives we can readily appreciate – and on what may be termed 'benevolence' and 'transparency'.

Hollywood narratives and codes are dictated by a desire to make the story readily comprehensible to the audience. This does not mean that techniques and structures are themselves simplistic; rather it means that a sophisticated set of conventions has evolved which aims to guide viewers through the story (in this sense they are 'benevolent'). The techniques are 'transparent' because they seek to keep viewers focused on the story; they are therefore unobtrusive, so that audiences remain absorbed in *what* is happening, rather than become distracted by *how* the story is told. Part of the sophistication of Hollywood narratives and techniques lies in their invisibility, in the effort involved in appearing effortless.

It is in Hollywood narratives where the principle of cause and effect is adhered to most rigidly, since it is this which produces story clarity. It is usually character which provides the causal elements, driving the story forward and providing connections between the elements which the plot places side by side. For this reason most Hollywood films feature heroes who have definite goals: the central character desires something, seeks to achieve something, and the story consists of the actions the character undertakes to fulfil such aims. In most cases the story is 'closed'; that is, the ending offers a complete conclusion to the character's goal (obvious exceptions to this include where a film is part of a franchise, so that the ending sets up the scenario for a sequel). The narrative will end with the character's goal having been met, or the attempt having failed – although the industry's aim of giving pleasure has led to the predominance of the former outcome.

Sometimes heroes have more than one goal, although usually such multiple goals will coincide and reinforce each other. In *His Girl Friday* (Howard Hawks, 1939), for example, Walter (Cary Grant) seeks to prevent Hildy (Rosalind Russell) from marrying Bruce (Ralph Bellamy), because he wants regain his star 'newspaper "man"' at the *Washington Post*, and because he wants to marry her for a second time himself. Thus his professional goal and his romantic goal result in his pursuing a single course of action. In *Grosse Pointe Blank* (George Armitage, 1997), meanwhile, contract killer Martin Blank (John Cusack) pursues two different courses of action when he is forced into taking on one last 'hit', while trying to win back the love of his former girlfriend Debi (Minnie Driver). However these two goals intersect when Martin discovers that the man he is supposed to kill is Debi's father, and he is able to gain her love by changing his approach to his professional goal, killing his employers instead. Most mainstream movies contain a romantic story-line of some kind, and the interweaving of romance with another story-line represents a common type of multiple-goal narrative. In mainstream narratives characters' methods of achieving goals are shaped by personality 'traits' which are clearly identified: in *LA Confidential*, for example, Bud is motivated by a need to protect women from violent men. Characters provide direction for the story, and the narrative provides clear delineation of what characters are like, and what they want.

For an illustration of classical narrative see Case study 1.

• Plate 3.1
The goal-oriented hero of *Gladiator* (Ridley Scott, 2000)

Art cinema narratives

Because art films are not governed to the same degree by a commercial imperative to provide entertainment and pleasure, their narrative conventions differ from those of mainstream films. Art films are not shaped by the formulaic approach to story-telling described above, although in their oppositional position to mainstream cinema they offer recurring characteristics that suggest broad guidelines in terms of conventions.

Art films are not governed by the narrative strategy of cause and effect: coincidence, chance and random sequences of events are common in their narratives. Frequently the story connections offered by the plot are jarring and confusing rather than elucidatory: thus Bernardo Bertolucci's *The Conformist* (1969) does not make clear for some time that early scenes in a radio station are a flashback in relation to the plot's opening car journey, and our sense dislocation is furthered by the presence of flashforwards within the flashback sequence. The film's structure is highly fragmented, with individual story moments repeatedly interrupted by other moments in a disorientating fashion. Similarly the motivations of characters are also not readily discernible, and they cannot be relied on to explain the logic and direction of the story. In *Le Mépris* (1963), for example, Camille (Brigitte Bardot) vacillates between reassuring her husband Paul (Michel Piccoli) that she still loves him, and angrily voicing her contempt for him. Art films do not necessarily invite us to like their heroes and heroines: Godard's *A bout de souffle* (1959) presents us with an arrogant central protagonist (played by Jean Paul Belmondo) who repeatedly insults his girlfriend; *The Conformist*, more radically, depicts a character who spies for the fascists, and passively colludes in murder.

In many art films characters are not particularly active, and typically the story moves more slowly than in Hollywood films, with plots assigning long portions of running time to scenes showing little story progress. In *Le Mépris* much of the film's first seventy-two minutes are taken up with little more than Paul's indecision about whether he will accept film producer Prokosch's (Jack Palance) offer of a job, and Camille's indecision about whether she will accompany him. François Truffaut's *Baisers volés* (1968) contains a scene in which Antoine Doinel (Jean-Pierre Léaud) sends a love letter, and there follows a series of shots of the letter as it is sucked down the vacuum-tubes of the postal system and delivered to its destination. This sequence constitutes a plot dramatization in which no significant action takes place, and is pointedly superfluous to the unfolding of the story.

Art cinema also tends to avoid closed endings, favouring instead a sense of irresolution and indecision. Many art films give the impression that they have 'stopped' rather than 'ended' – that the plot has ceased to dramatize rather than resolved the story's dilemmas. Famously, François Truffaut's first Antoine Doinel film, *Les Quatre cents coups* (1959), ends with a freeze frame as Antoine is in the process of running away, while *Le Mépris* cuts short the marital conflicts of its protagonists with a shocking car crash.

For further discussion of the French New Wave see Chapter 15, pp. 398–428.

All these properties may be related to a number of broad preoccupations which art cinema explores. While in mainstream narratives the characters and their traits are put in service of telling the story, in art cinema the logic, progress and resolution of the story are often subordinate to the exploration of character. Characters' subjectivity and mental states become a key focus, and it is not uncommon to find characters who are emotionally unbalanced – or even psychotic – acting as the principal focalizers of the narrative (as in, for example, Robert Wiene's *The Cabinet of Dr Caligari* (1919) or Roman Polanski's *Repulsion* (1965)). The subjectivity of characters is one way that we may account for the films' fragmented structures and dramatic ambiguities, although such readings are not usually confirmed for us by the narrative.

Implicit in these uncertainties is the idea that human behaviour and human stories cannot be as readily resolved in life as they are in mainstream narratives: our experience of the world is not one of neat cause and effect, nor do we necessarily approach our lives with clear-cut goals in mind and an understanding of our motives. Art films suggest that characters cannot control events, and that the action will not necessarily reward us with satisfying answers. *The Conformist* constitutes an exploration of the idea that people and causes can never be understood, in that initially it seems to suggest that it will uncover why people become fascists; however, its fragmented structure seems to bury rather than reveal explanations, implying that the causes of history and human behaviour can never be fully comprehended.

Just as story is put in service of character, it is also subordinate to plot. Art cinema prioritizes the question of *how* narrative is presented rather than *what* is told. Despite the fact that many of its archetypal films were released decades after the era of Modernism, art cinema is Modernist in that it takes up a self-conscious position in relation to its own aesthetic forms, seeking to explore the properties of cinematic expression itself. This may take the form of jarring, fragmented or superfluous narrative devices, which make the operations of the plot conspicuous as opposed to transparent; it may also take the form of experimental cinematic codes, such as the **jump-cuts** of Godard's *A bout de souffle*, which again force us to notice, rather than enjoy, cinematic technique. A number of art films, such as *Le Mépris* and Federico Fellini's *8½* (1963), are also more blatantly self-referential in that their stories are themselves concerned with filmmaking. In such instances it is often the limitations of the medium which are explored, as the frustrations of undertaking fictional film projects serve as metaphors for the fractured narratives of the films themselves – and perhaps also for the impossibilities of achieving any satis-factory communication.

jump-cut
An elliptical cut, where the transition between one image and the next is disruptive because it is in some way spatially or temporally inconsistent, or because the two images involved are very similar.

Art cinema is sometimes – problematically – associated with the personal expression of the director in ways that Hollywood cinema is not. This is in part because the production contexts of art films mean that the director's role is likely to be more prominent than it is in larger, commercial ventures. In addition, the self-consciousness of art cinema encourages us to associate the films with a particular artist, since the invitation to notice techniques draws our attention to the possible creative presence behind them. The figure of the auteur originated in European cinematic discourses and has been central to much critical writing on European cinema, although more recent interest in European popular genres has eroded this dominance (see Dyer and Vincendeau 1992). However, since auteurism has also featured prominently in critical approaches to Hollywood, and has been subject to considerable revision and critique, it is an approach towards art cinema which should perhaps be treated with caution.

For further discussion of auteurism see Chapter 8, pp. 91–108.

For further discussion of British cinema see Chapter 13, pp. 302–34.

Some critics also define art cinema in terms of a tendency to engage in political and/or social commentary (see Street 1997: 47). This does not typify all art cinema but there are certain national movements (such as Italian Neo-realism or the British New Wave) where this criterion does apply. It is also the case that the art cinema of certain countries displays a preoccupation with questions of national politics and history. This is particularly apparent where countries have turbulent national histories, as in the case of new German cinema which seeks to explore Germany's Nazi past and legacy.

CINEMATIC CODES

Critical accounts of cinematic codes have tended to differ in the ways they have broken down, or categorized for analysis, cinema's key communicative procedures. This chapter considers three basic areas – two visual codes (mise-en-scène and editing) and one audio code (soundtrack).

Mise-en-scène

The term 'mise-en-scène' originated in the theatre. Meaning literally 'putting into the scene' it referred to the staging of a drama within theatrical space. The term as it has been applied to cinema may be understood in two ways. For some critics it has retained its theatrical connotations, and is used only to refer to those elements of the shot which are staged in front of the camera at the time of filming. These elements comprise setting, props, costume and make-up, lighting and performance. For others the term has broader significance, and is used to refer to everything which appears within the frame of the finished film. According to this definition cinematography and special effects are both aspects of mise-en-scène, even though the former is performed by, rather than placed in front of, the camera, and the latter are often added to the image during post-production. For the purposes of this study I will adopt this second definition, but will maintain the distinction between the different 'phases' of mise-en-scène by dealing first with what takes place in front of camera at the time of shooting, then with what the camera does, and finally with what is added to the image afterwards.

Setting

Setting is a crucial part of film's expressive capabilities, and because it is subject to the techniques of other aspects of mise-en-scène (it may be lit strikingly, or elements may be shown in close-up) it constitutes much more than simply a backdrop for the action of a story.

A filmmaker may select a setting from a pre-existing environment, or may construct a set within a studio lot or sound stage. Films may also use a combination of construction and pre-existing environments: the Roman scenes of *Gladiator* (Ridley Scott, 2000), for example, were shot in a Napoleonic barracks in Malta to which additional structures were added.

In many instances the primary aim of the setting is to suggest authenticity, and the content and style of the set are dictated by what is appropriate to the story's time and place. Period dramas are often marketed on the basis of the setting's visual pleasure, and also on the efforts undertaken to provide accurate re-creations of the past. Setting is central to bringing plausibility and clarity to the narrative **diegesis**: in *Bladerunner* (Ridley Scott, 1984) the film's elaborate futuristic skylines with its postmodern architecture and flying 'cars' combine with rainy, chaotic, street-level marketplaces and squalor to suggest a fictional world which is at once startling and convincing in its scope and coherence.

Setting may also be used to imbue the image with graphic properties which comment on story and characters: in *The Conformist*'s fascist ministry, for example, the patterns

diegesis
The fictional world in which we presume the story takes place.

• **Plate 3.2**
The city of Los Angeles in Ridley Scott's *Bladerunner* (1984)

of straight lines provided by windows, pillars and staircases are strongly suggestive of prison bars. Setting, particularly in art films, may also create a sense of alienation from the story, or draw attention to the narrative's artificiality: in *Le Mépris*, bold, vibrant colours recur in ways that make the narrative and its environment feel staged even where real exterior locations are used. Clearly for films shot on colour film stock, colour shades and contrasts are important ingredients of the mise-en-scène; the film *Pleasantville* (Gary Ross, 1998) bases its narrative premise around the effects of colour, using **CGI** to turn a black and white world into a colour one as the knowledge and freedom of the central characters grow.

The German Expressionist movement of the 1920s took the metaphoric possibilities of setting to their furthest extreme, making sets representative of the psychological disturbances of characters. Thus in *The Cabinet of Dr Caligari* the exaggeratedly canted, angular backdrops are conspicuously artificial in that they are painted sets (even 'light' and 'shadow' are painted on), and are ultimately revealed to exist only inside the mind of one of the characters. In other Expressionist films, such as *Destiny* (Fritz Lang, 1921), the setting, though not the product of a character's imagination, nevertheless takes on non-naturalistic, often nightmarish appearances, which reflect characters' experiences or inner torment. With the financial take-over of the German studio UFA in 1927 and the rise of Nazism in 1933, key Expressionist directors such as Lang and F.W. Murnau, along with many members of their creative teams, left Germany for Hollywood; this assisted in the spread of Expressionist tendencies in mainstream cinema – most obviously in Universal Studio's horror cycle of the 1930s and in the film noir cycle of the 1940s and early 1950s.

Props

The term 'props', short for 'property', refers to movable objects within the set, specifically those which take on a significant function within the story. Thus props are more than simply 'things' which are used to dress the set: they may serve as iconographic demonstrations of genre (we associate stakes, crosses, coffins and silver bullets with horror films, guns with westerns and so on); they may also be used to drive the narrative forward, and, crucially, may also take on metaphoric significance.

Props can provide narrative drive in a number of ways. Most obviously they may contribute to character motivation: in *Pirates of the Carribean: Dead Man's Chest* (Gore Verbinski, 2006), the story is structured around competing characters' desires to possess four related artefacts – the magic compass which may point the way to the 'dead man's chest', the key which opens the chest, the chest itself, and the still-beating heart which is the chest's contents; the possession of these four props is what motivates all the leading characters (though each character has a different reason for this need), and each prop is in turn (often comically) abandoned as the importance of the next prop is revealed. Props may also contribute to the unfolding narrative by shaping the staging of action across time and space: in *His Girl Friday*, for example, the constantly ringing telephones of the newsroom contribute to our sense of the environment's frenetic pace, but they also contribute the pace of the plot itself, continually interrupting one event with news of action taking place off-screen, and providing reasons for characters to enter and depart, often at high speed.

Props may also take on metaphoric significance, depending on how attention is drawn to them through cinematography or dialogue. In *Rebecca* (Alfred Hitchcock, 1940) our unnamed heroine (Joan Fontaine) and her husband (Laurence Olivier) forget to take their wedding licence with them after they are married; it is dropped down to them from the registry office staircase, and is shown floating downwards in a way that suggests a downward spiral in the couple's future marriage. This example provides a clear illustration of why props are highly significant to film's ability to signal metaphor and connotation, since one of the most common, and expressive, forms of cinematic metaphor is metonymy (see Metz, 1982). Metonymy refers to a figure of speech whereby

CGI
An acronym for 'computer-generated imagery', meaning the use of digital software to create, change or enhance aspects of mise-en-scène.

an object or detail associated with an idea is substituted for the idea itself (thus, in *Rebecca*, the marriage licence stands in for the entire conjugal relationship). In cinematic metonymy, therefore, props play a key role in suggesting a whole array of meanings beyond what is shown; they are a rich, and extremely economic, source of connotative expression.

Crucially, the prop as metaphor may also draw on metaphorical associations which exist outside the film itself: when, in *Pleasantville*, a black and white Margaret (Marley Shelton) plucks a bright red apple from a tree and gives it to David (Tobey Maguire), the moment takes on significance because it references, and renders positive, the biblical connotations of picking forbidden fruit. Props are more likely to imply metaphorical significance if they are shot in ways which draw attention to both the prop and the cinematic techniques used to shoot it: in *Pleasantville* the shot of the apple stands out as unique, and therefore symbolic, because once the apple is picked it reveals the moon through the branches behind it (the camera refocuses quickly so that we see first a blurred orb, then a clear, glowing, full moon). Similarly props tend to take on symbolic meanings when they are repeated in the narrative and mise-en-scène: in *The Draughtsman's Contract* (Peter Greenaway, 1982), for example, fruit is a recurring motif, and is piled high in opulent displays and frequently eaten by the characters. The visual properties of the fruit suggest multiple metaphoric possibilities (which we draw from both specific narrative contexts and wider cultural connotations), such as sexual pleasure, the luxuries of aristocratic life, and the urgent need for wealthy women to 'bear fruit' in the form of male heirs.

Costume

Costume and make-up have similar expressive and symbolic capabilities to the other graphic properties of mise-en-scène, but are also explicitly connected to characterization. Costumes may be used to indicate to us information about the personality or status of the character. In *His Girl Friday*, for example, Hildy Johnson's pin-striped suit and jaunty hat (which resembles the trilbies worn by the film's male journalists) indicate

• **Plate 3.3**
Fast talking in *His Girl Friday* (Howard Hawks, 1939)

that she is better suited to the cut-throat environment of the *Washington Post* than to child-rearing in Albany, despite her own protestations to the contrary.

As with props, costumes may draw on existing cultural connotations: thus in *William Shakespeare's Romeo and Juliet* (Baz Luhrmann, 1996) our hero and heroine first meet at a fancy-dress ball at which Romeo (Leonardo DiCaprio) is dressed as a knight and Juliet (Claire Danes) as an angel. Here the inclusion of a story occasion involving dressing up is used to establish clear associations of goodness and innocence which stand out in an otherwise corrupt world. At the same time, the bold symbolism of the costumes also subtly suggests that the characters' sudden, extreme infatuation with each other may be attributed in part to a teenage propensity to 'play-act' certain roles.

Costume can function to signal a change in a character's status, as in *Trading Places* (John Landis, 1983) where Winthrop Winkle's (Dan Ackroyd) privileged life is indicated by his elegant suit and tie, and his change in fortune is accompanied by comical, humiliating changes in clothing – culminating in a filthy, soaking-wet Santa outfit. Changes in costume may equally reflect alterations in a character's psychology: in *The Madness of King George* (Nicholas Hytner, 1994), the king's mental disintegration, as well as his medical torture, are emphasized by his ragged appearance in undergarments and straitjacket. In *Metropolis* (Fritz Lang, 1926), meanwhile, although the evil Robot Maria frequently wears the same costume as her virtuous human counterpart, their differences in morality are connoted by the heavier, darker, eye make-up worn by the robot. Costume may also take on significance in its relationship to other elements of mise-en-scène: in German Expressionist cinema costume and setting as well as lighting and performance are complementary, creating the impression of a single, coherent visual design in which people and environment merge together. Similarly in *The Draughtsman's Contract* the characters' elaborate wigs often seem to complement the displays of fruit in ways suggestive of ludicrous extravagance and vanity.

Performance

Performance is an extremely rich area of cinematic expression. As with narrative itself, many elements of cinematic performance have their origins in conventions imported from the theatre. Thus the vaudeville tradition informs the types of performance often found in musicals and comedies, where physical dexterity – in the form of dancing, acrobatics, slapstick or mime – may be required. The more high-brow theatrical tradit-

• **Plate 3.4**
Costume, props and lighting in *The Draughtsman's Contract* (Peter Greenaway, 1982)

ions of repertory theatre inform many performances which seem more naturalistic (that is, closer to the way we feel people behave in 'real' life), particularly those where emphasis is placed on the actor's voice – as in Philip Seymour Hoffman's performance in *Capote* (Bennett Miller, 2005). In the 1950s Lee Strasberg's 'Actor's Studio' had an important influence on Hollywood cinema through its promotion of 'method acting', in which actors were encouraged to explore their own psychology and personal history as a means of producing performances. In practice 'the method' often produced highly mannered, 'visible' acting styles, such as Marlon Brando's in *A Streetcar Named Desire* (Elia Kazan, 1951).

However, it is important to note that notions such as 'naturalism' and 'visibility' are relative terms, in that they operate in relation to existing conventions and audience expectations. Thus what may, to one generation of movie-goers, seem like a highly naturalistic performance, might, to their children, seem overtly stylized and exaggerated, because these judgements are based not so much on how people actually behave in life, but on what audiences are used to seeing on stage and screen. Having said this, it is clear that certain performance styles do seek to draw attention to their own artificiality. German Expressionism falls into this category, with actors – many of them trained by theatre director Max Reinhardt – adopting highly exaggerated gestures derived from theatrical melodrama (as when, in *Metropolis*, Maria clutches her hands over her heart to signify anguish).

Any analysis of performance involves breaking down what it is an actor does into constituent elements. This can be difficult, since we are accustomed to decoding performances in terms of the motivations and emotions of characters, rather than the techniques of the actor. Richard Dyer, however, has identified the following performance 'signs': 'facial expression; voice; gestures (principally of hands and arms, but also of any limb, e.g. neck, leg); body posture (how someone is standing or sitting); body movement (movement of the whole body, including how someone stands up or sits down, how they walk, run, etc.)' (Dyer 1979: 134). These categories allow us to make distinctions between how characters behave and what actors do. Thus, for example, in *Rebecca*, when our heroine encounters the housekeeper Mrs Danvers (Judith Anderson) on her first morning in her husband's stately home, we see that she feels out of place – that she is lonely, inexperienced and extremely nervous. The actress, Joan Fontaine, meanwhile, conveys this through the following performance signs: she wraps her arms around her body and turns her head jerkily as she walks; she slumps into a chair, and jumps and recoils when she is interrupted; her hands shake when she answers the telephone and she stammers and swallows as she speaks; she gives short, twitching half-smiles and she licks and bites her lip. As this list suggests, actors' performances and our decoding of them are shaped by our everyday shared understanding of human body language, which alerts us to the possibility that the act of chewing a lip, for example, may signify anxiety.

Lighting
Lighting is clearly crucial in that it shapes how we respond to all of mise-en-scène's other properties, providing compositional emphasis through illumination and shadow. Lighting may come from sources that we see on screen (lamps, torches, candles and so on which are part of the setting or props), but more typically they come from off-screen sources. Conventionally in mainstream cinema lighting set-ups are designed to be consistent with the light sources we see on-screen, so that we are not distracted from the action of the story by shafts of light which seem to come from nowhere (again, therefore, our attention is directed towards story rather than techniques). However, inconsistencies between on- and off-screen light sources are sometimes used to disturbing effect (for example, in horror films). Colour also provides an important stylistic variant within lighting set-ups: in Wong Kar-wai's *Chungking Express* (1994), for example, scenes are frequently illuminated by blue, yellow and green tinges of light.

Classical Hollywood lighting traditionally involves either a two- or a three-point system, in which a key light is the primary light source, and normally corresponds to visible light sources on-screen. A fill-light, frequently placed just over 90 degrees from the key light, serves to soften the effect by cancelling out some of the shadows cast by the key light. In some cases a back light is also used; normally this is placed behind actors to highlight their shape and make them stand out against the setting. Thus lighting set-ups are usually dictated by the position of actors in relation to the camera; where more than one actor is in shot, one actor's key light may serve as another's fill, and vice versa; each new camera position, however, demands a rearrangement of the lighting. The precise nature and arrangement of the lights determine whether or not the overall lighting effect of an image is **high-key** or **low-key**.

Lighting is also important to characterization: backlighting, frontlighting, toplighting or underlighting may influence the light (in the metaphorical sense) in which we view characters. In Carl Dreyer's *La Passion de Jeanne d'Arc* (1928), for example, toplighting shines down on the face of Joan of Arc (Renée Jeanne Falconetti), intensifying our impression of her holiness. By contrast, in *The Draughtsman's Contract*, underlighting serves to exaggerate protagonists' facial features, so that our sense of their debauchery is heightened. (Underlighting is also a staple technique in horror films, giving an other-worldly air to monstrous or psychotic villains.)

Crucially, lighting also creates shadows, and these play an important part in the expressive properties of mise-en-scène. Setting and props may be transformed by shadows cast by, and on to, them: in the ministry scenes of *The Conformist* it is not only the structural elements of the setting which suggest prison bars, but also the long shadows cast on the floor. Several genres, most noticeably German Expressionism and film noir, owe much of their stylistic properties to the effects of light and shadow, and the use of low-key lighting. Film noir is a cycle of thrillers and detective films of the 1940s and 1950s, adapted from hard-boiled fiction of the the 1930s. The lighting in film noir is low-key and evokes a dangerous world, in which characters (especially **femmes fatales**) are not what they seem. In *Out of the Past* (Jacques Tourneur, 1947), for example, the character of Kathy (Jane Greer) is frequently shrouded in shadows, and when she and Jeff (Robert Mitchum) first kiss, we scarcely see her face at all, which sets an ominous tone for their relationship. Later, when Jeff and his business partner fight, their movements throw a series of shadows over Kathy, so that we see her watching (and enjoying) the violence in a pool of erratically flickering light. This serves at once to illuminate her true character while also implying her continued threat. The device of minimizing fill lighting, so that a character's eyes remain in shadow, is frequently used to alert us to a character's untrustworthiness – as in Hitchcock's *Sabotage* (1936), where the saboteur's hat casts a shadow across his face when we first see him. Film noir, in particular, has had a lasting impact on cinema as a whole in terms of lighting techniques, and lighting as a tool in shaping characterization and tone.

Cinematography

The precise parameters of what 'cinematography' refers to have been defined differently by different critics. It is used here to refer to all those elements of cinematic expression which are performed or controlled by the camera. These include framing and shot scale, camera angle and movement, and depth of field and focus. Clearly the presentation of all elements of mise-en-scène are shaped by the way they are treated and recorded using camera and film stock; thus, although it is important to be aware of the distinction between what the camera photographs and what it does, in the processes of film analysis these elements are often considered in terms of their relationship to one another.

The basic component of film is the **shot,** or take, which may constitute a static **framing** or a mobile one. In a mobile framing the image within a single shot may change radically as the camera moves. The frame itself is crucial to the presentation of the image, since all aspects of mise-en-scène are subject to their placement within the rectangular space of the flat screen. The composition of an image may be balanced or

high-key lighting
This term refers to a lighting design (normally using a three-point system) where there is little contrast between the light and shadowed areas of the frame.

low-key lighting
This term refers to a lighting design where there is a stark contrast between the light and shadowed areas of the frame. Frequently it is produced using only one light source.

femme fatale
A term which originated in critical discourses on film noir; it refers to dangerous, seductive female characters who are normally literally 'fatal', in that they cause the death of the hero.

shot/take
One uninterrupted (uncut) image on-screen whether it is shot with a mobile or a stationary camera. During shooting, a 'take' refers to a single, uninterrupted recording of the camera before the director calls 'cut'.

framing
The choices made about what to include within the frame and what to exclude.

depth cues
These are provided by the arrangement of setting, lighting and props within the frame, which determines the degree to which the space depicted in the cinematic image appears to recede backwards and to take on three-dimensionality. Converging lines, size diminution, and the suggestion of different 'planes' in the fore-, middle- and background of the shot all accentuate the sense that there is a lot of space between the camera and the farthest visible object in the frame.

shot scale
This refers to the range of shots which suggest the apparent distance of an object from the camera; it is conventionally defined according to the framing of the human form.

close-up
A framing in which the object shown takes up most of the screen (as in a shot where a person's face is shown from the neck up).

extreme close-up
A framing in which the object shown takes up virtually the whole screen (as in a shot of a body part, such as a leg or an eye).

long shot
A framing in which the object shown (typically a human body shown from head to toe) fills around three-quarters of the height of the screen.

extreme long shot
A framing in which the object shown (typically a human body shown from head to toe) fills a small fraction of the screen.

medium long shot
Also known as the 'plan Américain' because of its frequency in classical Hollywood, this is a framing in which the human body is shown from mid-calf or knees upwards.

medium shot
A framing in which the human body is shown from the waste upwards.

two-shot/three-shot
A framing containing two or three people.

• Plate 3.5
The femme-fatale in *Out of the Past* (Jacques Tourneur, 1947)

unbalanced, depending on whether the right and left, and top and bottom of the frame offer matching, harmonious, or mismatched, uneven patterns. A shot may also appear 'shallow' or 'deep' depending on whether the mise-en-scène is framed in a way that suggests few or many **depth cues**. *The Draughtsman's Contract*, which features an elaborately landscaped, seventeenth-century garden, is an exercise in such aspects of framing: shots of the garden emphasize deep space, with lines of trees, shrubs, ornaments and pathways receding backwards, or else crossing the screen horizontally to suggest planes, or layers, to the space. We also see the garden shot through the grid which the draughtsman uses to compose his drawings, so that the frame itself is divided into sixteen rectangles. This helps us to recognize the compositional balance created by elements of the mise-en-scène, which are distributed in precise geometric patterns within the cinematic frame. The film provides a Modernist demonstration of the picturesque possibilities of cinematic space.

Shot scale is another crucial element of cinematography, and is measured according the following categories: the **close-up**, the **extreme close-up**, the **long shot**, **the extreme long shot**, the **medium long shot**, and the **medium shot**. These framings are crucial in depicting characters and their interactions: the medium long shot is the scale frequently adopted in Hollywood films for **two-** or **three-shots**, while the close-up affords the opportunity for intimate scrutiny of characters, and has facilitated approaches to screen performance not possible on stage, since the smallest changes in expression (such as eye movements and flinches) may be witnessed by viewers. A predominance of certain shot scales may serve to convey particular aspects of character or situation: the accumulation of close-ups in *La Passion de Jeanne d'Arc* creates a proximity between viewers and Joan of Arc which heightens our sense of her suffering. In *North by Northwest* (Alfred Hitchcock, 1959), meanwhile, when Roger Thorwald (Cary Grant) is under attack from the crop-duster aeroplane, his vulnerability is stressed through a number of extreme long shots conveying his remote location; in particular, the opening shot of the scene is a **high-angle shot**, in which the vastness of the landscape is accentuated by the converging lines of the road, crops, fences and telegraph poles.

Camera angle is another key element of framing, and the crop-duster sequence in *North by Northwest* also contains a number of **low-angle shots**, in which we see the plane from below as it swoops down to attack, as well as **straight-on shots** as we watch Thorwald scanning the horizon or taking cover. Camera angle can also be instrumental in conveying character and establishing (literal and figurative) point of view: thus in *Oliver Twist* (David Lean, 1948) we frequently either look up at adults from Oliver's eye-level, or we look down at Oliver from the perspective of adults; both angles enhance our sense of Oliver's helpless, disempowered position in a dangerous world. **Canted framing** is also important in conveying mood and point of view: thus in *The Third Man* (Carol Reed, 1949), repeated canted framings suggest Holly Martin's (Joseph Cotton) fear and confusion, as well as the structural disintegration of post-war Vienna, and sometimes also Martin's literal view as he hides amidst the rubble.

The camera also has four basic types of mobility – the **pan**, the **track**, the **tilt** and the **crane shot**. The latter, especially in conjunction with distant framing, is particularly useful for the narrative convention of the **establishing shot**. Camera movement can again be used to suggest character point of view, as in *North by Northwest*'s crop-duster sequence, when Thorwald hesitatingly approaches a man at the bus-stop, and the camera produces his viewpoint by tracking in on the man. This cinematic code makes the moving camera a powerful tool for the horror genre: in *Halloween* (John Carpenter, 1978) the camera's pans and tracks follow Laurie (Jamie Lee Curtis) as she walks to school, creating the uneasy impression that someone is stalking her. Camera movement, since it results in a continuous change in the space occupying the frame, can make us powerfully aware of the area outside the frame, a property again exploited in horror films, where characters may seem continually under threat from things we cannot see. A number of art films also use camera movement to draw our attention to cinematic space: *Jules et Jim* (François Truffaut, 1961), for example, employs **whip-pans** and fast tracks to jarring effect in the scene where the two friends visit a statue; both *Le Mèpris* and *The Draughtsman's Contract*, meanwhile, stage conversations with the camera tracking slowly between speakers in ways that emphasize the distance (literally and emotionally) between characters, and the dimensions of the space they occupy.

Depth of field is another key aspect of cinematography. This is the distance between the farthest and nearest point from the camera at which subject details will be recorded in sharp focus. Depth of field is determined by the **aperture** and **focal length** of the camera lens: in order to obtain a wide depth of field a shorter focal length lens is used, and/or a smaller aperture; in order to use a smaller aperture, either more light is required in the mise-en-scène, or a **faster speed film stock** may be used (or a combination of the two). *Citizen Kane* (Orson Welles, 1941) was highly influential in its use of large depth of field (or 'deep focus'), achieved by the use of fast film stock, short focal-length lenses and powerful lighting set-ups. The effect in Welles's film was to create extremely rich images in which cavernous spaces are clearly defined in sharp focus and contrasting tones of light and dark. Another important function of the camera lens is its capacity to **zoom**. The abrupt change in framing brought about by the zoom tends to make its effect jarring (as in the end of *North by Northwest*'s crop-duster sequence where Thorwald is nearly hit by a truck, and his alarm, as well as the vehicle's speed, is signified by a sudden zoom in on Grant).

high-angle shot
A framing where the camera looks down from above on to the objects or scene filmed.

low-angle shot
A framing where the camera looks up from below at the objects or scene filmed.

straight-on shot
A framing where the camera is at the same level as the objects or scene filmed.

canted framing
A framing where the camera is not level, causing the mise-en-scène to appear slanted within the frame.

pan/whip-pan
A 'pan' is a camera movement in which the camera itself remains in the same place but swivels round horizontally; a 'whip-pan' is a very fast pan.

track/tracking shot/ dolly shot
A camera movement in which the camera moves horizontally by travelling along the ground (originally on 'tracks' on which a wheeled support – or 'dolly' – for the camera could be mounted).

tilt
A camera movement in which the camera remains in one place but swivels up or down.

crane shot
A camera movement in which the camera moves above the ground in any direction (for which it is mounted on the arm of a special 'camera crane').

establishing shot
A shot at the start of a film or scene which establishes spatial relationships within the mise-en-scène and locates the story within the diegesis.

aperture
The opening within a lens controlling the amount of light that passes through the lens to the film; the smaller the aperture, the less light will hit the film.

focal length
This refers to the ability of a lens to bend the incoming light on to the film plane; a shorter focal length will provide a wider angle of view (which dictates what appears within the frame); a longer focal length will provide a narrower field of view but greater magnification of what is shown; for any given set of conditions a shorter focal length will provide a larger depth of field.

faster speed film speed/speed of film stock
Sensitivity of the photographic emulsion of the film to light; a higher speed of film will require less light (i.e. a smaller aperture may be used) in order to produce a properly exposed image; faster speed film stock tends to provide greater contrast in tone than a slower film stock.

zoom
A shot in which the lens alters the angle of view (either from narrow to wide or wide or narrow); the effect is a sudden change in shot scale within one take.

superimposition
The process by which more than one image is exposed on the same frames of the film stock.

matte shot
A type of shot in which aspects of mise-en-scène are photographed separately and then combined into one image in post-production. Opaque images mask out certain areas of the film negative, and subsequent passes through the camera allow the initially matted-out space to be exposed with another image. Nowadays, matting is often achieved using 'blue screen', a process where action is filmed in front of a blue screen; this footage is then used to create an image of the performers in front of a dark background, and a silhouette of the performer against a clear background, which is used to 'cut out' space for the performer in the scene on to which the action is to be matted.

Special effects

'Special effects' is a broad term referring to image manipulations that change the appearance of other aspects of mise-en-scène: it includes **superimposition**, **matte shots** and CGI. While digital technology has seen radical advances in the possibilities of such manipulations, special effects are not in themselves new to cinema: at the turn of the twentieth century, for example, George Meliés used such techniques as hand-tinted film stock in his fantasy films. Nowadays most special effects are achieved by 'laboratory' work which takes place in post-production.

Among the effects which the advent of CGI has heralded, two important techniques are digital matting and motion capture. Digital matting enables shots to be stitch together out of a series of other images, some of which may be photographed, some of which may be designed and animated using computer software. In *Gladiator*, aerial shots of Rome were created by matting computer-drawn buildings on to a helicopter shot of the production's Malta location; the stone and brick textures of these 'virtual' structures were then matted on to the image using photographs of existing buildings.

Motion capture is a technique which combines live-action performances with computer-generated animation: in *The Lord of the Rings: The Two Towers* (Peter Jackson, 2002) and *The Lord of the Rings: The Return of the King* (Jackson, 2003) the character of Gollum was created by recording the performance of actor Andy Serkis while he wore a suit with nodes identifying key parts of the body. The movements of these nodes were scanned into a computer, and used to define the movement and posture of the wholly computer-generated Gollum. This enabled the expressiveness of the individual actor's physical performance to be replicated by the virtual character. The case of Gollum is interesting, in that it suggests that advances in CGI utilize, rather than usurp, the craft that actors bring to films.

Because of such technology it is becoming increasingly difficult to distinguish between effects achieved during shooting and those of post-production: in *Gladiator*, for

• **Plate 3.6**
The crop-dusting sequence of *North by Northwest* (Alfred Hitchcock, 1959)

example, there is a sweeping pan across a battlefield; however, the shot was achieved using three 'locked off' (stationary) cameras, whose images were scanned into a computer and joined together digitally. The panning motion was then performed during post-production in the computer rather than on location using a camera. This enables the film to show in one fluid, mobile shot, a battle featuring many more times the number of soldiers than there were extras employed on the production.

Editing

The actual process of editing involves the joining together of separate pieces of film. Each take consists of one or more exposed frames on a length of film stock, and it is the task of film editors to review all recorded footage, 'cutting' unwanted material, and joining the wanted strips of film in the desired order. Formerly, editing took place in the laboratory, the join being achieved with either a dry splice, using tape, or a wet splice, using liquid cement. Nowadays editing is undertaken digitally, using specialist hardware and software, such as those developed by Avid Technology, Inc during the 1990s. Digital editing involves the importing of a film's rushes on to hard disk, after which the material may be edited in a non-linear fashion, with each cut saved on an 'edit decision list', so that no alteration is irreversible and no material is destroyed in the process.

Unlike mise-en-scène, which inherited and developed its codes from other art forms, the practices of film editing are unique to cinema. Without editing, the expressive and narrative capabilities of the moving image would not be anything like as rich as they are. The power of editing lies in its ability to create juxtapositions, which in turn may change the impact and meaning of each individual shot. Soviet filmmakers of the 1920s sought to explore the possibilities of such juxtapositions (in the movement known as Soviet Montage cinema), and in a now famous experiment filmmaker Lev Kuleshov cut together shots of actor Ivan Mosjoukine's face with three other images – a bowl of soup, a child at play and a body in a coffin. Kuleshov claimed that audiences 'read' the actor's performance as being different in each case, their responses shaped by the shot with which the face was juxtaposed. Kuleshov probably overstated his case: the experiment undervalues the role of performance, the footage has not survived, and several attempts to re-create it have not produced the decisive results to which Kuleshov laid claim (although a reconstruction using shots of actor Bruno Ganz, posted on the University of Alabama website by the Department of Telecommunication and Film, is not unconvincing). Regardless of its precise veracity, the story remains suggestive of editing's potential to shape and override the content of a single shot.

The juxtaposition between one shot and the next may be presented in a number of ways: a **cut** provides an immediate change from one image to the next, while a dissolve offers a more gradual transition, as does the **fade**. Early filmmakers made use of other types of transition, such as the wipe (offering a similar change-over to 'magic-lantern' slide shows), and the **iris-in** and **iris-out**. These were intended as additional attractions to the phenomenon of the moving image (see Salt 1992: 53 and 84), and are nowadays used most often for comic effect, or as the type of self-conscious device found in Modernist narratives: Tony Richardson's *Tom Jones* (1963), for example, uses its wipes and iris shots to add to the ironic playfulness of its tone. In narrative cinema different transitions have come to signify particular types of plot organization; thus fades in and out often signal breaks between scenes. Dissolves sometimes suggest story ellipses: in *Stand by Me* (Rob Reiner, 1986), for example, the night the boys spend out in the forest is rendered using dissolves to show snippets of their aimless, comical, camp-fire conversation. The scene is a variant of the montage sequence, in which segments of story are summarized through the editing together of images which 'typify', or symbolize, events: thus in *Jules et Jim* a montage of shots of the two men (and various women) in cafés, forests and river boats sums up their early romantic relationships. Dissolves and fades are useful for rendering ellipses in that their slow transitions provide visual metaphors

For further discussion of Kuleshov and montage editing see pp. 369–71.

cut
The joining of two strips of film in the editing room, and the resulting immediate change from one image to another on-screen.

fade
An editing technique in which one of the juxtaposed images is a black screen. With a 'fade-out' the image slowly darkens; with a 'fade-in' the image slowly emerges out of darkness.

iris-in/iris-out
Editing techniques in which the transition from one image to another is marked by the closing and reopening of an 'iris' or circular hole in the centre of the frame.

for missed out portions of story-time; however, it should be noted that such techniques do not automatically signal specific plot devices, the narrative function of editing being shaped by the content of the shots involved and the context in which they are placed.

In that editing itself involves the cutting together of images filmed at different times and of different spaces, it is clearly instrumental to how films plot stories in time and across space. The development of **cross-cutting,** for example, pioneered by D.W. Griffith, enables films to imply that two different actions, dramatized alternately on screen, take place simultaneously in the story. Because editing imbues sequences and scenes with particular rhythms in cutting, it can also be highly influential in generating mood: the shower scene in *Psycho* (Alfred Hitchcock, 1960), for instance, contains seventy-eight separate shots (see Maltby 1995: 218), with aggressively rapid cutting that emulates the slashes of the knife; in this scene the editing forms a kind of visual assault on the viewer, chopping up the time and space of the film with a violence of its own. By contrast, Hitchcock's *Rope* (1948) was shot entirely in ten-minute takes that were edited together to disguise the joins so that the film appears to have no cuts at all. This, combined with very mobile framing, produces tension in that the camera seems to probe unremittingly the space of the story. Long takes may suggest tranquillity, however: the beginning of *Pride and Prejudice* (Joe Wright, 2005) features a one-and-a-half-minute take which follows Elizabeth (Keira Knightley) as she walks home, tracks through the house, out of a window, then back into the house. The effect is a serene opening, allowing viewers time to observe the dilapidated charm of the Bennets' home, and the pastoral aimlessness of the girls' lives.

Editing also creates juxtapositions between all the aspects of the mise-en-scène, and may be used to suggest matches, or contrasts, between setting, costumes, props and performances. Soviet montage director Sergei Eisenstein used montage's potential for spatial juxtaposition to maximum metaphoric effect in his use of 'non-diegetic inserts' – that is, shots which do not belong to the narrative context, but serve to commentate on (or symbolize) narrative content: *October* (1927), for example, features cuts between Kerenksy and images of Napoleon and of a peacock, which imply the tyranny and vanity of the leader of the Provisional Government. Eisenstein wrote extensively on editing, and his films abound with striking montage innovations, from jump-cuts, fast, rhythmic editing (most famously in the Odessa steps sequence of *Battleship Potemkin* (1925), **impact editing** and **overlapping editing**. His films are powerful demonstrations of the potential of editing as a tool of expression and persuasion.

Continuity editing

The conventions which govern editing in classical Hollywood cinema, and which have come to dominate much filmmaking outside Hollywood, are known as 'continuity editing'. Continuity editing developed early in cinema's history, and most of its key features were in place by around 1919. The purpose of continuity editing is to maintain the viewer's understanding of, and engagement with, the story. As with Hollywood's treatment of plot, the guiding principle is transparency – that is, the rendering of techniques unobtrusively so that audiences retain their focus on what is happening, and not on how things are shown.

This means that shots are generally juxtaposed in ways that minimize the disruption inherent in editing. Cuts are designed to avoid confusing ellipses, or disorientating changes in screen space. The convention of the establishing shot assists this in making clear the layout and parameters of a scene; the closer shots which follow may then be understood as framings within this larger space. Another frequently employed technique is the **180° rule,** which ensures spatial consistency across successive shots, preventing aspects of mise-en-scène which appear on one side of the frame in one shot from appearing on the other side of the frame (as if in mirror image) in the next. The **30° rule** operates in a similar way in that it ensures sufficient change in framing from one shot to the next so that jump-cuts are avoided. Also central to achieving smooth, coherent

cross-cutting
Editing that alternates shots occurring in different story locations to imply that the events shown are occurring simultaneously.

impact editing
Editing that produces violent contrast between images, most often by switching between close and long shot scales.

overlapping editing
Editing where shots repeat part or all of the action shown in the previous shot.

180° rule
An editing technique which dictates that the camera should remain on one side of an imaginary line drawn through a scene.

30° rule
An editing technique which dictates that the camera should be stationed at an angle of at least 30° from its location in the previous shot.

eyeline match
A cut in which one shot shows a person looking at something off-screen, and the other shot is thereby posited as the object of that person's gaze. More usually the shot showing the gazing person comes first, although cuts which show the gazer second are by no means uncommon.

match on action
A cut which joins two spaces together by virtue of the fact that an action shown in the first shot is then completed in the second.

spatial juxtapositions are techniques which 'match' successive shots – such as the **eyeline match** and the **match on action**. These map out for us the spatial position of one framing in relation to the next, using the story itself – its characters and actions – to link shots together.

As is implied by eyeline matching, editing is central to the cinematic construction of characters' point of view (meaning, literally, what they see, as opposed to the metaphorical connotations implicit in the term 'focalization'). Conversely the phenomenon of on-screen characters who look at things is also extremely valuable in conveying intelligible links between shots. This may be seen in another recurring technique of continuity editing, namely **shot–reverse shot** constructions. These are used most frequently for the staging of conversations between two characters, in which the camera looks at each character in turn over the shoulder of the other character. The technique offers us a clear understanding of where each speaker stands and what each sees, while also affording intimacy in the staging of character interactions.

The opening of *His Girl Friday* provides a demonstration of the operations of continuity editing: the film's establishing shot is a track through the newsroom of the *Washington Post*, which makes clear both the bustle of this environment and the relative locations of the editor's office (on the right of the set), the journalist and typist pool (in the middle) and the elevators (on the left). Following a dissolve to bring us to a closer shot, Hildy and Ralph exit an elevator; their subsequent exchange is depicted in an over-the-shoulder, shot–reverse shot sequence, which contrasts the previous mobile framings and seems to place the two in a world of their own amidst the newsroom commotion. A series of tracking shots then follows Hildy, and a match on action is used as she leaves the pool and enters Walter's office. Hildy at first stands in the doorway looking slightly to the right of camera, and there follows a shot of Walter and Louie, whom we identify as the object of her gaze. Hildy announces herself, and a cut introduces a medium long shot showing all three characters, which in turn establishes the layout of this new room.

Following initial greetings and an interruption by Duffy, a medium long two-shot introduces a prolonged exchange between Hildy and Walter, during which Hildy crosses to sit behind Walter: she is now to the right of the frame with Walter on the left. Walter responds by swivelling his chair so that he sits facing her with his back to the camera; there follows a cut so that Walter is now facing us. Although this cut involves a transition from Walter with his back to us to Walter facing us, the camera has moved less than 180°, as is made clear by the fact that the first shot has Walter slightly to the left of camera, while the second has him slightly to the right; there follows a point-of-view shot of Hildy, in which the spatial relations of the earlier medium long shot are retained, with Hildy still on the right and Walter's shoulder on the left.

This scene adheres to continuity editing and shows how variety is available within continuity rules. We might also note that Hildy's move to sit behind Walter serves to alter the position of the imaginary line governing the 180° rule: while the scene contains four people, three of whom enter or leave, the line runs from the door to the window; once the scene involves only Walter and Hildy, Hildy effectively realigns the scene along an axis which runs straight through the characters, thus expanding the number of camera positions possible overall. This also subtly uses editing to signal a shift in the character interaction as Walter and Hildy embark on a bantering, bickering reminiscence. Throughout the scene the editing is unobtrusive, serving and enhancing our appreciation of story in ways that, normally, we scarcely notice.

While continuity editing remains central to film 'language' in mainstream and art cinema, it is also the case that audiences' increasing film literacy has enabled such rules to be broken with greater frequency. The 180° rule, in particular, is frequently discarded in action sequences, for example, where camera mobility and variety in framing complement dynamic mise-en-scène. Art films also frequently disrupt editing continuity (as in Godard's use of jump-cuts) as part of their self-conscious exploration of film technique.

shot–reverse shot
A cut which switches between complementary spaces, sometimes with the camera stationed in almost opposing/facing positions within the confines of the 180° rule.

For further discussion of Godard's filming technique see pp. 405–20.

Sound

Sound was introduced to cinema in 1927, and is now an extremely rich element of cinematic expression. Its properties and possibilities extend beyond the scope of this chapter, but some key considerations are noted here.

Although sound played an important role in cinema exhibition before 1927, in the form of live musical accompaniment and sometimes commentating 'showmen', the advent of the recorded soundtrack had a profound effect on the stories films told and the possibilities of cinematic narration. Synchronized sound, of course, brought speech to cinema, and this allied cinema more closely with theatre than previously. New cinematic genres arose, such as the musical and the screwball comedy, which had their roots in theatrical traditions, and which offered sound as a key attraction. While recorded speech is clearly crucial to screenplays, it is not the only element of sound to have significantly shaped cinema's development, and we might divide film sound into three basic areas – speech, music and sound effects.

Sound in film narrative may be identified as either diegetic or non-diegetic – in other words, it either belongs within the story 'universe', or we attribute it as originating from outside the fictional world inhabited by characters. The film's musical score is the most common form of non-diegetic sound, although it is not the only one: we might distinguish, for example, between diegetic voice-overs spoken by characters – as in *The Big Sleep* or Amy Heckerling's *Clueless* (1995) – and non-diegetic voice-overs, which originate from seemingly omniscient 'narrators' – as in *Jules et Jim*. Films may blur the distinction between diegetic and non-diegetic sound, sometimes for comic effect and sometimes as an element of aesthetic innovation. Early sound films frequently introduced non-diegetic score unobtrusively by including melodies diegetically first. This occurs in Jean Vigo's *L'Atalante* (1934), where the melody played by Père Jules (Michel Simon) suddenly becomes a non-diegetic accompaniment to two singing voices as we see the honeymoon couple embrace. Diegetic and non-diegetic sound should not be confused with on- and off-screen sound: a sound may originate off-screen (as when a person not in shot speaks or cries out) but still belong within the diegesis. Off-screen sound has the effect of changing our relationship with the image, drawing our attention specifically to the space outside the frame (making it another staple technique of horror films).

The presence of sound alongside the image creates a whole series of possible relationships between sound and editing, and sound and mise-en-scène: the rhythms of noise and music, for example, may seem to match the rhythm of editing or of movements within the mise-en-scène, or they may seem at odds with them; sound-effects may appear faithful to the sources we assume produced them, or may seem incongruous with them. In *The 39 Steps* sound and editing are used to create a striking scenic transition, in which there is a cut from a woman who is about to scream to a train exiting a tunnel; the train's screeching whistle is substituted for the woman's cry, making the human reaction to the story's murder scenario seem piercingly acute. Sound, in the form of **sound-bridges**, may also be used as a means of smoothing over divisions between scenes.

sound-bridge
An audio connection between scenes, where sound from one scene continues into the beginning of the scene which follows, or where sound belonging to the opening of a scene begins during the close of the scene which precedes it.

The distinction between sound which seems faithful to image and sound which does not may be extremely subtle: in *The English Patient* (Anthony Minghella, 1996) the soundtrack of the desert scenes includes a whole series of effects – clicks suggesting insects, rubbing noises representing grains of sand – many of which would not, realistically, be picked up by the human ear. However, these noises evoke the desert terrain, and paradoxically give us an eerie sense of 'a space that is silent' (Ondaatje 2002: 118). Thus the sounds, though not precisely true to what we might hear in this location, do not strike us as out of place, since they enhance both the mood of the setting and the metaphors of emotional isolation within the narrative. As with performance, therefore, our assessment of the verisimilitude of noise is as much shaped by cinematic conventions as it is by our experiences of real life. In terms of sound volume in relation to image, we conventionally expect some degree of 'sound perspective', so that loud sounds represent actions depicted in close-up or near depth planes, while quieter sounds represent actions depicted in longer shot scales or distant depth planes. However, films may subvert this rule, as Godard does in *Weekend* (1967), where the characters' indoor conversations are sometimes drowned out by the outdoor noise.

The selection, generation, recording, distortion, amplification and mixing of film sounds create an array of possibilities for films' audio tracks, which means that we may consider them as 'soundscapes' – as a sophisticated orchestration of multi-faceted techniques comparable to the production of the film's visual elements. Technological advances that originated in the music industry have led to the advent of soundtracks where speech, music and noise may overlap and fluctuate in highly complex ways: in *Apocalypse Now* (Francis Coppola, 1979), for which the chief sound editor was, as with *The English Patient*, Walter Murch, sounds of war, jungle, speech, diegetic and non-diegetic music are mixed in a disorientating, multi-layered fashion which evokes the (drug-enhanced) terrors of the soldiers in Vietnam; the degree of multiplicity within the audio track is aptly demonstrated by the trouble Murch and his team went to in producing the sound of crickets: one cricket was recorded close to a microphone, the sound was electronically multiplied and all the resulting noises were then all overlaid on top of each other; this mix was then itself mixed with other elements of the soundtrack. The effect is to produce a cricket noise which is not so much a lifelike version of how many crickets sound as it is a nightmare rendition of a jungle cacophony.

Sound in cinema fluctuates not only in volume and rhythm, but also in **pitch** and **timbre**. These properties are particularly important to music, although they also characterize vocal performance and sound-effects: in *His Girl Friday*, for example, Cary Grant's voice frequently veers to a high pitch suggestive of urgency (or even megalomania), while in *L'Atalante* Père Jules entertains Juliette (Dita Parlo) with series of toys that produce noises and notes of contrasting timbre (ranging from tinkling glockenspiel to a hollow rattle). A film's non-diegetic music conventionally matches timbre, pitch, volume and rhythm to the action depicted on screen – so, for example, Alfred Newman's score for *Wuthering Heights* (William Wyler, 1939) has soaring strings accompanying its love scenes. Thus music guides and enhances our responses to the story. In *Jaws*, for example, John Williams's rhythmically monotonous score, with its modulation between only two notes, alerts us in advance of imminent danger, heightening our fear of the seemingly relentless predator.

In his economy of melody, Williams was heavily influenced by film composer Bernard Herrmann, whose work with Alfred Hitchcock has been particularly influential in shaping and advancing approaches to film music. In Herrmann's score for *Psycho*, for example, three notes recur and form the basis of the violent chords of both the opening theme and the shower scene's screeching violins. Timbre, as well as pitch, play a role in the score's insistent menace, in that Herrmann omitted both the woodwind and brass sections from his orchestra, limiting the tonal 'colour' of the music only to strings. Herrmann, throughout his career, made innovative, unexpected choices in his allocation of musical instruments to particular visual motifs, as, for example, in Hitchcock's *Vertigo* (1958), where the 'vertigo effect', achieved by the camera's simultaneous track in and zoom out, is accompanied in Herrmann's score by harps. Herrmann demonstrated that considerable expressive possibilities are opened up through the selection or composition of seemingly incongruous non-diegetic music: thus *2001: A Space Odyssey* (Stanley Kubrick, 1969) transforms our impression of space flight into something balletic and peaceful through its appropriation of Johann Strauss's *The Blue Danube*.

pitch
The height or depth of a musical sound as it is determined by its frequency relative to other notes.

timbre
The tonal quality of a musical sound; timbre is what makes a saxophone sound different from a clarinet, for example.

□ CASE STUDY 1: CLASSICAL CONVENTIONS IN *GLADIATOR* (RIDLEY SCOTT, 2000)

For a case study on the production process of Gladiator see pp. 44–7.

At first sight Ridley Scott's *Gladiator* (scripted by David Franzoni, John Logan and William Nicholson) may not seem to conform to mainstream conventions, in that our hero, Maximus (Russell Crowe), dies at the end. However, the film constitutes a persuasive demonstration of the dominance of classical story-telling, in that its norms persist even in this tale: all the hero's goals are met, and the film is so ingeniously plotted that death itself is presented to us as a 'happy ending'.

The film opens with intertitles that set the scene as AD 180 during the reign of Roman Emperor Marcus Aurelius; the plot begins prior to the last battle between the Roman Empire and Germania; however, the battle is preceded by a fleeting moment of tranquillity achieved by shots of golden cornfields, which are then posited as Maximus's imaginings. With the battle won, the significance of this becomes clear: Maximus, the great Roman general, wants to go home. This is the character's primary, overarching goal, but almost as soon as it is established a second goal is presented which must delay the achievement of the first: Marcus Aurelius charges Maximus to 'give Rome back to the people', a task he will undertake as 'Protector of Rome' after the emperor's death. Marcus Aurelius gives Maximus until sunset to decide his course of action, but before then the emperor is murdered by his son, Commodus. Commodus orders Maximus to be murdered also, but Maximus escapes and returns to his farm in Spain. At this point the narrative seems to thwart, permanently and horrifically, Maximus's goal of returning home, because his wife and son have been crucified, and his farm ransacked and burnt. It seems therefore that this goal, motivated by love, will be replaced by one motivated by hate, namely revenge against Commodus. However, even this goal is thwarted, because at the end of the first act, an injured, distraught Maximus is captured by slave-traders.

In this opening, the motivations for characters' actions are made clear: Marcus Aurelius wants to rid Rome of corruption and leave behind a noble legacy; he chooses Maximus because he loves him as a son and because he is untainted by politics; Maximus, because he is uncorrupted, wants only to return to his family and a quiet, country life; however, he is also motivated by his sense of duty towards Rome and by his love for the emperor. Commodus's motives, meanwhile, are at once psychologically complex and childishly simple: he is ambitious, but this in itself is rooted in a desire to be loved; we see his desperate longing for his father's approval, and his hatred of Maximus is a product of both political rivalry and 'fraternal' jealousy; Commodus wants to be emperor because he seeks to substitute the love of the people for the father's love he cannot win, and because his love for his father makes him want to live up to him.

At the start of the next act Maximus is sold to Proximo, a gladiator 'impresario', and so becomes a gladiator. All the goals of the previous act are therefore left hanging, and are replaced by new ones necessitated by his changed circumstances: he needs to stay alive in the arena, and he also seeks to avoid the humiliation of becoming an 'entertainer', of turning the fighting skills which once brought glory to Rome into a public spectacle. Maximus's reluctance to win over the crowd posits his character as the exact opposite of Commodus's, and the plot now switches between Maximus in Zucchabar, and Commodus in Rome, who conceives the idea of 150 days of gladiatorial games as a means of winning the people's love. An ironic cause-and-effect pattern is therefore set in motion, in that Commodus's desire to be loved leads directly to the arrival in Rome of Maximus, Commodus's former rival for his father's affection. Maximus learns that Proximo used to be a gladiator, and that he was granted his freedom by Marcus Aurelius; this conversation changes Maximus's goals, because he realizes that by winning over the crowd as a gladiator 'entertainer' he may meet Commodus again. Thus Maximus and Commodus are again rivals (this time for the love of the Roman people) and Maximus's goal of killing Commodus is made clear.

We are now presented with the first spectacular fight at the Colosseum, and the plot turns this into a high point in character interaction too, because Commodus realizes that Maximus is alive. Maximus postpones killing Commodus because Lucius, the son of Commodus's sister Lucilla, is present, but the scene marks a turning point in the narrative, in that Maximus's popularity blatantly renews his status as Commodus's rival: the two men now pursue parallel goals of murdering each other. Lucilla visits Maximus, and a third source of rivalry is now spelled out, in that Lucilla, for whom Commodus has an incestuous love, was once romantically involved with Maximus. Motivated by grief for her father, attachment to Maximus, duty towards Rome and, above all, fear for her son's life, Lucilla urges Maximus to meet with Senator Gracchus and plot the overthrow of Commodus. Maximus refuses, saying that he is a slave, and not the man he used to be. This establishes a path for Maximus which he himself does not acknowledge – namely to rise to be again the man he once was. From now on the narrative charts the recovery of his former goals, a process initiated by Maximus's reunion with Cicero, a friend whose loyalty convinces Maximus that his former regiment will fight for him. Cicero's absence from, and return to, the story is explained by the fact that Maximus was previously assumed dead; his return reminds us of Maximus's former, foremost goal – to return home – in that he restores to Maximus keepsakes of his wife and son that he used to carry. Maximus now agrees to Lucilla's scheme, but Gracchus is subsequently arrested. Commodus threatens Lucius, thereby forcing Lucilla to confess their plans, but a cause is now picked up from much earlier in the plot, in that Proximo frees Maximus, motivated by loyalty towards Marcus Aurelius, the man who freed Proximo himself. Maximus is captured, however, owing to Lucilla's confession, and the scene is now set for a final showdown between Maximus and Commodus; as Commodus says: 'People want to know how the story ends.'

Although Maximus still wishes to kill Commodus, his motives have been transformed in the second half of the film: he is no longer driven primarily by revenge, but is now fulfilling the goal of 'giving Rome back to the people' set for him by Marcus Aurelius. He retains our sympathy through his restoration to a man fulfilling a duty out of love, as opposed to a man bent on murder as vengeance. Commodus, of course, still wishes to kill Maximus, but his difficulty is that if he kills such a popular man, he will fail in his other goal of securing the people's love. This dilemma motivates Commodus to fight Maximus himself in the Colosseum, since he is seeking precisely the adulation accorded to gladiator 'entertainers'; the plot therefore utilizes Commodus's weaknesses as a means of accommodating its implausible dramatic climax. Commodus's willingness to battle a champion in public is further explained when he stabs Maximus in secret before the fight. In the Colosseum a dying Maximus kills Commodus with the concealed dagger Commodus used to stab him, and asks Lucilla to free Gracchus and honour her father's wish of re-establishing a republic. The film's recurring motif of the golden cornfields which are Maximus's farm accompany his death, and kneeling by Maximus's body, Lucilla whispers, 'You are home.'

Thus the film offers Maximus's death as his longed-for reunion with his lost wife and son. The plot signals this trajectory right at the start, when Maximus, briefing his soldiers before battle, tells them, 'If you should find yourself alone, riding in green fields with the sun on your face, do not be troubled, for you are in Elysium and you are already dead.' The story's end is also anticipated through the scenes Maximus shares with fellow gladiator Juba, with whom he discusses the wife and son who are 'waiting for him'. The evocation of Maximus's family as at once dead but waiting is both moving and convenient, since it offers a romantic story of marital fidelity which does not conflict with the more intriguing unfulfilled romance with Lucilla. The plot's ingenuity rests in the way it manages to pull off the story it promises at first but then seems irretrievably to subvert: Maximus does exactly what Marcus Aurelius says he will do – he performs one last task for his emperor and Rome, and then he goes home.

The above analysis demonstrates the film's goal-oriented, cause-and-effect plot structure. It seeks, not to tell the story, but to show the logic by which the story is told. However, we may also use it to draw out other aspects of the film, namely its meaning, or 'themes'. These operate on several levels: most simply, the narrative promotes love over hatred in its depiction of a man who rises above revenge to do his duty and is rewarded with eternal happiness; the narrative also promotes democracy over tyranny, and its repetition of Marcus Aurelius's lament that 'there once was a dream that was Rome' aligns Maximus with an American 'dream', and Rome's republican future with contemporary Western conceptions of 'democratic freedom'. Moreover, the film demonstrates a preoccupation with 'entertainment', and since the gladiators fight for their lives for spectacle and profit they provide an obvious metaphor for both contemporary sports industries and the film industry, where 'players' are 'owned' by huge corporations. We might conclude that the film critiques such dehumanization, but this message is subtly undermined by the way that the gladiatorial arena increasingly becomes the political arena: Commodus and Maximus fight there over the future of Rome, and the gladiators who formerly fought for sport are transformed into Maximus's 'real', loyal army. Thus the film offers us a celebration of Commodus's games and of itself, where 'truth' and true heroism are represented by 'the entertainers'.

☐ CASE STUDY 2: ART AND ARTIFICE IN *WILD STRAWBERRIES/SMULTRONSTÄLLET* (INGMAR BERGMAN, 1957)

Ingmar Bergman wrote, as well as directed, *Wild Strawberries*, and its cast includes recurring Bergman collaborators – Ingrid Thulin, Max von Sydow, Gunnar Bjornstand and Bibi Andersson (who was Bergman's mistress) – as well as Lena Bergman, Ingmar's daughter. The film stars Victor Sjöström, a film director of the silent era, whose status as a towering figure in Swedish cinema has been usurped only by the status of Bergman himself. Thus *Wild Strawberries* presents itself as art cinema through Bergman's insistent creative presence and through the film's self-conscious cinematic referencing.

A pre-credits scene introduces Isak Borg (Sjöström), whose voice-over narration establishes him as a cynical, 78-year-old widower who spurns human company. However, he confesses to loneliness and is surrounded by photographs of his family (his son, his mother, his dead wife). We learn that tomorrow he is going to Lund to receive a 'jubilee doctorate', an honorary accolade awarded fifty years after a doctorate. The narrative then depicts Isak's one-day journey, on which his daughter-in-law, Marianne, accompanies him. Journey motifs are common in fiction (as in the road movie), and there is generally a correlation between physical travel and metaphorical, spiritual odyssey. Bergman's film, however, is ambivalent in its employment of this symbolism, leaving us uncertain how much Isak learns or changes at the story's end.

After the credits the voice-over recurs, but it has now changed tense: while Isak spoke previously of the journey as taking place 'tomorrow', he now looks back at a dream he remembers having the night before departure. A technique we associate with reliable exposition, therefore, is used here to create uncertainty about 'when' the story is being narrated to us, and whether or not what is to come constitutes a memory. There follows an enactment of Isak's dream, whose nightmarish, random images draw heavily on the avant-garde movement of Surrealism: Isak wanders down a lonely street, sees a clock with no hands, a 'faceless' man who disintegrates into blood, and a hearse which spills its coffin on to the road; Isak sees himself in the coffin, and this alter ego tries to pull him into the coffin as well. The dream sequence makes clear that the subject of the film is Isak's troubled psyche, and the symbolism suggests either that he is a member of the 'living dead' (a fear he will later voice) or that he is literally about to die. Isak assumes the latter possibility and, with uncharacteristic superstition, decides to drive rather than fly to Lund.

The first stop he makes (at his childhood summerhouse) provides further narrative confusion: Isak's voice-over tells us that he began to reminisce; however, the reliability of the flashback that follows is undermined by the fact that during the family gathering depicted, one of Isak's sisters remarks that Isak is out fishing. Isak is therefore 'remembering' a scene that he never witnessed, and which possibly never took place. The flashback features Isak's childhood love Sara (Bibi Andersson), who picks strawberries, flirts with his brother and talks about Isak's 'sensitivity'; this suggests that the youthful Isak was very different from the cold Isak of today, although since the memory is unreliable we cannot be sure if this is merely a representation of himself that the old Isak wishes to imagine. The flashback also breaks cinematic conventions in that the older Isak is physically present within it, watching, and walking among, his family of the past.

Isak and Marianne then pick up three young hitch-hikers, one of whom is also called Sara (and is also played by Andersson). This spilling over of the past into the present remains unexplained, although one possibility is that Isak's memories of his lost love are clouding his impression of a pretty girl whom he meets in old age. This further renders the story's non-flashback scenes unreliable. During the course of the day the five travellers have several encounters – with a fighting couple, a garage attendant and Isak's mother – and Isak has another dream. The enactment of this dream lasts a full seventeen minutes of the film's running time, and its mise-en-scène evokes the artifice and artificiality of German Expressionism through its low-key lighting, cast shadows and grotesquely gnarled trees. In the nightmare, Isak is tormented by the Sara of his youth, fails an examination, and is made to watch his wife having sex with another man

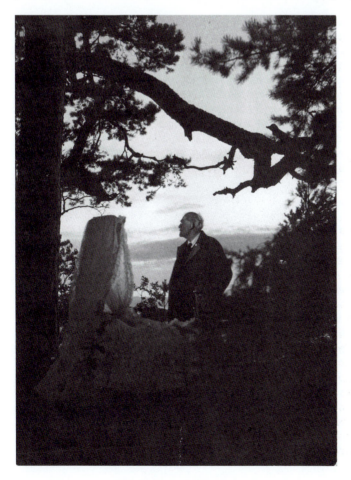

• **Plate 3.7**
Isak's nightmares in
Wild Strawberries
(Ingmar Bergman, 1957)

(or possibly being raped); we are told that this is a memory, but since this information comes from a character within a dream it is again dubious. When Isak awakes, Marianne tells him that she is pregnant and that Ewald, his son, does not want to be a father. In contrast to Isak's earlier behaviour towards Marianne, he now appears concerned and caring.

At the end of the film we are given some indications that Isak has changed as a result of his mental journey: he embraces Marianne, tells her he is fond of her, and possibly attempts to cancel the financial debt Ewald owes him. However, Ewald simply repeats, 'You'll get your money', and Isak does not pursue the matter; this leaves the reconciliation between father and son half-finished, and suggests that relationships cannot be healed as readily as narratives often have us believe – particularly since Ewald is himself the product of Isak's uncompromising approach to human intimacy. The narrative of *Wild Strawberries* makes reference to conventional, cause-and-effect structures through the motif of the linear journey, but fractures this with flashbacks and dreams whose status and reliability are unclear. Furthermore, the entire plot may, or may not, be circular in construction since the past tense of most of the voice-over suggests a narrative 'frame' outside the story from which Isak is remembering. Thus the whole narrative may constitute a memory of past memories of events which never took place. The voice-over is also troubling in that it sometimes downplays the importance of flashbacks ('It is possible I became a bit sentimental') and seems unable to comprehend the dreams; thus it does not seem to belong to a future Isak who has really achieved self-knowledge. We are left with the impression that Isak's learning process has been only partial and semi-honest.

The film finishes with a flashback that the voice-over introduces as memory, though its veracity is again doubtful: the old Isaac is seen among the family of his childhood, and Sarah takes him by the hand and leads him to where he can see his parents, who sit tranquilly on a distant shore. The combination of extreme long shot, idyllic setting and picturesque composition suggests that this not an image of his parents as they were, but instead symbolizes Isak's unattainable ideal of them. The narrative finishes by rewarding Isak and us with this moment of bliss, while also undermining our capacity to believe in it. Bergman's film, therefore, suggests the impossibility of reconciliations, full self-knowledge and dying at peace. It is characteristic of art cinema in its exploration of character subjectivity, its irresolvable plot links and its opposition to mainstream narratives, where fathers and sons forgive each other, and lives and stories end in unproblematic happiness.

☐ CASE STUDY 3: POSTMODERNISM AND PLAYING GAMES IN *RUN LOLA RUN/LOLA RENNT* (TOM TYKWER, 1998)

Director and script-writer Tom Tykwer has described *Run Lola Run* as 'an experimental film for a mass audience' (Halle and McCarthy 2003: 401), which suggests that it seeks to break down some of the conventional distinctions between mainstream and art cinema. Its two opening-intertitle quotations – one by T.S. Eliot, the other by the former coach of former West Germany's national football team Sepp Herberger – reinforces this blurring of boundaries. In its mixing together of styles and forms from high and popular culture, and its frequent use of **pastiche**, *Run Lola Run* constitutes a 'postmodern' narrative.

The film tells three stories, or rather it provides three alternative sets of outcomes all proceeding from the same opening. The narrative premise makes use of a plot technique known as a 'time lock' (Hunter 1994: 51), or story deadline; this is a common means of generating suspense in mainstream film narratives which makes use of the audience's experience of cinematic running time. In *Run Lola Run*, Lola's (Franka Potente) boyfriend

pastiche
From the Italian verb 'to paste', this refers to a patchwork of references from, or imitations of, other works of art.

Manni has lost DM100,000 (the proceeds of a stolen car deal with which a gangster, Ronnie, has entrusted him) on the Berlin underground, and Lola has twenty minutes to replace the money and deliver it to him. Over the phone, Manni tells her that Ronnie will kill him, and that if she does not deliver the money by noon he will commit robbery to obtain it. The film plays out the story three times. Lola always chooses the same solution (to ask her bank-manager father) but for each version a different cause-and-effect chain is set in motion and so the outcome changes: first she dies, then Manni dies, then she obtains the money legally while Manni recovers the lost funds. The final version is the happy ending on which the film finishes.

The film does not explain the links between the stories, and its ambiguity, coupled with the themes of fate and all-conquering love which are suggested, seem to align it with art cinema. However, the narrative also offers us the possibility of another explanation which draws on contemporary popular culture, namely that this constitutes a live-action enactment of a computer game: thus Lola keeps playing until she overcomes all obstacles and 'wins'. Several aspects of the film point to this: when Lola runs down the stairs the camera zooms in on a television set on which an animated Lola is seen; Lola also sometimes seems to learn from one story to the next as if through trial and error (as when she releases the safety catch of the gun in the second story, or when the cartoon Lola takes a huge leap over the dog in the third). The narrative is also free of any ethical consideration of Manni's actions, as if the story exists in the 'virtual moral vacuum' of, for example, *Grand Theft Auto*: as the film's opening football metaphors attest, this is all a game.

Run Lola Run is one of a number of recent films, such as *eXistenZ* (David Cronenberg, 1999) and *The Matrix* trilogy (Andy and Larry Wachowski, 1999, 2003, 2003), which draw on the phenomenon of computer games to construct narratives where 'reality' and illusion are blurred, or where 'the real' emerges as a type of fictional construct. These films draw on the work of postmodern theorists such as Fredric Jameson and Jean Baudrillard, for whom the pervasiveness of contemporary mass media and popular culture has led to an obliteration of 'reality' and history, in favour of an endless production and recycling of images (of 'reality' and history). Tykwer's film invites us to invest in the urgency of Lola's story without identifying which outcome is 'real', or if the stories themselves are a story (or game) within a story. This suggests the absence of 'truth' which is again central to postmodern thought, whereby there are no overarching 'grand narratives' (such as religion, patriarchy, Marxism, science), only different ways of telling stories. Thus the narrative's imitation of a computer game becomes a metaphor which expounds postmodern philosophy.

Run Lola Run, with its frenetic plot, dizzying camera mobility, split-second montages, split-screen framings and pounding soundtrack, also draws on the style of the music video, a postmodern pastiche which functions simultaneously as a Modernist critique of the benevolent, transparent codes of classical cinema. Finally, the film offers us a self-reflexive exploration of mainstream narratives. The operations of cause and effect are demonstrated, so that, for example, when Lola runs more slowly in the second story than she does in the first, because she trips down the stairs, her slightly later arrival at each subsequent encounter shapes the different events shown. Similarly the film draws our attention to classical narrative's focus on central characters, through its 'snapshot' montages of what happens next to three people whom Lola encounters (these stories too are different each time, suggesting an endless web of possible outcomes). However, the film eschews 'grand narratives' and single answers, and this extends to its self-reflexivity, since it does not always demonstrate cause-and-effect logic: in the third story Lola jumps over the dog, does not hesitate on the stairs, and so, we assume, is slightly ahead of 'schedule' this time; nevertheless, she appears to arrive in front of Herr Meyer's car slightly later than she does in the first story, and what follows is shaped by this unexplained variation. Thus, as with Modernist narratives, a 'single' reading of this narrative of multiplicity is not possible. The film incorporates popular culture into a

European tradition of innovation and ambiguity. It blurs the categories of mainstream and art cinema and at the same time affirms their cultural distinction and importance, since we can only appreciate what *Run Lola Run* does through our familiarity with film's form and its various narrative traditions.

FURTHER READING

Bordwell, David, *Narration in the Fiction Film*, Routledge, London, 1997; originally published Methuen, London, 1985.

Bordwell, David and Thompson, Kristin, *Film Art: An Introduction* (7th edn), McGraw-Hill, Boston and London, 2004.

Bordwell, David, Staiger, Jenet and Thompson, Kristin, *The Classical Hollywood Cinema*, Routledge, London, 1985; reprinted 1994.

Chatman, Seymour, *Story and Discourse: Narrative Structure in Fiction and Film*, Cornell University Press, Ithica, NY, 1980.

Dyer, Richard, *Heavenly Bodies* (2nd edn), Routledge, London, 2004.

Maltby, Richard, *Hollywood Cinema*, Blackwell, London, 1995.

Monaco, James, *How To Read a Film* (3rd edn), Oxford University Press, Oxford, 2000.

Neupert, Richard, *The End: Narration and Closure in the Cinema*, Wayne State University Press, Detroit, 1995.

Smith, Murray, *Engaging Characters: Fiction, Emotion and the Cinema*, Oxford University Press, Oxford, 1995.

FURTHER VIEWING

All film viewing constitutes appropriate study activity for the subject of this chapter. In order to understand further the differences and relationships between mainstream and art cinema, careful viewing of the examples cited in the chapter – such as *His Girl Friday*, *Bambi*, *Le Mépris* and *The Conformist* – is recommended. You will also find the films cited in the sections on film form useful. Some further examples – chosen for the conspicuous and/or unusual use they make of particular techniques – are listed below.

Setting, props, costume and make-up
Black Narcissus (Michael Powell and Emeric Pressburger, 1947)
The Fifth Element (Luc Besson, 1997)
Orlando (Sally Potter, 1992)
Ying xiong/Hero (Yimou Zhang, 2002)

Performance
All About Eve (Joseph L. Mankiewicz, 1950)
Rebel Without a Cause (Nicholas Ray, 1955)

Lighting
Double Indemnity (Billy Wilder, 1944)
The Man Who Wasn't There (Joel Coen, 2001)
Nosferatu (F.W. Murnau, 1922)

Cinematography and special effects
Citizen Kane (Orson Welles, 1941)
Heavenly Creatures (Peter Jackson, 1994)
The *Matrix* trilogy (Andy and Larry Wachowski, 1999, 2003, 2003)
Vertigo (Alfred Hitchcock, 1958)

Editing
JFK (Oliver Stone, 1991)
The Man with Movie Camera (Dziga Vertov, 1929)

Sound
Blackmail (Alfred Hitchcock, 1928)
The Conversation (Francis Ford Coppola, 1974)
Singin' in the Rain (Stanley Donen and Gene Kelly, 1952)

RESOURCE CENTRES

http://www.filmeducation.org
http://www.bfi.org.uk
http://www.screensite.org
http://www.ukfilmcouncil.org.uk

Chapter 4

Approaches to cinematic authorship

Paul Watson

■ Approaches to cinematic authorship

INTRODUCTION

This chapter sets itself the task of defining what is at stake when we claim that certain films are authored, that is, the creative expression of an individual artist, in a way more or less analogous to the way we speak of the author of a novel, a letter, a poem or a painting. In other words, we will examine the contentious idea that both a film's meanings and its significance may be attributed to a single creative source who stands behind it as its creator. But already, right here, we confront the theoretical dilemma of cinematic authorship, where traditional and common-sense conceptions of the author fail to describe the inherent complexity of filmmaking, a process which director Peter Bogdanovich describes as involving '300 different opinions and 500 alternative possibilities' (Bogdanovich 2002: 9). So, even if it is possible to make a case for a writer or painter to be the author of a work on the grounds that it might be entirely generated by a single individual, who out of more than 250 people credited for working on *Brokeback Mountain* (2005) shall we single out as its author? Because, as we will see, the question of cinematic authorship has routinely been posed as a question of directorial control over visual style and narrative themes, precisely as a question of a director's individual vision, the paradigmatic reading of *Brokeback Mountain* posits Ang Lee as its author only insofar as it is possible to impute to him, as its director, considerable control over textual operation and meaning. Indeed, the dominant view of cinematic authorship has been that, like novels and paintings, films have a single author usually held to be the director. And, of course, when we speak of seeing the latest Quentin Tarantino or Martin Scorsese film we are, at least on a basic level, rehearsing this romantic notion of authorship as origin, a model in which the figure of the film director is stitched together with the notion of free authorial agency.

THE THREE PARADOXES OF CINEMATIC AUTHORSHIP

Boiling down the notion of cinematic authorship to such commonsensical simplicity, however, belies not only the theoretical and methodological complexities which bear on the study of authorship, but also the controversies that have attended the history of the concept in film studies. In other words, while Adrian Martin is right when he says that cinematic authorship is 'quite a simple principle' with a twofold emphasis on *the art of film production* and a method of *understanding films as legitimate artworks*, this in itself tells us little about the implied relationship between human material activity, creativity and the critical processes involved in defining and valorising films as art. Nor for that matter does it necessarily shed light on the political economy of filmmaking in terms of either the commercial frameworks in which any putative creativity takes place or the ways in which directors/authors often function as marketable commodities in their own right (see Martin 2001). Indeed, despite the recent attempts, which I address below, to variously overcome, fix or dodge them, a number of stubborn dilemmas continue to dog theories of cinematic authorship.

For instance, given that the concept of authorship has been consistently defined and redefined in different historical periods, what does the term actually refer to? As Tag Gallagher points out, 'even those who admit that some movies have an "author" disagree about what the term means' (Gallagher 2001). Similarly, how do accounts of cinematic authorship sit with accounts derived from other disciplines? What models of authorship most adequately describe creative agency in relation to cinema? Can models be imported from elsewhere, say, literature or architecture, or are we impelled to devise a bespoke theory attuned to the specificities of the form? On another note, where is the critical efficacy of authorship to be found? Is authorship, as Janet Staiger argues, a question of 'causality for the film', one sensitive to the 'material reality of human actions' (Staiger 2003: 28,49), or does it, as Jonathan Rosenbaum suggests, 'exist largely for the convenience of critics ... [as] a way of reading movies, not explaining how they're made' (Rosenbaum 2000: 84)? Approaching the same issue from the other end, if authorship is no longer the *raison d'être* of film studies then what is the purpose of author/director studies? Is it specific to the disciplinary purview of film studies or should it be hooked up with the political concerns of cultural studies? Moreover, can authorship survive the theoretical challenge brought by developments in structuralist, post-structuralist and postmodernist thinking, and if so where is the author to be found – still embodied in the figure of the director; in other creative personnel such as producers, screenwriters, actors and so forth; as a distinctive outcome of collaborative working practice; or as markers of institutional or corporate identity? As we proceed, we will, by necessity, begin to unpick this theoretical knot in order to tease out the threads required to plait a model of cinematic authorship which is by turns pragmatic, flexible and, above all, useful, that is to say, one that is attuned to both the authoring practices of real individuals and the various socio-economic contexts which always frame such practices. However, one thing is clear. The notion of cinematic authorship is paradoxical, and paradoxical in three distinct, albeit related, ways. Nevertheless, paradox can be productive insofar as it directs attention towards points of intellectual friction which, if probed with care, can often ignite the critical imagination and generate fresh thinking. As such, before turning to a consideration of the history of cinematic authorship and its subsequent development, it is worth entertaining paradox for the sake of progress.

The paradox of collaboration: 'Get me my agency!'

If on the one hand it is now commonplace to speak of the director as the author of his or her films and those films as the direct expression of individuated agency (the idea that 'a Spielberg film' implies a coherence of expressive techniques and meanings in a way that, say, 'a Dreamworks picture' does not), on the other hand, it is also a given of academic film studies to acknowledge that the overwhelming majority of filmmaking, and Hollywood studio production as a whole, is a fundamentally collaborative practice, and collaborative in crucial ways which affect the textual operation and meanings of a film. This is the first paradox of cinematic authorship: given the fundamentally collaborative working dynamics of industrial filmmaking, is it possible, or indeed plausible, to attribute authorship to a single creative source? Underpinning this problem is the question of the suitability of models of authorship developed in relation to literature and the arts for explaining film signification, and that while authorship may be a fuzzy concept generally, when grafted on to the study of cinema it becomes particularly slippery. For simply transposing the primary terms of traditional authorial analysis to the study of film may not only belie the intrinsic differences between the traditional arts and film, but more worryingly conceal more complex axes of art-making practice and expressivity that characterise cinema's mode of production. Either way, it is far from clear whether the assumed analogy between the collective and collaborative nature of most filmmaking and the individual novelist or painter is an appropriate one.

This already vexed issue is further complicated when we take into account the various strategies adopted by film scholars to deal with the implications of the first paradox of cinematic authorship. In attempting to fix that paradox by adding progressively finer detail to the concept of the film author, the level of complexity required to sustain the idea becomes incrementally geared up. As Berys Gaut observes:

It has been held that the film author is the director, the screenwriter, the star or the studio; that the film author is an actual individual, or a critical construct; that there is not one film author, but several;

the claim of film authorship has been held primarily as an evaluative one, or an interpretive one, or simply as the view that that there are authors of films as there are authors of literary works.

(Gaut 1997: 149)

Indeed, Gaut himself argues that while there is 'a core truth' to claims of cinematic authorship and that it 'should not be rejected in the cavalier fashion in which some critics have dealt with it', the fact that commercial films are typically the result of the work of many agents leads him to conclude that the notion of 'multiple-authorship' is a more 'theoretically sound and critically fruitful' model than the dominant view of singular authorship (Gaut 1997: 149, 150). Other critics have addressed this same paradox by uncoupling the agent of enunciation from the flesh-and-bone figure of a biographical self so as to 'squeeze out' the author 'from his position of prominence and transform the notion of him [sic] which remains' (Wollen 1973: 84). What remains, depending on which critical position one adopts, is a picture of the author as variously: a source/product of discourse; a function of ideology; an unintentional 'signature' traceable across a number of films; a position or voice constructed by/within the narrative; or a construction produced by the spectator in the act of reading/comprehending a film or group of films. Either way, it is this degree of elaboration and contradiction which leads Catherine Grant to argue that 'despite the continual attention accorded to film directors during the last four decades, film authorship has rarely been considered a wholly legitimate object of contemplation' (Grant 2000: 101), and David Gerstner to suggest that the 'pleasures and politics associated with authorship studies' must to some degree 'remain suspect' (Gerstner 2003: 21).

The paradox of theory: the immortal monster

The scepticism directed towards the idea of cinematic authorship prompts the second paradox of authorship. On the one hand, in turning away from authorship and towards such theoretical concepts as semiotics, structuralism and psychoanalysis that are abstracted from the actual practices of filmmaking, film theory either confined the author to the sidelines of its debates, or simply ignored the question of cinematic authorship altogether. On the other hand, however, and in the face of such stubborn indifference, authorship continues to survive as a going academic concern with major academic publishers commissioning series after series of books dedicated to the work of single directors. It is in this respect that John Belton describes cinematic authorship 'not so much a theory as it is a crime scene to which critics and theorists seem to be drawn again and again. The bodies on the floor change but the scene remains the same' (Belton 2005: 62). He goes on to discuss the notion of the author as a 'monster who will not die, the mesmerizing figure that the field of film studies has been unable and unwilling to exorcise' (Belton 2005: 60). It is this theoretical peccadillo, the seemingly irrepressible urge to scratch the author-itch, which accounts for the fact that the idea of the director-as-author 'remains probably the most widely shared assumption in film studies today' (Bordwell and Thompson 1994: 38). Indeed, not only do writers and publishers continue to organise output around the work of directors/authors, but, as chapters such as this one attest, authorship studies are firmly ensconced in curricula at all levels of film and media education. So while there seems to be a tacit agreement among professional film scholars, even those who have in recent years attempted to resuscitate and reinvigorate authorship approaches, that the work of individual filmmakers is best understood as a thread in a much more complex tapestry of technological, social, historical, institutional, cognitive and cultural practices, this stance accounts for neither the individuated creative crafts involved in film production in the first instance, nor, in the final instance, the continued fascination and identification with the figure of the cinematic author by the film industry, film critics and film audiences.

The cultural paradox: authors, authors everywhere

Claims that the author is somehow dead, or a theoretical irrelevancy, appear out of step not only with our intuitions, but more crucially with contemporary media culture. For instance, it is possible to argue, with Timothy Corrigan, that far from being supplanted by the apparently more rigorous approaches of semiotics, structuralism, psychoanalysis and audience studies, the figure of the cinematic author may in fact be 'more alive now than at any other point in film history' (Corrigan 1991: 135). With the rapid proliferation of convergent media platforms and the corresponding exponential increase in the number and variety of media texts, it seems that the *visibility* of the author is now more pronounced than ever. For example, in the shift from videotape to DVD, it is now common after watching a movie to watch it again in order to listen to the director's commentary. Perhaps we will then watch the accompanying 'Making Of' documentary, or the director's personal video diary of the shoot, read the script and production notes on the DVDROM, or follow the hyperlinks to a further range of web-based material. Indeed, the time it would take to watch the panoply of special features contained on the two-disc set of *War of the Worlds* (2005) would far surpass the viewing time of the film itself.

For more detailed discussion of the impact of new media on film see Chapter 2, pp. 42–8.

Notwithstanding the significance of the sheer amount of material that is now routinely jam-packed on to DVDs, both Parker and Parker (2005) and Alex Cox (2001) attach particular salience to the 'director commentary' as a means of both analysing individual authors and making a case for the continuing relevance of authorship studies in the cultural moment. The former argue that such commentaries can not only articulate the 'specifics of intention' (that is, the local and specific decision-making processes carried out by a director from scene to scene, and the 'suppressed' or 'residual' intentions of other potential authors such as screenwriters or cinematographers), but also the 'limits of intention', the way contingency, expediency, chance and luck can all bear upon the final film's style and effect (Parker and Parker 2005). The latter agrees that the change in the way movies can be now watched and comprehended on DVD 'can provide some sort of film literacy, even insight'. More important for Cox, however, is the potential of the director commentary and other bonus features to breathe new life into debates about cinematic authorship. He argues that such 'additional elements' may 'represent the Return of the Director.... The idea that a film director is an 'author' is maintained by a tiny band of believers: the Director's Guild, people who live in Paris, and ... the buyers of DVDs' (Cox 2001: 10).

The recent release of *King Kong: Peter Jackson's Production Diaries* (2005) may perhaps be seen as a new stage in the role of the DVD extra as, almost literally, an extra-textual conduit for authorial voices. This special edition two-disc set was packaged and marketed as an 'unprecedented behind-the-scenes filmmaker's journey' offering 'an exciting, exclusive first-hand account of the intense eight month production process of the most anticipated motion picture of 2005'. The two discs contain fifty-four production documentaries and are accompanied by a fifty-two-page 'Scrapbook of Drawings, Photographs, Images and Notes from Peter Jackson', four 'Exclusive Production Art Prints', and, a 'Letter of Authenticity'. Crucially, however, and what sets it apart from the gamut of similiar DVDs, is that it was released approximately six months in advance of theatrical release of the movie proper. In other words, what *Peter Jackson's Production Diaries* presents us with, and sells to us, is strictly speaking not an extra-textual commentary about intentionality, however conceived, but more precisely a *pre-textual* prolegomena centred around the figure of the heroic author/director. So even if Parker and Parker are right in their diagnosis that the availability and commercial viability of a storage capacity which exceeds that required to contain the film is 'a secondary benefit of digitization, not the goal that drove development of the medium itself', it is becoming less certain that this 'spare' space 'cannot provide a rationale for creating' the kinds of additional materials one routinely finds on DVDs (Parker and Parker 2005). Indeed, in the case of *Peter Jackson's Production Diaries*, the materials usually produced to pad out this excess capacity have themselves become not only the primary content but also

• **Plate 4.1**
King Kong: Peter Jackson's Production Diaries (2005, Universal Studios). A 'Collector's Edition' DVD package released in advance of the movie itself which contains a panopoly of special features and 'limited quantity' materials relating to the production of the film

the focus of pleasure. In addition, of course, the nature of those pleasures is intimately entwined with, and to a significant extent predicated precisely on, the *presence* of the knowable author.

This, then, is the third paradox of cinematic authorship: that at a time when many critics would like to think that film theory has finally wriggled free from its fascination with the figure of the cinematic author the discourse of authorship seems once more to present itself as a vital node in understanding the relationship between the film industry, the film and its audience. Indeed, as borne out by the commercial and cultural complexities bound up with the director commentary phenomenon, there remains what Dana Polan has recently called a simultaneous 'desire *of* the director' and 'desire *for* the director' (Polan 2001). The first of these terms refers to a director's 'recourse to filmmaking as a way to express personal vision', and the subsequent attempts by critics to identify and understand their 'primary obsessions and thematic preoccupations' as the product of individual artistic desire. The second term, the desire *for* the director, directs attention away from what the director wants and instead focuses it on the activities of fans, critics and scholars who continue to want to 'understand films as having an originary instance in the person who signs them' and who arbitrate on the relative worth of film based on who that signature belongs to (Polan 2001). It is in these respects, then, that if authorship is a fiction, it is, as Thomas Elsaesser notes, a necessary one insofar as it names a pleasure 'that seems to have no substitute in the sobered-up deconstruction of the authorless voice of ideology' (Elsaesser 1981: 11). Indeed, this pleasure seems to have at last regained some academic respectability in recent years with a number of scholars beginning once again to see the task of theorising cinematic authorship as both possible and worthwhile. Much of that work has attempted to reincarnate, recast or rethink what is variously referred to as classical authorship or vulgar **auteurism**. It is to a more detailed examination of those approaches, their origination, development and efficacy, that we now turn.

For further discussion of auteur theory and the French New Wave see pp. 399–404.

auteurism
see **auteur**

auteur
A French term that originated in the pages of the film journal *Cahiers du cinéma* in the 1950s to refer to directors who infused their films with their distinctive personal vision through the salient manipulation of film technique. Auteurs, seen as genuine artists, were contrasted with **metteurs-en-scène** who were held to be technically competent directors who merely executed the processes of filmmaking without consistently stamping their 'personality' on the material from one film to the next. To study film as if it were the creative expression of a single individual, usually held to be the director, is often called **auterism**.

WHAT'S THE USE OF AUTHORSHIP?

In spite of its troubled theoretical career, the common-sense position – that a film bears traces of its creator(s) – has proved remarkably durable precisely because it addresses a number of crucial questions, questions that refuse to go away, about the role of cinema as an art form, a commodity and a communicative practice: exactly how are the makers of film and the audience bound together in the activities of creation, communication and comprehension; what kind of communication is this and are there really any grounds for erecting theoretical boundaries between the practices of filmmaking and the experience of watching movies; and why, in the final instance, do audiences and critics continue to hanker for the cinematic author when 'the challenge to the concept of the author as source and centre of the text ... has been decisive in contemporary criticism' (Caughie 1981: 1)?

As we shall see, the emergence of authorship outfitted film critics with a set of tools with which to:

- Argue for the artistic and academic legitimacy of cinema by claiming that there are film artists just as there are literary or visual artists and that the work of these artists should be afforded the same intellectual scrutiny as the traditional arts.
- Interpret films as the creative expression of those who made it by shifting the critical focus away from film narrative (what happens) towards film style (**mise-en-scène** and thematics).
- Evaluate the relative artistic merits of both a film and its maker(s) and make more precise differentiations between individual films and filmmakers.

mise-en-scène
Refers both to what is filmed (setting, props, costumes) and to *how* it is filmed (cinematographic properties of the shot such as depth of field, focus and camera movement). In an attempt to counter the imprecision of the term, this latter aspect is sometimes called 'mise-en-shot'.

It is these three principal critical procedures which continue to make cinematic authorship not only a controversial idea, but a useful critical tool as well. There are, however, two important implications that emerge from these various dimensions of authorship. First, we cannot assume that authorship means the same thing in every context. For the question of how authorship relates to a film's meanings and enunciative techniques is not the same as how an author creates value in a film. And second, we may have to look for a more pragmatic definition of film authorship which recognises the importance of the distinct contribution of a broader range of cinematic roles to the meaning and value of films. This would involve, on the one hand, a reconsideration of the *critical function* of authorship theory (what we expect its yield to be in the way of results), and on the other, a reconsideration of *how and where we look for evidence of authorship*, and with it reconsideration of some of those elements that have, up until now, tended to be assigned to the director. Before doing so, however, it is first necessary to review some of the most salient steps in the history and development of authorship theory in order to: (1) locate the above discussion of the paradoxical nature of the authorship debate in its proper historical context; (2) identify the useful aspects arising from the various incarnations of authorship theory; and (3) establish how it may be possible to shape those aspects into a critical method for analysing contemporary cinema that chimes with both current theoretical concerns and our intuitive attraction to the author.

The emergence of the auteur

Today, both filmmakers and critics take for granted cinema's status as an art form. Some fifty or so years ago, however, when not altogether ignored by scholars as beneath serious critical attention, cinema was often vilified along with other forms of mass culture as a blemish on art, or worse, a dehumanising agent of cultural oppression. Despite attempts to designate film as 'the seventh art', and notwithstanding the work of such prototypical auteurists as Parker Tyler and James Agee, cinema's search for artistic legitimation was more of a hope than a prospect. Cinema, and Hollywood cinema in particular, was seen first and foremost as a business governed by economic logic and the conventions of product marketability. And, as Gallagher notes, 'conventions have nothing to do with art. Art is original, individual. Conventions are collective – what everyone knows' (Gallagher 2001). As such, the origins of cinematic authorship may be understood as a response to three simultaneous lines of argument which conspired to exile film from artistic and intellectual respectability. First, cinema's technological means of production preclude individual creativity. Second, the collaborative nature of industrial filmmaking and the specialised division of labour it entails forestalls self-expression. Third, the need to entertain a large audience necessitates a high degree of standardisation and conventionality which are incompatible with original artistic expression. In all of these propositions the blanket rejection of cinema as artistically illegitimate depends on the idea that art is necessarily the result of the creative activities of an individual, and can be appreciated and understood as such.

Within this context, therefore, authorship offered first and foremost a ready-made strategy for vindicating film as an art form precisely by installing in cinema the figure of the individual artist. Moreover, to a significant extent the infant discipline of film studies was underwritten by the theoretical legitimacy and disciplinary vocabulary associated with the ideas of authorship and individual artistic expression which had already been well rehearsed in literary criticism and art history. Richard Dyer neatly summarises this idea, stating that authorship

made the case for taking film seriously by seeking to show that a film could be just as profound, beautiful and important as any other kind of art, provided, following a dominant model of value in art, it was demonstrably the work of a highly individual artist.... The power of authorship resided in its ability to mobilize a familiar argument about artistic worth and, importantly, to show that this could be used to discriminate between films. Thus, at a stroke, it was proclaimed that film could be art (with all the cultural capital this implies) and that there could be a form of criticism – indeed, study – of it.

(Dyer 1998: 5).

So although film had been discussed as art before the notion of the film author had taken shape, in borrowing some of the academic legitimacy from more established disciplines by making the author-as-artist a necessary sufficient condition of the serious study of cinema, cinematic authorship entwined the notion of the value of film with the person who was deemed aesthetically responsible for it. As such, at the heart of the various complexities associated with authorship lies the idea that films are valued when they are deemed to be the work of an artist, traditionally identified as the director. In other words, the critical strategy on which this move is predicted is to assume the 'director as the creative source of meaning' and their 'output as an oeuvre'; that is to say, 'a repetition and enrichment of characteristic themes and stylistic choices' which bear traces of individual personality (Bordwell 1989: 44).

These ideas were initially cultivated in the pages of the French journal *Cahiers du cinéma* during the 1950s and were subsequently formulated into what became known as 'auteur theory' by the American critic Andrew Sarris in the 1960s. While the idea that a film's director should be considered its author certainly did not originate in the pages of *Cahiers du cinéma*, the central role which the journal played in propagating and disseminating that thesis cannot be underestimated. Likewise, despite the critical venom subsequently directed towards Sarris's contribution, especially by Pauline Kael in her scathing 1963 essay 'Circles and Squares', it is his work that is chiefly responsible for publicising ideas of cinematic authorship in America and shaping it into a critical method for analysing and evaluating the particular art of Hollywood production.

The *Cahiers* critics, as they became known, writers such as François Truffaut, André Bazin, Jean Luc-Godard, Claude Chabrol and Eric Rohmer, not only formulated the inaugural principles which Sarris later recast into auteur theory, but also implicitly and explicitly outfitted the study of cinema with an analytical method and critical vocabulary. In what is often seen as the founding document of cinematic authorship, 'A Certain Tendency of the French Cinema', François Truffaut chides the inclination of the dominant mode of French cinema of the 1940s and 1950s for its bourgeois values and dependency on literary sources for its inspiration. For Truffaut this notion of 'quality cinema', motivated by traditional models of high culture and leaning on 'respectable' literature for its value, offers little in the way of art besides the technical transposition of literary scripts to the screen. Indeed, on this account the merits of a film are relatively unconnected with the practices of filmmaking, but are rather determined by the putative literary pedigree of the script. In contrast, Truffaut argued for the recognition, in terms of both filmmaking and its critical reception, of the 'audacities' specific to the medium of film: an attention to the cinematographic properties of film style, especially the way mise-en-scène was deployed by a filmmaker (see Truffaut 1976). This manifesto for seeing film *qua* film through an attention to the *craft* of filmmaking found perhaps its most well-known expression, somewhat ironically, in the title of Bazin's 1957 article, 'La Politique des auteurs'. It is ironic insofar as Bazin's essay simultaneously provides not only the titular 'policy' that Sarris would later recast as 'theory' and the terms of authorship analysis which would subsequently be used to both teach auteurism and conduct studies of specific auteurs, but also one of the strongest cautions against the excesses of auteurism. Indeed, after warning against the dangers of, on the one hand, ignoring the work of directors deemed not to be auteurs and, on the other, side-stepping consideration of the material conditions in which directors produce their work, he concludes with the reproof, 'Auteur, yes, but what of?' (Bazin 1996). Nevertheless, the foundations of 'auteur theory' had been laid and its propositional cornerstone – the recognition of the director as a film's principle creative source – set squarely in place. For, generally speaking, the Cahiers critics believed that film ought to bear the personal stylistic signature of its director; that is, to announce what William D. Routt has called the 'auteurprints' of its creator. Indeed, Routt goes so far as to suggest that 'La politique des auteurs' evinces 'perhaps the most radical assertion of the shaping power of one individual in popular art' (Routt 1990). In this way, then, auteurism's first provocative move was to locate the author and creative centre of a film not as its writer but as its director insofar as it is the director who orchestrates the visual aspects of cinema.

Auteurism's second and perhaps most provocative intervention was the championing of certain Hollywood directors as genuine, even exemplary auteurs. Indeed, to a significant extent, the idea that it is possible, even desirable to adopt a serious, critical stance towards Hollywood cinema became knotted together with the auteur approach. For in the work of directors such as Alfred Hitchcock, Howard Hawks, Nicholas Ray, Orson Welles, John Ford and Douglas Sirk the Cahiers critics detected a style and purity of technique undiluted by the cultural dead-weight of literary heritage. It is in this sense, then, that auteurism's most profound and influential critical tactic is not the mere attribution of individuated creative agency in what is a collaborative medium, but rather the exaltation of Hollywood directors, hitherto seen as mere cogs in a vulgar commercial machine, as auteurs. Indeed, Bill Nichols argues that 'a frequent tenet of auteur criticism is that a tension exists between the artist's vision and the means at his [sic] disposal for realizing it: studio pressure, genre conventions, star demands, story requirements. These constraints are also seen as a source of strength, imposing discipline and promoting cunning subversions' (Nichols 1976: 306) As such, it is precisely the industrial restrictions and formal constraints that were previously evoked to define Hollywood studio productions as anonymous genre fodder that, ironically, the Cahiers critics valorised as the background of conventions against which the great directors' ingenuity and personal vision take shape and can be discerned. Hitchcock, Hawks and others were championed as auteurs because they realised personal expression in the face of the industrial constraints imposed on them. Their work was valorised not despite the barriers to its expression, but precisely because of them. More crudely, if it could be demonstrated that auteurs exist in the most restrictive filmmaking system in the world, then they can exist anywhere.

Auteurism as method

Auteurism, as it emerged from the pages of Cahiers du cinéma, thus not only imbricated cinema with the traditional arts through the ascription of director-as-author, but evolved into a critical strategy for sorting the artistic wheat from the generic chaff of Hollywood cinema. The principal method by which this was achieved was the establishment of the hierarchical distinction between those directors dubbed mere '**metteurs-en-scène**' and genuine auteurs. While metteurs-en-scène were deemed technically competent directors, film-to-film their work nevertheless evinced little or no stylistic coherence or thematic consistency. By contrast, the auteur infused their work with a personal vision, leaving behind a distinctive signature across a significant number of films. Unlike the tradition of 'quality' filmmaking in France, for the auteur the script was merely a pretext for engaging in the proper practices of filmmaking – *the intentional and salient manipulation of cinematic techniques for communicative and/or expressive ends*. Privileged among

metteur-en-scène
See **auteur**

these stylistic techniques was mise-en-scène. For, it is through the specific organisation of mise-en-scène, critics argued, that a director leaves behind the footprints of his or her vision, individual stylistic touches that accrue to resemble the unique personality of the auteur. John Caughie argues that 'it is with the mise-en-scène that the *auteur* transforms the material which has been given to him or her; so it is in the mise-en-scène ... that the auteur writes his or her individuality into the film' (Caughie 1981: 12–13).

Of course, such a fundamentally evaluative critical method not only enabled cinema's great works and the great film artists to be ranked alongside the great works and artists from the classical arts, but it also presented critics with a methodology and vocabulary for studying cinema. Armed with such a method, it was possible for the critic to contribute to the task of winkling out traces of authorship in a range of filmmakers' work. As Robert Stam notes, 'one of the pleasures of auteurist criticism was discerning style and individuality where it had not been detected before' (Stam 2000b: 2). Thus, the critic skilled in auteur archaeology roves across the surfaces of a director's work brushing away the dust of conventionality until aspects of film style and technique deemed salient are unearthed, aspects which can then be explicated and retroactively strung together into a coherent vision of the director-as-auteur who is positioned behind them as their originator. In other words, the critic's work is that of ferreting out the unique marks, flourishes and touches of a director so that they may be credited back to or projected upon their source: the auteur. As such, figures like Hitchcock and Welles were deemed significant in the first instance not necessarily for advancing cinema technically, but rather for a certain aesthetic consistency and salience.

It is this avowedly evaluative form of cinematic authorship that Andrew Sarris translated into North American film criticism and in so doing added a false veneer of rigour to the approach in modifying 'auteur policy' to 'auteur theory'. In other words, what started out in the pages of *Cahiers du cinéma* as a polemic calling for the art and artists of cinema to be recognised became, with Sarris, a prescriptive method for evaluating the worth of directors and championing the putative supremacy of American film. In a much quoted essay, 'Notes on the Auteur Theory in 1962', Sarris sought to shake both art criticism and film criticism out of its blindness towards Hollywood cinema and was willing, in Janet Staiger's phrase, to 'out-auteur' many of the French critics in order to do so (Staiger 2003: 36). In further refining the distinction between metteurs-en-scène and auteur, he argued that 'the way a film looks and moves should have some relationship to the way a director thinks and feels'. Moreover, he advocated 'wrenching' directors from 'their historical environments' in order to subject them to an aesthetic analysis which could both discern their 'personal signatures' and be used to determine their proper place within his pantheon. Sarris proposed three criteria for establishing the auteurist credentials of a director which correlated with the 'circles' of that pantheon: technical competency; distinguishable personality; and the 'interior meaning' of a film arising from the tension between the director's personality and the material. While the first two of these premises were criterion of value, the latter, for Sarris, 'is the ultimate glory of the cinema as an art' (see Sarris 1963, 1996). On the one hand, the lineage to the *Cahiers* critics is clearly visible in this strategy inasmuch as the worth of a film remains firmly indexed to the director's ability to inscribe his personality across a series of films in spite of the limitations imposed on individual creativity by the industrial and commercial pressures of filmmaking. On the other hand, however, Sarris's legacy to the auteurist debate resides in the slippage from the *evaluative* method established in 'La Politique' into a method explicitly based on *value judgements*. For in *The American Cinema* Sarris not only deployed the principles of auteurism to recast the history of American film as a pantheon – a nine-part hierarchical system which ranked films top to bottom according to his own criteria for determining value – but went further in declaring that, film for film, American cinema was superior to that of 'the rest of the world' (Sarris 1996).

Sarris's regressive use of auteur theory to reconstruct film history, however, represents only one snag in the frayed theoretical principles of cinematic authorship. Indeed, it is not surprising that such an anachronistic move – the installation in the cinema of the romantic figure of the artist – would provide a broad enough, and easy enough, target to attract a range of far-reaching criticisms.

THE PROBLEMS OF AUTEUR THEORY

For a discussion of Warner Bros Studio as auteur read pp. 32–5.

If, as Dyer suggests, auteurism is film studies' 'greatest hit', then it is also perhaps its most criticised and controversial idea (Dyer 1998: 5). Indeed, as Routt argues, the 'absurd pretences' on which the entire notion of cinematic authorship is founded 'are easy to see, and to reject, as all sober folk of good intentions have rejected and continue to reject them' (Routt 1990). For while the desire to forge a critical method capable of bestowing intellectual and artistic credibility to cinema, that is, to interrogate cinema's distinctive contribution to the arts, does not in itself invoke essentialist or romantic conceptions of the artist and all the elitist dead wood thus entailed, its significance nevertheless does lie in the foregrounding of a specific relationship between cinematic signification and the creative activities of individuals. And it is here that the difficulty of cinematic authorship continues to replay itself, raising uncomfortable questions about the relationship between the film text and the spectator implied by the model of communication that underpins it. For a number of crucial problems become clear once we view auteurism through the lens of subsequent developments in film theory.

First, and most obviously, auteurism was attacked for belying the collaborative conditions of cinema's mode of production. As discussed above, the analogy between writer or painter and the auteur becomes difficult to sustain when one takes into account the material realities and creative diversity of the filmmaking process in which collaboration is standard and undeniable. A corollary argument to this is the idea that auteurism was insufficiently rigorous or simply whimsical, that at best it depended on the taste of a few specialised critics who pronounced on a film's worth by appealing to the already shop-worn principles of the traditional arts, and, at worse, resembled personalised and impressionistic conjecture. This prompted critics to try to correct some of these charges of imprecision by grafting auteurism on to the quasi-scientific methodology of structuralism. In an effort to counter the individualist paradigm of the Romantic artist axiomatic to its predecessor, auteur-structuralism, as it became known, was an attempt to probe beneath the surfaces of individuated agency into the 'deep' underlying socio-cultural structures which imbued a film with significance and meaning. Its apparent sophistication resided in its conception of the auteur not as the biographical figure who intentionally 'put the meaning into the film' so to speak, but as a structure identifiable in the text. As such, the concept of the auteur was, in the final instance, neither necessarily the director, nor even a person, but a indeterminate structure unearthed in the critical process of reading a film. Peter Wollen's (1972, 1973) work formed a central pillar in this line of thinking inasmuch as he recast the author from an a priori figure responsible for putting the meaning into a film to 'an a posteriori construction produced by the spectator to identify the particular bundles of oppositions that structured a group of texts associated with the author figure' (Belton 2005: 60). In other words, auteurs no longer produced films intentionally, rather films produced auteurs unintentionally.

intentional fallacy
A phrase coined by Monroe Beardsley to describe the difference between a text's meaning(s) and what its author intended. As such, criticism dependent on or directed towards uncovering the intentions of the author/artist falls foul of the 'intentional fallacy' insofar as the meaning of a text is not fixed within it, but created in the historically situated act of reading.

Passing through various other theoretical modifications, this line of thinking progressively diluted auteurism's theoretical respectability to the point where Roland Barthes' 1968 article announced 'The Death of the Author'. Underscoring Barthes' argument, as well as most of the above objections, is the suspect notion of 'ideal' comprehension, where the director's intentions coincide with the spectator's/critic's reading of a film. Often referred to as the **intentional fallacy**, the model of communication implied by the classical auteurist approach is one in which spectators are subjected to the vision of the director, a vision they reconstruct more or less faithfully in line with the map provided by the author through the film's stylistic salience. In other words, communication and signification become a closed circuit with authors jam-packing films full of meaning and spectators subsequently unpacking that meaning at its ultimate destination. This is a problematical model for a number of reasons. Not only is it at odds with cognitive models of cinematic comprehension which attribute a far more important stake to the spectator in actually creating meaning, but specifically in terms of cinematic authorship it tends to confine the significance of the auteur to the evidence of his or her activities left behind in the film text itself. To put it another way, auteurs now have an increasing cultural visibility which, in the last instance, is not tied to their role as director. Timothy Corrigan calls this extra-textual notion of cinematic authorship 'the commerce of auteurism' (Corrigan 1991). For Corrigan, auteurism has become 'a *commercial* strategy for organizing audience reception, as a critical concept bound to distribution and marketing aims' (ibid.: 103).

A BIOGRAPHICAL LEGEND: THE COMMERCE OF AUTHORSHIP

Corrigan's intervention in the debate is to locate auteurism's critical and performative impetus not with filmmaking but rather with film consumption. He argues that 'in today's commerce we want to know what our authors or auteurs look like or how they act' and that, accordingly, the concept of auteurism is now defined by institutional and commercial agencies 'almost exclusively as publicity and advertisement' (ibid.: 106). This is the idea of *auteur as star* and, like film stars, auteurs peddle their celebrity currency in the promotion, marketing and publicity of the film to the extent that our primary access to the auteur is not through the film itself but through the numerous interviews, talk shows, reviews, trailers, websites, award ceremonies and guest appearances the auteur undertakes in selling the film to us. In other words, instead of struggling against the system in order to express their personal vision, authors are located as a function of the system, summoned up by the industrial forces and mobilised according to institutional needs. As such, to study an auteur one no longer focuses exclusively on the markers of individual style left behind in the film, but rather their 'biographical legend' – the term David Bordwell (1988) uses to describe the *image* of a director that one constructs not only from their films, but from the full range of extra texts in which they appear.

Once again, the role of DVD, and especially the 'director commentary', may be seen as particularly significant in this respect. As with its videotape processor, DVD is first and foremost a means of re-promoting and reselling the film to us on a different platform. Indeed, yields from DVD sales now far exceed those derived from the theatrical release of films to the extent that they are responsible for keeping many major studios afloat. Moreover, this income is boosted by the ability to exploit the economic potential of the studios' back-catalogue – simply stated, the practice of selling old films to us in a new format. Increasingly this not only involves reissuing classical films, or films made before the uptake of DVD, but more complexly the repackaging of both classical and contemporary films, some of which may already have been released on DVD, to include a range of special features that had not been previously made available. For example, Paramount Pictures recently rereleased *Mission: Impossible* (1996) and *Mission: Impossible 2* (2000) as a two-disc 'Special Collector's Edition' DVD to accompany the theatrical release of *Mission: Impossible III* (2006), only this time, of course, it was chock-full of new special features relating to all three movies in the series. The main point here, however, is the function of the director's commentary within the package not simply as mediator of intentionality or as marketable asset, but rather as a *performance* of authorial agency which implies yet exceeds both. In other words, both on general and specific levels, the director commentary exposes an interesting slippage between textual and extra-textual models of cinematic authorship.

While the director commentary is intimately related to the film it annotates, it nevertheless complicates how we experience it and how we understand it. But it is not just the experience of 'watching' director commentaries that reveals the performative act of the auteur but also the process of producing them, a process described by filmmaker Alex Cox as 'sitting watching a video of a film made, usually, several years previously. As the film plays, [the director] is expected sagely to regale a microphone with anecdotes about the making of the film. It helps if the director has managed to snag someone as "back-up" – the producer, the writer, an actor or the composer. Quite often, their recollections will be completely different' (Cox 2001: 10). Cox's anecdote prompts two observations. First, there is no a priori reason to believe that the director is the most knowledgeable, reliable or even honest commentator about either their own role in the filmmaking process or the finished film itself. Indeed, with DVDs which have an audio track with multiple commentators or multiple audio tracks with a single commentator a range of possible descriptions become available of the same events and processes. This has the potential not only to complicate the dynamics of authorial intentionality and possibly unseat the director from the assumed position as the film's controlling centre, but also to prompt consideration of instances where authorship might be more plausibly conceived as collaborative or multiple.

Second, and perhaps more complexly, the director commentary deliberately foregrounds authorial agency through a network of extra-textual relationships not only as a method of representing the artistic worth of a film and thus differentiating it within the market, but also as a way of stabilising the possible ways in which it is received. That is to say, if the conception of the auteur developed in the pages of *Cahiers du cinéma* and circulated by Sarris depended on the discernible textual evidence of artistic agency, auteurs are now 'placed before, after and outside a film text ... in effect usurping the work of that text and its reception' (Corrigan 1991: 106). Access to a blow-by-blow account of a director's intentions, influences and ideas – that is to say, evidence of the relationship between individual agency and aesthetics – short-circuits the critical need to unearth those intentions since they are already provided as part of the package. In this respect, developments such as the directorial commentary are a logical extension or complement to the model of commercial auteurism outlined by Corrigan in which a *refusal of interpretation* becomes tied in with cinematic pleasures. He argues that many of the pleasures of contemporary cinema lie 'in being able to already know, not read, the meaning of the film in a totalising image that precedes the movie in the public images of its creator' (ibid.: 106). In this sense, the notion of authorship functions as *a precept of aesthetic expectation* insofar as the extra-textual construction of the auteur implies a particular mode of consumption and endorses a range of possible understandings *in advance* of viewing a film. The logical destination of this line of thought, therefore, is the idea that it is possible to understand and consume the work of an auteur without seeing the films, an idea literally played out by *King Kong: Peter Jackson's Production Diaries*. Viewed from the other end, this means that *the principle* of authorship in cinema is predicated neither on the vagaries of spectatorship nor even on the 'fact' of the film text itself, but is rather redirected through the institutional circuits of extra-textual mediation which surround a film and which act as a pre-condition to its reception.

TOWARDS A PRAGMATIC CONCEPTION OF CINEMATIC AUTHORSHIP

While on the one hand it is undeniable that auteurs are increasingly sustained and understood extra-textually through the journalistic practices of reviewers and critics, as well as through the institutional commodification of the director precisely as a signature, on the other hand *the films* those people make remain irreducible to the commercial process of mediation and branding. In other words, it is one thing to agree that cinematic authorship is a perplexing, far from coherent theory, but it is quite another to deny or unduly discard its usefulness as a critical tool for helping us understand cinema as both an art form and a cultural phenomenon. The persistence of auteurism testifies to that, and although its meaning and function are historically malleable, at times ambiguous, this is no reason to dismiss it *in toto*. Indeed, for every good reason not to pursue authorship studies there is equally good reason to do so. For instance, whatever else it may or may not do, auteurism remains cued into the creative practices and aesthetic achievements of cinema and, as such, 'is a formidable approach for comprehending style, technique and expression' (Gallagher 2001). The question of causality for film, however, is not simply an aesthetic matter but, as Staiger argues, a political one: 'taking studies of the author off the table can eliminate the politically crucial question of causality for texts – something highly undesirable from the point of view of critical theory' (Staiger 2003: 29). For social groups who have historically been denied authorship, those whose voices have been variously ignored, marginalised or silenced, for those people who seem finally to have won a position from which they can speak and be heard, the claim that the author is dead seems to be not only an act of supreme authorial privilege itself, but also political sabotage. In this respect, then, authorship matters greatly to those 'in non-dominant positions in which asserting even a partial agency may seem to be important for day-to-day survival or where locating moments of alternative practice takes away the naturalized privileges of normativity' (ibid.: 27).

For these reasons, then, as well as a host of others, all of the attempts to twiddle and tweak conceptions of cinematic authorship in the wake of the post-structuralist challenge to it never really stuck. Indeed, it seems that the more authorship was recast as a 'sub-code', 'a discourse', 'a signature', 'a reading position' or whatever, the less the figure of the author seemed to matter. And all such machinations tended to dodge the material reality of human actions; that is to say, the activities of real people in real socio-historical situations which effect both the art and politics of cinematic representation. Given this, the notion of cinematic authorship needs to be revived and recast to take account of agency in such a way as to avoid the twin pitfalls of romanticism and erasure. The question, then, is: What model of cinematic authorship is able to account for both the artistic and commercial concerns of filmmaking while simultaneously acknowledging the political dynamics which frame all authorial claims?

The recent renewal of interest in cinematic authorship has produced a number of answers to this question which, albeit in different ways, attempt to negotiate a critical position somewhere between simply resurrecting the tenets of older approaches and total reinvention. For instance, whereas classical auteurism tended to rest on assumptions about the working practices of a director, a number of critics are now focusing squarely on the concrete material conditions which structure creativity. This work tends to privilege the craft of filmmaking, that is to say, the ways in which a director deploys film technique in precise ways within specific conditions to achieve innovation. A second, though related, move has been to direct attention to the business of filmmaking. This shifts the point of study away from the 'art' of the finished film and locates it in the political economy of film production. Third, as we have already noted, work by Corrrigan and Bordwell suggests that authors/auteurs may be understood as marketable commodities that are produced by, and fulfil the needs of, commercial and institutional demands. Yet other strategies for rethinking authorship in the current moment have focused on unearthing authorial voices ignored or marginalised by classical auteurism. In some cases this has involved studying directors who have been previously hidden from history, in particular the work of women directors, and elsewhere it has led to a discussion of sources of creativity other than the director.

The answer to that question I want to pursue here, however, is non-partisan insofar as it does not adhere to any one of these approaches at the expense of the others. It does not think that one approach is necessarily better than another and, more precisely, that the approach one employs should be determined on a case-by-case basis in relation to the specifics of the research question. For example, starting out from the same predetermined theoretical/methodological position is of little use if we want to study on the one hand directors/auteurs such as Jim Jarmusch, Sofia Coppola, Jane Campion, Paul Thomas Anderson or Ang Lee, or on the other hand, corporate authors such as Disney, Pixar or Industrial Light and Magic. In other words, it accepts that cinematic authorship is an untidy concept but sees that untidiness as grist to its mill. It is an approach I call pragmatic. Like the word 'author' itself, pragmatism is an overworked word which is used to mean any number of different things. I use it here, however, to suggest a model of analysis which stops asking the question 'Do authors exist?' and starts from such questions as 'Is it useful to study this or that film *as if* it were the product of a creative agency?', or 'Might it be useful to study this or that person *as if* they were an author?' In other words, the theoretical question of whether the notion of authorship in cinema is plausible *per se* is different from the piecemeal approach which asks how individual agency relates to film style. The result of such an approach will not settle the debate about whether or not authors exist, but produce a rather more modest and useful *enrichment of our understanding of cinema and our experience of it*. So, what does a pragmatic conception of cinematic authorship look like?

The first move is to shake off some of the unnecessarily convoluted aspects of the critical vocabulary associated with cinematic authorship that have tended to sink auteur analysis even before it has begun. For what is lost at the more dizzying levels of abstraction associated with much theoretical writing on auteurism is precisely the ability to make critically interesting and useful judgements about the relative artistic and aesthetic merits of a film and its makers. As such, instead of searching for the intangible evidence of a film's unifying figure, it is perhaps useful to think of *creativity as constitutive at every level of cinematic activity*. To put it another way, the question of cinematic authorship can usefully be posed on a range of labour, creative and commercial levels. In this respect, director Alexander Kluge's observation that 'auteur cinema is not a minority phenomenon: all people relate to their experiences as authors – rather than as managers of department stores' provides a useful starting point (quoted in Corrigan 1991: 118). Kluge's quip alerts us to three important ideas: first, that the people who make films understand their respective roles and practise their individual crafts in ways that can meaningfully be thought of as art-making; second, that the material reality of human actions has genuine consequences for the way a film looks and sounds as well as for how we experience it; and third, that we need a more useful way of engaging with the question of the link between individual agency, self-expression and authorial function in order not only to liberate the notion of cinematic authorship from 'director studies' and thus open up the possibility of finding other, potentially more complex authorial voices, but also to remain sensitive to the politics that determine the limits of self-expression.

A first step, here, is to identify the terms on which auteurism was founded and which, despite all efforts, refuse to be exiled. It is not surprising, moreover, that these are also the terms which we cannot abandon if we want to discuss cinema as art:

- Art
- Aesthetics
- Artist
- Craft
- Agency
- Technique
- Practice
- Style
- Expression
- Experience

In pruning back our vocabulary to focus on these core ideas and attending to localised descriptions of how specific artistic, creative and institutional practices relate to both a film's style and its particular comprehension, it is possible to find an exit route from the excesses of the romantic conception of auteur-as-creator as well as from the equally counterintuitive claim that the author is nowhere to be found, or worse, dead. For these tendencies are the recto and verso of the same theoretical argument which sees auteurism as a conceptual dead-end.

As such, a more plausible method for discussing cinematic authorship entails tracking back and forth between the various practices of film production and the film text to see how these concepts may be deployed to help us describe and better understand those practices and their relationship to how we experience the film. Indeed, It is just such a paired-down approach to film authorship which allows us to explore Jim Jarmusch as a particularly persuasive case for the contemporary director-as-author. More specifically, the stylistic and expressive significance of his films may be usefully explained through an analysis which interrogates the interrelations between aesthetics and his individual agency. For instance, Jarmusch's character-centred working practice, the idea that he 'starts from a basic perception, sometimes not even accurate, of a person, an actor, a quality of that personality' and then builds characters around it' helps us to understand the episodic, character-driven form of his films (in Keogh 2001: 128). In short, all the principal characters in *Broken Flowers* (2005) were written for the actors who play them on the basis of their specific personal and performative traits. As such, the film was developed, and develops, not around the demands of a story, but rather as a series of character vignettes. By the same token, the fact that Jarmusch not only plays a significant role in raising the money for his films but insists on retaining ownership of the negatives allows us to make more concrete and plausible claims about the link between financial independence and authorial control. Of course, none of this is to suggest that Jarmusch's name and the biographical legend it invokes are not figured within institutional forces and commercial discourses every bit as much as Spielberg's.

We should not expect, however, to be able to deploy this model of analysis with equal success in every case, or that the results will necessarily be comparable. For individual films may be marked by the presence, but also the absence of a coherent authorial voice. Indeed, attention to the pragmatics of film production, to the web of crafts and industrial contingencies that interact in filmmaking, will determine which, if any, notions of authorship are on the table. Such a paired-down and modest theory of cinematic

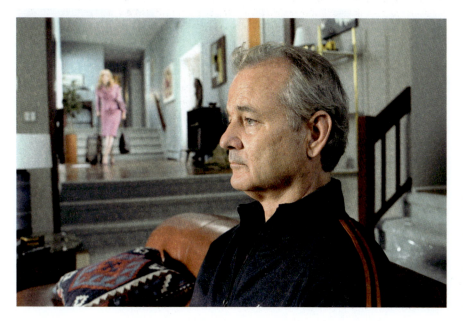

● **Plate 4.2**
Broken Flowers (Jim Jarmusch, 2005). Bill Murray plays Don Johnstone, an emotionally insulated middle-aged roué who goes travelling in search of his romantic past

authorship is built from piecemeal accounts of how the images and sounds made by a film hang together in meaningful and expressive patterns, one which can be fitted into or contrasted with other accounts of the technological, institutional and social contingencies which intersect in any film. As Richard Shusterman argues, conceived in this pragmatic fashion, theory is 'understood as critical, imaginative reflection on practice, emerging from practice' and also 'judged pragmatically by its fruits for that practice' (Shusterman 2000: 59–60).

Moreover, if we accept that there are a range of criteria available to us for deploying ideas of authorship in the effort to better understand film, then auteurism is not neutralised but refurbished by the absence of singular and transcendental notions of the artist. For once we let go of such essentialist notions of art-making, a whole host of potential auteurs emerge from the theoretical sidelines: creative personnel, agencies, even corporations whose influence on the art of cinema cannot be recognised by the stifling romanticism of previous conceptions of auteurism. For instance, Andrew Darley argues that in an age of digital visual culture, creativity and innovation become 'first and foremost a technical problem' in which 'technique, technicians and technology itself take command' (Darley 2000: 141). Within this context, it is significant that a set of company names such as 'Industrial Light and Magic' (ILM) and Pixar now operate as an index of artistic style alongside or in front of individual creative agency. Indeed, one implication of this situation is not only that authorial agency might usefully be located with creative personnel other than the director, but that it becomes possible, even desirable, to locate authorship at an institutional or corporate level. As such, Pixar and ILM may be seen as corporate authors precisely to the extent that the company name acts as a sign which organises and executes highly specialised and distinctive forms of industrial aesthetic practice within cinema beyond the scope of any one of the individuals it employs, and functions as a pre-condition to the film's realisation in the first instance and as a corporate agency through which key enunciative and expressive techniques are executed and cohere in the final instance.

Paul Wells argues in relation to animation that the notions of the 'supra-auteur' and the 'intra-auteur' throw into relief two further models of cinematic authorship elided by the obsessive focus on directors. In this respect, Walt Disney may be understood as a supra-auteur insofar as even after his death he fundamentally denied authorial

For further discussion of Disney, ILM, Pixar and computer technology in animation read Chapter 9, pp. 199–217.

• **Plate 4.3**
In the Mood For Love (Wong Kar Wai, 2000). Chris Doyle's multi-textured cinematography and distinctive framing are key contributors to the look and feel of the film, and may be read as salient markers of his role as an intra-auteur

inscription to anyone else and created 'an identity and mode of representation which, despite cultural criticism, market variations, and changing social trends, transcends the vicissitudes of contemporary America' (Wells 2002: 90). By contrast, Ray Harryhausen's stop-motion work in films such as *The 7th Voyage of Sinbad* (1958) and *Jason and the Argonauts* (1963) figures him as an intra-auteur 'by in effect authoring a text from within its ostensible live-action boundaries' (ibid.: 101). This latter concept, the notion of intra-authorship, is a particularly useful one for attending to sources of creativity other than the director. For instance, the densely textured collages so often evident in Chris Doyle's cinematography, or the balletic grace of Yeun Woo-Ping's wire-work fight choreography, or the mixture of formal experimentation and pathos found in Charlie Kaufman's screenplays, not to mention numerous others, may all be usefully seen as specific examples of the work of intra-auteurs. The main point here, however, is that in locating the study of film authorship in a *practice-based model of art* it is not only possible but desirable to study the work of stunt directors, production designers, visual effects supervisors, concept illustrators, computer animators, costume designers, sound engineers, fight coordinators, composers, specialist post-production houses, studios as well as screenwriters, producers, editors, actors and directors in terms of film aesthetics and comprehension.

CONCLUSION

The model of auteurist analysis which emerges from this pragmatic redescription of cinematic authorship, then, recognises two necessarily simultaneous practices: (1) the particular creative, expressive and artistic activities of the personnel who collaborate in varying degrees to make a film and whose respective individual agencies determine in complex ways film style; and (2) the socio-cultural practices of contemporary media culture which construct the auteur as a commodity, a logo so to speak, which stands not behind the text as in Romantic notions of authorship, but rather in front of it precisely to explicate, expand and legitimise the marks of individuality, expression and style in a film.

In accepting the 'intentional fallacy' as the last word on romantic notions of auteurism, such a pragmatic reconfiguration of cinematic authorship, attuned to the primacy and complexities of filmmaking *practice* as well as to the *commercial imperatives* of media culture, affords us the opportunity of capturing some of the continued allure of the auteur while locating the focus of our critical gaze back in the art of filmmaking. Indeed, in negotiating the moment between the textual and the extra-textual activities of the auteur, a pragmatic approach to the question of authorship confronts itself back where it began: as a tool for helping us look for the art in cinema.

FURTHER READING

While it is neither possible nor necessary to list them here, there are many books and articles which discuss the work of individual auteurs. As such, most of the works listed below tend to deal with cinematic authorship as a theoretical problem.

Key texts

Caughie, John (ed.) (1981) *Theories of Authorship: A Reader*, London: Routledge. Despite its age, Caughie's book remains a useful resource in terms of both the seminal work it anthologises and his own commentary on that work.

Gerstner, David A. and Staiger, Janet (eds) (2003) *Authorship and Film*, London: Routledge. A very useful collection of essays which both contributes to the recent resurgence of interest in authorship studies but also puts forward a number of ways for thinking about issues of agency, identity and politics within auteur analyses.

Wright Wexman, Virginia (ed.) (2003) *Film and Authorship*, New Brunswick, NJ: Rutgers University Press. This collection anthologises a number of influential works produced since the publication of Caughie's book. Indeed, the essays span a number of approaches to authorship including post-structuralism, feminism, post-colonialism and cultural studies.

Useful anthologies

Braddock, Jeremy and Hock, Stephen (eds) (2001) *Directed by Allen Smithee*, Minneapolis: University of Minnesota Press.

Tasker, Yvonne (ed.) (2002) *Fifty Contemporary Filmmakers*, London: Routledge.

Useful Compendiums

Allon, Yoram, Cullen, Del and Patterson, Hannah (eds) (2002) *Contemporary North American Directors: A Wallflower Critical Guide* (2nd edn), London: Wallflower Press.

Murphy, Robert (ed.) (2006) *Directors in British and Irish Cinema: A Reference Guide*, London: BFI.

Online reading

Film-Philosophy, Vol. 10, no.1 (2006), 'Reanimating the Auteur' [online at], http://www.film-philosophy.com/

Screening The Past, Issue 12 (2001), [online at] http://www.latrobe.edu.au/screeningthepast/current/cc0301.html.

Two online special issues dedicated to rethinking aspects of cinematic authorship.

FURTHER VIEWING

The auteurist method is largely founded on mapping similarities of technique and style across a number of films by the same director. As such, use a resource such as the Internet Movie Database (http://www.imdb.com) to compile a filmography of a director and then watch a sample of his or her films and note any consistencies of style and/or theme that occur across more than one film. See if it is possible to detect a 'personal statement' or 'worldview' in the films. Of course, this method is not limited to directors. Repeat the exercise using a cinematographer, actor, fight choreographer, or even a studio such as Disney or Pixar to see if other figures/agencies can be usefully analysed 'as if' they are an auteur. Finally, auteurs now exist as much outside the film text as inside it. Try watching a film on DVD while listening to the director's commentary. How does this effect, delimit or anchor the possible meanings of the film around the director's putative intentions? Moreover, in relation to the release of a new film, track the director's performance of 'being an auteur' across the full range of media – chat show appearances, interviews on radio, in newspapers and on the internet, and public appearances at premieres and other related events.

Genre theory and Hollywood cinema

Paul Watson

■ Genre theory and Hollywood cinema

INTRODUCTION

Common questions we ask each other before going to the cinema or renting a movie are: 'What sort of film shall we watch?'; 'What kind of film do you feel like seeing?' Alternatively, in making our selections we might say things such as: 'I don't like horror films'; 'I'm not in the mood for a weepie, let's watch a comedy'. These kinds of questions and statements identify, at least on an informal level, a film's *genre*, a French term imported to film theory from literary studies meaning 'type' or 'class'. The result of such deliberations is, say, the choice of watching a thriller over a western, a comedy over a musical, a science fiction film over a crime movie or, more generally, the idea that we have particular likes or dislikes for certain types of film. Moreover, the issues that underpin such deliberations and discriminations – issues of taste, preference, identity and pleasure associated with particular kinds of film – are, of course, precisely the issues that producers of film need to take into account in the effort to make their product appealing to audiences, and, by implication, a contained economic risk. Likewise, attention to those same issues provides the film reviewer with a tactical means of evaluating a film's relative merits in terms of the way it may be said to be a classic of its genre, or, moreover, if it affords particular pleasures by extending, usurping, challenging or reworking particular generic elements. On this everyday level, genre resembles a golden thread that knits the concerns of industry together with the desires of audiences.

Seizing on this sense of continuity, much genre criticism is underpinned by the assumption that genre is a conceptual prism that allows critics to simultaneously address the activities of industry, audience and culture insofar as it functions as: (1) a financial security blanket for the industry by providing a logic, or framework, for organising its output so as to capitalise on previous models of success and thus minimise financial risk; (2) a set of precepts and expectations for audiences to organise their viewing; and (3) a critical framework for reviewers to arbitrate between the distinctiveness and putative success of the product and the taste of its implied audience. In this way, Peter Hutchings argues that 'part of the appeal of studying genre is that it offers the opportunity to deal with cinema, and Hollywood cinema in particular, as both an industrial and popular medium' (Hutchings 1995: 61).

GENRE THEORY AND HOLLYWOOD CINEMA

Partly because of its promise of theoretical ubiquity, and partly due to its apparent affinity to Hollywood cinema, genre has been a key concept in the development of film theory, and, in return, cinema has provided an important staging ground for the broader discussion of genre in relation to mass entertainment and media culture. For genre criticism is marked by the possibility it affords critics to analyse the cinema as an *industrial form of aesthetic practice;* that is, precisely as a major form of mass entertainment.

In this respect, it is important to note that genre's more extravert and inherently inclusive critical disposition contrasts sharply with auteurism's introversion and intrinsic exclusivity. Indeed, the emergence of genre criticism in the late 1960s and early 1970s is usually understood as either a development, qualification, corrective or outright rejection of auteurism. Whereas auteurist criticism was overwhelmingly trained upon the work of relatively few directors which could be distilled from the general category of cinema by appealing to Romantic conceptions of the artist, genre, in casting its critical net wider, seemed to offer critics a far more inclusive and democratic method, one which was attuned to the industrial and commercial imperatives of Hollywood. It is in this sense that Gledhill sees genre as a 'conceptual space' in which 'issues of texts and aesthetics ...

intersect with those of industry and institution, history and society, culture and audiences' and describes the term as reclaiming the 'commercial products of Hollywood for serious critical appraisal' (Gledhill 2000: 221, 222). Stam talks of genre as the 'crystallization of a negotiated encounter between film-maker and audience, a way of reconciling the stability of an industry with the excitement of an evolving popular art' (Stam 2000: 127). It is this holistic approach to studying cinema that seemed to early genre critics capable of extending and advancing critical interest in popular cinema in a way auteurism could not. For in trying to skim the cream off Hollywood's output, auteurism tended to either construct popular cinema as the insignificant counterpoint to genuine art, or worse, to simply ignore it altogether. In short, the logic of much auteurist writing runs that it is not the film but in fact the artist that is important, and by implication that it is a few individual creative geniuses who are the proper focus of film studies rather than the industrial, historical and social nexus that frames the cinematic process. Or, to put it another way, auteurism valued the exception rather than the rule inasmuch as it threshed the artistic wheat from the generic chaff, while genre criticism, on the contrary, set itself the task of understanding precisely the 'rule'-governed practices of cinema as a mass entertainment medium.

In trawling deeper and wider than auteurism, genre criticism may be seen as an attempt to deal with Hollywood cinema as an industrial mode of film production which is itself bound up with, not to mention limited by, a much broader economic system governed by the imperatives of commodification and commercialism. For a generic analysis of cinema offers not only the possibility of describing the systematic nature of Hollywood as an industry in which differentiation between individual films occurs only within an overarching logic of product standardisation, but also prompts consideration of different genres in terms of their collective significance or deeper meanings. In other words, exactly the same value judgement that sees Hollywood cinema as, first and foremost, a cinema of genres which served to marginalise the *standard* practices of Hollywood in the hands of auteur critics provided genre critics with a critical vocabulary appropriate to the art of those practices.

Genre theory and contemporary cinema

Ironically, such has been the success of genre criticism in describing popular cinema that Hollywood is now often equated with generic filmmaking. As Tom Ryall argues, 'whatever else it is, Hollywood is surely a cinema of genres, a cinema of westerns, gangster films, musicals, melodramas and thrillers' (Ryall 1998: 327). However, such an equation tends to hide as much as it reveals. For such claims tend to emerge from analyses of Hollywood's classical period and cannot automatically be transposed to the contemporary situation. Indeed, since the assimilation of Hollywood studios into larger conglomerates and the concomitant shift away from the factory-like manufacture of films towards what has been described as the 'package-unit' model of film production, genres are no longer associated with specific studios in the way they were in the heyday of the **studio system**. In addition, cinema-going nowadays is for most people a relatively infrequent event in comparison to the time devoted to other media forms. In fact, the majority of film viewing itself now revolves around our television sets, whether that is tuning into a movie broadcast on terrestrial networks or one of a proliferating number of dedicated satellite and cable channels; hiring a DVD from a rental outlet; or watching a movie from our own personal collection. Indeed, at a time when movies resemble less the self-contained entities often implied by notions of classical Hollywood, and more 'multi-purpose entertainment machines' (Schatz 1993: 9–10) that initiate 'an endless chain of other cultural products' (Wasko 1994: 4), it is perhaps not surprising that the film text itself is only one among many possible sites where genre condenses. Likewise, much contemporary cinema evinces a variety of technological, formal, thematic and stylistic affinities with other media forms as well as itself spawning a host of other media commodities.

For further discussion of the studio system see Chapter 1, pp. 25–35.

studio system
Usually seen to have developed *circa* 1920 and lasting until *circa* 1950, the studio system indicates the period of Hollywood history in which the major studios controlled all aspects of the production, distribution and exhibition of their products.

postmodern
Used by critics in a
number of different
ways, it can refer to the
contemporary historical
moment (the period
after modernity); an
artistic or aesthetic
style which privileges
surface appearances
over 'deep meaning' or
'truth' (characterised
by strategies of irony,
intertextuality, pastiche,
bricolage, **eclecticism**,
self-reflexivity); and
a theoretical position
which adopts a sceptical
attitude towards
totalising notions of truth,
reality and progress.

intertextuality
This term, strongly linked
with **postmodernism**,
designates, in its narrow
sense, the ways in which
a film either explicitly
or implicitly refers to
other films (e.g. through
allusion, imitation,
parody or pastiche), or
in its broader sense, the
various relationships
one (film) text may
have with other texts
(see also **eclecticism**,
palimpsest).

eclecticism
An aesthetic style in
which a new composition
is composed wholly or
in part from elements
selected from a range of
previous styles, forms,
texts, genres drawn
form different periods
and from both high and
popular culture. This
is one of the principal
aesthetic strategies of
postmodern art (see
also **intertextuality**,
palimpsest (p. 121),
self-reflexivity).

taxonomic
See **taxonomy**

taxonomy
The practice of
classification. In this
sense, the practice
of classifying films
into groups based on
similarities of form and/
or content.

Given these cultural changes, some critics have recently become less convinced of the security of genre for describing Hollywood's industrial mode of production. Steve Neale, for instance, maintains that it is not genres that are Hollywood's primary commodity, but rather narratives inasmuch as 'the system of narration adopted by mainstream cinema serves as the very currency of cinema itself' (Neale 1980: 20). On this account, genre is simply a mode, albeit a key one, of Hollywood's narrative system. More recently, Andrew Darley has suggested that in a **postmodern** culture of institutionalised **intertextuality** and radical **eclecticism** brought about by new technological developments, genre, while not entirely disappearing, has 'a far more limited structural role to play', perhaps reliably referring to nothing more than 'the general level of a form itself – narrative cinema' (Darley 2000: 144). Such a move divests genre theory of precisely the critical dexterity that distinguishes it from other critical approaches to studying popular film, while some critics even suggest abandoning the term itself in favour of other terms that more plausibly describe Hollywood's commercial activities within the global mediascape – terms such as repetition, seriality, cycle, trend and mode.

Simply disposing of the term, however, or replacing it with other cognate terms, not only seems counterintuitive on an everyday level but also risks unnecessarily jettisoning some useful conceptual tools for thinking about cinema on a range of theoretical levels. For if on the one hand we do need to rethink and expand our conceptions of film genre by looking beyond the film text for our inspiration, to place the question of film genre squarely within broader multi-discursive formations, on the other hand it is precisely the complexity of those formations, the thoroughgoing intertextuality of contemporary media culture, that makes genre not less but more pertinent to understanding contemporary Hollywood. In other words, we need to stop seeing genre as a one-dimensional entity descriptive of Hollywood's output and to recast it as a ubiquitous phenomenon common to all instances of discourse. And, as Steve Neale argues, one implication of this multi-faceted (re)conceptualisation of genre is that we must modify both the perception and location of Hollywood genres: 'No longer the sole or even the principal site of genre in the cinema, Hollywood instead becomes just one particular site, its genres specific instances – not necessarily paradigms – of a much more general phenomenon (Neale 2000: 31). Clearly, then, much turns on how we choose to define genre.

DEFINING GENRE(S)

At a general level work on genre seeks to understand film as a *specific form of commodity* and at a more refined level attempts to disentangle *different instances of that commodity*. In other words, genre is addressed as a system for organising production as well as groupings of individual films which have collective and singular significance. It is important to note, however, that a number of approaches have developed that address Hollywood's generic structures, all of which are underpinned by different assumptions about the purpose of genre criticism. It is possible to trace three key lines of theoretical development here: firstly, the **taxonomic** view of genre which attempts to map the boundaries between generic classes; second, the view of genre as an economic strategy for organising film production schedules; and third, the view of genre as a function of cognition, as a contract between producers and consumers which renders films intelligible on some level.

Genre as taxonomy

Tom Ryall argues that 'if genre criticism were simply a matter of constructing taxonomies and allocating films to their places in the system, then the intellectual basis of the exercise would certainly be open to doubt' (Ryall 1998: 336). While Ryall is right to caution against viewing genre criticism *merely* as a question of fitting films into their appropriate generic hole, it nevertheless remains the case that the question of genre routinely emerges as a border dispute: defining the boundaries between one genre and another. For whatever else it might be, genre implies a process of categorisation; that is to say, sorting cultural products into discrete groupings based on similarities and common properties. Here, defining genre involves a twofold process: describing the differences between individual genres, that is, between thrillers, westerns, musicals, horror films, gangster films, action movies and so forth, as well as mapping the common elements that members of any one genre share. Indeed, the notions of *difference* and *sameness* that taxonomies imply are, albeit in various ways, central to all generic criticism. As such, Richard Maltby argues that the genre critic seeks to 'place movies into generic categories as a way of dividing up the cinematic map of Hollywood into smaller, more manageable, and relative discrete areas' (Maltby 2003: 75). Critics have attempted to map the contours of genres in a number of ways, using a variety of methods, often producing corpuses of vastly differing size and complexity.

Theoretical taxonomies

In *Poetics*, perhaps the *locus classicus* of genre studies, Aristotle sets out to categorise poetry into its 'various kinds' on the basis of the apparently incontrovertible properties of the poetic text. As Rick Altman points out, this move 'set genre theory on to a virtually unbroken course of textual analysis' (Altman 1999: 2–3). Moreover, it is founded on certain problematic assumptions to do not only with the model of genre it implies – that genre is somehow already 'out there' as an essential structure of texts – but also to do with the activity of 'doing genre studies' – the application of theoretical and analytical rigour in the description and coding of texts in order to uncover their distinct internal characteristics. While the former assumption rests on the ahistorical premise that genre exists in itself and that it inevitably has essential qualities that can be revealed through proper analysis, the latter assumption tends to mask the productive role of critics/ scholars in the definition of generic categories and the institutional frameworks within which such practices take place. Nevertheless, despite these problems, problems which Altman argues have had the effect of 'narrowing genre theory ever since', Aristotle's model of genre analysis has by turns proved remarkably influential and durable (Altman 1999: 2). So, in the same way that Aristotle identifies the epic, comedy, tragedy and so forth as essential genres of poetry insofar as they are seen to exist in themselves as 'pure' categories of literature, Alan Williams has identified the principal film genres as the narrative film, experimental/avant-garde film and the documentary (Williams 1984: 121). For Williams, these categories are the conceptual equivalent of, and thus share the same sense of permanence as, those described by Aristotle. He argues that, in reserving this general or theoretical level for the term genre, 'then film genres will by definition have the staying power seen in literary genres' (ibid.: 122). On this account, the labels we ordinarily use to distinguish between films of various kinds – thriller, horror, comedy, romance, and so on – actually refer to sub-genres of the narrative film.

There are, however, a number of problems with imposing theoretical generic categories onto cinema. First, and most obviously, it is counterintuitive in the sense that genre becomes abstracted from both industrial and cultural usages of the term. Second, ascending to this level of theoretical abstraction tends to belie the inherent complexity of cinematic forms. For instance, animation doesn't fit comfortably into any of Williams' categories in the sense that animation's fundamentally graphic economy permits it to straddle Williams' categories which are clearly erected to describe photographic modes of enunciation. One answer would be to put forward animation as a fourth principal genre, yet this simply compounds the fundamental problem of theoretically instigated cinematic genres insofar as the complex and highly productive relationship between animation and narrative, non-fiction and experimental film, would be further obfus- cated behind discrete generic walls. A similar problem arises in the distinction between narrative and documentary film in that narrative is every bit as important and complex in documentary forms as in fictional forms. Indeed, as Alan Renov notes, the distinction between fiction and documentary genres is an unsustainable one given that 'nonfiction contains any number of "fictive" elements' to the extent that 'it might be said that the two domains inhabit one another' (Renov 1993: 2, 3).

Historical taxonomies

Given the problems of defining genre and drawing classificatory boundaries using a set of theoretical principles, most critical writing has adopted a more historical stance to genre in seeking to map more selective 'groupings of actual films inductively linked on the basis of common themes, styles and **iconography**' (Ryall 1998: 329). Instead of asking questions such as 'What markers of cinematographic representation differentiate one genre from the next?', an historical approach to genre asks, 'What distinguishes a western from a gangster film, a thriller from a crime movie?' and so forth, and 'how does an individual western film relate to the broader category of the western?', and 'why are certain genres popular at particular times, but not at others?' In short, unlike the essentialism implied by purely theoretical definitions of genre, this model of genre criticism attempts to cut cinema at its generic joints precisely by acknowledging the historical contingency of generic forms. A variety of tactics have been used to make the dissection ranging from attention to a genre's relation to history; to common subject matter, themes and content; to the presence of certain shared formal elements; to their intended affect on the audience; to looser groupings around stylistic or cinematographic properties. Table 5.1 schematises some of the different ways in which genres may be seen to be held together.

If such schematisation does demonstrate *possible* criteria for differentiating genres, it also belies the inherent complexity and mutability of generic definitions. For example, as indicated below, film noir could quite easily sit in any one of three groupings, or all

iconography
A term used to describe and categorise visual motifs in films. It is usually associated with genre insofar as visual patterns of setting, dress, props and style have been used to classify and analyse films generically, but it also shares similarities with **mise-en-scène**.

Genre	Defining criteria	Differentiating criteria
Western		American West
Gangster film		1920s urban America
Epic	**Historical subject**	Biblical or ancient history
War film		Specific historical conflicts
Film noir		Postwar America
Horror		Intended to horrify
Thriller	**Intended affect**	Intended to thrill
Comedy		Generation of laughter
Musical		Presence of diegetic song and dance performances
Action movie	**Formal criteria**	Presence of action set-pieces
Pornography		Presence of sex acts
Science fiction		Futuristic technologies/future worlds
Fantasy		Impossible worlds/fantastical characters
Disaster		Natural or man-made catastrophe
Crime film	**Subject matter**	Criminal and investigatory activities
Melodrama		Domestic drama and heterosexual romance
Road movie		Journey or road-trip, usually across America
Film noir		Crime and institutional corruption
Children's films	**Target audience**	Stories designed for consumption by children
Family movie		Stories designed for consumption by family groups
Blockbuster	**Style**	Spectacular events
Film noir		Chiaroscuro lighting/dark mise-en-scène

three simultaneously depending on which criteria one chooses to privilege. Alternatively, we could make the case, as many critics have done, that film noir is, in fact, not a genre at all but merely a particular stylistic inflection of the crime film. Moreover, and notwithstanding a host of further possible objections one might raise, not only is it possible to relocate, say, the western and gangster film to the category demarcated by formal criteria on the basis of the presence of 'the gun fight' and 'the shoot-out' respectively, but we might also collapse all categories into the one which sees differences exclusively in terms of subject matter. It is also possible, for that matter, to locate all of the above groups as subcategories of the feature film – Hollywood's principal product – and to therefore argue that all films are fundamentally multi-generic.

Part of the problem with this method of genre building, of course, is that genres are defined in a number of different contexts. So while some genres such as the western and the musical are established industrial categories of production readily recognised by both filmmakers and audiences, others, such as the 'gross-out comedy', are constructed by critics only after the film has been released. Moreover, generic labels generated by critics are often appropriated into studio production cycles and marketing materials while the most long-standing generic categories continue to act as a key point of reference in the critical evaluation of a film.

By the same token, such highly schematised generic classifications suffer from what Stam calls the problem of extension – the implied scope of a generic category (Stam 2000: 128). For example, herding films together under the generic banner 'comedy' seems straightforward enough, but actually tells us very little about individual films beyond the intention to incite laughter. For if the 'generation of laughter' is the comedy genre's definitive convention then not only does it, by definition, mark all modes of comedy – slapstick, screwball, farce, satire, parody – but also encompasses the comic elements or funny moments that routinely appear in most if not all other genres. Indeed, the co-presence of laughter and fear is common to the horror film, while compound generic categorisations such as romantic comedy, sex comedy and gross-out comedy address at promotional and journalistic levels precisely comedy's nomadic generic existence. Approaching the same problem of extension from the opposite end, if comedy seems too broad as a class, then 'funny films about a motley police force', or 'science fiction films concerning time travel' seem too narrow. Either way, the issue of extension betrays the fundamental difficulty of demarcating generic borders in any reliable way, a problem telescoped by the extreme eclecticism and **self-reflexivity** of much of contemporary Hollywood. To take just one example, *Moulin Rouge* (Baz Luhrmann, 2001) is simultaneously distinguished historically (its depiction of *fin-de-siècle* Paris); formally (the performance of song and dance routines); stylistically (an exemplar of postmodern filmmaking); and in terms of its organisation of subject matter (quasi-melodramatic narrative of heterosexual romance).

Visual taxonomies

From the late 1960s critics attempted to refine the ways of defining the criteria which policed generic boundaries. Derived from art history, and in particular from the work of Erwin Panofsky, the notion of iconography seemed to offer an empirical methodology more suited to the task of classifying cinema's visual terrain. As Ed Buscombe writes, 'since we are dealing with a visual medium we ought surely to look for our defining criteria at what we actually see on the screen' (in Neale 1980: 12). Thus, strictly aesthetic criteria – variously referred to as 'motifs', 'visual conventions', 'patterns of visual imagery' and 'sign-events' – were seen as essential indicators of generic differentiation. Simply stated, an iconographic approach to genre analysis involved the identification, description and interpretation of cinematic objects, events, figures in order to see how one type of film was marked off from another on the basis of differences in visual conventions. As such, the western was distinguished by its settings, both specific and general (the West, the frontier, deserts, mountains, Monument Valley, saloons, homesteads); costume (the

self-reflexivity
Used to describe films or texts which self-consciously acknowledge or reflect upon their own status as fictional artefacts and/or the processes involved in their creation. This is one of the principal aesthetic strategies of **postmodern** art (see also **eclecticism**, **intertextuality**, **palimpsest**).

Stetson, waistcoat, gun belts, boots, chaps and spurs of the cowboy; the facial paint, feathered head-dress of the Indian; the tight-bodiced dress and gartered stockings of the Saloon whore); specificities of props (Colt 45, horses – especially pintos – bows and arrows); even individual actors (John Wayne, Gary Cooper, Clint Eastwood).

However, if an attention to iconography worked well for the western and gangster film, it proved difficult to translate such a visually specific methodology to other kinds of films. For instance, it is difficult to isolate distinct iconographic systems for crime films, thrillers, film noirs and most action films with any clarity. Guns and weaponry are common to each and, unlike the western and gangster film, there is not necessarily any historically specific criteria to regulate aspects of setting and costume. Moreover, consideration of comedy and animation once again tends to blunt the usefulness of iconography as a generic arbitrator. In the case of the former there is no connection between the comic elements of a film and specific iconography beyond the incidental deployment of resources (verbal, physical and material) in gag-specific scenarios, while the self-enunciating visual language of animation has an abstract or arbitrary relation to the concept of iconography insofar as the notions of setting, costume and props are always provisional.

Multi-dimensional taxonomies

In criticising tautological approaches to genre devoted to the discovery and analysis of individual genres, Tom Ryall argues that 'by and large genre criticism has confined itself to producing taxonomies on the basis of "family resemblances", allocating films to their position within generic constellations, stopping short of what are the interesting and informative questions about generic groupings' (Ryall 1975–76: 27). A decade later, Rick Altman made a similar complaint in suggesting that, following the logic laid out by Aristotle, genres continue to be 'treated as if they spring full-blown from the head of Zeus' and that even some of the more sophisticated attempts to understand generic texts 'still hold on to a notion of genre that is fundamentally ahistorical in nature' (Altman 1984: 8). Both authors called for a less reductive approach to genre, one which was both theoretically plausible and sensitive to the historical conditions in which genres circulated and were consumed by audiences. Indeed, Ryall himself put forward what he termed a new 'master image for genre criticism' consisting of 'a triangle composed of artist/structures/audience'. From this basis, he argues, 'genres may be defined as 'patterns/forms/styles/structures which transcend individual films, and which supervise both their construction by the film maker, and their reading by an audience' (Ryall 1975–76: 28). On this account, each genre is a rule-governed territory, one which shares a conventionality not only of visual imagery, but more complexly of particular expectations of plot and narrative structure, and how these, in turn, motivate and justify the specificities of props, costume, milieux and subject matter within and across the generic spectrum. Thus, guns are common to westerns, thrillers, gangster films, action films, film noirs, war films and science fiction films, but their significance, function and consequences differ depending on a host of other contextualising factors established in the narrative and thematic structures of genre films. For Ryall, therefore, genre is not a transhistorical property of the film text, but rather a complex socio-cultural negotiation between the film industry and film reviewers on the on hand, and audience expectations and competencies on the other.

Despite the more nuanced approaches to genre suggested by Ryall (1975–76) and Altman (1984), as well a Neale (1980, 1990), it nevertheless remained the case that critics tended to mobilise the expanded definitions they put forward for taxonomic ends. There are two complementary and contradictory aspects to this. On the one hand, given that the checklist of generic markers had apparently been broadened, more films could be added to encyclopaedic lists of genre films. On the other hand, however, in the face of such an inexorable growth of generic corpora, critics could once again become preoccupied by the desire to find generic exemplars; that is to say, those films which are deemed to represent a specific genre more completely and more faithfully than others. These responses, of course, are really only two sides of the same taxonomic coin: the first aims to produce an *inclusive* list of all possible instances of a genre while the second concerns itself with an *exclusive* list of classical instances in the hope of discerning the 'true' structure and meaning of a genre.

The limits of generic taxonomies

Even if a taxonomic approach to genre offers a way of managing, organising, and interrogating vast numbers of films and can, as Gledhill argues, operate as a useful 'empirical tool for collating the range of cultural knowledges' which genres assume, this kind of approach inevitably privileges the analysis of the structural components of individual genres, however defined, over the more general theoretical questions relating to the nature and operation as genre (Gledhill 1999: 140). Moreover, in the end, all taxonomic writing on genre suffers from what Andrew Tudor calls the 'empiricist dilemma' – the inescapable circular logic which means that to study, say, a western in order to define its distinctive generic characteristics the critic must *already* know what those characteristics are in order to identify it as a western in the first place, yet such an identification ought surely to be made on the evidence of the film *after* it has been watched. Thus, the genre critic is 'caught in a circle which first requires that the films be isolated, for which purposes a criterion is necessary, but the criterion is, in turn, meant to emerge from the empirically established common characteristics of the films' (Tudor 1974: 137). The result of this logic, for Tudor at least, is that 'genre is what we collectively believe it to be' (ibid.: 139).

GENRE AS ECONOMIC STRATEGY

If taxonomic approaches to genre ask questions such as 'How do we cut cinema at its generic joints?', and 'Have we drawn our lines in the correct places?', then an economic approach to genre asks 'What functions does genre perform?' This refocusing directs attention to the role genre plays within the industrial practices and structures of Hollywood. Indeed, genre criticism is often justified precisely on the grounds that, unlike most other approaches, it is plugged into Hollywood's commercial practices in the first instance and that there is a correspondence between its object of inquiry – genres – and the ways in which Hollywood seeks to organise its output in the last instance. So even if, as Neale points out, film companies rarely planned or plan their production schedules in terms which correspond exactly with traditional critical conceptions of genre, and notwithstanding reductive histories of the studio era which attempt to simply equate specific studios with the production of specific genres, it nevertheless remains the case that genre serves as a useful tool for understanding the capitalist business practices in which films are both produced and consumed (see Neale 2000). Simply put, despite the 'facelessness' of contemporary American genre filmmaking identified by Wheeler Winston Dixon, and the 'more of the same' logic which he suggests now drives Hollywood production schedules, what is incontestable is that every film *is* different (Winston Dixon 2000: 1, 8). As such, production and promotion are governed not simply by the need to employ familiar ingredients and recycle previous products in order to secure maximum capital returns, but also by the need to celebrate and sell difference. Indeed, it is precisely in respect of this tension between the 'tried and tested' and the 'new and unknown', that is to say, between formula and innovation, that Hollywood's generic regime performs two crucial interrelated functions: to guarantee meanings and pleasures for audiences; and to offset the considerable economic risks of industrial film production by providing cognitive collateral against innovation and difference. Let us consider these one at a time.

Generic pleasures

Genre works to stabilise or regulate particular desires, expectations and pleasures offered by the cinema. On this account, while genre is not simply an institutionalised strategy to delimit choice, if we choose to watch, say, a horror film, then we expect certain pleasures in return: to encounter a monster of some description; that some characters will be killed by the monster while one, usually the lead character, will kill it; and so on. By the same token, each genre implies its own set of desires, expectations and pleasures. Indeed, Neale argues that much of the pleasure of popular cinema lies precisely in the process of 'difference *in* repetition', that is, both in the recognition of the familiar elements of a generic framework *and* in the way individual instances of that genre introduce unfamiliar elements or orchestrate familiar elements in more or less original ways. This process perhaps finds its most refined expression in films such as the *Scream* and *Scary Movie* series which transpose certain familiar elements across successive sequels while at the same time incorporating new material into each individual film. Yet the same pull between familiarity and difference is no less crucial to looser generic groupings. For the success of, say, any individual action film, both in terms of the profit it generates and the pleasures it affords audiences, is rooted not simply in its promise to deliver action set-pieces but, more accurately, in the expectation that *the way it delivers its action* will be, at least on some level, notably distinct from other action films.

Genre as insurance policy

The capital-intensive nature of Hollywood film production requires a market of sufficient size to generate surplus revenue in order to both satisfy investors and plough back into future productions. This means that, as far as possible, the economic risk associated with any individual film must be contained insofar as its potential market must be predictable. Genres, on this view, allow the film industry to offset some of its financial investments against the cognitive collateral of presold generic expectations and pleasures. Neale writes that genres are crucial to industrial modes of film production inasmuch as they 'serve as basic and "convenient" units for the calculation of investment and profit, and as basic and "convenient" categories in which to organise capital assets so as to ensure that their capacity will be utilised to the maximum' (Neale 1980: 53). While this economic logic does not account for the existence of mass-produced genres *per se*, nor the emergence and popularity of any one genre at any one time, it nevertheless does, at least in part, explain why Hollywood is a cinema of genres.

However, Darley argues that in an age of visual digital culture characterised by aesthetic and economic synthesis between media formats we cannot regard genre in the same way, that cultural production is now organised around principles other than generic ones. He refers to this shift as a 'poetics of repetition', a situation in which 'old categories and boundaries are breaking down, blurring in the face of self-referential impulses spawned by new technological development' (Darley 2000: 142). Darley argues that, while the modifying variable, or differential element of the 'difference in repetition' model of commodity production, 'is even more vital today, precisely because of the apparent de-differentiation that is under way', at the same time the markers of difference become 'smaller in scale and simpler in operation: a mechanism for miniscule formal or surface distinctions' (ibid.: 143). Within this intensified mode of commodity production, he claims, the idea of genre is merely nominal, and, moreover, that the notion of *seriality* is 'coming to replace or subsume genre in more recent manifestations of mass visual culture' (ibid.: 126):

Seriality is akin to genre … and yet it is subtly different from it. The serial mode appears to operate and organise – in the first instance at any rate – at a more general or inclusive level than does genre, whilst at the same time being more precise and prescriptive in terms of the processes it defines. Lacking the more open (and involved) character of genre, it appears to be tied as much to the demarcation and regulation of *forms and modes* within material production processes as to the

sucess depends on
↳ promise to deliver
conventions of genre
↳ meet expectation
to be distinct in
same way

distinguishing of types or kinds (along with their aesthetic delineation) in aesthetic ones. It seems thereby, to be more intimately bound to the standardisation involved in commodification itself.

(ibid.: 126)

This is instructive for a number or reasons. First, the notion of seriality directs our attention towards Hollywood's predilection for sequels, prequels, series, follow-ups and franchises not in terms of their putative aesthetic paucity, but rather as the most potent distillation, besides rereleases, of the economic imperatives of genre described by Neale. Second, the notion of 'mode' is a more persuasive description of contemporary Hollywood production trends. That is, notions of the blockbuster, special effects movie, event cinema, spectacle cinema, summer movie, even action cinema which tend to fall outside of, or in between, traditional generic groupings, are more plausibly described as *modes* of filmmaking which, in turn, entail particular modes of viewing. Third, subsuming genre within a broader poetics of repetition which frames contemporary cultural practice permits us to see cinema as an *intermedia*, that is, as thoroughly implicated in a bi-directional system of aesthetic commodification exchange which extends far beyond its own textual and formal borders through merchandising, product tie-ins, product place-ments, franchise deals, branding, sequels, TV spin-offs, video games, novelisations and so on. In this sense, the notion of film genre dissolves into much more multiple and diverse commercial configurations of *themed entertainment*.

It would, however, be premature to entirely abandon the notion of genre to seriality in an economic analysis of Hollywood cinema. While the term *genre* struggles to cope with much of contemporary Hollywood in terms of both manufacturing principles and aesthetic classification, the prominence of generic motifs within marketing and promotion campaigns seems to be increasing in importance insofar as, today, 'the commercial drama surrounding a movie's promotion can say as much as the fictional drama of the film itself' (Watson 1997: 79). Indeed, the idea of film as merely a pretext or staging ground for a much more extensive commercial venture often goes hand in hand with marketing strategies which foreground generic discourses in a hypervisible display of its attractions. On this view, the modal seriality of contemporary Hollywood production and the primacy of generic imagery in promotional material can be seen as two sides of the same process – the institutionalisation of exploitation cinema: a mode of film production in which textual considerations are subordinate to the considerations of marketing and promotion (see ibid.).

GENRE AS COGNITION

Neale argues that 'genres are not simply bodies of work, however classified, labelled and designed' (Neale 1990: 46). On the contrary, he sees genre as being equally constituted by 'specific systems of expectation and hypothesis which spectators bring with them to the cinema and which interact with the films themselves during the course of the viewing process' (ibid.: 46). The clear implication of this observation is that the question of film genre can be posed not merely along industrial and aesthetic axes of the cinematic process, but as a question of film comprehension insofar as cognitive primacy is afforded to the spectator in the act of reading a film. Another way of making this point is to say that the question of film genre is, in fact, part of much broader questions to do with cultural cognition and structures of visual communication. As such, the purpose of genre criticism may be regarded as an inquiry into how we make meaning from film.

On this cognitive view, textual conventions are important not as a means of dissecting cinema into discrete categories, but instead for the way they activate certain mental processes in what Jonathan Culler calls the 'operations of reading'. He argues that 'the function of genre conventions is essentially to establish a contract between writer and reader so as to make certain relevant expectations operative and thus permit both compliance and deviation from accepted modes of intelligibility' (Culler 1975: 147). As Culler suggests, acts of communication are rendered intelligible only within the context of a shared, conventional framework of expression. Ryall notes that for Hollywood films this communal framework is provided by the generic system which constructs a framework for comprehension, an 'ideal world' or 'fictional reality' through which the individual film 'sustains at least some of its levels of comprehensibility and maybe its dominant level of comprehensibility' (Ryall 1998: 336). Genre, here, becomes understood not as a corpus of approximate films, but as provisional and malleable conceptual environments: a cognitive repository of images, sounds, characters, events, stories, scenarios, expec-tations and so on. Genre may thus be seen as part of a cognitive process which delimits the number of possible meanings of any individual film by activating certain conceptual constellations while leaving others dormant.

Such a cognitive view of film genre not only forestalls the taxonomic impulses of earlier genre criticism by reformulating genre as fundamentally an intertextual process, but is more sensitive to what Jim Collins calls the **'sophisticated hyperconsciousness'** of contemporary Hollywood cinema (Collins 1995: 133). Collins argues that in the same way that television changed the production, circulation and consumption of popular entertainment during the 1950s and 1960s, contemporary Hollywood cinema marks a 'new form of entertainment', one which is simultaneously a response and a contribution to media-saturated culture (ibid.: 156). 'Genericity' is the term he coins in order to describe the shift in production and consumption initiated 'by the ever increasing number of entertainment options and the fragmentation of what was once thought to be a mass audience into a cluster of "target" audiences' (ibid.: 128). Indeed, the eclecticism and appropriationism of popular cinema today involves levels of hybridity and intertextuality that work 'at cross-purposes with the traditional notion of genre as a stable, integrated set of narrative and stylistic conventions' (ibid.: 126). In short, many contemporary Hollywood films are composed almost entirely of generic elements hijacked from the image banks of both popular and high culture and reassembled in ways that either circumnavigate, short-circuit or contradict singular generic understanding.

sophisticated hyperconsciousness
A term used by Jim Collins to describe the extreme 'knowingness' and high degree of media literacy evinced by both contemporary cinema and its audience.

FROM TEXT TO INTERTEXT: GENERICITY AND *MOULIN ROUGE*

As a number of critics are now rightly pointing out, it would be a mistake to assume that generic hybridity, intertextuality and allusion are simply products of either the post-studio era or the postmodern film. Indeed, genre mixing is not a recent fad but is both a crucial aspect in the creation and evolution of genres themselves and a long-standing economic and stylistic strategy used by Hollywood to produce and promote new products. However, it is also the case that an increasing number of contemporary films display not only a flagrant disregard for generic boundaries, but also seem to revel in blatant referentiality. For instance, about half-way into *From Dusk Till Dawn* (1996), at the precise moment when Salma Hayek's character transforms from a border-town showgirl into a vampire, the film shifts genres from a thriller to schlock-horror. The robbery–hijack premise which motivates the first half of the narrative is thoroughly recast around different generic conventions: the loot cannot buy them safety, guns are rendered defunct as, in the battle against the undead, impromptu crosses and crucifixes are the order of the day. Similarly, generically and stylistically speaking, *The Chronicles of Narnia* (2005) owes as much to the impossibly epic battle sequences and warrior heroism of *The Lord of The Rings* trilogy as it does to C.S. Lewis's children's story. Moreover, the intertextual overload that characterises *The Matrix* trilogy (1999, 2003, 2003) defies singular generic description. Indeed, its various generic echoes are not simply *mixed* together, but *remixed* into an eclectic techno-aesthetic comprised from cinema, of course, but also video games, anime, comic books, pop videos, cyberpunk novels, postmodern philosophy, all rendered through a seamless fusion of live action and computer animation.

However, in looking to identify exemplars of the way certain contemporary Hollywood films operate through intertextual aesthetic strategies we could do worse than start with *Moulin Rouge* (2001). Indeed, to ask what genre the film belongs to we have to be ready to say 'feature-length music video' as readily as 'musical', 'blockbuster' as easily as 'a Baz Luhrmann film', 'postmodern film' as quickly as 'American film', and 'romance' as swiftly as 'star vehicle'. For *Moulin Rouge*'s giddy assemblage of cinematic references, historical intertexts and cultural allusions simultaneously *defies* singular generic categorisation yet *implies* a high degree of prior orientation with precisely those generic formations in order to comprehend their disorientation and rearticulation. So while on one level the film may be described generically, and was promoted generically – as a musical which tells of the tragic love affair between a penniless writer and a starlet showgirl – this actually tells us very little either about the semiotic excess of the film or the cultural literacy it demands of its audience. Likewise, if, as many critics have hinted, *Moulin Rouge* redefines the film musical it does so partly by wrenching itself free of musical conventions and hooking up with a range of other generic formations, most obviously the music video and MTV, but also Bollywood, television advertisements, computer animation and virtual reality. Indeed, almost every shot is an ironic collage of popular cultural images and sounds, conjuring up a highly eclectic range of intertexts from the past and the present in a sophisticated **palimpsest** image. The result is a text which is simultaneously *decorative*, demanding to be looked at, and *dense*, demanding to the read *through*.

We can begin to apprehend the film's exhilarating eclecticism through analysis of the way it first introduces us to the Moulin Rouge. Indeed, while on a general stylistic level the sheer excess of the scene not only recalls the set-piece dance extravaganzas of Busby Berkeley's Warner musicals and the graphic energy of many of Toulouse Lautrec's studies of Cancan girls, but at a more specific level the entrance of Satine (Nicole Kidman) begs comparison to Lola-Lola, the Cabaret artist played by Marlene Dietrich in *The Blue Angel* (1930) (see Plates 5.1 and 5.2). Moreover, as Satine begins to sing the opening lines of 'Diamonds Are a Girl's Best Friend', a song made famous by Marilyn Monroe's performance of Lorelei Lee in *Gentlemen Prefer Blondes* (1953), it is not only the song which is 'out of time', but also Kidman's raspy vocal performance. However, when she later shifts style and launches into the chorus of 'Material Girl', it is not simply the image of Madonna which the film inherits, but that of Monroe once again, since in the video for the song Madonna is dressed as Monroe in her pink gown from the 'Diamonds' number (*see Plates 5.3, 5.4 and 5.5*).

palimpsest
Defined literally, a palimpsest is a manuscript written over a previous text that has been entirely or partly erased. In a figurative sense, however, the term is often used to describe a film or text with multiple levels of meaning created through dense layers of **intertextuality**. In this way, the term has become associated with **postmodern** aesthetics.

• **Plate 5.1**
Moulin Rouge (Baz Luhrmann, 2001). As Satine (Nicole Kidman) descends towards the drooling punters on a swing, she is dressed in a manner which closely resembles Marlene Dietrich in *The Blue Angel* (1930)

• **Plate 5.2**
Der Blaue Engel/The Blue Angel (Josef von Sternberg, 1930). Marlene Dietrich plays nightclub songstress Lola-Lola – an image which is appropriated in Luhrmann's *Moulin Rouge* (2001)

• **Plate 5.3**
Moulin Rouge (Baz Luhrmann, 2001). As Satine (Nicole Kidman) begins to sing 'Diamonds Are a Girl's Best Friend' the film recalls the image of Marilyn Monroe performing the same number in *Gentlemen Prefer Blondes* (1953)

• **Plate 5.4**
Gentlemen Prefer Blondes (Howard Hawks, 1953). Lorelei Lee (Marilyn Monroe) performs the famous 'Diamonds Are a Girl's Best Friend' song and dance number. This sequence is summoned up as part of *Moulin Rouge*'s multi-layered intertextuality

• Plate 5.5
Material Girl (Mary Lambert, 1985). When in *Moulin Rouge* Satine segues from 'Diamonds Are a Girl's Best Friend' to 'Material Girl' it is not simply Madonna who is inscribed but Monroe again, since Madonna has already hijacked Monroe's image from *Gentlemen Prefer Blondes* and reactivated it in this video

Moreover, not only does the scene itself unfold around a melody, or more precisely a remix, of 'classic' popular music, but much of the film's dialogue is a montage of lines literally hijacked from the lyrics of popular ballads, love songs and well-known literature. 'Love is a many-splendoured thing, love lifts us up where we belong, all you need is love' Christian (Ewan McGregor) waxes lyrical to Satine. Indeed, if on the one hand the film may be seen as a relatively 'old-fashioned' love story then, on the other, the pathos that attends the tale, if in fact there is any at all, is entirely generated through the co-option and rearticulation of romantic sentiments that have *already* been said and which are *already* familiar because they are in constant circulation in the imaginative landscape of popular culture. It is in this respect that McGregor's rendition of Elton John's 'Your Song' functions simultaneously as the film's authentic emotional refrain and clearest marker of its thoroughgoing inauthenticity.

In these ways, then, *Moulin Rouge*'s textual articulations are, in fact, always double articulations insofar as its images and sounds relate to both the internal narrative and aesthetic 'life' of the film as well as to their external 'lives' in popular culture. The fact that the film's textual and emotional economies proceed almost entirely through quotation reflects not just the increasing sophistication of the genre text *per se*, but also a change in terms of audience competence and the kinds of pleasures associated with contemporary manifestations of genre. For the co-presence of generic traces from a number of different forms of popular culture, as well as from a number of specific different generic texts assembled from a range on different historical periods, results not in the collapse of genre into an 'anything-goes' version of postmodernism, but more precisely in a kind of meta-genre. In other words, individual generic features are not the property of specific genres but rather mediated *artefacts* which circulate through popular culture, retaining traces of their past articulation but which are reinscribed in the present moment. *Moulin Rouge*, then, may be understood as an extreme version of what Collins calls a 'techno-palimpsest', that is to say, a film in which a whole host of generic traces can be 'immediately called up, back to the surface to be replayed, or more precisely, recirculated' (Collins 1995: 139). And, of course, if judged by the referents of the 'classic film musical', then many of its quotations, allusions and appropriations seem inappropriate. However, the main point is that they are entirely appropriate to a culture in which past and future co-exist in/with the present and in which an increasing amount of popular entertainment is predicated on profound intertextuality and the reactivation of past generic artefacts. In this way, then, *Moulin Rouge*, like so much of contemporary Hollywood, presents us with a generic paradox: simultaneously being *post-generic* in the sense that the hyperconsciousness of its text spills over singular classificatory boundaries yet attaining intelligibility precisely in relation to those generic formations.

RETHINKING GENRE: MULTIPLICITY AND METAPHOR

Most of the more interesting recent work on film genre picks up on this expanded and more complex configuration of textuality, history and economics that bears upon the operation and meanings of both individual films and the concept of genre as such and has sought to situate the study of genre within the broader 'inter-textual relay' in which cinema is figured (see Neale 2000). In other words, in departing from traditional notions of genre as a stable system for classifying films into their proper grouping, a system untroubled by historical and cultural change, this work has approached genre as a multi-faceted discursive system involving not only the films themselves but also a whole range of other **extra-textual** and cultural phenomena. For some critics this has meant paying much more careful attention to the historical conditions which give rise to a genre in the first place and in which any given instance of a genre film circulates and is understood by its audience. This (re)turn to history no longer prioritises the film itself as reliable evidence for the definition and circulation of genres, but affords primacy to institutional categories, marketing materials and journalistic practices which are seen to provide original and contemporaneous testimony to generic configurations. Indeed, in recognising the limitations of his earlier text-centred work, Neale argues that not only do such industrial, cultural and journalistic labels constitute crucial evidence for understanding both the significance of genre to industry and audiences in the present moment, they also offer 'virtually the only available evidence for a historical study of the array of genres in circulation, or of the ways in which individual films have been generically perceived at any one point in time' (Neale 1990: 52).

In *Film/Genre* (1999), Rick Altman maps out a similar, yet distinct, model of generic analysis, one he calls a 'semantic/syntactic/pragmatic approach'. In refusing the textual determinacy of previous work and basing his own analysis on a general theory of meaning, he argues that 'what we call *genre* is in fact something quite different from what has always been supposed' (Altman 1999: 214). Indeed, his work stresses precisely the multivalence of the term *genre*, a term used differently by different users for different purposes and which can mean multiple and often conflicting things depending on the context in which it is being used. 'While genres may make meaning by regulating and co-ordinating disparate users', he writes, 'they always do so in an arena where users with divergent interests compete to carry out their own programmes' (ibid.: 215).

The expanded, more flexible approach to genre recommended by Altman (ibid.) and Neale (1990, 2000) has many advantages. For example, it recognises that the way in which audiences 'use' genre in the comprehension of a film's textual and extra-textual codes is by no means a stable or uniform process, but one which is capable of embodying significant differences between one historical period and another, or even between one spectator and another. By extension, critics are prompted to interrogate not only those moments of 'user agreement' in which the generic labels of production and promotion unproblematically coincide with their understanding by critics, reviewers and audiences, but also those moments of conflict in which there is a distinct lack of agreement about the attribution and comprehension of generic labels. So even though it is impossible, and for that matter undesirable, to completely extract textual structures from the institutional and cultural discourses that frame them, it is nevertheless remains the case that they cannot simply be collapsed into each other: to say that neither can speak independently of the other is not the same as saying that they inevitably say the same thing. One further advantage of this kind of approach is that the notion of generic evolution, so often treated as a natural and inevitable property of genre itself, can be mapped more precisely against not only trends in cinema itself but social and historical shifts and developments more generally. Either way, the picture of genre which is emerging from work of this kind differs considerably from earlier taxonomic conceptions of the term insofar as it is concerned less with establishing a clear and stable definition

extra-textual
In a broad sense, designates the 'outside' of the film/text, the range of cultural texts which relate in some way to the film/text, but in a narrower sense refers to the non-filmic intertexts which in varying degrees relate to the film/text (such as marketing and promotional materials, film reviews).

of the term than with the attempt to capture and understand its multiplicities in a critical vocabulary that is simultaneously theoretically motivated and historically grounded.

It is at this point that we are able to rethink film genre not as a literal concept – as either inventories of comparable films or as an economic explanation for Hollywood's production trends – but as a *metaphorical process.* Describing film genre as a *web of metaphorical expressions* allows us to capture in our analyses some of the 'liveness', volatility and malleability of contemporary (post)generic configurations by hooking understandings of film cognition up with aesthetic and industrial aspects of the cinematic process. Another way of putting this is to say that it helps us explain *why* genre can only ever be what we collectively believe it to be. For metaphors in themselves do not tell us anything, but rather draw attention to a *relationship* between things and prompt us to start looking for ways of making meaning. Indeed, the basis of metaphor is a process of *transference*: the transference of aspects of one object to another object so that the second object has an *implied resemblance* to the first object, yet is an original expression. It is precisely the ideas of *transference* and *implied resemblance* that help us describe genre as a metaphorical process. Thus film genre becomes understood as a metaphorical redescription, reworking or redeployment of cinematic and cultural vocabularies. Individual films, likewise, become original in precisely the ways they *interfere* with those vocabularies; that is to say, in the ways they deviate from the implied intertexts which form the reservoir of cognitive resemblances that make comprehension possible. Such a metaphoric conception of film genre focuses attention on the *nature* of textual transference and the process of *interference* between intertexts; that is to say, on the ways in which a film deploys familiar things in unfamiliar ways.

To see the operations of genre not as a literal, circumscribed process but as a metaphorical process is to stop asking questions such as, 'To what genre does *Moulin Rouge* belong?', and to restrict ourselves to more pragmatic questions such as, 'What other cultural objects does *Moulin Rouge* resemble?', and 'How does it cause us to compare it to other experiences?' So while on the one hand we can say that *Moulin Rouge's* opening shot of Montmartre looks *as if* it were shot by the Lumière brothers, and that Kidman sounds *like* Madonna and Monroe, on the other hand these are not literal transferrals – it is not Lumière footage and it is Kidman's voice we hear – but metaphorical expressions that alter the meanings of those extrapolations in the specific relationship of their rearticulation. It is here that a metaphorical conception of genre chimes with cognitive approaches in the sense that the spectator has to *do* something: to explore the nature of the assemblage, transferrals, and interferences in the act of comprehending the film.

Equally crucial, here, is the idea that metaphors are constantly being renewed, with old ones dying off and forming part of the cultural 'memory bank' which itself serves as the foil for the creation of new ones. In other words, *Moulin Rouge's* kaleidoscope of generic metaphors are themselves unrepeatable, but will be assimilated into our shared cognitive frameworks which then serve to throw future metaphors of expression into relief. For instance, the recent mini-movie advert for the perfume Chanel No. 5 (2004) really only coheres if understood as a post-*Moulin Rouge* film. Directed by Baz Luhrmann and starring Nicole Kidman, the advert works as a generic reprise of *Moulin Rouge's* narrative and stylistic features, and rearticulates and recirculates many of its generic metaphors which, of course, are themselves already hijacked from elsewhere. So, not only do we get Nicole Kidman playing Satine, playing 'the most famous woman in the world', playing Nicole Kidman all played *by* Nicole Kidman, but in the same way that the Parisian rooftop cityscape becomes both the location and the backdrop for *Moulin Rouge's* fairy-tale romance then an equally stylised geography frames much of the action of Luhrmann's advertising film.

On this account, then, genre not only becomes a cognitive mechanism of film comprehension, but also one of the most important principals by which cinema advances, changes and develops. For metaphors stretch cultural expression by casting

about for unpredictable resemblances, surprising relationships and unexpected associations so that, in the process of watching a film, we have to constantly revise our
hypotheses and expectations to fit the new material. And, of course, the notions of
'transference' and 'implied resemblance' are not only useful for explicating the film text
but can be mapped in relation to other industrial and commercial practices as well, from
the way a producer assembles a production package; to the way a film is promoted to
its audience; to the broader commercial ventures it entails. Indeed, rethinking genre as a
metaphorical process allows us to situate the textual analysis of film within the context
of a hyper-commodity culture of symbolic exchange which sees cinema's product both
being derived from, and exploited across, the full range of information and entertainment
platforms.

FURTHER READING

Although it is impossible to list them here, there
is a multitude of books which address individual
genres from a variety of historical and theoretical
standpoints. The following works, therefore,
represent some of the key attempts to conceptu-
alise film genre.

Introductory texts
Frow, John (2005) *Genre*, London: Routledge.
    Part of Routledge's *New Critical Idiom* series,
    Frow's book serves as an excellent intro-
    duction to the notion of genre generally as well
    as offering some fresh ideas on the ways in
    which genres actively generate and shape our
    knowledge of the world.
Keith Grant, Barry (2006) *Film Genre: From
    Iconography to Ideology*, London: Wallflower
    Press. This book forms part of Wallflower
    Press' *Short Cuts* series and, like many of the
    books in that series, combines an excellent
    survey of the field as well as introducing some
    new ideas.

Selected key works
Altman, Rick (1999) *Film/Genre*, London: BFI.
Langford, Barry (2005) *Film Genre: Hollywood
    and Beyond*, Edinburgh: Edinburgh University
    Press.
Neale, Steve (1990) *Genre*, London: BFI.
Neale, Stephen (2000) *Genre and Hollywood*,
    London: Routledge.

Useful anthologies
Grant, Barry Keith (ed.) (1986) *Film Genre Reader*,
    Austin: University of Texas Press.
Grant, Barry Keith (ed.) (1995) *Film Genre Reader
    II*, Austin: University of Texas Press.
Grant, Barry Keith (ed.) (2003) *Film Genre Reader
    III*, Austin: University of Texas Press.
Neale, Steve (2002) *Genre and Contemporary
    Hollywood*, London: BFI.
Winston Dixon, Wheeler (2000) 'Introduction', in
    Wheeler Winston Dixon (ed.), *Film Genre 2000*,
    Albany, NY: State University Press of New
    York.

FURTHER VIEWING

One approach to the study of film genre is to track
the ways in which any one genre has changed
over time. As such, watch a range of films of the
same genre from different periods. For example, if
you were to investigate the western film then the
following would give a good indication of both the
continuities and changes that have occurred within
the genre.

The Great Train Robbery (Edwin S. Porter, 1903)
Stagecoach (John Ford, 1939)
My Darling Clementine (John Ford, 1946)
Shane (George Stevens,1952)
High Noon (Fred Zinnemann, 1952)

Johnny Guitar (Nicholas Ray, 1954)
The Searchers (John Ford, 1956)
A Fistful of Dollars (Sergio Leone, 1964)
Billy the Kid Versus Dracula (William Beaudine,
    1966)
Butch Cassidy and the Sundance Kid (George Roy
    Hill, 1969)
The Wild Bunch (Sam Peckinpah, 1969)
Little Big Man (Arthur Penn, 1970)
McCabe and Mrs Miller (Robert Altman, 1971)
Blazing Saddles (Mel Brooks, 1974)
The Outlaw Josey Wales (Clint Eastwood, 1976)
Back to the Future III (Robert Zemeckis, 1990)
Dances with Wolves (Kevin Costner, 1990)

Unforgiven (Clint Eastwood, 1992)
Dead Man (Jim Jarmusch, 1995)
The Quick and the Dead (Sam Rami, 1995)
Last Man Standing (Walter Hill, 1996)
Shanghai Noon (Tom Dey, 2000)
Open Range (Kevin Costner, 2003)
Brokeback Mountain (Ang Lee, 2005)
The Proposition (John Hillcoat, 2005)
The Three Burials of Melquiades Estrada (Tommy Lee Jones, 2005)

Another approach to the study of genre is to map the range of intertexts that intersect in any one film. So, if it is possible to see *Moulin Rouge* as a complex remix of opera, melodrama, music video and Hollywood musical, is it possible to track a similar range of referents in other contemporary films? To adequately understand the various generic configurations which coalesce in *The Matrix* trilogy, for example, it may be necessary to watch and research:

- Japanese Manga and Anime
- Hong Kong action cinema
- Hollywood action-adventure films
- Postmodern philosophy
- Cyberpunk novels
- Music videos
- Computer games

Chapter 6

Stardom and Hollywood cinema

Paul Watson

■ Stardom and Hollywood cinema

INTRODUCTION: THREE APPROACHES TO STARDOM

In December 2005 readers of the UK film magazine *Empire* voted Tom Cruise the 'biggest film star of all time' (*Empire*, December 2005). More recently, Cruise emerged from *Premiere* magazine's 2006 list of the most powerful people in Hollywood as 'the most powerful actor in the world' (*Premiere*, June 2006). How do we understand such claims and what models of stardom might they imply? In the case of the *Empire* poll, does the idea of the 'biggest film star' mean the 'best' film star, the most popular star, or that Cruise is the most accomplished actor of all time? Alternatively, does it mean that audiences have consistently enjoyed the films in which Cruise stars, or that the action-adventure genre that he is often associated with is a hit with readers of the magazine? This situation becomes further vexed when we take into account the fact that the readers of the same magazine who voted Cruise the 'biggest star of all time' also named him the world's most irritating star (*Empire*, December 2005). In terms of the *Premiere* rankings, what are we to make of the idea that Cruise is the world's most powerful actor? Does it mean he is able to get more films 'green-lit' simply by attaching his name to the project? Is it that, in relation to other actors, he has unrivalled influence in Hollywood, or is it simply a question of wealth – that he can command multimillion-dollar sums for his performances? Moreover, if Cruise is the highest ranked actor at number thirteen on the 'power list', then what are we to make of the observation that the highest ranked actress, and for that matter the highest ranked woman, Reese Witherspoon, only manages number twenty-nine?

Even if the kinds of issues which emerge from such polls and lists are on one level clearly a product of the terms and conditions which govern the list-making process itself, on another level they do serve to throw into relief a number of important questions and confusions which bear upon the study of stardom: When is an actor also a star? What is the relationship between performance and stardom? What stake does the star hold in the processes of film production? Does the idea of a star mean the same thing across different historical moments and production contexts? Is there a difference between stardom and celebrity? Why are film stars so fascinating to us and what are the pleasures we get from them? Do male and female stars operate in the same context and can we understand them in the same way? These are, of course, some of the questions we will ask in this chapter. Yet, while these questions have always proved troubling to rigorous academic scrutiny, in cinema's third century the answers to such questions become even more complex. However, before attempting to unravel some of these questions we shall begin by surveying the three principal approaches developed for discussing stardom in the cinema.

Star as commodity

The first of these approaches locates the star within the economic contexts of film production and film marketing. During the era of the **studio system**, where creative and technical personnel were tied to long-term contracts, stars 'provided one of the principal means by which Hollywood offered audiences guarantees of predictability' by embodying a set of particular expectations and, by extension, particular kinds of pleasure (Maltby 2003: 145). Since the collapse of the studio system in the 1950s, stars have become arguably the key element of the unit-package around which movies are produced. Susan Hayward explains that 'producers will put up money for films that include the latest top star' and 'stars can attract financial backing for a film that otherwise might not get off the ground' (Hayward 2000: 350). Moreover, even a cursory glance at the promotional material surrounding a film's launch – posters, trailers, interviews in

studio system
Usually seen to have developed *circa* 1920 and lasting until *circa* 1950, the studio system indicates the period of Hollywood history in which the major studios controlled all aspects of the production, distribution and exhibition of their products.

For further discussion of the star and Hollywood read pp. 31 and 43.

print, on TV and online, as well as a host of further merchandising products – reveals the considerable stake stars hold in announcing its presence and generating an audience of sufficient size to recoup costs. On this account, then, the star is understood as a specific form of *industrial commodity* not only insofar as, like genre, stars function to 'differentiate films within the market' (McDonald 2000: 104) but also insofar as they are often the key 'mechanism for selling movie tickets' by guaranteeing certain pleasures and functioning as a commercial strategy for marketing films (Maltby 2003: 142).

However, a star's commercial capacity is inextricably bound up with his or her ability to 'be liked' by large amounts of people from a range of cultural and national contexts. The remaining two approaches to studying stars are sensitive to these more social and psychical aspects of stardom inasmuch as they turn away from industrial questions, focusing instead on the ways in which the figure of the film star generates specific meanings and pleasures.

Star as text

intertextuality
This term, which is strongly linked with **postmodernism**, designates, in its narrow sense, the ways in which a film either explicitly or implicitly refers to other films (e.g. through allusion, imitation, parody or pastiche), or in its broader sense, the various relationships one (film) text may have with other texts.

Given this, the second approach seeks to understand the star as a sign, that is, precisely as an *image* constructed through a network of **intertextuality**. This blend of semiotics, sociology and ideological criticism is the most familiar approach to questions of stardom and is associated most strongly with the seminal work of Richard Dyer (1979). Indeed, so influential is Dyer's work that the critical vocabulary it proposes for discussing stars has provided the centre of critical gravity for almost twenty-five years inasmuch as it is virtually impossible to discuss stardom without nodding in its direction. Central to this approach is the idea that stars are not reducible to flesh-and-blood actors but are conceived of as 'complex personas made up of far more than the texts in which they appear' (Tasker 1993: 74). There are two important implications of this observation. First, while on the one hand stardom is literally *embodied* in real human beings and is, to a significant extent, therefore anchored by that person's name, physical appearance, voice quality and specific performance skills, on the other hand 'we never know them as real people, only as they are found in media texts' (Dyer 1979: 2). The second, and related, point is that stardom manifests not only in the films in which a star appears, but across all kinds of other 'official' and 'unofficial' media texts in which the star may or may not appear in person: publicity and marketing materials, newspapers, magazines, television, websites, DVD 'special features', biographies and so forth. Indeed, within this web of intertextuality 'the star' itself becomes understood, and thus *understandable*, as a specific form of text just insofar as stardom is only accessible to us through texts, and thus only *exists* as a text. The crucial point here, however, is, as Paul McDonald notes, that 'the study of stars as texts ... cannot be limited to the analysis of specific films or star performances' since they are precisely 'the product of intertextuality in which the non-filmic texts of promotion, publicity and criticism interact with the film text.... In other words, the star's image cannot be known outside this shifting series of texts' (McDonald 1995: 83). On this account, the aim of star studies is not to peel away these layers of textuality in order to reveal the *true* self of the star, but to analyse the explicit and implicit meanings of precisely that mediated image and to read it in the context of wider ideological and social discourses.

Star as 'object of desire'

Whereas the intertextual approach focuses on the ways in which stars are realised in and through texts, the third principal approach addresses the *consumption* of stars. Indeed, if the audience remains *implicit* in the 'star as text' approach as the locus of meaning, the point where the star image is (re)constructed through the act of reading, then the politics of spectatorship and the pleasures of 'star-gazing' form the explicit foci of work which theorises the star–spectator relationship. James Donald argues that while spectatorship 'is the most hotly disputed question in the whole study of stars' there is, nevertheless, 'a good case for starting not with the return on capital invested in film production, but with the unquantifiable returns on our emotional investments in … those moments of erotic contemplation of the spectacular figure of the star' (Donald 1999: 39). By the same token, in pointing out some of the limitations of ideological approaches to stardom, Alan Lovell argues for a framework of analysis based on aesthetics and performance that 'should be concerned with … beauty, pleasure and delight' (Lovell 2003: 270). On this account, the star is seen, first and foremost, as an object of desire and is studied in terms of the ways in which spectators identify with, find meaning in, and gain a certain fulfilment from his or her image.

Perhaps the most influential strain of this approach is an offshoot of feminist psycho-analytic work on gender which theorises the orchestration of visual pleasure in cinema. Classically, the female star is held to be a sexualised spectacle that disrupts narrative momentum in moments of erotic exhibitionism which exceed the bounds of the story, while, on the other hand, the male star/hero is located as an ideal ego who controls the narrative and is thus the central mechanism for audience identification. More recently, work such as Jackie Stacey's *Star Gazing* (1994) and Rachel Moseley's *Growing Up with Audrey Hepburn* (2003) has attempted to ground this attention to pleasure and spectatorship in the study of *actual audiences*; that is to say, historically situated movie-goers. For example, in contrast to the general, theoretical explanation of why audiences like stars offered by psychoanalysis, Stacey develops an ethnographic approach to the star–spectator relationship which uses a combination of interviews with, and surveys of, viewers, as well as information drawn from personal letters and diaries. From this primary data, Stacey catalogues the different ways in which female viewers respond to, identify with and use images of stars. As such, unlike the universalising tendencies of psycho-analytic methods, Stacey is able to distinguish between various modes of identification and different types of pleasure.

WHEN IS A STAR NOT A STAR?

Three approaches to stardom, then, have held sway in film studies since the late 1970s. And as Geraghty (2000) notes, the definition of stardom that has emerged from these approaches has tended to turn on a series of dualities: between a star's performing presence and their off-screen existence, between actor and character, glamour and ordinariness, and between public and private spheres. As such, she argues that, generally speaking, 'the model for work on stars and their audiences has been that of an unstable and contradictory figure, constructed both intertextually (across different films) and extratextually (across different types of material)' (Geraghty 2000: 85). Indeed, it is precisely this putative instability of the film star, that is to say, the way a star might mean a number of potentially conflicting things, that has underwritten academic work on stars to the extent that, until recently, hardly anyone has noticed that such work has almost entirely been forged in the shadow cast by the star system and the stars who were deemed to exemplify its operations. So although the practice of tying stars into long-term fixed contracts which ceded overall control over their public and private image to the studio was over by the 1950s, the subdiscipline of star studies remains heavily influenced by the critical vocabulary used to analyse figures such as Marilyn Monroe, James Cagney, Humphrey Bogart, Marlene Dietrich, Greta Garbo and so on.

Today, however, the question of stardom is considerably more vexed than it was in the 1970s when the groundwork for star studies was being laid. In the first instance, the term 'star' itself is now culturally hierarchised alongside the celebrity, the superstar and the megastar. As such, the notion of stardom has undergone significant broad-ening in the sense that we now routinely speak of pop stars, rock stars, soap stars, star footballers and stars of sport generally, star DJs, star artists, star buildings, star fashion designers, star models, star politicians, even star academics. If cinema once provided 'the ultimate confirmation of stardom' (Gledhill 1991: xiii), then the growing number of Hollywood films which co-opt stars confirmed in other areas of the entertainment industries (pop princesses Jennifer Lopez, Madonna, Britney Spears, Beyoncé Knowles, Whitney Houston, Jessica Simpson, and Christina Milian; WWF champion The Rock; ex-fashion models Cameron Diaz and Charlize Theron; as well as a host of talent drawn from television, George Clooney being perhaps the most visible) certainly seems to question cinema's presumed privileged relationship to stardom.

In the second instance, in the information age and in the wake of transformations brought about by digital image-making technologies and computer animation, 'the definition of "film" as an object of study has not only broadened considerably but has also been destabilized as an object and form' (Sobchack 2000: 301). In this way, not only is there now a new breed of **synthespians** or computer-generated stars to contend with (in this respect figures such as Buzz Lightyear and Woody from the *Toy Story* (1995, 1999) films, Sullivan and Mike from *Monsters Inc.* (2001), Shrek and Donkey from the two *Shrek* (2001, 2004) films, the entire family of *The Incredibles* (2004) and Jar Jar Binks from the latest instalments of the *Star Wars* franchise (1999, 2002, 2005) are perhaps the apotheosis of the economic logic of the star system – fully contracted, entirely reusable, totally manipulable, and not subject to the ageing process), but increasingly the 'star' of the movie is more plausibly described as a digital entity or special effect (a twister, tsunami, volcano or storm; prehistoric dinosaurs, extraterrestrial invaders or mutant reptiles; a mythical, spiritual or fantastical force; or an earth-threatening or city-destroying catastrophe of either natural or alien doing). Thus, in uncoupling the filmic image and the cinematic process from photographic technology, the notion of the film star is now neither necessarily a flesh-and-blood human, nor for that matter even a character in the traditional sense of the term. As such, the guest appearance at the 2002 Academy Awards® of Sullivan and Mike from PIXAR's *Monsters Inc.*, and Donkey and the titular star of Dreamworks' *Shrek* not only marked the arrival of a dedicated Oscar® for the 'Best Animated Feature', but also highlights these more complex articulations of stardom in contemporary popular culture, articulations which cause us not to entirely supplant the dominant models for analysing stars, but to rethink the concepts and descriptions we use to account for these *different modes of stardom*.

CONTEMPORARY HOLLYWOOD AND 'MODES OF STARDOM'

Geraghty argues that while the term *star* should not simply be abandoned because of its non-specific, catch-all nature, we do, however, need to examine contemporary configurations of film stardom within the broader contexts of popular entertainment and media culture: 'Film stardom … has to be seen in the context of the drive in the media to create and exploit the status of being famous across the whole range of entertainment formats' (Geraghty 2000: 188). The notion of *being famous* is important, here, since it allows us to see the notions of star, superstar, megastar, as well as celebrity and actor, as points on the same fame continuum, a continuum which is itself bound up with, and fuelled by, the operations of mass-mediated culture. In other words, it permits us to speak of different modes, forms or degrees of stardom, which is to say, different articulations of 'the star' become differences of kind not circumscribed or delimited by the specificities of different media or different forms within individual media. In other words, contemporary configurations of film stardom must be seen as inextricably entwined with broader orchestrations of fame across and through all media platforms. It is in this sense that Geraghty attempts to rethink stardom through the categories of 'celebrity', 'professional' and 'performer' inasmuch as 'these distinctions better help us to understand what film stars have in common with and how they differ from other media public figures' (ibid.: 187). Let us take these categories one at a time.

---

synthespians
A recently coined term which describes 'virtual' or non-human actors. The term relates to digitally scanned or motion-captured versions of 'real' actors, as well as entirely computer-generated characters.

Star-as-celebrity

Celebrity is a mode of stardom relatively unconnected to the sphere of professional work. In other words, celebrity is sustained not by someone's talent or ability in their chosen profession, but almost entirely by notoriety and infamy. In this sense, Geraghty argues that celebrity privileges biographical information about a star to the extent that his or her stardom is almost entirely rooted in, and constructed through, 'gossip, press and television reports, magazine articles and public relations' (ibid.: 187). As such, titbits about a film star's latest failed relationship, his or her love of Chihuahuas or favourite designer circulate alongside similar morsels about musicians, sportsmen and women, royals, soap stars, It-Girls, socialites, designers, TV presenters and so forth. For instance, the 29 May 2006 edition of *New!* (see Plate 6.1), a British weekly magazine devoted

• Plate 6.1
New! magazine cover (Issue 165, May 2006), a British weekly celebrity gossip magazine. The image indicated ways in which film stars interact and vie with celebrities from other areas of the entertainment world

explicitly to celebrity reporting, leads with a feature about the impending birth of Brad Pitt and Angelina Jolie's baby. Yet 'Brad and Ange's' story struggles for prominence alongside not only the tale of ex-pop star Kerry Katona's 'fight to keep her kids' and superstar footballer David Beckham and his ex-Spice Girl wife Victoria's celebrity party, but also vies with the 'saucy secrets' of the celebrity wannabes who comprise the house-mates of *Big Brother 7*. Indeed, a cursory glance at the covers of any of the seemingly ever increasing number of photomagazines dedicated to peddling stories of celebrities' private lives simultaneously reveals how 'knowledge of the star's "real" life is pieced together through gossip columns and celebrity interviews' and how film stars 'literally interact with those from other areas' of the entertainment world (ibid.: 188). In this respect it is easy to track, for example, the trajectory of Tom Cruise's romantic relation-ships – from his divorce from his first wife Mimi Rogers, his role alongside Nicole Kidman as one half of Hollywood's first couple, to its demise and his subsequent relationship and marriage to Katie Holmes – just by looking at the covers of such magazines. The main point here, however, is the idea that attention is directed towards the drama of the star's 'private' life, not his or her public work as a professional actor.

Generally, then, we can identify three interrelated aspects to the star-as-celebrity. First, it is the public circulation of information about the putative 'real' private life of the star that sustains the celebrity. Second, the notion of intertextuality is not only descriptive of the *form* and *practice* of celebrity, but also *analytic* in the sense that such intertexts, in this mode of stardom, provide a primary focus of research precisely insofar as 'it is the audience's access to and celebration of intimate information from a variety of texts and sources which are important' (ibid.: 189). Third, and perhaps most crucially, whereas traditional models of stardom emphasise the film text as the primary site of stardom, or at least the place where the star image is completed (see Ellis 1982), the celebrity mode forestalls the primacy of the films themselves inasmuch as it constitutes a mode of stardom which does not necessarily involve spectatorship. In other words, it is not just that 'the star can continue to command attention as a celebrity despite failures at the box office' (Geraghty 2000: 189) but rather it is quite possible to be a fan of, to admire, or simply to 'like' a star *without watching the films in which he or she appears*. In short, it is not simply that the image of the star-as-celebrity exceeds the film text, but instead that it is dislocated from it altogether and dispersed across a range of extra-filmic texts.

Indeed, the adaptability and ubiquity, as well as the centrality of 'celebrity culture' to media culture *per se*, make 'celebrity' perhaps the key mode of contemporary stardom.

Star-as-professional

If star-as-celebrity is understood as part of the much broader operations of media consumption which are relatively divorced from the cinematic text, then the star-as-professional is, at least in the first instance, rooted squarely in the film text itself. So while on the one hand it appears increasingly the case that film stars are appreciated independently of their professional work, on the other hand 'it is quite possible to understand and enjoy the meaning of the star without the interdiscursive knowledge which the star-as-celebrity relies on' (ibid.: 189).

Crucial to the star-as-professional mode of stardom is the degree of 'fit' between the specificities of a particular star image and the corpus of professional roles played by the actor. In other words, the star-as-professional makes sense when it *appears* that the actor's 'real' personality corresponds more or less accurately and more or less consistently with his or her performed personas; that is to say, the idea that the actor him or herself is *personified* in their professional roles. Maltby argues that 'classical Hollywood's star system engineered a correspondence between star and role' to the extent that 'scripts were written specifically to exhibit already established traits and mannerisms in their stars' (Maltby 2003: 385). As such, 'the fact that a star's persona circulated in the media as part of the promotion of specific movies allowed for a considerable interaction between the star's performance and offscreen persona, and in many respects substituted for variation in the roles a star undertook' (ibid.: 385). For example, on-screen and off-screen, Marilyn Monroe embodied the persona of a beautiful yet innocent sex goddess, thus dissolving her 'real' personality into her professional performances. Indeed, the idea that we can detect Monroe the star in and through her roles, that her repertoire of gestures, expressions and movements are her own and not the property of any individual character, is central to the economy of pleasure associated with this mode of stardom.

More recently, in light of the dissolution of the star system and the change in the distribution of films brought about, in particular, by the video/DVD rental markets, the star-as-professional mode has become reconfigured with the star now being associated or identified with a particular genre. In organising the vast amount of titles available to audiences in rental outlets, 'video stores tend not to use the more specific genre categorisations of westerns, gangster films and horror genres and employ vaguer descriptions … such as "action movie", "comedy" and "drama"' (Geraghty 2000: 189). It is within these broader groupings that individual stars delineate more precise sets of expectations and pleasures. For instance, Jackie Chan, Jet Li and Steven Segal are closely linked to specific forms of martial arts/action cinema; Jim Carrey is associated with a certain form of physical comedy while one would expect different comic pleasures from a film featuring Chris Rock or Eddie Murphy; and despite the glut of male stars of the action film, figures such as Bruce Willis, Arnold Schwarzenegger, George Clooney, Tom Cruise, John Travolta, Nicolas Cage, Keanu Reeves, Harrison Ford and Jean Claude Van Damme arguably indicate relatively precise variations of masculine agency and thus provide a quite distinct set of expectations within the overarching category of action cinema. Indeed, Geraghty suggests that 'a stable star image' is crucial for the star-as-professional insofar as 'too much difference from established star image may lead to disappointment for the intended audience' (ibid.: 189). This perhaps accounts for why actors such as Clooney, Cruise, Willis and Cage, actors whose star image, though related to their physical appearance is not in the end predicated primarily on the display of muscularity or physical force, have been able to successfully work in a number of genres while similar generic transitions for Schwarzenegger, Stallone, Van Damme and, more recently, Jet Li have proved less successful. In this way, then, Geraghty suggests that stars who inhabit the star-as-professional mode 'operate for cinema and video in the same way as a character in a television series, providing the pleasures of stability and repetition and the guarantee of consistency in the apparent plethora of choice offered by the expanding media' (ibid.: 191).

Star-as-performer

In a reversal of the star-as-celebrity, Geraghty's final category shifts the emphasis away from biographical aspects of a star's private life towards notions of *performance* in deliberately focusing attention on the job of acting and the nature of performance. Thus while to some extent stars have always been understood in relation to their acting abilities and style, Geraghty suggests that the discourse of performance 'now takes on particular importance as a way for film stars to claim legitimate space in the overcrowded world of celebrity status' (ibid.: 192). If in hypermediated culture film stars are often levelled down to celebrities and have to struggle for exposure alongside footballers, pop stars and royals, then the concept of star-as-performer may be understood as perhaps the primary mechanism for reinscribing some of the cultural prestige of film stardom precisely by redirecting attention towards the film text as a privileged site for the art of acting. Indeed, such an emphasis on performance not only serves to distinguish certain film stars such as Marlon Brando, Robert De Niro, Al Pacino, Sean Penn, Johnny Depp, John Malkovich, Jodie Foster, Meryl Streep, Philip Seymour-Hoffman, and to a lesser extent, Brad Pitt, Charlize Theron and Edward Norton from the tittle-tattle of celebrity, but also operates as a key way of 'claiming back the cinema for human stars' from special effects and a growing number of non-human or animated stars (ibid.: 192).

It is possible to identify two principal ways in which film stardom is legitimised through this appeal to the craft of performance and acting talent. The first concerns a particular tradition of acting associated with the Actor's Studio in New York known as the Method, an approach to acting which Maltby argues has become 'the dominant account of how actors create naturalist performances' (Maltby 2003: 394). Method acting, on the one hand, is rooted in the presence of the actor's self as the emotional and psychological basis of *all* performance. As such, in order to be able to 'get inside' the mind of a character, the Method actor must first investigate his or her own anxieties, repressions, motivations and drives 'as the mine from which all psychological truth must be dug' (Vineberg 1991: 6). On the other hand, however, the authentic performance can only be fully realised and understood when the distinction between actor and character is abolished in the seamless fusion of performer and role. It is in this sense, then, that Method acting reclaims a degree of cultural prestige for the star-as-performer precisely 'by making the celebrity trappings part of the detritus which has to be discarded' if the performance is to be 'real' and thus worthwhile (Geraghty 2000: 192). Accordingly, it is not simply that actors such as Brando, De Niro and Penn often threaten to disappear into their roles, immersing themselves in the complex psyches of their characters, but, moreover, that their cultural status as performers is enhanced in rejecting the 'vulgar commercialism' of Hollywood. Brando was for many years renowned for being a semi-recluse, while James Kaplan writes that Penn 'gives interviews sparingly and reluctantly' while being a performer who 'has consistently taken roles in challenging films, as opposed to films that earn big money' and has 'effectively turned himself into an actor's actor, a remote star with a lingering air of menace and inaccessibility' (Kaplan 2001).

The second way in which film stardom becomes legitimised through a collocation with performance is related to a particular actor's *selection of projects*. This works on two levels, the first reconfirming the primacy of the film text to the star-as-performer noted by Geraghty, the second diluting such a primacy by acknowledging the rhetorical construction of the actor as a serious artist precisely through an extended circuit of mediation. In the case of the former, actors such as Penn, Depp, Pitt and Foster have tended to resist roles which might compromise their pretensions towards serious acting, instead choosing parts which enable them to put on display the highly visible and recognisable mannerisms of the Method. In the latter case, the star-as-performer reclaims cultural value for his or her work through a route of extra-filmic mediation which complements and commentates on both his or her performances and choice of roles. Often through a combination of star interviews, public pronouncements and self-authored articles, the star-as-performer sets him or herself apart from the vacuities of celebrity and the cold commercialism of Hollywood. For instance, Kevin Spacey's much publicised decision to take on the role of artistic director at London's historic Old Vic theatre shifts the emphasis from his star image to his creative talents. In other words, if, as Andrew Higson observes, 'acting and stardom are ... by no means necessary to each other' inasmuch as stardom depends 'as much on image as technique', then Spacey's move, at least in part, is one way of rejecting the image and promoting technique (Higson 2001: 71–2). Similarly, the recent glut of Hollywood stars, Julia Roberts being perhaps most notable among them, who have taken up roles in West End or Broadway productions beg to be considered, for better or worse, not in terms of their star persona, but rather in terms of the way they demonstrate the craft of acting.

One final example will serve to highlight the complex ways in which on-screen and off-screen, textual and extra-textual, images of a star can interpenetrate to produce a relatively sophisticated version of stardom. Sean Penn, while perhaps the contemporary epitome of the rhetorical construction of the 'serious actor', also provides us with an example of the way in which the two aspects of the star-as-performer often inform each other. For on the one hand, after declaring that he doesn't like acting and announcing a number of pseudo-retirements, he 'came back' 'determined to attach himself only to projects of impeccable aesthetic integrity' (Pulver 2001). On this level, his performances in such films as *Carlito's Way* (1993), *Dead Man Walking* (1995), *U Turn* (1997), *The Thin Red Line* (1998), *Hurlyburly* (1998), *Sweet and Lowdown* (1999), *21 Grams* (2003), *The Assassination of Richard Nixon* (2004), *The Interpreter* (2005) and *All The King's Men* (2006) have earned him the reputation of being 'the most powerful actor of his generation' (Ebert 1996), 'all fireworks and brooding Method' (Pulver 2001). On the other hand, however, Penn complements the status of his on-screen performances with a series of public tirades against the 'trash ethos' of Hollywood in which 'everything is about entertainment and no politics' (Penn, cited in Gibbons 2001). 'The one thing you can count on in Hollywood – across the board – is cowardice' (Penn, in Kaplan 2001) Penn has said, and if 'you are willing to put two ideas into a picture you are ahead of the game' (Penn, cited in Gibbons 2001). At the 2001 Edinburgh Festival, Penn made perhaps his most controversial public outburst when he accused certain big-name directors of 'raping society' and claimed that they 'should be sent running home screaming with rectal cancer' because 'they don't care about the films they make, or about what is going on around them or the effect they are having on their audience .... The definition of a good film now is one that makes the bank happy – not one that shines a light on people's lives' (Penn, cited in ibid.). As such, Penn's prestige as an actor is not only claimed through his performances in the film text, but through a more or less self-conscious rhetoric of prestige constructed extra-textually. So while 'the claim to stardom as a performer depends on the work of acting being put on display', such a display is not necessarily limited to the films in which an actor appears but can extend, as in the case of Penn, Spacey and others, to series of extra-filmic performances which serve to reinforce their putative distance from either 'stars-as-celebrities who can become famous for "being themselves" and stars-as-professionals who act as themselves' (Geraghty 2000: 193).

'THE ONLY THING I CAN'T PLAY IS A WEAK, DITZY WOMAN': ANALYSING JODIE FOSTER

Jodie Foster offers a particularly interesting and nuanced example of the contemporary film star. In part this is because, at some point in her career, she has embodied all three of Geraghty's categories of stardom, but it is also because she has been, for a number of years, one of the few female Hollywood actors who are considered able to 'carry a film' as well as being a member of that even rarer breed of female producer–directors that can wield a degree of power in Hollywood. Indeed, despite dissolving her production company Egg Pictures in 2002, telling *Premiere* magazine that 'producing other people's movies is just hard on your soul', Foster has, since the early 1990s, regularly appeared on lists of the most powerful people in Hollywood (Smith 2002: 48). Moreover, following the success of *The Silence of the Lambs* (1991), Foster has become 'one of the very few contemporary actresses who combine fairly consistent box office appeal with the power to make films … largely to her own designs' (Krämer 2003: 201). These latter observations, as well as the simple longevity of her career (she is still able to open mainstream movies after turning 40, often seen as the point of no return for Hollywood actresses), are crucial insofar as Geraghty notes that 'it is important to recognise that women stars do operate in a different context from their male counterparts' (Geraghty 2000: 196). Perhaps most interesting, however, is the way in which the various modes of stardom overlay one another in Foster's star persona and interpenetrate to produce a sophisticated image of **postfeminist** heroism and womanhood both on- and off-screen.

   Linda Ruth Williams's (2002) discussion of Foster as Meg Altman in David Fincher's *Panic Room* (2002) draws attention to the ways in which she has, since her first screen appearance in an ad for suntan lotion aged just 3, straddled the three categories of stardom identified by Geraghty. As Ruth Williams's analysis highlights, despite a 'veneer of ordinariness that encases her extraordinary success' and a private persona characterised by 'reserve rather than reclusiveness', Foster's career is not untouched by rumour and gossip about her private life that fuels the star-as-celebrity (Williams 2002:12). Indeed, her accomplished performances as a child star in such demanding roles as Audrey, the streetwise alcoholic kid in *Alice Doesn't Live Here Anymore* (1974), the 12-year-old prostitute Iris in *Taxi Driver* (1976), the child broad Tallulah in *Bugsy Malone* (1976), and Rynn the child murderer in *The Little Girl Who Lives Down the Lane* (1976) were thrown further into relief by publicity which sought to compare such 'fallen angel' roles with her real-life broken family. Latterly, this attention on Foster's family life has been replayed through a series of 'scandals' which have attempted to 'out' her as variously lesbian or bisexual, and, despite not being able to identify 'a single person she has ever dated' (Smith 2002: 86), journalists have repeatedly attempted to 'name' the father of her children. Moreover, since John Hinckley Jr attempted to gun down the President of the United States, Ronald Reagan, after apparently becoming obsessed with her role in *Taxi Driver*, the press have shown a persistent interest in claiming that Foster was acutely traumatised by her association with Hinckley and have often interpreted her subsequent 'woman as victim' roles as a kind of autobiographical cathartic response to victimisation. This interest was reignited in 2000 when Foster eventually broke her silence on the Hinckley Jr case, angrily denouncing as 'grotesque' the 'fascination that people have with celebrity' and that it made her feel as she 'was being used' (cited in Abramowitz 2000). The main point here, however, is that despite her virtually unrivalled ability to protect her privacy, and while being able to determine the agenda for much of what is written about her, it nevertheless remains the case that Foster's stardom is caught up in, and partially constructed through, the erosion of the public–private boundary on which notions of celebrity are predicated.

   However, while generally the category of celebrity 'works well for female stars' inasmuch as 'the common association in popular culture between women and the private sphere of personal relationships and domesticity' (Geraghty 2000: 196) chimes

postfeminism
The notion of postfeminism is a contested term used by different people, in different ways to mean different things. It is used here to indicate a version of popularised, and to some extent individualised feminism that is different from (mainly in the sense that it comes after) the highly politicised feminism of the 1970s.

For further discussion of feminism and feminist film theory see pp. 220–36.

with celebrity culture's thirst for gossip, the balance of Foster's stardom lies in her abilities as a performer and a professional. As a performer she is generally seen as 'the most respected actress of her generation' (Ruth Williams 2002: 12), 'a preternaturally gifted star' (Benson 1988: 4), 'not only a wonderful actor but an intelligent one' (Ebert 1999), and someone 'whose skill and presence seem to increase with each picture' (Turan 1997). Such critical eulogies are important precisely to the extent that they focus not on the glamour and beauty of the female star, nor on the ups and downs of her private life, but rather on her intellect, craft and sheer professionalism. So it is not simply Foster's refusal of celebrity that sets her apart from the overwhelming majority of contemporary female stars, but, more complexly, that her stardom is exemplary of what Hilary Radner calls Hollywood's new women, a rare breed of female actor who defies 'the Hollywood machinery that all too often reduces femininity to her image, the flattened body that functions as a projection of masculine desire' (Radner 1998: 260). In this respect her 'Californian golden-girl looks' *are* significant precisely to the extent that they don't reduce Foster to mere 'bimbo fodder', but actually inform a reading of her as articulating a new space within feminism in which feminine and feminist identities are no longer seen as mutually exclusive possibilities. As Ruth Williams charts, on screen Foster has portrayed femininity as 'riven by dark desires rather than erotic availability', playing a number of 'feisty "women on the edge"' who 'single-handedly carry mainstream productions' (ibid.: 12). In such roles as rape victim Sarah Tobias in *The Accused* (1988), single parent of child genius Dede Tate in *Little Man Tate* (1991), FBI agent Clarice Starling in *The Silence of the Lambs*, radio astronomer Ellie Arroway in *Contact* (1997), trapped parent Meg Altman in *Panic Room* (2002) and propulsion engineer Kyle Pratt, searching for her kidnapped daughter in *Flightplan* (2005), Foster has created a series of psychologically complex yet potent women who, despite their neuroses, are nevertheless 'effective agents, firmly grasping the symbolic order as they strive to wield public power' (ibid.: 14). Indeed, in both *Panic Room* and *Flightplan*, Foster is forced to combine courage and intelligence to defend her child against a set of male aggressors who, at least on the face of it, seem to hold all the cards. In the case of the former, Meg has to overcome her own claustrophobia and outwit the three intruders who apparently have her trapped inside her own impregnable hideaway in order to save her fast-ailing diabetic daughter. In the latter, Kyle not only has to suspend her own grief following the death of her husband and control her subsequent 'queasily rising hysteria' (Barnes 2005: 61) on discovering that her daughter, Julia, seems to have implausibly gone missing on a flight from Berlin to New York, but also the crew's and passengers' perception of her as simply mad – that somehow her story is a fantasy evoked by her traumatised imagination. Indeed, the film's plot turns precisely upon both her level-headedness in the face of panic and her superior knowledge about the construction and operation of the aircraft. In short, as with so many of Foster's characters, forced to confront her own worst nightmares and with no one else to turn to, it is her own psychological resourcefulness, acute intelligence and sheer single-minded determination to succeed that enable Kyle to survive and rescue her child.

At the level of Foster's performance, this pull between public social agency and the internal emotional traumas that rage behind the eyes of her characters is registered both verbally and visually in mesmerising 'displays of mumbled and humble inarticulacy' (Ruth Williams 2002: 13). Similarly, Roger Ebert has noted that so often when she speaks, 'we can almost feel each word being wrung out of her emotions' (Ebert 1988). But it is perhaps her trademark expression of strained fear, the look David Ansen describes as 'marvellously controlled fury' (Ansen 1988: 74), that defines Foster's persuasiveness in conveying 'intelligence and single-minded passion to the point of confrontational anger' (Turan 1997). Indeed, whether it is playing a game of psychological *quid pro quo* with Hannibal Lecter in *The Silence of the Lambs* in order to solicit a profile of the serial killer Buffalo Bill in return for her own traumatic childhood memories (Plate 6.2), or facing the extraterrestrial (re)incarnation of her long-dead father in *Contact* (Plate 6.3), or the deter-

• **Plate 6.2**
The Silence of the Lambs

• **Plate 6.3**
Still from *Contact*

• **Plate 6.4**
Panic Room (David Fincher, 2002). Meg Altman
(Foster) displays determined level-headedness in
overcoming her claustrophobia and protecting her
daughter from their male aggressors

• **Plate 6.5**
Flightplan (Robert Schwentke, 2005). Jodie Foster
as the grieving widow, Kyle Pratt, in Foster's most
recent performance of 'queasily rising hysteria' as she
tries to discover the whereabouts of her kidnapped
daughter

mined level-headedness she displays in outmanoeuvring her assailants in *Panic Room*
(Plate 6.4) and *Flightplan* (Plate 6.5), Foster's performances of grown-up contemporary
womanhood always contain traces of half-buried family sadness and repressed desires
in her tongue-tied delivery and desperate eyes.

In this respect, the final jaw-clenching scenes of *The Silence of the Lambs*, which
pit her head-to-head against Buffalo Bill, evince the powerful combination of these two
elements. Barely able to speak, yet sufficiently articulate to carry out her job, and with
terror etched into her forehead and visible through her nervously wide stare, Clarice
remains sufficiently composed and amply quick-witted to succeed in her task of neutral-
ising a version of masculinity which regards women merely as objects that can literally
be tailored to fit the excesses of male desire.

Although she is not a Method actor in the strict technical sense of the term, much of
Foster's prestige as a star derives from the emotional and psychological authenticity with
which characters such as Sarah Tobias, Clarice Starling, Dede Tate, Nell, Meg Altman
and Kyle Pratt develop. However, Ruth Williams suggests that there is another strand of
Foster's work in which the distinction between actor and role is less distinct, and that,
in a manner akin to the star-as-professional, it is possible to read these roles as Foster
performing herself. This idea focuses on Foster's exploration of characters either side of
the parent–child divide that are 'struggling to cope with the repercussions of an incomplete family' in a way that, to a greater or lesser extent, mirrors Foster's own experience

as both a child raised by a single parent and as a single parent herself (Ruth Williams 2002: 13). This is most obvious, perhaps, in *Little Man Tate*, Foster's directorial debut about a gifted child from a single-parent household whose mother is involved in a fight over the fate of his education and who struggles to get her voice heard amidst the various authorities which claim to 'know what's best' for her son. Although Foster herself admits that the film has some autobiographical elements to it, one critic argues that 'there is reason to believe that Jodie Foster – raised by a single mother, child performer from age three, teenage movie star, Yale graduate – might have a special affinity for Frank Scott's screenplay' (Brown 1991: 66). Moreover, the idea that Foster's characters are, in fact, really only manifestations of her own life and personality has been consistently employed by critics to interpret and evaluate her films. So, J. Hoberman saw the titular character of *Nell* (1994) as a product of 'Foster's own fantasy' while Richard Corliss thought the film 'was all about Foster herself, with Nell as her alter ego' (both quoted in Krämer 2003: 210). Hoberman also thought that her depiction of Clarice Starling as a 'mixture of beleaguered cool and intense isolation' took on 'additional resonance' because Foster was herself, in respect of the Hinckley Jr case, 'a victim of American pathology' (in ibid.: 204). This weaving together of the (auto)biographical Foster with Foster's roles may also be mapped through the reviews of *Contact*, *Anna and the King* (1999) and *Panic Room*, and has had its most recent airing in relation to *Flightplan* which the critic for the *Village Voice* has described as containing a 'shocking and raw performance' which milked 'the screenplay's uncomfortable echoes of her own life' (Holcomb 2005). Ironically, perhaps, the final confirmation of the desire to equate the off-screen Foster with her on-screen personae is to be found in the reviews for her most recent film, *Inside Man* (2006), which variously celebrate or criticise her performance of Madeleine White, a high-flying corporate fixer, for not 'fitting' either the 'courageous woman' or 'child victim' paradigm. So, on the one hand, Todd McCarthy thinks that Foster 'seems to be having fun … as the elegant, far-more-superior-than-thou intermediary' (McCarthy 2006) and Kevin Maher describes her performance as exploring 'a hitherto unseen smugness that provides a surprising counterbalance to the saintly mom persona she's perfected in recent roles' (Maher 2006: 57), a performance that David Ansen thinks is 'deliciously coldblooded' (Ansen 2006) and Kenneth Turan thinks is 'picture stealing' (Turan 2006); on the other hand, Roger Ebert thought that despite being 'smart and tough' she 'does more or less nothing' (Ebert 2006).

CONCLUSION

In these ways, then, Foster inhabits all three modes of stardom described by Geraghty; yet Foster's stardom is somehow more than the sum of these parts: more alluring, more intense and more unknowable than either category reveals alone. For it is the ways in which these various layers of stardom interpenetrate that not only make Foster a particularly complex version of contemporary stardom *per se*, but also position her as an interesting embodiment of postfeminist womanhood, or what Jacinda Read refers to as a popular, common-sense feminism (Read 2000). Read argues that 'film is one of the sites on, through and against which meanings of feminism are *produced*', and that to fully understand such meanings we should 'read films historically through the discourses surrounding them and to explore the complex ways in which such discourses intersect and negotiate with each other' (ibid.). In this sense, it is the very complexity of Foster's stardom – not only the fact that she is a successful professional woman in a male-dominated industry, or that she is herself a single parent trying to sustain a career while raising her children, or that some aspects of her private life may be glimpsed in certain of her roles, or that a number of her performances reconcile femininity with feminist agency, nor even that she is one of the few serious female actors deemed capable of carrying mainstream productions, in fact not any single facet of her stardom – that aligns her with a feminist identity not centred on a structural conflict between career and personal life. Indeed, in many ways, both Foster's on- and off-screen representation of a successful, professional woman who is able to make her way in a 'man's world' while not sacrificing either her femininity or aspects of her vulnerability, someone for whom family is important but not necessarily all-important, simultaneously acknowledges the politics of second-wave feminism and moves beyond them. For when we look at Foster and her films, a fulfilling private life is no obstacle to a successful public identity, having good looks and being feminine does not mean that you cannot be taken seriously, demonstrating doubt, fear, frustration or anger is not a sign of weakness or irrationality, and the desire to succeed professionally is not at the expense of personal happiness. As such, perhaps at the heart of Foster's appeal is the way, in dramatising many of the tensions and contradictions associated with being a working woman/mother today, she offers multiple points of identification. In short, the totality of Foster's star image turns not on the *choice* between her career and a private life, but rather the desire and the struggle to hold them together.

In discussing Foster's eleventh-hour replacement of Nicole Kidman for the lead role in *Panic Room*, the film's director David Fincher distils the significance of Foster's stardom. He says that 'Nicole Kidman makes you make a different movie. . . . It's about glamour and physicality.' With Foster on the other hand, 'it's about what happens in her eyes. It's more political. Jodie is someone who has spent 35 years making choices that define her as a woman and define women in film. Jodie Foster is nobody's pet, nobody's trophy wife' (Fincher, quoted in Brooks 2002: 16). It is for this reason that perhaps the only role Foster is incapable of playing is 'a weak, ditzy woman' (Foster, quoted in Krämer 2003: 209).

FURTHER READING

Introductory texts

McDonald, Paul (2000) *The Star System: Hollywood's Production of Popular Identities*, London: Wallflower Press. A relatively short but excellent introduction to the historical emergence and development of the star system in the American film industry.

Selected key works

Dyer, Richard (1998) *Stars* (2nd edn), London: BFI. Since its first publication in 1979, Dyer's book has been the key critical work in the field of star studies to the extent that it is virtually impossible to find any work since that doesn't take stars as its point of departure. The updated edition also features a useful supplementary chapter by Paul McDonald which traces more recent developments in star

studies. It is also worthwhile consulting Dyer's later book, *Heavenly Bodies: Film Stars and Society*, London: BFI (1987).

Gledhill, Christine (ed.) (1991) *Stardom: Industry of Desire*, London: Routledge. This anthology contains many seminal essays in the field of star studies.

Useful anthologies

Austin, Thomas and Barker, Martin (eds) (2003) *Contemporary Hollywood Stardom*, London: Arnold.

Moseley, Rachel (ed.) (2005) *Fashioning Film Stars: Dress, Culture, Identity*, London: BFI.

Willis, Andrew (ed.) (2004) *Film Stars: Hollywood and Beyond*, Manchester: Manchester University Press.

FURTHER VIEWING

Sean Penn

Dead Man Walking (Tim Robbins, 1995)
Hurlyburly (Anthony Drazan, 1998)
The Thin Red Line (Terrence Malick, 1998)

Sweet and Lowdown (Woody Allen, 1999)
I Am Sam (Jessie Nelson, 2001)
Mystic River (Clint Eastwood, 2003)
21 Grams (Alejandro González Iñárritu, 2003)

The Assassination of Richard Nixon (Niels Mueller, 2004)
The Interpreter (Sydney Pollack, 2005)
All the King's Men (Steven Zaillian, 2006)

Jodie Foster
Taxi Driver (Martin Scorsese, 1976)
The Accused (Jonathan Kaplan, 1988)
Little Man Tate (Jodie Foster, 1991)

The Silence of the Lambs (Jonathan Demme, 1991)
Nell (Michael Apted, 1994)
Contact (Robert Zemeckis, 1997)
Panic Room (David Fincher, 2002)
Un Long dimanche de fiançailles/A Very Long Engagement (Jean-Pierre Jeunet, 2004)
Flightplan (Robert Schwentke, 2005)
Inside Man (Spike Lee, 2006)

RESOURCE CENTRES

Online reading

Dargis, Manohla (2000) 'Ghostin the machine', *Sight and Sound*, Issue 7 (July): http://www.bfi.org.uk/sightandsound/feature/46

An essay which examines aspects of Tom Cruise's star and screen persona.

Feasey, Rebecca (2004), 'Stardom and distinction: Sharon Stone and the problem of legitimacy', *Scope*: http://www.nottinghamac.uk/film/scopearchive/articles/stardom-and-distinction.htm

An essay in the online film studies journal *Scope*, which discusses Sharon Stone.

Grieveson, Lee (2002) 'Stars and audiences in early American cinema', *Screening the Past*, issue 14: http://www.latrobe.edu.au/screeningthepast/classics/cl0902/lgcl14c.htm

Chapter 7

Spectator, audience and response

Patrick Phillips

■ Spectator, audience and response

INTRODUCTION

A central reason for studying film is to better describe and explain our response to the film experience. In a response study, we ask how and why we react as we do – both emotionally and intellectually. We may extend this to consider reasons for the uniformity or diversity of reactions among a group of people.

Film studies has distinguished between the response of social groups, collectives of people – an *audience* – and the response of the individual – a *spectator*. This chapter will consider some of the ideas that have informed thinking about the film spectator and the cinema audience and it will use these as a springboard for an introductory examination of *response*.

THE FILM SPECTATOR

Film studies has assigned great importance to spectatorship. The following are some of the working assumptions that have underpinned this work since the 1960s. Here are three, each of which may be considered open to dispute or be in need of considerable qualification:

■ spectatorship is primarily concerned with the way the individual is positioned between projector and screen in a darkened space
■ the audience ceases to exist for the individual spectator for the duration of the film
■ although the spectator is singular, a figure alone before the screen, spectatorship studies tries to generalise about how *all* spectators behave

Let us consider each of the above.

Spectatorship is primarily concerned with the way the individual is positioned between projector and screen in a darkened space

You or I are referred to as spectators when we position ourselves in front of a screen to watch a film. It has been argued that the cinema experience is much more completely separated from the rest of our lives than the act of watching a film on a television screen. We enter a public space having paid an admission charge. We are predisposed to a certain level of investment of ourselves in the film screening – if only because we have paid for it. The fact that we have paid also indicates that we have certain expectations which will further increase our willingness to concentrate. The cinema is, in a peculiar way, both more public and more private than our own homes. As a public place it offers us the chance to enjoy a different set of comforts and facilities from those at home. While the lights are up and the advertisements or trailers are playing, we are aware of the other members of the audience. The popcorn being crunched and the drinks being slurped don't annoy us particularly. When the lights go down and the film credits appear we are suddenly alone. Now the crunchers and the slurpers run the risk of seriously annoying us – we realise we have come here to lose ourselves in the images and sounds of the film.

The technology of cinema exhibition holds us much more powerfully than does television. The size (and shape) of the screen, the quality of the images, the clarity of the sound all invite much more attention – indeed they demand it. We are held in our comfortable seats; all around us is near-darkness except for exit signs. We have no control over the film. If we go to the toilet we can't put the film on 'pause'. Not only that; we can only engage in the briefest of whispers about what has happened in our absence.

It is important to consider the upturn in cinema visits at a time when DVD systems, multi-channel satellite/cable TV and online entertainment dominate the domestic space. The cinema 'experience' is acknowledged as special and different – and is considered as worth taking seriously as a topic of study. Of course, much of the above begs the question whether we therefore need to develop quite different approaches to spectatorship when we watch a film on television or on a computer screen where the scale is so much smaller and where, most often, we cannot lose ourselves in the dark (see Ellis 1992); and more than this, whether we need to revise our ideas of spectatorship in relation to digital projection as part of a 'home cinema' system. Certainly other explanations seem to be required for the viewing of a film or video work as an installation within a gallery space.

The audience ceases to exist for the individual spectator for the duration of the film

Do we lose ourselves in the dark? It could be argued that the public and social nature of cinema-going works against this experience. After all, we enter the auditorium as a member of the audience, our expectations possibly enhanced by the chat around us. Many people go to the cinema with one or more other people and their physical proximity is something that cannot easily be put out of our mind. Even if alone, we are conscious of shared reactions during a screening; sometimes this takes audible form – laughter, groans, screams – any of which can be infectious, altering the individual spectator's response (see Hill 1997).

On a broader front we may say that we exist as audiences for a movie well away from the cinema. We are constructed as members of a 'potential' audience in at least two ways. We become exposed to the promotional and marketing hype designed to create expectations. We are also drawn into conversation about issues relating to a movie which may be circulating within our culture, resulting particularly from the profile the film enjoys in other media. In moving from 'potential' to 'actual' audience member, we have both an individual and a collective sense of what we are doing – we are self-aware.

After the screening we may well engage in yet another expression of audience membership as we discuss our reactions in a variety of contexts – on the bus, in the pub, online – maybe for days afterwards. Nevertheless, for better or for worse, theories of spectatorship have tended to isolate the self that exists more or less alone with the film for the duration of its screening. We will have more to say about this later.

Although the spectator is singular, a figure alone before the screen, spectatorship studies tries to generalise about how *all* spectators behave

Even though theories of spectatorship isolate the self, this self is an abstract concept, rather than a self with individuality and differences from other spectators. In other words, interest is not in observing and explaining the response of actual people but rather in the attempt to generalise about a 'state of being' common to all people when they position themselves before a screen and watch a film. Generalisations about this theoretical spectator show some very interesting shifts. In the 1960s and 1970s the dominant model was of a 'passive' spectator controlled by the overwhelming mechanisms and physical presence of the film screening, so that they were made vulnerable to the assumed **ideological effects** of the film experience. The emphasis more recently has been much more on an 'active' spectator who makes meaning and 'negotiates' with the film in the act of consuming it. Either in conceiving of a 'passive' or an 'active' spectator, what we find are attempts to generalise about the complexity and significance of the film – spectator interaction.

ideological effects
Has political significance, manipulating the spectator into specific ways of thinking about and relating to the world.

THE FILM AUDIENCE

For further discussion of
the film audience in US
and UK cinema see
pp. 49–53.

The study of film audiences has emerged from a quite different academic base to that for spectatorship. Audiences exist in the culture, as social phenomena, and it is through media sociology and cultural studies that much of the work on audiences has developed. Here are three characteristics of film audience studies which, like those outlined above in relation to spectatorship studies, are open to question and debate:

- the audience is primarily of interest as an object of study *before* and *after* the film
- audiences are seen as constructed by mass-media institutions and exist in a dependent relationship with these institutions
- audience study, even though concerned with large collections of people, is now less likely to generalise than is spectator studies; it is concerned rather with local and specific factors that may explain audience behaviour

Let us consider each of the above.

The audience is primarily of interest as an object of study *before* and *after* the film

The audience disappears when the lights go out. Spectatorship theories, as we have already seen, kick in at this point, with the audience de-aggregated into individuals alone before the screen. This may seem odd – audiences certainly remain 'whole' at other spectator events such as music concerts and football matches. In film studies it seems that, on the one hand, the audience is the 'immanent' audience, the one forming for the event, constructed by a range of factors ranging from the influence of advertising to fan obsession. On the other, the audience is the 'virtual' audience, existing after the film, a group which remain a collective because of what they do in their wider cultural lives with the film experience they have shared. What audiences 'do' with a film is often expressed in terms of *uses and gratifications* – which is another way of talking about what needs in the audience are met by the film experience.

One concept that holds on to the audience as a collective during the film screening is that of the 'film event'. The film as an 'event' has been developed from a variety of contrasting perspectives. At one end of this spectrum we find political activist cinema, such as that of Latin America in the 1960s, where the film is something that can be stopped and argued over, where active participation in debate is the very purpose of the event. At the other end of the spectrum we have what might be called the 'carnival' film event, such as when an audience dresses up and sings along, as to *The Rocky Horror Show* or *The Sound of Music*.

The very exceptional nature of these 'events' relative to the standard movie-going experience reminds us of how oddly obedient the audience are within the standard film screening. The audience remain more or less silent, more or less unmoving in the seat they have chosen or been allocated. The experience remains remarkably similar to that of going to the theatre. In light of this it is perhaps not surprising that studies have focused on the *before* and *after* of this act of social conformity.

Audiences are seen as constructed by mass-media institutions and exist in a dependent relationship with these institutions

Audiences, especially fans-as-audience, may be seen to be very dependent on the media institutions that produce, promote and sell the product they consume. Just as the spectator may be seen as engaged in a symbiotic (and dependent) relationship with the film text and cinema apparatus, so the audience may be seen as engaged in a similar kind of relationship with the cinema institution. The demands of the audience are met (sometimes? always? hardly ever?) by corporations who supply the films that occupy the multiplex screens and meet the 'home cinema' market in video and DVD formats.

One interesting debate here is the extent to which audience demand for films, particularly as expressed through fan behaviour, determines supply, that is, the actual films produced by the industry. Certainly as an industry dependent on consumer choice, it might be expected that extreme sensitivity is required in interpreting indicators of audience preference. In practice, the audience is potentially so vast and diverse in its preferences that responding to audiences often means responding to a 'core' audience – the so-called 'avids' who go to the cinema most often. Of course, the more a market strategy is designed around these 'avids' the more they will dominate the audience in a closed circle of mutual interest to the exclusion of other audiences and their film preferences (see Dale 1997).

What we find here is indeed a parallel between the way spectatorship is managed by forces outside the control of the spectator and the way audience is managed by the power brokers of production, distribution and exhibition, operating within an international commercial market.

Audience study, even though concerned with large collections of people, is now less likely to generalise than is spectator studies; it is concerned rather with local and specific factors that may explain audience behaviour

From the earliest studies of film audiences it is clear that the routine methods of social science research could tell us a great deal. In these audience studies and in many others like them since the 1910s, what we have are deductions made from the collection of quantifiable information – information about, for example, frequency of visits to the cinema and genre preferences. (This contrasts with the inductive approach of spectatorship, which starts with a theory and then projects it on to the object of study – the person in front of the movie screen.)

The purpose of audience studies has usually been to identify – and then interpret – broad tendencies. So although information comes from actual individuals who describe their real behaviour, the interest in collecting this data has been in order to see larger patterns of behaviour. More recently, under the influence of cultural studies, there has developed an increased sensitivity to local conditions and circumstances; a move towards what are sometimes referred to as 'thicker' studies. A 'thick' approach to audience study respects the diverse backgrounds and motivations of subgroups who constitute the larger audience.

RESPONSE STUDIES

Who is it that we should talk about as responding to a film – the spectator or the audience?

Perhaps neither, so much as you or me as an individual, not quite contained within theories of the spectator or general sets of observations about the audience (both of which we will look at further in this chapter). film studies, influenced by Cultural Studies, is increasingly likely to centre on local, small-scale and precise groups of people who share, perhaps, some social or political 'formation'. Their behaviour both as individuated spectators and as a collective of people forming an audience is likely to be better understood if we respect and try to understand the importance of the particular life experiences and social attitudes they bring with them to the viewing situation.

Here is a very literal example. We could carry out a study of former members of the Women's Land Army, 'land girls', women who were sent to work on farms in Britain during the Second World War to make up for the labour shortage. These women who

Bill Nichols writes:

The goal of providing explanations for cultural forms and social practices loses its appeal in favour of an emphasis on the (preferably 'thick') interpretation of specific forms, practices and effects. It is in particulars rather than abstractions that larger generalities take on forms that have emotional impact, social effect and ideological import.
(Gledhill and Williams 2000: 38)

• **Plate 7.1**
Land Girls (David Leland, 1998). What is the audience's starting point: romance, nostalgia or history? A simple film may produce wildly varied responses

would now be in their eighties are invited to a screening of David Leland's *Land Girls* (UK, 1998). They form a 'community of interest', that is, a group of people who though not living in physical proximity to one another are identifiable as a community due to a shared interest. In fact we would discover many individual differences, as well as collective similarities in their response. For example, they may all experience to some degree a nostalgic glow for the period of their youth and for the romance of their contribution to the war effort – even if in reality they had very varied experiences as land girls from that represented in the film. On the other hand, their sophistication as film-goers may vary enormously, with some more able to see how the film is constructed at least as much around other films of a similar kind as it is constructed around any attempt at historical accuracy. As a result, tolerance levels for what is perceived as not very 'realistic' in the film may prove very varied.

It may soon become clear that even this approach, involving an apparently homogeneous group of women watching a film that locks into a key moment in their personal histories, is too big, too likely to produce fairly crude generalisations. We quickly become aware that the 'formation' of each person is only partly the result of their public and social selves. Each of us brings to the film event an interior self, a self of countless memories and desires, some scarcely acknowledged let alone understood. Major themes in *Land Girls*, for example, revolve around female friendship, sexuality and personal relationships. We can well imagine how, for each woman in our study, very specific memories and associations may be stimulated by these themes.

In this light we may have to consider that not only does every individual have a unique relationship with the film he or she is watching, but that this relationship is likely to change in subtle ways from one viewing of the film to the next. Response draws in the whole of the self, a self that includes:

■ a social self who can make meaning in ways not very different from others with a similar ideological 'formation'

- a cultural self who makes particular intertextual references (to other films, other kinds of images and sounds) based on the bank of material she possesses
- a private self who carries the memories of her own experiences and who may find personal significance in a film in ways very different from others in her community of interest
- a desiring self who brings conscious and unconscious energies and intensities to the film event that have little to do with the film's 'surface' content

The land girls of history came from different class backgrounds, enjoyed different educational opportunities and would subsequently have lived very different lives from one another (indeed, this is captured in Leland's film). Each of them would watch a fiction film loosely based on their experiences of the 1940s with different needs and thus different levels of personal investment in the viewing experience.

My example is a simple one – but it raises a problem of response study that is more or less the equal and opposite one to that raised in spectator study. If spectatorship study risks losing itself in the 'master narrative' of a generalising and theoretical account of how we watch films, response study can lose itself in the very particularity of each interaction between film and spectator.

WHAT WE CAN LEARN FROM EARLY CINEMA

We tend to take film viewing and our behaviour as consumers for granted, and so theories of spectatorship and studies in audiences can alert us to the complexities of our own response to film and the cinema experience. Very often the best way of trying to understand something we are so familiar with that we take it for granted is to take an historical perspective. Certainly one of the most fruitful ways of understanding the relationship between mainstream commercial film, spectatorship and audience construction is to study how they evolved in the period referred to as 'Early Cinema', dating from around 1895 to 1915. Here we may ask not only how spectatorship and audience developed but reflect on how they could have developed differently.

For further discussion of early Hollywood cinema see pp. 25–8 and early British cinema see pp. 305–12.

Film historians tend to agree that by about 1917 nearly all the fundamental features of what we now consider mainstream film 'language' were in place. Film had, in just twenty years, evolved ways of managing time and space, particularly through editing, and of managing the distance between object and audience, particularly through camera movement, which made the experience of cinema very different from that of the theatre. We must remember however that films still very clearly showed their relationship to popular forms of theatre such as melodrama and vaudeville, especially in their story-lines and character types.

The evolution of film form in Early Cinema

In very early films the camera is static before action and character. This can be accounted for purely by reference to the technical limitations of the equipment. However, there is also an assumption being made about spectator viewing position – the camera 'eye' assumes the position of a member of the audience sitting in the middle of the stalls of a proscenium arch theatre. The theatre spectator cannot move closer to a key character or observe a key event in more detail. Early films seem particularly clumsy to our eyes in that they often include shots full of people and a variety of action without any guidance as to which action or indeed which character is particularly significant for the development of the plot.

For discussion of film form in classical Hollywood and contemporary cinema see pp. 61–82.

Not only do early films not offer us close-ups but they fail to offer any guidance as to what we should give our attention to within the mise-en-scène. Also undeveloped is any systematic organisation of point-of-view shots which just a little later became so important as a means of drawing us into the action and emotion of an event.

• **Plate 7.2**
The Birth of a Nation
(D.W. Griffith, 1915).
A rider in Ku Klux Klan
garb rides at full tilt
towards the camera. It is
difficult to study Griffith's
film. On the one hand,
it is the most important
single advance in the
development of narrative
film and mainstream
film form. On the other
hand, it is obnoxiously
racist, and images such
as this one appear to
have contributed to the
increased recruitment
to the Ku Klux Klan
throughout the 1920s

It is useful to list some of the ways in which the spectator began to be drawn into a particular relationship with the screen through control exercised by camera movement, mise-en-scène and editing:

- camera movement towards and away from an object – usually the camera fixed to a train or a car – in order to give the spectator a greater sense of physical involvement
- camera position nearer or further from an object – long, medium and close shots motivated by a concern to 'direct' the spectator's attention and increase engagement with the emotions of characters
- mise-en-scène organised to enhance the meaning and emphasise the significance of particular actors or objects through positioning, set design and lighting
- the frame of the mise-en-scène exploited to create interest and desire in what cannot be seen beyond the edges of the frame
- editing used as the means by which shots can be organised and, thereby, the means by which the spectators' seeing is 'managed', for example:
  - parallel editing so that two events can be followed simultaneously encouraging the spectator to make and respond to assumed dramatic and thematic connections
  - editing used as montage – to encourage a particular interpretation of one shot by the influence exercised on the spectator's mind by the shots on either side of it
  - editing used particularly to move the spectator between different points of view within the mise-en-scène

the look
Developed as a central concept in relation to the control of the spectator. Cinematic looking has also been associated with theories of desire and pleasure, theories often founded in psychoanalysis.

A way of pulling much of the above together is by reference to the concept of **the look**.

The evolution of film spectatorship in Early Cinema

Early Cinema needed to find ways of controlling the look of the spectator as part of a move towards producing a more appealing and standardised 'product' for commercial exploitation. For example, it became essential to try to:

- ensure that the meanings intended by the film's makers were those taken by the members of the audience
- replicate for realism of effect the ways in which we engage in the act of looking outside the cinema
- provide greater pleasure in the act of looking

It is possible to talk about developments in the use of the camera, mise-en-scène and editing as ways of *controlling the look*. The camera offers a particular 'eye' on the world of the film. This 'eye' may be the camera as the impersonal storytelling device or it may be the 'eye' of a character within the film as represented by the camera. These are literally 'points-of-view'. Even when the camera is not aligned with the viewing position of a particular character but is 'objectively' pointing at a mise-en-scène, the spectator look could be directed by the looks and glances exchanged by the on-screen characters in order to draw attention to a significant plot detail. Editing allows the spectator to adopt different viewing positions; to share in an exchange of looks, most commonly in a shot-reverse-shot dialogue sequence.

One spectator 'effect' of the development of film form is particularly important. It is the way in which the spectator is drawn into the world of the film, caught inside and between characters. This is achieved through editing and point-of-view and results in the **interpellation** of the spectator who is drawn inside the psychic, and physical life of the fiction. This 'effect' is at the heart of so many debates around spectatorship and manipulation in popular cinema.

Of all the ideological aspects of spectatorship, none have received as much attention as those around notions of voyeurism – the look of the peeping tom, able to see without being seen. Early Cinema very frequently represents the female, dissected by the close-up into a fetishised object of the male look. It is certainly interesting in relation to ongoing debates around the proposition that overwhelmingly in mainstream cinema the 'camera is male', that the evolution of this out of crude peepshow technology should be so evident from the beginning of popular cinema. Two of the most famous films exploring voyeurism are Hitchcock's *Rear Window* (1954) and Powell's *Peeping Tom* (1960).

Practical solutions, common sense or ideology?

It is fascinating to study these developing strategies in Early Cinema, especially as they do not appear to have been systematic. Some are used, then discarded, then used again. Through trial and error, filmmakers found a set of procedures that worked – aesthetically, emotionally, intellectually and, most of all, commercially. There are different ways to account for how mainstream commercial film form developed the way it did by 1917.

It may be interpreted as entirely 'natural':

- a set of practical solutions to the problem of making the film more intelligible to an audience, motivated by commercial considerations
- a common-sense set of solutions to problems of replicating how the spectator engages with the real world through the act of looking

Alternatively, it may be interpreted as ideological:

- a reflection of the ways of seeing of Western culture and particularly of the male within Western culture
- a recognition of the medium, if only for commercial reasons, as a powerful manipulative medium, capable of controlling representation and response

In fact these two positions are not opposed: what appears 'natural' and 'common sense' is rooted in a set of **hegemonic** choices and constructions. The very naturalness of these choices simultaneously provides spectator/audience pleasure and a largely invisible and, therefore, particularly effective form of spectator/audience control.

A study of Early Cinema forces us to ask questions, the most fundamental of which is this: Could film have been different from what it is and still have attracted a mass

See Chapter 10 for more on the idea that the look is male. The idea was proposed by Laura Mulvey (see Mulvey 1975, 1981).

interpellation
Refers to the distinctive way the film spectator is, as it were, placed inside the fiction world of the film, placed by the apparatus and by the conventions of film form (such as in shot–reverse shot dialogue editing). Literally we are 'hailed' or called into a place we have no control over.

hegemony
Captures the idea that a set of ideas, attitudes, practices become so dominant that we forget that they are rooted in the exercise of power – and that we could choose differently. Hegemonic ideas, attitudes, practices appear as 'common sense' and any alternatives appear odd or potentially threatening by comparison. Hegemony is the ideological rendered invisible.

audience? Those frustrated by the way a particular conception of cinema came to dominate (the mainstream Hollywood-type film) sometimes look to the period of Early Cinema which may be seen as a kind of Garden of Eden – a period of innocence and infinite possibility. Studies in Early Cinema often encourage us to think what other ways film form – and, therefore, spectatorship – could have developed from the way in which they did. For example, a model for a radical alternative form of cinema might be conceived as one which does not guide us every step of the way through close-up, shot–reverse shot and so on. In a static camera long shot, for example, we are given freedom to choose for ourselves what we wish to focus upon. In not being interpellated, we are free to engage more objectively and thoughtfully with what we see and hear. There is not the space here to explore these arguments. However, it is necessary to recognise that much of the interest in Early Cinema is motivated precisely by a desire to reflect on other kinds of spectatorship possibilities than that established by the kind of cinema which Hollywood (and not just Hollywood) had evolved into by around 1917.

The evolution of the film audience in Early Cinema

In the introduction to this chapter, the interrelationship of spectator and audience studies was pointed out. With regard to Early Cinema, just as interesting as the study of the development of film form as it relates to spectatorship is the development of film exhibition as it relates to audiences.

Film gradually emerged from a fairground attraction of 1895 to the nickleodeons of the early 1900s. Audiences were overwhelmingly working and lower-working class. The medium of cinema had a very low cultural status. In the USA the move from nickelodeons, usually just small dark rooms with benches, to movie theatres, which accelerated in the early 1910s, was both cause and result of the move to make cinema-going more 'respectable' and controllable.

The commercial concern was to raise the social image of movies and this had to involve both making them into more sophisticated products and placing them within more 'theatrical' auditoria. A key objective was, as the founder of Paramount, Adolphe Zucker, said, 'to kill the slum tradition in the movies'. An anarchy in film response had to be contained if film-going were to be more appealing to the middle classes. This anarchy derived in part from the fact that the films were silent. This gave them a wonderful 'universality' on the one hand, but also offered them as particular to different audiences – for example, to the vast diversity of immigrant groups arriving on the East Coast of the USA. More specifically this anarchy derived from two factors. First, the lack of a controlled viewing position prior to the development of a standardised film form, as described in outline above, meant that the spectator was much freer to make meaning from the images presented on the screen. Second, the 'untrained' behaviour of the audience who used the cinema space as a noisy, interactive meeting place meant that the movie-going experience was held in very low regard by those sections of the middle classes that took it upon themselves to 'police' social behaviour. Neither the film's textual operations nor cinema's organisation of the viewing event was able to isolate and control the spectator. The peculiar nature of the film experience as both isolated (in spectatorship) and collective (in audience membership) was itself evolving – or rather, being constructed – towards greater uniformity.

The fact that film audiences were socialised into a particular cinema practice (e.g. sitting quietly) at the same time that film form had been evolved to manage the act of spectatorship (e.g. control over the look) is highly significant. The standardisation of both film form and of cinema exhibition from very early in the history of cinema has encouraged film theorists to develop ideas based on:

■ a normative spectator unified as the 'subject' addressed by the film

■ the viewing situation as a constant (rather than as variable according to who is the spectator, when and where they are and what they are watching)

The strengths and shortcomings of this approach to spectatorship, already highlighted above, are further considered in the two sections that follow our first case study, which focuses on the early cinema audience and response to a particularly controversial film.

□ CASE STUDY 1: THE RESPONSE TO *THE BIRTH OF A NATION* (D.W. GRIFFITH, 1915)

The purpose of this case study is to reflect on the most spectacular early experience of film – the discovery of the power of the medium to generate intense response both inside and outside the cinema auditorium. D.W. Griffith's film of 1915, *The Birth of a Nation*, is of great significance in the history of cinema. It brought together most of the developments of the previous years in film form in order to cement them in place in what we now sometimes call the **Institutional Mode of Representation (IMR)**. At the same time it offered the kind of film spectacle that accelerated the move of cinema into 'picture palaces'. The fact that the film remains one of the most racist films ever made offers a third key area of interest. In what follows, the emphasis is on the evolution of audiences and the idea of the film event, and on the increasing cultural (and political) significance of cinema within a developing industrial-commercial 'public sphere'.

Griffith was a perfect figure for social reformers of early cinema to have as an ally because of his commitment to what may loosely be described as Victorian, conservative values combined with his brilliant understanding of the potential of the medium. He carried forward a complex project intended to advance cinema as an art form to be respected by the arbiters of culture and simultaneously to rein it in so that it might be experienced as a more standardised commodity. Perhaps a little harshly, Larry May describes Griffith's achievement as not one of aesthetics 'but simply size, scale, prestige'. In other words, Griffith's achievement was to synthesise developments over the previous years and turn this into a more spectacular product. The complication to this neat narrative is that the most historically significant of Griffith's films, while certainly conservative in ideology and while certainly laying down a benchmark for the standard narrative realist film form, produced a disruptive social effect on a national scale far beyond anything in the short

Institutional Mode of Representation (IMR) Captures the idea that a normative set of ideas about what constitutes a 'mainstream' film became established around 1915 to 1917. The IMR may be seen as an example of hegemony – establishing an apparently 'common-sense' notion of how a film should be constructed and how it should communicate with an audience.

• Plate 7.3
The Great Train Robbery (Edwin S. Porter, 1903). This still illustrates the static camera of Early Silent Cinema. For a spectator accustomed to the 'standard' film language established twelve to fourteen years after this film, Early Cinema provides major problems. For example, the static camera does not create the expected involvement or draw attention to significant objects in the frame which might help create narrative clarity

history of cinema up until that point – or arguably since then (May 1980: ch. 4). In fact Griffith may appear as a very contradictory individual. His conservative values centred on ideas of the home, the family and on an essentially patriarchal sense of leadership by wise, enlightened men. At the same time, his defence of the freedom of speech (especially in defending his own work!) seems to put him in a much more liberal camp. His eye for sensational images of sex and violence certainly seems to fly in the face of any sense of him as a Victorian prude.

The Clansman, as the film was first known after the title of Thomas Dixon's novel, started production on 4 July 1914 and was completed at the end of October. The initial $40,000 budget was spent on just the battle scenes – the film finally cost an unbelievable $115,000 – a scale of production which tells us much about the 'invention' of cinema as fantastic spectacle. The film was previewed on 8 February 1915 at Clunes Theatre, Los Angeles. The event was unprecedented as the entire Los Angeles Philharmonic took up their places to accompany the film. Here, Karl Brown, assistant to Griffith's great cameraman Billy Bitzer, describes in a 1976 interview the moment the film began:

[A]nd when [the conductor] raised his baton and held it for a moment – down it came and everything blew just straight out of the can – oh it was the most tremendous gust of sound I'd ever heard.

It was renamed *The Birth of a Nation* before formally opening on 3 March 1915 at the Liberty Theatre, New York with usherettes dressed as southern belles. What it meant to go to the cinema was redefined by the scale of the film both as a film and as a cultural event – it changed people's idea of what cinema was, how it could be experienced, what effects, visceral, intellectual, moral, it could have on a society. The film had a lot of firsts – the first to run for three hours, the first to have a musical score played by a seventy-piece symphony orchestra, the first to have scheduled performances, the first to have an intermission, the first to charge $2 for reserved seats. It has also been described – flying in the face of what we might think of as 'silent cinema' – as one of the noisiest films ever made. A small army of people was employed backstage in the big city screenings to produce a complete range of sound effects.

The audience was constructed by national advertising and promotional campaigns. It was the first film to use large billboards, the first to take full-page ad space in newspapers. It was the first full-length film to be screened at the White House. No one could fail to know about it as an 'event'. It made huge profits – most famously making the future founder of MGM, Louis B. Mayer, his first fortune – simply by owning the distribution rights to *The Birth of a Nation* in the New England area.

This commercial hype was, of course, compounded by the controversy the film created. Many people were outraged by the film's racism and yet caught in a double bind – as liberals, many of these people were also against censorship. So *The Birth of a Nation* may also be regarded as the earliest example of a film demanding a collective response and yet dividing people as to what that response should be. Karl Brown, in his 1976 interview, recounts how when told that showing the film in Atlanta would cause race riots, Griffith replied, 'I hope to God they do'. Brown continues:

It wasn't that he was particularly anxious for a riot or people to be hurt or anything of the sort. But it's the old story that if someone gives you a tremendous pat hand, you're going to play it.

This confirms a view that Griffith was engaged in an act of provocation. Apologists for Griffith would argue that his main motive was not to promote racism but to prove and promote the idea that cinema was a new cultural form of great significance. However naive or calculating, what is clear is that Griffith was locked into a social formation in white, male, southern states culture that made it almost inevitable that the hegemonic form of representation of African Americans – a racist representation – would manifest itself in his film.

This and the other testimony quotes in this case study come from *D.W. Griffith – the Father of Film*. This is a three-part documentary produced by Keith Brownlow and David Gill in 1983.

The National Association for the Advancement of Colored People (NAACP) organised nationwide protests against the film, starting immediately after the Los Angeles preview one month before the New York premiere – even though members were in principle against censorship. There was plenty to be upset about – from the intertitle in Griffith's 'Prologue' which stated that 'The Bringing of the African to America planted the first seed of disunion' to the crudely racist representation of black men, especially in the post-Civil War second half of the film. Several screenings of the film were delayed and the Film Boards in some US cities required changes to the film in response to the protests. An Epilogue, paid for by the Hampton Institute, was made to show the positive contri-bution of African-Americans and this was first tagged on to the film at Boston's Tremont Cinema in 1916. A near riot broke out when a larger number of black people arrived to a screening to establish how useful the Epilogue was in correcting the damaging effects of the film – and were refused admission.

The effect of the film on black audiences, still at this time subject to segregation in cinemas, cannot be understated. Here is William Walker speaking in the early 1980s about his experience of having seen *The Birth of a Nation* in a blacks-only movie theatre in 1916:

[S]ome people were crying. You could hear people say, 'Oh, god' and some 'damn'…. You had the worst feeling in the world. You just felt like you were not counted, out of existence. But I tell you, I just felt like there could have been some way so they couldn't see me so I could kill some of them. I just felt like going out to kill every white person I saw in the world.

Between 1915 and 1973, the right to screen *The Birth of a Nation* was challenged in the US courts at least 120 times. However, the very controversy surrounding the film was a key incentive for those wishing to develop the full-length motion picture as a powerful and significant form of mass entertainment. The film showed that cinema could produce 'effects' for both individual spectator and collective audience on such a scale that there was no turning back. The commercial and cultural significance of cinema was proven to a very large degree by this one film.

This brief case study (much more could be said if space were available) demon-strates that a focus on audiences and the film 'event' draws together key areas of film studies. *The Birth of a Nation* is uniquely able to force the following questions: What kind of experience does cinema offer, and what kinds of social and cultural effects can a film have? What competing ideological forces are put into circulation by a film which dares to offer such amazing spectacle on the one hand and such pernicious messages and values on the other? *The Birth of a Nation* established that cinema matters. It demonstrated that some films at least enter into the public sphere, are experienced by audiences coming to the event with their different personal and community formations in ways that tell us not just about the movies but about the force-fields at work within the society.

In looking at issues of film reception, it shows us how issues of spectatorship and audience are difficult to untangle. Here is Karl Brown talking about the Ku-Klux-Klan rescue sequence with Wagner's 'Dance of the Valkyries' as accompaniment. Brown's construction by the film text as spectator is clear – but so, also, by implication at least, is his predisposition to a certain response determined by his own ideological formation and his construction as a member of an enthusiastic audience, expectant of the kind of thrills provided:

It was like a call to arms – you just couldn't let go. You weren't watching people ride, you were riding with them and you weren't riding with them to rescue somebody but you were riding on a stern determination for vengeance, vengeance for the death of that little girl you'd learnt to love so much…. And the fact that the showing of 'The Clansman' started riots and put blood on the streets was proof beyond proof that this was a great picture – regardless of what critics might have to say about it. The proof was there.

The Birth of a Nation was hugely significant in the evolution of both film spectatorship and the audience experience. However, like all historical case studies it needs to be considered in its specificity – as a unique case – as well as in its function as establishing a precedent which changed people's perceptions of what a movie was and what an evening at the cinema could offer.

This case study of audience responses to *The Birth of a Nation* suggests a very active audience. A film is resistible – both its content and its effects. The mechanisms of spectatorship are not all determining. *The Birth of a Nation*, even today, provides an excellent example of the peculiar tension between the power of spectatorship and the power of audience solidarity. These mixed messages about 'active' and 'passive' are the subjects of the next two sections.

THE SPECTATOR OF THEORY

What mental and emotional activity goes on in a spectator during the watching of a film? So much has been written on this – indeed, it has probably been the single most recurring area of investigation for film theory – that it is impossible to do more than summarise some of the main lines of thought.

The fact that spectatorship has been a subject of theory is itself an issue. There is a significant difference between a theoretical and an empirical scientific approach. After the dominance of theory in the 1970s and 1980s, in which hypothetical 'models' of spectatorship were built, based on then fashionable ideas emerging from linguistics and psychoanalysis, the period from the mid-1990s has tended to be dominated by 'post-theory'. This latter approach has attempted to undermine the spectator of theory, arguing that we should seek explanations much more in scientific theories of how the brain functions in response to stimuli and in processing information. In practice post-theory approaches to film spectatorship have not been very much more empirically based than what went before, although they are based on a science – cognitivism – which does make use of 'hard' empirical observation and testing. It is interesting that the battleground over different ways of trying to make sense of spectatorship has been broadly divided between academics from Western Europe, particularly France, and academics from the United States.

Structuralist and post-structuralist theory

The acronym SLAB has been created around the names of these four theorists. This rather derogatory term suggests how the theory that defined film studies in the 1970s and 1980s is now open to serious attack. For a sense of the arguments against SLAB theory, see Bordwell and Carroll 1996).

What derived from France (and the UK) was a combination of Saussurean linguistics, Lacanian psychoanalysis, Althussarian neo-Marxism and Bartheian semiotics which produced a very powerful intellectual framework that dominated film studies when it was first establishing itself as a serious academic subject in universities. What resulted was a model of spectatorship and the effect of films, especially mainstream films, that was very deterministic. From linguistics came the idea that language did our thinking for us – so that as we enter into a language system (and film was seen as language-like), we can only operate on its terms. From psychoanalysis was developed the idea that as we sit in front of the screen we regress to the narcissistic 'mirror phase' of very early childhood. The spectator was seen as locked into the 'cinema apparatus', somewhere between projector and screen. At the same time he or she was interpellated into the world of the film according to the controlling operations of the film's formal systems of editing, point of view and so on. From neo-Marxism came the idea that surrender to the apparatus and to the formal mechanisms of cinema also had powerful political effects. The spectator was tied into the invisible relationships of power and control that replicated the deepest levels of Western ideology. In brief, the spectator was vulnerable to a kind of waking dream experience that was stupefying. The pleasure was in the surrender, in the comfort the cinematic experience offered in playing out our fantasies and at the same time controlling them.

This first phase of structuralist theory gradually became modified as it was clear that the results of applying it were too deterministic – both in explaining films and spectator behaviour. There was the need to produce a lighter touch model that allowed for greater complexity, greater variation. Often it seemed that this model of the spectator was produced by cinephobes, that is, people with a hatred of cinema, in order to demonstrate how dangerous cinema is, politically and psychically! In its post-structural phase, theory became more open to variation. Psychoanalysis remained central, but instead of the spectator being seen as fixed in place by an (imaginary) unified self-image projected on to the screen, he or she was now considered capable of 'playing' or 'struggling' with different positions. He or she could occupy different and contradictory roles – male/female, hero/villain/protagonist/victim – and thus was able to exercise conflicting fantasies within the self. In addition, semiotics increasingly emphasised different kinds of response within an audience (see more below, p. 160), as individuals decoded audio-visual material according to their own situation and needs. The political dimension of theory became more flexible too, especially through adopting the concept of hegemony, emphasising how in society (as in a film) we can adopt one of several positions that are available to us within a social order that seems to evolve through consensus rather than through stark exercises of power and control.

Cognitivism

In opposition to explanations of spectator activity deriving from structuralist and post-structuralist theory, approaches to spectatorship, especially in the United States, have tended to prefer a much more pragmatic view of how, moment-by-moment, the brain works with the stimulus it is bombarded with by the film in order to make sense and gain emotional experience. This can be described, in broad terms, as a cognitivist approach. Rather than focusing on unconscious activity and the 'subjectification' of the spectator by the 'apparatus' of cinema, this approach takes as its starting point the idea that response can largely be tracked and explained by reference to conscious and routine activity. The brain works to recognise, process and 'place' the stimulus in such a way that it becomes possible to 'read' the film's meaning and manage its effects. This emphasis on cognition certainly supports the idea of an 'active' spectator, even if much of the mental processing seems entirely automatic. For example, we learn to read a film in all kinds of ways – through recognition of the familiar aspects of narrative, genre conventions and the common audio-visual techniques of film's communication system (such as continuity editing and synchronised sound). We do this by bringing our knowledge and experience of previous films to bear in responding to a new film experience.

One way to explain how spectators make meaning is by reference to **schemas**, a concept used in studies of the human thinking process. When we are confronted by a new experience, we look for familiar patterns that allow us to orient ourselves and make sense of what is in front of us. In the experience of watching a film we automatically look for the schemas we have become accustomed to from our previous experience of film. As well as narrative and genre mentioned in the previous paragraph, we may find, for example, that an auteur schema or a star schema is useful in mentally processing what we are being presented with by a film.

This may suggest that competence in carrying out these cognitive procedures takes many years to learn – well, some may – such as learning to recognise an auteur structure/schema. However, the fundamental schemas relating to, for example, narrative and genre, do not – and certainly learning to 'read' the basic communication system of film does not. One explanation for this ease with which we 'read' a film was provided

schema
Refers to a familiar pattern recognised by the mind that allows us to orient ourselves and make sense of what is in front of us. In the experience of watching a film we automatically look for the schemas we have become accustomed to from our previous experience of film. By extension we can talk about auteur, genre and star schemas.

Cognitivism may be seen as an instrument of hegemony by providing 'normal' explanations for phenomena and experiences that might otherwise seem to lie outside and challenge the way we think and see. Again I quote Bill Nichols:

Analytical philosophy and cognitive psychology cling to the same assumptions of abstract rationality and democratic equality that led to a politics of consensus (based on the denial of bodily, material difference) and the repression of a politics of identity.
(Gledhill and Williams 2000: 42)

as early as 1916 by a psychologist, Hugo Munsterburg (see Langdale 2002). He pointed out that what was remarkable about film was that it seemed to be organised to allow us to respond using the kinds of cognitive processes we bring to our everyday lives. Indeed, going back to the evolution of narrative film in Early Cinema, it may be argued that filmmakers were evolving by trial and error a form of cinema that made mental processing as 'natural' as possible. If cinema can be described as 'realist', then it is most profoundly so in the way it replicates mental activity rather than physical reality. Our brains effortlessly (but not passively!) function to make meaning from and manage response to the kind of stimulus the film throws at us second by second. Cognitivism could therefore be described as a 'realist' approach to spectatorship and response.

However, a major criticism of cognitivist approaches is that in relating the film experience to everyday routines of mental processing, it can only emphasise the similarities rather than the differences between the film experience and other kinds of 'everyday' activity. What, for example, of the very particular ways in which films provide us with moments of intensity, mobilising our desires, triggering memory in the dark of the movie auditorium? The activity of the 'active' spectator of cognitivism involves working to make safe the film experience, repeating conventional ways of thinking and processing stimulus material – in this case stimulus produced by a film. It would appear to elaborate on what in Chapter 1 was referred to as a 'sensory motor mechanism' (see p. 12). The real challenge for the film maker is to create a different kind of film experience, encouraging or even forcing the spectator to look and think differently; to celebrate difference.

Affect and excess

The different approaches to spectatorship outlined thus far all appear to derive from a strong need to explain how the potential waywardness of seeing and listening and responding in multiply different ways is managed – whether by the cinema apparatus, the formal features of the film itself or by the normative procedures of the mind. A very different approach to spectatorship is one that confronts this waywardness – where cinematic effects produce complex and diverse affects.

The theory deriving from Lacanian psychoanalysis emphasises 'lack'. It proposes that from early childhood we are aware of incompleteness, and our fantasy lives are driven by the need to complete this lack. Cinema may, in this context, be seen as a perfect machine for doing so. And for doing it endlessly, since desire can never be fulfilled by a film, as it is just a film – it can only enact our desire, encouraging us to come back for more. This theory suggests that as desiring subjects driven by lack, we fit into the regimes of seeing and hearing that are provided for us. The film experience is too little, indeed almost nothing at all at the material level – just the play of light on a screen. Even in relation to the imagination, we are placed within one or more systems that contain our fantasy lives within its structures.

Arguably, the experience of cinema is not lack, despite the undeniable fact that we never leave the cinema with anything other than memories of projected images. Perhaps it may be said that far from giving us too little, film gives us a huge excess of stimulus – more than we can manage, more than we want to manage. Steven Shaviro writes:

But is it really lack that makes images so dangerous and disturbing? What these theorists fear is not the emptiness of the image, but its weird fullness; not its impotence so much as its power. Images have an excessive capacity to seduce and mislead, to affect the spectator unwarrantedly. What is the source of this mysterious power?

(Shaviro 1993: 17)

Shaviro answers his own question by saying that an image is like a 'residue' of something that existed – and what disturbs is not its absence but the fact that it just won't go away! It exists not as a lack, but as something too much.

> The fleeting insistence of weightless images, of reflections and projections, of light and shadow, threaten to corrupt all standards, to exceed all limits, and to transgress every law
>
> (ibid.).

Is our desire for the visual, indeed for the audio-visual, actually excessive, always overflowing the controls and containments described above? Perhaps rather than focusing on how the cinematic apparatus is contributing to the endless reproduction of 'given' ways of experiencing our world, ways that fold us back into mechanisms of control, we could run with a very different kind of theory which is entirely affirmative of cinema as an imaginative medium in which an image, a sound, is always more than what it represents, what its narrative function might be. This is not to suggest that we have any control over this experience, but that we can rethink what we do with it. Shaviro writes: 'My own masochistic inclination is to revel in my bondage to images … rather than try to rectify it'.

A shift in emphasis away from the concept (meaning, system of representation) to the affect (feeling, emotion) becomes important. An affect is what lingers, what was described earlier as a 'residue', something we feel which is in excess of the representational system that produced it. So, for example, a film which at a 'conceptual' level appears rather conventional, even simple-minded, may leave me with a profound sense of loss or sadness. Thinking about affect forces us to question what we think of as knowledge. As Clare Colebroke writes:

> What we can acknowledge is that art is not about knowledge, conveying 'meanings' or providing information. Art is not just an ornament or style used to make data more consumable. Art may well have meanings but what makes it art is not its content but its affect, the sensible force or style through which it produces content. Why, for example, would we spend two hours in the cinema watching a film if all we wanted were the story or the moral message?
>
> (Colebroke 2002: 24–5)

Much of film studies has been dominated by representation, by concepts. In fact a film has the capacity endlessly to free sounds and images from their referents (their 'thing' – in the world), they become not something less (a lack, an absence) but something more. Shaviro argues that what in fact the apparatus of cinema does is 'deterritorialize' the image, that is, remove it from its routine, conventionalised place in the world, in the order of things, and this 'leads directly to the visceral immediacy of the cinematic experience.' (Shaviro 1993: 36).

This may appear as a retreat from the political priorities of theory, towards some kind of decadent surrender to pleasure. Perhaps it would be more accurate to say that it is a different kind of politics. Rather than one based on diagnosing 'symptoms' and ascribing negative effects for the purpose of increasing our wariness of the film experience, Shaviro's approach, which derives from the writings of Deleuze, is about foregrounding the imagination and its 'lines of flight'. Certainly this is a more liberating approach and more congenial to a cinephiliac – someone who loves cinema and who wants to share that love with others.

Melodrama is a good example of a genre where the gap between the conceptual and the affective is very pronounced. An ideological analysis of a 1950s, American melodrama may reveal all the ways in which it promotes a particular value system, one that is highly conventional and working to support ideas of social stability and coherence. However, at the level of affect, the experience may be very different, especially for the target audience – women. Here is what Jeanine Basinger writes about her own experience of growing up with 'the Woman's Film':

We grew to understand and accept the great secret of the Hollywood film: its ambivalence, its knowing pretence. You were a fool to believe any of it, but you were a fool if you didn't. You could have it both ways, neither way, one way or the other. It didn't matter, because movies were really only about one thing: a kind of yearning. A desire to know what you didn't know, have what you didn't have, and feel what you were afraid to feel. They were a door to the Other, to the Something Else.

(Basinger 1993: 4–5)

The following section is primarily an exploration of possible 'lines of flight' in our response to a particular film sequence.

RESPONSE

How we respond to a film is very complex. film studies has long moved away from a 'transmission' model based on the idea that meaning and emotion is all bottled up in the film itself. We bring so much to the interactive experience of film-watching, both as spectators, defined in our isolated relationship to the film, and as audience members, enjoying a shared experience.

One influential idea that emerged from post-structuralism, particularly from the work of Roland Barthes, was that of the 'death of the author'. Rather than hold to the view that the reader/spectator is entirely at the service of the producer of the work, the opposite was argued. A text (a book, a film, a painting) only comes into existence in the act of 'reading' it. In this way the reader of the text is, in a way, simultaneously its creator. The actual author (writer, filmmaker, painter) is 'dead'. Each of us comes to a film with our own personal 'formation' – the result of all our life experiences. These will predispose us to certain interpretations of character, certain attitudes towards moral and political issues and certain emotional responses to events. In its most dramatic form this suggests that there are in fact as many 'readings' of a film as there are spectators – and that an audience will typically be made up of people reacting in very different ways.

With mainstream commercial cinema, three factors work against this diversity of response. First, the audience will have been attracted to the film for broadly similar reasons to do with narrative and genre and star expectations – they will already be in some ways a collective defined by the 'promise' of the film. Second, the film most usually reflects ideological values that are generally accepted as 'common sense' by the majority of the audience. Within a given society people share a very similar constructed sense of social reality, what is sometimes described as a shared social imaginary. Third, the operations of the film will tend towards triggering a processing system that is common to all members of the audience – whether we call this the operations of cognitive processing or the sensory motor mechanism (see p. 12).

See Lapsley and Westlake 1988. This book gives a good overview of SLAB theory.

This idea of 'openness of meaning yet determinacy of effect' is a useful compromise in explaining how individual spectators form a collective called an audience. What needs to be added to the mix is what has been said in the last section about affect. Cognitive responses – making meaning – may be broadly similar but affective response may vary considerably. In addition, less conventional films, films that break with some of the features of the typical mainstream commercial film, are likely to produce greater diversity of response. First, expectations will be more varied, with the audience less singular in its make-up. Second, aspects of the taken-for-fragmented social imaginary are likely to be disturbed, leaving individual members of the audience to make what they can of the experience. Third, the film may deliberately deny the easy mental processing, as it breaks with the mechanisms of conventional representation and narrative development.

• Plate 7.4
Jungle Fever (Spike Lee, 1991). Spike Lee directs provocative films that produce a range of responses. Lee seems to be teasing out the ways in which different spectators within an audience go with the apparent messages of the film, adopting the 'preferred' response or whether they oppose that meaning – or whether they find themselves negotiating between these two positions in some way

Towards 'thicker' approaches to response

Another useful idea to emerge from semiotics is the distinction between four different kinds of response.

A '*preferred* reading' of a film is one in which the spectator takes up the intended meaning, finding it relatively easy to align with the messages and attitudes of those who have created the text. An '*oppositional* reading' is one that rejects this intended response. Generally, a 'preferred' response will be associated with the pleasure of reassurance that comes from the comfortable and familiar. Most often an oppositional response refuses some aspects of what the film has to offer. This can lead not simply to a lack of pleasure, but possibly to a different kind of pleasure – one that is based on using the film to reinforce the spectator's sense of independence. More crudely, there may be the temptation to associate a 'preferred' reading with the 'passive' spectator and an 'oppositional' reading with an active spectator.

Generally, the spectator attempts to work with those who have produced the work, best-guessing what they were intending, and sometimes compensating for perceived deficiencies. This *negotiated* response is the result of a particular kind of interaction between the spectator and the film, possibly motivated by a genuine sense that there is a mixture of appealing and unappealing elements. Perhaps a negotiated response arises from an over-compensation by the spectator in a situation in which the film is unappealing but where some justification is needed for having bought a ticket!

If we take early Spike Lee films such as *Do the Right Thing* (1989) or *Jungle Fever* (1990), we can identify strong differences in response which may be described in relation to 'preferred', 'oppositional' and 'negotiated' readings.

Lee's films are clear in the positions they adopt. Some films, especially those which use irony, are much more difficult to define in terms of their 'preferred' reading. Coppola's *Apocalypse Now* (1979) was intended by its director to be an anti-war movie. However, its spectacular battle sequences could be seen as celebrating war – if the irony is missed. Is 'I love the smell of napalm in the morning' spoken by a character called Kilgore really meant to be taken at face value? Films which are ambiguous or subtle or plain confusing are likely to lead to a fourth kind of response, the *aberrant*. While it may be said that there is no single 'right way' to respond to a film – an aberrant response is so far off track that it may simply be described as 'wrong'.

Looking at particular films and the range of responses possible allows a move away from theoretical generalisations about the spectator, towards an approach which takes account of diversity – both among different spectators within a single audience and between different audiences in different locations or in different historical moments. This 'thick' study is increasingly informing film studies from the broader discipline of Cultural Studies.

The words used here – recognition, alignment and allegiance – are taken from Murray Smith's *Engaging Characters – Fiction, Emotion and the Cinema* (Oxford: Clarendon Press, 1995).

In a three-part process we 'recognise' a character quite literally – that is, we know how to place him or her from experience as a particular type, maybe with a particular narrative function – and this is usually an automatic process.

Second we become 'aligned' with a particular character in that we experience some of the story through this figure. Film theory would say that this alignment is involuntary, as we are placed by the complex and powerful technical and textual mechanisms.

'Allegiance' describes how we choose to associate imaginatively with a character based on our assessment of their worth and appeal. As with alignment, film theory would tell us that allegiance is constructed by forces outside our control and that we

☐ CASE STUDY 2: PLEASURE AND EVALUATION – *PULP FICTION* (QUENTIN TARANTINO, 1994)

In this two-part case study we will consider the moment-by-moment response to a well-known sequence from Tarantino's *Pulp Fiction*. In the first part Vincent (John Travolta) picks up Mia (Uma Thurman) on the instructions of his gangster boss, Mia's husband, and takes her out to a diner. In the second part he has to cope with her overdosing, resorting to some rather shocking emergency treatment.

In exploring the first part of the sequence, the emphasis will be on responding to character and situation. In the second part, my emphasis will be on cinematic shock. In both parts, there is the opportunity to reflect on how we make meaning and obtain pleasure from the details of a film as we engage both intellectually and affectively in the act of spectatorship. What will also become clear is that central to response are judgements that we must make constantly – judgements that express favour or disfavour, and which may be deeply rooted in our personality, in our formation as a human being.

Thirty minutes into *Pulp Fiction* we have established that Vincent is a ruthless hitman but also a rather ordinary guy, appealing, even slightly vulnerable, in whom the audience can take an interest. (He is also John Travolta – a fact that significantly colours our sympathies.) Immediately before his arrival at Mia's house he has taken drugs. We have no significant knowledge of Mia, although our expectations based on the gangster genre (what cognitivists in particular refer to as the schema we rely upon to 'navigate' through fictional films) may lead us to expect a typical 'moll' or 'femme fatale'. So, in different ways, we are already working as spectators, either in placing and coming to terms with a character we have some knowledge of or in anticipating one we have yet to get to know.

Part one: Picking up Mia and Jack Rabbit Slim's

Vincent approaches the house of his employer Marsellus Wallace. The spectator follows him from behind, first in long and then in medium shot. As he takes a message from the door, there is a cut to close-up and we hear what we assume (from our familiarity with film conventions) is the voice of the person who has written the note, Mia. The voice invites Vincent to enter. There is a cut to the interior as Vincent feels his way gingerly – he's on unknown territory; he's high on heroin. The spectator is then presented with a shot of Mia from behind as she sits in front of four televisions relaying close-circuit surveillance pictures of Vincent. During the rest of the two-minute sequence, until Mia's fingers pick up the stylus, Dusty Springfield's version of 'Preacher Man' provides an accompaniment to what we see, generating a distinctive feel to the sequence and also opening up the affective dimension of our response. There is next a big close-up of Mia's lips at a microphone. Her call 'Vincent' startles him. All his movements seem to require additional thought. The spectator processes a range of information contained in the mise-en-scène: soundtrack, dialogue and performances. The information is controlled by the film's maker. To this extent the spectator is in a dependent situation. However, it is precisely because of this limited access to information that the spectator becomes active.

In the twenty-two shots before the couple leave the house, we do not see Mia's full face. The spectator's curiosity is increased, partly for this general reason, partly for the specific reason that she has been in control throughout. She is in a position of power because: (1) she is the boss's wife; (2) she controls camera and sound technology; and (3) Vincent's condition is not likely to produce assertiveness! Our alignment is increasingly with Mia, all the key point-of-view shots are hers, including ones where she prepares and then snorts cocaine. Our allegiance, however, is with Vincent. He is the object of the camera's look – which becomes the object of the female look. Our recognition is based on what we know of him from the first thirty minutes of the film. If an allegiance has formed, it is based in part on the attributes of the Vincent character as already established, in part on the attributes of the Travolta star persona. We quite literally do not recognise Mia yet (although it is almost certain that we will have an image already in our minds from publicity material in circulation outside the space of the cinema auditorium) and must move towards forming an allegiance based only on her behaviour, voice (and lips).

An evaluation of the two characters will, for experienced film spectators, depend less on judging them against a set of moral criteria from the real world than from those that are operative within the world of Tarantino's film. The recognition given by someone with no awareness of Travolta and with little ability or willingness to engage imaginatively within the terms of the film's genre and form may well be very different. In other words, we can anticipate the spectrum of 'preferred', 'negotiated' and 'oppositional' responses. Another way of discussing this is in terms of the competence of the individual spectator. This refers to the skills possessed by the spectator, most obviously their 'cine-literateness'. One could imagine a spectator who is either too inexperienced in

are manipulated into these allegiances. However, this seems to sell short the spectator's ability (indeed opportunity) to align with different characters within a fiction film, to 'try out' identities.

• **Plate 7.5**
Pulp Fiction (Quentin Tarantino, 1994). Uma Thurman in medium close-up

• **Plate 7.6**

Pulp Fiction (Tarantino, 1994). Travolta and Thurman in two-shot. The diner scene between Mia (Uma Thurman) and Vincent (John Travolta) is made up in large part of a classic shot-reverse-shot rhythm which 'sutures' (stitches) the spectator into the space between the characters producing intense involvement. Plate 7.5 is a typical Vincent point-of-view shot of Mia. However, Tarantino can surprise us as in the side-on two-shot (Plate 7.6). Suddenly the spectator is on the outside in much more of an observer role

• **Plate 7.7**

Pulp Fiction (Tarantino, 1994) Travolta and Thurman re-enter the apartment after Vincent returns Mia to her home. The spectator has been drawn into alignment and allegiance with these two characters. As a consequence of our involvement further anticipation and tension is created. After their very flirtatious night out, will Vincent risk taking things further with the boss's wife? Our privileged information on Mia's condition leads us to consider a different scenario. We care because we have been drawn into the situation by the calculated use of film techniques in the previous scenes. An unusual feature of *Pulp Fiction* is that our caring, our allegiance, is sometimes set up only to be wiped out by some turn in the plotting or structure of the film contemporary popular cinema or too unsophisticated to pick up Tarantino's tone and his attitude towards his characters.

There is a cut from the Wallace residence to a red Chevrolet. The camera pulls out and pans left to establish that Vincent and Mia have arrived in the diner car-park. We see Mia full face for the first time. Tarantino has used one minute seventeen seconds of screen time to establish the world of Jack Rabbit Slim's diner and get the two characters to their seats.

In looking at the sequence from Mia's 'What do you think?' to when she goes to 'powder her nose', we are presented with a very familiar shot–reverse shot dialogue sequence. As is typical of such a sequence, there are a large number of edits: seventy-five in five minutes thirty seconds of screen time with an average shot length of 4.4 seconds. The spectator is very much drawn into ('stitched' into) the space between the two characters. However, there is no obvious sense in which this involves spectator passivity. In terms of processing the visual and verbal information with which we are provided, very considerable 'active' processing is taking place. This is in part a consequence of the specific nature of this shot-reverse-shot dialogue: the characters are themselves objectifying the person opposite them, weighing them up. It is intended that the spectator becomes fascinated by the complex forces put into play: Mia's power over Vincent; Vincent's odd mix of coolness and vulnerability; the separate knowledge we have of the state of mind of each of them. This becomes particularly apparent during the 'comfortable silence' when the spectator is shifted from point-of-view shots to side-on 'observer' views of each character separately. The sequence, and its continuation after Mia returns from the ladies, requires the spectator to be both caught up within the exchange of looks and yet remain observant, responsive to the character information being revealed.

The spectator is very often both 'privileged' in possessing information which an on-screen character lacks and 'restricted' in that key information is withheld. Both are ways in which our interest is created and maintained. We may feel we have limited access to information at various points in this episode but in one important way we are in a position of superior knowledge: we know that *both* of them are high on drugs. Relative to Vincent, the spectator is 'privileged' on three separate occasions: before, during and after the trip to the diner we see Mia taking cocaine. Not only does this inform our understanding of and positioning with the Mia character, it also significantly shifts the spectator's expectations on what dramatic results are likely to follow. Having returned from Jack Rabbit Slim's, Vincent is observed in a bathroom of the Wallace home telling himself not to become sexually involved with Mia but to go home. This is a darkly comic situation, intensified by the Vincent/Travolta performance and made dramatically ironic by the knowledge given to the spectator that Mia is in the sitting-room with very different preoccupations.

There is then a sudden shift in tone after Vincent's bathroom monologue:

So you're gonna go out there, drink your drink, say 'Goodnight, I've had a lovely evening,' go home and jack off. And that's all you're gonna do.

(Tarantino 1994: 69)

We do not expect a close-up of Mia's face, suddenly deathly white, sick coming from her mouth, blood from her nose.

Part two: OD'ing

After Mia has overdosed, there is a two-minute ten-second sequence involving Vincent driving towards the house of Lance, trying all the while to communicate the desper-ateness of his situation on his mobile phone (while the Three Stooges play on Lance's TV). There then follows just under two minutes of frantic activity, much of it filmed using a handheld camera. (Tarantino's script offers the following description: 'everything in this scene is frantic, like a documentary in an emergency ward, with the big difference here being nobody knows what the fuck they're doing'.) There is then a quieter but hardly calmer one minute twenty-five seconds spent preparing for and giving the adrenaline shot to the heart that causes Mia's instant recovery.

The entire six minutes ten seconds before we see Mia, ghostly white, being driven home by Vincent is simultaneously suspenseful, shocking and comic. It is a rollercoaster ride of affect. In the act of spectatorship there are undoubtedly some responses which are involuntary just as there are in our responses to shocks and surprises outside the cinema. In this sequence, the most obvious illustration of this involuntary response is when Vincent, after a long pause, takes aim and plunges the syringe into Mia's heart. The shock of an entire audience is audible! However, for most of an action sequence, spectator involvement is far from involuntary. We need to *care* what happens – and this is directly related to the allegiances we have formed with the two central characters, specifically here as a result of our 'participation' in the previous long sequence in the diner. In considering some of the alternative ways of responding to the 'OD'ing sequence', it is first necessary to list some of the alternative ways of responding to the episode as a whole:

A   primarily at the level of character and the emotions generated by their circumstances – a very 'affective' response
B   primarily at the level of genre/form in which characters and situations are understood in relation to familiarity with the 'schemas' of different kinds of cinema – a 'cine-literate' if usually quite automatic response
C   primarily at the level of the film as 'construct' in which there is a strong awareness of the film's makers – an 'intellectual' response

These can be mapped against pleasure (1) and displeasure (2). In the abstract the alternatives look like this:

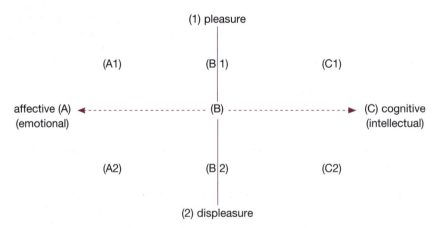

One way of interpreting these divergent responses is by reference to 'preferred', 'oppositional' and 'negotiated' readings.

In relation to the particular sequence, different responses may include the following:

A1   intense concern for Mia (that she recovers) and for Vincent (that he does not suffer the consequences of Mia's death)
B1   amusement at the mix of black comedy and farce
C1   delight in the way Tarantino mixes melodramatic intensity (1) with comedy and farce (2)

A2   distaste for Mia and Vincent, their behaviour and the values they represent

B2   disorientation at the mix of black comedy and farce in a situation involving a drug overdose, and possibly outrage as a consequence

C2   irritation at the 'smart' way Tarantino mixes melodramatic intensity (1) with comedy and farce (2)

Of course, these can be mixed: A1 could operate alongside B2 and C2, for example. And, of course, these are not the only responses.

The tone of *Pulp Fiction* needs to be carefully measured. It is most appropriately approached as a black comedy – arguably the 'preferred' response. So, for example, Mia is hardly treated with respect or care after her overdose. She is unceremoniously dropped on the grass outside Lance's house while Vincent begs for help for his *own* survival. 'That was fucking trippy' is the summary offered by Jody, Lance's girlfriend, at the end of the 'emergency', and, in relieving the tension of the situation, is meant to speak on behalf of the spectator. By contrast, one could well imagine a spectator who finds the world of the characters, the attitude towards drugs in particular, so disturbing as to 'oppose' the film. Some fairly hard 'negotiating' would be required by the spectator who is simultaneously delighted and shocked by the characters and events, and the manner in which they are depicted. We could also imagine a different kind of spectator, one who is committed to crime, violence and drugs. In seeing the film as endorsing criminal lifestyles, would they be closer to a 'preferred' reading?

A complementary way of trying to explain different responses is again in relation to the concept of spectator 'competence'. In some respects 'competence' and evaluative judgement are clearly separable from one another. For example, I may be perfectly capable of appreciating artistically and cinematically what Tarantino is doing – while despising it morally and ideologically!

In other respects, however, it is more difficult to disentangle competence from evaluative judgement. For example, the inexperienced spectator may not be able to engage with fictional characters in the kind of playful, imaginative way a film such as *Pulp Fiction* clearly requires. The film invites us to take pleasure in all of A1, B1 and C1 as identified above. It is only possible to do so if the spectator is simultaneously 'inside' and 'outside' the fiction, able to empathise with character, imagine the situation and yet still recognise its fictional nature. The active spectator, like the active reader of literature, is able to use fiction to expand their experience, become capable of new insights, more mature judgements – beyond the limitations of their actual experience in the 'real' world.

The most notorious example in *Pulp Fiction* of the mixing of tones is the accidental shooting of Marvin by Vincent as he sits in the back seat of a car – which then has to be meticulously cleaned!

In a variety of formulations this remains the key debate running through the whole of this chapter:

Films do have 'effects' (otherwise we would not bother to go and see them). These effects are the product of powerful communication processes. These effects will be handled by different spectators differently – on the basis of their 'formation' and their 'competence'. Most spectators, constituted as an audience, behave in more or less the same way because, other than in personal details, their social formations and their mental formations are very similar within a given community. However, film effects create 'affect'. The affective dimension of film response is much more personal, difficult to predict and to account for.

So, is the spectator 'passive' or 'active'; 'worked upon' or 'working'?

• **Plate 7.8**
Arrivée d'un train en gare à la Ciotat (The Lumière Brothers, 1895). Movement towards the camera thrilled and terrified the first cinema audiences. There are a number of examples of the sadistic delight taken in 'running down' the audience; for example, in R.W. Paul's *The Motorist* (c. 1902), a car 'hits' the spectator head-on

Imagining

While the last paragraph attempts to summarise much of what has been said thus far, there is the need to say a little more about the imagination. The 'passive' spectator is seen as one who somehow surrenders completely to the film experience in a form of imagining which can only be compared to some sort of infantile regression. The 'active' spectator is seen as one who is able to be simultaneously inside and outside the world of the film. A somewhat different way of expressing this is by considering two different kinds of imagining.

In *The Thread of Life* (1984), Richard Wollheim makes a fundamental distinction, corresponding to a big divide between two modes of imagination: '*central*' imagining and '*a-central*' imagining. A rough guide to the distinction may be found in linguistic clues. While central imagining is often expressed in the form 'I imagine ...', a-central imagining is expressed in the form 'I imagine that ...' (see Smith 1995: 76).

There are certain times when a spectator experiences central imagining, particularly when a film recreates a physical sensation such as falling or walking in a daze. The move towards ever more spectacular forms of visual and aural cinema – such as with the IMAX technology – we are being offered are forms of cinema providing more opportunities for central imagining: 'I imagine sitting on the rollercoaster ... I imagine the sensation of para-gliding over mountains ...'. What is being created is the effect recorded as early as 1896 of spectators imagining a train coming towards them in the Lumière Brothers' *Arrivée d'un train en gare à la Ciotat* and made fun of as early as 1901 in Paul's *The Countryman and the Cinematograph*.

Most of the time the spectator operates in the 'I imagine that ...' mode. *I imagine that it must be pretty scary to have a gangster's wife overdosing in front of you when you are responsible for her! I imagine that having to plunge a syringe into a woman's heart in order to bring her out of a coma must be, well, quite stressful and I can't imagine that I could ever do such a thing!*

In practice it seems wisest to approach spectatorship as a complex mixture of central and a-central imagining, especially in films that combine narrative with spectacle, using the full powers of digital technology.

Staying with *Pulp Fiction* a little longer, consider two further details in the 'Vincent Vega and Marcellus Wallace's Wife' episode which draw particular attention to the film as a construct rather than as a film trying to disguise its construction so that we may 'suspend our disbelief'.

The first is a brief moment when Vincent and Mia are still in the car having just arrived outside Jack Rabbit Slim's.

Vincent: Come on, Mia, let's go get a steak.

Mia: You can get a steak here, daddy-o. Don't be a …

Mia draws a square with her hands. Dotted lines appear on the screen forming a square. The lines disperse.

Vincent: After you, kitty-cat.

(Tarantino 1994: 51–2)

This is a particularly blatant admission to the spectator of the film as a construct. It is a characteristic particularly common in 'postmodern' art. The spectator is invited to take pleasure in a certain complicity with the filmmaker – this is a 'game' made possible due to the coming together of the 'playful' imaginations of both.

The second incident is when Mia demands that Vincent join her to dance the twist. The spectator is confronted with a fine distinction between John Travolta's role and his star identity as the dancing star of *Saturday Night Fever* (1977). The relationship between film and extra-film information is clearly being exploited here in order to acknowledge the star 'myth'. A model of spectatorship which presents the interaction between spectator and film as closed off from wider contexts of audience and culture seems particularly inadequate in explaining what happens at moments such as these. Again, this may be described as a characteristic moment of postmodern cinema, this time involving a 'play' between the role of a character within the fiction and the persona-image of a star who exists outside that fiction. Tarantino mobilises a knowledge and a set of associations held by the spectator, not to enhance the fiction but to intensify a sense of the spectator and director making meaning and generating affective response together.

Maybe we can talk of two tendencies in contemporary cinema. One is the ever more costly attempts to produce the spectacular realist illusion, especially in action movies – moving towards the kind of IMAX experience discussed above. The other is towards an ever more 'playful' kind of cinema – such as that exemplified by *Pulp Fiction*. Maybe we need different conceptions of spectatorship for each. 'I imagine …' for the first. I imagine that …' for the second. Whichever way one looks at things, the point holds: for the majority of films it seems wisest to approach spectatorship as a complex mixture of central and a-central imagining.

MIXING APPROACHES

There has not been space in this chapter to do more than outline a variety of approaches to the study of spectators, audiences and the responses they produce to films. The first section tried to outline some working assumptions about spectator and audience study which you may now wish to revisit and question or add to. The second section encouraged a study of Early Cinema in order to gain a better appreciation of the evolution of the spectator and audience. The remainder of the chapter has set out a 'menu' of issues and ideas that may provide you with the basis for further work in this broad area of film studies. What should be clear is that no particular theoretical or methodological approach has been particularly promoted. Rather, it is perhaps most useful to think in terms of an eclectic approach, taking whatever seems useful and productive.

FURTHER READING

Overview of shifts in film studies/film theory

To track the shift from 'subject–apparatus' approaches, through American pragmatism/cognitivism, to cultural studies perspectives, these three books provide a chronological map:

Bordwell, David and Carroll, Noel, *Post-theory: Reconstructing Film Studies*, University of Wisconsin, Madison, 1996.

Gledhill, Christine and Williams, Linda (eds), *Reinventing Film Studies*, Arnold, London, 2000.

Lapsley, R. and Westlake, M., *Film Theory: An Introduction*, Manchester University Press, Manchester, 1988.

Spectatorship and film

The following are accessible, with Judith Mayne's the most useful summary of the area:

Ellis, John, *Visible Fictions: Cinema, Television and Video*, Routledge & Kegan Paul, London, 1982; repr. 1992.

Mayne, Judith, *Cinema and Spectatorship*, Routledge, London, 1993.

Phillips, Patrick, *Understanding Film Texts*, British Film Institute, London, 2000.

Stacey, Jackie, *Star Gazing: Hollywood Cinema and Female Spectatorship*, Routledge, London, 1993.

Turner, Graeme, *Film as Social Practice*, Routledge, London, 1988; repr. Routledge, London, 1993.

The following are more demanding:

Shaviro, Steven, *The Cinematic Body*, University of Minnesota Press, Minneapolis, 1993.

Smith, Murray, *Engaging Characters – Fiction, Emotion and the Cinema*, Oxford University Press, Oxford, 1995.

The ideas of Deleuze, particularly important in the shift towards the study of affect, may be found in:

Colebroke, Claire, *Gilles Deleuze*, Routledge, London, 2002.

The following give a sense of a cognitive approach – though both are quite difficult:

Person, Per, *Understanding Cinema: A Psychological Theory of Moving Imagery*, (Cambridge University Press, Cambridge, 2003.

Plantinga, Carl and Smith, Greg, M (eds), *Passionate Views: Film Cognition and Emotion*, Johns Hopkins University Press, Baltimore, MD, 1999.

On Early Cinema and the development of spectatorship

The first two volumes of the University of California History of the American Cinema series are particularly useful:

Bowser, Eileen, *The Transformation of Cinema 1907–1915*, University of California, Berkeley, 1994.

Musser, Charles, *The Emergence of Cinema: The American Screen to 1907*, University of California, Berkeley, 1994.

The following are also very readable:

May, Larry, *Screening Out the Past: The Birth of Mass Culture and the Motion Picture Industry*, Chicago University Press, Chicago, IL, 1980.

Robinson, David, *From Peep Show to Palace – The Birth of American Film*, Columbia, New York, 1996.

The Silents Majority: On-line Journal of Silent Film; online at http://www.silentsmajority.com

Other books referred to in this chapter include:

Basinger, Jeanine, *A Woman's View: How Hollywood Spoke to Women 1930–1960*, Chatto & Windus, London, 1993.

Hill, Annette, *Shocking Entertainment*, John Libby, Luton, 1997.

Wollheim, Richard, *The Thread of Life*, Yale University Press, New Haven, CT, 1999.

Case studies

Birth of a Nation:

The script and a range of essays are contained in:

Lang, Robert (ed.), *D.W. Griffith – Birth of a Nation*, Rutgers University Press, New Brunswick, NJ, 1994.

An educational site with useful links may be found at: http://webster.edu/fatc/birth.html

Pulp Fiction:

Polan, Dana, *Pulp Fiction*, British Film Institute, London, 2001.

Tarantino, Quentin, *Pulp Fiction – The Screenplay*, Faber & Faber, London, 1994.

FURTHER VIEWING

Clearly all films raise issues in relation to spectatorship and response. The following twelve films, listed chronologically, are suggested for study purposes, as they raise particular questions or issues:

Early Cinema – Primitives and Pioneers (BFI compilation, DVD, 2005)
The Birth of a Nation (Griffith, US, 1915)
Man with a Movie Camera (Vertov, USSR, 1929)
Rear Window (Hitchcock, US, 1954)

Peeping Tom (Powell, UK, 1960)
Blow Up (Antonioni, UK/Italy, 1966)
Klute (Pakula, US, 1972)
Man Bites Dog (Belvaux and Bonzel, Belgium, 1992)
Natural Born Killers (Stone, US, 1994)
Festen (Vinterberg, Denmark, 1998)
Fight Club (Fincher, US, 1999)
Memento (Nolan, US, 2000)
Timecode (Figgis, US, 2000)
Hidden (Haneke, France, 2005)

RESOURCE CENTRES

http://www.geocities.com/Hollywood/7606/pulp.html
A site with most things a fan could wish for.

Part four

Other genre forms

Chapter 8

The documentary form

Paul Ward

■ The documentary form

INTRODUCTION

This chapter offers an overview of one of the most important and enduring forms of cinematic expression – the documentary. The past decade or so has seen something of a renaissance in terms of documentaries finding an audience in cinemas – big-screen successes such as *Hoop Dreams* (1994), *Touching the Void* (2003), *Murderball* (2005), *Etre et Avoir* (2002), *Supersize Me* (2004) and *Fahrenheit 9/11* (2004) attest to the potential popularity of documentary films. Likewise, there has been a major expansion in critical and scholarly attention to the form particularly concerning how documentary addresses its viewers, makes meaning and the relationship it has to fictional filmmaking. I use a more or less chronological framework to outline some of the key moments in documentary's history and examine the key figures involved. The most important questions addressed are:

■ How do we actually *recognise and define* documentary as a distinct form?
■ What *types* of documentary are there, and how do they overlap and interact with each other?
■ What relationship does documentary have with *fiction*, *drama* and *reconstruction*?
■ In what ways does the notion of *performance* problematise documentary as a form?

I begin by discussing some different definitions of documentary and then move on to examine the documentary status of early nonfictional films (**actualities**). These apparently simple recordings of a slice of life contrast with the more overtly constructed, narrativised films of Robert Flaherty, and the 'creative interpretation of actuality' as espoused by John Grierson, the person at the forefront of the British documentary movement of the 1930s. Central to understanding all of these films as 'documentary', however, is the relative level of intervention by the filmmakers: it has to be stressed at the outset that all documentary – despite its sometimes 'unmediated' appearance, its apparent capturing of life as it happens – is a construction. This needs to be kept in mind when discussing the work of the post-Second World War US filmmakers of the so-called **Direct Cinema** movement, as they are more guilty than most of professing a naïve belief in documentary's ability to simply 'capture' reality. The consideration of this movement is contextualised by comparing it with the more 'interventionist' **cinéma vérité** filmmaking, before moving on to consider the issues raised by overtly 'authored' or 'performative' documentaries. The questions raised by considering performance in documentary lead on to a consideration of drama and documentary, and the sometimes fractious relationship between these two modes.

Before proceeding, I will briefly comment on television. Although there are important debates to be had about the institution of television and the place of documentary within it, especially the role of **'reality TV'** and its impact on documentary as a form, these have been sidelined from the current discussion to a great extent. This is not to deny their importance, but rather to retain more of a focus on what are considered to be the most important issues for film documentary. Some discussion of television's influence is inevitable, but it cannot be the main focus of this chapter.

WHAT IS DOCUMENTARY?

There is much debate over what exactly defines a 'documentary', stemming from the overlaps and hybridity exhibited by different modes. We examine some of the more

actualitie
Derived from the French term *actualité* given to the short nonfictional films made in the early period (1895–1906 or so). These films often consisted simply of people going about their everyday business, or of particular events (sporting contests, visiting dignitaries).

Direct Cinema
A type of documentary filmmaking that emerged in the US in the 1950s, associated with Robert Drew, Richard Leacock, Don Pennebaker, Frederick Wiseman and the Maysles Brothers. Direct Cinema films often have a 'fly on the wall' aesthetic, linked to the strong belief that the filmmakers were mere observers of the reality they were filming. This apparent detachment and neutrality has been as controversial as it is influential.

cinéma vérité
The French term, literally meaning 'cinema truth', is sometimes confused with a US kind of filmmaking which is actually closer to **Direct Cinema**. The confusion stems from the common 'immediacy' that the films have – filming people with handheld cameras and portable sound recording equipment – but cinema verité properly has a foundation of interaction between filmmaker and filmed, rather than the detachment seen in Direct Cinema films. Nevertheless, it is common to see a range of different films referred to as 'cinema verité' (or sometimes just 'verité'), and it is important to distinguish between them.

reality TV
A relatively recent development in television, a form of highly structured programme using observational material of ordinary people. The programmes have a 'documentary' basis in the sense that they use actuality footage, but they are often shaped to fit specific formats (neighbours from hell, the rise of a successful business, a game show involving weekly tasks). In this respect, reality TV is a good example of how documentary can be taken and recontextualised by contemporary television to suit its schedules.

rhetorical
Designed to persuade. Rhetorical strategies in documentary are those that relate to the film's or programme's argument. This may be explicit (e.g. a voiceover or presenter actually stating what the argued points are), or it may be less immediately obvious (e.g. a filmmaker might cut from an image of a political leader to a library shot of a firing squad; this could be seen as an argument against the politician).

commonly accepted modes or subtypes of documentary as a form, but first of all we need a working definition of the term 'documentary'. Documentary is, broadly speaking, a subcategory of nonfiction – it is a form that tells stories, makes assertions or observations about the real historical world, rather than the fabricated worlds of fiction. It is often believed that a documentary must use literal 'actuality' footage – images and sounds recorded as they happened – and it is certainly the case that a great many documentaries do rest on this foundation of things observed and recorded. However, it is entirely possible for a text to be considered a documentary, even if it consists predominantly of reconstructed or re-enacted scenes. (Of course, those documentaries that *do* function in this way have been labelled with some other name – e.g. drama–documentary – something we return to below.) Documentary, in this sense, is a very broad church; the key defining factor is that the film or programme in question makes assertions about the real world, and provides audio-visual evidence to back up such assertions. This 'assertive' stance and 'evidential' basis need not necessarily mean that documentaries are explicitly laid out as 'arguments' (as we shall see, this is the preserve of a specific kind of documentary, the expository). Documentaries can and do use a variety of techniques as fits their aims and purpose – explicit argument, more allusive or associative connections between things, dramatic reconstruction, and different levels of filmmaker 'intervention' in the reality they are interpreting.

The most useful delineation of documentary modes has been provided by Bill Nichols (2001). He identifies six modes 'that function something like sub-genres of the documentary film genre itself: poetic, expository, participatory, observational, reflexive, performative' (2001: 99). We briefly consider each of these in turn. The poetic mode will seem more allusive and use 'associative' editing to capture a mood or tone rather than make an explicit argument about a subject. The so-called 'city symphony' films, such as Walter Ruttmann's *Berlin: Symphony of a Great City* (1927), Alberto Cavalcanti's surrealist portrait of Paris, *Rien que les heures* (1926) or Ron Fricke's epic environmental visual poem *Baraka* (1992) may all be seen as 'poetic' documentaries – they evoke a mood rather than stating or asserting things directly. Expository documentaries on the other hand do use explicitly **rhetorical** techniques in order to make points about aspects of actuality. The expository mode often uses voiceover and has a relatively straightforward

• **Plate 8.1**
Nanook of the North
(Robert Flaherty, 1922).
The film presents
man's struggles with
nature in a narrativised
documentary format

'show and tell' structure to guide the viewer through the material. Many television documentaries follow this template, where the voiceover provides the connection, the logic, between what might be disparate shots. Such films and programmes that are labelled 'expository' are often didactic in nature – for example, the *Why We Fight* (1943–45) series of films about the Second World War 'tell the story' of the War (and make a case for US involvement) using voiceover and other expository techniques such as maps and diagrams. Such direct address may be contrasted with the observational mode, where the documentary appears to take a detached and thereby 'neutral' (or 'objective') stance towards its subject matter – overtly 'interpretive' techniques such as editorialising voiceover or music (which are common in other modes of documentary) are eschewed in favour of an apparent capturing of reality as it unfolds. The films of Frederick Wiseman are excellent examples of this mode in that Wiseman presents his material in a detached, observational style with no voiceover, thereby seeming to allow viewers to make up their own mind. The fact that Wiseman's subject matter is generally US institutions – for example, education in *High School* (1968), the military in *Basic Training* (1971) – gives this seeming detachment a cumulative power; rather than offering an obviously didactic viewpoint on what he is representing, Wiseman allows the people and situations shown to apparently 'speak for themselves'. However, it is possible to discern a critical 'voice' running through Wiseman's films; in his editing and shot decisions we can discern that even the seemingly detached observational mode involves choices, juxtapositions and contrasts. The participatory (sometimes referred to as the 'interactive') is a documentary mode where the filmmaker does *not* remain aloof from the subject matter, but actively engages with it – by openly participating or interacting with the people and institutions on show. Michael Moore's first film for the cinema, *Roger and Me* (1989), exhibits many participatory characteristics: Moore is directly implicated in the subject matter (he is of course the 'me' of the title) and arguably many scenes would not unfold in the way they do without his specific participation. This results in a documentary form which is very far removed from the detached or straightforwardly didactic. The reflexive mode is a mode that attempts to offer a commentary on the means of representation itself. A reflexive documentary is a film which uses techniques that encourage the viewer to question the very idea of 'documentary' as a category or mode; this questioning can also lead to a critique of larger categories such as cinematic realism. For instance, in Errol Morris's *The Thin Blue Line* (1988), the story of a miscarriage of justice, the highly stylised reconstructions and repetitions of scenes from different viewpoints are reflexive strategies that Morris uses to encourage the viewer to think about relative levels of 'truth' and self-deception. Finally, the performative is a mode that raises all sorts of questions about filmmaker and subject 'performance' – not simply in the commonsense meaning of 'performing' in front of the camera (which is often referred to in the negative, as if it detracts from the essential truth of what is going on), but the notion of the filmmaker and their subjects *actively creating* the documentary by performing certain social actions. As Stella Bruzzi has noted, there are some documentaries that are 'given meaning by the interaction between performance and reality' (2000: 154); far from berating some documentaries for containing self-conscious performances, it follows here that such performances are actually *central* to this specific mode of documentary filmmaking. The films of Nick Broomfield are central to the performative mode, and are discussed below.

The most important thing to note about this typology of different modes is that it is constantly evolving. In addition, these modes are not mutually exclusive, and they can and do overlap across the history of documentary as a form, and co-exist, sometimes within the same documentary. It is entirely possible for a single documentary to use expository, poetic and observational techniques as suits its purpose at any one time. It is also important to remember that, despite some overviews of documentary (including this one) taking a roughly chronological form, this way of constructing history is precisely that – a construction. The vibrancy of documentary as a type of filmmaking resides in the ways that practitioners and audiences engage with different films about the real world of actuality.

'PROTO-DOCUMENTARY' – THE CASE OF EARLY FILM ACTUALITIES

For further discussion of early British cinema see pp. 305–12.

Arguably, the first 'documentaries' were the actualities of the first filmmakers, such as the Lumière Brothers in France or Sagar Mitchell and James Kenyon in the UK. The camera was used much like a stills camera would have been, to mechanically capture a slice of reality. Such films are of intrinsic interest, not just for film historians but for historians in general: they document the specificities of a particular milieu. There is however a paradox of sorts here, in the sense that the apparently simple and straightforward representing of actuality was played up as a 'novelty' – come and see the moving pictures! – and even the simplest of these films can show some evidence of directorial intervention. As Bill Nichols points out, it is therefore problematic in one sense to 'trace back' the beginnings of documentary film to its 'mythic origin' in early cinema (2001: 82–7). We need to be careful not to construct a simple 'lineage' from early nonfictional actualities to the later more complexly structured documentaries, as such a 'linear' view of history tends to ignore other potential avenues (e.g. the use of film technology for scientific rather than cinematic purposes). Having said this, a lot can be learned from examining how these proto-documentaries are similar to or differ from other forms of nonfictional output.

Despite the fact that these short actualities may be seen as what Noel Carroll (2003: 231) calls 'paradigmatic documentaries' – i.e. they exist as a model or prototypical example of the form – their original exhibition context was one of novelty and wonderment. Dai Vaughan notes that the soon-to-be-famous filmmaker Georges Melies, who was present at the first ever Lumière screening in Paris in 1895, drew specific attention to details like rustling leaves in the background of one film (Vaughan 1999: 4–5). In other words, despite the tendency for future commentators to emphasise the naivety of those first viewers – the oft-repeated tale of people flinching as the train approached in *L'arrivee d'un train en gare de la Ciotat* (1895) – they were fascinated by the ability of the cinema to accurately render (or 'document') an appearance of reality. It is also worth remembering that, although we can now look back on these early cinema films with a sense of their quaintness, their raw and unpolished appearance as 'mere recordings' of a slice of actuality, in their original exhibition context they would doubtless have been accompanied by some contextualising remarks from the exhibitor/showman; the equivalent of a voiceover in a 'proper' modern-day documentary. The point here is not to suggest that these early actualities are the same kind of documentary as later and clearly more complex films, but to draw attention to the fact that seeing them just as simplistic recordings is equally inaccurate.

☐ CASE STUDY 1: THE FILMS OF MITCHELL AND KENYON

Mitchell and Kenyon, a pair of entrepreneurs from Blackburn, certainly used the novelty factor of capturing real people and events as the selling point for their films, to increase interest. They filmed everyday events (or **'topicals'**) in and around Lancashire and Yorkshire during the 1897 to 1910 period and the 'hook' for getting people to come and see their films was that the viewer might well see themselves on the screen. Their company mottos – 'Local films' and 'We take them and make them' – attest to their desire to capture the specificities of local life, but do so in a way that could be sold to the subjects of the films. As Dan Cruickshank, the presenter of the BBC television series *The Lost World of Mitchell and Kenyon* (2004) says, 'they weren't meant to be documentary records of the time but were made for purely commercial reasons'. He later quotes the tagline of one of the posters of the time advertising such films: 'Nothing is so great a draw as a local subject.'

These original Mitchell and Kenyon films may be termed 'proto-documentaries' or at the very least be referred to as nonfictional films. On the face of it, the films are completely observational in the sense that the camera appears to merely observe events unfold and there is no 'shaping' of the material in the ways we might expect of a 'proper' documentary. To say that there is no shaping at all would be inaccurate, though, as all of these early nonfictional films show some signs of 'authorial' shaping. There is even one point in the series *The Lost World of Mitchell and Kenyon* when we see Kenyon caught on camera actively directing a crowd of workers by hurrying them along a pathway. Even the most naturalistic slice of life required some directing, in the same way as a 'natural' photographic portrait required some posing. Another good example is the scene of some miners, many of them with faces and clothes blackened with coal dust, emerging from work in *Pendlebury Colliery* (1901). As the scene progresses – with the by-then conventional glancing into the camera by many of the passers-by – a black miner wanders past having a good-natured jostle with another miner. The black miner, in pristine white shirt-sleeves, stands out like the proverbial sore thumb. It is hard not to discern some level of directorial shaping of the material here; indeed, Cruickshank speculates that the black man may have been a fairground worker planted in the film, precisely to draw out such visual contrasts.

One fascinating thing about these short actualities is their *changing status*: they have moved from being simple, short actualities, with arguably no pretence at 'documentary' status, to having sociological and historical importance. The way the original films have been mounted and recontextualised within the three-part series *The Lost World of Mitchell and Kenyon* is interesting because the original footage, shot for specific reasons, takes on new meanings and resonances; in short, it takes on a documentary status as opposed to arguably being a 'mere' document. For instance, the moment from *Pendlebury Colliery* is part of a wider commentary in the television series, examining attitudes to black people in Edwardian Britain.

topicals
The name given to nonfictional 'news' items in the early period. A royal visit, the opening of a factory, a sports event – anything that could be of interest to a local audience – could be labelled 'a topical'. As documentary developed as a form, topicals were subsumed into newsreels and other forms of film reporting.

This film may be viewed online at http://www.movinghistory.ac.uk/archives/bn/films/bn7colliery.html.

The reason he speculates about a 'fairground worker' is that the fair would have been one of the original exhibition sites for Mitchell and Kenyon's films, as there were no cinemas at this point. Indeed, a number of the Mitchell and Kenyon actuality films were commissioned by fairground operators – see http://www.bfi.org.uk/features/mk/about.html

• **Plate 8.2**
Pendlebury Colliery (Sagar Mitchell and James Kenyon, c. 1901). The capturing of everyday 'actuality' footage apparently as it happened – though with some signs of mischievous directorial shaping in the positioning of certain characters

Now, of course, the majority of people who view these films do so in the recontex-tualised format of the documentary series about the films. In this respect, the 'natural material' of the original films is 'creatively interpreted' by the makers of the documentary series. For example, there is one sequence where a man named Mick Judge views a video copy of one of the Mitchell and Kenyon films, a rugby game from 1901 where one of the players was Judge's great-grandfather. As he views the footage on his home television set, his own son playing in the background, Judge marvels at being able to see someone from all those years before running around, flesh and blood. The ordinariness, the everydayness is accentuated here, as Judge points out that his relative was not a famous person – underlining the ways in which historical traces of things are usually biased in favour of certain types of people. What is important here though is the fact that the original Mitchell and Kenyon film is placed in a context, a 'frame' that draws out some of the peculiarities of it as a piece of film, and this is done in such a way as to emphasise the contrasts with the modern day. Certain assertions are made by virtue of the clever juxtaposition of historical 'moments'.

It is this 'ethnographic' or 'anthropological' dimension to the footage that is interesting in terms of its status as documentary film. In another sequence, Cruickshank speaks in voiceover while we see the original Mitchell and Kenyon film of Nottingham town centre *circa* 1901. This footage is cross-cut with present-day footage of the same places; the viewer is actively encouraged to see what has changed in the intervening century. What was originally shot as something that was meant to be little more than an ephemeral crowd pleaser, of little or no interest to anyone but those who actually appear in it, has become an important social document. Again, though, it is in the creative juxtaposition of this footage with something else (the modern-day footage) that specific points are made.

THE SHIFT TO NARRATIVE STRUCTURE IN DOCUMENTARY

Despite their historical importance and the possibility that they can be read as 'proto-documentaries', however, such early film actualities lack the decisive creative shaping that distinguishes documentary from other forms of nonfictional filmmaking. It is in the dramatic narrative structures imposed on real material by a filmmaker such as Robert Flaherty (1884–1951) that we first see the move to a more immediately recognisable type of documentary form. Flaherty's work is often held up to be among the most influential of the early documentary filmmakers. Apart from anything else, films such as *Nanook of the North* (1922), *Moana* (1926) and *Man of Aran* (1934) were a huge influence on John Grierson, who went on to become an important figure in the British documentary movement of the 1930s and 1940s (and, later, founded the National Film Board of Canada). As with many of the most influential documentary filmmakers, Flaherty's work is both important and controversial for its methods.

Flaherty was not interested in merely recording reality – instead, his films were dramatically structured, with clear narrative goals and expectations set up for the viewer. Richard Meran Barsam points out that 'it would be misleading to think of Flaherty as the originator of the documentary film as we know it: the socio-political didactic film ... [instead, his filmmaking] poetically celebrates man and his life; his films are humanistic statements, not political ones' (1974: 124). Time and again in his films, Flaherty focuses on real people in real situations, attempting to draw out some of the mythic resonance of certain lifestyles. This approach has not gone uncriticised however – there are issues relating to Flaherty's methods and the romanticising of his subject matter that raise problems for much contemporary documentary practice.

In *Nanook of the North* (1922), for example, Flaherty immersed himself in the lifestyles of the Inuit people, spending a year living with them. Such a method perhaps implies a **participant observation** approach, where the filmmaker observes unobtrusively and creates as objective a record as possible. However, when it came to the construction of the documentary, Flaherty was not averse to fabricating events. It is often remarked that he constructed a special open-sided igloo to allow filming of interior shots; even more contentious is his filming of Nanook hunting with traditional harpoon rather than the more modern weapons that he actually used. Flaherty's *Moana* (1926) also included scenes of the Polynesian natives performing for the camera rituals they had long-since stopped doing in everyday life.

Such methods are in fact central and arguably unavoidable techniques in documentary production, and most certainly were in the period where filming on location, with handheld cameras and portable sound recording (things that were to become common-place in the post-Second World War era) was simply not possible. However, the 'justifiable' use of reconstruction has remained as controversial as it is important in the intervening years since Flaherty, and is something that links into debates about drama and re-enactment, discussed below. It also raises the spectre of **ethics**: is it *ever* admissible for a documentary filmmaker to fabricate things in order to achieve the 'higher' aim of revealing the 'inner truth' of the subject matter? Flaherty certainly thought so, as he consistently (re-)constructed things before the camera in order to reach what he saw as the essence of what he was portraying. As Jay Ruby points out, for instance, '"family members" in *Nanook of the North*, *Man of Aran* and *Louisiana Story* (1948) are not related to each other; they were selected because they suited Flaherty's conception of what makes a good Eskimo, Irish or Cajun family' (2005: 215).

JOHN GRIERSON AND THE BRITISH DOCUMENTARY MOVEMENT

As noted above, Flaherty's work was a direct influence on John Grierson. Grierson was born in Scotland in 1898 and went on to have a profound influence on the documentary form, especially those films produced at the Empire Marketing Board and General Post Office in Britain in the 1930s and 1940s. Although Grierson himself directed only two films (1929's *Drifters* and 1934's *Granton Trawler*) he is often credited with bringing together a diverse set of filmmakers to work under the aegis of these governmental organisations as well as industry sponsors. Films such as *Coal Face* (1935), *Night Mail* (1936), *Housing Problems* (1935), *Spare Time* (1939) and *Song of Ceylon* (1934) used a variety of techniques and modes of address to inform and educate. Grierson's view, influenced

participant observation
A social science methodology where researchers immerse themselves in the social context/group they are studying, often for years at a time. In documentary terms, such an approach arguably leads to more 'natural' responses, as the subjects have become used to the filmmakers and cameras.

ethics
Concerning morality, or codes of conduct. There is a strong ethical discourse running though the history of documentary, and debates to be had about the ethical dimension of things like reconstruction, filming people without their consent, informing the viewer of the extent of filmmaker intervention, and so on.

• **Plate 8.3**
Housing Problems
(Edgar Anstey and Arthur Elton, 1935).
Housing Problems
offers insights into a social problem by using real people to directly address the audience – an innovation for the time

by the mass media theories of Walter Lippmann (whose ideas Grierson encountered when he spent some time in the US in the mid-1920s), saw cinema as a potential tool for informing and educating the masses. At the same time, however, Grierson saw filmmaking as an art form – documentary filmmaking especially so. This perhaps explains the sometimes disconcerting combination of techniques within some of these British films. *Coal Face* is at times the expository documentary *par excellence*, with a robotically informative voiceover furnishing the viewer with facts about the coal industry, accompanied by maps and other graphic devices. At other times, though, it is more overtly 'poetic' in its evocation of the spaces, textures and sounds of the industry and the people who work within it. (These people remain little more than ciphers, however.) *Housing Problems*, on the other hand, appears more straightforward in its exposition of slum dwellings, the people who live in them, and the houses' clearance to make way for new homes. The film, directed by Arthur Elton and Edgar Anstey (with some involvement from Ruby Grierson, John's sister – see Macdonald and Cousins 1996: 122) nevertheless also uses what was for the time extremely unusual location shooting of interviews with ordinary people. The film was sponsored by the Gas, Light and Coke Company (i.e. the gas industry), who also funded *Enough to Eat?* (1936), a film about malnutrition in Britain. The potentially radical edge that these films had is somewhat reduced when they are viewed in a wider context, however. Rather than openly questioning the social structures that *caused* slums and unequal food distribution, we instead see the gas industry perhaps unsurprisingly positioned as the height of progress in slum clearance and construction of new dwellings, complete with gas supply. The causes of the problems are not really examined, and the real people involved here are arguably mere fodder for what Brian Winston labels 'the tradition of the victim in Griersonian documentary' (1988: 269–87).

There were, then, strong links between the British documentary filmmakers of this period and industry sponsors or government departments, with the consequence that there is a strand of discourse about documentary that sees it as mere propaganda (though that term should not be seen as simply pejorative; Grierson certainly saw propaganda as potentially positive and educative). This assumption that documentary must rely on sponsorship or governmental support is pervasive; as already noted, Grierson saw the role of documentary as a kind of mass educational tool, and saw the term documentary as one that, while not ideal – he is on the record calling it 'a clumsy description' (1966: 145) – at least had its uses. Alberto Cavalcanti, one of Grierson's colleagues in the 1930s, did not like the term 'documentary' as a description for the kinds of films he made. Grierson's response, Cavalcanti recalled, was: 'I have to deal with the Government, and the word "documentary" impresses them as something serious' (quoted in MacDonald and Cousins 1996: 117). We can also see in a film like *Housing Problems* that the social problem is constructed as something that can be easily 'answered' or remedied by the actions of the film's sponsor.

As already noted, a key conceptual distinction that needs to be made is that between films which simply record, with little or no discernible authorial shaping, and those which intervene, dramatise and editorialise in some way. Such a distinction is one that Grierson was at pains to make when he suggested that there were 'lower categories' of nonfiction film, such as 'lecture' films, which lacked the organisation that characterised documentary proper (1966: 145–6). Grierson famously coined the phrase 'the creative interpretation of actuality' (1932: 8) to emphasise that documentary films should not simply record material. Despite the fact that documentary cinema is 'an art based on photographs, in which one factor is always, or nearly always, a thing observed' (1966: 199), to qualify as a documentary there has to be *more* than mere observation. For Grierson, although documentaries will in all likelihood be based on recorded footage (or 'natural material' as he terms it (1966: 145)), it is in the *creative interventions* made by the filmmaker (specific use of sound, certain edited juxtapositions) that the 'documentariness' resides. The distinction, as Grierson points out, is between 'a method which describes only the surface values of a subject, and a method which more explosively reveals the reality of it' (ibid.: 148). This echoes the point made earlier about Flaherty, who fabricated events (albeit ones that would be perceived as 'probable' or likely to have actually happened) in order to represent what he saw as the essential truth. Grierson's point is similar: it is through creative juxtaposition and interpretation, rather than simply 'capturing' that any truth or meaning will emerge. It is via the filmmaker's *shaping* of the natural material, through whatever means, that the 'reality' of the subject matter is communicated.

However, one of the thorniest issues to trouble documentary since its inception has been the *extent* to which events are shaped or directed by the filmmaker (and/or the participants themselves – something that will be discussed in some detail below). A simplistic, but abiding, school of thought is that documentary footage can *only* have a claim on the real if it is somehow captured 'unawares'. As we shall see, this was never true and is certainly not true now. All documentaries rest on a shaping or creative treatment of the material, though that material may have a direct indexical link to a pro-filmic reality. We are now going to move on to examine some of the post-Second World War developments in documentary – developments that incorporate debates about the objectivity and neutrality of the filmmakers, and the extent to which they creatively interpret their material.

POST-WAR DEVELOPMENTS IN OBSERVATIONAL DOCUMENTARY

Alongside the influential Griersonian idea of documentary and the more narrative-driven films of Flaherty, the most dominant form, especially in the post-Second World War era, has been the observational documentary. This arguably covers a number of styles, but it is easy to see why the notion of a more or less detached observationalism might pervade ideas about what constitutes documentary. There is a sense that it distils all the ideas about the camera (and film) as a recording device that can capture an unmediated slice of actuality, with attendant beliefs in accuracy, objectivity and impartiality. The fact that there are distinct problems with an overly naive belief in the ability of the camera to objectively record things that happen before it has made the various types of obser-vational film and their proponents hugely controversial. The immediacy and apparently unvarnished nature of the images and sounds produced in such documentaries are emphasised by the technological developments of the era – more portable cameras and (crucially) sound-recording equipment made filming on location more feasible, without recourse to reconstructing scenes or dubbing the sound in post-production.

It is important to make a distinction between different types of filmmaking practice that are often lumped together and referred to as 'cinema verité' (or sometimes just 'verité' or 'fly on the wall'). The original cinema vérité practitioners were the French anthropologist Jean Rouch and sociologist Edgar Morin. Their approach was not one of simple, detached observation, but involved much more interaction between filmmaker and subject. In this respect, a cinema vérité film like Rouch and Morin's *Chronicle of a Summer* (1960) would come under Nichols's category of the 'participatory' rather than 'observational'. The adaptation of the notion of cinema vérité in the US context saw it transformed into so-called 'Direct Cinema', as exemplified by the work of filmmakers such as Richard Leacock, Robert Drew (founder of Drew Associates) and Don Pennebaker. Films such as Leacock's *Primary* (1960), on the campaign trail with John F. Kennedy and Hubert Humphrey, and Pennebaker's *Don't Look Back* (1967), a behind-the-scenes look at Bob Dylan on tour, had an unobtrusive style far removed from that of Rouch and Morin. The direct cinema practitioners believed that the presence of the camera and filmmakers did not have an impact on the subjects – or not much of one, at least. As Leacock said in an interview when asked about the differences between him and his colleagues and Rouch:

We don't think that [the filmmaker's presence] affects people very much, at least I don't. Let me add that, of course, it affects them in Jean Rouch's films, since the only thing that's happening to them is the fact that they're being filmed. There's nothing else to think about. How can they ever forget it?

(quoted in MacDonald and Cousins 1996: 256)

This comment touches on one of the abiding distinctions between different types of documentary – the relative 'obviousness' of the filmmaker's presence and the extent to which they are acknowledged by their subjects. It was noted earlier how in Frederick Wiseman's films, even though the viewer might discern some level of authorial 'voice' or critique stemming from Wiseman's choice of shots and how they are combined, what really comes across is that the subjects of his films do tend to carry on with their business *as if* the camera is not present. This is the key signifier of direct cinema and what marks it out as very different from cinéma vérité.

As with all these categories, though, there are grey areas, overlaps and hybrids – this is what keeps documentary developing as a field. Even with filmmakers such as the Maysles Brothers, often described as proponents of Direct Cinema, we can discern in their work some tensions between different documentary modes, and it is worth exploring these tensions, since they help us to understand the documentary field more fully. The Maysles Brothers, Albert and David, began working with Drew Associates in the late 1950s but formed their own production company in the mid-1960s. They directed some of the most memorable documentaries produced in the US in the 1960s and 1970s, including *Salesman* (1969), which follows a travelling Bible salesman, *Gimme Shelter* (1970), which documents the notorious Rolling Stones concert at Altamont in 1969, and *Grey Gardens* (1975). We are going to focus on the last of these films, as it is an interesting example of what happens when different documentary modes meet.

☐ CASE STUDY 2: *GREY GARDENS* (MAYSLES BROTHERS, 1975)

Grey Gardens is available on DVD from the Criterion Collection. It is also a film that has attracted a cult following – see the 'fan site and homage' at: http://www.greygardens.com/.

Grey Gardens is a very famous 'fly-on-the-wall' documentary about Edith Beale and Edie Beale, Jackie Kennedy's aunt and cousin, who live in the East Hampton mansion of the title. Over the years, their eccentricities and obsessions have led to the house becoming more and more dilapidated, and the film appears to revel in their oddness and squalor. The film begins in a seemingly 'random' fashion, a classic signifier of fly-on-the-wall transparency: over shots of the ramshackle house, and a montage of Hampton locations, two female voices argue about a cat. The title 'Grey Gardens' appears over a shot of the house itself, a shot which then transforms into a newspaper image, leading to an expository/scene-setting sequence where the backstory to the documentary is told via newspaper clippings. We learn that the two women have been told to clean up the mansion or face eviction, and that they resent such interference in their lives. In one shot of a clipping, the Maysles themselves are mentioned, along with the fact that they are making a film about the women.

Despite the fact that the Maysles are often celebrated as one of the main proponents of US Direct Cinema, this film is a far cry from simple, unobtrusive observation. The filmmakers are implicated throughout. After the opening scene-setting, we hear Edie's voice screech 'It's the Maysles!!' and there is a cut to a photograph of the two brothers with camera and sound equipment. We then see Edie chatting to the off-screen filmmakers. She says: 'What do you wanna do now? Where do you wanna go? Upstairs? You wanna go up and photograph it from the top porch?' Later still, there is one very odd sequence where Edie is standing on the porch, in long shot, adjusting her head-dress. Not speaking at this point, she almost seems to be waiting for a signal. Off-screen, Albert Maysles says 'Dressed for battle, Edie?!', and she then starts walking off the

• **Plate 8.4**
Grey Gardens (Maysles Brothers, 1975). A compelling combination of fly-on-the-wall observation and more overt 'participatory' techniques by the Maysles, where they directly interact with the subjects of their film

porch, talking as she goes. She sashays up to a medium close-up and talks straight into the camera. There is a sense here that the creative shaping, the directing of events for the camera, is being emphasised; the sequence plays out as if an off-screen voice had shouted 'Action!', and Edie's behaviour echoes that of the Gloria Swanson character in *Sunset Boulevard* (Billy Wilder, 1950), melodramatically approaching the camera saying, 'I'm ready for my close up now, Mr De Mille.'

In other words, far from being a straightforwardly observational record of these two eccentric women, this is a cleverly structured (some might say highly manipulative and ethically suspect) <u>film that engages with notions of performance and (self-)represen-tation.</u> The two women (especially Edie) interact with the Maysles, playing up to the cameras. In one scene they pore over old photographs – some of which are shown to the audience via rostrum camera shots – and reminisce about the old times. As the camera lingers in close-up on some of the photographs, there is a nice disjunction between the images and the bickering women on the soundtrack. At one point they fight over one photograph, Edie grabbing for it and tearing it while shouting, 'I wanna show it to Al!'

Such self-conscious performing for the cameras, in the context of a kind of observational filmmaking, is very interesting. In many ways one can see *Grey Gardens* as a precursor to contemporary 'reality TV' material, where people invite the cameras into their lives and appear to be playing to the filmmakers and the audience. One of the criticisms of a great deal of reality TV output is that the participants are 'not being themselves' or are in some way exaggerating certain characteristics to make the film or programme more entertaining. In the case of *Grey Gardens*, one gets the impression that these women are actually like this (though Edie certainly appears to do some things that she would not otherwise do, for the benefit of the camera). However, it is the case that the film resembles more recent reality TV output in some respects (though it does not have a voiceover, which is standard-issue for most reality TV formats). *Grey Gardens* is therefore better understood not as a simple exercise in fly on the wall observational filmmaking, but as a film where the filmmakers are interacting with their subject matter; where *both* filmmakers *and* subjects are revelling in their respective performances.

THE MOVE TO PERFORMATIVE AND REFLEXIVE DOCUMENTARY

There are, then, different degrees to which the subjects of a documentary might be perceived to be performing for the cameras. From the very first actualities, through apparently purely observational films such as *Primary*, to more recent films that foreground the notion of a self-conscious performance, the playing out of social roles has always been central to the documentary project. Likewise, there have been degrees of self-consciousness or recognition by the filmmakers of the role they are performing in the construction of a documentary. The categories of reflexive and performative documentary filmmaking are arguably where the most interesting current work is being produced. The reflexive refers to those documentaries where the actual process of representation and construction is somehow foregrounded. The performative may be seen as a subcategory of the 'reflexive'. Due to the fact that documentaries will always be about the real world, real people and real issues, the notion of performance within them is potentially radical and reflexive, as it seems opposed to notions of authenticity and unvarnished reality. As Stella Bruzzi has pointed out though, it is important to see this in context: there have always been films of this kind, documentaries that foreground those elements of construction (and reflexivity) and draw attention to the varying types of performance going on within them. As she says about the work of Nick Broomfield, he is 'acting out a documentary' (2000: 155). His very presence suggests that the objective, detached observer is a myth and his 'performance' as 'documentarist' implicitly (and sometimes explicitly) draws attention to the performances of his subjects. For example, his interventions in his two films about convicted killer Aileen Wuornos (*Aileen Wuornos: The Selling of a Serial Killer* (1992) and *Aileen: Life and Death of a Serial Killer* (2003)) consistently and self-consciously draw attention to his role as filmmaker and mediator of meaning. This means, ultimately, that his films are as much about him and the process of image-making as they are about Wuornos; this, in fact, works very well, as there is a sense that the 'truth' behind the Wuornos story was never going to be definitively told, and the Broomfield films end up being a savage indictment of the media circus and a legal system gone mad (see Ward 2005: 40–8). Broomfield's films therefore foreground the role of the documentarist, and the ways in which the filmmaker's inter-action with the reality they are filming impacts on the resulting footage. In *The Leader, His Driver and the Driver's Wife* (1991), a documentary about the South African white supremacist leader Eugene Terreblanche, Broomfield uses (deliberate) miscommunication and foregrounding of 'hitches' in the filming process to draw out and emphasise the ludicrousness of Terreblanche, his beliefs, and his inflated sense of his own importance. This is a technique that results in a strong critique of Terreblanche (as well as being highly amusing) – but would not have been possible without Broomfield's explicitly 'performative' strategies. In many respects it is Broomfield's bumbling attempts to act like a documentarist that so infuriate Terreblanche and lead to most of his outbursts.

☐ CASE STUDY 3: *GRIZZLY MAN* (WERNER HERZOG, 2005)

A very interesting recent example of such 'performative' tendencies in documentary is Werner Herzog's *Grizzly Man* (2005). Rather than the deliberately clumsy, knowing style of Broomfield, however, this film consists of its main character assuming a specific role in front of the camera, and seeming to believe it himself. At the film's heart is a strong belief in the ability of documentary footage to act as evidence; ultimately, however, the footage is recontextualised and made to say something other than its creator intended. This raises interesting questions about how actuality footage can be (re-)interpreted in different contexts.

Grizzly Man tells the story of Timothy Treadwell, a self-mythologising 'eco-warrior' who took it upon himself to live among the various communities of Alaskan grizzly bears each summer for thirteen years, spending the rest of the year touring and lecturing on the subject. In 2001, Treadwell (and his female companion, who is virtually absent from any of Treadwell's footage) was attacked and eaten by one of the bears. While living in Alaska, Treadwell amassed a vast archive of footage of the bears, and some of this remarkable footage features in the film. However, what is most interesting about this film as a documentary is the way in which Treadwell's original footage of him and the bears is taken and recontextualised by Herzog. There is little doubt that Treadwell was a somewhat delusional, odd character, who saw 'saving' the bears as his vocation. There are countless scenes in *Grizzly Man* where Treadwell appears in front of the camera and speaks at (repetitive) length about how much he 'loves' the bears. As Herzog points out in one of his laconic voiceover moments, Treadwell's view of nature was 'sentimentalised'; he constantly anthropomorphises the animals, in the way that some people talk about their domesticated pets. At one point, for example, after some stunning close-up footage of two male bears fighting, Treadwell surveys the battleground after the two bears have departed and exclaims of one of them: 'Sergeant Brown went to the bathroom, did a number two during his fight' while pointing at a pile of bear dung.

The film is interesting therefore because the vast amounts of footage that Treadwell shot (100-plus hours), with the presumption or knowledge that he would edit this into some sort of documentary shape, actually falls into the hands of someone else. In a sense, then, there are two documentary 'voices' at play in *Grizzly Man* – that of Treadwell, who consistently appears in front of the camera presenting his version of events; and Herzog, whose ironic editorialising voice permeates the film, on the soundtrack and via some of the strange interviews he sets up (e.g. with the coroner, Treadwell's friends). On the one hand, we can see that Treadwell did indeed film some remarkable footage. But he is also shown to be grossly manipulative of the material, often filming and refilming particular speeches to camera to get just the right tone of weepy indignation. On one level this is not a problem – many documentaries will film some shots a number of times, or use some other kinds of 'justifiable' re-enactment or reconstruction. But there is something disconcerting about watching Treadwell (whom we now know to be dead) obsessively re-enact and perform certain scenes. As Herzog opines at one point on the soundtrack, as we move into a sequence which shows Treadwell emoting straight to camera, it was as if the filming process had become a 'confessional' for him. After a tearful moment, where he states, 'I will die for these animals … I had no life. Now I have a life', Treadwell disappears behind the camera, emerging again as he says, 'Now, enough of that!' He then strikes a pose and delivers an exaggeratedly upbeat 'continuity style' line straight to camera ('We've gotta find Banjo! He's missing!') – clearly meant to provide an edit point and link for a completely different section of his film.

These shifts in gear – something that gives a glimpse 'behind the scenes' as it were, and would of course have been excised by Treadwell, or at least recontextualised as he creatively interpreted or shaped his material – are what give the film its tragi-comic or ironic tone. Treadwell, far from the committed and steadfast activist he sees himself as, comes across as a buffoon and a narcissist, with little or no real understanding of the workings of nature. At one point, the film cuts to him sitting next to a dead fox cub. The cub, we learn from Treadwell, was savaged the previous night by some wolves. Instead of recognising that this is part of nature – predators and prey – Treadwell coos in a sentimental manner about the death of the cub: 'I love you … and I don't understand…. Expedition 2001 has taken a sad turn, but it's a real turn, and I mourn the death of this gorgeous baby fox.' As he says this, looking mournfully into the camera, a fly that has been buzzing around the corpse alights on the cub's eye. Treadwell's reaction is indicative of his overall stance: he petulantly waves at the fly, saying, 'Get out of his eye … frigging fly'. He then stomps off, frame left, with the parting shot: 'Don't do it when I'm around. Have some respect. Fucker!' He is clearly angered by this imposition of nature (a fly feeding on a dead body) as it contradicts his sentimental view of things. The viewer might also speculate that Treadwell is equally annoyed that the fly has ruined the perfect 'spontaneity' of his moment with the dead fox cub.

Clearly, Treadwell comes across in *Grizzly Man* as someone who is actively performing and playing a role. While also coming across as delusional, one suspects Treadwell knew that some of his antics in front of the camera were meant for the cutting-room floor (or for his own personal viewing only). This inflects the finished product in an interesting way, because Herzog is also 'performing' a role, that of the sage and measured documentarist who uncovers the 'truth' of what happened, and places Treadwell the man, and his footage, into some sort of context.

DOCUMENTARY, DRAMA AND PERFORMANCE

The discussion of a self-consciously performed documentary such as *Grizzly Man*, the knowing playing up to the cameras seen in *Grey Gardens*, as well as the questions raised by re-enactment and reconstruction generally, mean that we do need to examine documentary's relationship with drama. There are, of course, strong traditions of drama/documentary hybrids (the best discussion of these is Paget (1998)) and various reasons for filmmakers using these techniques. A recent film such as *United 93* (2006), for example, uses unknown actors and a highly naturalistic style to tell the story of what happened on the United Airlines flight that was hijacked on 11 September 2001; some of the passengers fought back and overpowered the hijackers. The events depicted on the screen are of course 'speculative', though based as much as possible on the available evidence (flight recorders and so on). On the other hand, a documentary such as *One Day in September* (2001) offers an account of the events at the 1972 Munich Olympics, where Israeli athletes were killed by terrorists, but does so using many 'dramatic' conventions. The events depicted in this film are more easily verified and a matter of public record, and the people we see are the actual people involved rather than actors as in *United 93*. Nevertheless, both of these films are in the grey area of the spectrum where documentary and drama meet.

One of the main reasons for a documentarist to use drama and reconstruction is due to the lack of any original footage of the events being depicted. This then takes us back to the notion of 'sincere and justifiable' reconstruction as arguably seen in the work of Flaherty and the Griersonians. If the events depicted may be said to be typical, probable, and a part of the subject's usual routine, does it matter that we reconstructed (i.e. fabricated) that specific scene? Clearly there is a difference between such scenes and those that have been reconstructed due to lack of any original footage – for example, the scenes we might see in a documentary about the Middle Ages, or the battle scenes in Peter Watkins's *Culloden* (1964) – but it really is one of degree. While dramatised and reconstructed scenes appear to fly in the face of documentary as a mode, it must be remembered that it is only really one type of documentary – the observational, and especially the direct cinema variant of this – that appears to rule them out without reservation. The dramatic rendering of events – even those events that have not happened yet, as seen in *The War Game* (1966), *The Day Britain Stopped* (2003) or the BBC series *If . . .* – can play an important documentary role.

There is also an interesting tendency in recent years for certain films to use documentary techniques but to do so in conjunction with improvised dramatic reconstruction, often using non-professional actors (real people who are more often than not an integral part of the milieu shown in the film). For example, in the made-for-TV film *Twockers* (part of the BBC Storyville strand, directed by Pawel Pawlikowski and Ian Duncan, 1998), Pawlikowski (a renowned documentary filmmaker) uses a cast of unknowns to play out the real drama.

☐ CASE STUDY 4: *TWOCKERS* (PAWEL PAWLIKOWSKI AND IAN DUNCAN, 1998)

In *Twockers*, we see the tale of a gang of feral children living near Halifax, West Yorkshire. They take drugs, engage in petty crime and vandalism, and commit breaking and entering and the 'twocking' of the title – 'twockers' is the acronymically derived name given to those who engage in 'taking without owner's consent', usually referring to car crime. Clearly, this is not a documentary in the accepted sense of the term, quite simply because it consists of 'acted' or 'performed' scenes where the characters engage in criminal activity. The general style of the film is highly naturalistic, observational, though it does have a focalised narrative following Trevor (Trevor Wademan) as he falls for a local pregnant girl, and tries to go straight instead of hanging out with his younger and even more out-of-control friend Steve. The film bears some similarities to *Tina Goes Shopping* and *Tina Takes a Break* (Penny Woolcock, 1999 and 2001), both films that explore the British underclass via improvised, highly naturalistic docudramatic technique. The Woolcock films use direct-to-camera address by some characters which *Twockers* does not, but the same people-playing-themselves points apply. *Twockers* includes some point of view voiceover from Trevor reflecting on his inability to go straight – he does take a job in a chicken-processing factory, but cannot stick with it – but for the most part the film unfolds in such a way that the characters behave as if the cameras are not present.

These films are in the tradition of Ken Loach and Tony Garnett's TV work such as *The Wednesday Play*. As with much drama-documentary, there are debates to be had about the extent to which these films actually have any documentary worth – that is, aren't they just highly naturalistic fictions? Pawlikowski was commissioned by the BBC to make a documentary, but worked with the young cast to make this improvisational docudrama instead. As Pawlikowski notes, 'the kids we found and improvised with knew what they

For further discussion of contemporary British cinema see pp. 324–33.

• **Plate 8.6**

Twockers (Pawel Pawlikowski and Ian Duncan, 1998). The use of non-actors – real people playing a variation of themselves – and authentic social settings result in a highly convincing documentary-like drama

were doing' (Gibbons 2001). It is evident that Pawlikowski is interested in engaging with social realities in such a way that a more 'conventional' documentary approach, one that merely observed or asserted things about these people in an expository framework, cannot. During the film there are recurring scenes of the town and its 'sink' estates, shot from a hillside where the gang of youths hang out; they have even placed a battered sofa on the top of the hill. These shots are reminiscent of what Terry Lovell, referring to fictional kitchen sink dramas, has called 'that long shot of our town from the hill' (1990: 369) – a particularly resonant image for British social realist films. It is hard not to see some sense of irony in *Twockers*'s recurring use of this shot.

A film such as *Twockers* is in a grey area with regard to documentary status – it cannot be dismissed as an out-and-out fiction, and yet it is clearly approaching its nonfictional/real life locations, events and characters in a very different way to a conventional documentary. There are things which happen in the film that one would never see in a 'proper' documentary – indeed, virtually all of the events depicted would be 'inadmissible' due to their criminal status. For example, what are we to make of a scene where Trevor and Steve break into a supposedly empty house, only to find an old man dead in a chair, and then proceed to burgle the house? The ethical and legal ramifications of course mean that this scene comes clearly 'indexed' as something that is being acted or performed (whereas there are some other scenes – for example, when the youths engage in petty vandalism or raucous behaviour – that could feasibly be viewed as 'actual' rather than 'acted'). The point is that docudramatic films such as this rely on the viewer's interpretive activity, but it is becoming increasingly difficult to distinguish with any certainty between specific modes. The ways in which actuality is mediated by documentary modes, their use of dramatic reconstruction and different types of performance, remains central to an understanding of the field.

SUMMARY

This chapter outlines some of the conceptual and practical issues involved in defining documentary as a form. The main issues discussed are: the relationship between documentary and nonfiction as categories; the ways in which early cinema 'actualities' may be seen as 'proto-documentaries'; the role of performance across a variety of documentary modes; the ways in which narrative and dramatisation can lead to a greater understanding of the intersecting range of films and programmes that are collectively gathered under this umbrella term.

FURTHER READING

Corner, John, *The Art of Record*, Manchester University Press, Manchester, 1996.

Nichols, Bill, *Representing Reality*, Indiana University Press, Bloomington, 1991.

Nichols, Bill, *Blurred Boundaries*, Indiana University Press, Bloomington, 1994.

Paget, Derek, *True Stories? Documentary Drama on Radio, Screen and Stage*, Manchester University Press, Manchester, 1990.

Plantinga, Carl, *Rhetoric and Representation in Nonfiction Film*, Cambridge University Press, Cambridge, 1997.

Rosenthal, Alan and Corner, John (eds), *New Challenges for Documentary* (2nd edn), Manchester University Press, Manchester, 2005.

Winston, Brian, *Claiming the Real*, BFI, London, 1995.

FURTHER VIEWING

Baraka (Ron Fricke, 1992)

Basic Training (Frederick Wiseman, 1971)

Berlin: Symphony of a Great City (Walter Ruttmann, 1927)

Biggie and Tupac (Nick Broomfield, 2002)

Bowling for Columbine (Michael Moore, 2002)

Capturing the Friedmans (Andrew Jarecki, 2003)

Cathy Come Home (Ken Loach, 1966)

Chronicle of a Summer (Jean Rouch and Edgar Morin, 1960)

Coal Face (Alberto Cavalcanti, 1935)

The Day Britain Stopped (Gabriel Range, 2003)

Don't Look Back (Don Pennebaker, 1967)

Drifters (John Grierson, 1929)

Early Cinema: Primitives and Pioneers (BFI DVD)

Etre et avoir (Nicolas Philibert, 2002)

Fahrenheit 9/11 (Michael Moore, 2004)

Forgotten Silver (Peter Jackson and Costa Botes, 1995)

Gallivant (Andrew Kotting, 1997)

Gimme Shelter (Albert and David Maysles, Charlotte Zwerin, 1970)

Granton Trawler (John Grierson, 1934)

Grey Gardens (Albert and David Maysles, 1975)

Grizzly Man (Werner Herzog, 2005)

High School (Frederick Wiseman, 1968)

Hoop Dreams (Steve James, 1994)

Housing Problems (Arthur Elton and Edgar Anstey, 1935)

In the Year of the Pig (Emile de Antonio, 1968)

Kino-Pravda (Dziga Vertov, 1925)

Kurt and Courtney (Nick Broomfield, 1998)

The Leader, His Driver and the Driver's Wife (Nick Broomfield, 1991)

Little Dieter Needs to Fly (Werner Herzog, 1997)

London (Patrick Keiller, 1994)

The Lost World of Mitchell and Kenyon (BBC, 2004)

Louisiana Story (Robert Flaherty, 1948)

Man of Aran (Robert Flaherty, 1934)

Man with a Movie Camera (Dziga Vertov, 1929)

Moana (Robert Flaherty, 1926)

Murderball (Henry Alex Rubin and Dana Adam Shapiro, 2005)

Nanook of the North (Robert Flaherty, 1922)

Night Mail (Harry Watt and Basil Wright, 1936)

Primary (Robert Drew, 1960)

Rien que les heures (Alberto Cavalcanti, 1926)

Robinson in Space (Patrick Keiller, 1997)

Roger and Me (Michael Moore, 1989)

Salesman (Albert and David Maysles, Charlotte Zwerin, 1969)

Super Size Me (Morgan Spurlock, 2004)

Tarnation (Jonathan Caouette, 2003)

The Thin Blue Line (Errol Morris, 1988)

Tina Goes Shopping (Penny Woolcock, 1999)

Tina Takes a Break (Penny Woolcock, 2001)

Touching the Void (Kevin MacDonald, 2003)

Twockers (Pawel Pawlikowski and Ian Duncan, 1998)

United 93 (Paul Greengrass, 2006)

Why We Fight (Frank Capra, 1943–45)

RESOURCE CENTRES

**http://www.screenonline.org.uk/film/
id/1084507/index.html**
Screenonline/BFI page listing details of Mitchell
and Kenyon films, including playable versions of
some.

http://www.dfglondon.com/
The Documentary Filmmakers Group, based in
London, but including details of training courses,
history of documentary and other material.

http://www.nd.edu/~igodmilo/reality.html
Documentary filmmaker Jill Godmilow in conversation with Ann-Louise Shapiro, a useful and
provocative discussion of some important aspects
of documentary.

Chapter 9

The language of animation

Paul Wells

■ The language of animation

INTRODUCTION

In the contemporary era, animation both constitutes a particular and distinctive form of cinema, and operates as a language of expression in a range of diverse forms on television, on the web, and in other delivery platforms such as computer games, mobile phones and electronic displays. At the very same time that animation has achieved prominence as a filmmaking practice, though, the speed of change in the digital era has once more rendered the form subject to a range of questions and challenges. Such was the nature of animation's neglected status it was once necessary to argue not merely that animation was 'different' from live action as a filmmaking process, but as a 'political' point, to resist those who would always dismiss it, and once more consign it to the margins of cinema history, art and popular culture. In the digital era, 'live action' – the process of photographic recording with a camera – is much more reliant on post-production processes, and arguably, a great deal of contemporary 'cinema' is constructed in the computer. At the very moment when the dominant aesthetic of feature animation is computer-generated imagery, the space between 'animation' and 'live action' is a narrow one, and sometimes indistinguishable.

But in many ways this has always been the case, and requires, as some writers such as Cholodenko and Manovich (see Cholodenko 1991; Manovich 2002) have argued, the acceptance of the view that all cinema has in some way been a variation on 'animation', and not the reverse. While this validates 'animation' as the core language of cinema *per se*, and seems wholly pertinent to the post-photographic digital era, it remains insufficient as a way of viewing animation as a form. The computer is really 'a red herring'. As John Lasseter, the key creative driving force at Pixar Animation has often noted, 'the computer is just a tool', and operates no differently from the range of approaches which have characterised animated shorts and features in the past, by implication suggesting that the 'definition' of animation resides elsewhere.

While we might very well see a great deal of 'animation' in feature films like *King Kong* (2005), and the films of Pixar, Disney, Dreamworks and Blue Sky are self-evidently 'animated', this does not take into account the thousands of animated films made with different styles and techniques throughout the history of animation and in the present day. Further, this merely demonstrates that history repeats itself. 'Animation' was profoundly prominent in film spectaculars like the original *King Kong* (1933), but few thought of it as such, and pioneers such as Willis O'Brien, whose stop-motion animation created the lovelorn gorilla, were not seen as 'animators' or 'auteurs' but as effects artists, their identity and their work made invisible and absorbed within the special effects tradition. This, like many aspects of animated film, is important work to recover because it has also been the case that 'animation' has been viewed merely as 'the cartoon', and for the most part, 'the American cartoon', and furthermore, the 'Disney' cartoon in too many contexts where the form has been scrutinised. For many years, Disney defined the history and identity of animation, and many American pioneers such as Winsor McCay and Otto Mesmer were forgotten, but perhaps even more importantly, work going on in many countries worldwide remained absent from animation history, and the sheer diversity of the form went unrecognised – this is especially significant when it is clear that the West's domination and interpretation of 'animation' has consigned it to secondary status as a film form whereas in the East, for the most part, it has always been viewed as a prominent aspect of the graphic and fine arts.

This chapter will once again seek to provide an analysis of its distinctive vocabulary (looking in the latter part of the discussion at the impact and affect of computer animation), and aspects of animation history, noting that with the increasing impact of animation from across the world comes more information about alternative animation histories and traditions; and different models of animation which reveal the intrinsic versatility and progressiveness of the form. One need only note that with the success of Hayao Miyazaki's *Spirited Away* (2005), Nick Park and Peter Lord's *Curse of the Wererabbit* (2005), Dave McKean's *Mirrormask* (2005) and Christopher Nielson's *Free Jimmy* (2006) – to merely note animated features – animation has been able to continually experiment aesthetically and technologically while it has increased its audience and popularity. This in itself makes it unique within entertainment forms.

WHAT IS ANIMATION?

In the post-photographic filmmaking era, the question of 'what is animation?' has taken on new meaning and prompted fresh debate. If 'live action' and 'animation' have in some senses been effaced by digital technologies, it is still the case that animation is somehow recognisable as 'different'. We still know animation when we see it, especially in its form as a cartoon, or a 3D stop-motion film, or even in its specific incarnation as a computer-generated phenomenon, and sometimes, even when it is at its most photo-realistic. So what is it, that still signals this 'difference' and 'particularity'? Animation is still the art of the impossible, and whether it be the fertile imaginings of independent filmmakers represented in vivid symbolic images of inner states, or the seamless interventions of visual effects animators producing spectacle in major movies, animation remains the most versatile and autonomous form of artistic expression. In the pre-digital era, it was comparatively easy to argue that animation was a process art in which pro-filmic materials (drawings, a puppet with malleable limbs, clay, sand or ink on glass) were filmed 'frame-by-frame', and in between each frame an alteration of the materials was made to create the illusion of movement in phases of imagined action, when the film was projected at twenty-four frames per second. For this kind of filmmaking such a definition remains pertinent. The determining aspects of this kind of practice, of course, are the self-conscious pro-filmic construction of 'motion' in figures, objects and so on, and the notion of 'the frame' as the presiding increment by which this illusion is created. In the digital era, it is still the case that animation mostly uses artificially created and previously conceived movement instead of transferring movement from the natural world, but the 'frame' is no longer the determining factor in the measure of the advancement of this movement.

Norman McLaren, one of the medium's acknowledged masters, suggested of traditional animation practices that 'Animation is not the art of drawings that move, but rather the art of movements that are drawn', noting that 'what happens between each frame is more important than what happens on each frame' (Solomon 1987: 11). McLaren is arguing that the true essence of animation is the manipulation of movements between frames, and his observation still provides an insight about how animation is made, even in the digital era. Fundamentally, it has always been a misconception that animators are wholly concerned with 'the frame'. Actually, they are only concerned with 'a space' in which the motion of artificial figures, objects and forms is sequentially constructed over time. The computer interface, while being less concerned with 'the frame', is absolutely concerned with 'the space', and it is in this that traditional and contemporary animation are one and the same. As animator and author Mike Wellins has observed: 'Motion is easy; making something move from one place to the next is as simple as two mouse clicks, but doing true dynamic motion that is sharp, quick, full of energy, responds to physics, and adheres to the rules is never easy. The computer does do a lot; it creates every frame, applies colour and shading, and keeps shapes consistent. However, it does not, for the time being, create animation' (Wellins 2005: 77–8). It is still the animator's pro-filmic investment in the artificially constructed modes of movement that is at the heart of animation.

It is important, too, to recognise that animation is essentially based on stylisation and abstraction to some degree, even in its most apparently photo-realistic form.

The animators of the Zagreb School in former Yugoslavia stressed these creative and philosophic aspects of the craft: 'To animate [is to] give life and soul to a design, not through the copying but through the transformation of reality' (quoted in Holloway 1972: 9). The Zagreb School wished to emphasise that literally 'giving life' to the inanimate was to reveal something about the figure or object in the process which could not be privileged or effectively achieved in live action. It was this distinctiveness in the form that John Halas, of the British Halas and Batchelor studio, sought to theorise in the immediate postwar period when he tried to convince industry, business and education of the value of animation as a specific language of expression and communication, and crucially one that could support serious messages. He suggested that animation's key characteristics were:

- symbolisation of objects and human beings
- picturing the invisible
- penetration
- selection, exaggeration and transformation
- showing the past and predicting the future
- controlling speed and time

(cited in Halas and Wells 2006: 160)

This is a very helpful 'check-list' of qualities specific to the animated form. Symbolism can work to clarify and simplify an idea – a flag can represent a nation; a moving arrow, the direction of an invisible force, like the wind; a single iconic soldier, the military ambitions of a whole country. Such devices can 'picture the invisible', too. Sound waves, magnetism, radar and other physical properties characterised by laws not visible to the eye can be rendered clear and apparent. Halas suggests that animation can also 'penetrate' interior workings of the body or a machine, or other kinds of complex inner state (dream, memory, consciousness, fantasy), and provide a literal and conceptual interpretation which enables them to be more readily understood. Further, by 'selecting' an aspect of a scene or scenario to be visualised this can be accentuated or brought into the foreground for effect; thus it may be 'exaggerated' or 'transformed' to better reveal its properties or significance. All of these elements can be contextualised within various time frames – things can be represented from the long past and projected easily into the future, perhaps on the one hand depicting extinct fauna and flora, or on the other, reimagining nature in a thousand years time as a consequence of current ecological issues and effects. The speed and time in which this is presented can also be varied – a split second can be extended while millions of years can be truncated into a minute or two. The animator can intervene in these time frames, also, accelerating or showing in slow motion particular details. Halas' theories reinforce the control the animator has in constructing an artificial world that can be determined on its own terms and conditions, and with varying degrees of 'realism' or to the point of complete abstraction.

Julianne Burton-Carvajal goes so far as to suggest that '[T]he function and essence of cartoons is ... the impression of irreality, of intangible and imaginable worlds in chaotic, disruptive, subversive collision' (Smoodin 1994: 139). Walt Disney himself endorses this point when he says, '[T]he first duty of the cartoon is not to duplicate real action or things as they actually happen – but to give a caricature of life and action ... to bring to life dream fantasies and imaginative fantasies that we have all thought of [based on] a foundation of fact' (Disney, quoted in Barrier 1999: 142). Animation can defy the laws of gravity, contest our perceived view of space and time, and endow lifeless things with dynamic, vibrant properties. In short, animation can change the world and create magical effects, but most importantly it can interrogate previous representations of 'reality' and reinterpret how 'reality' might be viewed – a point well understood by pioneer filmmakers such as Georges Melies, and early animators J. Stuart Blackton, Emile Cohl, Winsor McCay and Ladislaw Starawicz.

EARLY ANIMATION

Animation as a practice did not emerge fully formed and recognisable as a distinctive way of making films, but rather came out of the experimental approaches to making images move from the long distant past, and in the early technological innovations that eventually led to 'cinema'. As early as 70 BC there is evidence of a mechanism that projected hand-drawn moving images on to a screen, described by Lucretius in *De Rerum Natura*.

In the sixteenth century, 'Flipbooks' emerged in Europe, often containing erotic drawings which, when riffled, showed the performance of sexual acts. In 1825, Peter Mark Roget developed what was later to be called the persistence of vision theory, determining why human beings could perceive movement. Basically, the human eye saw one image and carried with it an after-image on to the image that followed it, thus creating an apparent continuity. This is crucial in watching moving pictures in general, of course, but is of particular significance for the kind of animated cinema achieved frame by frame. With developments like the **phenakistoscope** in 1831; the **kinematoscope** in 1861 and the **praxinoscope** in 1877, there was the eventual emergence of the cinematic apparatus. Intrinsic to these diversionary 'toys' was the idea of the moving image as something magical – a colourful, playful, seemingly miraculous practice.

Also in place by the 1890s was the comic strip form in the American print media industries. This is important because the comic strip was to provide some of the initial vocabulary for the cartoon film: characters continuing from episode to episode; speech 'bubbles'; visual jokes; sequential narrative and so on. By 1893, the *New York World* and *New York Journal* were using colour printing in their strips, and these may be seen as prototypes of later animated forms.

At the centre of the development of 'trick effects' in the emergent cinema was Georges Melies. His discovery of the 'dissolve' (that is, when one image cross-fades into another) led him to pioneer a whole number of other cinematic effects that have become intrinsic to the possibilities available to animators. These included stop-motion photography, split-screen techniques, fast and slow motion, and the manipulation of live action within painted backdrops and scenery. Melies was also a 'lightning cartoonist', caricaturing contemporary personalities, speeding up their 'construction' on screen by undercranking the camera.

By 1900, J. Stuart Blackton made *The Enchanted Drawing*. He appeared as a 'lightning cartoonist', drawing a man smoking a cigar and drinking some wine. By the use of stop-motion, one drawing at a time is revealed and the man's face is made to take on various expressions. Various similar films had preceded this, including *The Vanishing Lady* (1898) and *A Visit to the Spiritualist* (1899). These films may be classified as **proto-animation**, as they employ techniques which are used by later animators but are not strictly or wholly made frame by frame. The 'lightning cartoonist' became particularly established in the music-halls in Britain, and key figures who were to essentially develop the first British animation school, Lancelot Speed, Max Martin and Harry Furniss, all graduated from this performance context, though it should be stressed that each had worked in illustration, theatre design and fine art before undertaking 'lightning cartooning', and all were well versed in the long-established caricaturial and satirical traditions in Britain. Against this background they diverged from their American counterparts, and animation in Britain therefore took a different course. This is but one example of the way various indigenous arts contexts and traditions globally informed emergent animation styles and processes, which were ultimately different from the dominant form that was to emerge from the US.

J. Stuart Blackton, himself an émigré Briton, achieved full animation in *Humorous Phases of Funny Faces* (1906). Although using full animation in key sequences, the film was essentially a series of tricks. Primitive notions of narrative animation followed in the early work of famous comic strip artist Winsor McCay, who under Blackton's supervision

For further discussion of the early film industry read pp. 25–8.

Early developments in the moving image
The **phenakistoscope** was made up of two rotating discs which appeared to make an image move. The **kinematoscope** was more sophisticated, and employed a series of sequential photographs mounted on a wheel and rotated. The **praxinoscope**, pioneered by Emile Reynaud, was a strip of images mounted in a revolving drum and reflected in mirrors; a model later revised and renamed theatre optique, which may claim to be the first proper mechanism to project seemingly animated images on to a screen.

proto-animation
Early live-action cinema demonstrated certain techniques which preceded their conscious use as a method in creating animation. This is largely in regard to stop-motion, mixed media and the use of dissolves to create the illusion of metamorphosis in early 'trick' films.

incoherent cinema
Influenced by the
'Incoherents' artists
working between
1883 and 1891, a
movement principally
led by Cohl, this kind
of animation was often
surreal, anarchistic
and playful, relating
seemingly unrelated
forms and events in
an often irrational and
spontaneous fashion.
Lines tumble into shapes
and figures in temporary
scenarios before evolving
into other images.

character animation
Many cartoons and
more sophisticated
adult animated films,
for example, Japanese
anime, are still
dominated by 'character'
or 'personality'
animation, which
prioritises exaggerated
and sometimes
caricatured expressions
of human traits in order
to direct attention to the
detail of gesture and the
range of human emotion
and experience. This kind
of animation is related
to identifiable aspects of
the real world and does
not readily correspond
with more abstract uses
of the animated medium.

anthropomorphism
The tendency in
animation to endow
creatures, objects and
environments with
human attributes,
abilities and qualities.
This can redefine or
merely draw attention to
characteristics which are
taken for granted in live-
action representations of
these things, and literally
create original 'worlds',
which nevertheless
have a high degree
of familiarity and
identification.

at the Vitagraph Brooklyn Studio made an animated version of his most celebrated strip, *Little Nemo in Slumberland*, in 1911. Blackton clearly recognised that the animated film could be a viable aesthetic and economic vehicle outside the context of orthodox live-action cinema. His film *The Haunted Hotel* (1907) included impressive supernatural sequences, and convinced audiences and financiers alike that the animated film had an unlimited potential.

Primitive notions of narrative animation followed in the early work of famous comic strip artist Winsor McCay, who under Blackton's supervision at the Vitagraph Brooklyn Studio made an animated version of his most celebrated strip, *Little Nemo in Slumberland*, in 1911. In France, caricaturist Emile Cohl's *Fantasmagorie* (1908) created animation as **incoherent cinema**, less predicated on the comic strip and more related to abstract art. In Russia, Ladislaw Starawicz was making extraordinary three-dimensional puppet films. *The Cameraman's Revenge* (1911) features insects in a melodramatic love triangle and self-consciously shows the power of cinema itself to show human life.

It is Winsor McCay, however, who must be properly acknowledged for his influence on Disney and American cartoonal tradition. McCay's *The Story of a Mosquito* (1912) is a mock horror story of a mosquito graphically feeding on a man until it is so bloated with blood that it explodes! Such a film anticipates his development of personality or **character animation** through the creation of *Gertie the Dinosaur* (1914). The playful dinosaur, Gertie, gleefully hurls a mammoth into a lake in the film and clearly displays an attitude. McCay included this film as part of his touring revue show debuting at Chicago's Palace Theatre in February 1914, and appeared to be directly talking to and acting upon his character. This **anthropomorphism** is key within animation in general, but most significantly in the films of Walt Disney that were to follow.

While Disney is acknowledged as the main figure in moving animation towards an industrial process, this is to neglect, however, the work of John R. Bray who pioneered the cel animation process using translucent cels in 1913, and made a film called *The Artist's Dream*. The Bray Studios then released a series of cartoons with a continuing character, Colonel Heeza Liar, and demonstrated the viability of animation as a commercial industry capable of mass production. Cartoons emerged in the marketplace in the US principally from studios in New York, and Earl Hurd's *Bobby Bumps* series and Paul Terry's *Farmer Al Falfa* cartoons were soon very popular. As Felix the Cat, created by Otto Messmer and Max Fleischer's Koko the Clown in the *Out of the Inkwell* series became stars in the US, and Bonzo the Dog, created by George Studdy, became a popular character in Britain, having his own moving icon in Piccadilly Circus, London and a range of merchandising, more experimental abstract animation was beginning to emerge out of European avant-garde cinema practices, particularly through filmmakers such as Walter Ruttmann, Hans Richter, Viking Eggeling, Lotte Reiniger, Fernand Léger and Oskar Fischinger. The work of individual artists like these sought to explore the aesthetic boundaries of filmmaking, largely working out of fine art experimental practices, while rapid advances in filmmaking technologies in America encouraged the emergence of a variety of organisations making films, and the creation of a commercial industry. In Japan, Oten Shimokawa, Seitaro Kitayama and Jun-Ichi Kouchi had made innovative shorts, and the first studio, Kitayama Movie Factory, was established by 1921, mainly producing educational and instructional films for the government. Following the Tokyo earthquake and fire in 1923, the studio recovered to make folk-tales and erotic animation, and though the animation from the United States, was to make a major impact – as it did worldwide for those able to see it – it is useful to remember that models of animation 'production', 'industry' and 'output' did exist elsewhere.

In the US, after initially working at the Bray Studios, the Fleischers established an efficient streamlined animation process, and were one of the first studios to experiment with sound. It is Walt Disney, however, who remains synonymous with animation, through his radical technical and aesthetic innovation between 1928 and 1942, perhaps the 'Golden Era' of cartoon animation.

THE LEGACY OF DISNEY

Walt Disney Productions was founded in 1923. Disney himself was a draughtsman on his first 'Laugh-O-Grams' – fairytales like *Puss in Boots* and *Cinderella* – but soon realised that his greatest flair was as an entrepreneur and artistic director (see Wells 2002a: 77–90). His film *Alice in Cartoonland*, a mix of animation and live action, was successful enough to secure distribution and finance to develop his ideas further. Fundamentally, Disney wanted to move towards the establishment of an industrial process and a studio ethos and identity which was competitive with and comparable to the established Hollywood studios. In 1927, Disney began working on his *Oswald the Rabbit* series of cartoons and during this process he developed 'the pencil test' (i.e. photographing a pencil-drawn sequence to check its quality of movement and authenticity before proceeding to draw it on cels, to paint it and so on). In 1928, Disney premiered *Steamboat Willie* featuring Mickey Mouse, which was the first synchronised sound cartoon. Following continuing experiments in the use of sound effects and music in differing relationships to the visual images, the cartoon began to standardise itself as a form which moved beyond the illustration of different kinds of music into one which accommodated narrative and a series of related jokes. Disney introduced Technicolor, the three-strip colour system, into his silly symphony *Flowers and Trees* in 1932, which later won an Oscar.

All Disney's animators undertook programmes of training in the skills and techniques of fine art in the constant drive towards ever greater notions of **realism** in his cartoons. Even though Disney was dealing with a form that arguably was more suited to abstract, non-realist expression, he insisted on verisimilitude in his characters, contexts and narratives. He wanted animated figures to move like real figures and to be informed by plausible motivation. Former Disney art director and veteran of the 'Golden era' Zack Schwartz suggests that even though the figures moved in an anatomically correct way, they still required an element of caricature which ironically appeared to make them 'more real' on screen, and that what Disney really wanted was a state of conviction in the characters that reconciled the realistic with the caricaturial (see Wells 1997: 4–9). This level of 'reality' was further enhanced by the development of the multi-plane camera. Traditionally, in the two-dimensional image, the illusion of perspective had to be created by the artist. The multi-plane camera achieves the illusion of perspective in the animated film by having the relevant image painted on a series of moveable panes of glass placed directly behind each other. Elements of the image can be painted in the foreground; other elements in the mid-spaces; other elements in the receding background. In this way the camera can move through the elements, seemingly keeping them in perspective. This directly aped live-action shooting and was successfully demonstrated in another Oscar-winning silly symphony, *The Old Mill* (1937), with its most advanced aesthetic use in the first full-length, Technicolor, sound-synchronised animated cartoon feature, *Snow White and the Seven Dwarfs* (1937).

Animation had reached a position of maturity, acknowledged in this form as 'art'. *Pinocchio* (1940), *Fantasia* (1940) and *Bambi* (1941) only consolidated this prestige, moving the animated film into the contemporary era, effectively reconciling fine art, a sense of Classicism and a model of traditional American folk culture, ironically drawn from many European influences (see Allan 1999). The rise of Disney and the populist utopian ideology which appealed to the American mass audience has resulted in the neglect of other kinds of animation, but perhaps even more significantly, the popular cartoon, as exemplified in the work of Tex Avery, Robert McKimson, Bob Clampett, Frank Tashlin and Chuck Jones at the famous 'Termite Terrace' lot at Warner Brothers' Studios (see Wells 2002b). An analysis of Chuck Jones's classic cartoon *Duck Amuck* (1953) may usefully offer, however, some points which both valorise the art of the cartoon short, offer an oppositional perspective on Disney's dominance within the field, and provide a vocabulary by which 'animation' itself may be studied.

realism
Live-action cinema has inspired numerous debates about what may be recognised as 'realism'. This is really a consideration of what may be recognised as the most accurate representation of what is 'real' in recording the concrete and tangible world. Clearly, the animated form in itself most readily accommodates 'the fantastic', but Disney prefered to create a hyper-realism which located his characters in plausibly 'real' worlds which also included fantasy elements in the narrative. Crucially, Disney's version of 'realism' sought to properly reproduce perspective illusionism in the frame, and not the surreal and 'eccentric mise-en-scène' of the Fleischer Brothers' films. Overall, animated films have a tendency to create their own realms which obey their own 'inner logic', however, and though a film may be fantastical, abstract, non-linear, surreal and so on, it will probably obey its own codes and conventions which establish its own authenticity and plausibility.

□ CASE STUDY 1: DECONSTRUCTING THE CARTOON: *DUCK AMUCK* (CHUCK JONES, 1953)

Duck Amuck, directed by Chuck Jones, is the perfect example of a cartoon which is wholly self-conscious and reveals all the aspects of its own construction. Consequently, it is possible to recognise the cartoon as a mode of **deconstruction**. As Richard Thompson points out,

It is at once a laff riot and an essay by demonstration on the nature and conditions of the animated film (from the inside) and the mechanics of film in general. (Even a quick checklist of film grammar is tossed in via the 'Gimme a close-up' gag.)

(cited in Peary and Peary 1980: 221)

Daffy begins the cartoon in anticipation that he is in a musketeer picture and swashbuckles with due aplomb until he realises that he is not accompanied by suitable scenery. He immediately recognises that he has been deserted by the context that both he and we as the audience are accustomed to. He drops the character he is playing and becomes Daffy, the betrayed actor who immediately addresses the camera, acknowledging both the animator and the audience. Perceiving himself as an actor he localises himself within the filmmaking process and signals its mechanisms, all of which are about to be revealed to us.

Trouper that he is, Daffy carries on, adapting to the new farmyard scenery with a spirited version of 'Old Macdonald Had a Farm', before adjusting once again to the arctic layout that has replaced the farmyard. The cartoon constantly draws attention to the relationship between foreground and background, and principally to the relationship between the character and the motivating aspects of the environmental context. Daffy's actions are determined by the understanding of the space he inhabits. These tensions inform the basic narrative process of most cartoons: all Daffy wants is for the animator to make up his mind!

Each environment is illustrated by the visual shorthand of dominant cultural images (e.g. the arctic is signified by an igloo, Hawaii by Daffy's grass skirt and banjo!). The white space, however, becomes the empty context of the cartoon. Daffy is then erased by an animated pencil rubber and essentially only remains as a voice. However, as Chuck Jones has pointed out, 'what I want to say is that Daffy can live and struggle on in an empty screen, without setting and without sound, just as well as with a lot of arbitrary props. He remains Daffy Duck' (Peary and Peary 1980: 233; see also Furniss 2005). This draws attention to the predetermined understanding of Daffy as a character, and to the notion that a whole character can be understood by any one of its parts. Cartoon vocabulary readily employs the **synecdoche**, the part that represents the whole, as a piece of narrative shorthand. Daffy may be understood through his **iconic** elements, both visually and aurally. No visual elements of Daffy need be seen for an audience to know him through his lisping voice, characterised by Mel Blanc. We need only see his manic eyes or particularly upturned beak to distinguish him from Donald Duck and other cartoon characters, who all have similar unique and distinguishing elements in their design.

At the point when Daffy asks 'Where am I?', even in his absence the audience know of his presence. When he is repainted by the anonymous brush as a singing cowboy we anticipate, of course, that Daffy will sing, although the genre probably prohibits him singing 'I'm Just Wild about Harry', which remains one of his favourites! Initially, Daffy finds there is no sound and holds up a small sign requesting 'sound please', thus drawing the audience's attention to the explicit vocabulary of sound necessitated by the cartoon form, and one immediately familiar to the anticipated viewer. When Daffy attempts to play the guitar, it sounds first like a machine-gun, then a horn, then a donkey, thus simultaneously showing the necessity of sound and image synchronisation for

deconstruction
All media 'texts' are constructed. To understand all the components within each construction it is necessary to deconstruct the text and analyse all its elements. For example, the cartoon is made up of a number of specific aspects which define it as a unique cinematic practice (i.e. its frame-by-frame construction; its modes of representation and so on).

synecdoche
The idea that a 'part' of a person, an object, a machine, may be used to represent the 'whole', and work as an emotive or suggestive shorthand to the viewer, who invests the 'part' with symbolic associations.

iconic
The iconic is defined by the dominant signs that signify a particular person or object – Chaplin, for example, would be defined by a bowler hat, a moustache, a cane and some old boots, while Hitler would be defined by a short, parted hairstyle and a small 'postage stamp' moustache.

narrative orthodoxy, and the creation of comedy through the incongruous mismatching of sound and image. This is developed after Daffy breaks the guitar in frustration – a standard element of the cartoon is the process of destruction – and attempts to complain to the animator about his treatment, especially as he considers himself 'A Star'. He is given the voice of a chicken and a cockatoo, and, just when he is at his most hysterical in his attempt to speak, he is allowed his own voice, but at increased volume. Daffy is visibly humiliated and his attitude once again reveals to an audience his helplessness in the face of the power of the animator. The animator is at liberty to manipulate the image completely, and to create impossible and dynamic relations which need not have any connection with orthodox and anticipated relations.

This manipulation of Daffy's image and identity also tells an audience about his essential character traits – egotism, ambition, frustration, anger and wilfulness – which are constantly challenged in most of the narratives through the resistance offered by the world around him. In *Duck Amuck*, he is also defeated by the animated context within which he exists. He pleads with the animator for orthodoxy and is greeted with a child's pencil drawing for a background, slapdash painting for the scenery and an absurd reconstruction of his own body in wild colours and a flag tied to his newly drawn tail indicating that he is a 'screwball'. Despite protestations that he has fulfilled his contract, Daffy continues to be treated with contempt. Just when he seems to have been granted the legitimacy of 'a sea picture' – an obvious reference to both Donald Duck and Popeye – Daffy is subjected to the standard cartoon gag of recognising that he is temporarily defying gravity by standing in mid-air only to drop into the sea the moment he realises. Seconds later he is on an island, but the image is merely a small frame within the normal frame, this time drawing the audience's attention to the compositional elements of the cartoon and, indeed, of film language itself. We can hardly hear Daffy as he calls for a close-up, and receives one at rapid speed, only showing us his eyes.

Once again calling upon the audience's recognition of the frame as a potentially three-dimensional space, Daffy then tries to cope with the sheer weight of the black background scenery which falls upon him like a heavy awning. He eventually tears up the 'screen' in sheer frustration and demands that the cartoon start, even though it has already been running for several minutes. A screen card with 'The End' comes up, accompanied by the Merrie Melodies theme. Daffy then attempts to take control of the film by returning to the key notion of himself as an entertainer performing a vaudevillian soft-shoe shuffle. He is trying to reclaim the idea of the cartoon as a medium for entertainment rather than deconstruction. His song-and-dance routine is interrupted, however, by the slippage of the frame as it appears to divide the screen in half and expose the frames of celluloid the film is supposedly composed of. The two frames, of course, reveal two Daffys, who immediately start to fight and disappear in a blur of drawn lines – the fight merely becomes a signifier of cartoon movement, a symbol of kineticism unique in embodying character and signifying form.

Narrative life improves for Daffy as 'the picture' casts him as a pilot. This is merely a device, however, to demonstrate a series of conventional cartoon gags, including an off-screen air crash, the appearance of the ubiquitous anvil as a substitute for Daffy's parachute and an explosion as Daffy tests some shells with a mallet – by this time, however, he is a gibbering heap, devoid of dignity or control, the two qualities Daffy most aspires to. As he tries to assert himself one last time, Daffy demands to know 'Who is responsible for this? I demand that you show yourself!' The frame as we understand it is then completely broken as the scene changes and the camera pulls back to reveal the drawing-board and 'the animator' – Bugs Bunny, Daffy's arch-rival. As Thompson remarks, 'Duck Amuck can be seen as Daffy's bad trip; his self-destruction fantasies and delusions, with their rapid, unpredictable, disconcerting changes of scene and orientation, are the final extension of ego-on-the-line dreams' (quoted in Peary and Peary 1980: 233). This is an important point in a number of respects. It locates Daffy as a character firmly in a relationship between form and meaning. Each narrative

For further discussion of narrative, film form and meaning see Chapter 3, pp. 61–86.

establishes and develops the vocabulary which defines the underpinning imperatives of both character and the form the character inhabits. This leads to the cartoon
animation embodying a number of **ideological** positions. Disney's films, for example,
often play out an orthodox narrative form to reinforce an ideological status quo. In other
words, Disney's films support and illustrate what Robert Sklar calls 'the spirit of social
purpose, the re-enforcing of old values' (quoted in ibid.: 61). This idealised world is
often challenged by the anarchic worlds of Tex Avery (see Adamson 1975; Wells 1998)
and Chuck Jones, and, indeed, other kinds of animation which send complex and often
subversive messages.

The animated film reached maturity in the 'golden era' of the American cartoon,
and in doing so had established Disney as synonymous with animation. This has led to
animation being understood in a limited way. Disney perfected a certain language for the
cartoon and the full-length feature which took its model from live-action filmmaking. This
overshadowed other kinds of innovation and styles of animation which have extended
the possibilities of the form and enabled other kinds of film to be made. Disney's art
remains the dominant language of animation and we can term this 'orthodox animation'.
This notion of 'orthodox' animation needs to be addressed in the light of Disney's
aesthetic now being overtaken by the prominence of computer-generated animation,
and principally the work of Pixar Animation. Many of the Pixar staff are classically
trained Disney animators, and are also well versed in animation history. The work of the
studio has in essence sought to enhance the classical tradition defined in 'the Golden
era' through conscious use of the aesthetic and technological advances enabled by the
computer. Consequently, while the work may have a different aesthetic, and the process
by which it was made has significantly changed, the sense of 'orthodoxy' in the Disney
style remains fundamentally unaltered. There is still the preoccupation with character
animation, narrative cause and effect, aesthetic consistency, 'cartoonal' reference, an
apparently non-interventionist authorial voice (though all animation is essentially self-
reflexive and self-figurative – see below), and a reliance on dialogue and a traditional
musical soundtrack to drive and define the story. This kind of work can still be usefully
compared to two other areas of the form, which we may classify as developmental
animation and experimental animation, the former demonstrating degrees of divergence
from the dominant 'orthodoxy'; the latter, essentially seeking out alternative methods of
expression using the versatility of the form, and readily defined by non-representational,
non-objective, non-linear, 'visual music' and the stylistic pluralism of more abstract
works.

These kinds of animations operate in a way that echoes Maureen Furniss's view that
all forms of animated film have varying degrees of reference either to 'mimesis' (literally,
like 'realist' representation) or 'abstraction' (which abandons realist referents and
signifiers in preference to other models of representation) (Furniss 1998: 6). In despite of
such variation, animation remains a singularly enunciative language, literally announcing
its intrinsic difference on-screen from live-action work and other modes of artistic
expression. More importantly, in announcing itself, it further announces what Donald
Crafton has called its 'self-figurative' nature (Crafton 1993: 11); this is the particular
aspect of animation which suggests that the 'author' of the film is present on screen or
imbued in its text in a self-evidently auteurist way. This may be literally with the presence
of the animator seeming to actually draw or create the animation in films like those from
the Fleischer Brothers' *Out of the Inkwell* series featuring Koko the Clown, or more
complexly, in the way that the self-conscious handling of the distinctive language of the
animation text is used by the filmmaker. In embracing **metamorphosis**, for example,
the animator is resisting the model of record and edit that is the primacy of live action,
and specific to the ways in which image, text and narrative make literal, frame-by-frame,
special manipulations of motion construction, or on-screen transitions in animated film.
This highly self-reflexive medium enables animators to verify the freedoms of the form,
and foreground perspectives which serve as a comment on the act of filmmaking *per se*,

ideological
Although a complex
issue, ideology may be
seen as the dominant
set of ideas and values
which inform any one
society or culture, but
which are imbued in
its social behaviour
and representative
texts at a level that
is not necessarily
obvious or conscious.
An ideological stance is
normally politicised and
historically determined.
In the first instance,
cartoons seem especially
'innocent' in this
respect, but they are
characterised by implicit
and sometimes explicit
statements about gender,
race, nationality, identity
and so on which are
the fabric of ideological
positions, and require
interrogation and
inspection.

metamorphosis
The ability for a figure,
object, shape or form to
relinquish its seemingly
fixed properties
and mutate into an
alternative model. This
transformation is literally
enacted within the
animated film and acts
as a model by which
the process of change
becomes part of the
narrative of the film.
A form starts as one
thing and ends up as
something different.

but more importantly, as a revision of accepted or naturalised constructions of 'reality', and a reinterpretation of received knowledge. Virgil Widrich's playful narrative, *Fast Film* (2003) serves as a good example of this.

□ CASE STUDY 2: ANIMATION AS A SELF-REFLEXIVE LANGUAGE: *FAST FILM* (VIRGIL WIDRICH, 2003)

Virgil Widrich's extraordinary short *Fast Film* is composed of 65,000 photocopied stills from over 400 notable Hollywood feature films from the silent era to the present day. Widrich and his team viewed over 1,200 films selecting images and sequences, which in their photocopied form were folded into three-dimensional objects, and recomposed and animated into a narrative about the codes and conventions of Hollywood narratives. Simply, the 'story' is one in which a woman is abducted, a man seeks to find and save her, and confronts a villainous enemy who seeks to thwart him in a series of spectacular chases. This does not begin to describe the self-reflexive complexity of the piece, however, in which nominal figures of the 'hero', 'played', among others, by Humphrey Bogart, Sean Connery, Cary Grant and Harrison Ford, and a 'heroine', represented by Lauren Bacall, Janet Leigh and Audrey Hepburn among many, engage in typical 'live-action' scenarios of pursuit, threat, suspense, conflict, escape and resolution, but which are self-consciously executed in a deliberately rough-hewn animation style, in which digital still photographs were animated with post-production software. The images appear to 'boil', producing an 'authentic' sense of the frame-by-frame animation, while foregrounding recognisable images from a range of Hollywood genres, including the western, the horror film, the film noir, the spy film and so on. This apparently 'low-rent' style is conducted with state-of-the-art technology, and this points up the significant changes in the production process, while demonstrating the very conventions of the Hollywood classical narrative that animation customarily subverts and reworks. Widrich and his team carefully delineated the formulaic aspects of different kinds of action sequence; for example, a train chase is broken down into four elements : 'crossing a train', 'getting on a train', 'getting under a train' and 'splitting a train'. So, by cross-cutting newly configured elements, in animation, from films as diverse as *Sherlock Jnr* (1927); *The General* (1927); *The Lady Vanishes* (1938); *The Train* (1964); *Butch Cassidy and the Sundance Kid* (1969); *Runaway Train* (1985); *To Live and Die in LA* (1985) and *Broken Arrow* (1996), the construction of narrative events and emotive visual cues could be readily revealed yet reworked.

For further discussion of genre and rethinking genre see pp. 110–24.

The film may also be read as an implicit history of Hollywood, and cleverly shows the formulaic aspects of the hero's journey, informed by variations on spectacular action; the role of the heroine as a passive subject; the clichéd aspirations of the 'villain' or 'monster' in their alternative underground worlds; and the sense of resolution played out through chases and conflicts – here, in the images below, in the guise of an aerial 'dogfight' – and principally, in the romantic kiss and embrace shared by the hero and heroine. These conventions are highlighted, but ultimately revised through animation, and their limited resonance and meaning exposed and playfully critiqued. The self-figurative and self-reflexive nature of the piece invites the viewer to see the transparency, yet basic appeal of formula 'live-action' narratives, while acknowledging the self-conscious art, technique and intensity of suggestion in the animated form. Even the title is playful – 'Fast', in English, signals that this is a highly **condensed** version of the Hollywood movie, but 'Fast', in German, means 'almost'. Animation as 'almost film' suggests both its sense of differentiation and its revisionist agenda.

condensation
The compression of a set of narrative or aesthetic agendas within a minimal structural framework. Essentially, achieving the maximum amount of suggested information and implication from the minimum amount of imagery used.

• **Plate 9.1**
Individual frames from Hollywood movies are created as A4 images, which are then folded into particular shapes to be animated. Here, John Wayne, flying in a jet fighter, is re-presented as a paper plane

• **Plate 9.2**
Hundreds of 'paper planes' are created featuring the incremental movements of John Wayne flying his jet fighter, ready to be 'animated' in a new aerial sequence

• **Plate 9.3**
Wayne in his 'paper plane' is reconfigured against a new background featuring other fighter planes. This image shows how a traditional 'frame-by-frame' method is being used to create the new 'dogfight' sequence

• **Plate 9.4**
The playfulness of the sequence is readily signalled in reconfiguring the spectacle of a live-action sequence as a seemingly basic animated action played out through the use of the 'paper plane'. This simultaneously parodies the excesses and predictability of Hollywood chase sequences, and draws attention to the self-figurative and self-reflexive nature of the animation process

• **Plate 9.5**
An image from the final sequence from *Fast Film* featuring Wayne in his paper plane aircraft fleeing his pursuers

PERPETUAL 'MODERNITY'

Throughout its history, even in its most supposedly conservative and orthodox forms, animation has consistently sought to progress its art, resisting the notion of a dominant form created at the Disney Studios. While even in the contemporary period, Disney still casts a long shadow on the field of animation, it is clear that both in the US, and elsewhere, while there remained an extraordinary degree of respect for the art and culture of the Disney Studios, and recognition of its achievements and influence, there was always the desire to achieve different things in animation. For example, as a consequence of the strike at Disney Studios in 1941, Canadian animator Stephen Busustow left the company and established United Productions of America (UPA). He, along with other talented animators John Hubley, Pete Burness, Bob Cannon and Bill Hurtz, wanted to pursue a more individual style that the Disney 'look' could not accommodate. This led to work that was less specifically 'realist' in its approach, and, as Ralph Stephenson has suggested, 'the cynicism, the sophistication, the depth of adult attitudes are not ruled out' (Stephenson 1969: 48).

Ironically, this 'sophistication' was achieved through non-naturalist, fairly unsophisticated technical means. These included minimal backgrounds, 'stick' characters and non-continuous 'jerky' movements. The **squash-and-stretch** conception of movement in conventional cartoon characters, based on a design where the body is thought of as a set of circles, was replaced by the representation of a body as a few sharp lines. Backgrounds, which in Disney animation were positively voluptuous in their colour and detail, were defined by a surrealist minimalism, where stairs led nowhere and lights hung from non-existent ceilings. This kind of development expanded the vocabulary of the animated film and more readily defined animation's relationship to modern art, and the desired 'shock of the new' imbued in its form. More importantly, it challenged the ideological and aesthetic premises by which Disney animation came to define 'American' animation (see Wells 2002b). Crucially, the division that Disney had effected in separating the notion of 'art' from the 'artisanal' by insisting upon all of the essential 'collaborativeness' of a hierarchical production process being absorbed within the authorial 'brand' named as 'Walt Disney', was challenged by a more self-evidently and individually 'authored' model of the cartoon. UPA, though operating a studio system, nevertheless privileged the work of specific directors and artists, once more reuniting the art with the artisanal – those who produced the work were acknowledged as its intrinsic creators. In many senses, this was a more self-conscious model of what actually occurred at the Warner Bros studio, largely because UPA were prepared to name the cartoon as 'art' and not merely comic diversion. It is pertinent to recall, though, that it was the British studios Halas and Batchelor, and W.E. Larkins, who incorporated the idioms of modern art into their work much earlier, during the Second World War, prompted by the émigré sensibilities of their leading figures John Halas and Peter Sacks. Both had been powerfully influenced by the work of the Bauhaus, and principally Laszlo Moholy-Nagy, and though the films made by the studios acknowledged the art of Disney, their work embraced the aesthetic principles of Klee, Kandinsky and others (see Plates 9.6–9).

Halas and Batchelor and the Larkins Studios sough to operate essentially as renaissance studios, and like UPA, sought to resist Disney-style hierarchies of production. In championing a politicised 'auteurism' even within studio confines – in direct opposition to Disney's subjugation of individual styles to the established aesthetic – UPA also echoed a similar vision to that held at the Zagreb Studios in the former Yugoslavia, whose aesthetic was drawn from the same modernist sources as those championed by Halas and Sacks.

Influenced by UPA's *Gerald McBoing Boing* (1951) and *The Four Poster Bed* (1952), designed by John and Faith Hubley, the Zagreb animation industry developed around the two key figures of Dusan Vukotic and Nikola Kostelac. Initially making advertising

squash and stretch
Many cartoon characters are constructed in a way that resembles a set of maleable and attached circles which may be elongated or compressed to achieve an effect of dynamic movement. When animators 'squash' and 'stretch' these circles they effectively create the physical space of the character and a particular design structure within the overall pattern of the film. Interestingly, early Disney shorts had characters based on 'ropes' rather than circles and this significantly changes the look of the films.

• **Plate 9.6**

Balance, made in 1950 by the W.E. Larkins Studio, under the direction of Peter Sacks, was a detailed address of ICI's expenditure and profit, with a commentary by Roger MacDougal and a score by Halas and Batchelor stalwart, Francis Chagrin

• **Plate 9.7**

Predicated on simple modernist art forms, principally those advocated by Paul Klee, the film uses pertinent symbols, shapes and lines to present direct and accessible information

• **Plate 9.8**

Sacks's direction proved highly influential, as Steve Bosustow, Head of UPA, saw the film, and echoed its style and approach in *Fudget's Budget* (1952)

• **Plate 9.9**

The W.E. Larkins Studio, and particularly, the Halas and Batchelor Studio, created important work which represented a distinctively 'British' style that not merely influenced modernist animation in the US, but also provided a platform for the development of an animation industry in Britain, acknowledged by its most important successors, Aardman Animations, even in the contemporary era

reduced animation

Animation may be literally the movement of one line which, in operating through time and space, may take on characteristics which an audience may perceive as expressive and symbolic. This form of minimalism constitutes reduced animation which takes as its premise 'less is more'. Literally an eye movement or the shift of a body posture becomes enough to connote a particular feeling or meaning. This enables the films to work in a mode which has an intensity of suggestion.

films, the two progressed to making cartoons deploying **reduced animation**, which is described by Ronald Holloway:

Some films took an unbelievable eight cels to make, without losing any of the expressive movement a large number of cels usually required. Drawings were reduced to the barest minimum, and in many cases the visual effect was stronger than with twice the number of drawings.

(Holloway 1972: 12)

Liberated from the limitations of orthodox animation, these films increased the intensity of suggestion located in the images and moved towards a more avant-garde or experimental sensibility which was able to embrace aesthetic development as a model of ideological progress and political critique. Many developmental and experimental animators saw animation itself as a vehicle by which they could challenge established forms of filmmaking practice, privilege their own vision, and refresh any stagnation in the animated form, too. While Disney's work was undoubtedly a pinnacle in the form, it both marginalised other 'cartoonal' forms and their pioneer creators, and rendered more progressive work as somehow unrelated to the dominant aesthetic and cultural identity defined by the cartoon. Although explicit here, the ways in which animated films can simultaneously make statements and advance the self-reflexiveness and modernity of the form itself are many and varied. Crucially, these kinds of works have responded to the changing creative and cultural climate in which they were made, using animation as a vehicle by which both subversive and alternative perspectives may be maintained. Ironically, though, it was economic factors which prompted radical change in the American animation industry. As the major studios closed their animation production units, unable to support the rising costs of producing cartoons, the era of theatrically distributed shorts was at an end. Despite misgivings that this was somehow 'the end' for animation altogether, television became the new exhibition context, and Hanna Barbera perfected a method of reduced animation – not dissimilar to the Zagreb and UPA approach – which was based on a limited number of movement cycles, but enhanced with high-quality vocal performances by, among others, Daws Butler and June Foray, and sharp, gag-laden scripts. From the *The Huckleberry Hound Show* through to *The Flintstones*, Hanna Barbera defined the television cartoon and sustained the animation industry. Unfortunately, the television cartoon in the period between the 1950s, almost through to the emergence of *The Simpsons*, is still often denigrated, but this is to neglect important work, and to once more reduce the animated form to an art with connotations of innocence and undemandingness, but of course, in response, this has been readily exploited by animators knowing that the very 'cuteness' of their expression may be the mechanism by which they can position the viewers' expectations only to challenge them. John Kricfalusi, one of the key directors of the contemporary television era, is a case in point.

☐ CASE STUDY 3 : RECALLING AND REVISING ANIMATION TRADITION: *THE REN AND STIMPY SHOW*

For many years, television cartoons have only been perceived in the light of their 'process-driven' presence; a form seemingly without authorship; a variety of funny narratives in which the characters seemed self-determining rather than the product of known artists. This in itself is ironic given the intrinsic artifice of the form. A greater recognition of this artifice in recent times, however, has not merely recovered modes of authorship, but also a recognition that the enunciativeness in the form should operate as a signifier of the knowledge that repromotes the importance of animation as an art form and a social signifier. John Kricfalusi's *The Ren and Stimpy Show* becomes a significant example of this process, taking on the self-conscious approach of a 'creator-driven' project which sought to foreground the self-conscious nature of the cartoon to a known model of potential spectatorship in 'baby boomer' adults and children willing to embrace a more taboo-breaking model of expression.

In prioritising the inherent properties of the medium and speaking to a visual literacy in his assumed audience, Kricfalusi once more reoriented the television cartoon to reflect the contingency and aesthetics of 'the Golden era'. Kricfalusi cites Dave Fleischer's 1930s' 'Talkatoons'; Grim Natwick's 'Betty Boop' designs; movement cycles in the *Popeye* cartoons; Chuck Jones's incongruous comic juxtapositions of classical music and cartoonal slapstick; Bob Clampett's *The Great Piggy Bank Robbery* (1946) and Hanna Barbera's *Tom and Jerry* cartoons as the key cartoonal influences that underpin his work, and provoke his dictums 'Symmetry is ungodly', 'No sharp angles, points or straight lines' and 'Need [to include] shit-eating grin', the latter a recognition of the satisfaction the cartoon medium offers in breaking taboo areas through the artifice of the graphic medium – anything you see is not really happening, but demonstrates what happens if it might have.

The Ren and Stimpy Show may be viewed as Kricalfusi's stand against what may be regarded as the least successful television cartoon. His explicit role as author, and his application of classical cartoonal aesthetics as an 'explicit' art within a popular form, marks out *The Ren and Stimpy Show* even from successful contemporaries like Mike Judge's *Beavis and Butthead*. Kricfalusi simultaneously wishes to recall, reappraise and revive the work of Chuck Jones, Tex Avery, Bob Clampett, and most specifically, Joe Barbera, while critiquing both the production context and history of the late television cartoon. This is achieved by using the extremes of representational possibility available within the classical animation vocabulary, particularly as it was executed within the Warner Bros and MGM cartoons of the 1940s, to portray the potential extremes of behavioural conduct and cultural mores in the late millennial period.

Furthermore, this was also known by Nickelodeon, as they sought initially to exploit the retro-styling of the cartoon in the assured knowledge that the best animation had longevity – *Looney Tunes* and *Tom and Jerry* still play after fifty years – and that the adult/child cross-over audience would engage with the known constituency of established appeal. Kricfalusi's work, however, moved beyond the 'knowing' cultural critique of *The Simpsons*, or the 'dumbed down' irony of *Beavis and Butthead*, and sought to reconfigure the design and spirit of the cartoon as a comic tension between noir foreboding and surreal brutalism, which criticised 'television' and the culture that produced it. Kricalfusi's use of catch-phrases from cartoons – Mr Jinx's 'I hate meeses to pieces' or Elmer Fudd's 'I'm huntin' for a wabbit' – work as aural fragments which offer a casual reminder of the way in which the cartoon restates its credentials within an updated, self-conscious form. Kricfalusi takes this considerably further though, using the cartoon to challenge views about contemporary taste and decency.

Son of Stimpy, the saga of Stimpy's search for 'Stinky', his fart-child, in its scenario alone stretches notions of credibility and acceptibility. Kricfalusi opens the cartoon with Stimpy watching cartoons on the television (the audience can only assume this fact from the soundtrack, however, as no images are seen), and engaging with a ritualistic act of flatulence; in Stimpy's eyes, the protracted performance, and the small 'skidmarks' left on the floor, evidence of the 'birth' of a child. From here, sustained only by the internal logic of the cartoon itself, Stimpy's 'fart-child', Stinky, is assumed to be a real, living entity. The fart's status as a gas, however, means that it apparently disappears as soon as it is born, and it is only Stimpy's faith in the existence of his 'son' that transcends Ren's scepticism about Stimpy's 'stinky fantasies', and the patronising 'just-agree-with-him, he's-mad' sensibility of the 'magic nose goblins' still living beneath a chair under which they have been wiped, who Stimpy consults about Stinky's possible whereabouts. Stimpy slumps into protracted depression about Stinky's absence, provoking Ren to note: 'It's been three years, I'm starting to worry about you.' Ren tries to comfort Stimpy at Christmas, offering to kiss under the mistletoe, but Stimpy angrily rejects him, and heads off out into the snowy night to find Stinky. Putting up 'Have you smelled me' posters of Stinky, Stimpy lives through urban oppressiveness; false alarms – he thinks he has found Stinky at a stable selling fresh manure; and the excessive cold, ultimately returning home in an ice block. Stinky, meanwhile, is also searching, escaping two hobos who attempt to 'light' him – a reference to the schoolboy prank of attempting to ignite 'fart' gas – and living underground. Finally, however, he is reunited with Stimpy in the 'squelch' of an embrace, but almost immediately he claims his independence in order to be married to a dead cod-head. The marriage takes place, and Stimpy enjoys 'a happy ending'.

Kricfalusi legitimises his narrative by bringing the melodramatic 'lost son' motif to an otherwise taboo subject: the breaking of wind, and the intimation of the emission of bodily waste. Stimpy 'values' this reductive act as a productive act. The 'fart' is now a 'figure', and with this transformation comes the address of a 'subject', rather than the abstract retention of an 'object'. The central currency of the whole cartoon is predicated on things that were impolite to talk about, but actually the object of amusement for both children and adults alike in 'real life' – farting, nose-picking, body odour and so on. The 'Son of God' motif which underpins the cartoon, signalled in its title and its

Christmas setting and soundtrack, allies the sacred and profane in a way that some might find provocative. Kricfalusi does not make this a coherent analogy, however, but self-evidently uses the 'openness' of the animated vocabulary for subversive purposes.

A crucial point here is that animation can work as a language of **dilution** in some circumstances and **amplification** in others. Arguably, Kricfalusi uses the animation of the children's cartoon, and the supposedly innocent environment of children's programming to subversive ends because the seemingly unpalatable or challenging aspects of his work are diluted by the assumption that this is 'merely' animation – ink and paint, and no more – and that animation does not carry with it charges of difficulty and unacceptability. Clearly, Kricfalusi's eventual removal by Nickelodeon from his own vehicle was testament to the view that animation can be seen, though, as an amplification of challenging perspectives, equally legitimised and sustained by their artifice.

THE IMPACT OF ANIMÉ

dilution and
amplification
The simultaneous capacity for animation, by virtue of its intrinsic artifice to be viewed either as a language which dilutes its outcomes and effects, rendering them 'innocent' and 'dismissable', or as a language which inherently amplifies its literal, aesthetic and ideological perspectives, rendering them sometimes unacceptably challenging in their representational aspects.

The Ren and Stimpy Show was instrumental in proving that television animation could be progressive and revive recollections of 'the Golden era'. Hanna Barbera and Filmation, among others, created any number of 'Saturday Morning Cartoons', but television also provided the first platform for the emergence of Japanese animation in the West. Osamu Tezuka, 'the God of Comics' and 'the Disney of Japan', was a key figure in both the manga and animation industries in Japan, his Mushi Production Company, creating 'Astro Boy' which debuted in the US in 1963. Japan's first colour animation for television, Tezuka's *Kimba the White Lion*, was broadcast by NBC in 1966, and in recent years has become part of an ongoing dispute, where it has been alleged that Disney's *The Lion King* (1994) drew upon Kimba for its characters and story unacknowledged (see Patten 2004: 144–91). However this might be viewed, it is indisputable that Japanese animation has been extraordinarily influential, not merely in the field of animation but on Hollywood film in general. Mamoru Oshii's *Ghost in the Shell* (1995), for example, is an oft-cited forerunner of *The Matrix* series (1999–2003), while Hayao Miyazaki's *Laputa, the Flying Island* (1986) is a clear influence on Disney's 'Atlantis'. Indeed, Miyazaki's work in general, from *Nausicaa of the Valley of the Winds* (1984) to *Howl's Moving Castle* (2004) has not merely established Miyazaki as a major animation auteur but a key Japanese director likened to live-action masters Kurosawa, Ozu and Mizoguchi, and an established figure in world cinema *per se*.

☐ CASE STUDY 4: HAYAO MIYAZAKI

Miyazaki began his career at the Toei Doga Studio in 1963, but was soon established as a key animator on Isao Takahata's *The Little Norse Prince* (1968), and eventually directed his first feature *The Castle of Cagliostro* in 1979. Miyazaki, like Tezuka, was a talented comic book artist, and created a graphic novel called *Nausicaa of the Valley of the Winds*, which was serialised in Toshio Suzuki's *Animage* magazine, later resulting in an animated feature of the story in 1984, and Suzuki funding a new animation studio, Studio Ghibli, led by Miyazaki and his colleague Takahata. Critically acclaimed films like *My Neighbour Totoro* (1988) and *Kiki's Delivery Service* (1989) followed, but only when Miyazaki's characters were fully exploited in relation to merchandising – much to his disappointment – did a mass audience find his work. *Porco Rosso* (1992), *Princess Mononoke* (1997) and *Spirited Away* (2001) all broke box-office records, but also established Miyazaki's core themes and preoccupations.

Miyazaki has been consistent in his use of young heroines, arguing that stories are still largely determined by male sensibilities, and that the use of a central female character enables greater freedom in the narrative and points of emotional transcendence. Furthermore, the young heroine has special purchase in Japan, as there is a sense of a 'lost era' of innocence and intrinsic 'Japaneseness' represented in these girl figures for a certain generation, and which is often misinterpreted in the West in relation to its erotic and cultural charge. Miyazaki uses his heroines to explore not merely their own rites of passage towards maturity, but also the conflicting personal, social and ideological forces at large in cultural life which affect individual experience, and cannot necessarily be resolved. While many of Miyazaki's characters have moments of epiphany and revelation that empower them and enable them to come to terms with their difficulties – often through elevation and flight – they often exist in dream-like, supernatural or surreal alternative worlds which cannot be subjected to rational and civilised order, and the limits of everyday habit and routine. Consequently, Miyazaki can depict characters not merely in their local time and place, but as part of a complex, multifaceted, historically indeterminable space, which illustrates the spiritual, sociological and political dynamics of experience. Miyazaki's key preoccupation in this respect would be a concern for ecological issues, and the ways in which the particular abuses of nature by humankind operate as a betrayal of children and their future lives. Miyazaki's main focus therefore is to address the sometimes contradictory, ambivalent and violent aspects of the human sensibility in order to foreground – mainly through his heroines – the more positive and progressive human values and emotions.

While Katsuhiro Otomo's *Akira* (1988) can claim to be the first major 'cross-over' animé in the West, and along with Mamoru Oshii's *Patlabor* (1990) and *Ghost in the Shell* (1995) and its sequel, *Innocence* (2004), operate as key works in charting a more dystopic, apocalyptic agenda in postwar Japan, it is Miyazaki's vision, still mostly achieved through hand-drawn cel-animated processes, though more recently including computer-generated material, that prevails as an insightful engagement both with animation as a medium of expression and a model of story-telling seeking to express universal concern, while promoting love and hope as intrinsic human qualities necessary for survival and progress. Like many great animation directors and artists, and like the form itself, Miyazaki continues to experiment, while speaking to a mainstream audience.

Continuing to experiment

For further discussion of art cinema, narrative and film form, see Chapter 3, pp. 61–2 and 66–7.

Experimental animation, in its most readily understood form, embraces a number of styles and approaches to the animated film which inevitably cross over into areas which we may also term avant-garde or art films. A great deal of animation has been constituted in new forms (computer, photocopy, sand on glass, direct on to celluloid, pinscreen) and resists traditional approaches as they have been understood within the cartoonal realm. William Moritz has argued that this form of non-objective and non-linear animation is actually the purest conception of animation, as its language is significantly different from its live action counterpart and most explicitly reveals the distinctive range and extent of the animated vocabulary (see Canemaker 1988: 21–32). Fundamentally, such films exhibit the greatest degree of abstraction and are more concerned with rhythm and movement in their own right, rejecting logical and linear continuity, moving away from the depiction of conventional forms and the assumed 'objectivity' of the exterior world, enabling shapes and objects to move, and liberating the artist to concentrate on the vocabulary he or she is using in itself instead of giving it a specific function or meaning. As Leopold Survage wrote,

I will animate my painting. I will give it movement. I will introduce rhythm into the concrete action of my abstract painting, born of my interior life; my instrument will be the cinematographic film, this true symbol of accumulated movement. It will execute 'the scores' of my visions, corresponding to my state of mind in its successive phases.... I am creating a new visual art in time, that of coloured rhythm and of rhythmic colour.

(quoted in Russett and Starr 1976: 96)

This kind of subjective work has therefore necessitated a different response from audiences. Instead of being located in understanding narrative, the audience is asked to bring its own interpretation to the work. Colour, shape and texture evoke certain moods and ideas, and give pleasure in their own right without having to be attached to a specific meaning or framework. The audience may recognise the physical nature of the paint or physical materials themselves, the associations with the colours used, the sheer spontaneity in the work, which may recall the freedoms of expression in the pre-socialised child and so on. These films are largely personal, subjective, original responses, which are the work of artists seeking to use the animated form in an innovative way. Sometimes these 'visions' are impenetrable and resist easy interpretation, being merely the absolutely individual expression of the artist. This in itself, once again, draws attention to the relationship between the artist and the work, and the relationship of the audience to the artist as it is being mediated through the work. The abstract nature of the films insists upon the recognition of their individuality. Further, these films may aspire to the condition of the dream-state, or memory, or fantasy, which, of course, has its own abstract logic, but conforms to a common understanding of human experience which embraces these states of consciousness. Dreams, memories, fantasies and the interpretation of thought processes may be the vehicles for personal visions but they possess a universalised dimension. Such work often has a strong relationship to music, and, indeed, it may be suggested that if music could be visualised it would resemble colours and shapes moving through time with differing rhythms, movements and speeds. Some filmmakers perceive that there is a psychological and emotional relationship with sound and colour which may only be expressed through the freedoms afforded through the use of animation. Sound is important in any animated film, but has particular resonance in the experimental film as it is often resisting dialogue, the clichéd sound effects of the cartoon or the easy emotiveness of certain kinds of music. Silence, avant-garde scores, unusual sounds and redefined notions of 'language' are used to create different kinds of statement.

□ CASE STUDY 5: NORMAN MCLAREN

Norman McLaren is probably the most experimental filmmaker in the animation field. He has explored a number of different styles, including direct animation (drawing directly on to celluloid), paper and object animation (stop-motion frame-by-frame constructions of movement with objects and cut-outs and so on), evolution works (the gradual evolution of a pastel or chalk drawing) and multiple printing works (where movements are recorded as they evolve through the multiple printing of each stage of the movement). Beyond the implicit influence of his work, he also nurtured other artists, and maintained a pacifist, left-wing, humanitarian agenda in his creative practice, evidenced early in his student film *Hell UnLtd* (1936).

Educated at the Glasgow School of Art in 1933, he made his first experimental 'cameraless' film in 1934, having been inspired by Oskar Fischinger's *Brahm's Hungarian Dance* (1931), and seeking out a reel of film to scrub clean and paint on. He then entered two films, *Camera Makes Whoopee* and *Colour Cocktail* in the Glasgow Film Festival of 1936. Although he believed the former to be his 'calling card' to the creative industries, it was the latter that impressed documentary filmmaker John Grierson, who invited McLaren to work at the General Post Office (GPO) Film Unit. Initially undertaking live-action camerawork for *Defence of Madrid* (1936), McLaren was later encouraged by the new studio head, Alberto Cavalcanti, to engage in his own films, and to work in a more improvised, looser style, than that signalled in McLaren's meticulously prepared original scripts. Although many have only seen Grierson as a documentary filmmaker committed to left-leaning works of social record, and someone not especially concerned with aesthetics, this is to neglect his interest in the 'creative interpretation of actuality', and more importantly, the key purpose in engaging with a left-wing agenda – to ensure not merely that the disempowered might find proper representation, but that the core democratic principle of the freedom of expression was clearly demonstrated in the work itself. Thus Grierson's work with Len Lye and Norman McLaren was a ready example of redefining 'films of record' to capture the spiritual and creative freedoms of expression of the artist in its purest, non-objective, non-linear form. McLaren made *Love on the Wing* (1938) and *Many a Pickle* (1938); the former, like many of McLaren's works, an experiment in moving abstract images aligned with and counterpointing musical idioms – in this case, Jacques Ibert's *Divertissement* – which was banned by the postmaster for its apparent use of phallic imagery. McLaren traced his interest in this kind of filmmaking to his high school years in which he only possessed a radio, and cultivated his ability to mentally visualise images which supported the dynamics of the music rather than creating a literal narrative to illustrate it. This drew McLaren to pursue research in colour and form rather than the rigours of story-telling.

McLaren was then invited by the Museum of Non-objective Painting, later named the Guggenheim, in New York, to make a range of abstract loops, including *Allegro* (1939) and *Dots* (1940), though he managed also to make two other personal films – *Stars and Stripes* (1939), which used the US flag as its background, and an experimental electronic work with Mary Ellen Bute, *Spook Sport* (1939). By this time Grierson had moved on to establish the National Film Board of Canada (NFB) and McLaren joined him, becoming head of the newly formed animation unit in 1943. Embracing the creative freedom offered by the NFB, even though the Board was charged with making films about Canada and Canadians, McLaren embarked on a career that sought to advance animation as an art form, most notably by drawing upon its relationship to dance in such films as *Blinkety Blink* (1954) and *Pas de deux* (1968), but also the imaginative use of sound – for example, in *Begone Dull Care* (1949) and *Synchromy* (1971). McLaren's desire to transcend national and ethnic boundaries within his work, and to ensure aesthetic, technical and creative innovation, meant that he used little dialogue, and employed multilingual credits. Crucially, McLaren's work, in the extension of technique, sought to be *about* the animated form as much as it also signified an implied subject matter in the apprehension of particular feelings or moods. *Neighbours* (1952), his famous anti-war parable, was a more explicit expression of McLaren's preoccupations, and not only redefined the cartoon, the principles of live-action performance and the use of animation as a peacetime propaganda tool, but also embodied the philosophic, imaginative and

• **Plate 9.10**
Norman McClaren working directly on to film stock, prompted by the notations of his 'script' – essentially reference points about motion and music

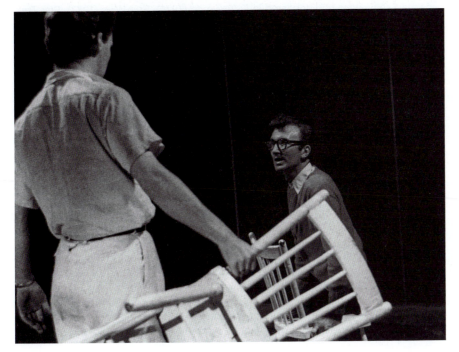

• **Plate 9.11**
One of McLaren's 'dope sheets' aligning proposed action with the intended rhythms on the soundtrack, essentially creating a model of 'visual music'

• **Plate 9.12**
McClaren working on the choreography for *A Chairy Tale*, in which a chair takes on a life of its own, part animated frame by frame, and part created through the use of invisible wires

humanitarian heart of Norman McLaren's vision. McLaren's playful engagement with the quasi-figurative, decorative and purely abstract forms in sensitive relation to the rhythmic dynamics of a variety of soundtracks both paid tribute to the European pioneers of the experimental form cited earlier, and encouraged generations of other animation filmmakers who wished to work with alternative techniques and approaches.

COMPUTERS AND CONVERGENCE

As has been suggested earlier in this discussion, experimentation has taken place in all forms of animation from the traditional cartoon to the explicitly avant-garde work. Animation can create the conditions to express new visions by devising a vocabulary which is both unlimitedly expressive and always potentially progressive because it need not refer to or comply with the codes and conventions of representation and expression that have preceded it. The three models of orthodox, developmental and experimental animation are constantly changing. Computer technology is enabling a new generation of animators to work with a different tool in order to both use traditional methods and invent fresh approaches to the animated form. Science, art and the moving image are conjoining to create a new digital cinema, enabling both a re-determination of the animated film and the enhancement of special effects in mainstream movies.

From the early experimental uses of computer animation at NASA and the Massachusetts Institute of Technology; the film exercises of James Whitney senior and junior; the proto-CG works of Stan Vanderbeek (*Poemfields*, 1967–69), Lillian Schwartz (*Pictures from a Gallery*, 1976) and Peter Foldes (*Hunger*, 1973); the work of the Halas and Batchelor Studio – both in the creation of pieces like Roger Mainwood's *Autobahn* (1979) for cult group Kraftwerk, the ground-breaking adaptation of Laslo Moholy-Nagy's modernist experiments in *A Memory of Moholy-Nagy* (1991) and in the prescient promotion of computer animation as a tool of the future (see Halas and Wells 2006); and in the early output of the PIXAR company, there is already a history of animation in computing which exhibits the continual development of a vocabulary that is extending the limits of the form.

Although a great deal of work had been done by the mid-1980s, and computer-generated sequences had appeared in *Futureworld* (1976), *Star Wars* (1977), *Star Trek: The Wrath of Khan* (1983), *Tron* (1983) and *The Last Starfighter* (1984), among others, it was three ground-breaking short pieces which ensured that computer-generated animation would transcend its extraordinary expense, long production cycle and lack of a standard software, to ultimately become the dominant form of expression in the form. First, Daniel Langlois' *Tony Le Peltrie* (1985), featuring an ageing lounge singer lamenting changing times, but even, despite its excessive caricature, proving that persuasive character animation could be executed in computer-generated form. Second, Robert Abel's *Brilliance* (1985), an advertisement, featured a '*Metropolis*-style' female robot, using the first primitive motion capture, and proving that computer-generated work could be visually attractive, create more sophisticated outcomes than common 'fly-throughs', and offer some form of dramatisation. Third, and most significant, ex-Disney animator John Lasseter's highly effective computer-animated shorts – *Luxo Jnr* (1986), *Tin Toy* (1990) and *Knick Knack* (1991), which, by emulating the character animation of Disney and the gag-structures of Warner Brothers and MGM cartoons, proved that computer animation could embrace 'the cartoon'. These film experiments culminated in the first full-length fully computer-generated feature *Toy Story* (1995), and its sequel, the equally engaging *Toy Story 2* (1999) which demonstrated what computer-generated images were initially uniquely able to offer. The toys were the perfect vehicle for the three-dimensional sense of smoothness and plasticity achievable using the geometric potentialities afforded by computer programs; further, the playroom space was fully exploited for the sense of dynamic movement through three-dimensional space also afforded by the computer. Inevitably, though – and this echoes the paradigm instigated by Disney – PIXAR continued to innovate in the area of computer-generated animation by pursuing ever greater degrees of realism (see Wells 2002a). If *Toy Story* is PIXAR's *Snow White and the Seven Dwarfs*, then *Monsters Inc* is PIXAR's *Bambi*, perfecting the fullest representation of 'hyper-realism' in the animated form (see Wells 2002c). This was compounded further in the brilliant undersea vistas of *Finding Nemo* (2003) and the extraordinary character animation in addressing the limitations of representing fish. While Dreamworks SKG have responded to PIXAR's work with the Warner-styled *Shrek* franchise, and Blue Sky have created entertaining pieces in *Ice Age* (2003) and *Robots* (2005), it was PIXAR's *The Incredibles* (2004) that created a watershed in computer-generated animation by being a fully realised piece of 'cinema' for children and adults, and setting a benchmark by which the quality of computer-generated films must be measured. Director Brad Bird's intention to 'break out' and create a narrative which could accommodate Bergmanesque domestic bleakness, Bond-style spectacle, and a genuine thematic conviction in addressing the redefinition of 'heroes' in the post–9/11 era; depicting the dangers of cultural conformism; and the powerlessness of humanity in the face of its social infrastructures, moved computer-generated features to the point where they can only be evaluated by what they are seeking to achieve rather than the 'awe' factor of their mere creation. Such has been the speed with which computer-generated features have become the orthodoxy in animation that a critical mass of production has now been reached where the 'technology' and its innovations is no longer sufficient in evaluating the progress of the form, and it is once more the traditional skills in innovative storytelling, persuasive character animation and inventive visual spectacle that will determine the next classic in the field.

Crucially, though, as more independent filmmakers embrace computer-generated animation, the dominant aesthetic established by PIXAR and its challengers will be changed and subverted. Already, Yoichiro Kawaguchi, in Japan, has sought to be more abstract and experimental in his computer-generated films – *Eggy* (1990), *Festival* (1991) and *Mutation* (1992) – by emulating organic forms and developing random systems which create different shapes, forms and colour combinations. British animator William Latham has also created software to execute designs in a similar spirit, for example, in *Biogenesis* (1993). Ruth Lingford has also successfully used computer animation to make more challenging work in the graphic starkness of *Death and the Mother* (1996) and *Pleasures of War* (1999) (see Wells 2001b: 338–9). Further, Johnny Hardstaff with *The Future of Gaming* (2001), Marc Craste with *JoJo in the Stars* (2004) and Chris Landreth with *Ryan* (2004) have already achieved works of high standing by once more revisiting and revising established vocabularies in the graphic and visual arts.

Hardstaff's controversial film, originally commissioned to promote Sony Playstation, is a sinister piece suggesting that the oppressive corporate intentions of the games masters, in keeping the masses amused and rewarded in facilitating a late capitalist system, have been challenged by a subversive global uprising prompted by the games themselves, which instigates everything from the release of uninhibited desire, the abuse of social convention, the dismissal of religious faith and the rise of arbitrary terrorism. Hardstaff's imagery draws upon a range of traditions in graphic design, illustration and decoration, and is used to make the familiar and formerly instructive a terrain of threat and subversion. His style resists any formalist tradition in animation, and consequently progresses the animated form in its graphic precision and social insight.

Marc Craste does something of a similar order in *JoJo in the Stars* by creating a romantic narrative in the half-light of a surreal and distant nightmare, based on the kinds of distanciating abstraction in films such as David Lynch's *Eraserhead*, and the understated perversity and unspeakable ambivalence in films such as Tod Browning's *Freaks*, and the Universal horror films of the 1930s. Such work recalls innovative aesthetic strategies, but further progresses them by divesting them of the 'camp' and 'kitsch' postmodern readings with which they are often attributed, and recalling the genuine sense of alienation and loss at their heart. This is computer animation with feeling and emotion which is

• Plate 9.13

Hardstaff's understanding of the symbolic and sign-led aspects of graphic design, contemporary gaming imagery and animation reinvigorates the form, creating a new hybrid of animated 'documentary' and graphic fiction

• Plate 9.14

Hardstaff's profoundly controversial imagery and its implications prove that animation should not be understood merely as an 'innocent' cartoonal form, but one able to embrace serious, subversive and challenging perspectives

• Plate 9.15

Animation is in essence 'moving graphics', but rarely have the imperatives of interior, product or industrial design strategies been used for narrative effects. Hardstaff's perspectives use all of these visual strategies and more, drawn from the history of art and design, to redraft the animation palette

not about the contrived sentimentalities of traditional classical narrative, but imbued in the aesthetic and motion of the piece. Chris Landreth's *Ryan* also seeks to prompt an emotive response, but his work, based on the life of former renowned animator at the National Film Board of Canada, now homeless street panhandler Ryan Larkin, uses a form of 'psychological realism' to redefine the documentary form. Landreth's command of the computer software enables him to create fragmented figures, seemingly in a state of atrophy and psychosomatic flux, and the characters themselves become readily symbolic of their disintegrating psychological states. Concerned with memory, addiction, compulsion and loss, the film defines aspects of the creative sensibility from the point of view of the subject – Larkin himself – and the maker of the film, Landreth. Once more, it is animation itself which is also enhanced as a language of illusion and artifice, but as the most appropriate medium to create a visual and aural terrain that extracts and literally depicts psychological and emotional truth.

These filmmakers merely exemplify the ways in which animation continues to develop, embrace change and push back the frontiers of creative expression. As the post-photographic era becomes increasingly consolidated, it is the language of future expression, drawing upon the rich legacy of its progressive past.

FURTHER READING

Barrier, M., *Hollywood Cartoons: American Animation in the Golden Age*, New York and Oxford: Oxford University Press, 1999.

Beck, J., *Animation Art*, London: Flame Tree Publishing, 2004.

Bell, E., Haas L. and Sells, L. (eds), *From Mouse to Mermaid: The Politics of Film, Gender and Culture*, Bloomington and Indianapolis: Indiana University Press, 1995.

Crafton, D., *Before Mickey: The Animated Film 1898–1928*, Chicago and London: University of Chicago Press, 1993.

Furniss, M., *Art in Motion: Animation Aesthetics*, London and Montrouge: John Libbey, 1998.

Klein, N., *7 Minutes*, London: Verso, 1993.

Leslie, E., *Hollywood Flatlands: Animation, Critical Theory and the Avant Garde*, London: Verso, 2002.

Manovich, L., *The Language of New Media*, Massachusetts : MIT, 2002.

Patten, F. *Watching Anime, Reading Manga*, Berkeley : Stone Bridge Press, 2004

Pilling, J. (ed.), *Women and Animation: A Compendium*, London: BFI, 1992.

Russett, R. and Starr, C., *Experimental Animation*, New York: Da Capo, 1976.

Wasko, J., *Understanding Disney*, Cambridge and Malden: Polity Press, 2001.

Wellins, M. *Storytelling Through Animation*, Hingham, MA: Charles Rive Media Inc, 2005.

Wells, P., *Understanding Animation*, London and New York: Routledge 1998.

Wells, P., *Animation: Genre and Authorship*, London: Wallflower Press, 2002a.

Wells, P., *Fundamentals of Animation*, Lausanne: AVA, 2006.

FURTHER VIEWING

Here are some key models of animated film which repay viewing and analysis:

Akira (1988) (Dir.: Katsuhiro Otamo)

Asparagus (1978) (Dir.: Suzan Pitt)

Bad Luck Blackie (1943) (Dir.: Tex Avery)

Binky and Boo (1989) (Dirs: Derek Hayes and Phil Austen)

Boy Who Saw the Iceberg, The (2000) (Dir: Paul Driessen)

Coal Black and de Sebben Dwarfs (1943) (Dir: Bob Clampett)

Dimensions of Dialogue (1982) (Dir.: Jan Svankmajer)

Dreams and Desires, Family Ties (2006) (Dir: Joanna Quinn)

Ersatz (1961) (Dir.: Dusan Vukotic)

Fast Film (2003) (Dir: Virgil Widrich)

Father and Daughter (2000) (Dir.: Michael Dudok de Wit)

Fatty Issues (1990) (Dir.: Candy Guard)

Give Up Yer Aul Sins (2001) (Dir: Cathal Gaffney)

Great (1974) (Dir.: Bob Godfrey)

Hand, The (1965) (Dir.: Jiri Trnka)

Hat, The (1964) (Dirs: John and Faith Hubley)

I Married a Strange Person (1997) (Dir: Bill Plympton)

Knick Knack (1991) (Dir.: John Lasseter)

Mona Lisa Descending a Staircase (1991) (Dir: Joan Gratz)

Morir de Amor (2005) (Dir : Gil Alkabetz)

Nose, The (1963) (Dir.: Alexander Alexieff)

Pas de deux (1967) (Dir.: Norman McLaren)

Popeye the Sailor meets Sinbad the Sailor (1936) (Dir.: Dave Fleischer)

Red Hot Riding Hood (1949) (Dir.: Tex Avery)

Springer and the S.S. (1946) (Dir.: Jiri Trnka)

Stain, The (1991) (Dirs: Christine Roche and Marjut Rimmenen)

Street, The (1974) (Dir.: Caroline Leaf)

Tale of Tales (1979) (Dir.: Yuri Norstein)

Tango (1981) (Dir.: Zbigniew Rybczynski)

The Incredibles (2004) (Dir.: Brad Bird)

Three Little Pigs (1933) (Dir.: Walt Disney)

Triangle (1994) (Dir: Erica Russell)

What's Opera, Doc? (1957) (Dir.: Chuck Jones)

RESOURCE CENTRES

The UK Directory, *Animation UK* is an invaluable resource in that it lists most animators, animation companies and facilitators, and courses running in Britain. Published annually by BECTU.

http: //www.aardman.com/
Aardman Animations

http: //www.annecy-animation-festival.tm.fr/
Annecy Festiva

http: //www.awn.com/
Animation World Network. The database section is pretty minimal and often incorrect; the best thing is the magazine's breadth of articles, mainly written by animators, critics or festival programmers. The What's New section in AWN is convenient for updates. The Animation Village has several listings and links to animators, organisations, festivals and so on. in the international animation world. Artists such as Caroline Leaf and Alison Snowden/ David Fine have their own home pages on AWN. The same has Nicole Salomon's AAA in Annecy, Folioscope, ASIFA Hollywood and ASIFA San Francisco, as well as the Society for Animation Studies, Motion Picture Screen Cartoonists Union Local 839 and the Writers Guild of America. There are also links to other similar home pages not hosted by AWN, such as ASIFA International.

http: //www.awn.com/asifa_hollywood/
ASIFA Hollywood

http: //www.awn.com/asifa-sf/
ASIFA San Francisco
ASIFA East and ASIFA San Francisco produce quite informative articles, and provide information on current (US-based) projects, both commercial and independent, as well as opinion pieces.

http: //www.awn.com/heaven_and_hell/
Animation Heaven and Hell. This site has nicely designed pages on model and stop-frame animation, including [0160]vankmajer and George Pal.

http: //www.awn.com/safo99/
Ottawa Festival

http: //www.chapman.edu/animation/
Animation Journal

http: //www.medios.fi/animafest/
Zagreb Festival

**http: //memory.loc.gov/ammem/oahtml/
    oahome.html**
Origins of American Animation web site

http: //www.nfb.ca/E/1/1/
National Film Board of Canada. The National Film Board of Canada has a really impressive site. You can go through their whole catalogue of films with descriptions; many of the most important filmmakers have their own biography; and the history of NFBC is extensively described. The main problem with the NFBC home page is that the entry page is too big, it takes minutes to download; skip it and go directly to the index.

http: //Samson.hivolda.no: 8000/asifa/
ASIFA International

http: //www.swcp.com/animate/
ASIFA Central

http: //www.yrd.com/asifa/
ASIFA East

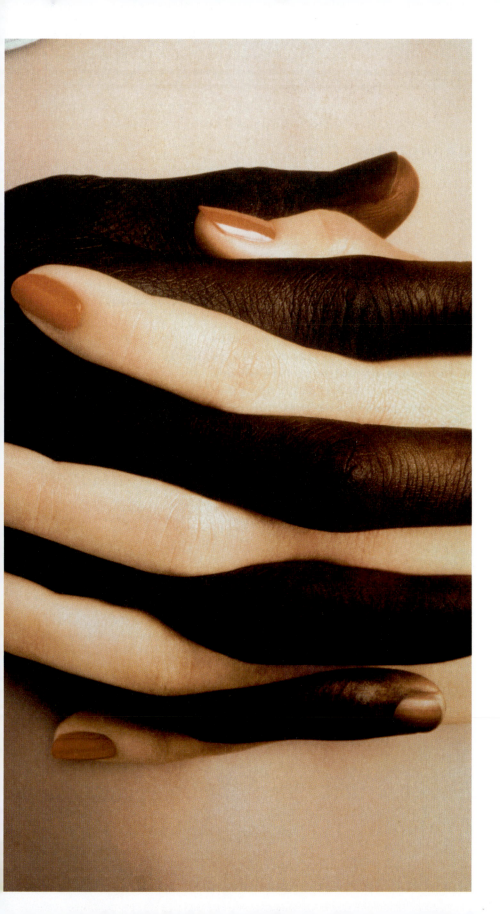

Cinema, identities and the politics of representation

Chapter 10

Gender and film

Jill Nelmes

■ Gender and film

INTRODUCTION

In the past decade there has been an increasing interest in examining how we understand gender and how gender may be understood in relation to film. In many ways this interest in studying gender has arisen out of feminist film studies research which brought the study of the representation of women in film on to the academic agenda, originally from a psychoanalytic perspective. At the same time, within the field of cultural studies, there has been a growing interest in looking at how we understand masculinity and femininity, and to what extent gender is culturally determined. The study of gender and film also raises questions about cross-gender issues and asks how our sexuality is defined.

The importance of feminist film theory in opening up debates around spectatorship, the male gaze and the role women play as 'object of the look' is evident from the influence it has had in many areas of academic study from art to literature and cultural studies. Although woman was originally the main focus of academic inquiry about gender and cinema there had been earlier discussion of masculinity: Joan Mellen in *Big Bad Wolves: Masculinity in the American Film*, for instance, wrote on the subject with some eloquence in the 1970s. Laura Mulvey's seminal article, 'Visual Pleasure and Narrative Cinema', published in 1975, was so influential that academic inquiry in the 1970s and early 1980s mostly focused on the representation of women in film. Little attention was given to the study of masculinity until the 1980s, when Steven Neale's essay, 'Masculinity as Spectacle', reopened the debate (see Cohan and Hark 1993).

Why study gender and film?

As humans we are interested in who we are and how we are defined. One of the primary, if not the primary, ways of defining ourselves is through gender. The physical characteristics which determine our gender are with us from the day we are born and are changeable only by surgery; exactly how much of gender is socialised, is constructed, is debatable however. We are usually aware that we belong to one gender or the other but sexual identity is more complex than simply being biologically determined male or female: the 'gender role' and therefore gender identity seem to be almost wholly learned. Judith Butler argues that the body is a 'variable boundary, a surface whose permeability is politically regulated, a signifying practice within a field of gender hierarchy and compulsory heterosexuality' (Butler 1990: 139).

How gender is portrayed on film does to some extent reflect concerns and anxieties in our society about who we are which are re-enacted through stories, through the narrative. The acting of male and female roles is a performance, a simulation, it is not fixed but constantly shifting. Film is a re-presentation of images, it is not reality but a series of shots with actors playing characters. These images are concentrated, symbolic and highly charged; they have a super-powered meaning. In mainstream film we are clearly intended to identify with and recognise certain character types and gender types. If film is to have resonance for an audience it must contain elements with which they can identify or empathise and, at some level, must say something about the world in which we live. It is both interesting and revealing to look at how film characters are made recognisable and how we understand them, what our culture portrays as being representative of masculinity and femininity, and what this tells us about our understanding of gender, sexuality and society.

In earlier feminist studies of classic Hollywood film, femininity is seen as spectacle, and masculinity as a sign and a performance. More recent studies of gender and masculinity have problematised this position and suggest that representations of masculinity and, as a consequence, femininity are far more complex.

• **Plate 10.1**
The Day I Became a Woman (Marzeh Meshkini, 2000). Films by Iranian women have been internationally successful

feminism
Based on the belief that we live in a society where women are still unequal to men; that women have lower status than men and have less power, particularly economic power. Feminists argue that the media reinforces the status quo by representing a narrow range of images of women; for instance, woman as carer, as passive object, as an object of desire. Many feminists argue that the range of representations for both male and female is limited and slow to change. In recent years feminism has become fragmented and it is difficult to argue that feminism is a complete area of study; but the relationship between gender and power relations in society may be seen as central to feminist thinking. For an interesting discussion on this area see Liesbet van Zoonen (1994).

This chapter addresses different approaches to studying gender and film, exploring how we understand the masculine and feminine in film. The first section outlines the findings of feminist film theory from early seminal articles to contemporary debates, and includes a discussion of feminist films which have been an intrinsic part of the feminist movement. In addition, a brief history of women working in mainstream film is given. The second section discusses how the study of masculinity has problematised and furthered debates around film and meaning, especially in terms of understanding sexuality and gender, ambiguity and anxiety with regard to masculinity.

WOMEN AND FILM

This section looks at the role of women in filmmaking and film theory. The focus is on British and American women filmmakers but women from other countries, such as Samira Makhmalbaf and Marzieh Meshkini from Iran, have also made a significant contribution to the form in recent years.

First, a broad background history traces women's place in filmmaking and looks at the difficulties women have encountered in gaining positions of authority and control in the industry. There are some grounds for optimism however, as an increasing number of women are given key positions in areas such as producing, directing and screenwriting within the film industry.

Second, the rise of **feminism**, the development of feminist film theory and the parallel rise of feminist filmmaking is discussed; in the 1970s feminist film theory and practice seemed to converge, but by the 1980s the links had become more tenuous; however, by the 1990s feminist film theory played an increasingly important role in many areas of academic study.

Finally, a selection of case studies of women filmmakers is given.

NO JOB FOR A WOMAN – A HISTORY OF WOMEN IN FILM

The early years

From the beginnings of the film industry in the late nineteenth century it was usual for women to work in non-technical areas such as continuity and make-up or as production assistants, but they rarely worked as producers, directors, editors or writers. Recent research suggests that the role of women has not been as silent as was once thought and some women did, both directly and indirectly, exert their influence in these fields.

The only recorded early women filmmakers were in France and America – there were apparently none in Britain. Two well-known Hollywood movie actresses, Mary Pickford and Lillian Gish, both directed films but did not want this known for fear of harming their image as stars.

France can claim to have raised the first woman director, Alice Guy Blaché, who gained access to equipment because she worked for Gaumont, a company that manufactured cameras. Her career began in 1896 with a one-minute short called *The Good Fairy in the Cabbage Patch*, which Blaché believed was the first narrative film ever made. After eleven years of working in the industry in France she left for America and the greater opportunities it would give her. There she wrote, directed and produced many films including *In the Year 2000*, a vision of the future in which women ruled the world. Blaché found working conditions in the USA much easier than in France, where a working woman was frowned upon. Her daughter, Simone Blaché, explained in an interview that: 'Mother was really cherished in the US. She used to say that people treated her so wonderfully because she was a woman, because she was a woman in film. The situation in France was quite the reverse' (Smith 1975: 6).

In the early 1900s the American film industry expanded rapidly and made large profits due to the vast audiences attracted to the new medium. Although the new industry was cut-throat and competitive, it was also much more receptive to change than the European film industry and there was significantly less discrimination against women. It has been estimated that there were at least twenty-six women directors in America before 1930, but there were probably many more who directed and acted or who were screenwriters and not credited with this role. One of the most highly paid screenwriters in Hollywood in the 1930s was female, Frances Marion. In the US between 1911 and 1925, women wrote half of all the films copyrighted, whereas in 2001 only 21 per cent of the scripts contracted were written by women.[1]

Lois Weber was the first female American filmmaker and probably the most famous, often writing, producing and starring in her films, many of which dealt with social issues such as abortion and divorce. Weber directed over seventy-five films.

By the end of the 1920s the talkies had arrived. This, indirectly, brought about the demise of many women's careers as filmmakers. Only the bigger studios could survive due to the expensive equipment needed in the change-over to sound, and it was generally the many small, independent companies (which employed the majority of women) that closed down, and with them went many jobs for women in the industry.

Only one woman director, Dorothy Arzner, really survived the transition to talkies. She went on to make many famous movies, for example, *Christopher Strong* (1933) with Katharine Hepburn and *Dance Girl Dance* (1940). At one time Arzner was ranked among the 'top ten' directors in Hollywood.

Ironically, the changes in America drove directors such as Elinor Glynn and Jacqueline Logan to Britain and Europe, which already had an extremely poor record of women working in film.

Britain did not give much encouragement to its indigenous women filmmakers; the earliest woman known to have directed British films was Dinah Shurey, though very little is known about her other than that she made two films, *Carry On* (1927) and *Last Port* (1929).

• **Plate 10.2**
Christopher Strong
(Dorothy Arzner, 1933).
Dorothy Arzner was
once ranked among
the top ten directors in
Hollywood

Until the Second World War, hardly any women in Britain could be termed filmmakers, but some played key roles in the filmmaking process: Alma Reville, married to Alfred Hitchcock, assisted him in many films such as *The 39 Steps* (1935) and *The Lady Vanishes* (1938). She also helped to write other scripts such as *Suspicion* (1941) and *Shadow of a Doubt* (1943). Mary Field worked in documentary from 1928 and became executive producer of children's entertainment for J. Arthur Rank from 1944 to 1950. Joy Batchelor worked mainly in animation from 1935 and co-directed the first British feature-length cartoon *Animal Farm* (1954), continuing to make animated films until the 1970s.

In Britain and the USA more women were able to work in documentary film. The British documentary film movement, of which John Grierson was the founder, had a huge influence on British film and has continued to exert its influence to the present day. Grierson's sister Ruby worked alongside him on a number of films and was involved in making films herself, such as *Housing Problems* (1940).

For further discussion
of Grierson and British
documentary see
Chapter 8,
pp. 181–3.

Many filmmakers involved in the early documentary movement went on to make propaganda films during the war. This was one area of film where a few women could be found working as directors and assistant directors. Some women were taken on in roles usually only open to men due to the increased demand for documentary propaganda film in wartime Britain and the shortage of available manpower.

Two female British fiction feature-film directors, Muriel Box and Wendy Toye, made a number of films in the 1940s and 1950s and gained an international reputation. Muriel Box made profitable mass entertainment films. Her most famous film, which she also scripted, is a melodrama, *The Seventh Veil* (1945), but she continued to make films up until 1964. The lesser-known Wendy Toye made such films as *Raising a Riot* (1957) and *We Joined the Navy* (1962), with Dirk Bogarde and Kenneth More.

Very few women filmmakers in Britain and the USA before 1970 could be termed commercially successful, Dorothy Arzner and Muriel Box being the outstanding exceptions. It was virtually unheard of for women to work in technical areas such as sound or camera, although women art directors and film editors were not so unusual – Ann V. Coates worked as an editor on Box's film *The Truth about Women* (1958) and David Lean's *Lawrence of Arabia* (1962). In general, however, it was rare for a woman to play a key role in filmmaking and, it could be argued, the rise of feminism in the 1960s was to be the great catalyst for change for women in film.

By the 1990s more women were working in previously male-dominated areas such as directing, camera, sound and lighting: Diane Tammes, Sue Gibson and Belinda Parsons are all respected camerawomen; Diana Ruston and Moya Burns work in sound. Surprisingly, they have come across little sexism and feel that with more and more women coming into the industry men have no choice but to accept them. Moya Burns comments in an article entitled 'Women in Focus':

The industry has changed a lot in the last ten years, there are not so many hard-boiled areas, like big-budget features. The features that get made today are financed differently, a lot of the money seems to be coming from bodies like Channel 4. They have a different emphasis on the type of film they want to make, and this filters right down to the type of crew they want to employ.

(Burns 1992: 4)

In the field of directing more women filmmakers seem to have broken into mainstream film, often from the independent sector, from TV or from the increasing number of film schools. Sally Potter, with some regularity, has made a range of feature films such as *The Gold Diggers* (1982), *Orlando* (1993), a film based on a Virginia Woolf novel (see Case study 1), and *The Man Who Cried* (2000), starring Johnny Depp and Cate Blanchett. Potter's latest film *Yes* (2005) has received much critical acclaim regarding its experimental style and use of poetic form. Gurinder Chada's first film *Bhaji on the Beach* (1993) takes a wry and witty look at life for Asian women in Britain, while *What's Cooking* (2000) is a rich and colourful film that has received international acclaim. Chada's film *Bend It Like Beckham* (2002) has been a huge success in Britain and the US, tapping into a need for feel-good films. *Bridget Jones' Diary* (2001), directed by Sharon Maguire, was a big hit in Britain while also doing very well in the USA and Europe. Internationally, more established women filmmakers such as Jane Campion and Kathryn Bigelow regularly produce feature films, but the box-office hits still generally come from male directors, and the biggest selling films worldwide last year were produced, written and directed by men.

A number of support agencies for women filmmakers have been established which aim to provide the female equivalent of the 'old boys' network': 'Women in Film and TV' helps women in the mainstream sector and in the independent and workshop sector by offering seminars and screenings, while 'Networking' provides information and support for all women interested in film and video.

Whether changing attitudes towards women working in the film industry will produce more positive, realistic and varied representations of women in film is open to question. Feminism has perhaps changed the way we look at film, and there is a greater awareness of how gender is represented in the media. *Thelma and Louise* (1991) was hailed as a feminist film (directed by Ridley Scott, but scripted by a woman, Callie Khouri), although a more cynical analysis of the film reveals that the women are filmed quite conventionally, as objects of 'the look'. *Charlie's Angels* (2001), while playing with conventions of the action genre and making the women protagonists active, uses the camera to focus on how they look and in particular the attractiveness of their bodies. *Baise-moi* (2000), a French film written and directed by Virginie Despontes and Coralie Trinh Thi, pushes the *Thelma and Louise* theme much further. The two women protagonists go on a sex and killing spree in a rape-revenge drama in which they have the power of the look. As more women writers and directors work in mainstream film, though, it does seem likely that there will be a widening out of representations of women both visually and thematically. Films such as Ang Lee's *Crouching Tiger, Hidden Dragon* (2000) have been internationally successful yet the central character is an action woman. The hugely popular *Erin Brockovich* (2000) was scripted by Susannah Grant. It stars Julia Roberts in the 'rags to riches' story of a woman's struggle to sue a multinational company while bringing up her children as a single mother. *Lovely and Amazing* (2001), directed by Nicola Holofcener, and Lisa Choldenko's *Laurel Canyon* (2002) received widespread critical acclaim. Both directors gained experience in US TV where there has been a move towards positive discrimination. Women's stories, told from a woman's point of view, are becoming more acceptable in mainstream cinema; hopefully this trend will continue as more women take on leading roles in the film industry and audiences enjoy watching their films.

\THE FEMINIST REVOLUTION

The women's movement did not suddenly arrive; since the days of the suffragettes an increasing number of women had seen the need for equality with men. A new political and social climate developed in the 1960s and early 1970s which questioned the established order, encouraged radical reform and produced conditions that were conducive to the rise of the feminist movement. Although this radical dissatisfaction with contemporary society began in America its message soon spread to Britain, and in both countries there was a questioning of woman's role in society. Betty Friedan's book *The Feminine Mystique*, published in 1963, touched a chord in many discontented women. The time was ripe for the spread of the feminist movement,[3] as Friedan explained:

… the absolute necessity for a civil rights movement for women had reached such a point of subter-ranean explosive urgency by 1966 that it took only a few of us to get together to ignite the spark – and it spread like a nuclear chain reaction.

(Cited in Banner 1984: 247)

patriarchal society
A society in which men have the power and control. Women are generally disadvantaged and have lower status. It could be argued that we no longer live in a patriarchal society, but in a society in which men and women have equal opportunities. For instance, in the USA, Sherry Lansing was head of Paramount Pictures and in the UK a number of women now have key roles in the media, particularly at the BBC, where there are now women heads of channel programming. But many feminists argue that we still have a long way to go in terms of politics, philosophy and economics before we live in a society in which men and women may be considered equal.

Representation and stereotyping of women in the media

Feminists generally believe that the media is a contributory factor in perpetuating a narrow range of **stereotyped** images of women. How women are **represented** in the media may encourage particular expectations of women which are extremely limiting; for instance, that women are always based in the home, that they are inferior to men, that they like men who are violent, are just a few of the myths that have been perpetuated by the media. As Molly Haskell points out:

From a woman's point of view the ten years from, say, 1962 or 1963 to 1973 have been the most disheartening in screen history. In the roles and prominence accorded to women, the decade began unpromisingly, grew steadily worse, and at present shows no sign of improving. Directors, who in 1962 were guilty only of covert misogyny (Stanley Kubrick's *Lolita*) or kindly indifference (Sam Peckinpah's *The High Country*) became overt in 1972 with the violent abuse and brutalisation of *A Clockwork Orange* and *Straw Dogs*.

(Haskell 1973: 323)

Film, particularly in the early feminist period, was seen as one area of the media that could become a battleground for the women's movement. Film would be used as an ideological tool, which would counteract the stereotyped images of women presented by the male-dominated media and raise women's awareness of their inferior position in **patriarchal society**, where women were generally relegated to a subservient role. For instance, in film, women, as the historical section indicates, have usually taken supportive roles rather than key, decision-making ones.

FEMINIST FILM THEORY AND PRACTICE

The influence of alternative, independent and avant-garde film

Alongside the expansion of feminism and the women's movement **alternative cinema** and **avant-garde cinema** were flourishing. **Independent cinema** could, at its simplest, be divided into two forms: documentary and avant-garde. British film has a strong documentary tradition, which has been to some extent socialist-influenced, and feminist film initially saw documentary as a way of presenting the 'truth' about the lives of women.

During the 1960s, American avant-garde filmmakers produced many innovative and controversial films, some of the most well known being 'gay' and 'camp' films that challenged traditional stereotypes of gender roles such as Andy Warhol's *Lonesome Cowboys* (1968) and Kenneth Anger's *Scorpio Rising* (1965). At the same time the avant-garde developed in Europe, the French filmmakers, Jean-Luc Godard and François Truffaut being its most famous exponents. Although gender roles in European films tended to be stereotypical, some feminist filmmakers saw the potential of avant-garde film as a means of breaking away from the constraints of traditional cinema.

The expansion of independent filmmaking in Britain during the 1960s encouraged the formation of a number of workshops aiming to make filmmaking available to all and to destroy the élitism often found in the industry. Many workshops made films that were outside the sphere of mainstream film and television, often being concerned with areas that were considered radical in politics or content.

stereotyping
A quick and easy way of labelling or categorising the world around us and making it understandable. Stereotypes are learned but are by no means fixed, yet are often resistant to change. They tend to restrict our understanding of the world and perpetuate beliefs that are often untrue or narrow. For instance, the concept that only thin women are attractive is a stereotype promoted by much of the media in contemporary society (though there are some exceptions, such as comediennes Dawn French and Roseanne). Stereotyping is not always negative, but tends to be very much concerned with preserving and perpetuating power relations in society. It is in the interests of those in power to continue to stereotype those with lower status in a negative light, thus preserving the status quo.

representation
The media re-presents information to its audience, who are encouraged by the mainstream media to see their output as a 'window on the world', as reflecting reality. Yet the process of re-presenting information is highly complex and highly selective. Many feminists argue that the way notions of gender are represented by the media perpetuates and reinforces the values of patriarchal society; for instance, men tend to take on strong, active roles, while women are shown as passive and relying on their attractiveness. There are exceptions to such narrow stereotyping:

the 'strong' woman shown by Ripley in the *Alien* trilogy and the two heroines Thelma and Louise may be seen as positive models, although rather more cynically they could be seen merely as 'role reversal' films and so as having purely novelty value. Representations often make use of stereotypes because they are a shorthand, quick and easy way of using information. It could be argued that the media production process encourages the use of stereotypes due to the pressure of time and budget.

alternative cinema
Provides an alternative to the codes and conventions of mainstream, narrative cinema, often both thematically and visually.

avant-garde cinema
Essentially non-narrative in structure and often intellectual in content, working in opposition to mainstream cinema. Avant-garde film is often self-conscious and frequently makes use of devices such as cuts to the camera crew, talking to the camera and scratching on film.

independent cinema
May be divided into two areas: first, independent mainstream cinema, which aims to compete with the big studios, although without any large financial backing finds it difficult to survive. Second, the term is used to describe filmmaking outside the mainstream sector, for instance, film workshops, avant-garde film, feminist film. The boundaries between these two areas are not always clear and may overlap.

The first women's film group

The combination of the expansion of the women's movement and the rise of independent filmmaking brought about the conditions in which feminist film could thrive. In 1972 the first women's film group in Britain was formed. The London Women's Film Group (LWFG) aimed to spread ideas about women's liberation and enable women to learn filmmaking skills otherwise unavailable to them.

In the 1970s there were no more women working in high-grade jobs in the film and television industry than there had been in the 1950s. Demystification of the learning of technical skills was considered vital, but it was also necessary to familiarise women with all the stages in the filmmaking process so that they had a large pool of knowledge, which they would never have been able to obtain from mainstream film. Many film groups worked co-operatively, giving all members an equal say in the production process and rejecting the strict hierarchy of roles used in mainstream film production.

The feminist film movement was intentionally political, aiming to give all women, but especially working-class women, a chance to work in film. The films were often shown to trade unions, in factories and housing estates, and it was hoped they would help to raise women's consciousness about their place in society. Many of the early feminist films fitted into the black and white documentary realist tradition, the dominant mode of alternative, political filmmaking in Britain. Linda Dove, of the LWFG, explained in an interview:

We tended to reject commercial films wholesale as the ideological products of capitalist, sexist, racist society.... Originally our aim was to change the context in which a film is seen – we wanted to break down the audience passivity by always going out with films and discussing them when they were shown.

(Dove 1976: 59)

Film as a 'window on the world'

The widely held view that the visual media presented a 'window on the world' came under question in the early 1970s. The media, it was argued, are manipulated by the ruling patriarchal ideology and what is seen as natural, as clear-cut and obvious, is in fact a construct produced by society. This ambivalence about the 'meaning' of films and other media suggests that its interpretation by the audience may be different from that intended by the filmmaker. For instance, *Women of the Rhondda* (1972), a documentary about women who live in the South Wales Valleys, has a naturalistic style with no voiceover and the images are intended to speak for themselves. The message, though, is somewhat ambiguous for a non-feminist audience because the text has so many possible readings.

Many feminist filmmakers in the 1970s appropriated ideas from avant-garde art cinema and applied them to discuss questions that were of concern to the women's movement, such as representation. The avant-garde had always been male-dominated and narrow in its representations of women (see, for instance, Jean-Luc Godard's films such as *Breathless* (1960), *A Married Woman* (1964) and *Weekend* (1967)). But the avant-garde's political/anarchist basis gave an alternative form to the traditional use of realism in both fiction and documentary film. This influence was most profound in filmmakers like Laura Mulvey and Sally Potter, whose films are discussed in more detail below.

Early feminist film theory

The ideological sense of purpose and political debate behind feminist filmmaking encouraged the development of a film theory. Feminist film theory was, in the early period, especially concerned with representation and sexuality, and its relation to the dominance of the male power structure within a patriarchal society. A number of women, often from an academic background, contributed to this development, but it was perhaps Laura Mulvey and Claire Johnston who were the progenitors of feminist film theory. Both wrote seminal articles which were to have a huge impact on the study of film and the media, and which will be discussed in this chapter.

Developing a counter-cinema

Claire Johnston's 'Women's Cinema as Counter-Cinema' (1973) is one of the earliest articles on feminist film theory and practice. Johnston shows how women have been stereotyped in film since the days of the silent cinema, and argues for a cinema that challenges such narrow conventions but which will also be entertaining. In mainstream cinema woman is seen as an extension of a male vision and Johnston criticises the narrow role she is given in film: 'It is probably true to say that despite the enormous emphasis placed on woman as spectacle in the cinema, woman as woman is largely absent' (ibid.: 214).

The work of two female Hollywood directors, Dorothy Arzner and Ida Lupino, is considered by Johnston, who suggests that their films partially subvert the patriarchal viewpoint. An understanding of how these films work could be important for feminist film practice in breaking through and challenging the ruling ideology. Johnston stresses the importance of developing a film practice that questions and challenges mainstream dominant cinema and its patriarchal basis. She terms it a counter-cinema movement, which will have links with avant-garde and left-wing film.

Pleasure, looking and gender

Psychoanalytic theory, particularly the theories of Freud and Lacan, has been instrumental in the development of a feminist film theory, although structuralist and Marxist theories[4] have also been influential to a lesser extent. Laura Mulvey's article 'Visual Pleasure and Narrative Cinema' (first published in 1975) emphasises the importance of the patriarchical viewpoint in the cinema; that the pleasure gained from looking (**scopophilia**) is a male pleasure and 'the look' in cinema is controlled by the male and directed at the female; this is often referred to as the 'male gaze'.

Scopophilia can be directed in two areas: first, voyeurism, that is, scopophilic pleasure linked to sexual attraction, and, second, scopophilic pleasure which is linked to narcissistic identification. Mulvey argues that this identification is always with the male, who is the pivot of the film, its hero, while the female is often seen as a threat. Film reflects society, argues Mulvey, and therefore society influences our understanding of film. This viewpoint is linked with psychoanalytical theory to demonstrate the influence of patriarchal society on film. Patriarchy and phallocentrism are intrinsically linked; the phallus is a symbol of power, of having (note how guns are used in film: guns = phallus = power). The woman has no phallus, she is castrated, which relates back to Freudian theory that the woman is lacking and therefore inferior because she has no phallus.

Freud's theories on scopophilia centre around voyeurism and the desire to see the erotic and the forbidden, yet this desire is male-centred. The cinema provides a perfect venue for illicit voyeuristic viewing because the audience is in a dark, enclosed, womb-like world. Mulvey argues that the power cinema holds is so strong that it can act as a temporary form of brainwashing (an argument which is still very much alive today!).

psychoanalytic theory
Based on the theories of Freud and, more recently, Lacan. Feminists argue that aspects of psychoanalysis are questionable because they are based on patriarchal assumptions that woman is inferior to man. Freud found female sexuality difficult and disturbing. Lacan argues that the mother is seen as lacking by the child because she has no phallus. Uncertainty about the role of the female in psychoanalytic theory has been picked up by a number of feminists such as Mulvey, De Lauretis and Modleski, who question the inevitability of Freud and Lacan's theories which emphasise the importance of the phallus, penis envy and patriarchal supremacy.

scopophilia
Freudian term meaning the sexual pleasure gained from looking, introduced to film analysis by Laura Mulvey, who pointed out that women are usually depicted in a passive role and are looked at, while men take on an active role and look.

structuralism
A movement founded on the belief that the study of society could be scientifically based and that there are structures in society that follow certain patterns or rules. Initially, most interest was centred on the use of language; Saussure, the founder of linguistics, argued that language was essential in communicating the ideology, the beliefs, of

a culture. Structuralists have applied these theories to film, which uses both visual and verbal communication, and pointed out that the text conveys an illusion of reality, so conveying the ideology of a society even more effectively.

Marxist theory
Argues that those who have the means of production have control in a capitalist society. The dominant class have control of the means of production and have an interest in perpetuating the dominant ideology. More recently, exponents of Althusserian Marxism, particularly post-1968, have argued that mainstream narrative cinema reinforces the capitalist system and that a revolutionary cinema is needed to challenge the dominant ideology.

REPRESENTATION OF GENDER AND SEXUALITY

The woman in Freudian theory represents desire, but also the fear of castration, and so there is a tension, an ambivalence towards the female form, and her 'look' can be threatening. As the male is the controller, taking the active role, the female is reduced to the icon, the erotic, but at the same time is a threat because of her difference.

Mulvey argues that woman has two roles in film: erotic object for the characters in the story and erotic object for the spectator. Recent feminist theory suggests that the representation of women is far more complex, and later theory, including Mulvey's, looks at films where women do play a key role as subject rather than object. Melodrama is one such area (see Mulvey 1981).

Mulvey refers to Hitchcock because of the complicit understanding in his films that the audience gains a voyeuristic pleasure from watching a film, from looking: 'In *Vertigo* (1958) in particular, but also in *Marnie* (1964) and *Rear Window* (1954), the "look" is central to the plot oscillating between voyeurism and fetishistic fascination' (Mulvey 1975: 813).

The denial of pleasure

Mulvey points out that devices used in the traditional Hollywood narrative film have trapped filmmakers into using certain codes and conventions which place the female in a subordinate, passive position, making her role as erotic object extremely limiting. Mulvey criticises the narrowness of this role and argues that to change woman's position in film a revolutionary look at cinema needs to be taken and the denial of voyeuristic cinematic pleasure be given a priority. The exclusion of woman as object, as provider of voyeuristic pleasure will then free her from the narrow limits she has been allocated in cinema. This may seem an extreme reaction to mainstream, narrative cinema, but in the early 1970s feminists felt that the only way to change female representation was to take extreme measures: a new radical cinema was needed, an alternative to the 'magic' of narrative cinema.

A new language

The importance of the creation of a female subject and the development of a new language is central to early feminist film theory, which argued that spoken, written and visual languages all placed women in a subordinate position and reflected a patriarchal ideology. A film theory and practice that had its own codes and conventions would replace the dominance of patriarchal cinema. Christine Gledhill echoes this desire in her article, 'Some Recent Developments in Feminist Criticism':

A feminist film-maker then, finds the root of patriarchy in the very tools she wishes to employ to speak about women. So what is required of her is the development of a counter-cinema that will deconstruct the language and techniques of classic cinema.

(1985: 841)

Classic narrative cinema was based on ideas that had been passed on from the literary realist tradition and many feminists felt that this realist tradition perpetuated a way of seeing, of understanding the world, which belonged to dominant patriarchal society, and feminists should break with this tradition.

Filmmakers such as Laura Mulvey and Sally Potter were interested in a film theory and practice which worked together and would produce a new feminist language. Avant-garde film was the ideal vehicle for these ideas because it broke the normal rules and conventions of mainstream cinema. Mulvey's article 'Film, Feminism and the Avant-Garde' (1979) explores this relationship, suggesting that both forms of film can be mutually beneficial, working towards similar goals. Mulvey's films, for instance, actively avoid any sense of being constructed for the male spectator, confronting the lack of representation of women in film; they are a mixture of avant-garde, melodrama and psychoanalytic theory.

For further analysis of avant-garde, feminist film see Case study 1: Sally Potter.

Many avant-garde films were termed 'difficult' and only attracted a small audience which tended to be those familiar with 'art film'. Even though avant-garde-influenced filmmakers such as Mulvey did much to aid the understanding of their films by producing hand-outs and giving lectures, some feminists felt that avant-garde film was élitist and would be of no interest to a mass audience of women. Mulvey's and Johnston's theories, they suggested, would be more useful for the development of a feminist film theory than as a guide on how to make feminist films. Kaplan (1983), for example, points out that it makes more sense to use familiar and recognisable cinematic conventions to explain that the 'realism' of mainstream cinema is a fabrication.

A period of optimism and defiance

Feminist film theory and practice in the period up to 1980 had presented a joint ideological struggle; film theory analysed the patriarchal conventions within which mainstream film worked and film practice was physically able to break these rules. But there was a very limited audience for feminist film during this period, even though there was an increasing interest in academic circles in feminist film theory. In the strongly male-dominated world of filmmaking, women were rarely seen as artists or filmmakers, and feminist art was seen as a possible challenge to patriarchal society. As Johnston (1973) explains, the female within patriarchy is seen as the 'other', and feminist art represented a threat to these narrow conceptions of gender.

By the end of the 1970s a feminist film theory and practice had been established, giving many women a new-found confidence and a belief that society could change. In the previous decade a number of influential articles on feminist film theory and practice had been written. A body of work had been formed by feminist writers and academics, Mulvey and Johnston being the founder writers who were to influence a generation of film and media critics.

At the beginning of the 1970s the focus was on representation in film and the media, but by the end of the decade attention was being diverted to the concept of 'pleasure' and whether this should be denied in film. Some feminists expressed the concern that by denying the pleasures of mainstream cinema feminist filmmakers might alienate their audience. Yet feminists generally agreed that feminist film theory and practice had an important role to play in raising consciousness as to the marginalisation of women in a patriarchal society.

A number of feminists still called for a counter-cinema and a deconstructive cinema in the early 1980s. Ann Kaplan and Annette Kuhn argued that there was a need to break down the dominant forms of cinema, and the audience should become active rather than passive, gaining pleasure from learning rather than the narrative.

Both Kuhn and Kaplan and filmmakers such as Sue Clayton were aware of the problems of using a cinema which rejects the mainstream; that is, which is anti-conventional and may alienate its audience. Kaplan suggested that a way forward would be to work within and manipulate the conventions of mainstream cinema.

REASSESSING FEMINIST FILM THEORY

In 1981 Mulvey published a response to 'Visual Pleasure and Narrative Cinema', which was so fundamental to the development of feminist film theory. Titled 'Afterthoughts on Visual Pleasure and Narrative Cinema', Mulvey presents two lines of thought: first, examining whether the female spectator can gain a deep pleasure from a male-oriented text, and second, how the text and the spectator are affected by the centrality of a female character in the narrative. 'Afterthoughts' marks a shift in attitude, a move away from representation to studying the female response, to asking how women watch films and questioning the role of melodrama, which has traditionally been viewed as the woman's genre.

Feminist film theory has been especially influenced by psychoanalytic theory and particularly by Freud and Lacan. Mulvey acknowledges her debt to Lacan who, she explains, has 'broadened and advanced ways of conceptualising sexual difference, emphasising the fictional, constructed nature of masculinity and femininity' (ibid.: 165).

Not all feminists supported a feminist film theory based on psychoanalytic theory. Terry Lovell, in *Pictures of Reality* (1983), criticised Lacanian theory because of its emphasis on the individual rather than the collective and argued that gaining pleasure from the text is rather more complex than a simple attribution to sexual desire.

In the latter part of the 1980s Freud's work was re-examined by many feminists due to its phallocentric basis. Tania Modleski, for instance, in her book *The Women Who Knew Too Much* (1988), argues for a less male-centred version of spectatorship and calls for the development of a feminist psychoanalytic theory which is challenging and inventive. Penley, in the introduction to *Feminism and Film Theory* (1988), states that much feminist film criticism questions the patriarchal roots of current psychoanalytic theories, especially those of Freud and Lacan.

Modleski applies her ideas to an analysis of Hitchcock's films, which have been of great interest to feminists due to his extreme use of voyeurism and the 'look'. Reassessing earlier theory, Modleski points out that Mulvey's article 'Visual Pleasure and Narrative Cinema' does not allow for the complex nature of representation and raises questions about the stereotypical, passive female object and the active male. Modleski states: 'What I want to argue is neither that Hitchcock is utterly misogynistic nor that he is largely sympathetic to women and their plight in patriarchy, but that his work is characterised by a thoroughgoing ambivalence about femininity' (1988: 3).

Many of Hitchcock's films are seen from the point of view of a female protagonist: for instance, *Blackmail* (1929), *Rebecca* (1940), *Notorious* (1946), or when the hero or heroine is in a vulnerable or passive, female position, as in *Rear Window* (1954).

Modleski re-examines aspects of Mulvey's work, especially the suggestion that the patriarchal order has banished a strong female presence. In *North by Northwest* (1959), Cary Grant's role is that of hero and sex object, the desirable male; in *Marnie* (1964), Sean Connery plays a similar role, which also serves to heighten the irony that Marnie,

• **Plate 10.4**
North By Northwest
(Alfred Hitchcock,
1959). Cary Grant –
irresistible to women

the heroine and his wife, is frigid. In Hitchcock's films both male and female can become objects of the 'look'.

The strong and powerful female can then exist within mainstream film, yet Hitchcock is patently not a feminist filmmaker and his films express Freud's assertion that the male contempt for femininity is an expression of the repression of their bisexuality – woman is a threat who must be destroyed. As Modleski concludes: 'the male object is greatly threatened by bisexuality, though he is at the same time fascinated by it; and it is the woman who pays for this ambivalence, often with her life itself' (ibid.: 10).

For further discussion of gender and sexuality, see Chapter 11.

Questioning psychoanalytic theory

In the 1970s and 1980s feminist film theory was dominated by a psychoanalytic approach. The tendency to favour a psychoanalytic approach had proven to be problematic, when applied to feminist film theory, because of its dependence on the Oedipal trajectory, in which woman is seen as not only 'lacking' but also as needing to be brought under control through the male gaze. If woman's role in film is to always be reduced to the 'other' by psychoanalytic theory, then it could be argued that there is little space to open up patriarchal narratives to account for the female spectator, other than through identification with the male.

Some feminist film theorists, such as Jackie Byars, have reworked psychoanalytic theory to give it a feminist perspective. Her analysis of melodrama suggests that the woman can exist as a spectator in a positive way. In *All that Heaven Allows*, Byars (1995) argues that the gaze is strongly female. Jackey Stacey's analysis of *Desperately Seeking Susan* points out that the film is not about sexual difference in terms of male and female but about the difference between the two women lead characters, a view which cannot be read in terms of Lacan or Freud whose theories are so phallocentric in nature (Stacey 1992). Psychoanalytic theory needs to develop a new framework which will view the woman as a positive force rather than suffering from a state of lack.

The reworking of psychoanalytic theory may provide a new model from which feminists could work. Mulvey's theories, based on Freud and Lacan, have had a considerable impact in enhancing our understanding of the role of the spectator in film and how media texts place the viewer in a particular position. These theories are useful when analysing a film such as *The Piano*, which gives the female the power of the look and, to some extent, reverses conventional filming practices (see case study on the support website at www.routledge.com/textbooks/9780415409285).

A cultural studies approach

In the past decade or so there has been a shift away from Freudian and Lacanian theory towards a cultural studies approach to the study of film. Black feminist film theory and lesbian feminist film theory, for instance, have both suggested new ways of understanding how women from different social and ethnic groups interpret cultural messages.

The emphasis has transferred from reading media texts, a move from the study of the encoding process which asks how messages are produced, to a study of the decoding process which asks how messages are received and understood by an audience.

Cultural studies theorists argue that **semiotic** and psychoanalytic readings of film tend to isolate the viewer from the text; cultural studies is more concerned with asking how cultural systems produce meaning and how ideology is replicated through cultural institutions, texts and practices. **Ideology** may be seen as the means by which we interpret and make sense of our lives, the viewpoint from which we see the world. Ideology, in a capitalist society, needs constant re-establishing, and this is carried out by what the critic Gramsci termed **hegemony**. This is the means by which a dominant social group maintains control of a subordinate group, a form of unconscious control, in which we take on certain beliefs, practices and attitudes as being natural or normal and carry those opinions with us; for instance, the belief that in a patriarchal society it

semiotics
The use of semiotics in film analysis has developed out of the theories of Ferdinand de Saussure, who argued that the meanings of words are not natural but learned and socially constructed; therefore the meaning of a word, or in the case of film, an image or sound, may be complex and layered.

ideology
The dominant set of ideas and values which inform any one society or culture, but which are imbued in its social behaviour and representative texts at a level that is not necessarily obvious or conscious.

hegemony
A set of ideas, attitudes or practices which have become so dominant that we forget they are rooted in choice and the exercise of power. They appear to be 'common sense' because they are so ingrained; any alternative seems 'odd' or potentially threatening by comparison.

is entirely normal for the woman to be the home-maker and to have a low-paid, menial job. Hegemony is constantly shifting; it is constantly negotiated and never fixed. From a feminist standpoint this means there is the potential for change in patriarchal society.

If cultural texts such as films are apparatus for transmitting cultural values, they are also sites for a struggle over meaning. The term given to describe the constant shifting and multiple possibilities of meaning a text may have is **polysemy**; that is, a text has no one fixed meaning. This then gives feminist film and cultural critics the opportunity to analyse audience response to texts as 'open' rather than 'closed', and the study of how gender differences work in the reception of texts becomes productive. Stuart Hall, in his early work, suggested there are three ways in which a text may be received: (1) as a *dominant reading*, as intended by its producer; (2) as a *negotiated reading*, when the text is generally accepted but is challenged in some areas; and (3) as *an oppositional reading*, when the viewer challenges the reading of the text.[5] In fact, recent research argues for the possibility of a much more complex relationship between the reader and the text than had previously been thought.

The audience may be accredited with entering into a viewing situation with a range of skills and competences and a background of cultural knowledge. The audience is therefore more of an active than a passive receiver of the message. This understanding has implications for feminist film theory, as it opens up the notion of the female as subject rather than as being permanently confined to the role of passive object. Christine Gledhill (1985) uses the term 'negotiation' of text, explaining that we negotiate with cultural texts at every level; from institutions, where feminists can apply pressure to negotiating the active meanings of texts, to the active process of reception.[6] Ethnographic research has proven to be of particular use when applied to studies of how women receive media texts. Janice Radway, in her research on romance fiction, found that the women whom she interviewed preferred a strong, independent heroine.[7] This contradicts previous feminist textual-based research which sees the romance novel as presenting women as passive and vulnerable. Jacqueline Bobo conducted group interviews to analyse the reception and interpretation of *The Color Purple*, the results of which she found surprising. The film contained many stereotypical images of black people and their culture and was filmed by a white, male director, Steven Spielberg, yet the black women interviewed saw the film as positive; they 'not only liked the film, but have formed a strong attachment to it. The film is significant to their lives' (Bobo 1988: 101). Bobo believes those interviewed were able to filter out negative aspects of the film and highlight areas they could relate to. Black feminist theory has found it problematic to apply what could be termed white, bourgeois film theory to an ethnic group which is so noticeably under-represented in film. bell hooks explains: 'many feminist film critics continue to structure their discourse as though it speaks about "women" when in fact it only speaks about white women' (hooks 1992: 123). Because black women are largely excluded from film or given an extremely limited number of representations, a film such as *The Color Purple* is of particular significance to the many black women who read the film favourably.[8]

Lesbian and gay studies is a developing area of cultural analysis. Lesbian writers point out that a theory of lesbian desire and its relationship to media texts and representation is needed; a theory separate from previous feminist film thinking which has been concerned with the relationship of the heterosexual woman to film and places lesbian desire as other.

An eclectic range of theoretical approaches is available to feminist film theorists in the new millennium: psychoanalytic, social historical, semiotic-based textual analysis, postmodernist and ethnographic study are just a sample of the tools available. Some feminists have been resistant to embracing cultural studies in its totality, arguing that it has been too concerned with examining class structure. Within cultural studies though there has been a shift away from concentrating solely on ideology and hegemony to studying identity and subjectivity; this may, at least in part, be attributed to the impact of feminism. Academics such as Sherrie Innes, Yvonne Tasker and Sharon Willis have

polysemic
A text with a multitude of possible readings.

See Chapter 11 for a more detailed discussion of lesbian and gay studies.

used this approach when studying gender and film. In *Tough Girls*, Innes discusses the strong woman in popular culture and asks why tough women with masculine qualities are popular in the media, where not only do they have to display toughness but they also have to have the right attitude and show 'little or no fear, even in the most dangerous circumstances; if she does show fear, it must not stop her from acting' (1999: 25). Yet even the tough woman is usually required to display a feminine side which would seem to diminish her toughness or, at least, put it under question. Innes argues that tough women are more acceptable than they were a decade ago and asks what does this mean for Western society? Do we want women to take on these attributes in a society that in so many ways is tough enough already? Innes's writing refers to the media prior to 1999 and so misses out on the huge success of the TV series *Buffy the Vampire Slayer* and films such as *Tomb Raider* (2001), *Kill Bill 1* (2001) and *11* (2003) and *The Matrix* (1999). Astrid Deuber-Mankowsky, in an insightful analysis of the role of Lara Croft in the Tomb Raider game series, analyses the popularity of Lara Croft, looking at her both as a cyber heroine and film heroine. She argues that Lara Croft, in the film played by Angelina Jolie, is a combination of the physically perfect fantasy female, the dream woman and the ideal male, her mental qualities are masculine, she has traditional male values; she is decisive, courageous, independent and heroic, cool at all times. Lara was modelled on the Indiana Jones character played by Harrison Ford and made female to be different. She is a male creation, a fantasy of the games' creator and, although a fusion of masculine and feminine qualities, her body is clearly fetishisised and seen as a combination of spectacle and action: Lara wears tight-fitting clothes that emphasise her curvy shape, she is a figure of desire, whilst at the same time she appears to be popular with women, who enjoy the fact that she is powerful and strong. Yet Deuber-Manksowsky argues, 'However much Lara Croft acts the role of the better male, she is still a woman. The hierarchy of

• **Plate 10.5**
Tomb Raider (Simon West, 2000). The perfect male/female fantasy figure?

values remains as unaffected as its underpinnings in the relation between the sexes. Lara Croft's femininity is reduced, in a very traditional manner, to her oversized female attributes' (2005: 47) As in the game, the films lens focuses on Lara narcissistically, she is always in the frame, both the film and the game play with voyeurism and exhibitionism. Lara is watched sexually, she is also on display for the viewer in quite a complex way, she may well appeal to the passive male as has been discussed by Carol Clover in her analysis of the horror film audience (see Clover 1992).

In concluding this section it is evident that feminist film theory has drawn on a wide range of analytical processes and these continue to contribute to our understanding of how women communicate, are communicated to and interpret film. The next section discusses theories of masculinity, and it may be that the study of gender is as likely to reveal fresh insights into how we understand femininity as well as masculinity.

The following case studies apply many of the theories, concepts and approaches on women and film discussed in this section to the following filmmakers and a selection of their films.

CASE STUDY 1: SALLY POTTER, FILMMAKER

Sally Potter is probably best known for three films: the film short *Thriller* (1979), the feature-length *The Gold Diggers* (1983) and the much-acclaimed *Orlando* (1993). Her recent films *The Tango Lesson* (1997), *The Man Who Cried* (2000) and *Yes* (2005) are experimental and her work has been termed avant-garde; nevertheless, while having many of the qualities of an 'art' production her films still contain a strong narrative drive.

Potter's earlier films are feminist in tone, but in more recent years she has found the term problematic, and in an interview with Penny Florence explains, 'I can't use the word anymore because it's become debased' (Florence 1993: 279). Potter, unlike many filmmakers, both male and female, has continued to make films with a strong personal vision, as Peter Greenaway and the late Derek Jarman have done. Potter is optimistic that there has been a change in attitude towards women filmmakers, that they are now seen as just directors.

Thriller is a feminist reading of Puccini's opera *La Bohème* (1895). Linking together feminist, Marxist and psychoanalytic theory, the film is a critique of the constraints of patriarchy, the lack of female voice and woman as object and victim. The film was funded by the British Arts Council, and although avant-garde in style was received with interest, although it was by no means a mainstream success. Ann Kaplan explains why the film aroused such interest: 'It is, first, an imaginative intervention in the dominance of a certain kind of classical narrative (the sentimental romance and the detective story) making a critique of such narratives into an alternative art form' (Kaplan 1983: 161).

The Gold Diggers (1983)

The Gold Diggers is a full-length film made with a grant from the British Film Institute (BFI). The film explores the relationship between women and power, money and patriarchy, and develops themes from *Thriller*. The film has two main characters, both women: the early nineteenth-century heroine (Julie Christie) and the modern heroine (Colette Lafone). Potter purposefully and ideologically chose an all-women crew to work on the film, including women musicians.

On its release in 1983 the film was poorly received, partly due to its complex yet plotless narrative which seemed to exemplify some of the problems of art and avant-garde cinema in the early 1980s – a lack of awareness of audience.

Potter has discussed the problems of the film, explaining the difficulties of working collaboratively with others (which was the case with *The Gold Diggers*). She has said that the film 'came out of a practice in the theatre of going with the moment, incorporating ideas, and not being completely text-bound' (Ehrenstein 1993: 3).

Imagery in the film often verges on the surreal, but the script is stilted, elliptical and difficult to follow, almost a series of vignettes. The modern heroine in the film plays the part of investigator and observer of events, an observer of patriarchy, which is seen as disempowering women. Patriarchy is threatening, bureaucratic, intimidating and ultimately ridiculous. In the scene when Colette is working at a VDU in an office with other women, the only male is the manager who imperiously surveys the scene. Colette asks him to explain what the information is on the screen, to which he patronisingly replies, 'Just do your job.'

The Gold Diggers was filmed in black and white, and is a rather bleak film suggesting that woman is either revered or reviled by man. *Orlando*, in contrast, is full of colour and optimism.

Orlando (1993)

Potter's film is an adaptation of a Virginia Woolf novel and was made by her own company, Adventure Pictures, formed with *Orlando*'s producer Christopher Sheppard. The film budget was £2 million, making it a medium-size British film, although the quality of the production gives it a much more expensive look. In contrast to *The Gold Diggers* in which the crew was all-female, a mixed crew worked on *Orlando*.

After the experience of *The Gold Diggers*, Potter took great care to ensure that the script was just right, doing endless rewrites until she was happy with it. The developmental process took years rather than months but ensured a clear narrative that powerfully drives the film forward.

The film is concerned with two central ideas: the concept of immortality and the fluidity of gender. Orlando travels 400 years, from the Elizabethan age (Queen Elizabeth is played by Quentin Crisp, introducing the theme of playing with gender) to the present day, changing sex in 1700. The mise-en-scène is sumptuous and exotic, richly coloured and textured, enhanced by the camera work; the scene when Orlando moves into the Victorian age, for instance, is full of movement and dynamism, the gorgeous costumes swirling forward into the future.

Aspects of feminism, gender, imperialism and politics are part of the narrative discourse – areas that are often anathema to a film's success. Yet *Orlando* has been received with much acclaim: David Ehrenstein in *Film Quarterly* compares the film to Orson Welles's *The Magnificent Ambersons*: 'Like no other film of the moment, it demonstates that art and pleasure are not mutually exclusive categories of experience' (Ehrenstein 1993: 2).

Potter is more concerned with gender than with feminism, although the vulnerability of women is a key theme: when Orlando becomes female she loses her home, her financial power. She then has only her body, her femaleness to bargain with, which she refuses to share in marriage with the archduke, who reminds her sternly she has no property and will suffer the ignominy of remaining a spinster.

The film has a strong sense of playfulness, from the knowing looks Orlando gives to the audience to the confusion of sexual identity. When Orlando becomes female in a beautifully filmed metamorphosis, she boldly states to the camera, 'same person, just a different sex'. Potter explains:

> I don't think the book so much explores sexual identities as dissolves them, and it's that kind of melting and shifting where nothing is ever what it seems for male or female that I think is the strength of the book and which I wanted to reproduce in the film.
>
> (Florence 1993: 283)

Potter put much thought into the development of Orlando's character. This led her to consider what it means to be 'male' and the dangers and difficulties of being masculine. At times gender differences are de-emphasised: for instance, the clothing worn by the young Orlando is not much less constricting than that worn by the female. However, when Orlando returns to Britain as a woman, her dress is used as a powerful symbol of her womanhood and the constraints and limitations that imposes. As a woman in the seventeenth century, Orlando must curb her sense of adventure and her enquiring mind. Orlando is offered the final insult when told that she may as well be dead as be a woman, and has to endure her house and wealth being taken away from her.

Orlando rebelliously enters the Victorian age, a heroine of melodrama ready to be rescued by a handsome, romantic hero who becomes her lover and fathers her daughter. Although Orlando has lost her home and refuses to follow her lover, she retains her independence and moves forward in time to successfully negotiate life in modern Britain.

The film finishes on a positive note. There is hope for the future in the form of a child and we are told, 'ever since she let go of the past she found her life was beginning'. Orlando is at peace.

Orlando, in style, has moved away from the avant-garde towards the mainstream while still playing with narrative form. Potter's film is a stimulating and rich attack on the senses and has a discourse that, although concerned with gender, suggests a blending of the sexes rather than a separation, which many of the earlier feminist films such as *A Question of Silence* (1982), *The Gold Diggers* (1983) and Lezli-Ann Barrett's *An Epic Poem* (1982) encouraged.

Yes (2005)

Potter was inspired to make this film in response to the attacks in the US on 9 September 2001. She explores the relationship between two lovers from opposite cultural backgrounds; a white American female played by Joan Cusack and a Middle Eastern male played by Abkarian. When differences in their cultural background begin to show, conflicts emerge and this divides them. They decide to part but are eventually reconciled in Cuba, a sort of no mans land of neutral cultural heritage. The themes discussed and the way the story unfolds are not especially unconventional but the format is; the characters speak in rhyming couplets, one actor speaks directly to the audience as in a Greek chorus. The producers are credited with getting the finance to make the

• **Plate 10.6**
Yes (Sally Potter, 2005).
The film debates
cultural differences
between East and West
in response to 9/11

film, an incredibly difficult task considering the content and form of the film. The actors worked on deferred fees and there was much support for the film in terms of unpaid labour due to the subject matter. In an interview, Potter explains that the poetry in the form of iambic pentameter came easily;

It came out in a torrent. It felt entirely natural a way expressing this strange blend of ideas; love and religion and war and death, which otherwise might have become rather heavy and direct everyday speech. They were big, big ideas to handle. But sometimes the form of verse, and iambic pentameter in particular, creates things that naturalises them.

(http://yesthemovie.com: 5)

GENDER THEORY AND THEORIES OF MASCULINITY

Masculinity as unproblematical

Laura Mulvey's essay 'Visual Pleasure and Narrative Cinema' focused attention on cinema spectatorship in terms of binary opposites of gender: woman is defined as object of the look and man as being in control of the gaze. The importance of Mulvey's conclusions and the implications of these findings initially resulted in little further questioning of the role of the male in film because he was seen as representing patriarchy in a straightforward way. Problems with defining femininity as passive and masculinity as active had become apparent by the 1980s because seeing gender in terms of binary opposites means there is then little space left for negotiation of these boundaries.[9] Defining the masculine as the 'norm' and the female as 'other' may be valid at a particular moment in classical Hollywood cinema, but if gender is a social construction then constructions of gender in film are not absolute and are therefore far more complex.

Steven Neale's essay, 'Masculinity as Spectacle', first published in 1983, is described by Cohan and Hark in *Screening the Male* as a 'pioneering attempt to put Mulvey's arguments in the context of those films that obviously represent a spectacular form of masculinity' (1993: 2).

Masculinity is associated with **voyeurism**, action, sadism, **fetishism** and the controlling narrative, while femininity is associated with passivity, exhibitionism, spectacle, masochism and narcissism. Yet these clear distinctions belie the acute anxieties and paradoxes which emerge when studying film; the binary opposites of masculinity and femininity are in fact much less opaque than may at first be apparent. The male image and the way it is represented is as complex and revealing as the female image, although it may appear 'hidden' and unrecognised, a natural part of patriarchy. Neale's essay examines identification, looking and spectacle using Mulvey's article as a reference point. He points out that how we identify with a character in film is a complex process. We do not always clearly align ourselves with either a male or female figure depending on our gender, otherwise why would females be able to identify with Clint Eastwood in *Unforgiven* (1992) or Bruce Willis in *Die Hard* (1988)?

The male hero in classical Hollywood cinema is usually recognised as powerful. He signifies omnipotence, mastering the narrative, being in control, sadistic rather than masochistic. Neale argues that the elements of violence, voyeurism and masochism in Anthony Mann's films in fact suggest a 'repressed homosexual voyeurism' (Cohan and Hark 1993: 13). The act of looking has a homoerotic quality and an anxiety which is produced as a result of the erotic possibilities that are repressed. The violence and mutilation present in these films are an expression of the anxiety which surrounds the suppression of homosexual desire that is evident in the looks between characters. Neale's discussion of looking and spectacle further develops Mulvey's division of active male, who controls the look, and the object of the look, the passive female. Neale argues that male figures can be the subject of voyeuristic looking also. In male-centred genres such as war, action, westerns and gangster films there are binary opposites in the form

voyeurism
The sexual pleasure gained from looking at others.

fetishism
Freudian theorists argue that fetishism is linked to the castration complex and is a form of male denial of the threat and fear of castration by the female. The female is made less threatening, more reassuring, by substituting her lack of a phallus with a fetish object such as high heels, long hair or turning her into a fetish object by exaggerating or fragmenting parts of the body such as lips or breasts.

See Case study 2: Fight Club (1999) for comparison.

of opposing forces which struggle for power and control. Mann's films use narrative outcome and spectacle to suggest male struggle, images of masculinity are fetishised and there is an emphasis on display and the spectacular.[10] Leone's westerns also work through an aggressive exchange of looks, another form of fetishisistic looking. But Neale points out that the male body is not shown purely for the purpose of erotic spectacle:

We see male bodies stylised and fragmented by close-ups, but our look is not direct, it is heavily mediated by the looks of the characters involved. And those looks are marked out not by desire but rather by fear, or hatred, or aggression.

(1983: 18)

The act of aggression takes the focus away from the spectacle and thus displaces the eroticism of the male body, while still suggesting this at a subconscious level. Some genres though, such as melodrama and the musical, do allow for the male body to be the object of the look; for instance, Rock Hudson in Sirk's melodramas and John Travolta in *Saturday Night Fever* (1977).

Neale points out the need to acknowledge and consider the eroticism and spectacle of the masculine image in terms of identification, voyeuristic looking and fetishistic representation. Mainstream cinema assumes there is a male norm, a male way of looking, while the female represents difference, that which requires investigation. But Neale argues that the male also requires investigation in the same kind of way, that masculinity is as much a mystery as femininity.

Neale's article is particularly important because he argues that the representation of the male is in no way straightforward or opaque. A number of academics researching in this area have further opened up the debate as to our understanding of masculinity and, indeed, gender in film, and this chapter will draw on some of their work in more depth. Neale's essay focuses on Freudian- and Lacanian-based psychoanalytic theory rather than cultural factors. This theoretical approach may be seen as white and phallocentric and it could also be argued, with some justification, that it is a rather limited method of study: racial and cultural differences, for instance, are ignored. There has been very little discussion of other masculinities such as the Mexican characters in Eastwood westerns or more recently the representation of Somalians in *Black Hawk Down* (2001). The focus has been on white masculinity to the exclusion of other identity-forming factors such as ethnic background, sexuality, nationality and so on.

The construction of identity, how and why we identify with a character, is complex, a fantasy we engage in when watching a film. Mainstream film is a site for questioning these rich and often ambiguous character identities, and the study of gender in film questions what these identities are and asks how they work.

Hollywood film is much more than a straightforward, easily read transmitter of the dominant ideology. It is complex in its construction and multi-layered in meaning and, to some extent, reflects the hopes and wants and desires of the cinema-going public.

Playing with gender

It has been observed by commentators in different disciplines that the strenuousness of the masculine identities is a pointer, not to their stability, but their fragility.

(Horrocks 1995: 16)

The myth presented regarding masculinity is that it is natural, normal and universal. This myth is repeated by stories and images we see in the media and especially in Hollywood film. Yet despite the certainty, the surety with which masculine identities are portrayed, closer examination reveals that masculinity is much less stable and much more easily undermined than previously thought.

• **Plate 10.7**
Gladiator (Ridley Scott, 2000). The general seeks to avenge the murder of this wife and children

Theorists such as Barbara Creed, Yvonne Tasker and Chris Holmlund have discussed the notion of masculinity as play, as performance and masquerade. Barbara Creed suggests that the muscle-bound hero of the 1980s cinema may be understood in terms of postmodernity, of playing with the notion of manhood, and argues that the muscular hero is a 'simulcra of an exaggerated masculinity, the original lost to sight' (1987: 65). The hero in action film is then a parody, a tongue-in-cheek play on the impossible role he has to perform. It is easy to apply this argument to Bruce Willis in the *Die Hard* films but does the same argument apply to Russell Crowe's role in *Gladiator* (2000)? Crowe's Roman general is a much more serious and weighty hero who has lost his family and is looking for revenge. He portrays a hypermasculinity but also evokes a sense of nostalgia, harking back to a time when men were strong and had a cause worth fighting for.

Whilst psychoanalysis has been used as a way of understanding the acquisition of sexual identity, postmodernism addresses the flexibility and ambiguity of popular culture. When put together, interesting ways of understanding gender emerge. Chris Holmlund combines these two approaches in 'Masculinity as Multiple Masquerade' (1993), in which she discusses the many ways that acting, playing a role on screen, is a masquerade; she argues that it is an act of gender pretence, a form of dressing up and putting on a show, and that heterosexuality is also a masquerade, a charade, in which there are often homoerotic overtones. Therefore masculinity, and thus gender, is a multiple charade of which the audience is aware yet not aware and much of the complexity of gender identity is understood by the audience at a subconscious level.

The male body

The action film, by being active, distracts from the eroticised male body on display. Dyer explains:

images of men must disavow ... passivity if they are to be kept in line with the dominant ideas of masculinity-as-activity.

(Dyer 1982: 66–7)

The masculine body as spectacle and performer, having a performative function, is a key theme of Hollywood film, particularly action films of the 1980s. Yvonne Tasker's analysis of the *Die Hard* films suggests that the particular representation of the male body in the 1980s reflects an anxiety about the roles men and women play in their everyday lives, both at home and at work, and their concerns regarding shifts in society and gender roles. *Die Hard* (1988) reflects on the lack of control for the male in the workplace, where the hero finds himself in impossible situations controlled by incompetent bureaucracies:

Anxieties to do with difference and sexuality increasingly seem to be worked out over the body of the male hero.

(Tasker 1993: 236)

For further discussion of the star in Hollywood, see Chapter 6.

In terms of stars and gender the star is an amplified sign of popularity. The star is larger than life in his physical abilities and looks. The usually white star/hero goes into a dangerous situation, and civilises and makes it safe. Again however, like gender, stardom is not fixed but unstable and shifting. Changes in the qualities of the male hero are evident from the 1980s to the 1990s; the male body in the 1980s was a spectacle of muscle, beauty, toughness and bravery, a body which could carry out extreme physical feats. In comparison the body of the early 1990s man is less a spectacle of male machismo associated with violence, but rather gentler, more questioning, allowed to show self-doubt, and existing in a world where love and family are important: films such as *Robin Hood* (1991), *Regarding Henry* (1991) and *Boyz N the Hood* (1991) try to work out these issues.

A comparison of *The Terminator* (1984) with *Terminator 2* (1991) demonstrates many of these changes in the representation of masculinity. Susan Jeffords argues that in *Terminator 2* the Terminator becomes the perfect father and mother and, therefore, Sarah's role as mother and saviour of the human race is diminished. Ironically, Sarah becomes a parody of the tough, fearless, 1980s action hero and, similarly, there is a fascination with her muscles and her body.

In *Terminator 2* there is a shift in position regarding violence and male machismo: a non-destructive, anti-killing morality is imposed. The Terminator is told by John Connor to aim for the knees when he shoots, and that killing is not good. Dyson, the creator of the Terminator, sacrifices himself for the greater good, to save humanity. John Connor, the son and future saviour of the human race, holds the real power in the narrative and the Terminator becomes a metaphor for the old Hollywood concept of masculinity.

Terminator 2, Jeffords argues, provides a new way for masculinity to go, not outward aggression

but inward, into increasingly emotive displays of masculine sensibilities, traumas and burdens. T2 offers an alternative way to resolve these anxieties about the ends of masculinity/territory through the manipulation of space and time via the male body.

(1993: 259)

The male body in the early 1990s is often damaged in some way, as in *Robocop 2* (1992), or, as in the case of the Terminator, it has to be destroyed. This damaged yet heroic body of the Terminator is the source of man's personal, emotional and social problems and appears to be past his 'sell-by date'. Films by black male directors, although concerned with families and masculinity, often do not have the same concern with the themes of internalisation and bodily betrayal. John Singleton's film *Boyz N the Hood* is much more

• **Plate 10.8**
Fight Club (David
Fincher, 1999). *Fight
Club* suggests a huge
anxiety about what it is
to be male

concerned with critiquing the culture and society in which black American boys are
brought up.

Tasker argues that muscles are signifiers of struggle, of hard physical labour, of the
working class. The importance of masculine muscles in the action film may be attributed
to a form of nostalgia or a need to identify with men who are clearly men. Although this
is a concern of the 1980s action film it is interesting to compare this with more recent
films which subject the male body to the gaze, such as *Fight Club* (1999) and the *Full
Monty* (1997). Yet different actors bring different qualities to the screen; Bruce Willis is
not just a working-class hero associated with muscles and a vest, he is part parody with
a wise-cracking voice. He gives a different performance from that of body builders such
as Stallone and Schwarzenegger, although by *Terminator 2* Schwarzenegger seemed to
have become a parody of himself.

The action-film narrative is a series of workings out to do with class and sexuality
situated within a cultural context in which masculinity has to some extent been
denaturalised. The use of military and police uniform in many action films appears to
relieve masculine anxiety, giving some stability in a society of changing values, and thus
raises self-esteem. The dress of the action hero gives an appearance of phallic power, a
substitute for the 'lack' feared; the muscular, phallic body functions as a powerful symbol
of desire and lack.

The action hero plays out a drama of power and powerlessness which is intrinsic to
anxieties about masculine identity and authority embodied in the figure of the struggling
hero. The action hero is tested; he has to undergo a set of narrative hurdles or challenges
to overcome which will often include suffering, torture and punishment, all tribal tests
of masculinity. Fight films such as *Rocky* (1976) and *Raging Bull* (1980), although very
different films, both focus on masochistic suffering and how much punishment the
masculine body can take.

Male anxiety: masculinity in crisis

The 1980s action hero is superficially a sign of masculine power, but on closer
examination an anxiety about masculine identity is revealed, an anxiety which has been
addressed in many films of the 1990s although in rather different forms. The arrogance

and certainty of many films in the boom periods of the 'Yuppie' Reagan years was replaced by uncertainty in the late 1980s and early 1990s as a result of economic depression, a downturn in the economy and a developing awareness that capitalism was not infallible. Films such as *Risky Business* (1983) and *Ferris Bueller's Day Off* (1986) are full of confident, masculine swagger while *Wall Street* (1987) reflects a much darker view of masculinity, capitalism and corporate greed.

Jude Davies's 1995 article 'Gender, Ethnicity and Cultural crisis in *Falling Down* and *Groundhog Day*', outlines how both films problematise white masculinity and links an American cultural and historical crisis with a crisis of masculinity. In *Falling Down* (1996), director Joel Schumacher makes the point that the pre-eminence of the white male can no longer be assumed. Michael Douglas as D-Fens plays a dysfunctional white male who is pushed to violence when he loses his job. *Falling Down* shows the tensions at work in mid-1990s America, a society affected by economic depression, gender and multicultural anxiety.

D-Fens is not portrayed as being typical of white masculinity; as the narrative progresses his behaviour becomes more extreme and further out of control. In the finale, however, D-Fens is transformed into the hero when we realise his death will give his young daughter insurance money: he sacrifices his life to help her.

Groundhog Day (1993) also features white masculinity in crisis but in a very different way. The film is a romantic comedy which shows the transformation of a cynical sexist into an enlightened sympathetic male. The film avoids any political gestures or comment and in terms of narrative Bill Murray's character has changed very little by the film's conclusion. Davies points out that *Falling Down* and *Groundhog Day*, while they are both

> in some senses critical of the white middle class masculinity which has occupied the default position in mainstream US culture, they reinforce the primacy of white males in making sense of, and responding to, a perceived crisis. Here when white masculinity seems most under fire it hogs the ground.
>
> (Ibid.: 229)

The new man?

See Chapter 7, pp. 143–71, for a case study of Pulp Fiction and the audience's interaction with the film. For further reference to The Full Monty and British cinema see Chapter 13, p. 324.

In early 1990s cinema white males are often presented as domesticated, feminised or paternal in a range of genres such as comedies, romances and action films; so much so that Quentin Tarantino was one of the few filmmakers in that period working in the gangster genre, probably the only genre in which macho masculinity remains intact. *Pulp Fiction* (1994) has levels of irony, self-reflexivity and parody; it also contains a homophobic construction of sexuality which belies the macho strutting of the actors. Films in the latter part of the decade and the new millennium, such as *The Full Monty* (1997), *Fight Club* (1999) and *Gladiator* (2000), in their very different ways, suggest an unease with taking on a feminised role and a desire for certainty in respect of what it is to be masculine.

The feminised, enlightened new man is more fiction than reality, according to Kathleen Rowe in her 1995 article 'Melodrama and Men in Post-Classical Romantic Comedy', in which she argues that there has been an increased use of melodrama to tell the story of men's lives and male suffering. There is a darker edge to these comedies which takes away the focus from the female heroine and transfers it to the male victim, the melodramatic hero; the female becomes, if not the villain, then the lesser character.

From the late 1970s onwards romantic comedy has tapped into an unease about the notions of romance: in *Sleepless in Seattle* (1993) the lovers don't meet until the end and have no sexual contact; Woody Allen's films are often discourses about broader cultural anxieties concerning romance and masculinity. These comedies suggest an underlying fear of the impact of the changes in the status of women and their effect on men. Rowe argues that they allow the male to determine the narrative outcome while the female is seen as lacking:

In these films it is the men who educate the women, not the reverse. Each of these heroines resists her male suitor less out of her inherent independence or recognition of his need to change than out of something wounded or underdeveloped in her – qualities which allow the hero to demonstrate his greater wisdom, charm or sensitivity.

(Kirkham and Thumin 1995: 187)

The classical Hollywood romantic comedies undermined masculine authority while melodrama was seen as the women's genre, a genre which appealed to women because it related to the sufferings they endured in patriarchal culture. Suffering and loss have been more often associated with the feminine; in women melancholy is seen as disabling and negative while in a man, for instance, Richard Gere in *Pretty Woman* (1989) or Tom Hanks in *Sleepless in Seattle* (1993), it is presented as positive, enabling the transformation of apparent loss into male power. These male transformation movies show a softer male but at the same time enhance and consolidate their hierarchical and patriarchal position by acquiring qualities traditionally regarded as feminine; in films such as *Regarding Henry* (1991), *The Fisher King* (1991), *Terminator 2* (1991), *Groundhog Day* (1993) and *Parenthood* (1989) men have emotions and are not afraid to display them but, apart from *Terminator 2*, in which Sarah Connor is sidelined in her role as mother, a role which is appropriated by Schwarzenegger, the woman's place is still in the kitchen.

Occasionally, Hollywood films overturn these conventions in an interesting or challenging way; in *Jagged Edge* (1989) Jeff Bridges plays the romantic hero but is finally exposed as the killer – the romantic hero becomes the villain.

Fatherhood and the family

Many films in the 1980s and 1990s have the role of fatherhood and the family as a central discourse. The family has been central to Western society and American national identity was founded on the patriarchal family structure. The contemporary American family, however, is not stable and many families divorce or separate. Action films such as *Die Hard* and *Lethal Weapon* (1989) reflect this uncertainty. Danny Glover's family, in *Lethal Weapon*, represents security, stability and paternal authority, while Mel Gibson plays the outsider who is emotionally lost after his wife's death, after the woman who gave him stability has gone.

The father replacing the mother or the mother being marginalised or ignored is a theme common to a variety of films from this period. In *Terminator 2*, the Terminator becomes the minder of John Connor (the son who has lost his father) and the 'hard' man learns to be gentle and how to nurture, while Sarah Connor is hardly involved with or even interested in motherhood. In *Three Men and a Baby* (1989) the men act as 'surrogate mothers' as well as fathers. The baby's mother is not reunited with her child until the end of the film and the audience view her as an outsider. Oliver Stone's *Wall Street* (1987) plays the 'good father' and 'the bad father' against each other, fighting to gain control of the good father's son; it is an exclusively male family scenario in which the women are either prizes or bought. More recent films such as *The Full Monty* (1997) and *Gladiator* (2000), in their very different ways, explore the role of the father as patriarch and how he reacts when the family is broken up and separated from the mother or the mother and family are destroyed.

Womb envy

A number of films, from genres as diverse as comedy in *Three Men and a Baby* to horror such as *The Fly* (1986), demonstrate an unease or discomfort which at times borders on envy regarding the reproductive powers of woman. Many horror films express a fascination with building a human such as *Frankenstein* (1930) or controlling reproductive power as does the scientist in *The Fly*.

Three Men and a Baby's central theme is about man's desire to take over and control the reproductive function. The film voices male concerns about fathering, birth and female sexuality, suggesting that fatherhood can be a collective male experience, rather than one man taking sole responsibility for the child. There is denial of a single responsibility for fatherhood while at the same time a desire to take the role of carer from the woman. A form of womb envy is apparent when one of the characters dresses as a pregnant woman.

Modleski argues that envy of woman and her procreative ability runs alongside a fear of feminisation and a wish to deny woman the role of childbearer and nurturer: 'it is possible, the film shows, for men to respond to the feminist demand for their increased participation in child rearing in such a way as to make women more marginal than ever' (2000: 525).

The protagonists in David Cronenberg's *The Fly* and *Dead Ringers* (1988) are so envious of female reproductive powers that they suffer feelings of impotence. The men in Cronenberg's films try to control the womb or gain knowledge that gives them power over female fertility as in the twin gynaecologists in *Dead Ringers*, while in *Videodrome* (1984) the central character gains a vagina in his stomach into which a video tape is inserted.

Masculine anxiety regarding paternity and reproduction is particularly evident in the horror film: in *Alien* there is a conflict between fear and fascination with the maternal. The film contains disturbing imagery regarding birth and the female sex organs: one of the crew gives birth through his stomach, the Alien is female, she eats men, consumes them; in contrast other imagery is comforting and maternal, the sleeping places are womb-like and the crew dress in nappies.

Hurt, agony, pain – love it: the masochistic spectator

Historically the male body is viewed as the norm and the female body as a deviation, as inferior, a poor copy. Yet many monstrous figures are, on closer examination, associated with aspects of femininity: Dracula has ruby-red lips, the werewolf's lunar cycle mimics menstruation and it is reborn in the process of transformation. More recently in *The Silence of the Lambs* (1991) Buffalo Bill hopes to realise transformation by covering himself in the skin of dead women.

Barbara Creed's article 'Dark Desires' (1993) argues that there are two types of horror film: the first explores man's desire for castration in order to become a woman, and the second, man's desire for castration as part of a male death wish. Creed examines the rape-revenge films *I Spit on Your Grave* (1978) and *Naked Vengeance* (1984), in which the male rapist is castrated and killed by his victim. A more recent equivalent is *Species* (1997), in which the female monster kills her victim after having sex with him.

It appears that who the audience identify with in terms of gender when watching film is rather more complex than outlined by Mulvey and by Metz (1983). Carol Clover examines the nature of the male monster and the identification of the audience with the female victim, and points out that the gaze of both the male and the female spectator is constructed as masochistic. In the horror film the victim is usually female and the audience mostly male. The horror film uses the female form not only for the male spectator to look at but for him to feel through and identify with, suggesting that the male viewer can easily identify with a different gender. He therefore takes on the role of masochistic spectator, identifying with the fear and pain of the hero/heroine. Clover argues that there has been a silence about male masochism and a silence about identification with the female, even though it is assumed that women identify with the masculine in film.

The title of this section 'Hurt, agony, pain – love it' is written on a sign at the beginning of *The Silence of the Lambs* (1991). The horror audience, whether male or female, does not have control of the look but is forced to take on a passive, classically feminine role, identifying with the pain and suffering of the protagonist: in the case of *The Silence of the Lambs*, the FBI agent Clarice Starling. Clover further argues that although the horror film is more overt in its manipulation of the audience, mainstream film makes use of similar tools to feminise the audience; we 'surrender ourselves' to a film, we expect to be manipulated, surprised and kept in suspense. Therefore the assumed dominant, sadistic role ascribed to the male viewer by Mulvey and by Metz is under question.

□ CASE STUDY 2: *FIGHT CLUB* (DAVID FINCHER, 1999)

Fight Club is a film about masculinity in crisis. It depicts the disaffected, feminised, young white American male and his frustration with late capitalism and late twentieth-century life. The film's central discourse suggests an uncertainty about man's role in society and a lack of purpose in life; Jack, the central protagonist, expresses this as:

We are the middle children of history with no purpose or place
We have no great war or great depression …
We were raised by television to believe that we'd be millionaires …
But we won't…. And now we're very pissed off.

These are the 'Lost Boys', a generation of men whose fathers have left home and have given no masculine guidance to their sons; they have no clear role or function in society and their lives are without meaning.

The crisis in identity exemplified by Jack's split personality is alluded to throughout the film, although not revealed until near the end. Tyler is Jack's physically perfect alter ego and also his dark side; a role played by Brad Pitt whose muscled body is often on display. In the first half of the film Jack has a homoerotic fascination with Tyler but in the latter section the two characters, facets of his personality, battle with each other for survival and Jack's sanity. Jack represents the passive, domesticated male and Tyler the fighter who is almost Neanderthal and ultimately destructive. As Henry Giroux points out:

The central protagonists, Jack and Tyler, represent two opposing registers that link consumerism and masculinity.… Jack exemplifies a form of domesticated masculinity – passive, alienated and without ambition. On the other hand Tyler exemplifies and embodies masculinity that refuses the seductions of consumerism.

(2000–1: 33)

The emasculated male, in need of testosterone, is evident from the beginning of the film, which opens with a phallic image of Jack with a gun in his mouth. There are many references throughout the film to fear of castration and phallic inadequacy. Jack is feminised, he is obsessed with decorating his flat with IKEA furniture and has an apparently lonely, meaningless but domesticated existence. There is clearly something wrong with Jack's life; he can't sleep, and tells a doctor that he's in pain. The doctor suggests he attends classes for the terminally ill to find out what pain really is. The first class Jack goes to is for testicular cancer, where he meets Bob who has breasts due to hormone treatment. Jack consoles him that 'we're still men'. Again these references suggest fear of castration, fear of losing masculine identity and fear of losing control of the body. Tyler shows Jack a way to regain his masculinity, his place in the world. There are a number of parallels with *Falling Down*, which depicts a man's extreme reaction to losing power and control in his life.

Identity is literally torn apart in the film and this is exemplified by the fight club; fighting is not only a spectacle but a test of one's masculinity and how much pain can be taken, can be suffered. The masochistic desire for self-punishment and the belief that pain through suffering is somehow redemptive or a transformative experience is a nostalgia for the past rituals of primitive societies; there is also a nostalgia for an age when the roles of masculine and feminine are imagined as being more clearly defined. Many male secret societies and fascist groups have used pain as a test for entrance to the group. The fights between Jack and Tyler are however later shown as delusions, and Jack's self-mutilation is presented as an aspect of self-hate, guilt, confusion and inner torment; we understand in retrospect that he is a deeply disturbed character.

The fight club is where men can rediscover their masculinity, can connect and overcome fear and pain. The club gives order and meaning to their lives; these men crave regulation, rules and clearly defined boundaries.

The film flirts with fascism; Jack watches in horror as the desire for a club of men and a new order is pushed to extremes. The fight club, the secret society, is transformed into an underground army which brainwashes its members who have to go through a series of masochistic initiations and tests to be considered 'man enough' to join. The paramilitary group has no real politics: Project Mayhem's aim is to destroy examples of modern art, architecture and coffee bars (the ubiquitous Starbucks?); its aim is to bring chaos and destruction. The film, through Tyler, offers a nihilist philosophy of destruction and negativity. As Tyler says: 'Self-improvement is masturbation, self-destruction is the answer.'

The film links self-abuse with regaining power over the body and one's life. Jack argues in voiceover that the fight club gives him power and the people who had power over him have less and less because of his new state of mind. This is undercut however when he says, 'by this point I could wiggle most of the teeth in my jaw', and we are made aware that he is actually destroying his body. The fight club pushes self-destruction and self-loathing to its limits as the men pound each other's bodies until one gives in. When Tyler pours lye on Jack's hand he tells Jack to feel the pain and not to avoid it; this ritual becomes a repeated image later in the film, an initiation test for new members of the club, another form of self-destruction and brainwashing.

A powerful desire for male bonding is repeatedly expressed, the need to be part of a group or movement which provides a reason for their existence. There is an element of homoeroticism in the images of dirty, sweaty, bloody men which is undercut by the action and violence that is so visceral at times (see above on men and action films). The uniform of muscles becomes the uniform of a terrorist organisation, and indeed there is a fetishism of the military which is very precise in its specificity of the clothing needed to join: two pairs of black socks and so on.

Women in *Fight Club* are, on first appearance, marginalised, non-existent, apart from Marla. Yet this is contradicted by some of Jack's first words: 'All this is about Marla Singer.' Much of the film is about denying or fighting against both the female within and the female figure of Marla. *Fight Club* gives a somewhat misogynist representation of women: Marla is defined as the cause of all Jack's problems – ' She ruined everything' – and women are a threat, representing fear of castration; Tyler says to Jack, 'a woman could cut off your penis and throw it out the car'. Jack is part of a generation raised by women and questions how this has affected his identity. He asks: 'I wonder if another woman is really the answer we need.' There is frequent reference to the negative effect women have on men in shaping their identities, in feminising them. Tyler tells Jack that men have lost their manhood because they have been feminised. Women are cast as binary opposites and defined in negative terms; even the woman dying at the beginning of the film is defined in terms of her sex and as being sexually unattractive. Marla's role in the film is that of an outsider and a threat to Jack's existence. She fulfils two roles, first, to make Jack unhappy, and second, to provide sex. Yet there is a paradox here: Jack says Marla has invaded his life but this is more the unconscious denial of a want than a real desire to get rid of her. Marla is a constant, always waiting in the background, and Jack is pushed to fight against Tyler partly because of his desire to save her.

On one level the film is a celebration of hypermasculinity and violence, revelling in the visceral physicality of the fighting scenes, for instance, and yet this destructive force is clearly satirised; the potential for and attraction to extreme violence by disaffected, alienated young men who have no place in society is made clear. It is rather chilling that the skyscrapers blown up at the end of the film were similar to the phallic symbols of American capitalism and wealth that were blown up on 11 September 2001 by extreme Islamic fundamentalists who were also alienated from Western society.

CONCLUSION

This chapter introduces the subject of film and gender. It is by no means a definitive study but presents a range of important viewpoints and key articles in this area of study. Mulvey's original article 'Visual Pleasure and Narrative Cinema' has inspired a whole range of theories concerning masculinity and femininity which try to unravel how meaning is produced in film. As more and more women are included in the filmmaking process, from writers to directors to cinematographers, it will be interesting to see if this means new theories will have to evolve to account for the new meanings and the new narratives produced.

NOTES

Full details of works cited in the notes section may be found in the consolidated bibliography.

1 For further information on women screenwriters past and present read 'What Happened to the Women?' by Nancy Hendrickson in *Creative Screenwriter*, July/August 2003, Vol. 10, 4, pp. 64–8.

2 See Donald and Scanlon's 1992 article on whether *Thelma and Louise* (1991) is a feminist film.

3 Suggested further reading: on the early feminist movement, K. Millett, *Sexual Politics* (1977) and G. Greer, *The Female Eunuch* (1971), and, more recently, M. Maynard (1987: 23).

4 Structuralism and Marxism have been, and still are, important concepts in the application of film theory and have historically affected film practice, particularly in the independent and workshop sector. For a good general background to these viewpoints read Chs 1 and 2 of Lapsley and Westlake (1988).

5 If you are interested in reading more about Stuart Hall's important input into cultural studies theory, a good starting point is 'Encoding/Decoding', in *Culture, Media, Language* (1980).

6 For further discussion of how we negotiate with cultural texts, see Gledhill's 'Pleasurable Negotiations', in Pribram (1988).

7 Janice Radway has thrown new light as to how women interpret fiction. Her theories may be usefully applied to other texts. For further details see *Reading the Romance* (1987).

8 For further reading on black feminist film theory and some excellent film analysis, see bell hooks, *Reel to Real* (1996) and Valerie Smith's *Not Just Race* (1998).

9 For a useful discussion of gender theories read Ch. 6, Bilton *et al.* (2002).

10 Neale's points about masculinity in Mann's film were originally referred to in a 1981 article by Paul Willemen entitled 'Anthony Mann: Looking at the Male'.

FURTHER READING

Berger, J., *Ways of Seeing*, Penguin, London, 1972. Although now old, this is still a very useful introduction to the visual image.

Betterton, R., *Looking On: Images of Femininity in the Visual Arts and the Media*, Pandora, London, 1987.

Brundsen, C. (ed.), *Films for Women*, British Film Institute, London, 1986. This book looks at a range of feminist films such as *A Question of Silence* (1982) directed by Marlene Gorris.

Bruzzi, S., *Undressing Cinema*, Routledge, London, 1997. An insightful look at dress in film with a focus on gender.

Clover, C., *Men, Women and Chainsaws: Gender in the Modern Horror Film*, British Film Institute,

London, 1992. An original and fascinating analysis of how we watch and understand horror film.

Cohan, S. and Hark, I. (eds), *Screening the Male*, Routledge, London, 1993. One of the first edited volumes to discuss masculinity and film. It contains many important articles which are well worth reading.

Cook, P. and Dodd, P. (eds), *Women and Film: A Sight and Sound Reader*, British Film Institute and Scarlet Press, London, 1993.

Deuber-Mankowsky, A., *Lara Croft – Cyber Heroine*, University of Minnesota Press, Minneapolis, 2005. Insightful discussion of computer games and film and gender.

Easthope, A., *What a Man's Gotta Do: The Masculine Myth in Popular Culture*, Unwin Hyman, Winchester, 1990. A good introduction to masculinity and myth.

Francke, L., *Script Girls*, British Film Institute, London, 1994. This book discusses the number of women who have worked as scriptwriters in the film industry, particularly Hollywood.

Hendrickson, N., 'What Happened to All the Women?', *Creative Screenwriter*, Vol. 10, No. 4, pp. 64–8.

hooks, bell, *Reel to Real: Race, Class and Sex in the Movies*, Routledge, New York, 1996. Well-written, insightful film readings of, among others, Spike Lee's *She's Gotta Have It* (1985) and *Crooklyn* (1991), and *Waiting to Exhale* (1995), directed by Forest Whitaker.

Horrocks, R., *Male Myths and Icons: Masculinity in Popular Culture*, Macmillan, London, 1995. A good discussion of masculinity.

Innes, S., *Tough Girls, Women Warriors and Wonder Women in Popular Culture*, University of Pennsylvania Press, Philadelphia, 1999. A great discussion of tough women in the media.

Kaplan, E.A. (ed.), *Feminism and Film*, Oxford University Press, Oxford, 2000.

Kirkham, P. and Thumin, J. (eds), *You Tarzan: Masculinity, Movies and Men*, Lawrence & Wishart, London, 1993. A good range of articles on issues of masculinity and film.

— (eds), *Me Jane: Masculinity, Movies and Women*, Lawrence & Wishart, London, 1995. A good range of articles on issues regarding masculinity, femininity and film.

MacKinnon, K., *Representing Men*, Arnold, London, 2003.

Modleski, T., *The Women Who Knew Too Much*, Methuen, London, 1988. A very accessible and original analysis of Hitchcock's films.

Pilling, J. (ed.), *Women and Animation: A Compendium*, British Film Institute, London, 1992.

Potter, S., www.yesthemovie.com, pp. 1–4.

Segal, M., *Slow Motion: Changing Masculinities, Changing Men*, Virago, London, 1997. This book has a very useful and approachable discussion of masculinity in its introduction.

Spicer, A., *Typical Men*, I.B. Tauris, London, 2001.

Tasker, Y., *Spectacular Bodies: Gender, Genre and the Action Movie*, Routledge, London, 1993.

— *Working Girls*, Routledge, London, 1998.

Thornham, S., *Passionate Detachments*, Arnold, London, 1997.

Van Zoonen, L., *Feminist Media Studies*, Sage, London, 1994. A good introduction to issues regarding feminism in the media.

Willis, S., *High Contrast: Race and Gender in Contemporary Hollywood Film*, Duke University Press, Durham and London, 1997.

Periodicals are extremely useful to refer to for further reading; they tend to be more topical and 'up to date'. Look out for articles on women and film in the following: *Feminist Review, Women: A Cultural Review* and *Sight and Sound*.

FURTHER VIEWING

This chapter has focused mainly on Hollywood and British film and is therefore a selective view. In terms of gender the analysis has concentrated mostly on Hollywood film, partly because so much research on masculinity and feminity is based on the study of popular culture. There are a number of British films which would be well worth further investigation: *Billy Elliot* (2000) and *Bend It Like Beckham* (2002), for instance, would both be revealing to study in terms of gender and the protagonists reaching out to achieve success in areas which are not considered appropriate (ballet and football respectively). More recent US films such as *American Beauty* (1999) and *Happiness* (1999) or *In the Bedroom* (2001) would be revealing

to study in terms of gender and family life. Films which portray women in powerful central roles such as *Erin Brockovich* (2000) and *Heartbreakers* (2001) are interesting to discuss as to whether the protagonists really are playing stereotypical roles: 'the tart with a heart' and 'the temptress', who is only after a man's money.

Worldwide women's cinema is rich and varied – countries as small and culturally diverse as New Zealand and Iran have contributed to this upsurge. As more women enter the film industry and take on key roles, the number of mainstream films made by women will hopefully increase.

Other chapters in this book refer to films by women: see Chapter 11. Unfortunately, many earlier films by women are difficult to obtain. The BFI and Cinenova (a film and video distributor that promotes films by women) hold a number of titles for rental. The latter's comprehensive catalogue is well worth looking through. The following films may all be hired through Cinenova at 113 Roman Road, London E2 0HN, tel: 0208 981 6828: *To Be a Woman* (UK, Jill Craigie, 1953); *Women of the Rhondda* (UK, Esther Ronay, 1972); *A Comedy in Six Unnatural Acts* (US, Jan Oxenburg, 1975); *An Epic Poem* (UK, Lezli-Ann Barrett, 1982); *Born in Flames* (US, Lizzie Borden, 1983).

The following films are all available for rental or sale from the BFI and provide stimulating viewing: *Orlando* (UK, Sally Potter, 1993) (see Case Study 1); *Wayward Girls and Wicked Women*, vols 1, 2 and 3 (1992) (various women animators, often witty, poignant and hard-hitting); *Sweetie* (Australia, Jane Campion, 1989) (it's anarchic, funny and strange!); *Dream On* (UK, Amber Films, 1992) (focuses on women on a north-east estate; realistic, hard-hitting with some lighter moments); any of Gurinder Chada's films are worth considered viewing and the latter two will be available on video/DVD: from *Bhaji on the Beach* (UK, 1993) which is the story of an Asian women's group's journey to Blackpool, to *What's Cooking* (2000), and *Bend It Like Beckham* (2002) about an Asian girl who wants to be a footballer.

RESOURCE CENTRES

www. bfi. org. uk
Has a very useful link to women in film and TV.

www. cinenova. org
A European feminist promoter of films by women. Well worth a look.

www. feminist. org
A useful site with lots of links to feminist subject matter.

www.Sallypotter.com

www. sistersincinema. com
An African-American women filmmakers' website with a resources list.

www. wmm. com
Women make movies website that aims to encourage the production of films by women. Has a good links section.

lib. berkeley. edu/ MRC/ womenbib. html

Chapter 11

Lesbian and gay cinema

Chris Jones

■ Lesbian and gay cinema

INTRODUCTION: REPRESENTATION

Representation is a social process which occurs in the interactions between a reader or viewer, and a text. It produces signs which reflect underlying sets of ideas and attitudes. In her essay, 'Visual Pleasure and Narrative Cinema', Laura Mulvey suggested ways in which a viewer of classic Hollywood films is addressed as male by being encouraged to adopt the viewpoint, the 'look' of the male protagonist. Although she later adjusted these ideas to cater for such female-orientated Hollywood genres as the melodrama, Mulvey's argument is based on the traditional psychoanalytic notion of male/female definitions and oppositions. Nowhere does she take into account the extent to which her argument is geared towards a **heterosexual** look. Nevertheless, her ideas about the positioning of the film spectator and filmmaker within the **gender** system have been very influential. They have led to much constructive critical investigation into how different kinds of filmmakers and viewers affect meaning-making processes according to their race and **sexuality**, as well as gender.

DEFINITIONS AND DEVELOPMENTS: CHANGING LANGUAGE

Men and women who relate sexually to members of their own **sex** have always existed, but the modern term 'homosexual' was invented in 1869 by a Swiss doctor. It was not commonly used in the English language until the 1890s, the decade that saw the birth of cinema. The term **homosexual** was partly inherited from nineteenth-century ideas of disease. Previously, same-sex relations had been predominantly characterised by notions of sin inherited from the medieval period. These commonly held associations continued into this century as German filmmakers produced a number of works campaigning for more enlightened attitudes in sexual and social matters. *Different from the Others* (1919) was a success on first release. Even though the main character, a homosexual musician, finally poisons himself, the dour storyline is countered by sections of the film in which Dr Magnus Hirschfield puts forward an affirmative view of homosexuality. Hirschfield was a sexual researcher and social reformer whose world-renowned Institute was later destroyed by the Nazis. Within a year of its release the film was subject to censorship and now exists only in fragments, although these have since been assembled and shown. *Girls in Uniform* (Leontine Sagan, 1931) is still seen today as a major portrayal of anti-authoritarianism, with the love of its two female protagonists for each other triumphing over the oppressive regime of their boarding-school.

During the Second World War, with its movements of population and large numbers of servicemen and women being thrown closely together in same-sex barracks, many people became aware of homosexuality on a personal and social level. This resulted in two parallel and contradictory developments in North America and Europe during the 1950s: increasing growth among communities of homosexuals and lesbians in big cities, and systematic attempts by those in authority to prevent such developments.

These communities began to demand and develop wider networks of meeting places and entertainment, including film. Early examples of films made with such audiences in mind are the physique films of Dick Fontaine, who worked in San Francisco from the late 1940s. Such film activity mainly took place within the art-film world, and involved small-budget production and viewing in clubs and homes. The pursuit of physical culture was an area that attracted homosexual men, especially in North America, as portrayed in Thom Fitzgerald's film *Beefcake* (2000). Jean Genet's *Un chant d'amour* (1950), with its sexually charged images of handsome male prisoners, became a cult film, as did

For further discussion of representation and feminism see Chapter 10.

For detailed discussion of spectatorship see Chapter 7.

heterosexual
A word used to name and describe a person whose main sexual feelings are for people of the opposite sex.

gender
A name for the social and cultural construction of a person's sex and sexuality. Gender, sex and sexuality can overlap but are by no means an exact match. It is this 'mismatch' which has generated a fascinating body of film production and criticism.

sexuality
A name for the sexual feelings and behaviour of a person. When applied to groups of people (e.g. heterosexuals) ideas of social attitude and organisation are implied.

sex
A word used to denote and describe a person's physical type according to his or her genital make-up. In academic discourse, this is primarily a scientific term.

homosexual
A word used to name and describe a person whose main sexual feelings are for people of the same sex. Mainly, but not exclusively, used in reference to males.

homoerotic
A description of
a text – prose,
poem, film, painting,
photograph – conveying
an enjoyable sense of
same-sex attraction.

gay
A description of strong,
positive sexual love
and attraction between
members of the same
sex, used by extension
to describe cultural
products, such as film
and video, concerned
with similar themes.
Mainly referring to
males, it may also be
used for any person.

lesbian
A word used to name
and describe a woman
whose main sexual
feelings are for other
women. Coined as a
medical term in the late
nineteenth century, the
word has been invested
post-Stonewall with new
ideas of openness and
liberation. It may also be
used to describe cultural
products, such as film
and video, dealing with
lesbian themes.

queer
Originally a negative
term for (mainly male)
homosexuals, this
word has been recently
reappropriated by critics,
artists and audiences to
describe a challenging
range of critical work
and cultural production
with emphasis on
diversity of race,
nationality and cultural
experience. The term
is deliberately used to
embrace a wider range
of sexualities: lesbian,
gay, bisexual and
transgendered people
and issues.

*See Chapter 7 for
further discussion of film
audiences.*

• **Plate 11.1**
Un chant d'amour
(Jean Genet, 1950).
Genet's erotic
imagery has inspired
generations of
filmmakers

Kenneth Anger's *Fireworks* (1947), a young man's sexual fantasy involving sailors. From the 1960s the **homoerotic** films of Andy Warhol and George Kuchar began to find wider audiences. It was during this period that the word **gay** began to be used to both denote and describe a male homosexual person.

The modern gay liberation movement developed after the Stonewall riots of 1969 in New York. Members of the new movement adopted the word 'gay' for its positive connotations of happiness, and because they wanted to use a term to describe themselves that had not been chosen by outsiders. For them, the term represented a way of demonstrating pride in their identity, the power of political organisation, and a distinct culture. The term was initially conceived as describing both men and women, but women soon began to feel marginalised within the movement, and the term **lesbian** came back into general use during the 1970s to signal the distinctness and strength of women.

It is the very different emotional connotations of these varying terms which led critic Vito Russo to say: 'There never have been lesbians or gay men in Hollywood films. Only homosexuals' (Russo 1987: 245). Since the 1990s, the term **queer** has become widely used as a critical term to describe both the kind of image production discussed in this chapter and the frameworks used by certain critics to produce, view and assess cultural production.

AUDIENCES

Gay men, like men in general, have on average more spending power than women, despite equal opportunities legislation in many countries. With gay liberation came a greatly expanded network of related commercial goods and services; nightclubs, shops, clothing, books and magazines, the majority of which were aimed at men. The same conditions apply in the developing structures of film and cinema aimed at lesbians and gays. Men constituted the main organised audience for this type of cultural production. Even those films with non-commercial financial backing, such as the work of Derek Jarman and Isaac Julien, tended to attract funds partly because of the perceived existence of this established gay male audience.

Lesbian film and video developed in parallel with the emerging women's movement, almost always with less finance than its male equivalent, and found a base in film clubs

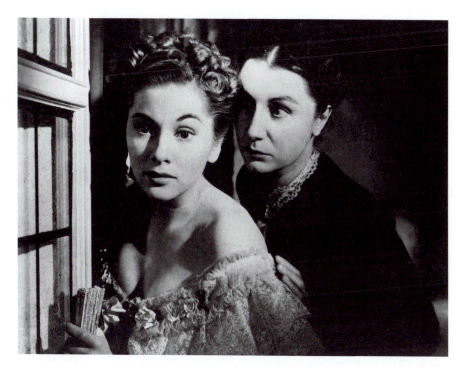

• **Plate 11.2**
Mrs Danvers (right) in
Hitchcock's *Rebecca*
(1940), making life
difficult for the woman
who seeks to replace
her beloved Rebecca.
This character is
arguably a touchstone
for the new queer
cinema spectator (Aaron
2004: 188)

and workshops. The American film and video artist Su Friedrich showed an active
preference for this type of outlet as a way of reaching lesbian audiences with films
such as *Damned If You Don't* (US, 1987). As a result of this production and viewing
background, and the modest financial levels this involved, many lesbian films of the
1970s and 1980s are less than feature-length. *Home Movie* (US, 1972) by Jan Oxenberg
is a modest but highly effective twelve-minute film, which edits home movie footage from
the director's own childhood with scenes of her adult life as a lesbian to make the viewer
amusingly aware of the conventions of family life. Her *Comedy in Six Unnatural Acts* (US
1975, twenty-six minutes) presents six short, staged scenes dealing with the foibles of
lesbian life, and debunking a few myths about **butch/femme** role-playing.

FILM FESTIVALS – AN HISTORICAL OVERVIEW

After 1945, film festivals became recognised across Europe and America as serving
several useful functions. They act as a marketplace for film distributors to view and
possibly buy new product and allow producers, scriptwriters and others to gather
and discuss new projects. Critics attending festivals alert wider audiences to new and
interesting work. Audiences can view and enjoy a wide range of films they would not
normally see in the cinema.

Since the 1970s a worldwide circuit of lesbian, gay and queer film festivals has grown
up. San Francisco was the first to start operating, followed by London, Paris, New York,
Toronto, Berlin and others. By the beginning of the twenty-first century, such festivals
were taking place outside Europe and North America in countries such as Korea and
Mexico. These events, often accompanied by lively lectures and discussions, serve all
the purposes already mentioned for lesbian and gay producers, directors, critics and
audiences. Their development has gone hand in hand with the flowering of gay political
consciousness. Rosa Von Praunheim's film *It Is Not the Homosexual Who Is Perverse,
but the Situation in which He Finds Himself* (Germany, 1970) is credited as a key text

butch
Description of behaviour
patterns – such as
aggression, sexual
dominance – traditionally
associated with
masculinity.

femme
Description of behaviour
patterns – such as
gentleness, sexual
passivity, concern with
dress and appearance –
traditionally associated
with femininity.

For further discussion
of film distribution and
exhibition, see Chapter 2.

in the awakening of the gay liberation movement, and was typical of the kind of work that found a viewing base in such festivals. In particular, these festivals have helped to bring small-scale film and video work and feature films from developing countries to the attention of wider lesbian and gay audiences. An example of the latter is the work of Lino Brocka from the Philippines (Murray 1998: 24), whose treatment of homosexual themes contains messages of tolerance and democracy not always acceptable to esablished authorities in his own country. Recent festivals have included work from Israel, Taiwan, India and Japan.

Another form of filmmaking given wider distribution through the festival circuit is feature-length documentary. *The Times of Harvey Milk* (Robert Epstein, US, 1985) chronicles the rise to power, and tragic assassination, of the San Francisco city supervisor who was one of the USA's first openly gay elected politicians. *Before Stonewall: The Making of a Gay and Lesbian Community* (Greta Schiller, US, 1985) vividly recalls gay and lesbian lives in the years during and following the Second World War. All these films wove together interviews, contemporary newsreel film and photographs. Through fostering cultural and historical consciousnes, such films as these aided the growing self-awareness of lesbian and gay communities in the USA and elsewhere (see Farmer (2000: Ch. 1) for ideas about performativity).

Much of this documentary material opens up new areas of awareness for its audiences. Showing at festivals tends now to be a first step towards wider exposure on TV. A recent example is the film *Queer and Catholic* (Peter Nicholson, UK, 2001) where current debates are explored through interviews with clergy and theologians in Britain, the USA and Rome.

As the AIDS crisis arose in the 1980s, this newly developed network of audiences and exhibition venues was particularly receptive to the wide variety of film and video work created in response to this situation, such as Rosa Von Praunheim's *A Virus Knows No Morals* (Germany, 1986). Short videos such as John Greyson's *The ADS Epidemic* (Canada, 1986) boosted morale by warning in a jokey way against ADS (Acquired Dread of Sex) while reminding people about safe sex. *Common Threads: Stories from the Quilt* (Robert Epstein and Jeffrey Freedman, US, 1989) is a full-length documentary chronicling the stories of a group of people who have lost loved ones to AIDS and contributed panels to the memorial quilt. We see moving interviews with, among others, the parents of a haemophiliac boy, a young drug-addicted widow and the gay critic Vito Russo.

See Chapter 11 for
further references
to lesbian and gay
documentary film.

Currently, the planetout website (see Resources at the end of this chapter) lists addresses and details of about 150 lesbian and gay film festivals around the world, including those devoted to such specialisations as documentary and experimental image production. See also the festival list in Daniel and Jackson (2003: 549).

GAY SENSIBILITY

In a book published by the British Film Institute to coincide with the first-ever Lesbian and Gay Film Festival at the National Film Theatre, London, in 1977, the critic Jack Babuscio wrote:

I define the gay sensibility as a creative energy reflecting a consciousness that is different from the mainstream; a heightened awareness of certain human complications of feeling that spring from the fact of social oppression; in short, a perception of the world which is coloured, shaped, directed and defined by the fact of one's gayness.

(quoted in Benshoff and Griffin 2004: 120)

In a key essay, 'Rejecting Straight Ideals: Gays In Film' (Steven 1985), Richard Dyer challenged Babuscio's emphasis on oppression as a mainspring for gay sensibility. He says this sensibility must be understood as 'something that has been and is produced and praised in history and culture' (Steven 1985: 287). For Dyer, oppression 'merely provides the conditions in relation to which oppressed people create their own subculture and attendant sensibility' (ibid.) and is not the defining factor as Babuscio perceives it.

In his essay, Dyer makes a convincing and clear argument based on the idea of what he calls 'the sexual **ideology** of our culture' (ibid.: 294); that is the idea that society and culture, through structures such as the family and artefacts such as film, impose a particular view of what it considers to be correct sexual behaviour. This view includes a dominance of the heterosexual viewpoint and antipathy towards the homosexual one. Homosexuality, according to Dyer, is predominantly seen from a heterosexual viewpoint in most mainstream films. As examples, he cites the image of homosexuality as a sickness and a problem in *Victim* (Basil Dearden, UK, 1961) and an endless succession of gay and lesbian characters as vampires, psychos and criminals which still continues today. However, as Dyer points out, ideology is contradictory and ambiguous, full of what he calls 'gaps and fissures' (ibid.: 294) through which filmmakers and audiences can make new, alternative meanings.

Critical awareness and discussion of gay sensibility and established sexual ideology, a concept that was later labelled 'heterosexism', started to be shared by increasing numbers of people: audiences, critics and filmmakers. Film production in this area continued to take place mainly within the structures of alternative or art cinema, although Hollywood made occasional attempts to exploit what was seen as an increasingly open gay audience, and a greater interest in gay themes by non-gays. Examples of products aimed at mainstream audiences are *The Boys in the Band* (William Friedkin, 1970), which exploited the sensationalistic stereotypes of emotional trauma, and *Making Love* (Arthur Hiller, 1982), an over-sweet romantic treatment of male love. *Cruising* (William Friedkin, 1980) equates homosexuality with pathological violence. These and many other mainstream films such as Jonathan Demme's *Philadelphia* (US, 1993) could profitably be examined using Dyer's notion of sexual ideology.

As a concept useful in the study of film, gay sensibility may be defined as a developed awareness of sexual variation. This does not automatically mean that a filmmaker or viewer has to be gay or lesbian to be able to present or appreciate themes and issues connected with gay people, but such awareness can open up rich creative possibilites. David Cronenberg's films, such as *Dead Ringers* (1988), make viewers uncomfortably aware of the fragile limits of conventional masculinity (see Chapter 10, p. 246). While one can debate what exactly constitutes a 'lesbian film' or a 'gay film', gay sensibility can enrich film production and appreciation for gays and non-gays.

CAMP AESTHETICS AND CINEMA

Dyer's ideas about searching for 'gaps and fissures' referred to above sometimes involves an attitude of conscious, ironic distancing on the part of a spectator known as **camp**, traditionally associated with gay audiences. In her famous essay, 'Notes on "Camp"', critic Susan Sontag states: 'the essence of Camp is its love of the unnatural: of artifice and exaggeration' (Sontag 1994: 275). She describes camp as 'one way of seeing the world as an aesthetic phenomenon … not in terms of beauty, but in terms of degree of artifice, of stylization' (ibid.: 277).

The concept of camp is useful when considering how lesbian and gay audiences often view mainstream representations but again the exercise of such sensibility is by no means confined to gays. The films of Ken Russell are considered to be very camp, as are many musicals, and muscle epics of the 1950s such as *Hercules Unchained*. In the latter, the exaggerated sexual signifiers of the hero (inflated muscles, heroic beard) and the main female figure (cleavage, diaphanous veils) come close to parodying gender

ideology
A set of ideas and attitudes held so much in common by most membes of a society that they are seen as part of the natural order.

For further discussion of the relationship between gender, film and ideology, see Chapter 10.

camp
A critical attitude which involves looking at texts less as reflections of reality than as constructed sets of words, images and sounds at a distance from reality. The attitude often involve irony or detachment when considering this distance. See 'Notes on "Camp"' by Susan Sontag.

stereotypes. Such exaggeration may also be seen in popular action movies, such as those starring Jean-Claude Van Damme, Dolph Lundgren, Vin Diesel and others, where camp elements intertwine with homoerotic subtext. Sontag suggested that 'Camp sensibility is disengaged, depoliticised, or at least apolitical' (ibid.). Camp continues to be a site of critical inquiry; see Farmer (2000: Ch. 3) where he argues cogently for the political subversiveness of camp sensibility, and the continuing discussion in the two compilations on queer cinema in the key texts.

CRITICAL RE-READINGS

The possible meanings of a film, as with all signifying practices, reside in the interaction between the viewer and the text. Much work has been done in recent years on how subgroups within the wider popular audience arrive at their own particular meanings when watching a mainstream film. Lesbian and gay critics have been at the forefront of such 're-readings'. Here are some examples. The books referred to are in the Further Reading section at the end of this chapter or in the Bibliography.

Tyler and Russo: early explorations

Parker Tyler's book *Screening the Sexes: Homosexuality in the Movies* opened up the field of study and analysis of lesbian and gay cinema in 1972, but Russo's *The Celluloid Closet: Homosexuality in the Movies* is now regarded as a major landmark. First published in 1981 and revised in 1987, the book has continued to influence later critical work in this area.

Russo combines a historical view of lesbian and gay people's contribution to cinema with an awareness of representation and audience. Although it deals mainly with Hollywood product, in contrast to Tyler's work, Russo's book is packed with examples and ideas that have formed the basis of further research by new generations of critics and academics. One example of insights Russo has to offer is his interpretation of the monster in the horror films of gay director James Whale. He sees *Frankenstein* and *The Bride of Frankenstein* as images of unnameable experiences and feelings outside normal society. These ideas were later developed by Harry Benshoff (1997).

Using cogently argued examples, Russo makes a powerful argument about how gay men derived particular subcultural messages from such films as *Rebel Without a Cause* when empathising with the relationship between Jim (James Dean) and Plato (Sal Mineo). Such tentative early explorations of spectatorial pleasure were to be greatly expanded by later gay and lesbian critics.

The emergence of neurotic, shadowy gay characters is discussed using *The Boys In The Band* and *The Killing of Sister George* (Robert Aldrich, US, 1968). Later critics were to investigate more fully the ideological underpinning of such representations. Russo's final argument, in the revised 1987 edition, is that worthwhile gay and lesbian cinema can only be developed and encouraged outside the traditional Hollywood power structures, and he outlines a range of examples of such positive work. An engaging documentary based on Russo's book, with relevant extracts, has proved popular and helped to bring his ideas to a wide audience (see Further Viewing at the end of this chapter).

Gay looking

Richard Dyer may be considered a major British figure in the critical and theoretical areas covered in this chapter. His book, *Now You See It* (2002) includes a comprehensive academic survey of the German films outlined above, as well as the work of Jean Genet and Kenneth Anger. It contains a particularly useful introduction to lesbian film and video-making of the postwar period.

Dyer is the author of many illuminating essays. His work on sexual ideology has already been mentioned, but he is perhaps best known for his work on stars. In his essay, 'Judy Garland and Gay Men' (1987), Dyer investigates the cultural associations between Judy Garland's star image and gay male audiences from the 1950s onward. He shows members of this audience strongly allying themselves with Garland's much vaunted ability to fight back against oppression and the status of outsider which her behaviour and personality often conferred on her (Benshoff and Griffin 2004: 153).

His essay 'Homosexuality in Film Noir' (Dyer 1993) shows coherently how gay characters in this classic Hollywood genre were negatively portrayed in both appearance and behaviour. He relates various homoerotic subtexts to film noir traditions and the dominant postwar view of sexual relations. This is an important genre to investigate because, as Dyer points out: 'Some of the first widely available images of homosexuality in our time were those provided by the American film noir' (Dyer 1993: 52). Dyer's essay 'Queer Noir' (Benshoff and Griffin 2004: 89) extends this examination.

Dyer's later studies of star image include a seminal essay on Rock Hudson in relation to public perceptions of sexuality, both before and after Hudson's homosexuality became public knowledge (Dyer 2002: 159). He demonstrates cogently how knowledge of Hudson's sexuality greatly enriches a viewer's appreciation of the gender play in the 1960s sex comedies in which he starred. He shows how such knowledge gives extra depth to Hudson's star performances in the famous sequence of 1950s melodramas directed by Douglas Sirk, such as *All that Heaven Allows* (US, 1955).

In North America, the critical writings of Thomas Waugh have been very influential. Read some of his key writings and ideas in the compilation entitled *The Fruit Machine* (Waugh, with a foreword by John Greyson (2000)). For a fruitful look at how close textual analysis can clarify alternative sexual insights into established cinema, the work of Alexander Doty is also of great importance, especially his book *Flaming Classics* (Doty 2000). Chapter 2 of his book *Making Things Perfectly Queer* is particularly recommended for his exploration of queer authorship (Doty 1993).

Some fascinating work on genre has been produced. A noteworthy example is Benshoff's thought-provoking book on homosexuality in the horror film (Benshoff 1997). Read also his essay in Benshoff and Griffin (2004) as well as Farmer's work on the musical (Farmer 2000: 69). Both of these critics demonstrate the use of excess and transgressive viewing strategies which challenge heterosexist norms.

Lesbian looking

The work of Andrea Weiss, like that of other writers on lesbian film such as Mandy Merck, B. Ruby Rich and Judith Mayne, was nurtured within the feminist movement. Weiss works primarily as a filmmaker. She was chief researcher on the documentary feature *Before Stonewall* and has produced an equally well-researched book on lesbians in film, *Vampires and Violets* (1993).

In her book, Weiss clearly tackles the critical problems asociated with identification and representation for lesbians. She states that:

identification involves both conscious and unconscious processes and cannot be reduced to a psychoanalytic model that sees sexual desire only in terms of the binary opposition of heterosexual masculinity and femininity; instead it involves varying degrees of subjectivity and distance depending upon race, class and sexual differences.

(Ibid.: 40)

This judgement reflects the questioning of Laura Mulvey's ideas on cinematic looking referred to above, a critical practice which has grown steadily since the 1980s. Weiss gives her readers a fascinating set of studies to show how lesbian audiences of classic

For further discussion
of Mulvey's theories
of gender and
spectatorship, see
Chapter 10.

Dorothy Arzner
The work of the only
woman to pursue
a career solely
as a director in
classic Hollywood is
currently undergoing
reassessment by
critics of lesbian
film such as Judith
Mayne. Here are
some key films:
The Wild Party
(1929)
Christopher Strong
(1933)
The Bride Wore Red
(1937)
Dance, Girl, Dance
(1940)

A lesbian auteur
Ulrike Ottinger
has been making
films for lesbian
audiences for a
number of years.
Read about her
(Kuzniar 2000: 139)
and watch some of
the following:
*Madame X – An
Absolute Ruler*
(1977)
Freak Orlando (1981)
Dorian Gray (1984)
*Joan of Arc of
Mongolia* (1989)

homophobia
Irrational prejudice and
hatred against a person
because of her or his
homosexuality.

Hollywood cinema have used their own interpretations to empower themselves, and how lesbian filmmakers have been able to make their own images.

These studies range across Dorothy Arzner's *The Wild Party* (US, 1929), star performances by Greta Garbo and Marlene Dietrich in the 1940s, lesbian vampire films, and 1970s radical lesbian films by Barbara Hammer. She offers fascinating, oppositional interpretations of the way in which lesbian audiences gained positive messages from the otherwise bleak and tragic lesbian characters and relationships in *The Killing of Sister George* (Robert Aldrich, 1968) and *The Children's Hour* (William Wyler, US, 1961).

Weiss clearly outlines the ongoing critical debate about the difficulties of representing autonomous female sexuality in a system of representation which continues to be focused on the male heterosexual look. A major part of this debate for lesbian film centres on the problems of producing scenes of woman-centred intimacy and lovemaking that remain satisfying for lesbian audiences while not falling into the traditional funcion of being a turn-on for heterosexual men.

In her section on the lesbian aspect of art film, Weiss uses some key films by Akerman and Ottinger (see Further Viewing at the end of this chapter) to show how their directors have dealt in various productive ways with the male heterosexist narrative and viewing strategies of this kind of film tradition. In her essay 'Transgressive Cinema: Lesbian Independent Film' (Benshoff and Griffin 2004: 43) she concentrates mainly on American production. She identifies as a crucial factor of this type of work how 'the power and intrigue of looking itself have become erotically charged' rather than the object of the look. She argues that a film such as Friedrich's *Damned If You Don't* (1987), and the work of Jan Oxenberg (see p. 255) have 'imagined lesbian cinema outside the pornographic parameters of dominant cinema' and have challenged patriarchal definitions of lesbianism. She goes on to suggest that such viewing strategies have had wide influence.

Weiss's critique of the traditional psychoanalytical approach and her outlines of alternative viewing strategies form the basis of many later textual explorations in lesbian criticism. An important and ground-breaking collection is *Immortal, Invisible* edited by Tamsin Wilton (see Further Reading at the end of this chapter). This was, as the editor points out in her introduction, 'the first collection, to my knowledge, of essays on lesbians and the moving image' (Wilton 1995: 2).

Wilton poses constructive questions about lesbian definition, then discusses a range of responses from the radical politics of Barbara Hammer's films to the playfulness of lesbian camp. As she says, 'the question of lesbian auteurism and context are debated in many chapters of this book' (ibid.: 5). Wilton's suggestion for viewing strategies is a crucial challenge to the domination of the psychoanalytic: 'I propose the notion of *cinematic contract*, by which the spectator tacitly agrees to make use of a variety of engagement strategies in order to "make sense of" the film in question'. She suggests that 'such engagement strategies derive less from the unconscious and more from the social location of the spectator' (ibid.: 16).

These ideas are developed in her essay 'On Not Being Lady Macbeth', where she looks at both the production and consumption side of the cinematic contract, and demonstrates the crucial importance of the image-consuming spectator in lively examples of her own viewing. She makes it clear that oppression is an ongoing factor in the social location of the lesbian spectator (ibid.: 143) and usefully discusses the idea of escapism for minority audiences: 'When the weight of **homophobia** (or racism, or sexism/misogyny) is present as a determining factor on the consumption side of the contract, the business of simple escapism takes on added significance' (ibid.: 159).

The contributors to Wilton's collection discuss a range of filmmaking from the work of Monica Treut to lesbian semiotics in the *Alien* films. Most important for subsequent developments, Wilton challenges the easy acceptance of 'queer' as a critical term: 'lesbians and gay men are not easily incorporated into a generic (gender resistant) queer' (ibid.: 9). Wilton is open-minded about whether feminist or queer theory serves lesbians better, a question still open to debate.

The work of Clare Whatling (1997) extends the process of lesbian intervention in classic psychoanalytic criticism. She also provides more discussion of Wilton's notion of location through investigation of lesbian spectator positioning along with readings of the star persona of Jodie Foster.

SOME QUEER FILMS

Stereotypes and characters

In his book *The Matter of Images* (1993a) Richard Dyer has pointed out the dangers inherent in thinking rigidly in terms of stereotypes when dealing with representation: 'a **stereotype** can be complex, varied, intense and contradictory, an image of otherness in which it is still possible to find oneself' (ibid.: 74). Stereotypes, he points out, are not always or necessarily negative, although some, such as the black mammy of Hollywood, are very limiting. The process of stereotyping involves power: the power of dominant groups to mould the accepted social view of themselves and of those groups they perceive as marginal. This view can change and develop as certain social groups, such as gays and lesbians, grow in self-awareness, expression and power, so that dominant groups have to modify their available images. As an example, Dyer cites the 'sad young man' stereotype common in popular film and literature of the 1940s and 1950s, an image of the passive, unhappy, sexually troubled outsider which grew into the ambiguously attractive and strong image of the social rebel as embodied in James Dean and Montgomery Clift. Are there any stereotypes in the following films that could be interpreted in several ways?

Dyer also suggests that replacing stereotypes with the traditional idea of 'rounded' characters may be an advance of sorts. However, he points out (in Steven 1985) that the 'well-rounded character', as advocated by theorists such as E.M. Forster, is in itself a limiting concept, for, in its strong preoccupation with individuality, it can obscure

stereotype
A set of commonly expected behaviour patterns and characteristics based on role (e.g. mother) or personal features such as race, age or sexuality. In society and cultural products, the depiction of a stereotype becomes a form of communicative shorthand, and often reflects the attitudes of dominant social groups.

For further discussion of representation and gender see Chapter 10.

key European films
These films by major European directors are important as gay texts and as such will reward further study using the insights of gay history, psychoanalysis and auteur theory:
The Color of Pomegranates (USSR/Georgia, Sergei Paradjanov, 1969)
Orphée (France, Jean Cocteau, 1946)
Ossessione (Italy, Luchino Visconti, 1942)
Querelle (Germany, Rainer Werner Fassbinder, 1982)
Theorum (Italy, Pier Paolo Pasolini, 1968)

The screenplay of *Go Fish*, by Rose Troche and Guinevere Turner, with an introduction by Lea Delaria, is available from the Overlook Press, New York, 1995.

• **Plate 11.3**
Go Fish (Rose Troche, 1994). A successful and engaging low-budget production about a group of lesbian friends which was promoted through the festival circuit. Guinevere Turner (left) became a lesbian star

awareness of the social groups to which that character belongs. A really useful study of representation can only take place within an overall awareness of the dominant ideology, the chief component of which, for the purposes of this chapter, is the assumption of heterosexuality as a dominant, structuring outlook and viewpoint (ibid.).

The film analyses offered are intended as sample case studies for an approach which may be applied to other films, to indicate ways in which wider ideological meanings and values may be examined through close analysis and awareness of representation. In this chapter you will find two analyses; the first is an example of a documentary in the tradition of art film about the poet Langston Hughes, and the second is a recent fiction film of transgender interest based on an actual individual. On the accompanying website I offer readings of two films of historical interest in the development of gay male imagery. *Victim* is regarded by many as a milestone in the sympathetic portrayal of gay men in the early 1960s. The dark comic tone of *The Living End* is based on the pre–1990s notion of HIV infection being a terminal condition, no longer the case of those with access to anti-viral drugs. There is a classic lesbian romance, *Desert Hearts*, which may be contrasted with a more edgy, queer offering of lesbian interest, *Go Fish*. *The Hanging Garden* reflects a growing movement in modern queer cinema to examine the position of gay and lesbian characters within wider family groupings. Finally, *Happy Together* reflects a developing strand of queer cinema in Asia.

☐ CASE STUDY 1: *LOOKING FOR LANGSTON* (ISAAC JULIEN, 1994)

Poetic meditation

Subtitled *A Meditation on Langston Hughes (1902–1967) and the Harlem Renaissance*, this film is a tribute to the American poet Langston Hughes, who lived in New York and whose writings formed a key part of the flowering of black culture in that city during the 1920s known as the 'Harlem Renaissance'. It is less than an hour long and was funded by Britain's Channel 4 TV. As the word 'meditation' suggests, the work is structured in a non-narrative way around a collage of visual images and a soundtrack of poetry by Hughes, Essex Hemphill and Bruce Nugent. It is dedicated to another outstanding American writer who was also gay and black, the novelist James Baldwin.

The current DVD of *Looking for Langston* from the BFI is accompanied by a booklet with contributions by several major black cultural critics from the US, including Henry Louis Gates Jr, bell hooks and Armond White.

The film opens with newsreel footage of Hughes's funeral. A female voiceover delivers an oration about the struggle of opposition, which no one undertakes easily. Later on, this idea of opposition is underlined when we see a modern article on Hughes entitled 'Black and Gay', and when we see a gang of fierce-looking skinheads attempting violence on the nightclub space occupied by the men. The skinheads are white, and when they invade the space they are seen to do so with white police officers looking on and doing nothing. The funeral footage immediately cuts to a modern re-creation, in sensuously crisp black and white, of the funeral, with large white lilies and the body laid out in its coffin. The black and white cinematography continues throughout the film as a homage and reference to famous gay images. The lilies recall the photography of Robert Mapplethorpe.

Male, black and gay

Images of the funeral recur and evoke respectful homage. They are interwoven with images of a nightclub peopled by handsome men dancing, drinking, talking and laughing together, images of enjoyment, sensuality and cultural solidarity. The men are in formal evening clothes and dancing to music which recalls the 1920s. One of the men is white and is later seen in intimate, loving surroundings with his black lover after displaying jealousy in the club. Later, the music and dancing become disco-style in a mix between 1920s and modern styles and scenes, a mix which recurs throughout the film to evoke the continuity of both black and gay culture.

• Plate 11.4
Looking for Langston
(Isaac Julien, 1988).
The beauty of this film's
images forms a vivid
tribute both to Hughes
as an artist and to the
culture that nurtured
him

The central figure in the club is a handsome man with a moustache who sees another very good-looking man. The two are attracted to each other, and the middle part of the film presents sensuous fantasy sequences of the two of them together. The man with the moustache is seen reflected in a pond in a spacious moorland setting. He comes across the other man, who is naked. His firm, well-made body is revealed to the viewer from behind, gradually, from the legs up. The poetry on the soundtrack talks of the man's 'dancer's body' and makes clear that this man is the figure of Beauty: 'Beauty's lips touched his.... How much pressure does it take to awaken love?' The shots of Beauty culminate in a scene of him lying naked in bed with the other man, their bodies intertwined. This memorable image recalls a famous photograph by George Platt Lynes, once again paying homage to a major figure of gay culture.

Cultural continuity

Fantasy elements underline the sense of meditation about Hughes and the cultural tradition of which he forms a part. The nightclub is first seen with the men in still poses. Male angels watch over the nightclub. At one point, a beautiful young angel is seen holding a large picture of Langston Hughes, then the camera pans slowly to a large picture of James Baldwin. At another point, the camera rises from the nightclub to a scene of funeral mourning situated on the balcony above. This establishes a spatial relationship between the two main movements and moods of the film, and the words of the poem on the soundtrack – 'Let my name be spoken without effect, without the ghost of shadow on it' – show that we are invited to celebrate with joy, not mourn with sadness, Hughes and the culture he represents.

Archive footage underlines cultural continuity. There is footage of Hughes reading his poetry in a TV programme, literary gatherings, jazz bands in Harlem, a football team, references to poets and anthologies and to the first production of the play *Amen Corner* by James Baldwin.

Throughout the film, Julien juxtaposes image and sound in order to provoke thought and emotion. What both the modern and the 1920s scenes have in common is a sense of danger for gay men in public spaces, outside the safety of places like the club, but at the same time a sense of going out into, of braving, those public spaces. A young man walks into the club, and the song lyric rings out:

You're such a beautiful black man,
But you've been made to feel,
That your beauty's not real.

To accompany this we see footage of a black sculptor working on a sculpture of a naked black man. The lyric, the footage of the sculptor at work, and the preceding homage to Beauty as a black man, provide a critique of sexual and aesthetic attitudes towards black men in a society dominated by ideas of beauty as white. Sound and image in collision are used to provoke questions and thoughts about how black men are sexually used by whites, black men as both objects and users of pornography, and the use of pornography for safe sex.

Strong, positive attitudes

This film takes on several controversial issues, including interracial sex and the questioning of the nature of black masculinity, and deals with them in an accomplished and stylish way. Such glamorously eroticised male images are, as Andrea Weiss points out, very different from the low-key approach taken by lesbian filmmaking, as in the film which Weiss and Greta Schiller made about the black lesbian jazz artist Tiny Davis, *Tiny and Ruby: Hell Drivin' Women* (US, 1988).

The final and dominant mood of *Looking for Langston* is elegiac. A male couple is seen to leave the club and walk across Waterloo Bridge in contemporary London. While a train passes and they look at each other, the voiceover poem is wistful: 'I love my friend. He went away from me. There's nothing more to say.' But life goes on, the angels overlook scenes of love and celebration, and a poem refers to Hannibal, Toussaint and other strong figures of black history. As the gang of skinheads advances down the street, the club erupts with disco music and we see the dancers enjoying themselves. The editing rhythm speeds up as it cuts between the skinheads, clubbers and police with truncheons. The expected clash is undercut when we see the police and thugs enter the club only to find it empty, followed by a shot of a laughing black angel. Is this a comment on the invisibility and/or oppression of black gay culture? Is it a demonstration of how prejudice and oppression can and will be deflected and dissipated? The final upbeat note is sounded when footage of the old TV programme is shown, with Hughes reading:

Sun's a risin'
This is gonna be my song.

☐ CASE STUDY 2: *BOYS DON'T CRY* (KIMBERLY PEIRCE, 1999)

Transgender considerations

The question of what makes a film 'gay' or 'lesbian' recurs throughout this chapter. Attempting definitions of a 'transgender' film blurs boundaries further. Within contemporary film studies, the term 'transgender' seems to cover a spectrum of work dealing with characters from those who wish to dress temporarily in the clothes of the opposite gender to those who feel the need for permanent changes in bodily configuration and social behaviour. Michele Aaron's critique of *Boys Don't Cry* (Aaron 2004) thus attempts to relate the film to a tradition of cross-dressing comedies such as *Some Like It Hot*.

Gender boundaries can thus be crossed in a variety of ways, and consideration of sexual orientation can add further complications. Judith Halberstam argues that 'the body in transition indelibly marks late twentieth century and early twenty-first century cinematic fantasy', citing examples such at the *Terminator* movies and *The Matrix*, then continues: 'Nowhere has the fantasy of the shape-shifting, identity-morphing body been more powerfully realised, however, than in the transgender film' (Daniel and Jackson 2003: 18).

There is an ongoing debate about the subversive potential of transgender representations: do they represent a radical blurring of the boundaries of gender and sexuality, or does the striving of certain characters to 'become' the opposite gender bring them back into a world of hetero-binarism, or **essentialism**? Halberstam cites *The Crying Game* (Neil Jordan, 1992) and *Boys Don't Cry* as tending towards a constricting binarism, with their leading characters who are 'represented as both heroic and fatally flawed' (ibid.) in their inability to enact a full transformation. It may also be worth pointing out that such films make clear societal prejudices about people with transgender identities, a critical viewpoint to be considered in this mix of arguments.

All of these elements and contradictions are reflected in a variety of films. The character Hedwig in *Hedwig and the Angry Inch* (John Cameron Mitchell, 2001) begins as a gay man and eventually finds happiness with her young male punk-rock lover. Conversely, the character Judy in *Better than Chocolate* (Anne Wheeler, 1999) retains her attraction to women after her male to female transition, and finds love with another woman.

In *Boys Don't Cry* the audience is left in no doubt that the character Brandon Teena feels himself to be male, and 'not a dyke', as he tells his supportive cousin Lonny. The film opens with a scene of Brandon dressing as a boy, in the words of director Kimberly Peirce, completely 'fulfilling his fantasy of himself'. The director wanted this kind of definite start to underline the film's alignment with the transformed Brandon (director's commentary on DVD). This film is itself highly unusual among those dealing with such issues in that its main character is a female to male transgendered person.

Narrative and mise-en-scène

Throughout the film, the viewer is kept aware of the main character's transgender state. We see a male personality contending with a female body. Brandon dresses in a conventionally male way and adopts consciously 'male' body language in Hilary Swank's

essentialism
A term describing the idea of a single, firmly fixed identity as regards gender, sexuality and other social elements. The opposite attitude is often described as **social contructionism**, implying that such identities are a product of one's society, attitudes and upbringing, and can vary or be changed.

Some transgender characters in film could be seen as metaphors for their political context. A critical examination of *The Crying Game* and *Hedwig and the Angry Inch* using such ideas could yield further insights.

The cabaret song, sung by the character Judy in *Better than Chocolate* is worth viewing as a memorable and entertaining transgender anthem.

• **Plate 11.5**
Lana and Brandon, the characters central to the narrative of *Boys Don't Cry* (Kimberly Peirce, 1999), fully acknowledge and love each other's individuality

skilful performance. He is even quick to deny a comment on the smallness of his hands. The contending factors in the character's life are made clear in a variety of ways, from dialogue discussion with his friend about affording a sex-change operation to scenes of Brandon desperately trying to cope with menstruation and flatten his breasts: 'Brandon's breasts and bleeding index sex characteristics, not gender' (Aaron 2004: 190).

The narrative indicates ongoing problems with the law for Brandon with the speeding ticket, and has a feel of inevitable trouble to come. Pre-publicity may have informed the audience that this is a story based on real life, and they may be aware of its violent ending, but the discordant soundtrack is used as a prefiguring device, and the vividly portrayed setting depicts a claustrophobic, small-town atmosphere which has no room for those who are different. Aaron comments on the 'sci-fi quality' of the setting which invokes 'a community of aliens and dreamers' (ibid.: 192). As cousin Lonny says: 'You know they shoot faggots down there.'

Tom and John, the two young men who Brandon befriends, are given clear signifiers of trouble and danger to come both in the narrative (violent bouts of anger, excessive drinking) and visually (angular close-ups, stubbly beards). At the same time they are not demonised, as the audience sees John's concern for the safety of Lara and his love for his child, and gets to know how both men are victims in their own right. The tragic feeling of the film is effectively countered by the central relationship between Brandon and his girlfriend Lana, who has the courage to accept him as he is after he has fully revealed his transgendered self. The discordant music is memorably replaced by lyrical sounds as the two eventually make love in complete knowledge of each other.

Audience complicity in the queer look

In this film we clearly see signs of physical and visual transformation in Brandon, but these are kept very much in the mode of realism rather than fantasy. Brandon's girlfriend comments on how pretty he is at the same time as he fights to suppress bodily signs of femininity. While being so aware of the character's ambivalent gender status, the audience is made conscious of conventional visual signs of masculinity in the way Brandon sits, combs his hair or smokes a cigarette, as well as the hair, clothing and facial expression. In this way the film is, in the words of Michele Aaron, about the 'spectacle of transvestism' (ibid.: 189).

In 'The New Queer Spectator' Aaron contrasts *Boys Don't Cry* with the traditional type of cross-dressing film such as *Mrs Doubtfire* (Chris Columbus, 1993) which is 'fuelled by heterosexual imperatives' where 'the narratives progress towards the climactic disclosure of the protagonists' "true" identity' (ibid.: 189). In such films, she points out, the gender signifiers tend to serve as reminders which 'reinforce the essentialism of gender even if the (relatively) easy disguise confirmed its **performativity**'. In *Boys Don't Cry* such traditional disavowal is withheld from the audience in a way that, Aaron argues, is a legacy of queer cinema narrative structures.

Not only is the audience implicated in knowledge of Brandon's passing himself off as a man, as indicated above, but this implication is underlined through the character of Lana, 'who comes to represent the spectator's own inevitably unfixed or queer response to the cross-dressed figure in general and to Brandon in particular' (ibid.: 191). Aaron goes on to point out that awareness of Brandon's identity is also set up through the reactions of other characters such as Lana's mother, and John. In addition, a blurring of gender roles is suggested through the casting against the grain of stereotype, where Lana is a big-boned beauty and Brandon looks petite and slim. Aaron writes: 'Meanwhile Tom, with his pubescent flourish of facial hair, and John, doe-eyed and long-lashed, cuddly, yet sociopathic, further promote the film's deliberate inscription of a spectrum of gender expression', and makes an argument for these two characters being part of 'an alternative network of implicated queerness' (ibid.: 192).

performativity
A concept derived from cultural studies whereby social groups develop self-awareness through shared actions that develop tastes, habits and attitudes in common. When applied to gender, you may wish to consider the popular conflation of masculinity and football, or femininity and shopping.

The climactic scene that underlines the separation of gender and the physical attributes of sex is the disclosure when John and Tom force Brandon to reveal his genitals. John shouts at Lana to 'look at your little boyfriend' and Lana's reply, 'leave him alone', effectively underscores the narrative's acceptance of Brandon's state. A short sequence of fantasy follows which 'reifies ... the distinction between gender and sex' as 'the divested Brandon splits from and stares at a clothed Brandon standing watching behind the other witnesses' (ibid.: 190). The tableau viewed is of a semi-naked Brandon supported on either side by Tom and John, with Lana kneeling below and looking up at him, a reference to Christ-like martyrdom that serves to strongly implicate the spectator yet again into complicity with Brandon. For Aaron, this film 'rescripts the cross-dressing narrative to avow the queerness not just of the characters in the film but the firmly implicated spectator' (ibid.: 192).

A QUEER DIVERSITY

Critic B. Ruby Rich described 1992 as 'a watershed year for independent gay and lesbian film' (Benshoff and Griffin 2004: 53), not only due to the number of shorts and features being made and shown, but because of the surge in critical interest which has accompanied them. During the 1990s such film and video activity came to be labelled 'Queer Cinema'. Lesbian and gay activists, critics, filmmakers and audiences started to imbue the previously negative term 'queer' with a range of new, exciting, positive meanings in politics, literature, art and filmmaking. This process of an oppressed group reclaiming and reshaping a previously negative word or idea is known as **reappropriation**. Critic Amy Taubin claimed 'American queer cinema has achieved critical mass (Cook and Dodd 1993: 176) with the release of features such as *My Own Private Idaho* (Gus Van Sant, 1991), using the Hollywood star system with Keanu Reeves and River Phoenix, and Tom Kalin's *Swoon* (1992).

The key ideas behind the queer cinema movement are diversity and fluidity: a range of (homo)sexualities manifested through a variety of character, situation, race, gender, sexual practice and film language. Rich defines the key ingredients as 'appropriation and pastiche, irony, as well as a reworking of history, with social constructionism very much in mind' (Beshoff and Griffin 2004: 54). Filmmakers are questioning the attitude, developed in the 1970s, that one must promote only positive images of lesbian and gay characters and situations. Lesbian and gay filmmakers see such ideas as constraints on creativity in an era where a much wider variety of lesbian and gay images is available.

In *Swoon*, Tom Kalin examines the infamous Leopold–Loeb case of 1924, where two rich, Jewish 18-year-olds kidnap and murder a 14-year-old boy. Unlike previous film versions such as Hitchcock's *Rope* (1948), Kalin concentrates on the homosexual relationship between the two young men, the poisonous effect of homophobia and anti-semitism on the mind of Leopold, and the hold that the pathological Leopold had over Loeb. In a discussion, Kalin stated: 'I think the necessary process of acknowledging all the different aspects of our identities is something that, for the most part, hasn't been allowed' (Bad Object Choices 1997: 277). Derek Jarman's *Edward II* (1991) doesn't hesitate to portray England's monarch as weak and vacillating while his male lover, Gaveston, is scheming and slimy. What Kalin's and Jarman's films do, in their very different ways, is make the audience aware of the political dimensions of homosexuality.

New techniques of expression: playing with genre

Diversity and experimentation in film language characterise those works regarded as part of the queer cinema movement. John Greyson mixes history in *Urinal* (1988) as famous figures of gay culture, including Langston Hughes and the Russian director Sergei Eisenstein, help to investigate police harassment of gays. In *Caravaggio* and *Edward II* Derek Jarman makes creative use of anachronism to underline the continuing relevance

---

reappropriation
The process whereby a previously oppressed group takes a negative term and turns it around to invest it with new meanings of power and liberation. Examples include 'black', 'virago' and 'queer'.

Derek Jarman
Painter, writer activist and acclaimed British gay/queer auteur Derek Jarman was a provocative figure and an inspiration for younger artists and filmmakers. Here are some key films:
Sebastiane (1976)
Jubilee (1978)
The Tempest (1979)
The Angelic Conversation (1985)
The Last of England (1987)

● **Plate 11.6**
Edward II (Derek Jarman, 1991). The love between Edward (left) and Gaveston, as queerly portrayed by Jarman, evokes mixed audience reactions

pink triangle
A symbol originally worn by homosexual prisoners in Nazi concentration camps which was later taken up by lesbian and gay people as a reminder of past oppression and an icon of liberation.

of his sexual and political themes. In the latter, we see Annie Lennox singing a Cole Porter song, vicars in dog-collars spitting on Gaveston after his banishment, and gay activists with placards and the **pink triangle** symbol invading the king's palace. In *Blue* (1993), Jarman's one-colour screen counterpoints the emotional range of the soundtrack's meditation on his life with, and approaching death from, HIV, and challenges received ideas about the visual portrayal of disease.

The documentary work of Stuart Marshall is challenging in subject matter and form. *Bright Eyes* (1984) presents the viewer with ever-relevant parallels between Nazi treatment of gays, Victorian medical practice and media coverage of the AIDS epidemic. Rosa Von Praunheim's *I Am My Own Woman* (1993) presents a portrait of Charlotte Von Mahlsdort (born Lothar Berfelde), a famous lifelong transvestite who is also gay (US DVD title: *I Am My Own Wife*). As well as using direct interviews with him, the film dramatises scenes from his life, including his anti-Nazi work during the Second World War. At the end of many of these dramatised scenes, he himself walks on to the set and is questioned by the actors about his thoughts and motivations, a productive Brechtian-style distanciation effect and perhaps an example of queer questioning.

Film genre and film style are mixed creatively in new queer cinema. Tod Haynes's *Poison* (1991) mixes 1950s B-film sci-fi and zombie elements with a homoerotic section styled as a homage to Genet. In *The Living End* (1993), widely considered to be a landmark of queer cinema, Gregg Araki offers a nihilistic gay road movie dominated by themes of AIDS and survival. In *Caught Looking* (1991), Constantine Giannaris takes the viewer on a journey through a spectrum of gay viewpoints with a character participating in an interactive video fantasy. John Greyson's *Zero Patience* (1993) subverts the conventions of the Hollywood musical to investigate attitudes to AIDS, once again using a figure from the gay past, the Victorian explorer Richard Francis Burton, in creative and amusing ways.

Gender, race and queer cinema

Monika Treut's feature-length *Virgin Machine* (1985) accompanies its heroine on a sexual odyssey in San Francisco, but the inequality of funding for men's and women's work means that many lesbian filmmakers continue to produce shorter films and videos. In *The Meeting of Two Queens* Cecilia Barriga has taken images of Garbo

• **Plate 11.7**
In *Poison* (1991) Todd Haynes pays homage to the homoerotic prison imagery of Genet. He later made good use of genre in *Far From Heaven* (2002)

and Dietrich and edited them together to produce a provocatively sensual play of eye contact and undressing between two screen goddesses. The video work of Sadie Benning, such as the ten-minute *Jollies*, intimately explores her own body, thoughts, memories and sexuality with a bold use of camerawork intricately interacting with the soundtrack.

Pratibha Parmar is a British filmmaker and critic of Asian origin who helped found the first group in Britain for black lesbians. For her, as for Julien Isaac, race is as important an issue as sexuality, and the intervention of both filmmakers contributes to the new kind of diversity within queer cinema. Parmar is concerned to disrupt and change the conventional images of Asians prevalent in British society. *Khush* (1991) is a television film she made for Channel 4 about the experience of being Asian and lesbian or gay. In this piece, interviews are interwoven with images of two women in saris relaxing and dancing together, and a classic Indian musical film is provocatively re-edited so that the dancing girl's glances interplay with those of another woman.

With videos such as *Orientations* (1985), Richard Fung helps give voice to North American lesbians and gays of Chinese origin. Marlon Riggs's feature-length poetic meditation on the lives of black gay men in the US, *Tongues Untied* (1989), is a beautifully constructed kaleidoscope of sound and image.

Queer and the mainstream – (mis)representation?

Consider varying attitudes to positive images of lesbians and gays. Should we condemn the conflation of homosexuality, violence and murder in such films as *Basic Instinct*? Or can we be confident that a wide enough variety of views of lesbian and gay life now circulates in society to balance out negative images, so that we may embrace the queer aesthetic?

Exactly how much of the queer aesthetic is being absorbed into mainstream filmmaking? Hollywood is still prone to attempt a 'normalising' process for its perceived mass audience. The publicity for *Philadelphia* (Jonathan Demme, 1993) presented the film primarily as a courtroom drama and deliberately played down its gay content. In *Gods and Monsters* (Bill Condon, 1998) the theatre actor and gay activist Ian McEllen played the famous gay Hollywood director James Whale. Mark Gatiss's biography of

Whale tells us that, during his last years, Whale enjoyed the company and devoted support of his young working-class lover and companion, Pierre Foegel. Yet the film version of Whale's life completely ignores this important relationship. Why did the writer/director Bill Condon make such an adjustment? Could it be that the image of a lonely old queen is more digestible for mainstream heterosexual audiences?

On the other hand, it could be argued that more diverse sexual perspectives have been flowing into the mainstream. Todd Haynes emerged as a noted cutting-edge queer director of the 1990s. He then went on to direct *Far From Heaven* (2002), a mainstream feature that makes ample use of its budget to re-create lush 1950s settings redolent of Douglas Sirk. At the same time the narrative plays in a post-queer way with Sirkian themes of sexuality and race. John Maybury is a British example of a queer cinema director undertaking a relatively mainstream project with *Love Is the Devil* (1998), a film biography of Francis Bacon which looks closely at the artist's relationship with his lover and muse, George Dyer.

Queerifications

In the early twenty-first century there is no consensus in the field of lesbian/gay/queer cinema, more a developed awareness of dissolving boundaries and multiplying identities. Critics, filmmakers and audiences are interested in a mapping of potentialities and possibilities. Criticism and debate is healthy, and is set to continue along with the wide, creative and growing range of this area of moving image production, work which will surely benefit anybody who seeks to widen and enrich their viewing experience.

The question continually hovers in the background: What constitutes a lesbian or gay film? Do the makers of such films have to be gay or lesbian themselves? Compare the portrayal of same-sex relationships in *Desert Hearts* and *Black Widow* (Bob Rafelson, 1987). Arguably, both involve homoerotic attraction and a certain gay sensibility in the play of looks on the screen and/or between the viewer and the text. In *Black Widow*, same-sex attraction and lesbian sensibility remain subtextual. Is *Desert Hearts* therefore more 'lesbian' due to its direct portrayal of sexuality in character, situation and action? Or is *Black Widow* equally powerful in this context? Apply a similar comparison to the male-orientated films *Jeffrey* and *Top Gun* (Tony Scott, 1986).

Consider the concept of 'queer'. Federico Fellini and Ken Russell, both heterosexuals, made some very queer films. What does the concept tell us about the portrayal of the boundaries of gender and sexuality? In this context, consider the fictional feature *The Adventures of Priscilla, Queen of the Desert* (Stephan Elliott, 1994) and the documentary *Southern Comfort* (Kate Davis, 2001) in the ways in which they present their transgendered central figures.

Essentialism – to label or not to label?

For many recent critics the term *queer* is to be preferred for its notions of opposition to mainstream representations. There are debates going on about exactly how conservative and fixed the terms *gay* and *lesbian* have become in both society and film. Have they become part of the mainstream against which the queer theorists strive? Such terms are seen by some as very fixed labels which form part of a rigid sexual system; in other words, as **essentialist** in nature. Those challenging this system assert that such labelling is inaccurate and misleading, in that it does not reflect either the realities of human sexuality or the fluid nature of film spectatorship. Such critics have become known as anti-essentialist.

On the other hand, defenders of gay and lesbian approaches claim that the term *queer* leads to an ignoring of lesbian and gay specificity, indeed, to the very kind of invisibility against which early critics like Russo fought. An essentialist position could be seen as historically specific and necessary. Barbara Hammer claims: 'Lesbian image-makers in the seventies were forced by critics into the "camp of essentialists" because

essentialism
A term describing the idea of a single, firmly fixed identity as regards **gender**, **sexuality** and other social elements. The opposite attitude is often described as social constructionism, implying that such identities are a product of one's society, attitudes and upbringing, and can vary or be changed.

● **Plate 11.8**
Khush (Pratiba Parmar, 1991). The title of this memorable film is the Urdu word for 'ecstatic pleasure'. In her look at some Asian lesbian and gay lives, Parmar mixed pleasurable dream sequences with interviews which recall oppression

of the extreme urgency of their need to make lesbian representation' (Gever *et al*. 1993: 71). Wilton points out: 'An anti-essentialist, social-constructionist perspective on sexual "identity" does not make "lesbian" a redundant label, rather it obliges us to recognise and deploy "lesbian" as an avowedly strategic sign' (Wilton 1995: 5). A clear introduction to these debates is provided by David Alderson and Linda Anderson (2000) (see Further Reading at the end of this chapter) where they talk about 'queer thinking, and the anti-essentialism that underpins it'.

From image-spotting to queer spectatorship: an overview

Vito Russo's pioneering book (1987) proved to be very popular and influential in the 1970s for those interested in challenging dominant views of film. The reasons for its popularity lay partly in the fact that, unlike its predecessor by Parker Tyler, *Screening the Sexes*, it concentrated almost entirely on the products of Hollywood and the question of gay invisibility, a major preoccupation of gay and lesbian campaigners at the time. Russo's critical method was to examine individual representations of gay and lesbian characters, situations and plotlines, and relate them to mainstream attitudes which we would now call homophobic. His method was a form of vigilant image-spotting, politically necessary at the time but ultimately, in the words of Ellis Hanson, concerned 'with only one gaze: the ubiquitous, prefabricated, gullible, voyeuristic gaze of homophobia'. Hanson goes on to say: 'Meanwhile, our own pleasure, that elusive gaze of delight, is left curiously undertheorised and at times inadmissible' (quoted in Farmer 2000: 4)

Whatever one may think about Hanson's judgement, critics who extended Russo's work have constructively investigated gay and lesbian viewing in terms of theory. Richard Dyer and Andrea Weiss have utilised auteur theory, star study, cinema history and ideas of audience reception. They, and other critics such as Judith Mayne, Tamsin Wilton and Thomas Waugh (see Bibliography), have contributed towards the forging of useful theories of gay, lesbian and queer viewing strategies. More recent critical work is moving towards theorising gay/lesbian/queer spectatorial pleasure. For a useful overview and development of this work, see Brett Farmer (2000).

In the introduction to his book Farmer points the way forward to the kind of theorisation that Hanson sees as vital in this area. He uses key concepts of *specificity* and *performativity* (Farmer 2000: 33–42) to ground a gay spectatorship theory that incorporates a synthesis of the social and the psychoanalytic. *Specificity* 'designates a space for the constitution of subjectivity, the arrangement of desire, and the productions of meaning in specific or particular ways' which he sees as 'a very different proposition from claiming gayness as an expressive, self-identical essence' (ibid.: 40).

CONCLUSION: THE WAY FORWARD

The best way forward I can think of is to encourage readers to diversify their viewing. Most films mentioned in this chapter are available on DVD, and the suggestions for further viewing on the website present a cross-section of the range of viewing experiences available in terms of nationality, historical period and sexual viewpoint.

Use the reading and viewing guides to investigate and develop the questions posed in this chapter. Watch and look into the films using the case studies as models. Above all, explore, enjoy and widen your viewing experiences.

FURTHER READING

Aaron, M. (ed.), *New Queer Cinema: A Critical Reader*, Edinburgh University Press, Edinburgh 2004. Helpful writings on context, Haynes and Araki as auteurs, lesbian perspectives, black queer cinema, nationality in relation to Australia, third cinema, art cinema, reception and spectatorship. The volume deals with a range of popular features from *The Talented Mr Ripley* (Anthony Mingella, 1999) to *Mansfield Park* (Patricia Rozema, 1999).

Alderson, David and Anderson, Linda (eds), *Territories of Desire in Queer Culture*, Manchester University Press, Manchester, 2000. An excellent summary, in the introduction, of the current debates about queer culture. A challenging essay on Jarman, and explorations of Spanish and Australian gay cinema. With an erudite historical overview, Jonathan Dollimore's concluding survey points the way to possible future developments.

Benshoff, H. and Griffin, S. (eds), *Queer Cinema: The Film Reader*, Routledge, New York and London, 2004. Crucial texts by Jack Babuscio on 'Camp and Gay Sensibility' and B. Ruby Rich on 'The New Queer Cinema'. Leading critics such as Dyer, Weiss, Doty and Waugh examine authorship, genre, reception and spectatorship.

Daniel, L. and Jackson, C. (eds), *The Bent Lens: A World Guide to Gay and Lesbian Film*, Roundhouse Publishing, Northam, 2003. An excellent reference which is prefaced by useful critical essays on lesbian and gay cinema in Europe, globalisation, nationality, representation and genre. The introductions to the gay, lesbian and transgender sections are clear and stimulating. The editors also list all their entries according to three useful categories: genre, which is an unusual approach for this kind of collection, director and nationality.

Dyer, Richard, *The Matter Of Images*: *Essays On Representation*, Routledge, London, 1993. An ideal primer for those starting to explore sexual representation in film. Dyer illustrates the power and complexity of images across a range of films, including film noir, the seminal British film *Victim*, and the 'sad young man' tradition which fed into the star persona of James Dean and others. A ground-breaking anthology. Read also his collection *The Culture of Queers,* which contains a selection of his key work on such topics as Fassbinder, Rock Hudson and film noir.

Farmer, Brett, *Spectacular Passions: Cinema, Fantasy, Gay Male Spectatorships*, Duke University Press, Durham, NC, 2000. Farmer closely questions the concepts of *gay* and *queer* and proposes a theory of gay spectatorship which aptly blends psychoanalytic ideas of fantasy, identification and pleasure with social notions of performativity. He then offers fruitful textual explorations based on his theory. This is an excellent way of coming to terms with the latest debates about essentialism and gay spectatorship.

Holmlund, Chris and Fuchs, Cynthia, *Between the Sheets, in the Streets: Queer, Lesbian and Gay Documentary*, University of Minnesota Press, Minneapolis,1997. Primarily US-centred, but an extremely fruitful exploration of the nature, form and address of documentary.

Mulvey, Laura, 'Visual Pleasure and Narrative Cinema', in *The Sexual Subject: A Screen Reader in Sexuality*, Rouledge, London and New York, 1995. Suggests ways in which a viewer of classic Hollywood films is addressed as male by being encouraged to adopt the viewpoint of the male protagonist. This must be read as the seminal first step, a work that helped give voice to the study of gender and sexuality in film. See also Jackie Stacey's key essay 'Desperately Seeking Difference' in the same volume, which helps to queerify Mulvey's insights.

Murray, Raymond, *Images in the Dark: An Encyclopedia of Lesbian and Gay Film and Video*, TLA Publications, Philadelphia, PA, 1996. An ideal sourcebook to make further investigations. International in its breadth, it covers mainstream and independent film and has separate sections on queer, lesbian, gay male and transgender interest, and on camp.

Index lists given according to film title, director and 'personality'.

Wilton, T. (ed.), *Immortal, Invisible: Lesbians and the Moving Image*, Routledge, London, 1995. Wilton's introduction and chapter 'On Not Being Lady Macbeth' are seminal in setting out the critical parameters on lesbian spectatorship and heterosexual ideology, and should be read by all students of film. This volume contains Julia Knight's essay on how Monica Treut seeks to transcend the category of lesbian and contains a set of insights applicable to a range of queer directors. It is also noteworthy for its textual explorations of camp and the lesbian semiotics of the *Alien* films.

FURTHER VIEWING

Aimée and Jaguar (Germany, Max Fäberböck, 1998)
A bold telling of an incredible but true story set in Berlin during the later years of the Second World War. Two women, Lilly and Felice, one a Nazi super-mum and the other a Jewish underground resistance member, meet, fall in love and remain devoted to each other through dangerous times, and Felice's capture by the Gestapo. The compelling narrative is framed by contemporary scenes showing the elderly Lilly, still honouring the memory of her lover.

Alexander (US, Oliver Stone, 2004)
A homoerotic subtext, present in so many big-budget Hollywood epics set in the ancient world (e.g. *Spartacus*), surfaces much more overtly here in the portrayal of Alexander's love for his boyhood friend. Interestingly, the director's cut plays down this subtext in comparison with the official release; a close comparison of the two would make a telling case study.

All About My Mother (Spain, Pedro Almodovar, 1999)
Featuring a search for a lost, transgendered father figure. A brilliantly queer, if rather phallocentric, reworking of the Hollywood classic *All About Eve*. Thanks to Almodovar's skilful work, the melodramatic storyline remains convincing. See also *Bad Education* by the same auteur.

All Over Me (US, Alex Sichel, 1997)
The story of a group of teenage girls, one of whom is lesbian, during the long, hot New York summers. They do the downtown music scene, dream and grapple with adult issues as the director slowly draws the viewers an intimate set of character portraits.

American Beauty (US, Sam Mendes, 2000)
A suburban comedy, very knowing in its portrayal of the repressed homosexual obsessions of the proto-fascist next-door neighbour, as well as the gay couple down the street who are pillars of the community.

Another Way (Hungary, Karoly Makk, 1982)
Said to be among Eastern Europe's first films dealing with a lesbian relationship, this is an intelligent and finely observed love story set just after the Hungarian uprising of 1956.

À toute vitesse (Full Speed) (France, Gaël Morel, 1996)
A bleak view of homophobia and racism among provincial French youth, contrasted with the bravery and loyalty of the central characters. Contains superb, compelling performances.

Beautiful Boxer (Thailand, Ekachai Uekrongtham, 2005)
Fact-based biopic of a leading champion kick-boxer from a poor backgound who uses his winnings to pay for a sex change. Caused controversy among Thai audiences not for the fact of its transgender leading character, but for its serious examination of the character's motives and outlook. See also *The Iron Ladies* (Thailand, Thongkonthun Youngyooth, 2000) a lively, real-life-based drama about how a gay volleyball team fought its way to become champions of the Thai league.

Beautiful Thing (UK, Hettie Macdonald, 1997)
Two young men find love and comfort in each other's arms on a Bermondsey council estate and start to explore the local gay scene. Mum is eventually won over, and the young woman next door lends a hand. Liberal clichés redeemed by skilful writing and acting.

Beefcake (Canada, Thom Fitzgerald, 2000)
An entertainingly camp and affectionate look at the activities of Bob Mizer's famous 1950s physique studio the 'Athletic Model Guild' through the eyes of a well-built country innocent learning the ways of the world in LA.

Before Night Falls (US, Julian Schnabel, 2000)
A powerful, engaging biopic of the Cuban Renaldo Arenas, whose gay sexuality, political activism and prolific writing are shown as inseparable aspects of his life. Spanish star Javier Bardem gives an excellent performance as Arenas. Also stars Johhny Depp as transvestite lover.

Being John Malkovich (US, Spike Jonze, 1999)
An enchanting, intriguing fantasy with a happy lesbian relationship entwined in its ending. Much loved by queer critics (Aaron 2004: 193).

Bent (UK, Sean Mathias,1997)
This film about the persecution of gays in Nazi Germany reflects the weaknesses of the stage play on which it is based. It is worth viewing, though, for its powerful performances and historically important subject matter. Features Mick Jagger as a transvestite cabaret performer, and Ian McKellen.

Bound (US, Andy and Larry Wachowski, 1996)
A post-queer lesbian private-eye film; two consciously stereotyped babes-with-brains in steamy union.

Brokeback Mountain (US, Ang Lee, 2005)
A mainstream, big-budget western about two cowboys whose love for each other changes their lives. Superb performances reflect the passionate feelings and social frustrations of their situation. 'A grand romantic tragedy' according to B. Ruby Rich, which has 'reimagined America as shaped by queer experience and memory'.

By Hook or by Crook (US, Harry Dodge and Silas Howard, 2000)
According to Judith Halberstom, an outstanding queer film in its portrayal of two gender outlaws in the San Francisco underworld (Daniel and Jackson 2003: 18).

Campfire (Belgium, Bavo Defune, 1999)
Four short portraits of young male relationships, replete with inspired use of a range of gay imagery which pays homage to the Athletic Model Guild, Jean Genet and the chic photo-homoerotics of Pierre et Gilles. The themes of sexual exploration and awakening are given unity across the four films through Defune's skilful use of his own range of visual metaphors: clouds, water and exteme close-ups.

The Celluloid Closet (US, Robert Epstein and Jeffrey Friedman, 1996)
Includes clips from about 100 films mentioned in Vito Russo's seminal book, and interviews with screenwriter Gore Vidal, director John Schlesinger and actors Tom Hanks and Whoopi Goldberg.

Coming Out (Germany, Heiner Carow, 1989)
A gay teacher is faced with coming out and coming to terms with himself when he falls in love with a man who he meets in a bar. The 'Coming Out Drama' is establishing itself as a recognisable queer genre; this is a superior example.

Conversation Piece (Italy, Luchino Visconti, 1974)
Burt Lancaster gives a remarkable performance as a retired, bookish professor reluctantly discovering his own latent homosexual passions. Visconti is, for me, a major queer auteur who is in need of close critical reassessment; see also *The Damned* and *Death in Venice*.

Daddy and the Muscle Academy (Finland, Ilppo Pohjola, 1992)
A well-made documentary presenting a range of insights into the social impact on gay men's identity of the homoerotic drawings of Tom of Finland. Includes interviews with the renowned artist himself, generous helpings of his images, along with personal comment from artist Isaac Julien and a number of leathermen. The DVD features extra interview footage and a picture gallery.

Defying Gravity (US, John Keitel, 1997)
Part of the growing gay genre of 'coming out' stories, this is set on an affluent American university campus, and involves a gay-bashing as well as racial, family and friendship issues. An engaging film with good use of flashbacks, although, annoyingly, not a single character in it ever manages to utter the 'g-word' or directly name same-sex issues in any way. For other genre examples see *Just Seventeen*, *Beautiful Thing* and *Trick*.

Desert Hearts (US, Donna Deitsch, 1985)
A rather idealised lesbian romance set in 1950s Texas, which has provoked a range of reactions from critics such as Richard Dyer, Mandy Merck and Barbara Hammer.

Dona Herlinda and Her Son (Mexico, Jaime Hermosillo, 1985)
An entertaining comedy of sexual manners where a perceptive mother arranges her son's love life to cater for his gay lover and her own desire for a grandchild. One of the first Latin American films to deal positively with a gay theme.

Drôle de Félix (France, Olivier Ducastel/ Jacques Martineau, 2000)
After his mother's death, a young gay man goes in search of the father he has never seen, supported by his lover. A complex sense of identity and love emerges from the unaffected performances of the chaotic couple.

East Palace, West Palace (China, Zhang Yuan, 1996)

A ground-breaking work in terms of homosexuality and mainland Chinese cinema. A macho cop apprehends a young gay man, and the ensuing interaction makes him question himself deeply. Remarkable for the gay character's assertion of selfhood. Slow-paced but elegiac, with excellent performances and cinematography. For a discussion of political considerations, see Chris Berry's essay in Grossman (2005).

Edge of Seventeen (US, David Morton, 1998)

Low-key coming-out story set in 1984 Ohio. Slow pacing and excellent performances serve to evoke very well the emotional ups and downs of the young protagonist Eric as he explores love, sex and being different. Evocative soundtrack of 1980s music.

Everyone (Canada, Bill Marchant, 2004)

This intelligent, bittersweet social comedy portrays the lives of a group of friends and relatives coming together to celebrate a gay union. Script and acting skilfully combine sophistication with earthiness and a touch of satire. As with all good films of this genre, serious issues hover behind the well-crafted dialogue.

Forbidden Love: The Unashamed Stories of Lesbian Lives (Canada, Aerlyn Wessman and Lynne Femie, 1992)

Wonderful to watch: a 1950s *Pulp Fiction*-style lesbian love story is interwoven with older women talking about their lives. Excellent docudrama.

Gohatto (Japan, Nagisa Oshima, 1999)

The title is Japanese for 'taboo'. Set in a samurai training academy in 1865. A beautiful young samurai warrior sets off a chain reaction of passions among his fellow trainees. Fascinating narrative tension in the depiction of how these passions conflict with strict samurai rules. Visually stunning, with excellent fight choreography.

The Hanging Garden (Canada, Thom Fitzgerald, 1997)

A gay man revisits his family and meets the image of his previous, repressed younger self which haunts his father. A drama that makes the viewer question the nature of queerness.

Happy, Texas (US, Mark Illsley, 2002)

A feelgood small-town comedy involving mistaken identity, a couple of gay designers and a lovelorn gay sheriff who eventually gets his man. For another feelgood gay-themed social comedy from the US see *In and Out* (Frank Oz, US, 2001).

Happy Together (Hong Kong, Wong Kar Wai, 1997)

Two young Chinese men try to patch up their relationship on an extended stay in Argentina. Particularly interesting for its use of sound, music and setting to portray and underline characters and relationships. For a discussion of political themes, see Chris Berry's essay in Grossman (2005).

Head On (Australia, Ana Kokkinos, 1998)

A powerful realisation of contemporary queer life in Australia. Centred on Ari, a young Greek–Australian battling to come to terms with his sexuality and his family. A salient product of queer cinema in its avoidance of any comforting character empathy or predictable narrative closure. See the essay on this film in Alderson and Anderson (2000).

Hellbent (US, David DeCoteau, 2005)

A gay horror film, 'the first to take its genre seriously, with gay characters played as honest-to-goodness people rather than for comic relief or cannon fodder' (Kevin Goebel, planetout.com).

High Art (US, Lisa Cholodenko, 1998)

A film that takes the lesbian sexuality of its main characters as natural and given, while looking at how they live their lives, make art and love one another. Much admired by queer critics such as Daniel Cunningham (Daniel and Jackson 2003: 12).

If These Walls Could Talk – 2

A notable and good-quality made-for-TV movie that traces lesbian lives and loves over three different generations in the late twentieth century. Features Vanessa Redgrave as an older 'lesbian widow' and Sharon Stone as a young adventurer.

Jeffrey (US, Chris Ashley, 1995)

Two beautiful New York men tread the rocky road to love in the age of AIDS, with the help of memorable supporting performances from Patrick Stewart as the arty older friend and Sigourney Weaver as a new-age guru.

Je, tu, il, elle (Belgium, Chantal Akerman, 1974)

This gently paced first feature by one of Europe's leading avant-garde filmmakers is captivating. A young woman hitches a lift to revisit her lover. The film is sensitively imbued with a woman-centred sensuality.

Law of Desire (Spain, Pedro Almodovar, 1987)

A gripping gay melodrama by one of Spain's leading contemporary directors. This was the precursor of several entertaining gay films from 1990s Spain – see the essay in Alderson and Anderson (2000).

Like It Is (UK, Paul Oremland, 1997)

A cross-class gay love story. Craig is a Northern boy who makes money from bare-knuckle boxing, and Matt is a smart, canny London record producer. Along the way Oremland takes a colourful look at the Blackpool gay scene and the Soho-based gay/music scene of the late 1990s. Roger Daltry gives a creepy and compelling performance as a sleazy promoter.

Longtime Companion (US, Norman Rene, 1990)
An AIDS melodrama of historical significance as an example of Hollywood's well-meaning attempt to tackle issues concerning a section of the gay community in the Western world of the 1980s. This has been criticised as simplistic, with a concentration on middle-class, white characters, but a strong message of community support and hope also comes across.

Love Is the Devil (UK, John Maybury, 1998)
A film biography of Francis Bacon which looks closely at the artist's relationship with his lover and muse, George Dyer. Maybury produced some notable experimental gay video work in the 1990s such as *Remembrance of Things Past* (1993).

Luster (US, Everett Lewis, 2001)
A quirky and engagingly perverse comedy about unrequited love and finding yourself, set in downtown LA. Gently satirises manners, big-city attitudes and life in the LA Anglo-queer community. The DVD includes an excellent interview with the director where he talks articulately about queer culture and independent filmmaking, plus helpful director commentary.

Ma vraie vie à Rouen (*The True Story of My Life in Rouen*) (France, Olivier Ducastel and Jacques Martineau, 2002)
Through audacious and skilful handling of its video diary structure, the film succeeds brilliantly in inviting the viewer to critically observe the elements of family life and heterosexuality surrounding the main character, Etienne. Skating sequences serve as a powerful symbol of growing self-confidence and a vivid portrait of a young man's growing self-awareness is presented.

Macho Dancer (The Phillipines, Lino Brocka, 1988)
A romantic and sensual, conventionally structured melodrama that portrays the young male central character struggling to survive financially and psychologically in Manila's gay underworld. Through his social realism and sympathy for the oppressed, the director was a leading force in the cinema of his country as well as a noted political dissident.

Madame X (Germany, Ulrike Ottinger, 1977)
An avant-garde lesbian feminist pirate adventure. Challenging viewing in its attempts to find new ways of presenting women in film, but rewarding.

Mandragora (Czech, Wiktor Grodecki, 1997)
'A riveting, brutally honest portrayal of male teen prostitution', said *Variety* magazine. A fictional feature version of Grodecki's documentary on the same subject, *Body Without A Soul* (1996), which places the subject in clear context. Neither film makes easy viewing; Grodecki is concerned to expose the exploitation happening since the opening up of the Eastern Bloc.

The Monkey's Mask (Australia, Samantha Lang, 2000)
A lesbian detective thriller. Jill, ex-cop and private eye, falls for Diane, a woman implicated in a murder. Makes good use of the interplay of cinematic looks through use of video evidence, and gently satirises Sydney's literary scene.

My Beautiful Laundrette (UK, Stephen Frears, 1986)
A well-made social comedy featuring a gay relationship between a white skinhead and a young Asian businessman.

Nitrate Kisses (US, Barbara Hammer, 1992)
A mixture of meditation and documentary, this richly textured film explores lesbian and gay sexuality through history, politics and poetry. Especially noteworthy for its lively portrayal of older lesbians, this is a feast for the eye and the mind.

No Skin Off My Ass (Canada, Bruce La Bruce, 1992)
New Queer Cinema with all its rough edges and unusual cinematic strategies; a punk hairdresser seduces a skinhead.

Okoge (Japan, Takehiro Nakajima, 1992)
A social comedy of love and compromise with graphic sex scenes and a background of Tokyo gay life.

The Opposite of Sex (US, Don Roos, 1999)
The queer aesthetic is engagingly woven into the plot here when pregnant teen Deedee goes to stay with her gay half-brother, a teacher and pillar of the local community, and causes havoc.

Pandora's Box (Germany, G.W. Pabst, 1928)
A beautiful and amoral femme fatale has several male lovers, but her lesbian lover proves to be the most devoted of her followers. A classic of early German cinema, and one of the first positive and sustained portrayals of a lesbian character.

Parting Glances (US, Bill Sherwood, 1986)
A beautifully made depiction of a group of people, gay and straight, in New York City. Nick, the central character played with gently compelling humour by Steve Buscemi, has AIDS, and enjoys the love and support of his friends.

Presque rien (France, Sebastien Lifshitz, 2002)
A portrait of a holiday affair between two young men. Captivating use of flashbacks to engage the viewer in the life and psychology of the characters.

Salmonberries (Germany, Percy Adlon, 1991)

A close emotional involvement between an Eskimo woman, played by k. d. lang, and a teacher fleeing her past. Compulsively watchable performances and locations.

She Must Be Seeing Things (US, Sheila McLaughlin, 1987)

This film touches on many uncomfortable aspects of lesbian sex, loving and looking. It does so in a stylish and articulate way. A key film in the history of lesbian representation, it provoked strong reactions among lesbian viewers; read Teresa de Lauretis (Bad Object Choices 1991: 223).

Skin Deep (Canada, Midi Onodera, 1997)

A male actor plays a woman passing as a man. This character, a transgender loner, becomes involved with a lesbian filmmaker and her long-suffering girlfriend. Overstuffed with incident, but fascinating.

Stonewall (UK, Nigel Finch, 1996)

A passionate and tragicomic version of the historically crucial gay riot of 1969, this film deserves particular credit for the way it puts drag queens, their music and their culture at the centre of it all in a historically accurate way.

Strangers on a Train (US, Alfred Hitchcock, 1951)

Hitch's directorial skill somehow evaded the censors here to present Bruno, one of the great gay characters of classic Hollywood. His psychological prey is played by gay icon Farley Grainger. Based on the thriller by noted lesbian writer Patricia Highsmith.

Sugar (Canada, Bruce La Bruce, 2006)

A young man learns about life through his love for a handsome, drug-addicted hustler. Superbly downbeat, convincing performances from the two leads as well as the understanding mother and the weird, compulsively watchable parade of clients who we see being serviced. The usual touch of Brucian humour comes through the character of the precocious younger sister. This outstanding queer filmmaker is well on his way to forging a distinct authorial voice.

Victim (UK, Basil Dearden, 1961)

A landmark early work in the portrayal of gay life and its difficulties in pre-liberation London. A detective story involving a memorable performance from Dirk Bogarde as a bravely honest gay lawyer. See the essay on Bogarde as queer film star in Griffiths (2005).

Virgin Machine (Germany, Monika Treut, 1988)

A journey of lesbian self-discovery and exploration for a young German journalist in San Francisco. Wacky and provocative views of that city's lesbian scene. See the essay on Treut in Wilton (1995) which discusses this director's emphasis on transcending the label 'lesbian'.

The Watermelon Woman (US, Cheryl Dunye, 1997)

Cheryl, an aspiring filmmaker who is making a documentary about a beautiful and elusive 1930s black film actress, is coolly seduced by the beautiful Diana. Fans of Dunye should recognise her quirky and attractive style in this feature, which seems set to widen her popularity. Stars Dunye herself and Guinevere Turner.

We Were One Man (Nous Etions Un Seul Homme) (France, Philippe Valois, 1981)

A beautifully crafted love story with a bittersweet ending set in rural France during the Second World War which chronicles an affair between a wounded German pilot and a young French peasant.

The Wedding Banquet (Taiwan/China/US, Ang Lee, 1993)

A cross-cultural comedy full of delightful characters. A Chinese gay man living in New York with his lover puts on a show wedding to keep visiting Mum and Dad happy. Themes of honesty, coming out and selfhood.

When Night Is Falling (Canada, Patricia Rozema, 1995)

A glossy and stylish lesbian romance with circus acts and a plot that closely echoes *Desert Hearts*. For a more quirky and attractively watchable film of lesbian interest see Rozema's *I've Heard the Mermaids Singing*.

Wilde (UK–US–Japan–Germany, Brian Gilbert, 1997)

At times simplistic in its account of the life and times of this great gay artist, the film offers a moving portrayal of the sexual passion that brought about Wilde's doom.

Young Soul Rebels (UK, Isaac Julien, 1991)

A gay murder is solved. In the process, two young DJs, one gay and one straight, fight racism, find romance and promote their brand of black soul music. A vivid evocation of the London club scene of the late 1970s set against the background of the Silver Jubilee, with a lively soundtrack.

RESOURCE CENTRES

Video/DVD availability is very variable. All the following offer helpful, up-to-the-minute information on currently available material.

www.amazon.co.uk

www.hmv.co.uk

www.play.com
Search under keywords 'lesbian' and/or 'gay' for a range of books, videos and DVDs for purchase. Other Amazon sites can be useful (you will need to enter titles/keywords in the native language), and subtitles in English are often available. Various formats available. Amazon has an excellent rental service. The play website requires specific titles.

www.bfi.org.uk
The British Film Institute website is especially useful for ordering their very comprehensive catalogues (UK Region 2 formats for DVDs), of which there is one devoted to lesbian/gay/transgender/queer material.

www.llgf.org.uk
This London Lesbian and Gay Film Festival website gives details of their presentations at the National Film Theatre in March/April. For a few months after that, the same programme of films and videos then tours various regional film theatres. All venues are indicated on the website.

www.millivresmultimedia.com
A commercial site from the publishers of *Diva* and *Gay Times*. Offers a selection from 'gentle romantic comedies, hard hitting coming out stories, arthouse experimental films to documentaries'. A variety of titles with helpful reviews available for sale (UK formats). You can also receive their newsletter by mail. Mainly UK DVD formats.

www.planetout.com
Go to the 'PopcornQ Movies' section for helpful information and reviews of festivals and individual films. North American (Region 1) formats only for DVDs.

www.qcinema.com
Excellent, clear, helpful databases on lesbian, gay, transgender and queer film, video, TV, actors, writers, producers. You can search for individual films and reviews, magazine articles and other material. North American (Region 1) formats only for DVDs.

Chapter 12

Ethnicity, race, and cinema – African American film

Terri Francis

■ Ethnicity, race, and cinema – African American film

INTRODUCTION

diaspora
Meaning dispersal, in the African American studies context, this term refers to populations of African descent around the world. Conceptually makes possible comparative studies of black people across national borders, while still accounting for significant cultural differences.

stereotype
Limiting perceptions about a group of people to just one aspect of them which is exaggerated.

constructed
The fact of not being natural or inevitable; having been assembled or otherwise created to appear natural or inevitable.

This chapter offers an overview of African American cinema and criticism. We emphasize films produced in the US. However, the African **diaspora** and Europe are critical contexts for understanding the history and interpretations of black American filmmaking for the following reasons:

- the historical confluences among imperialism, racial segregation, and the emergence of cinema
- the global circulation of the movies and their interaction with science, music, and other cultural forms
- the collaborative, capital-intensive nature of movie-making
- the flow of influences among individuals and groups, across and within national borders.

A taxonomy of cinematic **stereotypes** reveals that disturbing images of colonized and otherwise subjugated people have been and continue to be **constructed** in various ways while a complete history reveals how those people challenged caricatures of themselves and established filmmaking practices of their own.

African American cinema scholarship has two basic foci that span all periods and genres of cinema: (1) the 'ceaselessly shifting black image in commercial narrative cinema, attending to its insults and injuries, its momentary illuminations and insurgencies, and its rare narratives of black empowerment' (Guerrero 1993: 3), and (2) black independent film, examined within broad aesthetic (music, dance, theater, literature, painting, photography) and sociological fields. African American film cultures intersected with and were influenced by other cultural forms, particularly those of music and dance. Examination of black filmmaking alongside the history of black stereotypes presents a complex and more complete picture of both film history and African American experiences of cinema. Moreover, these phenomena did not occur in isolation. American racist imagery coexisted with European colonialist imagery. African American filmmaking developed differently but in many ways parallel to home-grown anti-colonial cinemas in Egypt, the Caribbean, and other parts of the world.

Not all cinematic images of peoples of color are racist portrayals, and not all examples of early film are uniformly complicit with the subjugation of Africans, Asians, Native Americans, and indigenous populations all over the world. Yet motion pictures did play a crucial role in generating, disseminating, and romanticizing the ideological aspects of European imperialism as well as America's expansionist projects and racial conflicts within its borders. Therefore, the study of race, ethnicity, and representation in the cinema is a central, if often overlooked, set of issues at the core of both formalist questions about how images are composed and social ones about how images make meaning in the world at large.

African American cinema is a case of the complex relationship among race, ethnicity, and cinematic representation. References to American history help to put the issues associated with these films into context but the constant migration of influences and people within the US and around the world makes attention to the African diaspora and colonialist representation essential. Although this chapter may not provide a thorough treatment of the colonialist situation, examining black images in American film can serve as a model for the greater understanding of how Africans, Asians, and other non-white ethnic/racial groups are portrayed in the movies.

Analyzing black roles in Hollywood, particularly contrasting the achievement of brilliant actors with the often demeaning roles they played, is perhaps the most common modality for examining images of African Americans on film. Scholars emphasize the tension or the gap between the actors, their intelligence and dignity versus the characters they were made to play on screen. The problem with the roles African Americans were asked to perform was precisely that they were so narrow and predictable. Outside the stereotypes, black actors rarely found emotionally rich, multi-dimensional characters to play. They were limited to specific stock roles as part of a greater social system. Over the past century, African American images have expanded to include a greater range of characters. The limitations and stereotypes that will be discussed later persist in certain ways, but they tend to exist on a continuum rather than in a dichotomy between positive and negative images. Moreover, gender, class, and other differences formed the basis for stereotypes within the black community. In addition to analyzing stereotypes and performance, three more rubrics through which to study African American cinema are: migration narratives, the city, and literature on film.

Since racism and stereotyping attack the worth of African American characterizations, both on screen and in the real world, the analysis of African American performances in film tends to revolve around the qualities of the characters and the personas associated with stars. Such emphasis furthermore reflects the weight that any one character bears amid the scarcity of black figures on screen.

Historically, the relationship between people of African descent and the film industry has been celebrated by recognizing the individual achievements of Hollywood stars such as Louise Beavers, Sidney Poitier, Dorothy Dandridge, Bill Cosby, and more recently Oprah Winfrey, Denzel Washington, Halle Berry, and Queen Latifah. Directors Spike Lee, John Singleton, and the Hughes Brothers have become film stars in their own right while behind the camera due to their unprecedented capacity to work consistently as writers/ directors within the Hollywood machine. Music videos have become a major way for young filmmakers to gain experience and some video directors such as Hype Williams have developed distinctive aesthetics. Like music videos, television shows provide a space for filmmakers to practice their craft. The small screen may seem a world away from the big screen but as consumers increasingly view movies at home on DVDs, the ways in which television and films share aesthetic and social codes become even more evident.

ETHNICITY, RACE, AND FILM

The major producers of cinema in the late nineteenth century were also imperial powers – Britain, France, Germany, and the United States. Meanwhile, in America, the highlight of international cinema's origins, which itself paralleled the expansion of the European imperialist project, coincided with the nadir of the post-Emancipation era. On April 23, 1896 in New York Edison demonstrated new technology for motion pictures: the projected film that could be viewed by a mass audience. Less than a month later in Washington DC, on May 18, 1896, the Supreme Court established the separate-but-equal doctrine through their decision on the *Plessy* vs. *Ferguson* case. 'Of all the celebrated "coincidences" – of the twin beginnings of cinema and psychoanalysis, cinema and nationalism, cinema and consumerism – it is this coincidence with the heights of imperialism that has been least explored' (Shohat and Stam 1994: 100). The relationship among the emergence of cinema, imperialism, and American Jim Crow is even more underexplored.

Although the idea of a mass audience implies unity, accessibility, and shared experience, the *Plessy* decision excluded blacks from participation in it. The ramifications of this case legalized and licensed blacks' marginalization within mainstream society, affecting all aspects of their labor and leisure experiences. As cinema quickly became the world's story-teller, filmmakers and producers drew screen caricatures of African Americans from the sources and precedents that vaudeville, blackface minstrel theater and literature provided. Generally, movies seemed to absorb caricatures of blacks and other people of color including Native Americans, Africans, and Asians, as well as plots that celebrated conquest and exoticized (or denigrated) racial difference from popular colonialist fiction, travel writing, and ethnographic explorations. Such stories aligned the cinematic gaze with an imperialist one.

The cinema 'was ideally suited to relay the projected narratives of nations and empires' (Shohat and Stam 1994: 101) because of the way that its audience functioned as a kind of imagined community (Anderson 1983: 41–64). Like the newspaper, which Benedict Anderson argues created a collective consciousness among disparate individuals, the movies provide members of an audience with a common experience. Projected cinematic narratives of heroes building nations and subduing so-called natives perhaps helped to suture audiences into an imperialist, racist gaze.

Particularly in American movies, black skin became associated with servility and stupidity, although this link shifted and changed over time and black people were not simply victims of these misrepresentations. 'Early American films depended unthinkingly on theatrical precursors, propagating racial caricature borrowed from the popular vaudeville and minstrel shows' (Snead 1988: 16). However, these images did not go unchallenged. The critical mass of financially and culturally connected African Americans in the north and the unacceptability of black film images created the conditions for a black independent film movement.

AFRICAN AMERICAN FILM HISTORY

blaxploitation
Movie studios'
exploitation of what they
believed were black
urban audiences' tastes
in film; beginning with
Melvin Van Peebles's
*Sweet Sweetback's
Baadasssss Song*,
concerned the years
1970 to 1974 in the USA;
usually black-cast action
films.

The history of black American cinema may be roughly divided into four periods: silent-era films and silent-era race films (1890–1928), soundies, race films, Hollywood melodrama on race, including passing films (1929–45); Postwar problem films (1945–60) contemporary films after 1960, including **blaxploitation** (1970–74), black independent film from the 1970s to the present, urban coming-of-age dramas of the 1990s, black women's filmmaking, black experimental films, and narrative feature films. The contemporary period is further divided among several auteurs who work in both documentary and fiction: Spike Lee, Charles Burnett, Julie Dash, Camille Billops, Cheryl Dunye, William Greaves, Kasi Lemons, Louis Massiah, and St. Claire Bourne.

The publicity and scholarly attention given to Spike Lee's 1986 film *She's Gotta Have It* created excitement around the idea of a black independent film movement. It revived interest in black film criticism. David Nicholson had founded the *Black Film Review* in the mid-1980s initially as a critique of black images in Hollywood film. However, writing in 1989, he said, 'In the four years since its founding, the focus of *Black Film Review* has changed. While *BFR* continues to report on aspects of Hollywood film, it now covers independent film from throughout the African Diaspora' (Martin 1995: 442). This shift in perspective reflects increased film production in the Caribbean, Africa, Europe, and the Americas during the 1980s and the way the film community's concerns expanded to include a greater understanding of how people of African descent imagined their worlds cinematically as well as how they were viewed by mainstream media. The majority of the studies cited in this chapter were published in the early to mid-1990s alongside a new wave of black cinema. In many ways early black films are as much products of the 1990s as the 1890s. The significance of Lee's work surely intensified attention on the black cinematic past. Forgotten or lost race films, such as Oscar Micheaux's *Within Our Gates* (found in Filmoteca Espanola in Madrid, Spain, and underwent inter-title restoration in 1993 by the Library of Congress) and *Symbol of the Unconquered* (found in Cinemtheque Royale in Brussels, Belgium, and restored in 1998 by Turner Classic Movies) re-emerged to take their place in film history. Classified as a race film, *Within Our Gates* is the earliest extant feature film by an African American director.

Race films are not films that address the concept of race or any particular race. Race films are black-cast movies that may or may not have been made by an African American director for African American audiences before 1950. They are a central part of considering the history of the intersection among images, art-making and aesthetics in black culture.

The years 1900 to 1930 saw the brief but significant efforts to create a black independent film movement. Bill Foster founded Foster Photoplay in 1910. Based in Chicago, this company specialized in black-cast comedy shorts, such as *The Railroad Porter* (1912) and *The Fall Guy* (1913). According to Mark Reid, these films are notable for portraying black community because they showed that 'black characters can not only be porters for whites but also waiters in respectable black cafés in middle-class African-American communities' (Reid 1993: 8). The Lincoln Motion Picture specialized in family-oriented movies: *The Realization of a Negro's Ambition* (1916), and *The Trooper of Company K* (1916) are two examples. An actor at Universal Studios, Noble Johnson, founded Lincoln in Los Angeles in 1916. Johnson served as president, director–scenarist and leading actor from 1916 to 1918. Clarence Brooks was the second leading actor and secretary. Dr. James Thomas Smith was vice-president and treasurer. Willes O. Tyler gave legal counsel, and Dudley A. Brooks was the assistant secretary. Harry Gant, Universal Studios cameraman, was the only white person in the organization.

Ebony Film Corporation was a white-dominated company that made black-cast comedy shorts from 1915 to 1919. Their product was not strictly race film and they were criticized in the black press for stereotyping. Colored Players' Film Corporation was a white film company that made black-cast dramas and comedies, including *Ten Nights in a Barroom* (1926), starring Charles Chenault and Charles Gilpin, who was a renowned stage actor. The Lafeyette Players' Dramatic Stock Company was a leading African American theatrical repertory company of the 1920s, which grew out of the Anita Bush Stock Company (founded in 1915). The company premiered in Lincoln Theater in Harlem and, when it moved to rival Lafayette, it became known as Lafayette Players. They aimed to present serious drama and direct opposition to minstrel comedy types. Many early members of the company such as Chenault appeared in films.

Micheaux was the most prolific of the race film writer/directors. He founded the Oscar Micheaux Book and Film Company in 1918. The officers included Swan Micheaux, secretary–treasurer; Charles Benson handled booking for Chicago-based distribution; Tiffany Oliver and W.R. Crowell operated the Roanoke, Virginia office and O.A. Adams, southwest region. Micheaux sold his autobiographical novels door to door and he developed this direct approach to his film's distribution as well. His films of this period include *The Homesteader* (1919) (novel – 1917), *Within Our Gates* (1920), and *Symbol of the Unconquered* (1920). Micheaux's company collapsed in 1928 and was reorganized with white financing in 1929.

Despite the strong entrepreneurial spirit these companies and their founders possessed, several forces worked against their ultimate success. In the late 1920s, the Great Depression and the high cost of sound equipment disproportionately affected financially vulnerable African American companies. The most devastating was the departure of actors and other creative talent for Hollywood. Major studios sought to capitalize on the coming of sound by featuring black voices and bodies in the movies. This opened up opportunities for African American entertainers and actors in mainstream productions. Evelyn Preer who starred consistently in Micheaux films went to Hollywood where she appeared in the minor role of Viola, a maid, in *Blonde Venus* in 1932. Most notably, Paul Robeson's first cinematic appearance was a dual role in Micheaux's *Body and Soul*. He went on to appear in many mainstream films. The trajectory of Robeson's career is an excellent example of the ways in which African American cinema history includes films by filmmakers of African descent as well as those that feature black performers. In many ways, African American cinema, while it may have nationalist impulses, is an interracial enterprise. The Micheaux Pictures Corporation had two notable features. *A Daughter of the Congo* (1930) was the result of a collaboration between Micheaux and Quality Amusements, a white company. Micheaux relied on Quality's distribution circuit. *The Exile* (1931) was the first all-talkie, feature-length, black commercial film.

With the exception of Micheaux and Spencer Williams, film history on black directing pauses and blacks seem absent from the scene as directors or writers in the 1930s. But they are present as characters, sometimes with stereotypical outlines. The year 1939 was significant for woman actors: *Imitation of Life* (Fredi Washington and Louise Beavers), *Gone with the Wind* (Hattie McDaniel), *The Green Pastures* (Rex Ingram). Black-cast commercial films were popular in the 1940s. Examples of some of the most important musicals include *Cabin in the Sky* (1943), *Stormy Weather* (1943), and *Song of the South* (1946). Films also took on a social conscience and many dealt with the race question. Among these are the 1949 pictures: *The Quiet One*, *Home of the Brave*, *Lost Boundaries*, *Pinky*, and *Intruder in the Dust*. The 1950s saw the rise of the black star on an unprecedented scale. As black stars in white films or black stars in black-cast films, Sidney Poitier, Dorothy Dandridge, Harry Belafonte, and Ethel Waters did much to revise existing types. Black art films are also an important part of African American canon: *Shadows* (John Cassevettes, 1961), *The Cool World* (Shirley Clarke, 1963), *One Potato, Two Potato* (Sam Weston and Larry Peerce, 1964), and *Nothing But a Man* (Michael Roemer, 1964).

Nothing But a Man is set between the 1954 ruling *Brown* vs. *Board of Education*, which led to desegregating public schools and was a first step in dismantling the separate but equal doctrine, established by *Plessy*, and the 1964 Civil Rights Act, which granted the US government power to prosecute discrimination in employment, voting, and education. The film is set in a small town outside Birmingham, which distances it from events in the city while the trajectories of characters' lives are still affected by them. The city of Birmingham was the site of the 16th Street Baptist Church bombing, which killed four girls. Spike Lee recounted the ordeal in his documentary, *Four Little Girls* (1998). *Nothing but a Man* represents an independent vision, which responded to a world seen in the television news but largely ignored by Hollywood. The story concerns the courtship and marriage of Duff (Ivan Dixon) and Josie (Abbey Lincoln) but centers in many ways on Duff's struggle with himself. His efforts to establish himself in his community put him in touch with the shifting definitions of black citizenship and masculinity on personal and social levels.

Sidney Poitier's stardom emerged in the 1950s and soared in the 1960s as a major way in which the studios responded to changes in race relations while packaging and containing them in the performer's masculine glamor. Poitier was criticized for playing on-screen characters that seemed to seek white approval or to be content as the official Other— the only black face in a sea of whiteness. In the era of black power, his roles in *Guess Who's Coming to Dinner* and *Lilies of the Field* may have seemed accommodationist. However, Poitier's stardom gained him power within Hollywood, which allowed him to direct his own films. These include the buddy films with Bill Cosby, *Let's Do It Again* and a *Piece of the Action*, romance films *A Warm December* (which he wrote) and *For the Love of Ivy*, starring Lincoln. These films and Poitier's western migration narrative *Buck and the Preacher* (with Harry Belafonte) comprise an aesthetically commercial yet financially independent layer of 1970s black cinema.

Blaxploitation concerned at most four years between 1970 and 1974 and it is best known for cheaply made, highly profitable action films. Blaxploitation was sometimes heralded as a new wave of black cinema. It has been discussed as having countered the perceived asexuality of Poitier's screen personas and in many ways translating black power rhetoric into black action screen heroes. But it was also decried as junk. The story of blaxploitation is only part of the story of African American cinema during the 1970s. At the same time, blaxploitation was a complex blend of auteurism and commercialism, recalling in many ways the example of Micheaux's film company.

For the most part, black cinema faded from the national view in the late 1970s and early 1980s, with the notable exceptions of Haile Gerima, Charles Burnett, and Michael Schultz. The 1986 release of *She's Gotta Have It* by Spike Lee then followed by the 1990s wave of urban dramas (i.e. *Boyz in the Hood*, 1991 and *Menace II Society*, 1993) returned African American film aesthetics and the politics of race and representation to the attention of movie audiences. Lee established his film company, calling it Forty Acres and a Mule, which referenced the broken promises that were made to ex-slaves during the short-lived Reconstruction period. The Freedman's Bureau had been established to oversee the transition of the ex-slaves into citizenship. Part of the restitution the government was prepared to offer was forty acres of land and a mule. However, this debt went unpaid. Lee recalls this economic and cultural history in the name of his film company while expressing his confidence and independence as a film author and entrepreneur.

For a list of films directed by Haile Gerima, Charles Burnett and Michael Schultz see Further Viewing on pp. 299–300.

AFRICAN AMERICAN MIGRATION NARRATIVES

African American migration patterns have resulted in a complex relationship between blacks and the cinema. First, 'the rise of the cinema as the predominant American entertainment during the first decades of the twentieth century coincided with the migration of hundreds of thousands of African Americans from their "traditional" homes in the South to increased social and economic opportunities in northern cities' (Stewart 2005: 2). These travelers were often spurred by violence in their home towns and were met by violence at their destination. Cities were spaces of both alienation and chances for better education and economic advancement for the migrants. Popular culture provided exhilarating opportunities for self-creation or re-creation. Yet it remains 'one of the bitter ironies of American history, then that motion picture technology, with its singular potential for good or evil, grew to perfection during the same time period (1890–1915) that saw the systematic, determined, almost hysterical persecution and defamation of blacks and other minority groups' (Snead 1988: 16). These years of racial violence against African Americans marked and, in many ways motivated, the Great Migration whose waves of travel from rural areas to cities and from the south to the north is known as 'the largest movement of Black bodies since slavery' (Gates 1993: 17). The Great Migration

• **Plate 12.1**
Daughters of the Dust (Julie Dash, 1991). Shot on location on South Helena Island, South Carolina in the USA, this film concerns migration. *Daughters* is a landmark of American independent filmmaking and shares stylistic features with Cuban and African films, including the use of realistic social space rather than idealized space

transformed America, African Americans, and their shared cultural institutions, including the cinema. Early motion pictures, which borrowed their aesthetic codes from literature and vaudeville, presented images, albeit problematic ones, of blackness and, in ways yet to be fully understood, consuming these and other cinematic images played a crucial role in forming the broad outlines of African American experiences in the urban north.

Black or African American identity is neither fixed nor essential, for it is continually reshaped by internal tensions and contradictions as well as by external pressures, such as migration. The 'variability of a Black "public" and the unpredictability of Black "experience"' (Stewart 2005: 13) are fundamental concepts in this discussion of African American cinema, despite scholars' necessary reliance at times on general notions of stereotypes, race, and racism. On the one hand a common-sense understanding that racism consists of negative views of one group by another group or between individuals is adequate. On the other hand, it is necessary to go beyond this superficial understanding to grasp the underlying dynamics of unequal power between groups and how they change over time. Migration is a recurring motif in African American cinema. Some examples are: *Girl from Chicago* (1932), *Buck and the Preacher* (1972), *Space Is the Place* (1974), *Daughters of the Dust* (1992), and *Down in the Delta* (1998).

'THE DOUBLE TRUTH, RUTH'

Concepts of truth and reality dominate the promotion and reception of black cinema, which, like black diaspora literature and music, is often celebrated for its perceived oppositional qualities. Although the discourse of African American cinema, embodied most emphatically by Spike Lee, concerns 'telling the truth' about the black experience and society at large, such claims need to be interrogated carefully against the specific realities a film or filmmaker references and the capacities and limitations of cinematic representation. Wahneema Lubiano writes that Lee's films *School Daze* (1988) and *Do the Right Thing* (1989) were 'discussed by most reviewers on the grounds of realism, authenticity, and relation to the "good" of the community represented in them' (Lubiano 1991: 260). Without denying Lee's claims explicitly, Lubiano asks, 'But compared to what?' and expresses concern over the dearth of African American films to counter or engage Lee's version of reality. Further, a realist reading of Lee's work obscures the surreal, imaginative qualities that inhere at the moments that seem 'authentic' and 'real.' The racial epithet sequence, titled on the DVD as 'Some Thoughts about Ethnicity,' provides a striking example of how surrealness and authenticity combine.

The sequence in which characters representing various members of Lee's Brooklyn community assault their neighbors and the mayor, and the viewing audience through direct address, with a rapid succession of racial slurs, can appear real in the sense that audience members may experience a greater connection to or awareness of racial tensions in their communities. The very idea of racial tension is 'real,' and urban blackness is often mobilized as a sign of the real. But the mode of address, though direct, also has a surreal quality, as the camera zooms in on characters that seem to float or become detached from their context for the length of the monologue. The quick rhythms and rhymes ('mida mida puerto rican') of the speeches, which string together a series of references to a group's physicality, preferred food brands, famous figures, music, shoe style preferences, and work habits, strikes a cord that is shocking as well as comical. The quick zoom that opens each monologue adds to the shock factor. The actors' accents and energy generate precise vernacular portrayals. The sequence and its apparent realism are delivered in a uniquely cinematic way. The characters seem to address each other verbally while they make eye contact with us. Such directness implicates the audience as receivers (you talking to me?) and as perpetrators (you read my mind) of the racial slurs. Lee's camerawork brings viewers into closer audio-visual contact with the film's characters and their world than might be possible otherwise, while also containing and intensifying that experience within the film sequence. This contradictory intimacy and distancing – suturing and alienation – raises the question of how 'real' Lee's filmic reality can be. *Do the Right Thing* may strike authentic notes and shape how audiences see the world but it is finally an imaginative work of fiction made potent by its surreal yet vernacular performances and mise-en-scène. The sequence ends when the local DJ, who in another moment of surreality has somehow heard the monologues which took place on the streets around Brooklyn from his radio booth, Mr. Senior Love Daddy, shouts to the players and the audiences in the theater: 'Yo, hold up ... you need to cool that shit out and that's the double truth, ruth.'

Lubiano points out that 'the reasons for "real" as a positive evaluation are tied, of course, to scarcity, the paucity of African-American presentations of facts and representations as well as desire for more of the first category, which in turn allows the second category to have its "selectiveness" forgotten in the rush to celebrate its mere presence.' What reviewers take for real consists of the vernacular – sights and sounds that are particular to a place and the people who live there. The vernacularity of Lee's film cannot be unquestioningly accepted as truth while the speech patterns, music, costumes, locations, and references to events that were reported in the media are all authenticating signs in the film. They blur the line between the film's diegesis and the real world. For 'telling the "truth" demands that we consider the truth of something compared to something else. Who is speaking? Who is asking? And to what end?' (Lubiano 1991: 264). The manner of filming and the vernacular quality of the racial epithet rant sequences in *Do the Right Thing* demonstrate the complex relationship between illusion and reality. At the same time, they offer a way of thinking about the ever-renewing power of stereotypes as shorthand for perceived reality.

STEREOTYPES

Stereotypes are ideas of one group about another group. They are part of a discursive phenomenon – specific names and images – that has implications for people in the real world. They function as tools used by institutions, groups or individuals within the ideological or cultural dimensions of racism. Often, stereotypes or negative caricatures are criticized in terms of a positive/negative dichotomy. But this morally driven analysis can obscure the processes by which stereotypes are created and how they function in a variety of media. Stereotypes themselves are recognizable yet multi-sided and unstable, hence the necessity of repetition where the types reassert their authority over our perception. Homi Bhabha writes: 'it is the force of ambivalence that gives the colonial stereotype its currency: ensures its repeatability in changing historical and discursive conjunctures' (Bhabha 1994: 64). Bhabha opens up ways to investigate rather than dismiss stereotypes. There is still, however, a bottom line in race relations on the discursive level because of what Elizabeth Alexander calls 'black bodily experience' (Alexander 2004: 179). She writes: 'there is such a thing as *bottom line blackness* with regard to the violence which erases other differentiations and highlights race' (ibid.: 180). In other words, while racial categories are constructed and tenuous, the effects of racism and its tools are concrete, too often experienced as physical violence or other non-discursive forms of discrimination.

The major stereotypes or tropes of racist depictions may be traced back to what is perhaps their most important manifestation as a group in Harriet Beecher Stowe's *Uncle Tom's Cabin*. This 1852 novel was an abolitionist text that used types to illustrate the effects of slavery on the slave. Donald Bogle enumerated them as follows: toms, coons, mulattos, mammies and bucks (1998: 3–10). Each stereotype has a specific meaning even as it resonates broadly depending on the narrative context, actor, and relationship to the surrounding characters. They have been revised over time, yet they endure, even if multi-dimensional, humanistic African American characters have also joined these types on the screen.

It is important to note that blacks were never totally invisible in the cinema but they were often misrepresented. Rather than being represented as the sum of many aspects, they tended to be limited to one or two, which were then exaggerated. While early film characters were often typed, the black types were generated by and supported a peculiarly racist regime beyond the movies. 'All were character types used for the same effect: to entertain by stressing Negro inferiority. Fun was poked at the American Negro by presenting him as either a nitwit or a childlike lackey. None of the types was meant to do great harm, although at various times individual ones did' (Bogle 1998: 3). **Racist iconography** was part of a greater social scheme.

The tom type is derived from Uncle Tom, the title character in Stowe's novel and its many incantations on stage and on film. He is 'the first in a long line of socially acceptable Good Negro characters' (Bogle 1998: 4). Tom was derided by blacks and praised by whites as docile, religious, and ever-faithful to his white owners, and thus seemingly too tolerant of the brutal circumstances he faced. Uncle Tom is usually middle-aged, long-suffering, and dutiful. He seems to avoid confrontation with politics.

The coon is both a plantation type and a stock character popular in minstrel theater. He is almost a comic version of Uncle Tom. The coon does not seem to have a care in the world. He is lazy and mischievous. There are a variety of coon types. Topsy was a 'wild child' that exemplified slavery's immoral impact on the young. The piccaninny was pictured with large, bulging eyes, red, large lips and was usually a comic character that was pictured eating constantly or as food for animals such as alligators. A common figure in racist or at least paternalist iconography is the quaint old man who disperses traditional-style tales, folk wisdom and, banjo-playing or other traditional Afro-American entertainment. Sometimes this figure is depicted as childlike or with children, and thus unthreatening. Examples include *Song of the South* and Bill Robinson's performances opposite Shirley Temple. The character of Medouze (Douta Seck) in Euzahn Palcy's *Sugar Cane Alley* (1983) is a counter-example to this type. A mentor and link to African traditions, Medouze is a grandfather figure for young Jose (Garry Cadenet), who is the film's protagonist narrator. Medouze challenges the history of framing black folk culture in Sambo stereotyping.

The term 'mulatto' is the archaic name for a person of mixed racial heritage. Historically, this person was said to have greater privileges than the darker skinned slaves; however, this idea is debatable. What is crucial to this type for our purposes is its placement in a tragic narrative mode. The tragic mulatta or mulatto is an ambitious, often sexually aggressive type, featured in a tragic narrative where his or her dreams cannot be realized because of the scourge of race. This stereotype carefully avoids making racism and white people the problem, instead casting the blame on the existence of racial difference, particularly the stain of blackness.

The mammy sometimes plays opposite a mulatta or in contrast to a white female star. Mammy was characterized by the warmth and cheerfulness she displayed for the white family she served, although she sometimes had a gruff voice (with which she would often make witty remarks). Mammy is recognizable by the combination of direct demeanor, large physical size, and dark skin. Her costumes tended to feature work clothes, including a headscarf and long, conservative dress. Her toothy grin also figured as part of her characterization. Mammy's fierce independence creates fruitful ambivalence, which may allow viewers to read her against the narratives in which she might appear.

The brutal buck cliché, returning to male stereotypes, was an aggressive, sometimes overly sexualized figure. The classic example of this figure is Gus the Renegade, as seen in *Birth of a Nation*, but the type is reprised in the 1970s blaxploitation films, such as the *Shaft* cycle of films. The instinctual black male renegade type who fights for his people's freedom but wants to marry a white woman was a powerful symbol of white fears about black participation in American democracy.

racist iconography
Images that accompany racist rhetoric or in racist contexts.

Certain stereotypes do have names but wielding them goes beyond the name-calling expressed between individuals or slurs slung in an institutional setting. Stereotypes are tools of denigration mobilized in power struggles. Most often they are used in a negative sense but, in rare cases, a group might attempt to capitalize on a stereotype's ambivalences in order to appropriate and redefine the negative stereotypes about their group through irony. In *Do the Right Thing*, racial epithets are deployed for the purpose of exposing racial tensions. Generally, a stereotype is a negative caricature that simplifies a group's identity by exaggerating a trait – be it physical or cultural. Stereotypes often seem totalizing in their insults but they are complicated and contradictory enough to be challenged and perhaps dismantled by their supposed victims. African Americans have not simply been victims of Hollywood's portrayals. Instead they have presented an ongoing challenge as audience members and participants in all aspects of the industry in a variety of ways. Racist imagery emerges as the result of interlocking forces of politics, economics, and aesthetics. The black image on film has been framed and challenged in various ways over time through a combined, synthesized set of efforts and issues. Ed Guerrero reminds us,

the ideology of racial domination and difference can never be permanently fixed in place as a complete or static 'thing.' Instead, it is a dynamic, shifting 'relation' defined and conditioned by social struggle, the demands of the historical moment, and the material imperative of an industry that privileges economics and short-term profit before all other human, aesthetic, or philosophic possibilities or concerns.

(Guerrero 1993: 2–5)

RACISM

Racism may be defined as 'the generalized and final assigning of values to real or imaginary differences, to the accuser's benefit and at his victim's expense, in order to justify the former's own privilege and aggression' (Memmi 1968: 186). In film, racism results in the construction of a privileged white gaze at the expense of other characters' points of view. The privilege of this gaze depends upon its presumed neutrality and transparency. The camera, the film's universal eye and/or the filmmaker's eye is aligned with the white hero or heroine's perspective. Examination of race and ethnicity in film entails not only attention to stereotypes of blackness or other groups dominated by colonialism, but also consideration of whiteness and notions of what is normal.

WHITENESS

Hollywood or other dominant cinemas normalize whiteness while subordinating other ethnic groups. Stereotypes play a role but whiteness itself is constructed in a particular way relative to blackness and other identities. The study of whiteness established in part by Richard Dyer and Daniel Bernardi has begun to lay bare this previously unseen identity. While stereotypes of non-white characters are limited to one, exaggerated characteristic, 'white people in their whiteness, however, are imaged as individual and/or endlessly diverse, complex and changing' (Dyer 1997: 12). The privilege and power of whiteness is its presumed neutrality and the way it represents what is normal. Unless he or she is a racial supremacist, and so does specify and make whiteness visible, the white character in a film presumes to speak not for any particular group but for all of humanity. Most portrayals of white people fall into the latter category. White privilege manifests as innocence when interacting with non-white others and the casualness with which they at gaze their cinematic world with total authority, distance, and objectivity. This gaze tends to dominate westerns as well as imperial action films.

Chris Harris' experimental film *Reckless Eyeballing* (2004) uses clips from *Birth of a Nation* and the blaxploitation movie *Foxy Brown* in order to challenge white

● **Plate 12.2**
Reckless Eyeballing
(Christopher Harris,
2004). Non-narrative
and formalistic, this
film features re-
photographed images of
Angela Davis' *Wanted*
posters, and excerpts
from a *Foxy Brown*
trailer (Jack Hill, 1974)
and *Birth of a Nation*
(D.W. Griffith, 1915).
Harris used solarization
to manipulate the light-
sensitive emulsion of
high-contrast black and
white film stock. This
process causes black
tones to become white
and the reverse; the
tonalities shift back and
forth continuously

cinematic authority and abstraction by positing a black abstraction. Harris's use of high-contrast black and white photography foregrounds his concern with the aesthetics and technologies of light and darkness, and how these are mapped ideologically onto white people and the dark skin color associated with African Americans. When he switches between the positive and negative versions of the same image, he seeks to deconstruct or at least demystify the ideological pull of whiteness. 'White' characters switch to black and black characters become white. This technique underscores the reality that white people are not actually white and black people are not actually black in color. In *Reckless Eyeballing*, whiteness is denaturalized and Harris reduces it to its technological elements.

The term 'reckless eyeballing' refers to the Jim Crow-era practice of criminalizing black men's gazes. A black man could be lynched for looking at or being *perceived* as looking at a white woman in a way that any white man felt was inappropriate. This instance of the white male gaze under Jim Crow is the ultimate in privileged white vision because in it a white man's perception of a situation determines the value of another man's life while policing white women at the same time. Black women and other people of color had peripheral roles in this scenario but were also affected by it. In the film, blackness seems to be disassociated from bodies and it becomes something resembling an independent aesthetic force. This move is significant because, through stereotyping, non-white characters tend to be subordinate to white characters. Thus they cannot act independently and are framed primarily in relation to the white character. With each shot, *Reckless Eyeballing* searches for the roots of this aesthetic and political phenomenon in cinema's visual grammar.

GENRE

How to define black film? Historian Thomas Cripps writes,

'black film' may be defined as those motion pictures made for theater distribution that have a black producer, director, and writer, or black performers; that speak to black audiences or, incidentally, to white audiences possessed of preternatural curiosity, attentiveness, or sensibility toward racial matters; and that emerge from self-conscious intentions, whether artistic or political, to illuminate the Afro-American experience. In the latter part of this century, this definition might be expanded to include major motion pictures and other projects made for television, as well as films that, despite foreign origins in, say, Africa, speak to Afro-American concerns.

(1978: 357)

Cripps goes on to note that very few films would meet these narrow criteria. Eloice Gist's early films might qualify. These were religious black-cast dramas written, directed, and produced by herself and her husband, and shown to black church audiences. But these were not made for theatrical distribution although they were made by and for a black audience. Obviously, such criteria are too limited to be useful and do not begin to account for the interracial, sometimes international collaborations that often make even the most humble film possible.

African Americans are not a nation unto themselves and, from a diasporic perspective, display wide differences among each other based on class, language, politics, and other factors. However, some shared experiences such as violence, discrimination, or celebrations such as Juneteenth can create the sense of a coherent or 'bottom-line,' if tenuous, community. African American cinema is a genre that contains other genres: documentary, fiction, and, experimental films that may be directed, produced, and/or performed by black people; such films may speak to African American historical issues, social concerns, and they may represent the community's rituals, cultural artifacts or spaces. Black films may be independently financed through grants or individuals, as well as by Hollywood or small production companies based in the US or abroad. They may be seen in museums, libraries, multiplexes, and arts events. Perhaps because of this ever-expanding diversity, with regard to the production, distribution, and exhibition of black film, the impulse to define and redefine black cinema persists. While black film cannot accurately be described as national, it often figures in nationalist discussions of black aesthetics and is seen as a site of African American self-definition and expression.

African Americans appeared in a variety of film types, including dance films, newsreels, and comedies. Some titles include: *The Pickaninnies* (1894), *The Watermelon Contest* (1896), *A Morning Bath* (1896), *Dancing Darkey Boy* (1897), *A Nigger in a Woodpile* (1904), *Who Said Chicken?* (1900), *Native Women Washing Clothes at St. Vincent, B.W.I.* (1903), *Cake Walk* (1903), and *Comedy Cake Walk* (1903). Some of these and other early images of African Americans may portray black Americans through what may be described as southern plantation imagery. These early cinematic tropes drew upon nineteenth-century minstrel theater, which featured white men in **blackface** make-up. They performed blackness as joke, stupidity, and as entertainment. (Over time, curiously but perhaps not unsurprisingly, African American actors also participated in the tradition and wore blackface make-up.) Literary and theatrical traditions in America and Europe, informed doubtless by travel writing and filmmaking about 'Africa,' provided the sources for the racist imagery found on a variety of household products and in the commercial media of the day.

Race/ethnicity and the reproduction of racial ideologies, in life as on film, are issues of perception and performance. Stereotypes represent not just individuals or groups of people. They demonstrate and influence ways of thinking about them; thus they represent how individuals and groups are viewed by society at large. While we assume that in society there are many ideologies at odds with each other, usually a dominant one and one resistant to it can be detected. The stereotypes described above are examples of American society's dominant racist ideologies of black American men and women of the nineteenth century but they persist into the present. These systems of thought, whether they are used intentionally or unintentionally, influence individuals' ideas about blacks. Even their ideas about themselves help to maintain an unequal power structure in society. Social inequality is symbiotic with stereotyping because they help to maintain the currency of well-used clichés, while the images perpetuate the view that the marginalized group is unworthy of citizenship and full participation in society. Filmmakers, performers,

blackface
Use of burnt cork or greasepaint to paint the face literally black; nineteenth-century minstrel theater; used by both white and black performers.

writers, producers, and others involved in film production, regardless of their racial, ethnic, or national identity, can operate within the film industry in a resistant fashion to offer characters, narratives, and history, often in the form of documentaries. Fiction and experimental films have expanded audiences' awareness of the ways that cinema shapes perception.

Over 100 and more years of filmmaking, stereotypes of African Americans have been occasionally revised, while often retaining their basic outlines, in response to shifts in the customs that shape discrimination and citizenship as well as growing intolerance for the invisibility and distorted visions of black people. For example, in the early 1940s the National Association for the Advancement of Colored People, under Walter White's leadership, initiated a series of meetings with film industry leaders. The subject of these conversations was the image of African Americans in mainstream motion pictures. White sought to influence the industry to not only eliminate black stereotypes but to integrate and normalize the presence of African Americans in films. When blacks were absent, the American cinematic world pictured an entirely white society as if that was the social reality. Invisibility worked in two ways: black characters were not there or, when present, black characters were there as only the servants and/or sidekicks of white stars (Cripps 1993: 35–63).

Hypervisibility refers to roles that emphasized blacks as spectacle. Two common forms of this mode are cameo appearances by famous performers or storylines that put a black character at the center of a social problem. Examples of social problem spectacularity include the documentary *The Quiet One* (Sidney Meyers, 1948), *Home of the Brave* (Mark Robson, 1949), and Sidney Poitier in *Guess Who's Coming to Dinner* (Stanley Kramer, 1967). In these films, the black characters have a well-defined role whose effectiveness depends upon the audience's recognition of them as stars, particularly in the second scenario, and as specifically black claimants on social justice in the other. While all three roles may be seen as 'positive' moves away from degrading stereotypes that mock black physical attributes or cultural practices, they tend not to be protagonists who move the story along and reflect on their own lives. For example, the boy in *The Quiet One* is the ostensible subject but, despite the film's stated concerns with his thoughts and feelings, his image is dominated by a voiceover narration.

□ CASE STUDY 1: *FROM ZORA NEALE HURSTON FIELDWORK FOOTAGE* (NATIONAL FILM PRESERVATION FOUNDATION, 2004)

Hurston's 1928 footage comprises forty minutes of extant images held at the Library of Congress in Washington D.C. (see Resources, p. 300). Archivists there have made some of this material available in a seven-minute compilation. The resulting short film highlights Hurston's careful composition of each shot. The footage provides a window into the unique and fragile communities she studied. The images do not have accompanying dialogue or sound; thus interpretation rests on the visual cues. In one striking shot, Hurston films the area around a labor camp from a moving train, perhaps as a humorous nod to the Lumière Brothers' image of a train pulling into the station. Hurston's image shows not only an object in motion, but it also shows the camera in motion and image itself as motion. Hurston makes movement itself a spectacle.

Hurston's brand of participant/observer anthropology is evident in the fieldwork footage. Hurston collected the stories, songs, and images in her fieldwork by living among her subjects, blending in as much as possible to learn to sing and talk as they did. A sequence with a woman who Hurston interviewed shows her complex relationship to her subject. The camera frames a house, so that the yard in front is visible. A woman walks toward the camera and presents herself for a portrait that emphasizes the details of her facial expression and suggests her subjectivity. Looking directly into the lens, she smiles, and an apparently personal connection is established between herself and the viewer. After a few seconds, as though taking directions, she turns her head to the right and then to the left, adopting the poses of classic anthropological display and racial science. There seems to be a clear distinction between a more collaborative mode and one of anthropological display. This difference is made all the more salient by the framing, which separates the subject from her environment and then switches from portraiture, almost personal engagement into an impersonal style. The framing does not change but the mode of presentation changes within it.

The following sequence complements the first by showing a group rather than an individual. Children are arranged in a circle and a boy dances in the middle while those watching clap in time to his movements. What is curious about this framing is that Hurston positions the camera so that while the dancer is centered, the arms and feet of those children on either side of the camera are also visible. Thus, Hurston and/or her camera are within the circle, which puts viewers of Hurston's film in the circle as well. This sequence is a metaphor of Hurston's complex double-consciousness and her position as insider and outsider.

When viewed in the context of Hurston's writing, it becomes clear that her images directly confront the problem of stereotypes. Aware of the black image problem, she wrote, 'It is assumed that all non-Anglo-saxons are uncomplicated stereotypes.... It is urgent to realize that minorities do think, and think about something other than the race problem' (Hurston 1979: 170). Her collaborative, community-centered filmmaking practice presents individual blacks in a community – not isolated caricatures. Because its purpose is to collect material for an anthropological study, Hurston's images serve as evidence of a coherent black culture within the US They are also complicated because they are representative of certain types in the community, which could play into broader stereotyping patterns of African Americans.

The Harlem Renaissance debates concerned the cultural role that people of African descent play within a broader American society as well as a global marketplace. They may be reprised to critique as well as celebrate today's black cinema. Hurston, who had been criticized for a perceived reliance on stereotypes in her lyrical portrayals of black rural workers, delivered an incisive contribution to the black arts debate as it continued into the 1940s. Published in 1947 in *Negro Digest*, Hurston's essay 'What White Publishers Won't Print' is an analysis of the American literary establishment and what she viewed as its overall preference for black stereotypes and other kinds of racialized (sometimes racist) literary shorthand. The essay is also a manifesto in which Hurston calls for 'intimate stories from the inside' that would not just counter but replace what she termed 'the museum dedicated to the convenient "typical"' (Hurston 1979: 171–3). In other words, Hurston wanted to see storytelling where audiences could hear a range of black voices instead of the 'notions' or clichés writers tended to use when denoting (and usually undermining) an African American character.

Hurston and her contemporaries devoted much energy to formulating, defending, and celebrating African American culture. But what she really seemed to want to do was to sanction telling the stories of everyday people. She wrote, 'For various reasons, the average, struggling, non-morbid Negro is the best-kept secret in America. His revelation to the public is the thing needed to do away with that feeling of difference which inspires fear and which ever expresses itself in dislike.' By replacing stereotypes (limiting ideas about a group of people to just one aspect of them, which is exaggerated) with **archetypes** (embodiments of a range of ideas and identities), Hurston was confident that 'this knowledge will destroy many illusions and romantic traditions which America probably likes to have around.' Hurston's camerawork, particularly the framing, manifests her awareness of her position inside and outside the community.

Although Hurston's images were taken in an anthropological context, they may now be viewed within the broader context of African American cinema.

archetypes
Embodiments of a range of ideas and identities.

☐ CASE STUDY 2: *THE HARDER THEY COME* (PERRY HENZELL, 1972)

'Third World' refers to the colonized, neocolonized, or decolonized nations and 'minorities' whose structural disadvantages have been shaped by the colonial process and by the unequal division of international labor' (Shohat and Stam 1994: 25). The term 'Third World cinema' first emerged in relation to the Cuban revolution and Cinema Novo in Brazil. Given the economic difficulties that filmmakers in this part of the world have to contend with, the term 'Third World cinema' might sound patronizing, as though it refers to a lesser, marginal cinema in third place, behind the Hollywood and European film industries. However, 'just as peoples of color form the global majority, so the cinemas of people of color from the majority cinema, and it is only the notion of Hollywood as the only "real" cinema that obscures this fact' (Shohat and Stam 1994: 27). Most of the world's films are produced in India, the Philippines, Indonesia and other Asian countries. These films sometimes have ideological as well as aesthetic agendas, which have changed over time. Owing in part to the migrations, whether forced or voluntary, almost every country in the so-called Third World has a diaspora film community which then interacts with other diasporas in centers such as New York, London, Paris, and Brussels.

Perry Henzell's film was a singular accomplishment for Jamaica in 1972 but it was also part of a small cohort of Anglophone Caribbean films. Harbance Kumar of Trinidad directed the first two feature films to be produced in the anglophone Caribbean. They were called *The Right and the Wrong* (1970) and *The Caribbean Fox* (1970). These were films that Keith Warner defines as 'those which are produced in the region by and

• **Plate 12.3**
The Harder They Come (Perry Henzell, 1972). Ivan (Jimmy Cliff) during the portrait sequence, accompanied by Desmond Dekker's 'Shantytown'. Ivan plans to circulate his image in the local newspapers, in a bid to finally achieve the celebrity this former country boy had hoped to find in the city. Filmed over two years at locations in Kingston, Jamaica, the story is drawn from 1940s news accounts of Rhygin, a criminal reportedly obsessed with westerns and who led police on an extended chase

white by and with a majority Caribbean personnel, and whose conception, realization, and flavour present a distinct Caribbean world view' (Warner 2000: 71). At that time, Jamaican film consisted of films shot in Jamaican locations but produced abroad and documentaries shot by members of the Jamaica Film Unit.

The Harder They Come took two years to make and premièred in Kingston on June 5, 1972. Known primarily for its musical score, which helped to introduce reggae internationally, the film is also visually remarkable. What is crucial about the presentation of music in the film as well as the sequence I will discuss here, is the way it shows creation and construction. The characters do not fantastically yet naturalistically burst into song as in a musical. The singing characters in *The Harder They Come* are musicians who write, record, and perform music. The film is partly about music as work and musical expression as both social and personal understanding. In the following sequence analysis we see Ivan (Jimmy Cliff), one of the musicians, creating or re-creating his persona in what is probably the most iconic set of images from the film. The images are destined for circulation in local newspapers.

The sequence works on many levels. It is certainly Ivan's shot at immortality but it is also Henzell's framing of Jimmy Cliff, the recording artist. Cliff takes on the persona of the stylish gangster Ivan, striking a variety of poses in images that suggest album covers. Desmond Dekker's recording of 'Shanty Town' accompanies the sequence. The song functions here as a kind of choral presence where the shanty town or Ivan's supporters gather around him and encourage him. (The sequence prior to this shows a confrontation between the detective and one of the ganja traders who has been hiding Ivan.) The sequence includes black and white still images taken in the studio, black and white motion pictures of Ivan getting into his poses and interacting with the photographer, and color snapshots of Ivan in other settings. The sequence thus also shows off a tension between stillness and motion. Ivan's expressivity is powerful to viewers as a phenomenon of motion, but how he commands space while standing still is also constitutive of the persona he is creating. However, in the film, Ivan circulates his image as a still photo. In an ironic twist, although Ivan asserts his celebrity status through visual presentation, he gains his celebrity status by evading police and disappears from public view. He disappears in the flesh only to re-emerge as an icon. Going to the movies provided formative experiences for Ivan when he first arrived in the city. And when all other routes to prosperity and celebrity have closed, he returns to self-representation and the bravado he had seen in westerns shown in Kingston at the Rialto.

□ CASE STUDY 3: *BAMBOOZLED* (SPIKE LEE, 2000)

In his satire *Bamboozled* (2000), Lee tackles the history of black images in the film, television, and music industries. Pierre Delacroix (Damon Wayans), a television writer, dreams up the most racist TV show he can in order to undercut his boss Dunwitty (Michael Rapaport), who has dismissed his previous efforts as culturally inauthentic. The idea was that the show – a minstrel show based on the variety format, featuring blackface, plantation scenery, physical comedy as well as song and dance – would be so obviously racist that no one could accept it. Delacroix and his assistant Sloan Hopkins (Jada Pinkett-Smith) hire a homeless tap-dance duo that had been performing regularly in front of his office building to play the lead roles. Delacroix calls the show *Man Tan, the New Millennium Minstrel Show*, featuring the tap-dancer Manray/Mantan (Savion Glover) and his comic sidekick Womack/Sleep-n-Eat (Tommy Davidson). *Man Tan* is a hit and Delcroix becomes trapped in his own joke because no one understands the show as satire. Various audiences receive his satire about minstrelsy and its cast of stereotypes as cutting edge, controversial, and entertaining.

The sequence where Delacroix pitches the show to Dunwitty is instrumental due to

• **Plate 12.4**
Bamboozled (Spike Lee, 2000). Dunwitty (Michael Rappaport) surrounded by photographs of famous African American sports heroes. 'African' or African-inspired sculptures are mixed in with his videotapes and CDs. The film touches on a range of media issues related to the representation of people of African descent

its place in the narrative. But it also centralizes and suspends the film's main concern – the question of authenticity in black cultural production. In the sequence, the viewer sees Dunwitty pictured with 'brothers on the wall' behind him. This mise-en-scène is a reference to a scene in Sal's Pizzeria from Lee's earlier film *Do the Right Thing*. Dunwitty's office is decorated with photographs of iconic African American athletes, African statues, and other cultural pieces. This space marks Dunwitty's self-perception as an authority on black American culture. By contrast, Delacroix is framed tightly by the desk, ceiling, and walls while he also appears to lack the kind of cultural backing Dunwitty seems to have. However, when he is shot in profile, he is neatly framed in a curious trinity with photographs of Muhammad Ali and Mike Tyson.

Enter Sloan, Mantan, and Womack. All are surprised to hear that the entertainers will be performing in blackface and Womack is taken aback by his new stage name: Sleep-n-Eat. All five characters sit at Dunwitty's desk/conference table, but creative power is far from evenly distributed. As Delacroix goes on to introduce the show's tagline, 'Mantan and Sleep-n-Eat, Two Real Coons,' the performers react with confusion and Sloan becomes angry. She interrupts Delacroix's presentation to remind him of negative precedents such as protests against the *Amos and Andy* television show. Delacroix presses on and describes a cast of characters that include Topsy and Aunt Jemima, classic black stereotypes. In many ways, this sequence repeats a familiar and straightforward litany of stereotypes. However, it becomes complicated when Dunwitty asks Mantan/Manray to demonstrate his dancing. When Mantan/Manray dances, his personal presence and evident dancing genius almost cancel out politically correct assumptions about his racist stereotypical TV role. For atop the conference table, Manray drops the 'Mantan' and seems to rise above the roles assigned to him. He is not

• **Plate 12.5**
Bamboozled (Spike Lee, 2000). Womack (Tommy Davidson) and Manray (Savion Glover) discuss the implications of their new-found success as stars of *The New Millennium Minstrel Show*, in which they perform in blackface. An American nineteenth-century phenomenon, blackface is both a theatrical make-up style (using burnt cork or greasepaint) and a performance genre that combined music and comedy to effect racist caricatures of African Americans

Sloan's social problem, nor is he Womack's sidekick or meal ticket. And he temporarily slips the yoke of Delacroix's minstrel type-casting.

In a sense, the viewer sees Manray suspended amid several distinct but interrelated points of view. The dramatic tension in the sequence arises from the coexistence of Manray's gifts as a dancer and the limited roles available to him for its expression. In this sequence, Manray references the history of black performance within stereotypical roles. And throughout the film, actors who performed within the entertainer's double-consciousness, such as Bert Williams, Bill Robinson, Stepin Fetchit (Lincoln Perry), and Mantan Moreland, are cited through clips and in the dialogue. The entertainer's double-consciousness is, as the actor–comedian Dave Chappelle put it, a question of dancing or shuffling. The audience's reception and the performer's self-view depend on a finely tuned ability to perceive the nuances of authorship.

In a revealing interview published in the Sunday May 15, 2005 edition of *Time Magazine*, Dave Chappelle struck the central problematic of African American cinema when he said: 'I want to make sure I'm dancing not shuffling.' With these words, Chappelle expressed the burden of his historical consciousness or, as W.E.B. Du Bois would put it, his double-consciousness. Building on this meaning, the actor's historical consciousness refers to his professional double-bind. At once a comedian and a member of an economically marginalized yet culturally influential minority group, Chappelle has a difficult public role to negotiate. His dancing/shuffling dichotomy evokes the blurry line that exists in comedy between jokes that he feels reflect his intelligent social observations and command of his craft, and those that merely play into the long-standing stereotypes and racist clichés reserved for and expected of both comedians of African descent and the community as a whole. It is the difference between having an audience laugh with him – that is, shocked, tricked, or persuaded to see the world through the eyes of a brilliant comic – or having them laugh at him when black identity or experience itself is seen as or made into a joke. The processes of viewing, producing, and performing cinematic representations of African Americans are all informed by Chappelle's problematic to some degree. Analysis of these works must take it into account as well. How to acknowledge or move beyond the troubling history of racist imagery in film without repeating or reinscribing it? How do performers honor the past without stifling their own creativity? How to recognize and analyze the tension between the person working as an actor and the persona that he or she creates for a public? In many ways, Chappelle's recent film *Dave Chappelle's Block Party* (Michel Gondry, 2006) seeks to return black performance to its community by both expanding and localizing a hip-hop sense of space. With Brooklyn as the site for the concert featuring The Roots, Jill Scott, Mos Def, and other 'conscious rappers' Chappelle seeks to create a home base for music that has become international and maybe rootless in some ways. His candid, desultory conversations with the musicians and a variety of his neighbors in Ohio breathe new life into a severely commodified aspect of black art – performance.

CONCLUSION

This chapter has explored a few of the major approaches to African American cinema and offers an introduction to the unique role of performance in this group of films. Moreover, it offers an innovative way to think about the representations of peoples of color on the complicated twenty-first-century screenscape. Performance studies, film studies, and literary studies all combine here to create an interdisciplinary humanistic method in order to gain a greater capacity to observe, describe, analyze, and explain the enactment or performance of ethnic and/or racial identity in cinema. Race and ethnicity are taken as cultural constructs that are normalized through repetition and circulation, often facilitated by media images. Film plays a central part in shaping perceptions of particular ethnic and racial groups due to its capacity for repetition and its realist claims and conventions. African American cinema, because of its diasporic position between Europe and America, provides a rich case for examining not only film's international circulation but also the intertwined social and aesthetic implications of its technologies.

FURTHER READING

Alexander, E., '"Can You Be BLACK and Look at This?": Reading the Rodney King Video(s)', in *The Black Interior*, Graywolf Press, St Paul, MN, 2004, pp. 175–205.

Alexander, G., *Why We Make Movies: Black Filmmakers Talk About the Magic of Cinema*, Harlem Moon, Broadway Books, New York, 2003.

Anderson, B., *Imagined Communities: Reflections on the Origin and Spread of Nationalism*, Verso, London, 1983, pp. 41–64.

Baldwin, J., *The Devil Finds Work*, Dial Press, New York, 1976.

Bhabha, H.K., *The Location of Culture*, Routledge, London and New York, 1994.

Billops, C., Griffin, A. and Smith, V., Black Film Issue, *Black American Literature Forum*, 1991, 25: 2.

Bobo, J. (ed.), *Black Women Film & Video Artists*, Routledge, New York, 1998.

Bogle, D., *Toms, Coons, Mulattoes, Mammies, and Bucks: An Interpretive History of Blacks in American Films*, Continuum, New York, 1998.

Bowser, P., Gaines, J. and Musser C. (eds), *Oscar Micheaux and His Circle*, Indiana University Press, Bloomington, 2001.

Center for Contemporary Cultural Studies, *The*

Empire Strikes Back: Race and Racism in 70s Britain, Hutchinson, in association with the Centre for Contemporary Cultural Studies, University of Birmingham, London, 1982.

Cham, M.B., *Ex-iles: Essays on Caribbean Cinema*, Africa World Press, Trenton, New Jersey, 1992.

Cooper, C., 'Slackness Hiding from Culture: Erotic Play in the Dancehall', in *Noises in the Blood: Orality, Gender, and the 'Vulgar' Body of Jamaican Popular Culture*, Duke University Press, Durham, 1995.

Cripps, T., *Black Film as Genre*, Indiana University Press, Bloomington, 1978.

—— *Slow Fade to Black: The Negro in American Film, 1900–1942* (2nd edn), Oxford University Press, New York, 1993a.

—— *Making Movies Black: The Hollywood Message Movie from World War II to the Civil Rights Era*, Oxford University Press, New York, 1993b.

Davies, J. and Smith C.R., *Gender, Ethnicity and Sexuality in Contemporary American Film* (2nd edn), Keele University Press, Edinburgh, 2001.

Diawara, M. (ed.), *Black American Cinema*, Routledge, New York, 1993.

Du Bois, W.E.B., *The Souls of Black Folk: Essays and Sketches*, Signet, New York, 1995.

Dyer, R., *White*, Routledge, London, 1997.

Ellison, R., *Shadow and Act*, Vintage International, New York, 1964.

Gaines, J., 'White Privilege and Looking Relations: Race and Gender in Feminist Film Theory', in S. Thornham (ed. and intro.), *Feminist Film Theory: A Reader*, New York University Press, New York, 1988.

Gates, H.L. Jr., 'New Negroes, Migration, and Cultural Exchange', in Elizabeth Hutton Turner (ed.), *Jacob Lawrence: The Migration Series*, Washington, DC, Rappahannock, 1993.

Guerrero, E., *Framing Blackness: The African American Image in Film*, Temple University Press, Philadelphia,1993.

hooks, b., *Black Looks: Race and Representation*, South End Press, Boston, MA, 1992.

—— *Reel to Real: Race, Sex and Class at the Movies*, Routledge, New York, 1996.

Hurston, Z.N., 'What White Publishers Won't Print', in A. Walker (ed.), *I Love Myself When I'm Laughing*, The Feminist Press, New York, 1979, pp. 169–173.

Julien, I., 'Black Is, Black Ain't: Notes on De-Essentializing Black Identities', in G. Dent (ed.), *Black Popular Culture*, Bay Press, Seattle, 1992.

Lanier-Seward, A., 'A Film Portrait of Black Ritual Express: The Blood of Jesus', in G. Gay and W.L. Baber (eds), *Expressively Black: The Cultural Basis of Ethnic Identity*, Praeger, New York, 1987.

Lee, S., *Spike Lee's Gotta Have It: Inside Guerrilla Filmmaking*, Fireside, New York, 1987.

Lee, S. and Jones, L., *Do the Right Thing*, Fireside, New York, 1989.

Lubiano, W., 'But Compared to What? Reading Realism, Representation and Essentialism in *School Daze*, *Do the Right Thing*, and the Spike Lee Discourse', *Black American Literature Forum*, Vol. 25 No. 2 (Summer 1991), 253–81.

Martin, M. (ed.), *Cinemas of the Black Diaspora: Diversity, Dependence and Oppositionality*, Wayne State University Press, Detroit, 1995.

Massood, P.J., *Black City Cinema: African American Urban Experiences in Film*, Temple University Press, Philadelphia, 2003.

Memmi, A., *Dominated Man*, Beacon Press, Boston, 1968.

Morrison, T., *Playing in the Dark: Whiteness and the Literary Imagination*, Harvard University Press, Cambridge, MA, 1992.

Pines, J. and Willemen, P. (eds), *Questions of Third Cinema*, BFI, London, 1989.

Reid, M., *Redefining Black Film*, University of California Press, Berkeley, 1993.

Rhines, J., *Black Film/White Money*, Rutgers University Press, New Brunswick, NJ, 1996.

Rony, F.T., *The Third Eye: Race, Cinema and Ethnographic Spectacle*, Duke University Press, Durham, 1996.

Sampson, H.T., *Blacks in Black and White* (2nd edn), Scarecrow, Metuchen, NJ, 1995.

Shohat, E. and Stam, R., *Unthinking Eurocentrism: Multiculturalism and the Media*, Routledge, New York, 1994.

Smith, S.M., *Photography on the Color Line: W.E.B. Du Bois, Race and Visual Culture*, Duke University Press, Durham, 2004.

Smith, V. (ed.), *Representing Blackness: Issues in Film and Video*, Rutgers University Press, New Brunswick, NJ, 1997.

Snead, J., 'Images of Blacks in Black Independent Films: A Brief Survey', in M.B. Cham and C. Andrade-Watkins (eds), *Blackframes: Critical Perspectives on Black Independent Cinema*, Cambridge, MA, Celebration of Black Cinema, MIT Press, 1988, pp. 16–25.

Snead, J., *White Screens, Black Images: Hollywood from the Dark Side*, ed. C. McCabe and C. West, Routledge, New York, 1994.

Stewart, J. N., *Migrating to the Movies: Cinema and Black Urban Modernity*, University of California Press, Berkeley, 2005.

Wallace, M., *Dark Designs and Visual Culture,* Duke University Press, Durham, 2004.

Warner, K., *On Location: Cinema and Film in the Anglophone Caribbean*, Macmillan Education., London, 2000.

Yearwood, G., *Black Film as a Signifying Practice: Cinema, Narration and the African American Aesthetic Tradition*, Africa World Press, Trenton, 2000.

FURTHER VIEWING

1915	*Birth of a Nation* (D. W. Griffith)
1920	*Within Our Gates* (Oscar Micheaux)
1929	*St. Louis Blues* (Dudley Murphy)
1933	*King Kong* (Merian C. Cooper and Ernest B. Shoedsack)
1934	*Imitation of Life* (John Stahl)
1939	*Gone with the Wind* (Victor Flemming)
1941	*The Blood of Jesus* (Spencer Williams)
1948	*The Quiet One* (Sidney Meyers)
1964	*Nothing But a Man* (Micheal Roemer)
1968	*Symbiopsychotaxiplasm: Take One* (William Greaves)

1973	*The Harder They Come* (Perry Henzell)
1973	*Wattstax* (Mel Stuart)
1976	*Car Wash* (Michael Schultz)
1977	*Killer of Sheep* (Charles Burnett)
1979	*Bush Mama* (Haile Gerima)
1984	*Hairpiece: A Film for Nappy-headed People* (Ayoka Chenzira)
1985	*The Color Purple* (Steven Spielberg)
1989	*Do the Right Thing* (Spike Lee)
1991	*Boyz in the Hood* (John Singleton)
1991	*Daughters of the Dust* (Julie Dash)
1997	*Dancehall Queen* (Rick Elgood and Don Letts)
1998	*Tree Shade* (Lisa Collins)
2000	*Bamboozled* (Spike Lee)
2001	*That's My Face* (Thomas Allen Harris)
2002	*String of Pearls* (Camille Billops and James Hatch)
2004	*Reckless Eyeballing* (Chris Harris)
2005	*Symbiopsychotaxiplasm: Take 21/2* (William Greaves)
2006	*Dave Chappelle's Block Party* (Michel Gondry)

RESOURCE CENTRES

http://www.Indiana.edu/~bfca/index/html
Black Film Center/Archive, Indiana University.

http://blackfilm,uchicago.edu/
Black Film Research Online, University of Chicago.

DVD, Zora Neale Hurston's Fieldwork Footage.
More Treasures from American Film Archives, 1894–1931. Program 3. National Film Preservation Foundation, 2004.

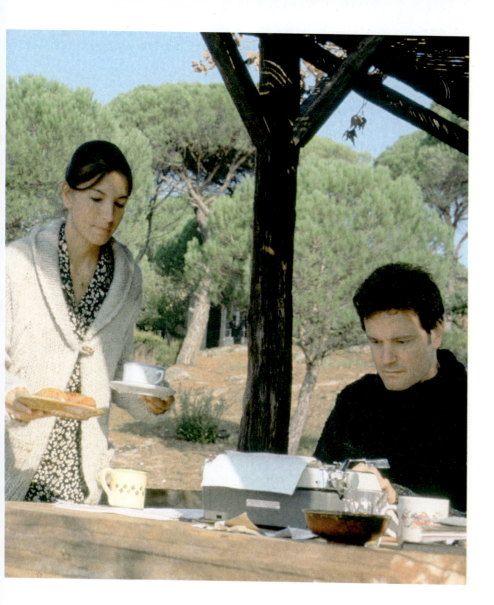

Part six

Cinema, nationhood and national identities

Studying national cinema: case studies

Chapter 13

British cinema

Lawrence Napper

■ British cinema[1]

DEFINING BRITISH CINEMA

What do we mean when we talk about 'British cinema'? Are we referring to a commercial industry, to a particular body of films made in Britain, or more abstractly to a particular style of filmmaking or set of narrative and thematic conventions?

This chapter will attempt to suggest some ways in which we might think about British cinema, both as a commercial industry, and as a set of films made by that industry from 1895 to the present. It will be arranged chronologically into sections, and organised thematically into two strands. The first strand will deal with filmmaking and film-going as a practice – a commercial industry involving **producers**, **distributors**, **exhibitors** and audiences. Recurrent themes in this strand will include the dominance of Hollywood films in British cinemas, different forms of state provision to protect and develop the British film industry, the production policies and economic fortunes of various companies, and film-going as a changing social habit. The second strand will deal with the films themselves as texts, both in terms of the ways in which they represent the nation, and in terms of their visual and narrative aesthetics. Recurrent themes in this strand will include representations of class, gender and ethnicity, 'realism' versus 'fantasy', individual desire versus consensus politics, discussion of key genres such as the working-class comedy, the adaptation and the historical film. The discussions will be designed to both evoke and interrogate key debates and accounts of British cinema, attempting to reframe some of the main assumptions about how films have engaged the film-going audience over the past century.

To begin with let us return to the question of how we define a film as 'British'. This has always been a knotty problem, partly due to the cultural proximity between Britain and America and the dominance of Hollywood films on British screens. While many other national cinemas have the ready distinction of language to mark their productions as nationally specific, the shared language of Britain and America means that the definition of a 'British film' is rather more leaky. The lack of a language barrier means that while on the one hand Britain represents Hollywood's primary export market, on the other hand British films sometimes have the opportunity to become mainstream popular hits in America. This 'special relationship' may be seen as both a blessing and a curse.

British films which gain successful distribution in America are often partly funded by American companies, raising questions as to how 'British' they really are. Many critics suggested, for example, that *Notting Hill* (Roger Michell, 1999) was effectively a Hollywood production as a result of its international funding structure, despite its British characters and setting, and its largely British cast and crew. The accusation of a Hollywood 'taint' appeared to be strengthened by the content of the film. The 'transatlantic' nature of the story, dealing with a romance between a glamorous Hollywood star and an unassuming 'ordinary' Englishman, and the sanitised nature of the film's portrayal of London as a set of picturesque tourist spaces, suggested that a primary concern for the filmmakers was to please American audiences by confirming their fantasies about what Britain was like. One might argue that these criticisms of *Notting Hill* stem from a long tradition of anxiety over American economic and cultural domination of British life which, as we shall see, has had important consequences for the history of the British film industry.

In fact, the funding structure of *Notting Hill* was more multinational than such criticism suggests, with funding coming from major European companies such as Polygram, as well as American distributors. The multinational nature of British film finance may be seen by looking at some of the other films in which *Notting Hill*'s production company Working Title has been involved. These include what seem like resolutely American films, such as

production
Division of the film industry concentrating on the making of film.

distribution
Division of the film industry concentrating on the marketing of film, connecting the producer with the exhibitor by leasing films from the former and renting them to the latter.

exhibition
Division of the film industry concentrating on the public screening of film.

40 Days and 40 Nights (Michael Lehmann, 2002), as well as films such as *Shaun of the Dead* (Edgar Wright, 2004) whose humour is built around apparently more specific British settings and characteristics.

How, then, can we define a 'British' film, and indeed, why would we want to? One might suggest that there are two possible ways of defining a film as British, as well as two possible incentives for doing so – economic and cultural. On the one hand, we can see a film as an economic product. The film industry in Britain employs technicians and actors, and it generates revenue from box-office takings both at home and abroad. As with any other industry, the government has an interest in maintaining this industry for the economic health of the nation. An economic definition of a British film might consider matters such as who financed it, how many British subjects were employed in making it, whether it was shot in British studios and locations, and whether the production company is registered in Britain. These kinds of definitions tend to be important *because* of the government's interest in encouraging the survival of the industry. Since 1928 a variety of schemes have been in place to support the British film industry, and each of these has had to come up with a workable definition of what constitutes a British film, to enable officials to determine which productions should enjoy the tax breaks and other incentives offered to such films.

On the other hand, we can see film as a cultural product. Films do not just make (or lose) money. They are also cultural objects which both 'reflect' the nation back to itself, and 'project' an image of Britain and what it means to be British to audiences at home and abroad. This 'cultural' definition of British films is not unrelated to the economic one. One of the most important 'invisible' results of successful British films is the extent to which they boost the tourist and travel industry – a fact which has been recognised since the mid-1920s. They also boost other industries, acting as a 'shop window' for British products as various as cars, clothes and music. Again this effect was recognised as early as the mid-1920s, and has been an important factor in the government's attitude to the film industry ever since.

As well as advertising British goods and landscapes though, films also advertise British 'values'. One might well debate exactly what British 'values' are, and it is a version of this debate which occurs whenever two people have a discussion about the relative merits of different British films. Is *Notting Hill* an adequate representation of our national life – is it how we want to see ourselves and be seen by others? Or is *Trainspotting* (Danny Boyle, 1996) a preferable example? Would we prefer to be understood through the restrained historical passions of *Pride and Prejudice* (Joe Wright, 2005) or the more contemporary exuberance of *Alien Autopsy* (Jonny Campbell, 2006)? Who are 'we' anyway? And who is the intended audience for these representations of 'us'?

British films are often criticised for portraying a very narrow view of British life – a tendency to show England over Scotland, Wales or Northern Ireland, and a tendency to show southern, white, middle-class England at that. One can identify similar biases in Hollywood films of course, although they don't tend to be discussed so urgently, and it is worth questioning why not. Nevertheless, with regard to British films, one might suggest though that over a century of filmmaking in this country has produced an enormous variety of representations, stories, narrative styles and visual aesthetics. It is difficult – probably impossible – to sum up an entire nation's filmmaking output in a single sentence, or even a few thousand words, let alone give a comprehensive account of how those films came to be made and were seen. In what follows I shall try to draw out the main historical changes to the industry, and some of the major traditions of representation which that industry developed. The chapter is intended to provide you only with an overview of British cinema. Many aspects of the material are contested and the Bibliography at the back of the book will point you to books and essays where some of the interpretations are debated and fought over, and where you can explore them in more detail. The account here is by no means exhaustive or unbiased – don't be afraid to find out new films for yourself, and use them to challenge my account. (For key essays on the historiography of British cinema, see Barr 1986; Higson 1989; Lovell 2003.)

For a case study on the films of Mitchell and Kenyon see pp. 178–80.

FROM PIONEERING TO PROTECTION

Fairground exhibition to picture palace

The recent discovery and restoration of over 800 films made by Sagar Mitchell and James Kenyon between 1900 and 1913 has created an enormous revival of interest in Britain's earliest filmmakers. Based in Blackburn, Mitchell and Kenyon and their agents worked throughout the North of England filming short local scenes of people leaving factories, processions, street scenes and sporting events. These '**actualities**' were often commissioned by showmen who were operating touring **cinematograph** shows in fairgrounds and wanted local scenes which would encourage audiences to pay to see themselves or their towns on the screen. Fairground exhibition – travelling cinemas – was a common way for people to see films in the first ten years of cinema from 1895 to 1905, when cinema itself was still a novelty, and a number of early films were made by travelling showmen. Film shows were also offered as part of the evening's entertainment at the local music-hall, as an interlude between live acts – although, of course, the presence of a 'lecturer' describing what was going on in the film, and of musicians providing accompaniment, meant that there was always an element of live performance as part of the cinematograph show. Alongside local actualities of the type produced by

actuality
Early term for a short, non-fiction film.

cinematograph
Early term for cinema. Initially it referred to the camera/projector, but soon came to be used to refer to the practice and the exhibition space.

• **Plate 13.1**
Mitchell and Kenyon – local films for local people

trick film
The generic term for the development of cinematic special effects using such techniques as **mattes**, **multiple exposures**, **proto-animation** and **substitution techniques**. Generally attributed to the pioneering French filmmaker George Melies.

Mitchell and Kenyon, audiences would have seen fictional and **'trick' films** as well as short narratives and reconstructions of current news events (Toulmin *et al.* 2004).

As films ceased to be a novelty, a number of key changes took place in the way they were both produced and exhibited. As the popularity of the pictures grew, it became financially viable to show films in a dedicated venue to which audiences returned week after week. Instead of touring the same films round to different audiences as the travelling showman had done, the proprietors of these fixed-site cinemas found it necessary to obtain new films every week to keep the audience coming back. It was no longer possible to buy a few films outright and make a living out of showing them again and again in different venues. Exhibitors began to obtain their films through a distributor, who supplied films on a rental basis, sending out new films each week. Thus the roles of film producers and exhibitors became more specialised, and the financial interests of each group became more divergent. Even as early as 1905 the demand for new films meant that the film industry was an international one. Distributors carried films made in France and America as well as British productions, and audiences were as likely to see foreign films as British ones. Indeed, this international film trade was fiercely competitive, American companies had formed a trade combine which sought to exclude European films from the lucrative American market, and European producers fought to protect their interests. Even at this early stage the British film industry was caught between America and Europe.

Until the mid-1950s, film was made from a material called silver nitrate which is extremely flammable – it burns very intensely producing a lot of heat, and is almost impossible to extinguish. Fairground cinematograph shows and early cinemas, which often contained the projector in the same space as the audience, were very prone to fires. Housed in a tent or a cheaply constructed wooden building, and often packed with people, fires in these venues were particularly dangerous, and after a number of high-profile disasters the government took action, passing the Cinematograph Act of 1909. This stipulated various stringent building safety measures designed to reduce the risk of fires and ensure adequate escape routes. The projector, for instance, had to be separated from the audience and contained in a fire-proof booth, and no cinema could operate without a licence from the local authority. The 1909 Act had three major effects. First, it meant that fixed-site, purpose-built cinemas became the dominant – if not the only – method of film exhibition. Second, it gave local authorities considerable power over exhibitors through the licensing system. Local authorities soon used this power to close down cinemas not only when they were contravening the safety regulations, but also when they showed films that local magistrates considered morally unsuitable. This led directly to the formation of the British Board of Film Censors in 1912. The BBFC was an industry body which sought to stabilise what had rapidly become an inconsistent and *ad hoc* local censorship system. Third, the 1909 Act, in demanding a specially constructed or converted building for film exhibition, forced exhibitors to invest much more capital in their businesses. As a result, exhibitors tried to safeguard their investment by attempting to attract more middle-class patrons to their 'well-appointed' cinemas – patrons who would pay higher admission prices if they felt they were partaking of a 'quality' leisure experience. The new censorship board was a useful tool in this drive towards moral and social 'uplift', breaking the association of film with cheap, working-class and morally suspect entertainment. The campaign was only partly successful however, and although it did gain some respectability among lower middle-class patrons, the cinema remained a resolutely mass entertainment. That distinction, though, is important for understanding some of the marketing strategies employed by British producers, as we shall see below.

newsreels
Films consisting of six or seven short topical news stories released to cinemas twice a week and shown as part of the full supporting programme. Newsreels were produced from the 1910s to the early 1970s by which time they had largely been overtaken by television news. They were also shown in specialist news cinemas, often located in or near big railway stations.

By the end of the First World War in 1918, the British film industry was roughly structured in a way that is still recognisable even today. Narrative feature films lasting around ninety minutes were the core of the cinema programme, although they were supported by a selection of shorts, **newsreels** and cartoons. Films were shown in specially built cinemas which were to be found in every town. The smaller cinemas of the 1910s were gradually being replaced by the picture palaces of the 1920s – much larger and plusher venues, sometimes boasting cafés, dance-halls, ushers, and even small orchestras to provide accompaniment for the silent films. Perhaps most importantly, as today, the vast majority of the films shown were made in Hollywood. Thus, while for British exhibitors the film trade was booming, this was mainly on the back of imported American productions (Eyles 2003; Higson 2002).

American films had come to dominate the British market during the First World War, and they were able to maintain this position for a variety of reasons. First, the American companies had already recouped the production costs of their films in their vast home market, so they could afford to offer British exhibitors the films at considerably lower prices than the British producers against whom they were competing. Second, from the early 1920s onwards they began to take advantage of this economic strength through an aggressive trade practice known as 'block booking'. Exhibitors were offered two or three films which were likely to be big box-office hits, but only on condition that they also booked a large number of smaller films of unknown worth. Effectively, exhibitors were forced to book an entire season from one distributor if they wanted to be sure of obtaining the most important and lucrative films. For the British producers this made life very difficult indeed. It was hard enough to raise the capital to make a film at all. With the vast American market closed to them, the films they made had to be relatively cheap so that they could ensure they covered their costs with box-office revenue from Britain alone. However, even once the film had been completed, it could be six to eight months before the film could be released to the cinemas, clogged up as they were with Hollywood films, which had been more expensively made but which were being offered to exhibitors at a cheaper price than their British competitors. The instability of this economic situation remained relatively unattractive to investors, thus undermining further the viability of filmmaking in Britain.

Despite these rather hostile conditions, British filmmakers persevered, adopting a variety of methods for making their films financially viable, distinctive and attractive to audiences. American executives at the time (and later) maintained that British films were not as successful because they were inferior to Hollywood productions, and until recently this judgement was accepted and repeated by both historians and critics (Low 1971). However, more recent accounts tend to stress the distinctiveness of British filmmaking in the 1920s not as inferiority, but rather as part of an explicit marketing strategy which sought to develop a 'national' style of filmmaking, understood to be purposely different from the more popular Hollywood product. To be sure, the films looked very different from the Hollywood productions against which they competed. They were slower, with less emphasis on goal-directed narrative, and more on pictorial composition. They tended to draw on representational traditions from outside cinema – literary and theatrical sources, painterly styles. The rhetoric around them emphasised the idea of preserving the best of British culture, of offering something more than the lowest common denominator. Another strategy adopted by British filmmakers throughout the 1920s, and in an increasingly organised manner from around 1926 onwards, was to forge alliances with European producing companies. During the silent period, language did not present the same kind of barrier to international European co-production as it does today, and this policy was enthusiastically pursued, particularly between Britain, Germany and France on the hope that a Europe-wide market would give producers a similar economic advantage to that enjoyed by Americans with their continental-sized home audience (Burrows 2001; Higson and Maltby 1999).

Nevertheless, throughout the 1920s concerns were expressed about both the weakness of the British film industry, and about the effect that exposure to so many American films might have on the British population. As ever, it was a combination of economic and cultural concerns which attracted the attention of the government. 'People are being taught to think and feel in ways that are not British', worried Sir Philip

Cunliffe-Lister in 1927. As President of the Board of Trade, his anxiety was not just confined to the people's thoughts and feelings – they were also being taught to desire American consumer goods and to buy them in preference to British ones. It was not only British audiences who were a cause for concern, Hollywood films dominated the exhibition sector throughout the Empire, and in various other international markets, where they acted as advertisements for American consumer goods to the detriment of British trade.

After a long period of consultation and lobbying from the various sectors of the film trade, the government finally passed the Cinematograph Act of 1927. This Act, which came into force in early 1928, is the most important piece of British legislation dealing with cinema, because it established the principle of governmental support for the British film industry. That acknowledgement of film as both an economic and cultural contribution to our national life which is worth supporting is one which (apart from a brief period in the 1980s) has been maintained by successive governments through a variety of different mechanisms ever since. The mechanism which was put in place in 1927 was that of the Quota. Each exhibitor was required by law to show a certain percentage of British films in their cinemas, and each distributor was required to carry a certain percentage of British films on their books. The percentages were set to rise year on year until the Act's renewal in 1938 when they would stand at 20 per cent, thus creating and maintaining a steady demand for British films. In addition, the practice of 'block' booking was outlawed. The Act also established a working definition of a British film as one made by a British subject or a company constituted in the British Empire, of which the majority of the directors would be British. All studio scenes were to be shot in the Empire, with no less than 75 per cent of the labour costs being paid to British subjects (excluding copyright payments and the wage of one foreign actor or producer) (Street 1997, 2003).

British scenes on British screens

Even before the discovery of Mitchell and Kenyon's films, British filmmakers of the earliest period were already regarded among film historians to be the most innovative in the world. Those working with film from 1895 to 1900 tended to have 'day' jobs in related activities. Chemists, photographers, inventors, showmen and magic lanternists, they came to film as genuine pioneers, experimenting with both the technology and the language of cinema. The films were initially single shots taken from a fixed camera position, and lasting only around a minute. They consisted of both actualities – filmed records of real places and events – and little scenes or 'attractions' staged especially for the camera. R.W. Paul, an engineer based in Hatton Garden, was one of the earliest of the film pioneers. His film *The Derby* of 1896 is a good example of an actuality. It was especially successful with audiences, recording as it did a celebrated win by the Prince of Wales's own horse. The *Strand Magazine* pronounced it a 'sensation', and described his process of 'lightening photography' in great detail, making clear that in this early stage the technology of moving pictures itself was as much an attraction as their subject matter. The article also emphasised the commercial aspect of Paul's work, describing how he processed the film overnight so that it could be shown the following day at the Alhambra Theatre. The Derby film survives, showing the horses rushing past the camera and the crowd running on to the course once they have passed – ineffectually supervised by a number of policemen.

A good example of an attraction staged purely for the camera is G.A. Smith's *The Miller and the Sweep* (1897). Smith, a showman and hypnotist, was one of a number of pioneers based around the Brighton and Hove area. His film, like many others around this period, is based on a scene or joke which was already popular as a subject for still photographs, cartoons and music-hall sketches. The miller (white with flour) and the sweep (black with soot) have a fight, covering each other with flour and soot. This extremely visual subject was given extra attraction by Smith, who staged it in front of a windmill whose moving sail increases the amount of movement in the frame. He also tacks on a chase at the end of the film, with the miller and sweep pursued apparently at random by a crowd of extras.

Such one-shot films quickly gave way to more complex, multi-shot scenes, and the variety of innovations and experiments evident in the various films of this period is immense. Two of Smith's later films give an indication of the speed of developments. In 1900 he produced *As Seen Through a Telescope* which introduces a brief narrative, involving editing and point of view – two of the cornerstones of narrative cinema even today. Our hero gets a closer look at a girl's ankle by the use of a telescope. We too are treated to the erotic spectacle, thanks to the insertion of a close-up point-of-view shot, although it is only the man who is subsequently punished. *Mary Jane's Mishap* (1903) again uses the close-up and various match-editing techniques to suggest links in time and space, as well as a **wipe** to indicate a temporal and spatial **ellipse**. Like *As Seen Through a Telescope* it suggests a mischievous moral ambivalence. Mary Jane, a lazy housemaid, tries to light the fire with paraffin. She gets blown up, but who has the last laugh?

Questions of ideology go hand-in-hand with developments in film language and narrative concerns. A famous example which combines all three areas is Cecil Hepworth's *Rescued by Rover* (Lewis Fitzhamon, 1905). A nursemaid is so busy flirting with a soldier that she fails to notice a gypsy stealing the baby in her charge. Rover, the family dog, however, is able to sniff out the culprit and victim. His search takes him from the posh end of town, over a river to a garret in the slum areas. Having made the discovery he returns home to alert the child's father and lead him back to his lost progeny. This film is widely celebrated for the sophistication of its spatial editing. Action is matched across the various scenes of Rover's journey, showing him moving repeatedly from top right to bottom left of each camera set-up, and vice versa for the return journey. The ideological centrality of the stable bourgeois family unit is emphasised not only in a narrative which sees it disrupted and then restored, but also in a final emblematic shot showing the

wipe
Transition between shots where a vertical line sweeps across the screen taking us from one scene to the next.

ellipse
A gap in the continuity of time and space of the narrative – usually indicated in editing by means of a **dissolve** or **wipe**.

reunited family group (and dog). Much is made of the apparent bourgeois morality of Hepworth's film, but it should be pointed out that there are plenty of examples of films at this time which take a positive delight in portraying criminals outwitting the forces of authority. See, for example, *Desperate Poaching Affray* (1903) made by William Haggar (a Welsh travelling showman), which is often cited as the inspiration for Edison and Porter's *The Great Train Robbery* (Edwin S. Porter, 1903) (Barr 2003).

Many of the pioneers of British cinema, including R.W. Paul and G.A. Smith, had dropped out of the industry by the outbreak of the First World War, moving on to other inventions, or back to their original trades. Cecil Hepworth, though, remained centrally concerned with filmmaking throughout the rest of his life. His company took its place among the growing number of British production companies of the 1910s organised along commercial lines to take advantage of the new mass medium. Hepworth's company was in the forefront of such developments as the rise of the **star system** and the development of fan magazines. In accordance with the movement for 'uplift' around 1910, Hepworth's company made adaptations of Dickens and Shakespeare, filming the famous actor Johnston Forbes-Robertson as *Hamlet* (Hay Plumb, 1913). By the early 1920s they were making feature-length adaptations of novels and plays, usually featuring his biggest star Alma Taylor, and set in well-photographed rural landscapes (Burrows 2001).

The collapse of Hepworth's company after *Comin' Thro the Rye* (Cecil Hepworth, 1923) in 1924 was until recently attributed to his 'backward-looking' cinematic style and business policy. When compared to American films circulating at the same time, Hepworth productions seem rather slow. Not a fan of Hollywood editing styles, he preferred to shoot scenes in long takes using quite frontal set-ups, rather than dissecting the space through structures such as the **shot-reverse-shot**. His films were, however, consistently praised for the quality of the photography, and his shooting style tended to emphasise the picturesque settings of the stories, which most often dealt with English rural life. Particularly good examples of this style include *Tansy* (Cecil Hepworth, 1921) which features Alma Taylor as a shepherdess forced to chose between two suitors, and *The Pipes of Pan* (Cecil Hepworth, 1923), a story inspired by a popular and much reproduced watercolour of the period by Estella Canziani. Both films deal with the threat to rural life presented by modernity, combining nostalgia with narratives about socially mobile characters whose personal fortunes threaten the stability of the social order (Gledhill 2004; Higson 1995).

It is now increasingly accepted that rather than evidence of naivety or incompetence, Hepworth's apparently idiosyncratic shooting style was a conscious attempt to differentiate his British productions from their American competitors, providing them with a distinctive 'national' filmmaking aesthetic which created a particular market appeal. As we have seen, Hepworth was not alone in this project. For instance, Stoll, the biggest British production company of the period, introduced a series of adaptations of popular novels under the banner 'Eminent British Authors'. Eschewing stars, Stoll's adaptations relied on the notion of the pre-sold popular literary property as the guarantee of wholesome entertainment. Exploiting more populist if no less distinctively British policies, George Pearson had a series of hits in the early 1920s with his star Betty Balfour in the role of *Squibs* (1921), a cockney flower girl with an irrepressible sense of humour and a persistent tendency to mock social pretension. The films were extremely popular with audiences, not least because of their East End settings and Balfour's considerable comic charisma. Other producers of the period pursued links with European companies in an attempt to increase the possible distribution for their films while also creating a product distinctive in style from Hollywood. Perhaps the most famous company founded during the latter half of the 1920s was Michael Balcon's Gainsborough Pictures. The success of Gainsborough was partly the result of the way it combined all three of the production strategies outlined above. The company is probably best remembered as the place where Alfred Hitchcock got his start at directing, first in Germany, and later in

See Chapter 6 for further discussion of the star system.

star system
The industrial apparatus which enables the building up of stars and their centrality to the advertising and promotion of films. This includes star contracts, ancillary advertising deals, fan magazines and so on.

shot-reverse-shot
Editing technique whereby conversations are filmed by cutting alternately between the faces of the interlocutors who are facing each other.

• Plate 13.3
Tansy (Cecil Hepworth, 1921). Showcasing the English rural landscape

Britain with his celebrated thriller *The Lodger* (1927) – a film whose 'German' influences have been much commented on. Gainsborough attracted a number of other talented directors, stars and writers, including Britain's top box-office attraction of the 1920s Ivor Novello, who appeared in a series of racy dramas as an apache underworld character known as 'the Rat' (Cook 1997; Napper and Williams 2001; Ryall 1996).

Maurice Elvey's *Hindle Wakes* (1927) made for Gaumont-British (a company which would soon combine with Balcon's Gainsborough) is a particularly interesting example of the kind of output being produced in Britain by the late 1920s. Adapted from a (then) famous stage play by Stanley Houghton, it tells the story of a Manchester cotton worker and her family. While on holiday in Blackpool she has a liaison with the son of the mill owner which threatens both families with shame and ruin. Negotiations among the older generations result in an agreement that the two young people should marry in order to maintain respectability. In a remarkable twist, however, the heroine rejects the arrangement, taking control of the narrative by declaring her independence both from the social mores of her community and from the hypocrisy of the double standard. 'I'm a woman, and I was your little fancy – You're a man and you were my little fancy. Don't you understand?' she explains to her ex-lover. A heroine with such a modern attitude is unusual in any film of this period, and certainly would not be found in any comparable Hollywood production. This is partly because she is the product of her northern social milieu of respectability over 'flash' which is culturally specific enough to be almost untranslatable. Elvey's direction seems designed to do for the industrial landscapes of the northwest what Hepworth was attempting with the rural south – distinctive British settings of the cobbled terraces, and extensive location shooting of the factory interiors and of the fun-fair at Blackpool create an almost documentary-realist feel to the first half of the film, the adaptation opening out the original play to a remarkable degree. Elvey's direction is certainly leisurely, and his emphasis on the details (particularly the use of footwear to indicate the distinction between work and leisure, wealth and poverty), belies a delight in **symbolism** at the expense of **narrative economy**. By Hollywood standards the film is slow, particularly in the later, more stagy scenes. Nevertheless, there are

symbolism
The means by which a filmmaker can assign additional meanings to objects/characters in a film. For example, in Dovzhenko's *Earth* and Eienstein's *Old and New*, the tractor is a symbol of progress.

narrative economy
The efficiency with which a film tells its story. 'Classical Hollywood' films have often been described as having a high degree of narrative economy, with few scenes or shots which do not contribute in some way to the telling of the story. Some genres such as musicals or epics, where spectacle is an important element of the film's pleasures, may be said to have a lesser degree of narrative economy.

some remarkably confident touches of direction. A scene where a next-door neighbour's grief at the death of his daughter is revealed to the family through the sound (visually represented) of his wooden leg as he paces the bedroom floor is every bit as striking and narratively efficient as Hitchcock's celebrated use of a glass ceiling to create a similar effect in *The Lodger*.

By the time the Cinematograph Act was being passed around 1927 then, British filmmakers had acquired the confidence and skill to create some remarkably accomplished and adult films, despite less than ideal financial conditions. Their achievement may have been undervalued or ignored by later film historians because the films were unfamiliar in two senses. Not only did they fail to conform to the expectations of good cinema created by the more dominant Hollywood product, but they were also difficult to access for many years. Only recently has a major re-evaluation of this cinema begun to understand it as striving to achieve a distinctive 'British' cinematic aesthetic. Meanwhile, that re-evaluation has only been possible as a result of their increased availability through archive prints, DVDs and internet resources.

DEPRESSION AND WAR

There is a persistent and often repeated myth that British films of the 1930s rarely contained working-class characters, and that such characters, when they did appear, only functioned as comic stereotypes. Such comments tend to reveal more about the cultural predilections of middle-class critics than the inadequacies of British film producers. Those critics tend to dismiss comedy as insignificant, preferring to see their working-class characters suffering in serious '**realist**' dramas such as the admittedly breath-taking *Love on the Dole* (John Baxter, 1941). Popular audiences, however, held comedy in much greater esteem. They valued the entertainment afforded by the sight of working-class stars cocking a snook at authority in anarchic narratives of social chaos, more than a realist reminder of the all-too-familiar dole queue. In fact the dominant British genre of the 1930s is the working-class comedy, and Britain's biggest stars of

realism/reality
The concept of the 'real' is problematic in cinema, and is generally used in two different ways. First, the extent to which a film attempts to mimic reality so that a fictional film can appear indistinguishable from documentary. Second, the film can establish its own world and can, by consistently using the same conventions, establish the credibility of this world. In this later sense a sciencefiction film such as *RoboCop* can be as realistic as a film set in a contemporary and recognisable world, such as *Sleepless in Seattle*.

• **Plate 13.4**
Millions Like Us (Launder and Gilliat, 1943). Women from disparate social and regional backgrounds come together for the war effort

the decade, George Formby and Gracie Fields, were presiding geniuses, their popularity enabling them to compete effortlessly with the best that Hollywood could offer, while remaining unequivocally specific in their Lancastrian cultural allusions.

Even before it had come into effect, the Cinematograph Act of 1927 produced a vast expansion of the British film industry. With the guarantee of screen space and the promise of a more stable economic future, financiers became much more confident about investing in film. Many new film companies were registered in the late 1920s, although this wave of confidence proved to be premature for many of them, since the coming of sound around the turn of the decade necessitated a huge re-investment both in technology and expertise. Not only studios, but also cinemas had to be converted to sound. Two of the most important companies to survive the transition were notable for being '**vertically integrated**'. Like their Hollywood rivals, British International Pictures and Gaumont British Picture Corporation both produced films, and owned the cinemas in which those films were shown. That was not a new phenomenon in Britain – the Stoll Company of the early 1920s had enjoyed a degree of vertical integration. Nevertheless, the capital investment these two giants put into their production facilities (at Elstree and Shepherds Bush respectively), and into their cinema chains was unlike anything Britain had seen previously, and would not have been possible without the steady flow of money which vertical integration allows. Alongside these two giants, there were various smaller producers operating with varying degrees of independence (Ryall 2003).

The Quota Act meant that all the major Hollywood distributors now also had to carry a certain amount of British films on their books. At best this meant that they were encouraged to make distribution deals with reputable British producers. The partnership between Alexander Korda's London Films and United Artists is the most famous example of such a deal, enabling Korda's film *The Private Life of Henry VIII* (Alexander Korda, 1933) to be distributed through United Artists in America with spectacular financial results. At worst the legislation encouraged US distributors to pay unambitious British producers a pittance to make films as quickly and cheaply as possible in order to fulfil the minimum requirements of the law, and the films that resulted became known as 'quota quickies'. The lamentable quality of such films has been exaggerated over the years with the myth that they were never meant to be seen and the story that they were habitually run in cinemas in the mornings for the cleaners, or last thing at night to chase the audiences home. In fact the evidence suggests that most of these films *were* intended to be seen and to entertain their audience, even if they were produced very cheaply. George Formby's first vehicle was a 'quota quickie', and the kind of broad music-hall humour which made him and Gracie Fields such massive stars was also being employed by Max Miller in a series of 'quickies' made for Warner Brothers at Teddington, as well as a host of other comedians working in both the quota and the 'legitimate' sections of the industry – Leslie Fuller, Will Fyffe, The Crazy Gang, Stanley Lupino and Will Hay to name only a few (Napper 2003).

Perhaps it is more appropriate to think of British films produced in the 1930s as being divided between those intended to compete with Hollywood's output – with high production values and stories which had a chance of appealing to an international audience, and those intended primarily for British audiences without any ambitions to be exported to wider markets. The Formby and Fields films would fit this latter category of '**inexportable**' films. As I have suggested, they were really only the tip of the iceberg of working-class comedies of the period, trading on cultural familiarity rather than attempting to compete with the more glamorous Hollywood productions.

Gracie Fields' popular nickname of 'our Gracie' indicates the kind of familiarity her star persona encouraged – a relationship with her fans which Jeffrey Richards describes as being akin to that of a big sister. Gracie's ordinariness was constantly emphasised in a string of narratives which placed her at the caring centre of her working-class community, whether as the social welfare officer of a factory in *Sing as We Go* (Basil Dean, 1934), the waitress in a local café in *Sally in Our Alley* (Maurice Elvey, 1931) or a successful

Compare the British film industry with Hollywood production in Chapter 1.

vertical integration
Where a company is organised so that it oversees a product from the planning/ development stage, through production, through market distribution, through to the end-user – the retail consumer. In the case of the film industry, this translates to a company controlling **production**, **distribution** and **exhibition** of its films.

inexportable
Critical term used to denote films of modest budget and ambition, only intended for distribution to their home markets. Adapted from Jean-Pierre Jeanncolas's use of the term with regard to certain French comedies.

music-hall star returned to help her family fight for the survival of the local market threatened with closure in *Look Up and Laugh* (Basil Dean, 1935). Several films contain scenes where her singing talent takes her out of her own community to perform for her social betters – a situation which leads to comic chaos as her authentic bonhomie is contrasted against their snobbishly polite codes of social interaction. The key register of these films is the tension between Gracie's personal talent leading to individual success, and her commitment to the ordinary community to which she belongs. This value is often embodied in an expressively sentimental song filmed using a motif which cuts between shots of her spontaneous community performance and the rapt, appreciative faces of the listening audience. Whether the listening figures are physically linked in space (for instance, around the street coffee stall in *Queen of Hearts* (Monty Banks, 1936)) or are in different spaces linked only by the editing (as in the 'Wonderful Love' number in *Sing as We Go*), they are nevertheless understood to be linked culturally to Gracie herself and the utopian sense of belonging which she embodies (Richards 1984).

Companies making more internationally ambitious films intended for export included Korda's London Films, which sought to repeat the extraordinary success of *The Private Life of Henry VIII* with a series of historical epics and Empire adventures conceived on a grand scale. These films tended to package British Empire history and landmarks as settings for adventure stories and romance narratives for both home and foreign audiences. In common with British International Pictures (whose films tended to be more modestly budgeted), Korda's product retained a distinctly international flavour as a result of using a range of émigré stars and technicians who had learned their craft in continental Europe. Indeed, it is often forgotten quite how cosmopolitan filmmaking in Britain was – a legacy of both the Film Europe policy of the late 1920s and the rise of European fascism in the mid-1930s (Richards 1984).

Michael Balcon at Gaumont-British also launched a concerted attempt to break into the American market, building up his star Jessie Matthews in a series of lavish modern musicals intended to compete in style and panache with the Astaire–Rogers cycle produced by RKO. A comparison between Matthews's films and those of Fields is instructive. If Fields was firmly rooted in a local community network with overtones of nostalgia, Matthews's character is always much more clearly independent, modern and unencumbered by the pull back to her roots. She was, in fact, rootless – always playing a bright, independent talent on the make in a series of modern urban settings beautifully designed to look glamorous in the Art Deco style by Alfred Junge. Many of her narratives involved her impersonating other people in order to achieve success (her own mother in *Evergreen* (Victor Saville, 1934), a rich society hostess in *It's Love Again* (Victor Saville, 1936), a male–female impersonator in *First a Girl* (Victor Saville, 1935), an international jewel thief in *Gangway* (Sonny Hale, 1937)). In such situations Gracie Fields always revealed herself immediately, sending up the pretence with her earthy Lancashire humour. More was riding on Matthews's impersonations, though, since an unmasking might lead to ruin. It never did, of course, but rather to a demonstration of her real talent, unencumbered by society's expectations. If Fields's films always reconfirmed her status as the moral heart of community life, Matthews' were more concerned with the meretricious rise of the talented individual – a narrative structure which was arguably more in tune with the **classical Hollywood** style. The Matthews musicals did achieve a measure of success in America, despite an unadvantageous distribution structure, and during the mid- to late 1930s it looked tantalisingly as though the dream of British films competing internationally with Hollywood ones might be achievable (Higson 1995; Street 2002).

The dream did not last long though, for despite the production boom, filmmaking in Britain remained an extremely risky investment. A series of financial scandals around 1937 brought about a collapse of confidence, and many of the companies which had pursued more ambitious production strategies (including Gaumont-British) were forced into receivership. The outbreak of the Second World War in 1939 saw the British film industry in a much more inward-looking mood.

classical Hollywood cinema

As described by David Bordwell, Janet Staiger and Kristin Thompson in their book of the same name, classical Hollywood Cinema is both a cinematic style (emphasising goal-orientated protagonists, particular form of economic narrative structure, continuity editing and a particular range of lighting and sound techniques) and a 'mode of production' (the studio system) which dominated American commercial filmmaking from around 1917 to 1960. Bordwell, Staiger and Thompson's account of classical Hollywood Cinema has been very influential, although it has many detractors.

Critics both at the time and since have often judged the Second World War as the period of British cinema's 'Golden Age' – a period where the national crisis seemed to give the project of filmmaking a purpose and an urgency which it had previously lacked. In fact, many of the more celebrated characteristics of wartime filmmaking may be traced back to traditions established during the 1930s, and it may be that the increased respect for British films was as much to do with a shift in the prevailing conceptualisation of the nation as with changes in the films themselves. The political and social divisions which to a certain extent had characterised national life during the depression of the 1930s had surfaced relatively rarely in British films of that decade, to the dismay of many critics who found the popular community optimism of the Gracie Fields cycle and the consensus politics of *The Good Companions* (Victor Saville, 1933) an inadequate substitute for political and social critique. By contrast, during the war both official propaganda and popular sentiment became dominated by the idea of the nation united in a consensus, with the old divisions and political grievances set aside in the face of the larger project of fighting both against Nazism and for a better future. In the popular phrase of the time, Britain was fighting a 'people's war' (Barr 2005; Ellis 1996).

A key film of this transition is John Baxter's *Love on the Dole* (1941), adapted from a Walter Greenwood novel of 1933 which had been considered too politically sensitive for a film treatment during the 1930s. It tells the story of a family living under the grinding poverty of unemployment during the depression of the early 1930s. No comic relief or uplifting community musical numbers are introduced to lighten the entertainment (although they abound in the director's other films). The downbeat ending of the film shows the daughter sacrificing her virtue to a man she doesn't like in order to vouchsafe the economic stability of her family. At the very close of the film this mood of hopelessness and despair is firmly placed in the past by a written title quoting A.V. Alexander (a Cabinet member in the wartime coalition government) which draws a wartime conclusion, pronouncing that 'Our working men and women have responded magnificently to any and every call made upon them. Their reward must be a new Britain. Never again must the unemployed become the forgotten men of peace.'

Forging a 'new Britain' through the necessary consensus of wartime struggle is an insistent theme of the most celebrated of the British films of the war period. Many such films share a narrative structure which brings together a range of individuals from different regions and social backgrounds, uniting them in the common public enterprise of the war, either as an army unit in *The Way Ahead* (Carol Reed, 1944), the crew of a battle cruiser in *In Which We Serve* (David Lean, 1942), a group of women factory workers in *Millions Like Us* (Launder and Gilliat, 1943), or a rural community of army trainees, land girls and village residents in *A Canterbury Tale* (Powell and Pressburger, 1944). The relationship between public and private life is a particularly important theme of such films, which often emphasise the sacrifice of individual desire to the greater benefit of the group, or the melding of individual and community goals. This theme is emphasised in all of the films through a mixture of aesthetic styles – a union between fiction and documentary techniques which was widely celebrated by critics. The tradition of British documentary films, begun in 1929 by John Grierson's *Drifters*, had been the most intellectually influential aspect of British filmmaking in the 1930s, and that documentary movement came into its own during the war period with the massive expansion in state sponsorship for documentary and propaganda films, particularly through the Ministry of Information (British documentary cinema is discussed in more detail in Chapter 8). The combination of documentary and fiction aesthetics (and personnel) in wartime British cinema is demonstrated, for instance, by the fact that *The Way Ahead* is a reworking of an earlier short training film, *The New Lot* (1943) made by Carol Reed for the Army Kinematograph Service, and by the fact that *Millions Like Us* began life as a commission from the Ministry of Information (Chapman 1997).

In its combination of melodrama and documentary realism, *Millions Like Us* is a particularly good example of consensus wartime filmmaking. As its title suggests, the film is concerned to tell the story of ordinary people and how they are affected by the war. The first half of the film introduces Celia, played by Patricia Roc, as simply one of a large range of characters responding to wartime conditions in short episodic scenes. Some of these scenes are pure documentary (the building of an aeroplane), and many show incidents and characters unrelated to the central lower middle-class family group to which Celia belongs. Only around forty minutes into the film does the heroine begin to take centre stage as she is transported out of her home to join a group of women from different social backgrounds at work in an aircraft factory. Her romantic fantasises of uniformed war service are firmly set aside by the ordinariness and lack of glamour in factory life. She does meet and marry an airman, but her personal happiness is cut short when he is killed in action. This narrative of personal desire and sacrifice is set against other scenes which show the initial class tensions resolving into a later unity between the disparate group of women working alongside Celia in the factory. An extraordinary final sequence set during a community concert in the factory canteen draws Celia (and us) back from her personal grief into the caring bosom of the newly formed social group, and through an editing motif already established earlier in the film, makes this process of accepting private sacrifice for public good a metaphor for the 'new Britain' that is being fought for. This is achieved literally through deflecting Celia's gaze into the camera upward through a visual and aural **dissolve** to the silhouettes of the bombers above, going out on another night operation. Personal and public sacrifice for the future are made one and the same act (Higson 1995).

Millions Like Us and the other consensus films were not naive about the impermanence of their wartime politics. In a telling and much cited scene immediately before its emotional ending, the characters speculate over whether the togetherness of the war period will remain once peace is achieved, or whether 'we are going to slip back'. Other films of the period continued traditions developed in the 1930s – the low-budget working-class comedy remained a staple, as evidenced by the continuing popularity of George Formby and figures such as Old Mother Riley – an anarchic washerwoman played by Arthur Lucan in a series of low-budget films. There was also a crop of new comedians transferring their talents from successful wartime radio comedies. Not surprisingly, many films and audiences of this period firmly turned their backs on the war as a subject, preferring escapist fantasies, and a particularly popular genre of the later war years was the historical melodrama, as produced by the Gainsborough Studios. In contrast to the consensus cycle, the Gainsborough melodrama resolutely privileged individual desire, ambition and sexuality over community responsibility or sacrifice. Commonly set in Regency England, the films provided an opportunity to revel in a sensuous visual aesthetic, particularly in the costuming and set designs, as well as in full-blooded narratives of sexual desire, jealousy and revenge. *The Wicked Lady* (Leslie Arliss, 1945), for instance, starred Margaret Lockwood as a bored aristocrat seeking thrills through a double life as a cross-dressing highwayman, killing off rivals and enjoying a torrid affair with the dangerously attractive James Mason. Her punishment and death at the end of the film seemed a small price to pay for ninety minutes of passionate adventure. These films were dismissed out of hand by critics of the period, but they were massively popular with audiences, regularly topping the box office charts, and feminist critics in more recent years have celebrated their frank portrayal of unencumbered female sexuality (Cook 1996; Harper 1994).

Box-office attendance was at its peak during and just after the war years, helped no doubt by fuel and food rationing, and a whole host of wartime hardships which made going to the cinema the most attractive of a very limited range of leisure options. As we have seen, British filmmaking was also enjoying a critical renaissance. American films still dominated British screens, of course. *Gone with the Wind* (Victor Fleming, 1939) was the biggest box-office attraction throughout the war years, although MGM's series of 'British' dramas, particularly *Mrs Miniver* (William Wyler, 1942) starring Greer Garson as a 'typical' English wife and mother coping in the early years of the war, were extremely

dissolve
Transition between shots with the first shot fading out to be simultaneously replaced by the second shot fading in. Often used to indicate an **ellipse**.

popular. It is worth comparing Hollywood's *Mrs Miniver* with British films dealing with similar subject matter, such as *Millions Like Us.* The differences, in terms of narrative, settings, characters and filming style, are very revealing of the different priorities of the two national film industries.

While the exhibition sector was enjoying a boom, the British production sector was going through a major period of transition following the financial collapse of the late 1930s. It was partly on the back of that collapse that J. Arthur Rank entered the industry, and quickly rose to become a key figure. Rank's fortune was originally in flour milling, and his initial interest in cinema had been as a means of Christian education – a staunch Methodist, Rank also proved to be an extremely astute businessman. During the late 1930s and early 1940s he made a series of key purchases until by the middle of the war he controlled enough of the industry for his involvement to be the subject of a monopoly enquiry. Rank's empire included not only the ownership of various studios, and interests in most of the major producing companies, but also importantly the Gaumont and the Odeon cinema chains. With a fully vertically integrated concern, the ambition to break into the American market, and the ability to invest heavily in that attempt, Rank quickly became the key figure of the British film industry both during and for a long while after the war.

GOLDEN AGE TO NEW WAVE

Filmmaking in Britain from the war to the early 1960s was dominated by the figure of J. Arthur Rank, whose company continued to juggle the two alternative attitudes to filmmaking in Britain established in the 1930s. Rank made various attempts to break into the American market with expensive quality British productions, yet he also funded a series of more modestly budgeted and culturally specific films intended for purely domestic consumption. The contrast between these two policies was most clearly marked in the mid- to late 1940s. The critical success of many British wartime productions both at home and in America led Rank to believe that with the lifting of restrictions in the postwar period, British films had a real chance of breaking into the lucrative American market. As early as 1944 he had opened a distribution office in New York which was designed to distribute quality British films in America under the descriptive trademark 'Eagle–Lion'. This was a period where Rank was investing heavily in British film production. He instituted a financing mechanism known as 'Independent Producers' which granted a remarkable degree of financial and artistic freedom to a small number of extremely talented British filmmakers working under several different production companies. It was through this arrangement that some of Britain's most prestigious and iconic films were produced, including *Henry V* (Laurence Olivier, 1944), *Brief Encounter* (David Lean, 1944) and *The Red Shoes* (Powell and Pressburger, 1948). These films, one might suggest, share a visual flamboyance and emotional expressiveness which may only be described as 'cinematic', belying British cinema's more usual reputation for social realism, literariness and emotional restraint (MacNab 1993; Petley 1986; Street 2002)

The narrative theme of *Brief Encounter*, for instance, is the repression of excessive romantic emotion, and yet the film employs a series of cinematic techniques in its lighting, camerawork and use of sound which can only be described *as* excessive. Consider an early scene where the heroine, Laura, is on a train with a talkative friend, beginning for the first time to reflect in voiceover on the extra-marital affair she has just ended. The cinematic shifts in emphasis – the slow, almost imperceptible movement closer to Laura's face, the darkening of the light around her, the fading-in of the music – all violently interrupted by the return to reality when her friend makes small-talk, contribute to provide us with an unequivocally subjective emotional viewpoint on the action, allied with that of the heroine. The film later makes fun of excessive romanticism in Hollywood films of the time, but in its meticulous way, one might argue, it is much more committed to 'violent emotion' than to the 'ordinariness' which it appears to foreground (Dyer 1993; Lant 1991).

While the Independent Producer system of finance led to films of high quality which certainly gained British cinema a critical reputation abroad, the freedom it gave filmmakers could also prove to be extremely expensive. For instance, due to its protracted shooting period, *Caesar and Cleopatra* (Gabriel Pascal, 1945) became an industry byword for wasteful and expensive filmmaking. Although they did find a market in America, on balance these expensive prestige films did not turn a large enough profit to justify Rank's investment and so the 'Independent Producer' system did not survive for very long.

By contrast, Rank also controlled Gainsborough Studios. Operating outside the 'Independent Producers' umbrella, Gainsborough was expected to continue producing its spectacularly successful historical melodramas and comedies within the context of tightly controlled budgets and production schedules. The films were intended to make their money back within the British market, so they were both more modest and much more culturally specific than the Independent Producers' films. Gainsborough's productions in the late 1940s took on a more contemporary flavour under the management of Sydney Box, whose sister Betty Box was put in charge of the company's studios in Islington. The production emphasis was on light comedies adapted from stage successes such as *Miranda* (Kenneth Annakin, 1948), and social problem films such as *The Good Time Girl* (David MacDonald, 1948). Perhaps the most indicative and indeed generative of the studio's films during this period was the series initiated by *Holiday Camp* (Kenneth Annakin, 1947) introducing the Huggetts, a lower middle-class suburban family who featured in a series of four films over the next two years. Modestly budgeted and not intended for export, the Huggett films had an episodic structure which made light comedy out of familiar contemporary situations and domestic tensions. Their continuity of casting and setting, and their episodic structure gave them a reassuring familiarity akin to later television soap operas. These features also give them an affinity with a range of later 'inexportable' comedy cycles which came to dominate the industry during the following three decades, beginning with Betty Box's biggest hit as a producer, *Doctor in the House* (Ralph Thomas, 1954). Looking back on her time at Gainsborough, Box ruefully compared the strict economy and box-office reliability of the studio's films with the high expense and uneven returns of those made under 'Independent Producers' (Ashby 2000).

One of the few studios not affiliated with Rank during this period was Michael Balcon's Ealing Studios. After his drive for international success at Gaumont-British had failed, Balcon had moved to Ealing where throughout the war he had produced modest, well-crafted films with a definite consensus flavour. The famous postwar series of 'Ealing Comedies' including *Passport to Pimlico* (Henry Cornelius, 1949), *The Lavender Hill Mob* (Charles Crichton, 1951) and *The Ladykillers* (Alexander MacKendrick, 1955) retain some aspects of the 'consensus' tradition, although they now have the reputation for cosy optimism. Possibly this characteristic has ensured their lasting popularity with certain American audiences, but as Charles Barr points out, the struggle between personal greed and community values which they dramatise is generally darker and more fraught than is often acknowledged, particularly in the work of directors such as Alexander MacKendrick and Robert Hamer. Ealing's distinctive production style, which owed much to the ethos of collaborative filmmaking encouraged by Balcon, was also evident in its non-comedy films, and might be summed up by Balcon's suggestion that in order for cinema to be international it must first be truly national (Barr 1998).

By the early 1950s it had become clear that Rank's ambitions to break into the lucrative American market were costing far more money than they were likely to generate, and the organisation began to steadily modify its ambitions and cut back its operating costs. As part of this strategy the Gainsborough studios were closed down, and most of Rank's production activities became concentrated at Pinewood Studios. The 1950s saw a steady decline in cinema attendances, as television became increasingly popular following the Coronation in 1953 and the introduction of ITV in 1955. Throughout the 1950s, in common with Hollywood producers, Rank retained a notion of cinema as 'family' entertainment in its attempts to compete with television. Comedies and war films predominated in the production schedule and at the box office, and Rank built up a roster of male stars whose appeal was curiously of the age. Kenneth More, John Mills and John Gregson would make unlikely stars today, but they were the epitome of masculine glamour in the 1950s, often playing tweed-clad, pipe-smoking, honourable war heroes in films such as *Reach for the Sky* (Lewis Gilbert, 1956) and *Above Us the Waves* (Ralph Thomas, 1955). These popular 1950s accounts of the war tended to emphasise individual heroism and action much more than the films made during the conflict itself, although always within the context of the 'group'. Rank was not the only company to draw on such material – the Associated British Picture Corporation, the other main, vertically integrated British film company at this time, was responsible for the highly successful *The Dam Busters* (Michael Anderson, 1954), for instance (Harper and Porter 2003).

Rank's most successful male star of the 1950s was even more unlikely. Norman Wisdom made an unexpected hit at the box office as the hapless stockroom boy of a department store in *Trouble in Store* (John Paddy Carstairs, 1953), and was immediately signed to star in a series of similar comedies. The Wisdom films continued the tradition established by Formby and Fields in the 1930s. Wisdom always played a character of low status, but with irrepressible energy, optimism and naivety, thrust into a world of deception which he didn't fully understand. The comedy revolved around the tension between his emotional honesty and the less innocent, more high-status figures around him. Like the Fields and Formby cycles, they also relied on an episodic narrative structure which gave full rein to Wisdom's anarchic slapstick humour (the window-dressing incident in *Trouble in Store* provides a perfect example), as well as containing a healthy dose of sentimentality. Norman always fell in love with a seemingly unattainable girl, who he serenaded with his surprisingly pleasant singing voice. Having found a magic formula of low production costs coupled with high box-office receipts in *Trouble in Store*, Rank sought to repeat the strategy with a string of similar Wisdom vehicles. The same may be said of their response to the box office success of *Doctor in the House* (Ralph Thomas, 1954), starring Dirk Bogarde as the diffident medical student Simon Sparrow. Bogarde's Sparrow was a more good-looking, well-heeled and well-mannered character than those played by Norman Wisdom, but the comic tension of the films was similar in that he was an innocent surrounded by heels, humbugs and buffoons. These comedy cycles enjoyed more success at the box office than they did in critical circles, and indeed the British films of the 1950s have generally been thought to be rather lacking in both social realism and cinematic value. In fact a number of films made during the period tackled serious social issues in an adult manner (it is worth noting the remarkable output of the director Basil Dearden in this light); however, the fact that both producers and censors still thought of cinema as primarily a family entertainment medium meant that the treatment of such subject matter remained too generically coded for later critical tastes (Sinyard and MacKillop 2003).

The decisive move away from attempts to appeal to a family audience marks an important transition from the 1950s to the 1960s. Shifts in cinema-going patterns, and in censorship regulations, as well as more general changes in cultural attitudes around the late 1950s, made possible the development of a range of new filmic styles which were directed at more specialised tastes. These films tended to be produced by independent companies, and by comparison with Rank's offerings of the early 1950s they certainly look surprisingly modern, and in many cases much more adult. Hammer Film Productions, for instance, had been making modest crime and science fiction films since the 1930s, but it was with the full-blooded and luridly coloured production of *The Curse of Frankenstein*

(Terence Fisher, 1957) that the company found real commercial success. A series of ground-breakingly graphic and expressive horror films followed. Hammer managed to combine commercial success with relatively small production costs through identifying themselves almost exclusively with the Horror genre – appealing to a niche market, and gaining a reputation for visual and emotional excess (Hutchings 1993).

The biggest critical breakthrough for an independent film, though, was with the production of *Room at the Top* (Jack Clayton, 1959), a film whose 'X' certificate rating indicated a clear rejection of the concept of the family audience as espoused by the Rank Organisation (at this period the Rank chain refused to show X certificate films). *Room at the Top* was hailed as the beginning of a 'new wave' in British filmmaking, and may be seen as initiating a cycle of realist films, including *Saturday Night, Sunday Morning* (Karel Reisz, 1960), *Look Back in Anger* (Tony Richardson, 1958), *A Kind of Loving* (John Schlesinger, 1962) and *A Taste Of Honey* (Tony Richardson, 1961), whose ordinariness of subject matter and settings earned them the description 'kitchen sink dramas'. These films tended to focus on the contemporary lives of ordinary working-class characters. Their settings in industrial northern towns, and their use of exterior locations, genuine working-class accents and understated lighting techniques gave them a much remarked-upon documentary quality, and indeed many of the filmmakers involved had begun as documentary filmmakers. Mostly adapted from the literary works of a new generation of writers and dramatists who had already made a reputation for themselves as 'Angry Young Men', the 'kitchen sink' films often dramatised the tension between their hero's entrapment within a traditional working-class culture, and his desire for something 'better'. The films may be seen as a response to the changes in postwar society engendered by the consumer boom and full employment of the early 1960s, which was beginning to ensure a higher standard of living for many ordinary people. However, they also share something of a nostalgia for old working-class values which they perceive as being under threat from the new consumer culture. This nostalgia, it may be argued, led them into a rather more reactionary political stance than one might expect, particularly around issues of gender. Films such as *Saturday Night, Sunday Morning* and *A Kind of Loving* associate both women and the new consumer culture with entrapment in a domestic sphere which threatens to restrict and feminise their male protagonists. Indeed, these films tend to fetishise the virile masculinity of their heroes at the expense of older characters, and women in particular. Nevertheless, the emphasis on resistance to consumerism – particularly characterised as coming from television, and from America – places the 'kitchen sink' cycle firmly within a tradition of British filmmaking that sought to differentiate itself from Hollywood standards and styles of production (Hill 1986; Murphy 1992).

The filmmakers of the 'new wave' were not the only ones to court a niche audience by apparently recasting the styles and themes associated with British cinema. The opening of *Summer Holiday* (Peter Yates, 1963) seems to deliberately evoke some of the realist clichés of the kitchen sink cycle, only to spectacularly reject them. In drab black and white, a traditional brass band stand on the beach under lowering skies playing the theme tune. It's the kind of traditional British working-class culture for which the kitchen sink cycle held a special affection. The heavens open, however, driving the band and the rest of the holiday-makers under cover. It looks like we might be in for a depressing two hours of realism, but soon Cliff Richard appears driving the London Transport bus in which he's planning to tour through Europe. At this point the film bursts into fabulous Technicolor while Cliff bursts into song, accompanied by the very large off-screen Associated British Studio Orchestra. Outrageous! The film was the first of a string of hits which took advantage of Cliff Richard's massive popularity for a teenage market who saw him as a rock-god to compete with America's Elvis Presley. In fact, of course, the film sounds much more like a conventional musical to us today, but its good-natured, full-colour travelogue through Europe, peppered with light romance and a host of songs, proved extremely successful, and provided a fitting antidote to the dominant image of

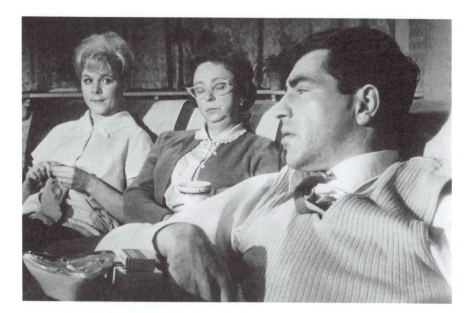

• **Plate 13.5**
A Kind of Loving (John Schlesinger, 1962). Alan Bates is emasculated by marriage and the television

British cinema as one of dour social realism. With prominent product placement for Dolcis and various other manufacturers of teenage fashions, *Summer Holiday* shows none of the anxiety over consumerism demonstrated by *A Kind of Loving*.

In fact, the most successful British film of 1963 was another picturesque Technicolor travelogue, although paradoxically it was made by the team responsible for many of the previous 'kitchen sink' cycle films. *Tom Jones* (1963), Tony Richardson and John Osborne's adaptation of Henry Fielding's eighteenth-century romp, combined the frank sexuality and innovative cinematic techniques of the British new wave with the good nature and colourful visuals of the Cliff Richard films. In order to raise the necessary finance to make such an expensive costume drama, the producers struck a co-production deal with United Artists, ensuring the film prominent distribution in America. The result was an international box-office sensation reminiscent of Korda's *Private Life of Henry VIII* in 1933. Osborne's playful adaptation of Fielding's novel encouraged a series of what at the time seemed like quite startling cinematic innovations – characters speak directly into the camera, chases are speeded up for comic effect, freeze frames are used as in a comic strip, and the pre-credit sequence pastiches the style of silent cinema. All of these techniques constituted an irrevocable break with classical filmmaking conventions, making the film appear both modern and daring. The success of *Tom Jones* in America was guaranteed when the film won the academy award for best film.

As had happened in 1933, the extent of the success of *Tom Jones* in the American market encouraged increased investment in British production during much of the rest of the 1960s. Indeed, with the Hollywood studio system breaking up, American producers themselves were looking more towards international co-productions as a way of funding large-scale projects, and Britain became an attractive option. MGM in fact had been operating a British production unit throughout the 1950s, producing costume dramas and historical epics with an international flavour. During the mid-1960s, with the success of the Beatles and the increasing perception of London as the centre of a fashionable youth culture, British films drawing on and reflecting this culture became an attractive investment proposition. The 'Swinging London' films, as they became known, tended to follow *Tom Jones* in combining elements of 'kitchen sink's' emphasis on sexuality, and youth, with modern, innovative, playful filmmaking techniques. The films were much less ambivalent about modern consumer culture than the 'kitchen sink' films had been, replacing that cycle's nostalgia for northern industrial spaces, with a delight in London as the centre of a happening, modern youth society. Nevertheless, 'Swinging London' films still articulated considerable reservations about the values of that society. Julie Christie as Diana in *Darling* (John Schlesinger, 1965), for example, is punished almost as severely at the end of her ninety minutes of amoral hedonism as Margaret Lockwood had been twenty years earlier at the end of *The Wicked Lady*. Similarly, while Michael Caine as *Alfie* (Lewis Gilbert, 1966) initially seems like a charmer, by the end of the film it is clear both to him and to us that he is less a lovable rogue than a selfish monster.

DECLINE AND REVIVAL

Despite the apparent boom associated with 'Swinging London', and the success of films directed at younger sections of the audience, cinema attendances continued to decline throughout the period from 1946 to the 1980s. The decline of the family audience is reflected in the fortunes of the Rank Organisation which continued to close cinemas in an attempt to rationalise their exhibition circuit. Rank began to diversify into other popular pastimes, and this is the period when many cinemas became converted into Bingo halls. Audiences for individual films became smaller, and it became more financially viable to have one cinema with several small screens, rather than the large single-screen picture palaces which had been in operation since the 1920s. Accordingly many cinemas were converted into multi-screen venues, while others fell into disuse or were converted into other uses.

For film producers as well, raising finance became increasingly difficult. Rank itself diversified away from film production, investing in the Xerox photocopying process – a far more lucrative long-term proposition than filmmaking had ever been. The government commitment to supporting the British production industry which had begun in 1927 remained, although during the 1950s the Quota had been replaced by the Eady Levy. This was a mechanism which diverted a percentage of box-office revenues to a special production fund controlled by the National Film Finance Corporation, which contributed finance to British film projects. Despite such measures, competition from television, the drop in overall attendance and the increasing emphasis on big-budget blockbusters rather than routine programme pictures meant that British filmmakers faced a difficult task (MacNab 1993).

As Rank had already discovered, trying to produce expensive international films that might compete with Hollywood's product was a risky production strategy, although some British films did attain international status, for instance, the James Bond series, which, like the 'Swinging London' films emphasised the modernity and sexual liberation of the hero. The first of the Bond films, *Dr No* (Terence Young, 1962) was made at Pinewood by Ion Productions – an independent production company which rented the studio space and personnel from Rank. Always a common practice, such an arrangement became increasingly dominant, meaning that today British studios often host the production of films which in every other respect are Hollywood products (Chapman 1999).

The international status of the Bond films forms a contrast with the less risky production policy adopted by other producers who placed an emphasis on modestly budgeted features which would reliably appeal to the home market through repeating a familiar and already successful formula. It comes as no surprise that such 'inexportable' film cycles became the mainstay of British production during the 1960s and 1970s. One might argue that the 'Carry On' films and the 'Confessions' series continue the tradition of working-class comedy established by George Formby and Gracie Fields in the 1930s. Made on rigorously small budgets, the 'Carry On' series eschewed stars in favour of a roster of familiar performers, and were reliant on an episodic format and a comedy style rooted in traditions of British music-hall. Beginning with *Carry on Sergeant* (Gerald Thomas, 1958) the series gently sent up British institutions, although later examples took advantage of relaxed censorship rules to use a more smutty and titillating form of humour than was possible on broadcast television at the time. This tendency continued in the 1970s with the rather ruder and less funny cycle initiated by *Confessions of a Window Cleaner* (Val Guest, 1974). The familiarity of the returning cast, the episodic nature of the films and the cycle, and their low production values gave these series an affinity with television aesthetics, and the association is borne out by the fact that the 'Carry On' series made the transition to television through various compilation shows, as well as *Carry On Laughing* (1975), a programme consisting of entirely new sketches made for Thames Television. The symbiosis between television and inexportable British cinema was also evident in the large number of big screen adaptations of familiar TV programmes during the 1970s, including *Doctor Who and the Invasion of the Daleks* (Gordon Flemying, 1965), and comedies such as *On the Buses* (Harry Booth, 1971), *Man About the House* (John Robins, 1974) and *Porridge* (Dick Clement, 1979). While enjoying a dolorous critical reputation, such films nevertheless provided evidence of British filmmakers catering to the comedy tastes of working-class audiences in a way that is often overlooked, even if some of their attitudes towards gender and race now seem embarrassingly primeval.

By the time Margaret Thatcher came to power in 1979, British cinema appeared to have settled into a definite decline. Thatcher's policies did nothing to allay fears for the British industry as it became clear that the legislative protection enjoyed by British filmmakers since the 1920s was anathema to Thatcher's doctrine of the free market. Accordingly, the Eady Levy was scrapped in 1985, and for the first time in sixty years British films had to fend for themselves in the marketplace. Thatcher's apparently philistine attitude towards British cultural life had the effect of dividing, galvanising and politicising the creative community, and British films of the 1980s reflect this in a renewed sense of urgent political purpose. Political, avant-garde and experimental filmmaking had in fact been going on throughout the 1970s, often on small-gauge formats and using miniscule budgets raised through the BFI's production board. An interest in formal experimentation and feminist politics marks the massively influential work of Laura Mulvey, whose films *The Riddles of the Sphinx* (1977) and *Amy* (1980) complement her remarkable critical writings on the representation of women in cinema. Similarly, Derek Jarman's work of the 1970s and into the 1980s, including *Jubilee* (1977) and *The Tempest* (1978), combined experimental techniques with an explicit political intent. During the Thatcherite period, this kind of politically inspired filmmaking became more mainstream, moving (as may be seen with Jarman's career) into a more accessible 'art-house' and festival exhibition context. Meanwhile, the relationship between cinema and television also began to alter as a generation of filmmakers trained in social realist television genres during the 1960s and 1970s tentatively made the transition to the big screen. Low budgets, intimate if political storylines and improvisational styles mark the work of directors such as Ken Loach and Mike Leigh, both of whose careers saw them move from television to film, culminating in a remarkable set of films in the early 1990s which commented on the state of the nation under Tory rule. *High Hopes* (Mike Leigh, 1988) and *Raining Stones* (Ken Loach, 1993) provide excellent examples of the kind of social realist cinema which is often understood to be one of the strongest traditions of British filmmaking (Leigh 2002; Lippard and Johnson 1993).

Perhaps the most significant element of the symbiosis between television and cinema was the launch of Channel 4 in 1982. As part of the new channel's commitment to innovation, 'Film on 4' was established to help fund the production of new British films which would be aired on television after a possible theatrical release. The quality and range of the films produced under this system was remarkable, although the ones which tend to be remembered today are the those which garnered criticism from right-wing critics for their unforgiving portrayals of contemporary life under Thatcher's government – films such as *Letter to Brezhnev* (Chris Bernard, 1985), *My Beautiful Laundrette* (Stephen Frears, 1985) and *Rita, Sue and Bob Too* (Alan Clarke, 1986). These

• **Plate 13.6**
Letter to Brezhnev (Chris Bernard, 1985). Struggling to have a good time in Thatcher's Britain

films adroitly mix comedy and social criticism, telling stories of ordinary people making enterprising choices in order to survive in the harsh economic environment of the period. *Letter to Brezhnev*, for example, celebrates the irrepressible spirit of its two working-class heroines as they determine to have a 'good time' on a night out in Liverpool, despite their poor jobs and lack of prospects. Theresa and Elaine steal money and drinks, and take a joyride, before picking up a couple of sailors from the USSR and spending the night with them. Elaine falls unexpectedly in love with her sailor, and the rest of the film chronicles her desperate attempts to leave Kirkby and join him in Russia, against the wishes of her family and of the British government. As she says, whatever is claimed in the press, 'life in Russia can't be any worse than it is here'. Famously made on a shoestring, but very successful at the box office when it finally achieved distribution, *Letter to Brezhnev* oscillates between broad comic optimism, intense romantic lyricism and, at its heart, an overwhelming despair at a society that can offer its resourceful heroines no alternatives other than a fantasy escape to the USSR, or a life of 'drinking vodka, fucking men and stuffing chickens' (Friedman 1993; Hill 1999).

By the mid-1990s with the advent of Tony Blair's New Labour government, representations of the northern working-class scene became slightly less politically embattled, although films such as *Trainspotting* (Danny Boyle, 1996) and *Brassed Off* (Mark Herman, 1996) still expressed considerable concern over the disenfranchisement of certain areas and industries. The ambivalence of Renton's position in *Trainspotting*, for instance – his initial rejection and then monstrous embrace of enterprise culture – provides a good indication of the mixed response to Blair's doctrine of the 'third way'. *Brassed Off*, by contrast, with its insistence on community solidarity and affection for traditional culture even in the face of a despairing acknowledgement of its imminent demise, shows a political conviction which even at the time of its release seemed old-fashioned. Indeed, in films of the 1990s it is possible to identify a shift away from a focus on class towards one on gender, and this is reflected too in the critical debates surrounding them. The massive success of *The Full Monty* (Peter Cattaneo, 1997) would seem to have had more to do with its fantasy about the repackaging of a masculinity understood to be in 'crisis' than with the structural unemployment of which its male characters were the primary victims. According to *Billy Elliot* (Stephen Daldry, 2000), the destruction of an entire industrial community and way of life is a small price to pay for enlightened masculine attitudes to the ballet. The film's setting during the 1984 miner's strike is used merely as a background, against which Billy's heart-warming story of individual achievement over adversity can be contrasted, and no actual discussion of the politics of the strike is allowed to mar the inspirational storyline. Nevertheless, it was partly this glossing of the political and cultural specificities of these stories that enabled their huge international appeal (Murphy 2000).

While such films attempted to deal with the contemporary realities of Thatcher and Blair's Britain, the other major cycle to emerge during the 1980s and 1990s appeared to look back nostalgically to a more elegant age. The massive international commercial and critical success of *Chariots of Fire* (Hugh Hudson, 1981) was reminiscent of the reception of *The Private Life of Henry VIII* and *Tom Jones* earlier in the century. As on those occasions, this success led to a great deal of optimism about a coming renaissance of British filmmaking, and a renewed confidence in the ability of British films to break into an international (and particularly an American) market. Like its predecessors, *Chariots of Fire* was a costume drama celebrating an aspect of Britain's cultural heritage – the story of the 1924 Olympic running team and the tension between the 'gentlemen' and the 'professionals'. The **mise-en-scène** of the film has since been widely discussed as central to its success – the beautiful cinematography creating an image of Britain as a 'heritage' site, with emphasis on the historic buildings of Cambridge, the country houses of the Home Counties and the wild mountains of Scotland. Certainly in its opening sequence the film establishes a visual aesthetic of well-composed shots containing beautiful objects and scenery which was repeated enough in subsequent British films for them to have been increasingly written about as a coherent genre which became labelled 'Heritage' films. These productions, which include later international successes such as *A Room with a View* (James Ivory, 1985), *Maurice* (James Ivory, 1987), *The Remains of the Day* (James Ivory, 1993), *Sense and Sensibility* (Ang Lee, 1995), *Wings of the Dove* (Ian Softley, 1997), *Elizabeth* (Shekhar Kapur, 1998) and *Shakespeare in Love* (John Madden, 1998) have been the subject of fierce critical debate over whether they are ideologically conservative or progressive. Visually, they certainly strive to present an image of Britain as a tourist opportunity, showcasing landscapes, houses and literary history as unchanging and available for inspection in a way that seems to reject the concerns of the social realist films. Nevertheless, as many critics have pointed out, the narrative of these films consistently offers criticisms of the British society they portray. *Chariots of Fire* itself was structured around the tension between those British runners who benefited from membership of the establishment, and those who were treated as outsiders as a result of being Jewish or Scottish Methodist. Many of the other heritage films contained narratives dealing with class and sexuality which would have appeared extremely radical given a contemporary setting; note, for instance, the argument for the acceptance of gay sexuality in *Maurice*, released at precisely the moment when the government was legislating against the acceptance of gay relationships as a 'pretend family relationship'. Critics have identified a widening of the 'Heritage' genre during the 1990s to include more expressive and less restrained filmmaking, particularly after the release of *Elizabeth* in 1998 (Higson 2003; Monk and Sargeant 2002).

The international success of *Chariots of Fire* encouraged its producers, Goldcrest, to fund a series of large budget productions designed to be exported internationally, and during the early 1980s a number of productions demonstrated that British filmmakers could gain a foothold in the international market. Films such as *Gandhi* (Richard Attenborough, 1982), *Local Hero* (Bill Forsyth, 1983) and *The Killing Fields* (Roland Joffe, 1984) drew on various traditions of British filmmaking, demonstrating the potential of British films, although all of their narratives had a significant international dimension. The company came to grief however, when two of its most ambitious and expensive productions failed at the box office. The musical pastiche of the 1950s *Absolute Beginners* (Julian Temple, 1986), and the epic treatment of the American war of independence *Revolution* (Hugh

Mise-en-scène
A theatrical term usually translated as 'staging' or 'what has been put into the scène'. In film, mise-en-scène refers not only to sets, costumes, props and the position of actors, but also to how the scene is organised, lit and framed for the camera. Mise-en-scène is one way of producing meanings in films which can be both straightforward and extremely complex, depending upon the intentions and skill of the director (the metteur-en-scène).

For more detailed discussion of mise-en-scène see pp. 67–77.

Hudson, 1985), had both been conceived on a particularly ambitious scale, and their failure demonstrated again the risky nature of international productions. Despite such risks, internationally ambitious cinema continues to be made in Britain, usually as part of international co-production deals. The success of a range of later international hits, including *Love Actually* (Richard Curtis, 2004) and the cycle initiated by *Harry Potter and the Sorcerer's Stone* (Chris Columbus, 2001) attest to the ability of British films both to reflect and to export British cultural values.

Having hit rock-bottom in 1984, cinema admissions figures began to rise again, and that upward trend is still continuing today. This may partly be the result of the development of 'multiplex' cinemas, the most common exhibition venue today. The advent of video during the 1980s, and more recently DVD, has given an added boost to cinema, both increasing the public's interest in film as an entertainment choice, but also allowing individual films a much longer money-earning life, and thus making them more attractive to potential investors. With the passing of the Thatcher government, some state support for the industry was reintroduced, with a complex system of tax incentives for filmmakers, and latterly through a production fund raised as part of the National Lottery and made available through the Film Council – a government agency created in 2000 to consolidate the administration of various filmmaking funds and initiatives designed to encourage and stimulate the British industry.

The creation of the UK Film Council in 2000 marked the latest in a series of government initiatives to assist the British film industry since the Cinematograph Act of 1927. The Film Council's remit combines commercial and non-commercial aims. On the one hand, it is concerned to support the commercial industry, providing financial and other kinds of assistance at key stages of production in order to ensure that potentially profitable films reach the screen. On the other hand, it has a commitment to widening the range of filmmaking opportunities available in Britain – enabling stories and representations to come to the screen which otherwise would not have been possible. This twin approach is broadly reflected in the two main funds which the Film Council manages. The Premier Fund is used for more potentially commercial projects, and has been instrumental in the production of internationally successful films such as *Gosford Park* (Robert Altman, 2001), *Vera Drake* (Mike Leigh, 2004), *Ladies in Lavender* (Charles Dance, 2004) and *The Constant Gardener* (Fernando Meirelles, 2005). At the time of writing, a number of films are in production with assistance from the Premier Fund, which clearly have international ambitions judging from their casting and storylines. For instance, *Closing the Ring*, directed by Richard Attenborough and due for release in 2007, boasts an international cast and a storyline which spans sixty years, set in Ireland and America. There is a clear tendency towards costume dramas, and dramas dealing with Britain's historical past among these films, although a comparison between films such as *Gosford Park* and *Vera Drake* reveals a very different treatment of such history. More contemporary stories being funded by the Premier Fund include the children's action-adventure film *Stormbreaker* (Geoffrey Sax, 2006).

The New Cinema Fund is designed to enable the production of more modestly budgeted films, with an emphasis on films which are original and innovative, or which represent minority, ethnic or regional communities which are underrepresented in mainstream commercial productions. Over recent years, films which have benefited from this fund include Ken Loach's controversial but award-winning Irish drama *The Wind that Shakes the Barley* (Ken Loach, 2006), *Bullet Boy* (Saul Dibb, 2005) and the mountaineering documentary *Touching the Void* (Kevin Macdonald, 2003). At the time of writing, an adaptation of Monica Ali's successful novel *Brick Lane* is in production with the assistance of the New Cinema Fund. Directed by Sarah Gavron, the story takes place in Britain and India, and focuses on two sisters and their contrasting experiences of the two cultures.

None of these films are funded solely by the UK Film Council – all are productions in partnership with commercial filmmaking organisations, and in many cases the vast majority of the production budget is raised commercially. Many other films of course are made without Lottery funding assistance, although these often tend to be international co-productions involving a consortium of multinational organisations. Nevertheless, such films often have an identifiably British address to audiences, and draw on British traditions of filmmaking. Films such as *Calendar Girls* (Nigel Cole, 2003) and *Kinky Boots* (Julian Jarrold, 2005) draw on specifically British subject matter, making use of British locations, characters and attitudes to tell stories which nevertheless have an international appeal. Indeed, one might see a film such as *Kinky Boots*, with its story of a small family firm fighting to save its future by balancing traditional and modern values, as drawing explicitly on the filmmaking traditions established at Ealing Studios in the early 1950s. The connection with television, established since the 1970s, remains strong, both in terms of funding from organisations such as BBC Films, and in terms of the range of acting, writing and production talent employed in many films. *Confetti* (Debbie Isitt, 2006) is a good example of a film which draws on television talent as well as providing a clever pastiche of popular television formats. One wonders what international audiences would make of its culturally specific humour, although it remains one of the best British films of recent years. Other films with more obviously international appeal – such as the sci-fi comedy *The Hitchhiker's Guide to the Galaxy* (Garth Jennings, 2005) and *Calendar Girls* – nevertheless take as their theme the effects of the exposure of unassuming ordinary 'British' characters – 'little Britons' – to modern international (and intergalactic) cultures. Perhaps the image of Martin Freeman (familiar to British audiences from television's *The Office*) as Arthur Dent, haplessly wondering about outer space in a dressing-gown in search of a nice cup of tea, sums up both the best and the worst of British film culture.

Filmmaking in Britain has always been subject to the dilemma of whether to try to compete with Hollywood's international cinema on its own terms, or whether to try to carve out a more distinctive and individual style, using the modest budgets which purely domestic distribution demands. The massive range of styles successfully adopted by British filmmakers since 1896, and the huge range of representations and pleasures which their productions provide, makes it impossible to talk about a singular national style. Rather, British film history should be understood to offer a range of representational traditions and strengths that can be both built on and added to.

☐ CASE STUDY 1: *LOVE ACTUALLY* (RICHARD CURTIS, 2003)

The poster for *Love Actually* presents it as a Christmas gift, wrapped in red ribbon complete with a tag reading 'From the makers of *Four Weddings*, *Bridget Jones* and *Notting Hill*'. The film is thus marketed as part of the distinctive cycle of British romantic comedies which began with the extraordinary international success of *Four Weddings and a Funeral* (Mike Newell, 1994), and which not only share creative personnel but also key generic characteristics. Richard Curtis as the writer of all the films, and Hugh Grant in a prominent starring role, are obvious similarities, but the films are also all co-produced by one of the most successful British production companies, Working Title. While *Four Weddings and a Funeral* was made in conjunction with Channel 4 on a relatively modest budget, its box-office success allowed the films which followed to be made with much more lavish budgets, and with increasingly international co-production partners. International appeal is very clearly a priority for these films, and indeed one might argue that they all self-consciously reflect on the cultural relationship between Britain and America. *Four Weddings and a Funeral* and *Notting Hill* (Roger Mitchell, 1999) are the most explicit in this exercise. Both films feature Hugh Grant as a diffident Englishman, marked out as 'ordinary' both through his professional and romantic failure, and through his association with a disparate group of 'ordinary' friends, who offer a range of identifications for the audience, not least through being played by actors primarily familiar from domestic television. Both films pair Grant with women who are successful romantically and professionally, and are initially understood to be beyond Grant's reach because of the glamour associated with their American nationality (they are, after all, played by Andie MacDowell and Julia Roberts respectively – a 'Hollywood' touch which is of course the explicit subject matter of *Notting Hill*). The narratives of the films present Americanness as glamorous and strange in contrast to the ordinariness and familiarity of Britishness.

However, like the films of the 'Heritage' cycle, these films also package Britain for an export audience. The London they present is a utopian fantasy of the actual city – it is clean and crime-free. Despite their apparent professional failure, the group of friends live in relatively affluent surroundings, moving between picturesque urban and rural locations, never experiencing material hardship or political disenfranchisement. This utopianism has proved a major sticking point for critics of the Curtis comedies, who accuse them of ignoring the reality of contemporary British lives, and instead presenting Britain as a sanitised, white, middle-class bubble unrecognisable to the majority of the domestic audience. Several commentators, for instance, have pointed to the fact that *Notting Hill* does not contain a single prominent black character, despite being set in an area of London otherwise most famous for its large multi-ethnic population and annual Caribbean carnival. While the issue of race remains unanswerable, one might suggest that concerns over the lack of 'social realism' in the cycle are based on a wilful misreading of the films' generic conventions. Romantic comedies by their very nature present a utopian vision of the city as an organic community. Representations of New York as a utopian community in Hollywood Rom-Coms such as *You've Got Mail* (Nora Ephron, 1998) and *Maid in Manhattan* (Wayne Wang, 2002) do not elicit anything like the same kind of ire as the Curtis cycle does among certain British critics, and it is worth reflecting on our heightened expectations of British films both to represent lives and spaces we recognise as 'authentic' (or as somehow to do with our everyday experience), and to offer us utopian fantasies of romance to which we might aspire.

Love Actually may be said to take some of the familiar aspects of the Curtis cycle to extremes, while at the same time it marks a major modification of the cycle's theme of British–American relations. The film refocuses the hero and group-of-friends structure of the earlier films, presenting instead a series of over ten narratives, each given more or less equal weighting, and each offering a variation on the theme of the love story. This 'portmanteau' structure is by no means unusual in British cinema, and as I have suggested, one of the most persistent traditions of British filmmaking is to emphasise the role of the community (often a metaphor for the 'national' community) over that of the individual hero. Many of the Ealing Comedies (such as *Passport to Pimlico*) are organised in this way, as are the most celebrated British wartime films, including (as we have seen) *Millions Like Us*. More recently, British romantic comedies such as *This Year's Love* (David Kane, 1999) have employed the same structure. *Love Actually* is perhaps the most explicit in suggesting that its disparate characters – loosely linked along a string of friendships, acquaintances and workplace colleagues – might stand as a metaphor for the nation as a whole. Not only that, but the film dares to fantasise a utopian version of that nation in which barriers of class, power and language are permeable in the face of love. This is perhaps most explicitly evident in the plotline involving Hugh Grant as the Prime Minister, falling in love with Nathalie the tea-lady (Martine McCutcheon). Her ordinariness is emphasised both by the actress' association with *EastEnders*, and by running jokes about her weight and her tendency to swear on inappropriate occasions. Through its string of connected characters, the film implies that the whole nation may be only six degrees of separation from the PM, and that coming across him and his family at our local state school Christmas play or carol singing down the road is entirely possible.

Despite this utopianism, the film does not shy away either from bleak storylines (Emma Thompson and Laura Linney act in the centre of narratives of personal sacrifice which offer little comfort for their characters) or from political comment. This political comment is at its most surprising for a film of this sort when it comes to the American–British theme previously so crucial to the cycle. One of the narratives reproduces and gently spoofs the previous films' faith in America as the source of glamorous female sexuality, as well as making gentle fun of the apparent fascination of female audiences in America with diffident English masculinity (a major factor, one might argue, in Hugh Grant's star status, and thus in the financial success of the earlier Curtis films). Kris Marshall plays Colin – a dweeb who cannot get a girlfriend at home and becomes convinced that his only hope is to cross the Atlantic, where American girls are all beautiful, easy, and find British geeks irresistible. On arriving in Milwaukee and walking into a random bar, he finds that all his fantasies are confirmed.

A more serious engagement with British–American relations is worked through the Hugh Grant plot. The first shots of the film show travellers greeting families at Heathrow, and Grant's voiceover comments on the scene, expressing optimism about the presence of love 'all around us'. He mentions the attack on the twin towers in the context of reaffirming optimistic faith in humanity and an explicit rejection of the principles of hate. The comment sets the tone for the whole film, but must also be understood in the context of the moment of the film's release at the end of 2003 – a year which had seen Tony Blair's government follow George Bush's lead in promulgating a war in Iraq, despite considerable domestic opposition, and international controversy over the legality of such an action. It is within the context of liberal anxieties that the Labour government was allowing itself to become a pawn of US foreign policy that we should read one of the key scenes of the film. Grant's PM observes the US president (played by Billy Bob Thornton) slickly using his status and power to place Nathalie in a compromised sexual situation – an act of casual arrogance and domination which stands in marked contrast to Grant's agonised reaction to his own more genuine feelings towards Nathalie. In a press conference immediately afterwards, the Prime Minister surprises the President and everyone else present by spontaneously 'standing up for Britain', suggesting that the 'special relationship' is no longer equal and that from now on Britain will not be bullied by America. The soundtrack in this scene can only be described as stirringly patriotic, and the delighted reaction of the other characters leaves the audience in no doubt as to the film's national loyalties. The scene is remarkable, particularly in a film whose production and marketing strategy is reliant on reaching a popular American audience.

The balance between appealing to domestic audiences and not alienating international audiences is a crucial element in British films with export ambitions, and it is worth thinking about each scene and storyline in *Love Actually* from the perspectives of both of these audiences. The specific cultural resonance of elements such as the appearance of Ant and Dec, the television star persona of Martine McCutcheon, the casual associations of mentions such as 'Wandsworth – the dodgy end', the Welsh accent of the Prime Minister's bodyguard when he starts singing carols, or the familiarity of the Victorian terraced houses where the character lives, all these elements have particular meanings and pleasures for British audiences which may be lost on audiences elsewhere. Is the loss of those meanings catastrophic to their understanding or pleasure in the film? Are there other elements of the film which are likely to carry specific cultural associations which British audiences don't share (Heike Makatsch for instance, is a celebrity in Germany with particular associations for that audience which she brings to her role as Mia) or which have been specifically inserted to increase the international appeal of it (the scenes set in France and America for instance)? Finally, while (despite its multiple narratives) the film does primarily represent a certain kind of Englishness – white, predominantly middle class, London-based – does this mean that British audiences who don't share those ethnic, class and regional affiliations are excluded from its 'national' pleasures? Victorian terraced housing of one kind or another is, after all, occupied by the full gamut of British citizens. Are we more demanding of the representations found in our national cinema than we are of those in international cinemas? What questions do international audiences ask about these films – and about their own cinema when it is designed for export?

☐ CASE STUDY 2: *BULLET BOY* (SAUL DIBB, 2004)

Discussing his ambitions for *Bullet Boy*, Saul Dibb has suggested that he wanted the film to have a 'really strong British flavour – I don't want it to have a glossy feel to it. I don't want it to be sentimental or glamorous.' In its rejection of gloss, sentiment and glamour, *Bullet Boy* may be understood to be the antithesis of the kind of internationally exportable popular film exemplified by *Love Actually*. As Dibb's comments imply, he is drawing on a long tradition of British cinema which, rather than competing with Hollywood, seeks to establish an alternative aesthetic of filmmaking, one which capitalises on the cultural specificities of life in Britain, attempting to tell stories drawn from everyday life in a realistic way. While the generic conventions of romantic comedy push *Love Actually* towards an optimistic and utopian vision of British society as a place of opportunity and goodwill, *Bullet Boy* is more concerned to highlight the specific inequalities and problems of the community which it represents. Many of its characters are trapped within situations which they work hard to resolve, but the odds are stacked against them. In this sense, the film could be seen as a political drama, although it contains no overt political speculation as to the causes of, or possible solutions to, the central dilemma. Instead it concentrates more on creating believable characters and situations, portraying those characters and their motivations as complex and contingent rather than generically coded. Nevertheless, while the film eschews the generic address of Rom-Coms such as *Love Actually*, or the cartoon-like glamour of crime caper gangster films such as *Lock Stock and Two Smoking Barrels* (Guy Richie, 1998), it still employs some generic narrative codes, balancing the demands of realism with those of entertainment. Furthermore, the casting of Ashley Walters in the lead role was a key strategy in marketing the film to young audiences who knew him primarily as Asher D, singer with the 'So Solid Crew', and his much publicised imprisonment for gun possession in 2002.

The film draws explicitly on the star persona of Walters who plays Ricky, a young man who at the opening of the story has similarly just emerged from prison, having served a sentence for a gun-related crime. The story is told through the eyes of his younger

• **Plate 13.8**
Bullet Boy (Saul Dibb,
2003). A low-budget
British feature which
successfully mixes
social realism and
entertainment

brother Curtis, who hero-worships Ricky but is also aware of his mistakes – 'You may find it hard to obtain work with a criminal record' he taunts his brother, reading from a government leaflet. Nevertheless, when the gun re-enters the house, Curtis is drawn to it as an object of fascination. Meanwhile Ricky, despite his best intentions, is drawn back into a cycle of violence between feuding gangs, sparked off by a characteristically trivial incident involving a broken wing mirror. *Bullet Boy* is careful to show Ricky as both trapped by a youth subculture but also integrated into a wider family structure and community network which is in opposition to that culture. He is torn between his street persona and his loyalty to his mother and brother, and the point at which those two worlds of street and family come together is the focus of the film's most emotional scenes, when his younger brother Curtis accidentally shoots a schoolmate. It looks as though, despite his mother's efforts, the cycle of gun violence might be passed from older to younger brother, as the schoolmate reminds Curtis that he has incurred a debt which may have to be repaid later in life, while admiring his gunshot wound as a battle scar. Nevertheless, towards its conclusion, the film holds out a moment of optimism and generic catharsis for the audience – suggesting in a key sequence that Curtis may have the strength of mind to reject his brother's legacy. He leaves his mother in church, inspired by the words of the preacher to finally get rid of the gun – the music of the gospel service on the soundtrack creates a clear emotional cue at this moment of narrative resolution. The use of the music in this scene might be considered in contrast to the gruellingly realist use of sound in an earlier scene where Curtis and his mother visit his schoolmates' parents and attempt to apologise for the shooting incident. The awkwardness of the visit is made viscerally apparent to the audience through the use of sound – and silence.

All of the principal characters of *Bullet Boy* are black – a striking contrast to the cosy tokenism of portrayals of ethnicity in more mainstream British films such as *Love Actually*, and one which reverses the impression given by much casting in Hollywood films. While the black figure of avuncular state authority is a cliché of Hollywood cinema, representatives of state power in *Bullet Boy* are in fact the only white characters in the film – teachers, probation officers, policemen. These characters remain peripheral to the story however, despite the raw power they wield over the lives of the main protagonists (particularly in the scenes of Ricky being released from prison, and with the probation officer). A scene of Curtis in his Hackney school, where the only white character is the teacher, demonstrates the film's commitment both to realism, and to the specificity of its story and location. Some critics have raised concerns about the appropriateness of a white director handling a story so firmly rooted within a black community, but the film is extremely confident both in its assumption that audiences will be able to identify with the principal characters regardless of race, and in the balance it strikes between telling a story which is specific to black urban experience, while nevertheless not producing that experience as an object for inspection 'from outside'. This balance is worth considering in the light of other, more celebrated films dealing with the experiences of British ethnic minorities. *My Beautiful Laundrette* (Stephen Frears, 1985), *Young Soul Rebels* (Isaac Julien, 1991) and *East Is East* (Damien O'Donnell, 1999) provide obvious examples, although the focus of these films tends to be more heavily on the notion of 'multiculturalism' than is evident in *Bullet Boy*.

The reach towards a specific cultural 'authenticity', of course, is part of a long tradition of British filmmaking, which as we have seen blends fiction narratives with documentary aesthetics and production practices. One might trace the impulse to put 'real people' on the screen right back to the early work of Mitchell and Kenyon, by way of the 'New Wave' cycle of the 1960s, the 'Golden Age' of wartime cinema and the celebrated documentary movement of the 1930s. Filmmakers working in this tradition more recently have often been influenced by television experience. Dibb himself has worked extensively as a television documentary-maker (although he is now also working in BBC drama), and *Bullet Boy* was primarily funded in a co-production partnership between BBC Films and the UK Film Council's New Cinema Fund. The film has some clear stylistic similarities to the work of other celebrated British realist filmmakers who began their careers in television, most notably Ken Loach and Mike Leigh. While works such as Loach's *Kes* (1969), *Ladybird, Ladybird* (1994) and *My Name Is Joe* (1998) were not worldwide mainstream box-office hits, they were critical successes which gained small-scale specialist distribution both in Britain and in America, proving the viability of this kind of modestly budgeted national cinema in the marketplace. Nevertheless, in a purely commercial environment, such specialist films would stand little chance of being made, and all to a greater or lesser extent rely on some form of non-commercial funding. They are also notable for their political commitment to showing communities and identities which are underrepresented in mainstream cinema, presenting life experiences in an apparently unmediated way.

Such films are often discussed in terms of realism or authenticity, and it is clear by comparison with a film such as *Love Actually* that there are a set of very different filmmaking principles and generic conventions in play. Working within a tradition established by the films of Loach, Leigh and others, *Bullet Boy* uses professional actors sparingly. The majority of its characters are played by non-professionals, people who live and work in the community being represented, often in the roles they are playing on-screen. Dibb and his co-writer Catherine Johnson devised a narrative based on their research within the community, but they also allowed the actors to improvise much of the actual dialogue in order to achieve a more realistic tone. The film is shot primarily on location in Hackney, using lightweight cameras and in real interiors. The result is precisely the lack of that 'gloss' which Dibb wants to achieve, and yet the film is also highly lyrical in many sequences, making particular use of shots of the landscape from the high-rise viewpoint of Curtis's home, and shots of wastelands and semi-rural locations in late sunlight. Much was made in the publicity for the film of the sense of 'ownership' over the story which members of the local community felt during its making and on its first release – a sense partly engendered by the production techniques of location shooting, use of non-professional actors, improvised dialogue and community research. Whether these techniques result in a heightened authenticity for other audiences, or whether they might be considered as just another set of generic conventions signifying a film aimed at a different kind of film-going audience is a matter for debate. *Bullet Boy*'s distribution history certainly suggests that it has been able to cross generic boundaries and address a range of audiences – originally circulated through festivals as an art-house product, the distributors were able to draw on finding from the Film Council to help them capitalise on the appeal of Ashley Walters to get the film released not just in independent cinemas but also in more mainstream Multiplex venues, particularly around London and other urban areas. Nevertheless, the film did not secure a theatrical release in America.

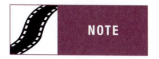

NOTE

1 The author would like to acknowledge the help of James Caterer, Amy Sargeant and Jane Bryan in the preparation of this chapter.

FURTHER READING

Ashby, J. and Higson, A. (eds) (2000) *British Cinema: Past and Present*, London: Routledge.

Babington, B. (ed.) (2001) *British Stars and Stardom: From Alma Taylor to Sean Connery*, Manchester: Manchester University Press.

Barr, C. (ed.) (1986) *All Our Yesterdays: 90 Years of British Cinema*, London: BFI Publishing.

Friedman, L. (ed.) (1993) *British Cinema and Thatcherism*, London: UCL Press.

Higson, A. (ed.) (2002) *Young and Innocent*, Exeter: Exeter University Press.

Murphy, R. (ed.) (2000), *British Cinema of the 90s*, London: BFI Publishing.

Murphy, R. (ed.) (2003) *The British Cinema Book, Second Edition*, London: BFI Publishing.

Sargeant, A. (ed.) *British Cinema: A Critical and Interpretative History*, London: BFI Publishing.

FURTHER VIEWING

This list highlights the films mentioned which are both most easily available and most likely to be productive or representative for teaching purposes. At the time of writing, all the films are available on DVD or (where indicated) on VHS. See also the note in the Resources section about key clips and films available online at www.screenonline.org.uk.

Most of the pre–1917 short films mentioned are available on DVD in the following collections:
Early Cinema, Primitives and Pioneers (BFI, 2005)
Electric Edwardians, The Films of Mitchel and Kenyon (BFI, 2005)

Hindle Wakes (Maurice Elvey, 1927) available on VHS
The Lodger (Alfred Hitchcock, 1927)
Sally in Our Alley (Maurice Elvey, 1931) available on VHS

Sing as We Go (Basil Dean, 1934) available on VHS
First a Girl (Victor Saville, 1935) available on VHS
Love on the Dole (John Baxter, 1941)
In Which We Serve (David Lean, 1942)
Millions Like Us (Launder and Gilliat, 1943)
A Canterbury Tale (Powell and Pressburger, 1944)
Brief Encounter (David Lean, 1945)
The Wicked Lady (Leslie Arliss, 1945)
Passport to Pimlico (Henry Cornelius, 1949)
Trouble in Store (John Paddy Carstairs, 1953)
Doctor in the House (Ralph Thomas, 1954)
The Dam Busters (Michael Anderson, 1954)
The Curse of Frankenstein (Terence Fisher, 1957)
Room at the Top (Jack Clayton, 1959)
Saturday Night, Sunday Morning (Karel Reisz, 1960)
Dr No (Terence Young, 1962)
Summer Holiday (Peter Yates, 1963)

Tom Jones (Tony Richardson, 1963)
Alfie (Lewis Gilbert, 1966)
Carry on Up the Kyber (Gerald Thomas, 1968)
Kes (Ken Loach, 1969)
Get Carter (Mike Hodges, 1971)
Jubilee (Derek Jarman, 1977)
Chariots of Fire (Hugh Hudson, 1981)
Letter to Brezhnev (Chris Bernard, 1985)
My Beautiful Laundrette (Stephen Frears, 1985)
Maurice (James Ivory, 1987)
Four Weddings and a Funeral (Mike Newell, 1994)

Ladybird, Ladybird (Ken Loach, 1994)
Brassed Off (Mark Herman, 1996)
Trainspotting (Danny Boyle, 1996)
The Full Monty (Peter Cattaneao, 1997)
Elizabeth (Shekhar Kapur, 1998)
East Is East (Damien O'Donnell, 1999)
Billy Elliot (Stephen Daldry, 2000)
Gosford Park (Robert Altman, 2001)
Calendar Girls (Nigel Cole, 2003)
The Constant Gardener (Fernando Meirelles, 2005)

RESOURCE CENTRES

The BFI library at Stephen Street in London is the main resource for those interested in further research. In addition, scholars of British cinema are remarkably lucky to have at their disposal an extensive website created by the British Film Institute to encourage study of British films – this includes detailed accounts of many individual films, filmmakers' biographies, interviews, company histories, as well as general thematic articles, and articles dealing with industrial and commercial matters such as censorship and distribution. There are links to the BFI special collections unit and to the BFI Stills, many of whose materials are also available online. For those working within licensed educational institutions it is also possible to download clips from a wide range of key films, many of which are otherwise unavailable. The site also contains considerable amounts of material on British television history. Go to www.screenonline.org.uk.

For current productions, and material about the contemporary British filmmaking scene, a good place to start is the webpage of the UK Film Council at www.ukfilmcouncil.org.uk.

Indian cinema[1]

Lalitha Gopalan

■ INDIAN CINEMA

INTRODUCTION

Even the most casual tourist in India resorts to hyperbole to describe the potency of this cinema that produces a thousand films in more than twelve languages each year. For the uninitiated, most commentators will list implausible twists and turns in plots, excessive melodrama, loud song and dance sequences, and lengthy narrative as having tremendous mass appeal but little critical value. For instance, in his travelogue *Video Night in Kathmandu*, Pico Iyer declares in a significant synecdoche that spills over its own rhetoric: 'Indian movies were India, only more so' (Iyer 1988). Other writers, such as Salman Rushdie, Alan Sealy and Farrukh Dhondy, have used various aspects of Indian film culture to spin fabulous narratives of success and failure, stardom and political life, love and villainy (Dhondy 1990; Rushdie 1988; Sealy 1990). Although the national audience has been its main address, Indian popular cinema or 'Bollywood' has long travelled across the world – the former Soviet Union, Latin America, Africa and Southeast Asia – entertaining audiences whose personal histories bear few ties to the subcontinent.[2] Sometimes, these travel routes are visible on video copies – Arabic subtitles on Hindi films, Malay on Tamil films – telling us of a global set of viewers who watch other national cinemas besides Hollywood. More recently, *Newsweek* reported that Japan is spellbound by Tamil films, especially those starring Rajnikanth, because 'Indian films are filled with the classical entertainment movies used to offer' (*Newsweek International* 1999).[3] In Britain, Indian films are steadily enjoying a cross-over audience which includes the diaspora as well as film-curious non-Indians: Star City, located outside Birmingham, opened on 26 July 2000 and is apparently the largest multiplex in Britain, with thirty screens of which six show Bollywood movies. In the last decade four Indian films have entered the UK Top 20 on release: *Dil Se* (1998), *Kuch Kuch Hota Hai* (1998), *Biwi Number One* (1999) and *Hum Dil de Chuke Sanam* (1999). In June 2000 the Indian equivalent of the Oscar ceremony was held in the Dome in London, hosted by the Indian Miss World Yukta Mookhey.[4] Besides the exhibition of these films characterised by a sensory excess, a range of extra-filmic events encourages us to read beyond the textual operations of individual films, cinematic aesthetics spilling into adjacent consumer economies. It is now commonplace to find the loyal Indian diaspora cultivating appreciation by sponsoring stage shows of film stars, events that read popular films as star-studded texts.

It is important to note, however, that these descriptions of excess cohere most intimately to popular cinema and not the other styles that include alternative, 'parallel', middle and documentary cinemas which also inhabit the cinematic landscape in India albeit in a struggling manner (more on this below). Although it has become common to group together all popular Indian films under the term 'Bollywood', it is important to note that often the production of popular Tamil and Telugu films outpaces that of Hindi, each producing about 150 to 200 films a year, in addition to a steady crop of films from Bengal, Kerala, Maharashtra, Gujarat and Punjab that also populate the regional markets. Among the three largest producers, the Tamil industry is located in Chennai, the Telugu in Hyderabad and Chennai, and Hindi films are produced in Mombai, Hyderabad and Chennai, each marked by its own star system, director, technicians and musicians with occasional cross-over from one industry to another: Malayalam cinematographers working on Tamil and Hindi films, Bengali or Marathi directors directing Hindi films and so on. Such a rich and varied national cinema requires a lifetime to understand its various contours; thus in this chapter we will limit our area of study to popular films produced in the 1980s and 1990s, and to Hindi, Tamil and diaspora productions. The task here is to understand and evaluate the form and address of popular Indian cinema so that even a rank outsider can appreciate its appeal. Such a focus reverses the standard

Bollywood
Bombay, the film capital of India.

study of national cinemas where all too often we are encouraged and even expected to understand the political, social and cultural movements of the nation and region before we can approach the films themselves. Among the many grand histories of Indian cinema, a couple of useful books spring to mind: Barnouw and Krishnaswamy's *Indian Film* (1980) offers a masterful introduction to the world of Indian cinema with its detailed history of cinema in India up until the 1970s, while Yves Thoraval's *The Cinemas of India* (2000) offers an updated version of this grand sweep. Their comprehensiveness and thoroughness provide a useful reference point. but it is impossible for a novice to counter their observations without undertaking similarly extensive archival research. On the other hand, this chapter suggests that an understanding of the form of Indian cinema as a 'cinema of interruptions' allows us to understand the histories of production and reception, albeit in a less sweeping manner. Using case studies to highlight the various critical debates in the study of Indian cinema, this chapter guides the reader through different reading strategies to come to terms with the varying contextual parameters that allow one to understand this national cinematic style within the economy of global cinematic styles.

PRODUCTION AND RECEPTION CONDITIONS

However expansive the influence of cinema, Indian filmmakers are acutely aware that most films fail at the box office. Their financial anxieties have increased in recent years with the rise of adjacent entertainment industries that threaten to diminish the power of films, even if cinema as an institution is not waning in the public imagination. Trade papers from the 1980s record industry fears of the growing video industry that many worried would eventually discourage audiences from going to the cinema. Nevertheless, the arrival in India of video shops also exposed the film-going public to world cinemas, an opportunity afforded previously only by film festivals and film societies. Suddenly films from other parts of Asia, Europe and America were easily available. Filmmakers were also very much part of this video-watching public, freely quoting and borrowing cinematic styles: for instance, director Ramgopal Varma started his career as the owner of a video shop. While a section of the urban rich retreated to their homes, trade papers reported an increase in film attendance in small towns and villages. Instead of assuming that one mode of watching would give way to the next evolutionary stage, we now find films coexisting alongside a robust video economy and satellite cable television. Ironically, both cable television and video shops are also responsible for renewing nostalgia for older films. Together, these different visual media have changed reception conditions by creating an audience which has developed a taste for global-style action films while simultaneously cherishing fondness for the particularities of Indian cinema.

In addition to video and satellite saturation of the visual field, American films (sometimes dubbed into Hindi) started reappearing in Indian cinemas after a new agreement was signed between the Government of India and Motion Picture Producers and Distributors of America, Inc (MPPDA) in April 1985, ending the trade embargo that began in 1971 (Pendakur 1985, 1990). Initially, Indian filmmakers protested against this invasion, but slowly reconciled themselves to the foreign presence after recognising that American films did not in fact pose a threat to Indian film distribution.[5] Occasionally we find characters in Indian films taking pot-shots at American cinema: in Ramgopal Varma's *Satya* (1998), protagonists purposely misread *Jurassic Park* (1993) as a horror film starring lizards; in Tamil films, cross-linguistic puns abound around James Cameron's *Titanic* (1997). These playful engagements with American culture confidently acknowledge that Indian cinema audiences belong to a virtual global economy where films from different production sites exist at the same level – a democratisation of global **cinephilia**. Perhaps I am exaggerating the dominance of Indian cinema, but the confidence of some Indian filmmakers does hold out hopes for unsettling the inequalities

cinephilia
The notion of cinephilia refers to an intense love of, even obsession with, cinema. It implies both a way of watching and a way of speaking about film beyond the standard relationship between cinema and its spectator. Cinephiles are people who, in Andrew Sarris's phrase, 'love cinema beyond all reason', and who engage with film in highly specific ways.

of the global marketplace where we are all too aware of American films unilaterally expanding into newer territories.

Although economic liberalisation opened up Indian markets to a range of television programmes and videos, it also facilitated, however slowly, access to state-of-the-art film technology for filmmakers. Within the industry there have been discernible changes in the production process. According to Manmohan Shetty, who runs a film-processing business, Adlabs, a sea change occurred in 1978 when Kodak introduced a negative film that could be processed at high ambient temperatures (105° Fahrenheit), improving colour resolution (Shetty 1994). At about the same time, professionally trained technicians in editing, cinematography and lighting began entering the commercial industry from film institutes in Pune and Chennai, vastly improving the quality of film production as well as increasing costs. Manjunath Pendakur (1985) notes that the rising costs of production since the 1980s not only includes huge salaries for film stars, but also higher wages for directors and technicians. Audiences seem attuned to these changes on screen. In Chennai, crowds get hysterical when cinematographer P.C. Sriram's name runs across the screen; directors have fan-supported websites competing with those on movie stars.

The profusion of filmmaking talent strengthened the Malayalam, Tamil and Telugu industries. Since 1979, film production in Tamil and Telugu has continued to keep pace with Hindi films, each producing about 140 films annually.[6] Increased production from regional industries has weakened the stronghold of Hindi films as the largest commercial industry in the nation while improvements in dubbing facilities have ensured a national audience for Tamil and Telugu films. In addition, filmmakers from the south such as S. Shankar, Sashilal Nair, Priyadarshan, Mani Ratnam and Ramgopal Varma have been making inroads into the Hindi film industry, once a prerogative of female stars (Chopra 1997). The migration of directors also means that narratives focusing on national themes – intercommunal love stories, war and terrorism – are no longer a prerogative of Hindi cinema, but also surface in regional cinemas. Concurrently, narratives in Hindi films have receded from national–secular themes addressing an urban audience, dabbling instead with regional stories resonating with preoccupations of the Hindi belt: Rajputs, Biharis and Punjabis now crowd the Hindi film screen.

Compare to the US and UK film industries discussed in Chapter 2.

Technical and aesthetic improvements in mainstream Indian cinema remind us that commercial filmmakers have benefited from narrative experiments introduced in the 1970s by independent filmmakers. Consciously setting themselves apart from commercial cinema, films by Adoor Gopalkrishnan, G. Aravindan, Mrinal Sen, Girish Kasarvalli, Kumar Shahini and Mani Kaul focused on social and political antagonisms to narrate their tales of disappointment with the post-colonial state, while conveying hopes for a different society.[7] Screened at film societies or special shows in large cinemas, their films drew the urban élite to cinemas and shaped filmviewing habits by encouraging the audience to focus more on the screen. A substantial number of commercial films made in the late 1980s borrowed from these filmmaking practices while continuing to improve on conventions of entertainment. Not unlike independent cinema, we now find directors gaining currency as auteurs in commercial cinema, controlling the production of their films and marking them with a unique cinematic style. In turn, the National Film Development Corporation (NFDC – the state body that finances independent films) started producing films which extensively incorporated mainstream stories and stars.

Further, Indian films have, on occasion, internationalised the production process: S. Shankar's Tamil film *Kaadalan/Lover* (1994), for example, polished its special effects in a Hong Kong film studio. Critics rightly focus on the film's playful commentary on upper-caste hegemony and its attendant economies of taste, but we cannot ignore how globalisation of the production process also influences this narrative of caste contestations (Dhareshwar and Niranjana 1996). The more conventional figuration of the world in Indian popular cinema – song and dance sequences set in foreign locales – is not only spruced up to arouse the spectator's interest in tourism, but also participates aggressively in the movement of global capital. These sequences not only bring the world home, they also acknowledge a loyal audience abroad that wishes to see its own stories of migrations and displacement written into these films. A number of Hindi films – *Pardes* (1997), *Dilwale Dulhaniya Le Jayange* (1995), *Dil to Pagal Hai* (1998), *Kuch Kuch Hota Hai* (1998) – index an audience straggling between national identities, harbouring longings for an original home or possessing the capital for tourism. Considered together, these narrative and production details place the viewer of Indian films in a global cinematic economy, finally catching up with a long history of global reception.

Since Independence, Indian films have travelled to the former Soviet Union, Latin America, Africa and Southeast Asia, entertaining audiences whose personal histories have few ties with the subcontinent. However, it is filmmakers in the diaspora who have been openly engaging with, and in the process teaching us a lesson or two in defamiliarising Indian film conventions. In both Srinivas Krishna's Canadian production *Masala* (1992) and Gurinder Chadda's British film *Bhaji on the Beach* (1994), we find lengthy quotations from Indian cinema: protagonists express desire by resorting to song and dance sequences. Inserted in films working with small budgets and relying on art-house distribution, such sequences serve as fabulous strands expressing immigration fantasies borne out of travel and displacement. In a more abrupt manner, Rachid Bouchareb's French–Algerian film *My Family's Honour* (1997) uses Hindi film songs on the soundtrack and even splices an entire musical number from *Hum Kisise Kum Nahin/We Are Number One* (1977) into his narrative on North African immigrants living in France. Displaying no diegetic link to the narrative, the jarring disjunction of this sequence conveys the disruption brought through immigration and displacement in Bouchareb's film. Terry Zwigoff's *Ghost World* (2000), narrating traumas of the summer after high school, opens with a song and dance sequence 'Jab Jaan Pechachan/When we got to know each other' from *Gumnaam* (1965), intercutting with the main narrative. The feverish cabaret and twist number offers the bored teenager the requisite degree of exotic abandon. Baz Luhrmann confesses to not only having seen Indian popular films but being mesmerised enough to deploy several song and dance sequences in his recent film *Moulin Rouge* (2000). Benny Torathi's Israeli film *Desparado Piazza*, also called *Piazza of Dreams* (2000), splices a song sequence from *Sangam* (1964) to map a different history of migration for ethnic Jews.[8] All these films celebrate these interruptions as a way of accounting for cinephilia even when the protagonists have to adjust to arduous conditions imposed through transnational migration, ennui-ridden teenagers or a courtesan's love story. These unexpected sites of reception allow us to see, from without, how Indian films are available for a wide range of readings, including camp and cult possibilities, based on their multi-plot narratives and multiple disruptions.

For further discussion of Moulin Rouge as an example of a film breaking genre conventions, see Chapter 5, pp. 120–3.

□ CASE STUDY 1: *MONSOON WEDDING* (MIRA NAIR, 2002)

A procession of colour, a clutch of garrulous Punjabis and a loving family crowd, Mira Nair's box-office success has emerged as the most successful Indian film to have cross-over appeal, as well as winning the Golden Lion Award at the 2001 Venice International Film Festival. Rumours have circulated that the wedding decor in the film has been imitated by non-resident Indians in the diaspora. Undoubtedly, Nair was aware of the appeal of the wedding film to audiences worldwide – *Four Weddings and a Funeral* (Mike Newell, 1994), *Hum Aap Ke Hain Koun*, *Dilwale Dulhania Le Jayenge* (*DDLG*) and so on – that include the doubtful bride, a cheating groom and a chorus of relatives whose own tribulations and desires make the wedding a sideshow. This film is no different, with the wedding as the central event, but in this the bride, Aditi, and groom, Hemant, are not the main draw in the film: the bride's parents Pimmi and Lalit exhibit an 'old-shoe' affection as Nair puts in it an interview; the bride's cousin Ria who is the same age faces her demons of sexual abuse at the family gathering; the bride's trysts with her older lover; her teenage brother whose voracious appetite for cooking casts aspersions on his masculinity; and a sideshow of uncles, aunts and cousins whose own desires criss-cross with others during the days before the wedding. While the upper-class, globally conscious Punjabi family holds centre stage in the film, Nair reels into it the budding romance and eventual union of the event manager Dube and the maid Alice.

In the official website for the film, Nair acknowledges her homage to Bollywood style, particularly songs from old films on the soundtrack; Dube's floral tribute to Alice is a nod to Raj Kapoor's *Shree 420* and the incorporation of song and dance sequences as part of the wedding festivities. It is worth noting, however, that Nair also engages with the small-film idea that has taken over film production with the advent of digital video, largely inspired by the low-budget aesthetics of the Dogma group. In fact, *Monsoon Wedding* seems to bear a structural similarity to *Festen/Celebration* (Thomas Vinterberg, 1998). In other words, the film's scale and its lack of obvious stars casts it as a small film incorporating particular elements from different world cinemas.

Having located Nair's film within the wedding genre, albeit in various global locations, it is useful to frame our reading of the film in terms of the discussion that has developed on this genre in Hindi cinema in the mid-1990s. In a productive reading of two such films produced in the mid-1990s – *DDLJ* and *Pardes* – Patricia Uberoi (1998) suggests we consider the aspirations of the Indian middle class, both within the nation and in the diaspora, that wishes to retain a certain configuration of Indian values while embracing the options offered by the global marketplace. Even if you haven't seen these particular films, you can imagine a series of conflicts: tradition versus modernity; arranged versus love marriages; individual desires versus familial obligations and so on. Uberoi suggests that these films offer the 'arranged love marriage' as the ideal, 'a style of matchmaking whereby a romantic choice already made is endorsed, *post facto*, by parental approval and treated thereafter like an "arranged marriage"'. What Uberoi attends to in these films is the particular problematisation of these various issues and their resolution, a framework that is equally useful for our purposes here.

WRITING ON INDIAN CINEMA

Within India, critical writing on cinema has blossomed in the past two decades, reporting a serious, sometimes cinephiliac, relationship to films. Published from Bangalore, *Deep Focus* combines interviews with directors from different regions of the world, film reviews and lengthy critical pieces. *Cinemaya*, based in Delhi, follows the festival schedule in Asia, brings its readers news of the latest films and interviews with directors, and addresses a pan-Asian audience from Turkey to Japan. These two magazines locate Indian cinema, both popular and alternative, and its audience, within a global network of cinematic styles.

The short-lived *Splice*, published from Calcutta, had an exclusive focus on alternative cinematic practices and excavated the correspondences between avant-garde practices in India and those from the former socialist republics. For a brief moment, *Splice* was an integral part of a blooming film scene in Calcutta which now includes a film archive at Nandan and a brand-new film studies department at Jadavpur University. The recently launched *Journal of Moving Images* from the Department of film studies at Jadavpur addresses an emerging academic audience. Published by the Film and Television Institute of India (FTII), Pune, *Lensight* addresses filmmakers with reports on state-of-the-art lab-processing techniques, editing equipment and cameras while also carrying lengthy interviews with filmmakers on their craft. Although pitched exclusively to filmmakers, *Lensight* carries a wealth of information on sociological conditions of production that are not widely available to a film critic.

Finally, publication of the *Encyclopaedia of Indian Cinema* (1994, with a revised edition in 1999) stamped the scholarly seal of approval on Indian cinema. Expansive in its scope, Ashish Rajadhyaksha and Paul Willemen's opus strings together biographies, film lists and plot summaries, providing a road-map of the different features of Indian cinema, from genres to independent film movements and regional cinemas.

The emergence of a field of Indian film studies against this backdrop has made it possible for critics to steer away from large-scale histories of the 'national cinema' towards more intensive readings of films and cinematic institutions. Although I will focus here on these different theoretical paradigms that privilege textual analysis, it is useful to be aware of the burgeoning field of extra-cinematic studies that combine ethnographic fieldwork and archival work to look at non-filmic objects. For instance, S.V. Srinivas's careful study of fan clubs in Telugu argues persuasively for a critical study of reception and not just close textual analysis of individual films (Srinivas 2000). Sara Dickey's ethnographic study of fan clubs in the South Indian town of Madurai and Steve Derne's study of film-going practices in the North Indian town of Shimla similarly provide us with a textured analysis of extra-filmic institutions (Derne 2000; Dickey 1993). Rachel Dwyer's reading of the popular star-zine *Stardust* urges us to consider the discourse of stardom as a mode of understanding the popularity of films (Dwyer 2000).

For further discussion of audience see Chapter 7, pp. 144–62.

These disparate details form the bedrock of material changes in the production and reception of Indian popular cinema. Spelling out these details undercuts a series of archaic oppositions that we find steadfastly held in the arena of film studies: between national and international cinemas overlooking alternative routes of film distribution; between Hollywood and other national cinemas casting the latter as bad copies instead of examining them as rejoinders to a hegemonic cinema; between national and regional cinemas, placing Hindi cinema at the helm of the national imaginary and ignoring a simultaneous move towards regional nationalisms; between national and global audiences by not anticipating audiences who also endow Indian popular cinema with meaning that exceeds its own intended horizon of address; between art and commercial cinema, repeating a high modernist division between high and low cultures without admitting to a more varied terrain of taste. Naming these mobile processes speaks to a post-colonial condition that according to Stuart Hall marks a 'critical interruption into that whole grand historiographical narrative which, in liberal historiography and Weberian historical sociology, as much as in the dominant traditions of Western Marxism, gave this global dimension a subordinate presence in a story which could essentially be told from within European parameters' (Hall 1996: 250).

GENRE AND FORM

For further discussion of Hollywood and genre see Chapter 5.

Some clarification of the concept of film genre is in order before I launch into particularities of Indian cinema. Identified as a narrative form developed by classical Hollywood commercial cinema, film theorists have developed a barrage of theoretical and methodological tools to understand the narrative structure, cinematic specificity and viewer's relationship to genre films. For instance, cinematic genres are differentiated by iconography: frontier landscapes in a western; city spaces in gangster films. At other times, we understand how genre verisimilitude derives from details in the mise-en-scène: monsters in horror films and horses in a western. Genre theory continues to benefit from psychoanalytical theories by allowing us to see how our viewing pleasures are dictated by a structuring of repetition and difference in films. Research on advertising and distribution practices of Hollywood films reveals that film producers were deeply invested in using genre categories to target and consolidate their audience: women's films, summer action films and so on. Instead of considering genre in either/or terms, Steve Neale (1980, 2000) suggests that we see genre films as a dynamic among industry, films and viewers to better understand cinema as a modern commodity form. In a book on American genre films and theory, Rick Altman (1999) proposes that far from being particular, Hollywood films are constructed as multiple, overlapping genres to reach a wider audience. Discrete genres, a predilection of critics, only surface after the fact. Whatever particular features film critics or filmmakers deploy to differentiate one genre from another or to see multiple genres in one film, American genre films broadly obey certain cinematic principles perfected in classical Hollywood cinema that frame the unfolding narrative: continuity editing, omniscient narration, internally coherent diegesis and character-motivated plot.

In contrast to the internally coherent narrative form generated by Hollywood genre films, genres in Indian popular cinema display a set of features that are akin to pre-classical cinema, especially several extra-diegetic sequences or sequences of attractions. Instead of concluding that these films stage the underdeveloped aspects of capitalism in the Indian economy, a different set of concerns nurtures this narrative form, including a desire to domesticate cinematic technology and develop a national cinematic style. For instance, writing on Dadasaheb Phalke's *Raja Harishchandra* (1913), Ashish Rajadhyaksha argues that the prevalence of frontal address in this film points to how narrative strategies in early cinema borrowed from painting, theatre and traditional arts to lure the viewer into this new technological apparatus (Rajadhyaksha 1993). In a similar vein, Geeta Kapur (1987) suggests through her reading of *Sant Tukaram* (Damle–Fattelal, Marathi, 1936) that frontal address in this 'saint film' was a calculated move by filmmakers to draw in viewers accustomed to watching theatre, yet the sequence of miracles mandatory in a saint film highlighted cinema's ability to produce magic. Both Kapur and Rajadhyaksha alert us to how cinema in India developed in a whirl of anti-colonial struggles that included an impulse to forge an independent cultural form by both reinterpreting tradition and making technology developed in the West indigenous.

Besides the direct address, other features of Indian popular cinemas similarly undercut the hermetic universe developed in Hollywood films, by interrupting it with song and dance sequences, comedy tracks and multi-plot narratives. Spectacular, and at times excessive, the elaboration of these attractions in this cinema has invited critics to dub them '**masala movies**' – a culinary term that seeks to define a medley of narrative strands in popular cinema. Naming the films made in the 1950s and 1960s as the 'feudal family romance', Madhava Prasad (1998) argues that this super-genre asserts

masala movie
Spicy Indian movie overloaded with emotions.

its dominance through narrative strategies of annexations whenever new sub-genres emerge. In short, Prasad suggests that instead of discrete genres a megalomaniac genre cannibalises the formation of sub-genres. Ravi Vasudevan (1995b), on the other hand, sees popular Hindi film as a discontinuous form that includes attractions such as song and dance sequences and comedic sub-plots. Instead of skipping over these moments that either break the diegetic universe or disrupt the linear trajectory of the narrative, we must simply face the fact that the most persistent narrative form found in Indian popular cinema includes several interruptions bearing a more or less systematic relationship to the narrative. In other words, we should start heeding production details that obsess over how Indian filmmakers expend considerable energy experimenting with the chore-ography and location of these sequences and, in the process, acknowledge how our viewing pleasure arises from these interruptions and the novel ways in which a popular film strings together these sequences.

Identifying these interruptions encourages us to start in the reverse direction; that is, by exploring how these films experiment with and fortify Indian cinematic conventions, rather than mulling over how these films are derived from Hollywood genres. Moreover, attending to these interruptions throws light on how the concept of a national cinematic style emerges at the conjuncture of state interests in quality cinema, the film industry's interests in profits and global circulation of popular cinemas. To account for how these disparate interests in production and reception shape the textual make-up of popular films, I will be looking at three different kinds of interruptions that brand the narrative form of Indian cinema: song and dance sequences, the interval, and censorship.

☐ CASE STUDY 2: *SHOLAY* (RAMESH SIPPY, 1975)

More than any of the above material conditions effecting the relationship between films and their viewers, Ramesh Sippy's *Sholay/Flames* (1975) was a landmark in Indian cinema, changing forever the production and reception of popular cinema. Coinciding with the State of Emergency declared by Prime Minister Indira Gandhi in 1975, *Sholay* was emblematic of a slew of films feeding off what political theorists refer to as a crisis of legitimacy of the Indian state (Vanaik 1991). Film critics, media activists and film scholars agree that the unrest in civil society marked by communal riots, police brutality, violent secessionist movements and assaults against women and minorities seeped into film narratives (Das 1992). Stacked with gangsters, avenging women, brutal police and corrupt politicians, these films resolve their narratives through vigilante actions that repeatedly undercut the authority of the state (Doriaswamy 1995; Rangoonwala 1993). Activist organisations such as Delhi's Media Advocacy Group argue that representations of brutality in contemporary commercial cinema have a direct and reinforcing effect on the level of violence in civil society (the Media Advocacy Group for the National Commission for Women, 1993).[9]

However, *Sholay*'s iconic status exceeds a mimetic relationship to reality, drawing in large part from its reconfiguration of the western.[10] Mixing a host of conventions from Indian popular cinema such as song and dance sequences, *Sholay* successfully produced an Indian riposte to the classic American western. Fans of this cult film exten-sively quote Salim Khan and Javed Akhtar's script back to the screen; rumours abound as to the existent variations of the closing sequence; and overnight the actor Amjad Khan, who plays the villain Gabbar Singh, became one of the most popular stars in the film world. Anupama Chopra's book *Sholay: The Making of a Classic* (2000) – a requisite read for any fan – revives cinephiliac obsession with this film by journeying to its origins of production. The film also spurred the first psychoanalytical critique of popular Indian cinema. In a much neglected essay, Madan Gopal Singh (1983) evaluates the tremendous success of this film by picking one scene as a symptom of the changing relationship between screen and spectator: the 'Mehbooba! Mehbooba!' song and dance sequence.

• Plate 14.2
Sholay (Sippy
Films–United
Producers–British Film
Institute)

According to Singh, in this sequence the camera gropes the dancer's body and, by extension, provides us with a point of view that was hitherto unavailable in popular Hindi cinema. Singh uses voyeurism as a conceptual tool to describe the altered relationship between screen and spectator in the film, an idea that draws extensively from certain cinematic principles found in Hollywood – omniscient narration, continuity editing, internally coherent narrative and the ideal spectator's identification with the camera – leading to the argument that the camera's groping mechanism fragments the female dancer's body and generates viewing pleasure. But he glosses over the fact that song and dance sequences explicitly distract the viewer from narrative flow and go against conventions of continuity editing. Overtly exhibitionistic, song and dance sequences break codes of realism that psychoanalytical voyeurism relies upon.[11] Nevertheless, Singh's cryptic formulation prods us to consider how even the most superficial and entertaining song and dance sequences carry an ideological charge, heightening our viewing pleasure.[12]

Singh's essay also tells another story, a story of the intellectual context of his critical engagement with Hindi films. Originally published in the avant-garde *Journal of Arts and Ideas*, Singh's essay echoes the opinions of alternative filmmakers such as Kumar Shahini, Mani Kaul and John Abraham, all of whom were writing and making a different kind of narrative cinema. Accounting for the hegemonic potential of Hindi commercial cinema, especially its ability to throttle radical filmmaking, Singh bemoans the loss of freshly minted student filmmakers from the FTII to the commercial industry, a move, he argues, that turns them into technicians of special effects. While *Sholay* affords Singh the occasion to critically assess the ideological manifestations of the consumerist cinema, his theoretical speculations helped shape an entire generation of film theorists working on Indian cinema.[13] In sharp contrast to Singh's critical essay, *Sholay* is a revered master text of success for filmmakers: Ramgopal Varma confesses to knowing every shot of two of his favourite films – *Sholay* and Francis Ford Coppola's *The Godfather* (1972); more recently, Rajkumar Santoshi allegedly watched *Sholay* every morning while shooting his own *China Gate* (1999) (Naseeruddin Shah, *Filmfare*, May 1998). Sholay is the mythical origin spurring an entire generation of filmmakers to borrow from globally circulating genres, yet reincorporating conventions from Indian popular cinema with great aplomb.[14] Spawning a number of B films throughout the 1980s, the full impact of Sippy's innovative cinematic style on popular Indian cinema – accommodating Indian cinematic conventions within a Hollywood genre – was fully developed a decade later by J.P. Dutta, Mani Ratnam, Mukul Anand, Ramgopal Varma, Rajkumar Santoshi and Shekhar Kapur.

These divergent readings of *Sholay* demonstrate a gap between critics writing on popular Indian cinema and filmmakers. Simply put, critics tend to take a moralistic view of mainstream cinema, seeing very little of the 'popular', while commercial filmmakers see themselves as entertainers and regard critics as élitists whose opinions rarely account for the working of the industry (Thomas 1985[15]). This stand-off between critics and commercial filmmakers is as old as the practice of narrative cinema itself, and has little new to add to debates on the differences between high and low, between mass and popular cultures that as cultural critics we have learned to make and then unmake. Finally we have settled on 'popular culture' as the most viable concept that absorbs the paradoxes of our trade: we can read resistance in its form, even as we continue to be mesmerised by it (MacCabe 1986). This shifty definition seems vastly superior to the polarised definitions of cultural taste plaguing readings of Indian films. There is no doubt that we learn a great deal from vigilant readings of cinema's hegemonic influence that reveal its power to affirm ethnic stereotyping, sexism and jingoism, and caution us against being taken in by its dazzling surface. But all too often we tend to pay little attention to questions of pleasure. Inasmuch as we assume that commercial films maintain the status quo, flattening all radical possibilities in their viewers, we must also admit that filmmakers are constantly invested in inviting us to return to the movies through novel cinematic conventions.

For further discussion of the relationship between film and the spectator, see Chapter 7.

Sholay exemplified the possibility of combining ever so deftly dominant genre principles developed in Hollywood films with conventions particular to Indian cinema. Recasting the linear trajectory of genre films to include several local cinematic conventions, Indian popular films often render the former illegible to the rank outsider. What I am suggesting is that it seems presumptuous to think that when Hollywood genres are appropriated by other national cinemas, we may find straightforward application of dominant genre principles instead of reading how local contexts of production and reception intervene and prevail over genre. The end-product of this encounter between global and local features may, at times, be read as a subaltern response to Hollywood, a strategy forwarded by Paul Smith in his reading of Leone's 'spaghetti westerns', or we can simply read it as a riposte that simultaneously reveals how Hollywood genres are also built around certain national cinematic styles (Smith 1993).

For discussion of narrative and non-narrative film, see Chapter 3, pp. 61–82.

SONG AND DANCE SEQUENCES

One of the most common and popular features of Indian films are its song and dance sequences. According to Barnouw and Krishnaswamy (1980: 69), Indian talkies always had songs: the first sound feature, Ardeshir Irani's *Alam Ara/Light of the World* (1931), had over seven songs; another early Hindi film had forty songs; not to be outdone, a Tamil film is counted as having sixty. By the 1950s 'the film song had become a key to successful film promotion' (ibid.: 157). Filmmakers continue to release audio tracks prior to the film's release and it is now widely believed that those sales alone can recover the production costs of a movie.[16] Music directors, choreographers and singers receive awards, and popular memories of these sequences often surpass the film's own story. Over the years, commercial filmmakers have tried experimenting with their absence, with varying commercial success: K.A. Abbas's *Munna/Lost Child* (1954), the Tamil film *Antha Nal/That Day* (1954), B.R. Chopra's *Ittefaq* (1969), P.C. Sriram's *Kurudhippunal/River of Blood* (1995), Ramgopal Varma's *Kaun/Who?* (1998) are some examples. However, since song and dance sequences guarantee a definite income, it has been difficult to dispense with them altogether. Song and dance sequences traverse radio and television, independently of the films themselves, a phenomenon encouraging critics to rush to the conclusion that they are inserted into films only as entertaining spectacles with tangential links to the narrative.

The first sound film, *Alam Ara* (1931), included seven songs, setting the standard for popular cinema. The first decade of sound witnessed a range of experiments with sound and narrative, including introducing a number of songs into films. Musicologist Bhaskar Chankravarkar (1989) names songs of one minute and forty seconds' length as 'songlets' that were rarely heard outside the cinema halls, and thus are unavailable on gramophone records of the film. Referring to films such as *Indrasabha* (1931), laden with seventy-one songs, or *Kalidas* (1931), a Tamil film with fifty songs, Ashok Ranade (1981) suggests that not all of these were strictly songs but verse-in-tune flowing between prose-based dialogue and a full-blown song, a convention that he suggests emerges from oral-based cultures. Bowing to pressures from the recording industries, songs were standardised to three to four minutes, emerging as discrete moments in films, a practice that has stayed intact for the most part. According to Theodore Baskaran (1996), dramatist P. Sambanda Mudaliyar suggested that 'ideally song sequences should take about one-fourth of the film's duration'. Besides pressures from gramophone industries that promised revenues from sales of film song records, experiments in sound recording, including pre-recorded song and lip-synching by playback singers, encouraged the consolidation of film songs as distinct modules. Overseeing the composition of lyrics, managing an orchestra and choosing playback singers fortified the role of the music director.[17] Allegedly, Nitin Bose's *Dhoop Chaon* (1935) was the first film systematically to use playback singing under the helm of music director R.C. Boral.[18] Film historians and musicologists suggest that the popularity and persistence of film songs points to Indian cinema's early links to conventions of nineteenth-century Parsi theatre as well as folk theatre which were similarly strung together with a number of songs. Besides these theatrical origins, Chandravarkar and Ranade point to a confluence of musical influences in the hybrid film song: Indian classical, folk and Western tunes (Chandravarkar 1989). In recent years, in addition to star music directors, choreographers such as Prabhu Deva, Saroj Khan, Farah Khan and others have been asserting their presence by grafting together Indian dance styles with Western dance moves.

Although musicologists have written extensively on the synthetic quality of Indian film songs, on the parallel economy of star music directors and singers, there is an absence of literature on song sequences, lending support to the assumption that the sequences are extra-diegetic or, in narratological terms, achronies, outside the temporal reckoning of the narrative.[19] A flamboyant example of such an instance occurs in S. Shankar's *Indian* (1994), where the film abruptly cuts from Madras to Australia as the preferred setting for the 'Melbourne' song and dance. Declaiming such practices, Baskaran writes: 'The flow of the film would not be affected in the least if song sequences were excised, wholly or partly' (1996: 48). However, indulgent song and dance sequences remain, and a close analysis of this interruption begs us to explore how they relate to the narrative time of different kinds of films.

In addition to attending to the ways in which song and dance interrupt the narrative in various ways, the iconography of these sequences of attractions calls our attention to other features that bolster a spectator's interest in Indian cinema. For instance, the abrupt cut to exotic locations sparks the tourist interests of the viewer, and similarly the object-laden mise-en-scène endorses consumerism. Not unlike the commercial imperative towards product placement in contemporary American cinema, song and dance sequences draw in a whole host of adjacent economies such as tourism and consumerism that are not so easily compartmentalised in Indian cinema. There is no doubt that the presence of several such sequences is reminiscent of a cinema of attractions found in early cinema where the spectacular aspects of such a scene override narrative

For further discussion of audience and early cinema see Chapter 7, pp. 149–56.

coherence. Even in their most exhibitionistic form, when their presence rarely furthers the narrative and its 'undatedness' or achrony is most visible in their ability to circulate as self-contained segments on music television or film previews, their iconography remains open to a wide range of ideological readings.[20] But they also solicit our interests as tourists, albeit virtual tourists travelling the world within the closed confines of the movie theatre. The connection between tourism and cinema is an old one – Lumière shorts of Egypt are some of the earliest examples – and in Indian popular films these excursions speak to the continued interest in the travel genre even if a particular film lurches towards a different kind of genre consolidation.[21] Thus what we often find on screen are hybrid genres: gangster films intersecting with travel genres and so on. This hunt for the perfect or the most exotic locale makes filmmakers sound like explorers. I have argued elsewhere that the iconography in the song and dance sequences comments on the relationship between the love story and national identity. For instance, the presence and absence of scenes from Kashmir alert us to the ways in which films stage contestations over cartography in the national imaginary (Gopalan 1997b).

In contrast to these assumptions that promote their extra-diegetic relationship to the narrative, or dismiss them as a 'sequence of attractions' reminiscent of early cinema, song and dance sequences deserve another look, differentiating their relationship to the diegesis: delaying the development of the plot, distracting us from the other scene of the narrative through spatial and temporal disjunctions, and bearing an integral link to the plot. Even in one film, there may be different articulations of these sequences, thus complicating the idea of a single diegesis or the valency of the extra-diegetic. The lack of uniform temporal sequencing across different films alerts us to consider genre differences and auteur signatures inflecting the choreography of song and dance sequences.

LOVE STORY

Although song and dance sequences surface in different genres of Indian cinema, their timing and elaboration in the love story genre has had the most success. Star-crossed lovers sing the same song across disparate spaces; lovers meet in a song and dance sequence; sylvan locales in Kashmir, Switzerland, Australia or South Africa ideally express the lovers' passion. The florid lyrics seem well suited to the lovelorn, ecstatic or the marooned lover, and in each such instance the sequence carries metaphoric possibilities that a realist narrative cannot completely deliver. Hence, in the following case studies we will explore how this interruption inflects the love story while at the same time examining how class, caste, communal and gender identities are staged in this genre.

☐ CASE STUDY 3: *BOMBAY* (MANI RATNAM, 1995)

The love story has always been a successful genre in Indian cinema. In fact, one can look at the different preoccupations of the love story over the past fifty years that press us to consider them as allegories of the nation state: inter-caste, inter-religious, inter-class stories and so on. Besides being available for political and social commentary, the genre has allowed its formula-ridden stories to be masterpieces in the hands of a competent director – the most obvious example being Raj Kapoor, whose experiments with this genre have set the standard for future generations of directors. However, the love story too has undergone considerable revision, at times so extreme that we often watch marriage and wedding tales rather than pursue stories of star-crossed lovers. In this cycle of revision, Mani Ratnam emerges as the master of the political love story with his well-known trilogy: *Roja* juxtaposes contestations over Kashmir against the happiness of a newly-wed couple honeymooning in the valley; in *Dil Se* a series of political contestations vie for attention with a doomed love story between a radio reporter

Compare to genre in Hollywood cinema in Chapter 5, pp. 110–26.

and a revolutionary/terrorist; and in *Bombay* – simultaneously produced in Tamil and Hindi – the durability of a Hindu–Muslim marital union is tested against the backdrop of communal riots in the city. Film critics have had a field day with Ratnam's films, and we can say that critical debates on Roja and Bombay have fundamentally changed the terms of debates on cinema in India.

Bombay traces the love story of a Hindu man, Shekhar, and a Muslim woman, Shailabano. Facing opposition from their parents, Shekhar leaves his village for Bombay and Shailabano flees her home to join him. It is in Bombay that they marry and have twin sons, Kamal and Kabir, but it is also in Bombay that they witness the rise of communal tensions marking the social fabric of India in the 1980s and 1990s. Provoked by Hindu fundamentalists demolishing the Babri Masjid in December 1992, communal riots in Bombay splinter the family. A miraculous reunion between parents and children also allows for an inter-generational reunion: Shekhar's father and Shailabano's parents arrive in Bombay and reconcile with their estranged children. Another round of riots in January ruptures the short-lived reunion, killing and scattering the family: older parents die in communal fires, and the twins are separated from each other and from their parents. As Bombay burns, Shekhar and Shailabano hunt for their children, only to be reunited with them at the very moment the leaders of the respective communities call a halt to the insane marauding.

Among the different critical and popular writings on the film, Ravi Vasudevan's landmark essay carefully maps the history of censorship, both public and state, surrounding the film as a way of understanding the relationship between a Hindu man and a Muslim woman, a union that seems peculiarly underdeveloped in Hindi cinema, acquiring a taboo-like status for directors and writers. Besides attending to the public outcry against the film from both the right and left coalitions, Vasudevan leads us to consider the film's own management of this social taboo through various cinematic strategies that he argues produces an incoherence identifiable as the form of Indian popular cinema – the disaggregate narrative (Vasudevan 1996).

☐ **CASE STUDY 4: *DIL CHAHTA HAI/WHAT THE HEART DESIRES* (FARHAN AKHTAR, 2001)**

For discussion of lesbian and gay cinema, see Chapter 11.

Although not a heterosexual love story, this first film by Farhan Akhtar focuses on the friendship between three men – Sameer, Aakash and Siddharth – and assumes the form of a love story. Akhtar is no stranger to the film world, having an accomplished father, Javed Akhtar, a scriptwriter and poet who wrote the catchy songs in this film, and a mother, Honey Irani, who has moved from child star to scriptwriter. Of course, pedigree alone does not account for the success of the film, which captures the lives of the three upper-class boys in the period following their college graduation. The conventional battles with traditional parents or parents insisting on finding the right girl for their sons are rendered inconsequential; in fact, the parents appear to be supportive, mildly admonishing and even indulgent of their sons' development into men. Given that the narrative does not seek to displace conflicts on to the parental generation, the precipitating crisis in the film is the friendship among the three boys and the ways in which it is affected by their erotic development. As in most heterosexual narratives, here too women interfere and force changes in what is often perceived to be a stable economy between men, a narrative conceit that has tremendous play in westerns and gangster films.[22] In a provocative reading of this film, Kimberly Ringler uses Corey Creekmur's essay, 'Acting Like a Male: Masculine Performances in My Darling Clementine', which extends Sedgwick's reading of the relationship between compulsory heterosexuality and homophobia, to argue that the mise-en-scène in this film suggests, yet at the same time disavows, the possibility of an erotic union between the three men (Ringler 2002). For instance, Ringler suggests that the film employs doors to ward off intimacy between men, at the same time suggesting the possibility of a homosexual union between them. Ringler's reading encourages us to consider the mise-en-scène as a rich site to mine for erotic desire, class aspirations, national longings and so on.

☐ CASE STUDY 5: GURU DUTT

The availability of a number of films in DVD format from previous decades has enabled viewers to finally watch films which were earlier only accessible in a film archive or retrospectives. Among the recent spate of DVD collections are those directed and produced by Guru Dutt, available for purchase at the website yashraj.com. While the poor quality of transfer from film to DVD is noticeable, the films nevertheless reveal Guru Dutt's reputation as a director who could produce a commercial hit without forsaking cinematic style. Accounts of his biography, available in the *Encyclopedia of Indian Cinema*, describe his birth in Bangalore in 1925, followed by early years in Calcutta. After being briefly employed as a telephone operator in Calcutta, Dutt embarked on a career in filmmaking by joining Prabhat Studios in 1944. Shortly thereafter, Dutt's collaborations with Bombay cinema's leading actors, lyricists, cameramen and music directors produced a number of box-office successes. Also playing the part of a producer under the banner of Guru Dutt films, Dutt experimented with a wide variety of genres and is seen retrospectively as one of the first Indian filmmakers to embrace a modern sensibility. Dutt committed suicide in 1964 leaving behind a rich legacy of films that continue to fascinate contemporary viewers.

Nasreen Munni Kabir's documentary *In Search of Guru Dutt* (1989) offers the most comprehensive understanding of Dutt's milieu between 1945 and 1964 as narrated by his colleagues in the industry and members of his family. Among the many aspects of his filmmaking style discussed in the documentary, Shyam Benegal, a renowned contemporary director in his own right and a cousin of the late director, identifies Guru Dutt's song picturisation as perhaps his greatest contribution to the cinematic style of popular Hindi cinema. Ably supported by lyricists, playback singers, choreographers and cameramen, the song and dance sequences in his films demonstrate a firm link to the narrative without ever appearing as superfluous additions. Kabir's ninety-minute documentary is widely available as a special feature in the Yashraj's DVD releases of Guru Dutt's films.

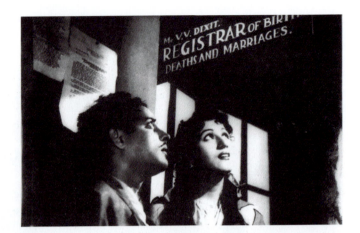

• **Plate 14.4**
Mr. and Mrs. 55 (Guru
Dutt Films Pvt Ltd–
Hyphen Films Ltd)

As part of this exercise to understand Guru Dutt's cinematic style through his song and dance sequences, view his film *Mr. and Mrs. 55* (1955) and Kabir's documentary *In Search of Guru Dutt*. Please remember that the DVD version of the film does not indicate the location of the interval, and the poor quality of the transfer fails to adequately convey Guru Dutt's cinematographic style.

Mr. and Mrs. 55 is immediately recognisable as a hybrid genre that combines elements of the romantic comedy with social drama. Anita is a rich heiress who lives with her aunt, Sita Devi, a strident feminist who is a leading proponent of the Hindu Code Bill which grants women a right to annul a Hindu marriage. While Sita Devi is campaigning for women's rights, Anita fritters away her days at tennis matches and pools where unbeknownst to her a poor cartoonist, Pritam, falls hopelessly in love with her. In the meantime, Anita discovers on her twentieth birthday that her inheritance carries the condition that she must marry within a month. Appalled by her late brother's stipulations, Sita Devi conceives of a way to subvert the condition by arranging Anita's marriage to Pritam in exchange for a fee, with the understanding that her niece will annul the marriage after a month. Pritam seizes the opportunity for pecuniary reasons, initially unaware that the girl in question is none other than the one he is in love with. Through a series of misunderstandings that are par for the course in a romantic comedy, Anita and Pritam finally reunite after having annulled their first marriage.

In her discussion of the film, Jyotika Virdi (2003: 76) argues: 'The film's narrative line manifests familiar symptoms of male anxiety about women repositioning themselves in society – symptoms that include publicly mocking women or trivializing and caricaturing their demands' (76).[23] Virdi suggests that the film casts Sita Devi as an eccentric who 'joins the ranks of a long list of spinsters, dowagers, prohibitionists, mothers-in-law, suffragettes, "battle-axes," career women, "women's libbers," and lesbians' (ibid.: 85).[24] While taking into account Virdi's critique of the film's misogyny, it is also worth considering how the genre of the comedy does not offer a clear moral resolution after having lampooned every rule and convention in the narrative. It is no accident that Anita and Pritam's reunion occurs after the annulment of their marriage and at considerable distance from Sita Devi's command, a closure that is fitting within the generic convention of the romantic comedy.

While the caricature of the Hindu Code Bill dominates one strand of the narrative, it locks us into the strict spaces of Sita Devi's dominion, the courts and her mansion. In the sections tracking Anita, Pritam and their friends, the camera wanders through buses, parks, pools, bars, restaurants, offices and airports, spaces that are particularly animated in the nine song and dance sequences. Since critics have repeatedly remarked on song picturisation as a hallmark of Guru Dutt's cinematic style, it is worthy of further exploration.

INTERVAL

The 'interval' is the ten-minute break in every Indian popular film taking place after eighty minutes of film screening. Lights are turned on, the projector is turned off and viewers step out of the theatre to smoke a cigarette, eat a snack or visit the bathroom. Unlike the strong imprint of song and dance sequences in the film-going experience, the location of the interval remains an elusive detail in the memory of even the most avid film-viewer. It is simply seen as a brief respite from the long screening. Trade papers, however, make passing references to which halves of the film were more, or less, interesting.

According to Theodore Baskaran, a historian of Tamil cinema, intervals have existed since the early 1930s when the feature film as a genre took root.[25] The term arises, in part, from the early years of film exhibition, when the constraints of working with a single projector would force the projectionist to stop the film more than once, in effect producing two or three intervals. Besides the whims of the projectionist, Baskaran notes that the films themselves referred overtly to this break in the narrative: in *Apoorva Sagodrigal/Strange Friends* (1949) a song and dance sequence set in a garden ends with the word 'Edivali' ('Interval' in Tamil) strung together by flowers dropping from the trees; and in *Velaikkari/Servant* (1949), Mani, one of the protagonists, devises a plan which he indicates will take place later – after the interval. Baskaran speculates that intervals probably persisted to pace the narrative which was laden with at least a dozen songs, a feature he thinks has retained this cinema in a primitive stage of filmmaking beholden to attractions.

The interval weighs in as a crucial punctuation, adjusting both opening and closing strategies of the film, in effect, producing two opening and closing sequences in every Indian film. As in the song and dance sequences, the interval is not randomly located but regulated by genre constraints and directorial style. Breaking the spell of the dark auditorium, the interval reminds us of early cinema's exhibition practices when a film was one of many instalments of the evening's entertainment. In its current form, the interval is a cinematic device that organises the dose of cinematic attractions mandatory in Indian cinema as well as serving as a punctuation mark that continually directs our anticipation in surprising ways by opening and closing certain narrative strands.

Both song and dance sequences, and the interval, attune us to their structural function in popular Indian films, particularly through their play on spatial and temporal disjunctions. Their articulation in specific texts highlights how films imbibe both global and local conventions: genre films adjust to song and dance sequences while the interval doubles the structuring of anticipation and pleasure found in genre films. In each case, they call attention to interruptions in the convention of the linear narrative with a single diegesis dominant in Hollywood or other commercial industries, with their attendant assumptions of realist codes.[26] The ideal spectator of film theory, cloistered from adjacent consumer economies, surfaces as a phantom figure in Indian popular cinema; the Indian spectator, in contrast, travels several circuits of pleasures generated by a multi-diegetic narrative.[27]

For comparison with Hollywood narrative structure see Chapter 3, pp. 62–6.

There is no doubt that the location of the interval is crucial to Indian filmmakers as an indispensable device to organise the narrative structure. For instance, when asked: 'Do you write a screenplay, like a play, in three acts?', the scriptwriter Salim Khan responds:

I need a simple nice plot in which I must have a definite beginning, a middle and a crucial end. The end must be clear in my mind and then I start working on the sub-plots and the characters. I go on developing material, then I arrange it till the interval point, and then further the progress of the story.

(*Screen*, 15 July 1988)

Sagar Sarhadi, another scriptwriter, answers similarly:

No. Normally I have two. There are two dramatic movements – the interval and the end. The screenplay is written to heighten these dramatic movements.

(*Screen*, 11 July 1988)

Unlike an arbitrary break at the halfway point, Indian films often use the intermission as a definitive break, linking it to the opening and closing segments of a film. This distinct punctuation emerges not only as a unique marker of 'Indian' cinematic style but also locates the place of innovation and authorial style. Considered in these terms, the interval stands out as an obvious strategy to pace the narrative, and instead of rationalising it as a moment of relief from the tedium of a long film, this unique form of cinematic punctuation is the corner-stone of inventiveness in Indian cinema, a structuring device that inflects our reading of this cinema. Since it falls between two moments in a film, I suggest that we can explore the ways in which it pilfers closing strategies usually anticipated later in the film, and, at the same time permits narrative strands to bloom in the second half. Rearranging narrative expecta-tions instructs us to reconsider the charge of derivativeness aimed at Indian commercial cinema, a charge that overlooks the different ways in which a film accommodates Hollywood genre features within the constellation of interruptions. Alternatively, the 'interval' seems to have seeped into films produced outside India – Stanley Kubrick's *Full Metal Jacket* (1987), Quentin Tarantino's *Pulp Fiction* (1994), Wong Kar-Wai's *Chunking Express* (1994), Milcho Manchevski's *Before the Rain* (1994), Alejandro Gonzalez Inarritu's *Amores Perros/Love's a Bitch* (2001), Marzeih Meshkini's *Roozi Khe Zan Shodam/The Day I Became a Woman* (2001) and Jeremy Podeswa's *Five Senses* (2000) appear to have hijacked the interval to heighten their narratives of disjunctions and dispersal.

GANGSTER FILMS

Although the gangster, often cast as the villain, has long been a fixture in the urban mise-en-scène in popular films – his death reinstating a moral universe in the diegesis – his exalted status as the protagonist gathers force in the mid-1970s when popular culture seemed to respond and absorb the crisis of state legitimacy set in motion by the State of Emergency of 1975. In place of the iconic masculine subject who directs the narrative from chaos to the restoration of law and order, this emerging masculine subject flaunts the conventions of law and order by railing aggressively against corrupt police and politicians through vigilante actions. Critics classify these films as the 'angry man' films that fortified Amitabh Bachchan's star status. In a compelling reading of Bachchan's films – *Zanjeer/The Chain* (Prakash Mehra, 1973), *Deewar/The Wall* (Yash Chopra, 1975) and *Sholay/Flames* (Ramesh Sippy, 1975) – Madhava Prasad formulates this shift in the popular cinema narrative as the 'disaggregation' of the super-genre, throwing up narra-tives teetering between the star persona on the one hand, and the role of the subaltern hero who mobilises the populist sentiments of the masses on the other. Tying Bachchan's stardom to that of the star scriptwriters Salim and Javed, Prasad identifies a shift in the production conditions towards a reinstatement of the dominance of popular cinema at a time when the state was vigorously involved in the production of small-budget films. Prasad's formulation allows us to explore how Bachchan's star status initiated changes at the formal register of the film through spectacular slow-motion shots of the star, fetish-isation of the masculine-star's body through extreme close-ups that willy-nilly revised the heterosexual paradigms of previous years or at least problematised the relationship between the masculine subject and social authority.

Although critics are quick to recognise Bachchan's stardom as the defining trope of the 1970s and 1980s, there is no doubt that the changing production conditions also made it possible for certain star directors such as Mukul Anand, N. Chandra, Manmohan

Desai, J.P. Dutta, Rajkumar Santoshi and Ramesh Sippy to emerge as auteurs and metteurs en scène, wresting control from distributors who by all accounts exercised undue authority over themes and stars of individual films. Centring the male protagonist – Amitabh Bachchan in the upmarket versions; other male stars such as Firoz Khan and Mithun Chakraborty in B and C productions – these films unfold around elaborate action sequences that bear a strong resemblance to Hollywood-style westerns and gangster films. As we have already seen, *Sholay* was one of the most successful ventures to combine generic themes borrowed from Hollywood with conventions developed in Indian cinema, a combination that permits us similarly to scrutinise their iconography, articulations of the city and figurations of masculinity, areas that will help us to better understand the populist thrust of such films.[28]

☐ **CASE STUDY 6: *SATYA* (RAMGOPAL VARMA, 1998)**

Ramgopal Varma's landmark gangster film is the perfect example of global and local cinematic conventions. Set against the backdrop of Bombay, the film narrates the rise and fall of Bhiku Mhatre whose range of activities include bankrolling politicians, bribing the police, and financing film production and prostitution, a range that makes it almost impossible for the police to arrest him. Its gritty portrayal of the Bombay underworld including the multilingual slang has made it one of India's most popular films, with gangsters offering encomiums to the actor Manoj Bajpai (Bhiku Mhatre). At the centre of the narrative is Bhiku's friendship with Satya, which, the film suggests, propels his meteoric rise in the underworld as well as his precipitous fall. The hyper-real narrative, however, does include song and dance sequences and the interval punctuates the narrative to heighten the relationship between gangster and state.

CENSORSHIP

For a discussion on censorship in the US and the UK see website, Chapter 2.

In addition to these two kinds of interruptions, viewers of Indian films are aware that the state monitors the relationship between cinema and society most visibly through film censorship. The most glaring manifestation of state intervention in film production is the Board of Censors' certificate that precedes each film. This inaugural moment of every film publicly released in India, whether imported or indigenous, informs the spectator that the film has been approved by the state and carries with it traces of censored cuts. The British colonial state introduced film censorship by passing the Cinematograph Act of 1918 for at least two reasons: first, to censor film footage that might incite anti-colonial riots; second, to avoid (mis)representations of the West, particularly images of Western women. These broad concerns targeted both Indian and imported films, and set a pattern for post-independence censorship practices, where the state perceives films as having a tremendous influence over its citizenry and thus directs its regulations towards the production and control of 'quality' films (see Razdan 1975; Sarkar 1982; *The Indian Cinematograph Code*, 1982; Vasudev 1978). However, instead of seeing censorship as post facto interference from the state, I suggest that filmmakers spend considerable energy incorporating censorship regulations *during* filmmaking in an attempt to pre-empt sweeping cuts that would drastically affect the flow of the narrative. Moreover, over the years, the relationship between the state and the film industry has revealed a spectrum of negotiations – from an obedient nationalism to a flagrant flouting of regulations that fuel the production of images on screen.

While the obscenity codes governing Indian cinema address a wide range of issues affecting both image and dialogue, in practice the object of greatest scrutiny is the female body. I use the term *coitus interruptus* to indicate the different ways in which the film industry negotiates the code to finally produce the female body on screen. This is not a gratuitous evocation of contraception, but rather a play on the structural similarity between two mechanisms – contraceptive regulations and censorship – suggesting how the state isolates the female body as the prime site of control and regulation in the public sphere. Among the several manifestations of *coitus interruptus*, the withdrawal-of-the-camera technique is instantly recognisable in various Indian films: the camera withdraws just before a steamy love scene ensues and the film replaces it with extra-diegetic shots of waterfalls, flowers, thunder, lightning and tropical storms. The varying configurations and recurrent use of *coitus interruptus* demonstrate how the film industry, despite its laments about state control, has been preoccupied with the withdrawal-of-the-camera technique as a crucial source of surplus pleasure. With its focus on dodging censorship prescriptions as well as maintaining its interests in the female body on screen, *coitus interruptus*, as a cinematic convention, captures an intimate and tense relationship between the state and the film industry predicated on attempts, however contradictory, to align the *national* subject with the film spectator. Far from aligning perfectly with the interests of the state and the film industry, the viewer is drawn into a fetishistic scenario where s/he oscillates between a cinephiliac mourning over lost footage on the one hand and, on the other, acknowledges that the state employs patriarchal law to produce limits on seeing.

THE WOMAN'S FILM

For further discussion of women filmmakers, see Chapter 10, pp. 223–6.

For further discussion of feminism and feminist film theory, see Chapter 10, pp. 226–36.

Inasmuch as cultural critics see popular films as staging social and political anxieties, the woman's film genre – which includes women-centred narratives, female protagonists undergoing political conversion, and more or less overt gestures towards feminist politics – has drawn responses and responded to the concerns of feminists, both in India and the diaspora. As mentioned above, Madhava Prasad notes that a fully independent woman's film struggled to develop in the 1960s, all too often annexed to what he sees as the 'super-genre', or the feudal family romance. Besides the obvious economic motives of the box office that carries bias against women ageing on-screen, we may conjecture that the inability of the woman's film to survive was the unavailability of representations of strong woman-centred narratives in the social terrain, as well as the absence of critical feminist voices evaluating popular films. In this context it is useful to browse through past issues of Manushi – the most important feminist magazine in India – to gauge the developing, yet shifting, feminist readings of popular cinema set in motion by a section on film reviews. Rather than dismiss popular cinema altogether and applaud the politics of 'middle', parallel or alternative cinemas, these reviews read regressive representations as well as seeing feminist possibilities in popular cinema.

In recent years, the burgeoning field of feminist criticism of Indian films has produced an array of reading strategies that we can bring to bear on popular films. For instance, Maithili Rao (1998) examines the avenging women films of the 1980s to reprimand popular cinema for canny representations of aggressive women that fall short of feminism. Charting a similar territory, I have argued that the avenging women genre is shaped by the ongoing tussle between the film industry's desire to mine the woman's body for a range of representations and Censor Board dictates on obscenity codes, a tussle that throws up a heady concoction between sex and violence in these narratives that are predicated on rape and revenge (Gopalan 1997a). Jyotika Virdi (1999) locates the avenging women genre within the genre of women's film of the 1970s that similarly mobilised feminist possibilities but prematurely foreclosed those very options by evoking traditional representations of the pure or good woman.

Although these readings focus on women-centred narratives in popular cinema, we can detect feminist modes of analysis in Tejawini Niranjana's (1994) reading of Mani Ratnam's *Roja*, in which she argues that the film uses the figure of the good-wife-in-distress to promote a Hindu nationalist imaginary. In addition to decoding the narrative, attending to point-of-view shots and responding to the modes of address, critics have isolated examples of feminist offerings that are even queer at times in popular cinema:

Radha Subramanyam sights a feminist consciousness in Kalpana Lajmi's *Rudaali/The Crier* (1992) that places the gendered subaltern within an erotic economy (Subramanyam 1996).

While critics have directed their energies at popular cinema, women filmmakers from middle or art cinema have long been experimenting with feminist aesthetics that include narrating the plight of Brahmin widowhood while giving them dignity (see e.g. Prema Karanth's *Phaniyamma*, 1983); centring on the loneliness of an Anglo-Indian teacher (see e.g. Aparna Sen's *36 Chowringhee Lane*, 1982) and so on. In the field of documentary filmmaking, Deepa Dhanaraj's careful documenting of communal riots, and policies on reproductive rights and population control, has expanded the field of feminist aesthetics beyond a women-centred narrative. Similarly, the women's film collective Media Storm, based in Delhi, has employed conventional and guerrilla tactics to propose visual interventions to the ongoing debates on right-wing nationalism, state brutality and feminist subjectivity.

This rich and complicated terrain of feminist film criticism provides a productive framework to examine two controversial films: *Bandit Queen* and *Fire*.

□ **CASE STUDY 7: *BANDIT QUEEN* (SHEKHAR KAPUR, 1994) AND *FIRE* (DEEPA MEHTA, 1998)**

Bandit Queen (Shekhar Kapur, 1994)

Produced in collaboration with British Channel 4 and based on Mala Sen's (1991) biography of the notorious dacoit Phoolan Devi, Shekhar Kapur's film details Phoolan's development from a child bride to an outlaw. Its release in India was stymied by the Censor Board that recommended excising the explicit scenes of sex and violence in the film. In addition, the film's claim that it was a true story provoked the late Phoolan Devi, by that time a newly elected Member of Parliament from a lower caste facing allegations from the upper caste in her constituency for a massacre in Behmai. The public debate on the film took Kapur to task for the prolonged rape scenes in the film, using the guise of feminism.[29] *Bandit Queen* was eventually released with no cuts but in several cities there were separate showings for women. Since the brouhaha surrounding its release two scholarly responses have allowed us to interrogate the film's politics: Shohini Ghosh's

• **Plate 14.5**
Bandit Queen (Channel 4 Films–Kaleidoscope Productions–British Film Institute)

essay 'Deviant Pleasures and Disorderly Women' places the film within the rubric of the outlaw films in popular films, questioning the film's feminist address; while Priyamvada Gopal assesses the context of its reception and questions the ethics of representation.

Fire (Deepa Mehta, 1998)

A Canadian–Indian co-production, Deepa Mehta's film sparked a similar debate to that on *Bandit Queen* because of its overt representations of sexual relationships between women. The right-wing Hindu party Shiv Sena called for a ban, propelling a heated debate on Hindu representations of women, lesbianism in the Hindu tradition and so on. Most of this is well recorded on several websites, including SAWNET (South Asian Women's Net). After the dust had settled there was further debate among feminists on the film's images of lesbian desire, Mehta's own distance from queer politics, the class politics in the film, and the relationship between audiences in the West and in India; such positions demand that we take a another look at this film.

FOUNDATIONAL FICTIONS OF THE POST-COLONIAL NATION

Critical writings on Indian cinema frequently dwell on how Indian films are intimately linked to questions of national identity and history. Sumita Chakravarty's *National Identity in Indian Popular Cinema, 1947–1987* (1993) for example examines the themes in Hindi popular cinema as contestations over national identity, including the shifting relationship between the gendered body and the nation state. Theodore Baskaran's pioneering work on Tamil cinema unravels the link between Tamil cinema and nationalist politics in Tamil Nadu, a focus that forces us to acknowledge regional nationalisms and cinemas (Baskaran 1981). The recent spate of overtly nationalist films has invited the ire of critics who have taken *Roja* and *Gadar* to task for espousing and condoning Hindu nationalist politics. It is in this context that we will look at two films in order to better understand how films stage battles over national identity.

☐ CASE STUDY 8: *HEY! RAM* (KAMAL HAASAN, 1999)[30]

Kamal Haasan's *Hey! Ram* (1999) tackles a nationalist narrative of epic proportions including Partition, Gandhi's assassination and contemporary communal politics in India. Rather than working as part of the backdrop, the film intimately ties these political and social events to the fate of the male protagonist Saket Ram. The twin preoccupations of the film produce an unruly narrative that avoids resolution of the knotty issues it sets in motion, yet urges us to consider the inextricable links between cinematic and national histories. Keeping pace with the narrative, the film deploys a number of formal strategies including monochromatic sequences for the contemporary scenes, digital images akin to video games, as well as a rich tapestry of quotations from world cinemas: elephants from D.W. Griffith's *Intolerance* (1916) and Pastrone's *Cabiria* (1914); dream sequences from Luis Bunuel's films; mise-en-scène from *Raiders of the Lost Ark* (Steven Spielberg, 1981) and so on. Simultaneously, it evokes these references to world cinema within a nationalist narrative and in effect revisits similar coincidences of interests in Griffith's *The Birth of a Nation* (1915), to a lesser extent in Mehboob Khan's *Mother India* (1957), and more overtly in S. Shankar's *Indian* (1996), a rich set of associations encouraging us to consider Mikhail Imapolski's (1998) suggestion that quotations in films gesture towards the past. *Hey! Ram* reconfigures the melodramatic aspects of these nationalist narratives by focusing exclusively on the male protagonist's relationship to the nation, a focus that dwells on the slow conversion of the South Indian Brahmin from a distant observer to a militant subversive by deploying digital technologies.[31]

To the consternation of critics lamenting the invasion of digital technologies, there is no doubt that digital morphing as a technique vastly improves the use of dissolves and cuts to suggest corporeal transformation on screen – wolf to man, man to woman and so on (Sobchack 2000). A similar pre-digital history obtains in Indian cinema, where cut-and-paste devices paper over the metamorphosis of a woman into a snake (see especially the genre of snake films including *Nagin* (1954) and *Nagina* (1986)); or the grafting of two separate frames to maintain the illusion of the multiple roles played by the same actor. In an instrumental sense, digital technologies advance the making of these illusions by rendering seamless transformations on-screen, in effect suturing us into the diegesis of the story. Yet this pull into the narrative cannot completely repress the history of innovations in digital technology imbricated in military experiments that are similarly plagued with issues of time and space.[32] It is therefore not surprising that we should find the most spectacular use of digital technologies in conquest narratives such as *Independence Day* (Roland Emmerich, 1996) and *The Matrix* (Wachowski, 1999), which heighten the relationship between cinematic and military modes of representations. Although *Hey! Ram* underplays military prowess, the film's use of digital technology to simulate a different story of origins consolidates the nationalist narrative and cannot help but remind us of the militant aspects of nationalism.

Kamal Haasan's film deploys digital technology to scramble linear chronology by moving back and forth between 1999 and the period 1946 to 1948. We see Saket Ram, a Tamil Brahmin, working as an archaeologist in Mohenjodaro in 1946; with his first wife Aparna in Calcutta during communal riots which ends in her death in 1946; a respite in Chidambaram and Madras where he marries Mythili, a little before Independence in 1947; visits to Maharashtra and his joining the ranks of right-wing Hindu militants between 1947 and 1948; and finally the denouement in Delhi when he tries to assassinate Gandhi in 1948. The temporal scrambling matches the spatial journey through pre-Partition India, allowing the film to draw a continuum from communal antagonisms during Partition to contemporary tensions set in motion after Hindu militants demolished the Babri Masjid on 6 December 1992. Saket Ram's conversion proceeds from his role as a disinterested scholar to a militant Hindu nationalist after encountering gorier aspects of communal riots in Calcutta, and finally to a Gandhian pacificist, a conversion narrative that rescues the film from wholly aligning itself with Hindu nationalism. Yet it is the middle sections, the parts spelling out Ram's entry into the ranks of the Hindu right, that are replete with the film's mastery over digital technology, especially morphing, relaying its own conversion from analogue to digital images.

One of the most flamboyant exhibitions of digital morphing takes places during Ram and Mythili's visit to a kingdom in Maharashtra – marking his definitive sympathies towards the right-wing Hindu party Rashtriya Sevak Sangha (RSS) – when the local king at the behest of Abhiyankar, a right-wing Hindu zealot whom Ram encounters during the riots in Calcutta – draws him into a scheme to kill Gandhi. After a fortuitous reconnection with his old friend Lalvani from Karachi, Ram and Mythili join the Ram Lila celebrations at the palace grounds where Abhiyankar offers Ram a drug-laced drink that induces Ram to conjure figures from the riot scene in Calcutta as well as heightening his sexual interest in Mythili. Seducing her away from a dance performance, he leads Mythili to their chambers. As they begin to make love, we see her morph into an enormous gun with Ram stroking its barrel. Undoubtedly this is a heavy-handed metaphoric substitution that carries a banal psychoanalytical association: the woman replaces the gun in a way that demands we understand how the libidinal drive severs itself from object identification. Clearly the excesses of the scene lead us to recognise how morphing showcases digital technology while providing only a tangential link to the narrative. Nevertheless, another reading also obtains here, one which takes us down a different road. Blinding us with technological prowess, *Hey! Ram* uses morphing to veil its relationship to censorship regulations. Instead of including a sexually explicit scene that may provoke the ire of the Board of Censors, the altered image allows us to view the scene through metaphoric

For further discussion of computer technology see Chapter 9, pp. 214–15.

substitution, a substitution that reconfigures the temporality of censorship. In its extreme form, popular films simply substitute the love-making scene with pastoral evocations, cut to a song and dance sequence to regulate the overflow of passion, or push the envelope to the limit. In all three possibilities available in the pre-digital era, we confront a linear unfolding of the narrative where a cut directs us to the next image. Morphing, on the other hand, maintains intact an old-fashioned relationship to censorship while distracting us with a show-stopping spectacle that morphs objects within the frame – a spatial transformation rather than a temporal one. Cushioned in a visit that highlights Ram's political conversion, morphing in this sequence overdetermines the connectives between political and sexual desire, an overlap that the film underscores during a secret meeting in the Maharaja's chambers when from Ram's point of view we see the Maharaja's face morph into that of Aparna. In other words, morphing allows a film such as *Hey! Ram* to expand the limits of what is permissible on the Indian screen through metaphoric substitution, a substitution that inverts the relationship between space and time between frames.

The second spectacular scene of morphing occurs soon after Ram's visit to Maharashtra, detouring through scenes of riots in 1996 composed in monochromatic colours mimicking black and white documentary footage – a burst of red fire undercuts the documentary gesture swaying it towards the diegesis of the film. These excursions to the monochromatic footage focus on an ailing Ram in the care of his grandson. Escorting Ram to a hospital through streets pocked by communal riots marking the anniversary of the demolition of the Babri Masjid, his grandson is halted by the police and escorted to the safety of a bunker. From an extreme close-up shot of Ram's left pupil the film dissolves into a digitally produced target. On the soundtrack we hear the police-officer's command to shoot – a sound-bridge connecting the two images. In the digitally produced scene, we see a muscular Ram at target practice; his attire clearly betrays signs of a Brahmin man including the sacred thread across his bare chest, an image that cannot completely sever its relationship to the real – Ram converts the handgun to a rifle by attaching a shoulder rest. This short scene of target practice celebrating the morphed muscular Brahmin body gives way to a simulated storm that sweeps over the entire screen. Undeterred by the ferocity of the storm he stands his ground.

Poised to function as an explanatory segment, morphing actualises Ram's metamorphosis from a reluctant spectator into a full-fledged member of a right-wing militant Hindu political party. Clearly the digital simulation of a muscular body adds further credence to popular representations of militant masculinities that surface in Amar Chitra Katha comic books and cable television.[33]

For further discussion of gender and masculinity, see Chapter 10, pp. 239–49.

In a compelling reading of masculinity and morphing in *Forrest Gump* (Robert Zemeckis, 1994), Joseba Gabilondo (2000) suggests that in the 1990s representations of morphing on screen usher in a different kind of masculinity, a resolutely heterosexual masculinity, constructed after or in response to both queer and feminist politics. Rather than the hard masculinities of the 1980s, according to him we find a masculinity that is self-involved, more narcissistic and more openly engaged with queerness without being queer.[34] Its response to feminism, however, has involved usurping reproduction, not through duplication but by inverting it – masculinity reclaims fatherhood as well as motherhood. This shift in representations, mobilised by morphing, according to Gabilondo, equally affects the conventional sadomasochism underlying masculinity:

The morphed and reproductive Masculinity of the 1990s show a new arrangement of this sadomasochistic economy: masochism becomes *avowed* by traditional filmic means (narrative and camera) while sadism is *disavowed* through morphing.

(Ibid.: 197)

Although great differences separate the unwilling male protagonist who suffers in *Forrest Gump* from the very deliberate action-oriented hero in *Hey! Ram*, both films engage with narratives of placing the common man in history, both officially and on the margins. Here too we find the sections preceding the morphing segment ripe with masculine inability: Ram watches helplessly as his wife Aparna is raped; bows to family pressures by marrying again; and even bears a sentimental attachment to women, home and domesticity. The communal riots do not immediately transform him into a militant Hindu nationalist. Rather, the narrative derives sufficient pleasure in his suffering, a convention familiar in several Tamil films starring Kamal Haasan: frontal shots of a body bruised by the police in *Nayakan* (1987) and *Guna* (1991); unrelenting masochistic narrative of the suffering male in *Mahanadhi* (1993) and so on. Morphing, on the other hand, provides the space to articulate a sadistic masculinity that is set in motion after Abhiyankar's death when Saket Ram is chosen to assassinate Gandhi. While we do find a fair share of masochism in the scene, morphing nevertheless constructs a hyperreal space outside the conventions of realism, allowing the passage from being subjected to a subject, from victim to agent. The narrative moves decisively towards action and resolution soon after the morphing segment: Ram leaves his wife and launches his participation in the assassination scheme. At closure, the film renders the excesses of militant masculinity as a futile excursion, choosing instead to close on a male subject whose place in history is assured after a journey through sadism.

Although *Hey! Ram* converts Kamal Haasan, the star, into a spectacular digital image that exceeds the star ideal, it is not the first film to do so. We find a more benign version of this digital simulation in *Magalir Mattum/Ladies Only* (1994), also starring Kamal Haasan. Frustrated by sexism at work, the women office-workers conjure a computer-simulated image of an ideal man who turns out to be the star Kamal Haasan. While *Magalir Mattum* unabashedly celebrates the star's image as the ideal poster boy for women office-workers, *Hey! Ram* accentuates this available image by severing its link to an indexical referent: the digital image is a vastly improved version of the star's body. However, the muscular body in the digital space does not abdicate its commitment to other referents but seeks to find its purpose within an older regime of filmic representation that continues to battle with notions of the real. In other words, the muscular militant body in the film services the cause of the ideal male image in Hindu nationalism and not that of the simulated battle on the screen. Yet Gabilondo's proposal that 'masculinity's masochistic renunciation of reality also represents a utopian possibility for other subject positionalities' (2000: 201) provides us with a way to imagine possibilities offered by the hyperreal digital images in *Hey! Ram*.

☐ **CASE STUDY 9: *LAGAAN/TAX* (ASHUTOSH GOWRIKAR, 2001)**

This highly successful film about cricket and politics has been the biggest cross-over film of the Hindi film industry to date, and was shown to packed houses in Britain in summer 2001. Set in the colonial period, the film sketches the trials and tribulations of the peasants of Champaner who are being subjected to British land tax during a long period of drought. The negotiations with the local British officers lead to an unexpected offer: if the villagers were to win a game of cricket, they would no longer have to pay taxes. Unlike the contemporary success of Indian cricket teams, the motley team put together by the protagonist Bhuvan, played by the star Aamir Khan, barely know or even understand the rudimentary rules of the game. This lacuna offers fodder for an Indo-English relationship to develop between the British captain's sister Elizabeth, serving as the peasants' coach, a move that allows us to imagine a romantic union between Bhuvan and the white memsahib. However, Gauri from the village, who has long harboured a desire for Bhuvan, prevents this reunion; hence a triangular erotic comedy unfolds. Besides managing these competing romantic interests, Bhuvan is focused on putting together a team that can

• **Plate 14.6**
Lagaan, Aamir Khan
Productions, courtesy
Hyphen Films Ltd

pulverise the British, an aspect of the narrative that the film succeeds in satisfying the cricket-crazed public in India by referencing stalwarts from Indian cricketing history. Thus, although a period film, the references to corruption and match-fixing resonate with contemporary overtones. The match itself is a good hour long with chance and talent pitted against each other. In a rather canny move, the film coaches the audiences in the finer aspects of the game through the figure of Elizabeth: we learn about the game as the villagers learn to play. There is no doubt that *Lagaan* successfully fuses, at least for the Indian audiences, two obsessions: cricket and movies.

CONCLUSION

The peculiar conditions of Indian commercial film narrative are constantly shifting, undoing our assumptions about some of its constituent elements. Defying the need to make sense by importing reading strategies inspired from either classical, early or contemporary American cinema, contemporary Indian movies compel us to employ several of these theoretical positions simultaneously to read *one* film. Despite being far removed from the central engine of capitalism and its accompanying realist narrative, Indian cinema mimics, copies and rewrites these forms while simultaneously maintaining a local quotient of attractions. In a curious twist in the history of appropriation and application of film theory across national cinemas, certain ontological questions surrounding narrative cinema – questions which Eisenstein raised in his famous essay on the 'montage of attractions' – find fertile ground in contemporary Indian cinema (Eisenstein 1997). An amalgamation of the different interruptions in Indian popular cinema throws up a picture bearing an uncanny resemblance to Peter Wollen's conceptualisation of the 'multi-diegesis' in Jean Luc-Godard's *Vent d'est/Wind from the East* (1969), a film that he claims undoes the narrative conventions of both Hollywood and Soviet films (Wollen 1982). We may be hard-pressed to see any immediate link between an overtly avant-garde practice and popular Indian cinema but, not unlike Wollen, viewers of Indian films do see its digressions and interruptions as intrinsic to enjoying and understanding these films as well as comprising the location of intense ideological struggles.

For detailed discussion of Eisenstein and Soviet Montage, see Chapter 15.

**http://www.mith2.umd.edu/WomensStudies/
FilmReviews/**

A database of film reviews of feminist films from
the University of Maryland, mainly written by Linda
Lopez McAllister. Some interesting and unusual
perspectives on American and British films.
Includes non-mainstream films.

http://www.virtualref.com/abs/882.htm

Women in Cinema: a reference guide. A discussion
of the role and impact of women on Western
cinema. Areas of discussion include: bibliogra-
phies and guides, biographical sources, reviews
and filmographies, electronic sources and subject
collections of film.

http://haze.customer.netspace.net.au

RML's movie page. A nicely organised collection
of information on directors, films and actors.
Described as 'international', meaning American
and European films.

http://imdb.com

The international movie database is comprehensive
and allows you to search for movies, including
Indian cinema, on title.

http://www.indiaplaza.com

Lists Hindi DVDs with English subtitles.

http://www.anytamil.com/php/home.php

Lists Tamil DVDs.

National cinemas: art, politics and the avant-garde

Chapter 15

The Soviet montage cinema of the 1920s

Mark Joyce

■ The Soviet montage cinema of the 1920s

INTRODUCTION: WHY STUDY THE SOVIET CINEMA?

As the lights went up at the end an emotion-charged silence reigned, broken only when Lunacharsky [the Soviet Union's Commissar for Education] jumped on his chair and began an enthusiastic speech: 'We've been witnesses at an historic cultural event. A new art has been born.'

(cited in Barna 1973: 102)

Anatoli Lunacharsky's response to Sergei Eisenstein's 1925 film *Battleship Potemkin* acknowledges the importance of a new wave of filmmaking. The films made by the Soviet directors of the 1920s are considered by many to be the most innovative and exciting to have been produced in the history of the cinema. The names of these filmmakers – Eisenstein, Pudovkin, Vertov and Kuleshov among others – are far from forgotten, and a number of the films and directors from this period score consistently highly in *Sight and Sound*'s critics'/directors' choice of the best ten films and directors.

This decade of intensive experimentation with film form produced techniques that have subsequently been widely emulated. In addition, the theoretical debates formulated by these filmmakers are still relevant today. For these reasons the **Soviet cinema** of the 1920s merits detailed analysis.

HISTORICAL BACKGROUND

The Soviet filmmakers of the 1920s reflect the **ideology** (the values and beliefs) and politics of the society in which they were produced. The early 1920s marked the end of a period of civil unrest, the causes of which lay in the great divide that separated wealthy landowning Russians from the peasants and workers.[1] For centuries Russia had been governed by the single figure of the Tsar, who had absolute powers. The Russian serfs were not granted freedom from slavery until 1861; this liberation, however, did not mean improved conditions, since they continued to live an existence of appalling poverty. Attempts had been made prior to the Revolution of October 1917 by various factions to undermine the Tsarist regime, all of which were unsuccessful. A wave of revolutionary activity in 1905 included a mutiny by Russian sailors at Odessa which formed the basis for Sergei Eisenstein's 1925 film *Battleship Potemkin*.

The First World War (1914–18) eventually proved to be disastrous for Tsar Nicholas II, since it consumed vast amounts of money and resources that were sorely needed at home. It was also unpopular with the Russian people as the reasons for fighting were unclear. The peasants and the workers were the worst hit by the impact of the war, either being killed on the front or starving at home as supplies became depleted. The landowning rich were protected by their wealth and were able to continue in their existing lifestyle.

These conditions provided the catalyst for the Revolution of 25 February 1917 which resulted in the formation of a liberal provisional government led by Alexander Kerensky and later supported by Menshevik and socialist revolutionary factions. This caused Nicholas II to abdicate on 4 March. The provisional government decided to continue the war, and for many (especially V.I. Lenin who was in hiding in Zurich) it appeared that the new government was in effect continuing the policies of the Tsarist order.

On 25 October 1917 the Bolsheviks, taking advantage of a situation of confusion and competition between the various factions, seized power by storming the Winter Palace.[2] The new Bolshevik government agreed to Germany's demands for control of areas of

Soviet cinema
This will refer to films made in the Soviet Union between October 1920 and 1991, although for the purposes of this chapter most Soviet films discussed will be confined to the 1920s.

See Chapter 3 for further discussion of film form.

See Chapter 7, pp. 151–2, for discussion of ideology in relation to spectatorship.

ideology
There are two key definitions of this term, one provided by the nineteenth-century German philosopher Karl Marx, the other by the twentieth-century French Marxist philosopher Louis Althusser, drawing on Marx's original ideas. For Marx, ideology was the dominant set of beliefs and values existent within society, which sustained power relations. For Althusser, ideology consisted of the representations and images which reflect society's view of 'reality'. Ideology thus refers to 'the myths that a society lives by'.

land previously under Russian administration and pulled out of the war. Almost immediately, however, a fierce civil war broke out between the Bolsheviks (known as the Reds) and those still loyal to the Tsarist regime (known as the Whites).[3]

By 1920 it was clear that the Bolsheviks had seized ultimate control of the country. The new Soviet government under the leadership of V.I. Lenin was faced with the task of convincing the population of Russia of the evils of the Tsarist regime and the positive points of the new communist one.

Selected historical dates

1905, Jan.	First revolution (abortive)
	Provides the backdrop for Eisenstein's *Battleship Potemkin*
1914, July	General strike organised by the Bolsheviks
	Outbreak of war and crushing of political unrest
	The war was a general disaster for the Russians; low morale and food shortages in the following years led to uprisings in 1917
1917, Feb.	Popular uprisings culminating in the overthrow of the Tsar and the setting up of a provisional government
1917, Oct.	The Bolsheviks overthrow the provisional government and seize political power
1918–21	Civil war between White and Red factions, as well as fighting of hostile troops sent from abroad in an attempt to restore the power of the Tsar. The continued fighting led to the destruction of trade, agriculture, industry and film production
1922–28	NEP (New Economic Policy) adopted by Lenin. A brief return to controlled forms of capitalism to help to rebuild the shattered economy
1922–23	Soviet feature film production resumes
1924	Sergei Eisenstein's *Strike* completed
1927	The tenth anniversary of the October Revolution. A number of films are made to mark the occasion including:
	October (Eisenstein)
	The End of St Petersburg (Vsevolod Pudovkin)
	The Fall of the Romanov Dynasty (Esfir Shub)

PRE-REVOLUTIONARY RUSSIAN CINEMA

The nature of Russian cinema

When discussing the Soviet cinema it is important to have at least an outline of the form and content of its antecedent, since although the majority of the Soviet directors had not made films prior to 1919, they would certainly have been familiar with the conventions of the pre-revolutionary cinema. Significantly, for a number of the Soviet directors, this cinema was the antithesis of their new approach to filmmaking. The **Russian cinema** (1907–17) was in fact markedly different from the Soviet cinema of the 1920s. The majority of the films that are available for viewing today[4] are between thirty-five and seventy minutes long and deal predominantly with the lives of the upper classes, centring quite frequently on their relationship with servants and/or the working class. Their subject matter, plot and preoccupations are often melodramatic; unfaithful husbands and wives, psychological states of mind and death predominate. The form of the films is also different, comprising slow-moving scenes containing a limited number of shots, with an emphasis on the **mise-en-scène** and in particular the expressions of the actors. A key director working in this period is Evgeny Bauer, who produced a large number of films including *After Death* (1915), *A Life for a Life* (1916) and *The King of Paris* (1917).

The Russian Revolution of October 1917 and the civil war that followed had a devastating effect on the Russian film industry, which was almost completely destroyed. Very

See Chapter 3, for further discussion of mise-en-scène.

Russian cinema
This will refer to the body of films made in Tsarist Russia between 1907 and 1917.

mise-en-scène
This literally means 'placed in the scene', and it includes all elements that are placed before the camera such as props, actors, costume, movement and position of actors, etc.

few of the Russian directors and stars remained in Russia after 1919, the majority having fled to Paris where they continued production. Initially it would seem that Russian cinema had little in common with the Soviet cinema that followed, and there appears to have been a clear break in terms of style between the two cinemas after the Revolution. The figure of Yakov Protazanov, however, provides an interesting example of a filmmaker who made films between 1911 and 1943.[5] His key films from the pre-revolutionary era include *The Queen of Spades* (1916) and *Satan Triumphant* (1917); these conform to the conventions of Russian cinema outlined above. His best-known film of the 1920s is *Aelita* (1924), a fantasy concerning a revolution on Mars. Protazanov was more concerned with mise-en-scène than with creating new meanings by juxtaposing images. A study of his films reveals that the Tsarist cinema continued into the Soviet **montage** era and was by all accounts successful with the public.[6]

montage
From the French word meaning 'to edit', montage means the assembling of pieces of footage to form a whole. In film studies it usually refers to the style of fast editing adopted by the Soviet filmmakers of the 1920s.

Russian cinema audiences and imported films

That Russian films had moderate success with native audiences is not surprising. What is significant, however, is that before the Revolution the most popular films with Russian audiences were imported from America, France and Germany. The first Russian film studio was not set up until 1907[7] and this may account in part for the success of these foreign films as audiences had grown accustomed to watching them. In the 1910s when native films vied for audiences with imported films, foreign films were clearly the more successful, and were perceived by Russian audiences as being more entertaining and having higher production values than Russian films.

SOVIET CINEMA AND IDEOLOGY: FILM AS AGENT OF CHANGE[8]

The October Revolution was the first successful revolution made in the name of Karl Marx (1818–83). For Marx, the key fact about any society was how it produced its livelihood. He saw capitalism as an economic system which, just like every other previous economic system, was based on exploitation. In capitalism the class with power was the bourgeoisie, the owners of the means of production, and the class subject to their power was the proletariat or working class. In addition, the bourgeoisie's economic strength was protected by the state and sustained by ideology. However, as capitalism developed, the workers, who survived by selling their labour for wages, would be squeezed more and more as competition between capitalists intensified. At the same time they would become aware that they would have everything to gain by replacing an economic system based on the ownership of private property with one based on the non-exploitative communal ownership of productive property. This awareness, or class-consciousness, would eventually produce a revolution. The October Revolution was seen as such a proletarian revolution in Russia and was celebrated in the films of the key Soviet filmmakers of the 1920s.

The revolution, however, was only the beginning of a process of radical social change, called the era of 'the dictatorship of the proletariat' because it involved the proletariat, or in this case its representative the Bolshevik Party, establishing its dominance. V.I. Lenin, writing in *Pravda*, outlined the situation:

Theoretically, there can be no doubt that between capitalism and communism there lies a definite transition period which must combine the features and properties of both these forms of social economy. This transition period has to be a period of struggle between dying capitalism and nascent communism – or, in other words, between capitalism which has been defeated but not destroyed and communism which has been born but is still very feeble.

(Lenin 1919)

See Chapter 8,
for discussion of
propaganda and British
cinema during the
Second World War.

propaganda cinema
A term used pejoratively
with reference to any
film that consciously
attempts to persuade an
audience towards certain
beliefs and values.

The transition to communism referred to by Lenin would have been a monumental task at the best of times, but the Bolsheviks had seized control of a country whose industry and agriculture were relatively underdeveloped. In addition, they had to confront internal and external opposition, civil war and famine. In such a situation artists and filmmakers were perceived as having a special role as proponents of **propaganda cinema.** Lenin declared in 1922 that 'of all the arts, for us the cinema is the most important'.[9] Prior to this, trains highly decorated with Soviet flags and paintings had been sent into the countryside in an attempt to educate and inform the peasants. Short, agitational films called *agitki* were made. Pre-revolutionary newsreels and foreign fiction films were also shown, with a Soviet commentator giving a 'new' reading to the material. Later most of the energy went into the making of new feature films that reflected the ideals of the new regime. Anatoli Lunacharsky (the People's Commissar for Education) had stated in 1924:

There is no doubt that cinema art is a first-class and perhaps even an incomparable instrument for the dissemination of all sorts of ideas. Cinema's strength lies in the fact that, like any art, it imbues an idea with feeling and with captivating form but, unlike the other arts, cinema is actually cheap, portable and unusually graphic. Its effects reach where even the book cannot reach and it is, of course, more powerful than any kind of narrow propaganda. The Russian Revolution, which is extremely interested in exercising the broadest possible influence on the masses, should long since have turned its attention to cinema as its natural instrument.

(Taylor and Christie 1994: 109)

The enthusiastic, young, educated filmmakers, who attempted to fulfil Lunacharsky's ideal of revolutionary cinema, responded by making innovative films which were revolutionary both in content and form.

ECONOMICS OF THE SOVIET FILM INDUSTRY

The pre-revolutionary Russian film industry had previously imported its film stock from abroad, and during the civil war most of the Russian filmmakers had fled to White-held areas (or abroad) taking their equipment with them. The reality facing the filmmakers of the newly formed state was that there was little in the way of film stock or equipment.[10]

The Soviet government attempted initially to ban the showing of all American and European films, as they were concerned about the public being exposed to films that reflected the values of capitalist societies. The Soviets, however, had little option but to show these films since they had no native film industry to produce their own. The cinema was seen by the new government as a means of keeping the public entertained at a time of hardship and general civil unrest.

From a Western perspective it is easy to underestimate the importance of imported films in the Soviet Union in the 1920s. Denise Youngblood (1992: 51), in *Movies for the Masses*, states that 'Foreign films accounted for almost two-thirds of the titles screened in the twenties.... Nearly as many American as Soviet films were shown in this period.' She continues: 'Sovkino's head, K.M. Shvedchikov, claimed in 1927 that Sovkino would be bankrupt were it not for the success of its import policy.'

The 1920s could be characterised as a period in which American and European narrative films were in effect directly subsidising the dramatic experimentation with film form undertaken by the Soviet filmmakers.

Innovation and experimentation frequently arise from a lack. In the Soviet Union the lack of film stock (and even film cameras) meant that certain groups of filmmakers worked on re-editing existing films (often European/American films and old Russian newsreels) to make them conform to the values of the Soviet state. Other filmmakers experimented with creating films from the small amount of negative available, which often only came in short lengths. Out of this experimentation came Soviet montage cinema.

FORM: MONTAGE

The roots of Soviet montage

The innovative use of montage in film by the Soviet filmmakers had its roots in art forms such as painting, literature and music from pre-revolutionary Russia. David Bordwell (1972), in 'The Idea of Montage in Soviet Art and Film', states that by 1910 a group of Russian painters had already experimented extensively with 'montage': 'the Russian futurists declared that conventional art must be destroyed and that a new art, appropriate to the machine age, must be created. Hence the futurists took their subjects from modern life and exploited a technique of shocking juxtapositions.' Poetry, in particular that of Mayakovsky,[11] was also 'shattering words and reassembling them into brutal images'.

The question needs to be asked: Why didn't the Russian filmmakers of the 1910s experiment with montage earlier? This lack of explicit montage experiment in Russian cinema compared to that taking place in other art forms may perhaps be attributed to economics. The crucial difference between film and many of the other arts at the time was that the small groups of experimental artists, writers and musicians were often privately funded by rich patrons. The film industry, however, was not.[12] The Revolution of October 1917 provided the right conditions for experimentation with film to take place. It is ironic that this experimentation had its roots in the élitist art forms of pre-revolutionary Russia.

The Kuleshov effect and its consequences

The montage technique is based on the theory that when two pieces of film are placed side by side the audience immediately draws the conclusion that the two shots must be directly related in some way. In other words, the audience tries to create meaning by combining the two separate images. The experimentation along these lines by Lev Kuleshov, a young Soviet filmmaker, culminated in what became known as the Kuleshov effect. Vsevolod Pudovkin outlined the experiment in a lecture given at the London Film Society in February 1929:

See Chapter 3, pp. 77–9, for reference to Kuleshov's experiments with editing, and discussion of editing in mainstream narrative cinema.

> Kuleshov and I made an interesting experiment. We took from some film or other several close-ups of the well-known Russian actor Mosjukhin. We chose close-ups which were static and which did not express any feeling at all – quiet close-ups. We joined these close-ups, which were all similar, with other bits of film in three different combinations. In the first combination the close-up of Mosjukhin was immediately followed by a shot of a plate of soup standing on a table. It was obvious and certain that Mosjukhin was looking at this soup. In the second combination the face of Mosjukhin was joined to shots showing a coffin in which lay a dead woman. In the third the close-up was followed by a shot of a little girl playing with a funny toy bear. When we showed the three combinations to an audience which had not been let into the secret the result was terrific. The public raved about the acting of the artist. They pointed out the heavy pensiveness of his mood over the forgotten soup, were touched and moved by the deep sorrow with which he looked on the dead woman, and admired the light, happy smile with which he surveyed the girl at play. But we knew that in all three cases the face was exactly the same.

(Pudovkin 1929)

Kuleshov carried out further experiments using editing in which he cut together separate shots of a walking man, a waiting woman, a gate, a staircase and a mansion.[13] When the shots were combined the audience assumed that the different elements were present at the same location. Kuleshov had discovered the cinema's ability to link entirely unrelated material into coherent sequences. He termed the technique 'creative geography'.

Hollywood cinema
In classical Hollywood cinema, the editing is designed to be 'invisible'. It is intended to allow the audience closer views and to see the point of view of different characters. The editing is used essentially to clarify what is taking place in the narrative. This type of editing had become dominant in Hollywood filmmaking by approximately 1920.

juxtaposition
In film studies, this usually refers to two different shots that have been joined together to make a contrast.

alternative
Alternative cinema is defined with reference to **dominant**: it is an alternative (both economically and formally) to the dominant form. In any study concerning an 'alternative' cinema, the films would not only have to be examined in their own right, but also compared to contemporary dominant Hollywood cinema. A number of questions may have to be posed when analysing these alternative films: In what ways is this group of films different to the dominant cinema of the time? What are the possible reasons for the difference: cultural? economic? social? political? Could this 'alternative' way of making films, given the right conditions, have itself turned into the dominant cinema? The Soviet cinema of the 1920s, when compared to the Hollywood cinema of the same era, could certainly be regarded as alternative. In other words, it offered a style of filmmaking that was radically different to the mass of films that was being produced in America.

Kuleshov's discoveries about the nature of the cinema medium provided a number of filmmakers with a new set of ideas about how film could manipulate and deceive an audience. Perhaps the most vital consequence of the Kuleshov effect, however, for later directors, was its recognition that the audience were not merely passive recipients.

Soviet montage cinema

In the 1920s a number of filmmakers carried out further experiments with editing techniques along the same lines as Kuleshov. It was discovered that when two shots were joined together meaning could be made by emphasising the difference between shots; that is, instead of trying to cover up graphic dissimilarities between shots, as with **Hollywood cinema**, the difference could be emphasised and indeed become the main way in which meaning could be created. This 'montage' cinema which demanded that audiences continually search for the meanings created by the **juxtaposition** of two shots may thus be seen as **alternative** to the continuity editing-based Hollywood cinema. One of the Soviet filmmakers who developed this idea into both a theory and a practice of filmmaking was Sergei Eisenstein.

Eisenstein believed that maximum impact could be achieved if shots in a scene were in conflict. This belief was based on the general philosophical idea that 'existence' can only continue by constant change. In other words, everything surrounding us in the world is as a result of a 'collision' of opposite elements. The existing world is itself only in a temporary state until the next collision of elements produces a completely new state. It is only through this 'collision' that change can be effected. This method of creating meaning from such collision of opposites is termed **dialectical**. When applying this idea to film, Eisenstein proposed the view that when two shots are combined a completely new meaning is formed. For example, shot A combined with shot B does not produce AB but the new meaning C. The formulation can also be presented as:

thesis + anti-thesis = synthesis.

Vsevolod Pudovkin, another key Soviet filmmaker, was opposed to the theoretical ideas of Eisenstein, although they both used innovative forms of montage in their films. Pudovkin, like Kuleshov, believed that shots could be likened to bricks in the sense that they could be used as building blocks to construct a scene. Pudovkin then did not see his shots as being in conflict. In Pudovkin's formulae shot A + shot B = AB rather than C. Pudovkin aimed at linkage rather than conflict in his scenes.

The montage technique was not only confined to fiction filmmaking. Soviet documentary filmmakers such as Dziga Vertov and Esfir Shub used montage extensively in a range of films in the 1920s, including Vertov's well-known *The Man with a Movie Camera* (1929). For Vertov much of the power of cinema came from its ability to record mechanically events that took place before the camera, but he also ensured that the audience was made aware of the constructed nature of his films. His films are a whirlwind of conflicting shots which disavow conventional ideas of narrative.

The montage technique for the majority of the Soviet filmmakers could also provide sequences with a sense of rhythm and momentum, which could be used to increase or decrease the speed of the action. Eisenstein, for example, frequently increases his rate of cutting prior to the climax of a scene. Violent actions could also be emphasised by using a succession of short conflicting shots from different viewpoints. Montage, the filmmakers discovered, could be further used to either compress or expand time, which could heighten the effect of certain actions or events.

Four different types of film montage[14]

The first two categories of montage outlined below are frequently, although not exclusively, used in Soviet film; the last two categories deal with montage techniques that are often to be found in mainstream films:

- intellectual montage (also called dialectical montage or discontinuity editing)
- linkage editing (also known as constructive editing)
- Hollywood montage
- fast cutting

Intellectual montage

In this type of editing, shots are placed together to emphasise their difference. They are in 'collision' with each other. For example, in *October* a shot of a mechanical golden peacock is placed next to a shot of a man (the peacock does not form part of the world of the film; that is, it is **non-diegetic**).[15] The audience draw the conclusion that the man is vain. In this type of editing the audience are not passive as they play an active part in producing meaning from the film.

Linkage editing

Mainly used by Pudovkin, who proposed a theory of montage based on this principle. In linkage editing individual shots are used to build up scenes. The shots are not in collision with each other, but are used as fragments or parts of a whole scene. This technique may be seen in *The Mother* and *The End of St Petersburg*.

Hollywood montage

Often used to show a quick succession of events over a period of time. For example, in *Raging Bull* (1980) Martin Scorsese shows the successful career of the boxer Jack La Motta by combining shots (mostly still photographs) taken from a number of different fights interspersed with home movie footage of La Motta's home life. The shots are clearly intended to flow into each other rather than to be in conflict. The music played on the soundtrack over the images reinforces the sense of continuity.

Fast cutting

In which editing is used primarily to build suspense or tension. For example, in the gunfight at the climax of *The Good, the Bad and the Ugly* (1966), Sergio Leone creates a dramatic effect by using a combination of music, tighter and tighter close-ups of the three characters, and a shortening of shot length.

Statistical analysis of Soviet films

Soviet films, because of the use of the montage technique, contain many more shots than Hollywood films of the same period. David Bordwell (1986)[16] claims that the Soviet films of the 1920s contain on average between 600 and 2,000 shots, whereas the films made in Hollywood between 1917 and 1928 contain on average between 500 and 1,000 shots. He further suggests that Hollywood films had an average shot length of five to six seconds while for Soviet films the average shot length was two to four seconds. The comparison provides concrete evidence of the unique nature of the editing used in the Soviet films during this period.

OTHER FEATURES OF SOVIET MONTAGE CINEMA

Aside from editing, these films have other features which separate them from the **dominant** Hollywood cinema. In keeping with a Marxist analysis of society, plots frequently do not centre on the individual; for example, in Eisenstein's *Strike*, *October* and *Battleship Potemkin*, individual heroes are replaced by a mass of people. The only characters that are individuated are those that wield power or have wealth. Events in the narrative therefore are not motivated by individuals. Films such as Pudovkin's *The Mother* and *The End of St Petersburg* and Dovzhenko's *Earth* (1930) do have central characters, but it is made clear that these characters are representative of the masses.

dialectical
A difficult term to define, as it has many different meanings. The *Collins English Dictionary* (2nd edn, 1986), for example, defines it as a 'disputation or debate, esp. intended to resolve differences between two views rather than to establish one of them as true'. The crucial factor to grasp in the context of Eisenstein's thinking, however, is the notion of change and the creation of a new order. Eisenstein would have defined dialectic with reference to Marxist philosophy, which believed that society was contradictory and in need of change.

non-diegetic
Refers to any element that remains outside the world of the film, such as voiceovers, credits and mood-setting music, that does not originate from the world of the film.

dominant
Refers to both economic strength and the dominant form or convention, which at this time is realism: dominant cinema in film studies is assumed to be Hollywood.

The audience is not interested in the details of the heroes, only what they represent. A number of the Soviet filmmakers (including Eisenstein and Pudovkin) also used non-actors to play key parts, believing that the external appearance of the character was vital to the performance. This idea is termed 'typage'.

The montage style also means that Soviet cinema relies more heavily on the use of the close-up than does Hollywood cinema. Not only are there more shots overall in a scene, but a greater proportion of them are close-ups. A number of Soviet films also rely on high levels of **symbolism** to achieve their aims. The audience must be culturally and politically aware to be able to decode the messages that are being presented. In Eisenstein's *October*, for example, great demands are made on the audience to create a 'reading' of the film which does justice to Eisenstein's political thinking. It may seem that many of the filmmakers ran the risk of making films that were not understood by their audience.

Several of the montage filmmakers combined the montage principle with other techniques that they believed would revitalise cinema. Lev Kuleshov, for example, placed great emphasis on the gestures and movement of actors. FEKS (Factory of the Eccentric Actor), formed by filmmakers Grigori Kozintsev and Leonid Trauberg, had similar concerns about the role of the actor, but also paid close attention to mise-en-scène.

symbolism
The means by which a filmmaker can assign additional meanings to objects/characters in a film. For example, in Dovzhenko's *Earth* and Eisenstein's *Old and New*, the tractor is a symbol of progress.

THE KEY SOVIET MONTAGE FILMMAKERS OF THE 1920s

Fiction
Lev Kuleshov
Sergei Eisenstein
Vsevolod Pudovkin
FEKS (Kozintsev and Trauberg)
Alexander Dovzhenko

Documentary
Dziga Vertov
Esfir Shub

A film directed by Eisenstein probably provided most viewers' first experience of Soviet montage. The history of the Soviet cinema of the 1920s, however, involves more than the work of this one director. In this section, although the work of Eisenstein is discussed in detail, the vital importance of Eisenstein's contemporaries is recognised by analysing the work of such directors as Kuleshov, Pudovkin, Kozintsev and Trauberg, Dovzhenko, Vertov and Shub.

Lev Kuleshov (1899–1970)

Key films
Engineer Prite's Project (1918)
The Extraordinary Adventures of Mr West in the Land of the Bolsheviks (1924)
The Death Ray (1925)
By the Law (1926)

Shortly after the Revolution, Kuleshov was recruited as a teacher by the State Film School where he set up an experimental film workshop. Kuleshov and his students carried out a number of experiments related to editing, partly inspired by a lack of raw film stock. One of these experiments included re-editing D.W. Griffith's *Intolerance* (1916), a film that had impressed Kuleshov due to its innovative use of editing. The experiments resulted in the formation of a number of principles of filmmaking that the group adopted. The underlying belief for Kuleshov was that 'Film-art begins from the moment when the director begins to combine and join together the various pieces of film'.[17] Kuleshov's ideas about how editing should work are similar to those of Pudovkin in that his shots, rather than being in conflict, may be seen as blocks out of which a scene can be constructed. Significantly, Kuleshov's students included Vsevolod Pudovkin and, for a brief time, Sergei Eisenstein. In Eisenstein's films and theoretical writing the influence of Kuleshov may be seen clearly.

Kuleshov's experimentation was not confined to editing, however, but also involved acting. He believed that theatre-trained actors, in particular those from the Moscow Arts Theatre,[18] were not suitable for the cinema. He also rejected the idea of using non-actors or 'types' chosen for their visual suitability for a role. He set up an acting laboratory dedicated to developing a style of acting tailored specifically to the requirements of the cinema and he carefully recruited would-be film actors who were 'endowed with natural beauty, good health, and the ability to show expediency and purpose on the screen without "acting" or "recreating", unaided by makeup, wigs, and props, of course' (cited in Zorkaya 1989: 52).

The techniques that Kuleshov adopted emphasised gesture and movement, the exact nature and timing of which had been practised rigorously in rehearsals. This style of acting was combined with close attention to the composition and framing of each shot to give maximum impact to the action. Kuleshov's opportunity to apply the principles that he had developed came in 1924 when he was assigned valuable imported film stock to direct the first feature film of the film school: *The Extraordinary Adventures of Mr West in the Land of the Bolsheviks*.

For comparison and contrast see Chapter 6, for a discussion of the star in Hollywood cinema.

□ CASE STUDY 1: LEV KULESHOV, *THE EXTRAORDINARY ADVENTURES OF MR WEST IN THE LAND OF THE BOLSHEVIKS* (1924)

The film is an action comedy which uses satire to expose the false attitudes and beliefs about the Soviet Union held by many in the West. The action centres on the fate of Mr West, an American visitor to the USSR, whose view of the Bolsheviks as savages is formed by reading the *New York Times*. Mr West falls into the hands of a group of petty criminals who frighten him into parting with his dollars by dressing up to look like the Bolsheviks who Mr West has seen in his paper. At the climax he is rescued by a 'real' Bolshevik who uncovers the deception. Mr West's stereotypical views of the Bolsheviks are dismantled and he sends a radio message to his wife telling her to hang Lenin's picture in the study.

The montage technique used in *Mr West* is largely based on a system of close-ups of the actors that emphasise facial expressions. Kuleshov frequently cuts from an action to a close-up reaction shot of a character's face. He begins the film with a separate shot of Mr West juxtaposed with another of his wife; it is only later that we see them together.

• **Plate 15.1**
The Extraordinary Adventures of Mr West in the Land of the Bolsheviks (Lev Kuleshov, 1924). Mr West is duped by the false Bolsheviks

Later in the film Kuleshov cuts between a shot of the 'real' Bolshevik and Mr West standing on a balcony, and another shot of marching Soviet troops taken at a different place and time (the film stock is markedly different).

Kuleshov here is using his technique of creative geography to make the audience construct a location in their minds that does not actually exist. The film also fulfils Kuleshov's ideas concerning acting. The movements of the actors are stylised and precise, and it is clear that attention has been paid to even the smallest action. The comical nature of the action and a plot based on individual characters meant that the film was popular with audiences.[19]

Sergei Eisenstein (1898–1948)

Eisenstein, as his age might indicate (he was just 26 when he completed *Strike*), did not emerge from the context of the pre-revolutionary Russian cinema. Prior to his filmmaking career, he had experimented with a number of different art forms, including the theatre. In this experimentation, the principles of his work in film may be found. In 1923 Eisenstein produced a version of a play by Alexander Ostrovky,[20] in which he attempted to communicate the messages of the play to the audience using a series of shocks which Eisenstein termed 'attractions': 'Emotions were expressed through flamboyant physical stunts … at the finale, firecrackers exploded under spectators' seats … [he] explained that the theatre could engage its audience through a calculated assembly of "strong moments" of shock or surprise' (Bordwell 1993: 6).

Eisenstein quickly abandoned experimentation with the theatre and turned to the more popular and accessible medium of film, to which he rigorously applied his theatrical principle of 'montage of attractions'.

☐ CASE STUDY 2: SERGEI EISENSTEIN, *STRIKE* (1924); *BATTLESHIP POTEMKIN* (1925); *OCTOBER* (1927); *OLD AND NEW* (1929)

Strike (1924)

Strike was the first of a proposed series of eight films[21] made by the Moscow Theatre of the Proletkult, under the general subheading 'Towards the Dictatorship of the Proletariat'. *Strike* is about the repression of a group of factory workers involved in an industrial dispute, which ends with the massacre of the strikers and their families by government forces. The six-part structure of *Strike* – (1) 'All Quiet at the Factory', (2) 'The Immediate Cause of Strike', (3) 'The Factory Stands Idle', (4) 'The Strike is Protracted', (5) 'Engineering a Massacre', (6) 'Slaughter' – is due in part to Eisenstein's theatrical background, but it would also have been vital for the film to be contained on single reels, as many cinemas had only one projector.

The plot of *Strike*, as in Eisenstein's later films *Battleship Potemkin* (1925) and *October* (1927), is not told using individual characters as heroes. Instead, any character that is individuated is deemed to be 'bad' or corrupt. The grotesque factory owner, for example, is shown completely isolated in a vast office. The workers themselves, however, are seen usually as a group with no one individual standing out to play the role of leader. In Part 3 these ideas are combined. The scenes depicting the four stockholders of the factory carelessly deciding the future of the strikers are intercut with images of strikers being attacked by mounted police; the individual concern of the capitalists contrasts with the collective concern of the masses. The effect of this montage is dramatic, as parallels can immediately be drawn by the viewer between, for example, the dishonesty, greed, deviousness and wealth of the management, and the poverty and honesty of the workers. The political implications of this are obvious. Eisenstein, through montage, is seeking to persuade his audience towards a certain view.

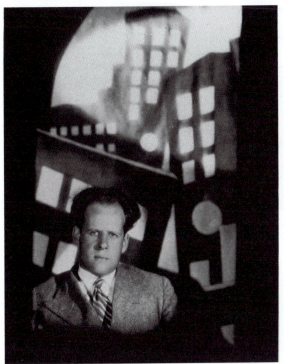

• **Plate 15.2**
Sergei Eisenstein
(1898–1948)

• **Plate 15.3**
Strike (Sergei
Eisenstein, 1924).
Mounted police enter
the factory district

The methods applied by Eisenstein in *Strike* are derived in part from a rebellion against what Eisenstein termed the 'Bourgeois Cinema' that was still the main form of entertainment in post-revolutionary cinemas. Eisenstein explains how this cinema was rejected in favour of his own approach: 'We brought collective and mass action onto the screen ... our films in this period made an abrupt deviation – insisting on an understanding of the masses as hero' (cited in Leyda 1983: 181).

• **Plate 15.4**
This sequence from *Strike* (lasting 25 seconds) illustrates Eisenstein's intellectual montage. An inter-title ('Rout') is inserted between shots 2 and 3

In terms of Hollywood cinema it is not difficult to imagine how the plot of *Strike* could have been adapted into a mainstream film: the story of one individual's fight against authority. The comparison may be trite, but it does emphasise the difference in approach and purpose between the two different modes of representation. Eisenstein's decision not to use individual heroes is of course deliberate: the film registers a political ideology that enshrines the notion of collective strength.

In *Strike*, Eisenstein applies his principle of 'montage of attractions' to the editing. He believed that by creating visual 'jolts' between each cut, the viewer would be 'shocked' into new awarenesses. In most sequences this approach involves juxtaposing shots that are in conflict with each other in some way, either cutting between different actions taking place in a scene or emphasising the importance of certain actions or events by fragmenting them into a number of shots taken from different viewpoints. At various points in *Strike* Eisenstein juxtaposes shots which need to be interpreted by the audience. One of the best examples of this type of 'intellectual montage' is in the last part of the film ('Slaughter'), in which Eisenstein juxtaposes a non-diegetic image of a bull being slaughtered with shots of factory workers being systematically butchered by government forces. The formula mentioned earlier may be applied: shot A (massacre of the workers) + shot B (bull being slaughtered) = NEW MEANING C (that the workers are being killed cold-bloodedly like animals in a slaughterhouse). It is the audience that is creating meaning here from the juxtaposition of the shots, thus becoming active political interpreters.

● **Plate 15.5**
Battleship Potemkin
(Sergei Eisenstein,
1925). Drama on the
quarter-deck (the firing
squad)

Battleship Potemkin (1925)

Eisenstein's second film, *Battleship Potemkin*, is based on the true story of a mutiny that took place on board the *Potemkin* in 1905.[22] As in *Strike, Battleship Potemkin* is split into a number of distinct parts: (1) 'Men and Maggots', (2) 'Drama on the Quarter Deck', (3) 'Appeal from the Dead', (4) 'The Odessa Steps', (5) 'Meeting the Squadron'.

The central scene of the film, 'The Odessa Steps', consisting of parallel lines of soldiers marching down the steps leading to the harbour systematically shooting the onlookers, provides a vivid example of the effectiveness of Eisenstein's montage technique.[23] A close examination of the sequence reveals that Eisenstein, by using montage to repeat certain key events, has expanded time.[24] The effect is to heighten the horrific nature of the slaughter as well as to hold the audience in suspense as the pram finally begins its descent. The furious and shocking climax to the scene demonstrates how Eisenstein is able to use montage to manipulate audience expectations, and to shock with violent juxtapositions and graphic images.

In the last part of the film in which the sailors aboard the *Potemkin* are nervously anticipating an attack by the rest of the Russian Fleet, Eisenstein builds up tension by increasing the number of cuts in a montage finale that maintains a consistently high rate of shots per minute. The scene provides an excellent example of the way in which montage could be used to create an event that did not exist as a whole, as according to Eisenstein the shots of the 'Russian' squadron were taken from 'old newsreels of naval manoeuvres – not even of the Russian Fleet' (cited in Leyda 1983: 195).[25] It also reveals how montage may be used for rhythmic effect, as the fast cutting between the different elements gives the scene a sense of urgency which would be impossible to achieve using any other method.

The opposition of critics at the time ironically stressed the difficulties of understanding *Potemkin*'s experimental form; ironic because it was through film form that Eisenstein hoped to make his political points. It was also declared that *Potemkin* was pitched far above the intellectual level of most peasants, a damning indictment for any propaganda/revolutionary piece. However, although *Potemkin* was not successful as a piece of popular propaganda, it did, like *Strike* before it, mark a major step in the progress of revolutionary cinema. It also represented the first film that achieved recognition and acclaim for Soviet cinema. The claim that the experimental nature of *Potemkin* was not

• **Plate 15.6**
Battleship Potemkin
(Sergei Eisenstein,
1925). The Odessa
Steps

• **Plates 15.7, 15.8, 15.9**
Battleship Potemkin (Sergei Eisenstein, 1925). Immediately after the massacre on the Odessa Steps, the sailors on
the battleship take their revenge by shelling the headquarters of the generals. As part of this sequence, Eisenstein
juxtaposes three images of stone lions in different stages of awakening as a symbol of the awakening of the
Russian people to political ideas and action

solely to blame for its unpopularity, and that it was badly let down by Sovkino's methods
of distribution, is a view that should certainly be considered.

Immediately after the massacre on the Odessa Steps, the sailors on the battleship
take their revenge by shelling the headquarters of the generals. As part of this sequence,
Eisenstein juxtaposes three images of stone lions in different stages of awakening as a
symbol of the awakening of the Russian people to political ideas and action.

October (1927)

October, made for the Tenth Anniversary celebrations of the Russian Revolution, depicts
the buildup to the October Revolution, ending with the storming of the Winter Palace by
the Bolsheviks. It is considered the most experimental of Eisenstein's films, especially in
its increased use of 'intellectual montage', which demands that the audience think critically and constructively about important political issues. A demonstration of this type
of montage may be found in the scene in which both Kerensky and General Kornilov
are depicted as Napoleons. By intercutting between the two men and the plaster-cast
figures of Napoleon, Eisenstein effectively exposes both the vanity and essentially
the lack of any power within the characters themselves to form a separate identity.
Eisenstein's 'intellectual montage' also involves **diegetic** material. For example, early in
the film, shots of a soldier cowering in a trench are juxtaposed with low-angle shots of a

diegetic
The elements of a film
that originate from
directly within the film's
narrative. For example,
a popular song being
played on the soundtrack
would be diegetic if it
was clear that it was
coming from a source
within the world of the
film such as a car radio.

• **Plate 15.10**
October (Sergei
Eisenstein, 1927).
Lenin's arrival at the
Finland Railway Station

vast cannon being unloaded elsewhere. The combination of shots points initially to the soldier being physically crushed, but then the assumption is swiftly reached that the war is oppressive, degrading and without purpose for the ordinary troops.

Eisenstein also combines montage techniques with visual puns and symbolism for political effect. At one point, in order to degrade the power of the Church, he swiftly cuts from the image of one deity to another, starting with a magnificent statue of Christ, and ending up with a primitive wooden idol, demonstrating that all religions essentially worship crude man-made objects. Eisenstein's use of such techniques was considered by many to be obscure, inaccessible in meaning and élitist. Victor Shklovsky, writing in *Novyi Lef* in 1927, records the responses of a man connected with the cinema:

After viewing some Eisenstein sequences a man who is intelligent and conversant with cinema said to me, 'That is very good. I like that a lot but what will the masses say? What will the people we are working for say?' What can you say to that?

(cited in Taylor and Christie 1994: 182)

Indeed, an examination of contemporary criticism of *October* reveals that far from being popular among Soviet audiences, the film was met with derision and apprehension.

Old and New (1929)

The adverse reaction to *October* prompted Eisenstein to produce *Old and New*, a film understood more readily by audiences. Despite employing a number of the techniques used in *October*, Eisenstein presents them in a simplified form. Juxtapositions, for example, are more obvious and on a less symbolic level.

• **Plate 15.11**
Old and New or *The General Line* (Sergei Eisenstein, 1929). The new tractor is eventually delivered to Martha's co-operative

The narrative of *Old and New*, concerned with the collectivisation of agriculture, unlike Eisenstein's previous films, is bound together by a central character or heroine 'Martha'. Despite its more conventional narrative form, the film contains one of Eisenstein's most effective montage sequences in which a cream separator is delivered to the collective farm. The new machine is eyed suspiciously by the peasants as milk is poured into it. In an ever-quickening flow of images, Eisenstein cuts between the glittering, spinning parts of the machine, the changing faces of the peasants and non-diegetic shots of fountains of water which symbolise the future flow of cream from the separator. The film is fascinating to study in the context of Eisenstein's earlier work and marks an attempt to address problems of understanding associated with *October*.

Vsevolod Pudovkin (1893–1953)

Key films
The Mother (1926)
The End of St Petersburg (1927)
Storm Over Asia (1928)

Editing is the language of the film director. Just as in living speech, so, one may say, in editing: there is a word – the piece of exposed film, the image; a phrase – the combination of these pieces.

(Pudovkin, cited in Perkins 1972a: 21)

Pudovkin believed that the power of cinema comes from editing. In the above quotation he claims that a 'shot' (or image) which is the equivalent of the single word in language has very limited meaning. However, when a number of words are combined together they form a 'phrase' which is dense with meaning. Pudovkin's equivalent of a 'phrase' was a number of shots edited together. He went further to support his claim by contending that

every object taken from a given viewpoint and shown on the screen to spectators, is a *dead object*, even though it has moved before the camera.... Only if the object be placed together among a number of separate objects, only if it be presented as part of a synthesis of different separate visual images, is it endowed with filmic life.

(Ibid.: 22)

It would seem initially that Pudovkin's theoretical position regarding the effectiveness of editing was in tandem with his contemporary Eisenstein. There are, however, important differences in the specific way each director thought editing should be used.[26] Pudovkin did not agree with Eisenstein's system of montage, which created visual 'jolts' between cuts. Instead, Pudovkin believed greater impact could be made by linking shots in a constructive way. Shots were to be used as individual building blocks, made to fit together exactly. Although seemingly theoretically opposed to Eisensteinian montage, Pudovkin made extensive use of devices such as 'intellectual montage' in *The Mother* and *The End of St Petersburg*. Pudovkin's juxtapositions, however, are much less symbolic, more clearly related to the diegetic world of the film and less intent on creating conflict than those of Eisenstein. Leon Moussinac, a French historian, summed up the differences between the two directors: 'An Eisenstein film resembles a shout, a Pudovkin film evokes a song' (cited in Taylor 1979: 142).

Pudovkin, like Eisenstein, cast according to 'type' and was concerned about the problem of 'stagey acting'. He stated:

I want to work only with real material – this is my principle. I maintain that to show, alongside real water and real trees and grass, a property beard pasted on the actor's face, wrinkles traced by means of paint, or stagey acting is impossible. It is opposed to the most elementary ideas of style.[27]

Unlike Eisenstein, however, Pudovkin uses individual characters that are cast in the role of hero or heroine to carry the narrative, and although he discouraged the use of professional actors some of his lead parts were played by professional actors of the Moscow Arts Theatre.[28]

☐ CASE STUDY 3: VSEVOLOD PUDOVKIN, *THE MOTHER* (1926); *THE END OF ST PETERSBURG* (1927)

The Mother (1926)

The scenario for Pudovkin's *The Mother* is based on the earlier play by Gorky of the same name. The plot is concerned with the political awakening of a mother after she betrays her son to the police, in the belief that he will be dealt with justly. The action is set (as in *Battleship Potemkin*) in the revolutionary context of 1905, with strikes, mass protests and a final brutal massacre of the workers.

With its focus on individuals, the film offers an interesting contrast to Eisenstein's approach to revolutionary cinema. In *The Mother*, the role of the individual is reinstated and emphasised. The mass struggle is thus registered through the lives and fates of separate characters involved in that struggle. It is important to note that the individual characters are not highlighted in such a way that the general struggle itself becomes obscured. The audience is encouraged to make connections between individual fate and the fate of the masses. Pudovkin is thus using individual characters to make his political points, believing that the audience would be able to relate better to separate identities than to an anonymous mass.

Pudovkin's use of 'linkage' editing (shot A + shot B = AB) may be illustrated in the trial scene at the mid-point of the film. The scene is composed of a large number of shots which tend to centre on single characters or pairs of characters. The fragmentation allows Pudovkin to draw direct comparisons between, for example, the uninterested and uncaring attitude of the judges, the accused Pavel, his mother and several of the gossiping onlookers. Close shots of the soldiers guarding the courthouse are also inserted in order to demonstrate that 'justice' is being upheld by a substantial force. Pudovkin clearly reveals the judges to be vain and self-interested by highlighting their overriding concern with attire and pictures of horses, rather than with the proceedings of the trial. If the same scene had been shot by Eisenstein the vanity of the judges might have been indicated in a similar way to that of Kerensky in *October* (that is, by juxtaposing him with a shot of a peacock).

The End of St Petersburg (1927)

Made to celebrate the Tenth Anniversary of the October Revolution, *The End of St Petersburg*, based on André Bely's 1916 symbolist novel *Petersburg*,[29] also uses individual characters to deal with the events preceding the Revolution. One is a young peasant boy who has come to St Petersburg to seek work, as his family can no longer support him at home. Despite initial involvement with strike-breakers, the boy quickly becomes aware of the corruption and injustice of the Tsarist regime. His political awakening, however, lands him in prison and he is forced to volunteer into the Tsar's army, where he is exposed to the horrors of trench warfare.

Using montage, Pudovkin draws a contrast between the suffering of the soldiers who are fighting for the Tsar and the greed of those who are benefiting financially from the war. Horrific images of dying soldiers in mud at the front-line trenches are intercut with scenes at the St Petersburg stockmarket. As the fighting gets worse and worse at the front, the higher the value of the shares becomes – thereby enforcing the point that people are making money out of suffering. The old order, by supporting and being supported by the stockmarket, is seen to be inhumane and preoccupied with the wrong values – the acquisition of wealth at whatever cost. Pudovkin at one point intercuts between the image of a soldier slashing ferociously at an opponent with his bayonet and the image of a stockmarket figure frenetically dealing at the stock-exchange. He thus likens the barbarities of war to the barbarity inherent in the centre of the capitalist structure. Earlier Pudovkin intercut between the images of death at the front and the words 'In the name of the Tsar, the fatherland, and the capital'. This is clearly ironic, as the soldiers have no idea what they are fighting for – certainly not for the Tsar.

Key films
The Adventures of Oktyabrina (1924)
The Cloak (1926)
The New Babylon (1929)

• **Plate 15.12**
The End of St Petersburg (Vsevolod Pudovkin, 1927). One of Pudovkin's central characters, a young peasant boy, is seen here demanding justice from the authorities

WE
CONSIDER ART AS A TIRELESS RAM SHATTERING THE HIGH WALLS OF HABIT AND DOGMA

But we also have our own ancestors! and lots of them

The brilliant creators of cinema posters, circus posters, music hall posters. Unknown designers of pulp thrillers who exalt the exploits of the King of the detectives or adventurers. In using your art, more magnificent than a clown's red nose, we spring up as if from a trampoline to perform our intripid somersault! Only the poster has escaped the pernicious scalpel of analysis and the intellect. Subject and form are indivisible, but what do they sing of?

Danger, Audacity, Violence, Pursuit, Revolution, Gold, Blood, Laxative pills, Charlie Chaplin, Catastrophes on land, sea and in the air. Fat cigars, Prima donnas of the operettas, Adventures of all sorts, Skating rinks, Tap shoes, Horses, Wrestling, Torch singers, Somersaults on bicycles and all those millions and millions of events which make splendid our Today!

THE 200 VOLUMES OF GERMAN EXPRESSIONISM DO NOT OFFER THE EXPRESSIVITY OF ONE SOLE

CIRCUS POSTER!!!

• **Plate 15.13**
Extract from FEKS
(Factory of the Eccentric
Actor) Manifesto, 1922

• Plate 15.14
The New Babylon
(Grigori Kozintsev and
Leonid Trauberg, 1929)

In the final part of *The End of St Petersburg*, in the storming of the Winter Palace sequences, Pudovkin intercuts images of the advancing Bolsheviks with both fast-moving clouds and crashing waves. This emphasises the power and inevitability of the revolution – revolution is unstoppable. Earlier in a Bolshevik's speech at the Lebedev factory, images of machinery slowing down are intercut with the speaker to point to the power of his words upon the workers.

Eccentrism of the FEKS: Grigori Kozintsev and Leonid Trauberg

FEKS (Factory of the Eccentric Actor), formed in December 1921 by a small group of theatre actors and directors, shared the common aim of reforming the traditional theatre and incorporating into their experimental work elements of the circus, music hall and puppet theatre. On 9 July 1922 FEKS published a manifesto which stated their aims as a group.[30] The poster on page 384 shows just a small sample of the material contained within the manifesto.

The extract makes it clear that FEKS valued the bold, dynamic and popular elements of circus and cinema posters. It was with these elements that they proposed to revitalise the theatre. Two of the founding members of the group, Grigori Kozintsev and Leonid Trauberg, became interested in the cinema, making a number of short experimental films between 1924 and 1927, including *The Adventures of Oktyabrina* (1924) and *The Cloak* (1926). The films primarily emphasised the artificial nature of the mise-en-scène and the stylised nature of the acting rather than the editing.

Kozintsev and Trauberg are perhaps best known for their 1929 film *The New Babylon*, based on the events building up to the Paris Commune of 1871. As in their previous films, artificial mise-en-scène combined with stylised acting were employed, but extensive use was made also of camera movement. At one point in the film the camera moves swiftly enough to blur the image, thus conveying the sense of confusion present in the scene. The response to the film was unfavourable, as audiences failed to understand its form.

□ CASE STUDY 4: ALEXANDER DOVZHENKO, *ARSENAL* (1929); *EARTH* (1930)[31]

Inspired by the creative and political possibilities of film, Dovzhenko had approached the Odessa film studio in 1926. At this point he had little knowledge of cinema, but within a few years he had made an outstanding contribution to Soviet revolutionary cinema with such films as *Arsenal* and *Earth* which, in addition to revolutionary fervour, displayed poetic qualities and provided a demonstration of his love for the Ukraine and its people.

Arsenal surveys the devastating impact of the First World War and the political struggles between the Social Democrats and the Bolsheviks during 1917. The opening sequences of *Arsenal* exemplify Dovzhenko's approach to filmmaking. There is little camera movement or use of establishing shots and, overall, there is less concern with a conventional rendering of space and time than with the emotional impact of the flow of images. In these opening and further sequences Dovzhenko reveals the loss and impoverishment of the people, as well as the unthinking callousness of the social order.

Arsenal shows that Dovzhenko is not concerned with personalised conflict between individuals, but with the ongoing struggle between opposing social forces. This concern is pursued further in *Earth*, which deals with class struggle in the countryside, although like *Arsenal* it features a strong, attractive male hero, Vasil. The latter is the operator of the tractor which will allow the collective farm effectively to rid the village of the self-seeking and more prosperous peasants, the kulaks. In the end Vasil is shot by Khoma, the son of a kulak, although what Vasil stands for will not be defeated. Vasil's father, hitherto hostile to the young revolutionaries of the village, commits himself to the cause of collectivisation and rejects a religious burial in favour of the village youth singing songs about the new life to come. The film, then, presents a strong case for the recently instigated policy of the collectivisation of agriculture. Commentators on the film, however, have argued that its formal and poetic qualities actually undermine the political message. Denise J. Youngblood, for example, states that:

• **Plate 15.15**
Earth (Alexander
Dovzhenko, 1930)

Dovzhenko's *Earth* (1930) is a much more curious example of the collectivisation film – the politically correct story of a handsome young village Party activist murdered by an evil and dissolute kulak opposed to collectivisation is undercut by a deeply subversive subtext related to its form. The lyrical imagery and slow-rhythms of this film, totally unlike Eisenstein's, belie the purported theme and in effect serve as a paean to a way of life soon to be no more.

(Youngblood 1992: 169)

The opening sequence in which Vasil's grandfather dies would certainly seem to bear out this interpretation. He dies contented, his last act being to enjoy a pear, a product of the fruitful Ukrainian earth. Next to him a baby plays and a boy eats an apple, while the adult members of the family await the inevitable. This portrait of pastoral abundance and peacefulness with its allusions to the cycle of life and death seem to undermine the necessity for revolutionary change, but it is made clear by the old man's friend Petro that his has been a life of hard work – 'Seventy-five years behind a plough'.

Dziga Vertov (1896–1954)

Dziga Vertov[32] (pseudonym of Denis Kaufman) was interested in the idea that the film camera had the potential to capture 'truth'; the camera could be seen simply as a mechanical device that was capable of recording the world without human intervention. Vertov led a group of filmmakers called *Kinoki* ('cinema-eye') who stated in their 1923 manifesto:

I am the Cine-Eye. I am the mechanical eye.

I the machine show you the world as only I can see it.

I emancipate myself henceforth and forever from human immobility. I am in constant motion. I approach objects and move away from them, I creep up on them, I clamber over them, I move alongside the muzzle of a running horse, I tear into a crowd at full tilt, I flee before fleeing soldiers, I turn over on my back, I rise up with aeroplanes, I fall and rise with falling and rising bodies.

I the camera rushed along the equilibrium, manoeuvring amid the chaos of movements, fixing movement to movement in the most complex combinations.

Freed from any obligation to 16–17 frames a second, freed from the restraints of time and space, *I juxtapose any points in the universe* regardless of where I fixed them.

My path leads towards the creation of a fresh perception of the world. I can thus decipher a world you do not know.

(cited in Taylor and Christie 1994: 93)

Vertov believed that the fiction film could not be used to reveal the 'truth' about a society. His films were based on documenting events around him; nothing should be artificially set up or staged for the camera. In 1922 Vertov had stated: 'WE declare the old films, the romantic, the theatricalised etc., to be leprous' (ibid.: 69) and in 1926 produced some 'very simple slogans' that summarised his approach:

1   Film-drama is the opium of the people.
2   Down with the immortal kings and queens of the screen! Long live the ordinary mortal, filmed in life at his daily tasks!
3   Down with the bourgeois fairy-tale script! Long live life as it is!
4   Film-drama and religion are deadly weapons in the hands of the capitalists. By showing our revolutionary way of life, we will wrest that weapon from the enemy's hands.
5   The contemporary artistic drama is a vestige of the old world. It is an attempt to pour our revolutionary reality into bourgeois molds.
6   Down with the staging of everyday life! Film us as we are.
7   The scenario is a fairy tale invented for us by a writer. We live our own lives, and we do not submit to anyone's fictions.

Key films
Film Truth (Kino-Pravda) (1922)
Kino-Eye (1924)
A Sixth of the World (1926)
The Man With a Movie Camera (1929)
Enthusiasm (1931)

For further and more detailed discussion of the documentary form see Chapter 8, pp. 175–92.

8   Each of us does his task in life and does not prevent anyone else from working. The film workers' task is to film us so as not to interfere with our work.

9   Long live the kino-eye of the proletarian revolution!

(cited in Michelson 1984: 71)

Vertov's techniques were based on experimentation caused by the general scarcity of film stock and also, when available, the short lengths of the negative film. His experiments included using old newsreels as part of his films, and he found that new meanings could be created by the conflict produced by the old material and the new. Vertov soon discovered that the conflicts produced by montage were a vital element in the construction of meaning in his films.

Perhaps one of the most interesting features of Vertov's films is that great effort is taken to ensure that the audience is made aware of cameraman, editor and the whole process of producing a film. In *The Man with a Movie Camera*, for example, Vertov shows the cameraman shooting the scenes that we see before us, and later we see shots of this same film being edited. This technique of acknowledging the nature of the filmmaking process can be linked to documentary filmmaking practice in the 1970s and 1980s (in the films of Emile de Antonio and Jean-Pierre Gorin, for example) which went against the **fly-on-the-wall** practice and attempted to show the presence of the film-crew and camera and the fact that the audience is watching a manufactured film rather than 'reality'. This style of filmmaking which draws attention to its own process is often termed 'self-reflexive'.

---

fly-on-the-wall
A term associated with a style of documentary filmmaking which attempts to present events as though the presence of the camera and film crew had not influenced them in any way.

☐ CASE STUDY 5: DZIGA VERTOV, *THE MAN WITH THE MOVIE CAMERA* (1929)

It was such a dazzling experience that it took two or three other Soviet films with normal 'stories' to convince me that all Soviet films were not compounded of such intricate camera pyrotechnics. But I hope to be forgiven for not bringing away any very clear critical idea as I reeled out of the Eight Street Playhouse – I was even too stunned to sit through it again.

(Leyda 1983: 251)

Leyda's experience of seeing *The Man with the Movie Camera* in New York in 1930 highlights three key issues:

- the film's sheer technical and intellectual brilliance and its status as a 'masterpiece'
- the challenge the film offered to audiences in terms of comprehension
- the extent to which the film fulfilled its role as Soviet propaganda

The Man with the Movie Camera, a celebration of Soviet city life, may be divided into six parts: Part 1: credit sequence, Part 2: the audience of the film, Part 3: the awakening city, Part 4: the working day, Part 5: leisure time, Part 6: the audience of the film. The credit sequence clearly outlines Vertov's experimental ambitions:

THE MAN WITH THE MOVIE CAMERA

A RECORD ON CELLULOID IN 6 REELS

PRODUCED BY VUFKU, 1929

(AN EXCERPT FROM THE DIARY OF A CAMERAMAN)

FOR VIEWERS' ATTENTION

THIS FILM PRESENTS AN EXPERIMENT IN THE CINEMATIC

COMMUNICATION OF VISIBLE EVENTS

WITHOUT THE AID OF INTERTITLES

(A FILM WITHOUT INTERTITLES)

WITHOUT THE AID OF A SCENARIO

(A FILM WITHOUT A SCENARIO)

WITHOUT THE AID OF THEATRE

(A FILM WITHOUT SETS, ACTORS ETC.)

THIS EXPERIMENTAL WORK IS DIRECTED TOWARDS THE CREATION

OF A GENUINE, INTERNATIONAL PURELY CINEMATIC LANGUAGE,

ENTIRELY DISTINCT FROM THE LANGUAGE OF THE THEATRE AND

LITERATURE

Part 2 establishes the self-reflexive nature of the project. We are shown shots of: the camera and cameraman (using a split screen), an empty cinema, a film projector and projectionist, the loading of film reels, the opening of the screen curtain, the audience being let in, the film orchestra ready to play, the film projector lamp being lit, the orchestra starting to play, the film moving through the projector.

Part 3 shows the city awakening. There are shots of: empty streets in the early morning, a woman lying asleep, a vagrant on a bench, shop window displays, a typewriter keyboard, various pieces of machinery (all static), cogs (not moving) and factory chimneys (not smoking). There is now some movement – shots of: a moving car, the odd pedestrian in the street, the car crossing some railway tracks and finally a quickly edited sequence of a train approaching and going over the camera. The woman awakes and gets dressed. The car travels with the cameraman filming. There are shots of: tram rails, streets and windows being cleaned, a blind opening, the camera lens, aerodrome doors opening, airplanes being wheeled out, the greasing of tram tracks, trains emerging from sheds and people travelling to work.

Part 4 documents the city's working day. Vertov demonstrates how the human life cycle, the work cycle and the daily life cycle of the city are inseparable by inter-cutting various elements together. The human life cycle is represented by shots of: a wedding registration, a divorce registration, a funeral and a birth. The work cycle is represented by shots of various industries: textile, coal, steel and film production. Vertov further demonstrates the interconnectedness of city life by emphasising both communication and transportation. Communication is represented by shots of: a letter being posted, delivery of mail, the answering of a telephone, a telephone kiosk, a telephone exchange and frantic typing. Transportation by shots of: trains, trams, cars and ships.

Part 5 deals with the leisure time of the city workers. A diverse range of activities is documented including shots of: a day at the beach, swimming, fairground rides, high jumping, horse riding, exercise machines, a magic show, dancing, netball, football, motorbike racing, a proletarian film theatre, beer drinking, playing chess, playing the piano and listening to the radio. Vertov blends all these activities together into a seamless sequence that highlights similarities rather than differences. Part 6 returns to the cinema and its audience – again emphasising the role of the camera, cameraman, editor and audience in the creation of the film.

Vertov's sophisticated montage techniques are present in all parts of the film but in addition he used a number of other devices that furthered his goal to create 'a genuine, international, purely cinematic language'. They included: super-imposition, freeze-frame, slow motion, accelerated motion, stop-motion trick photography, vertical and horizontal split-screen and reverse motion. Vertov, however, intended *The Man with the Movie Camera* to be much more than formalist experimentation. In his film proposal, dated 19 March 1928, Vertov provides a clear sense of how he intended the film to be read:

The man with the movie camera marches apace with life. To the bank and the club. The beer hall and clinic. The Soviet and the housing council. The cooperative and the school. The demonstration and the party-cell meeting. The man with the movie camera manages to go everywhere ...

Life's chaos gradually becomes clear as he observes and shoots. Nothing is accidental. Everything is explicable and governed by law. every peasant with his seeder, every worker at his lathe, every worker-student at his books, every engineer at his drafting table, every Young Pioneer speaking at a meeting in a club – each is engaged in the same great necessary labour.

(cited in Michelson, 1984: 287–8)

Vertov had clearly fulfilled his ambition of smashing through the moribund formal conventions of 'bourgeois' pre-revolutionary Russian cinema but he appears to have failed in his attempt to create *politically* revolutionary cinema, as *The Man with the Movie Camera* was not widely understood by Soviet audiences. Denise Youngblood claims that contemporary commentators were critical of the film with one condemning it for its 'narrow formalism' and 'technical fetishism' (1991: 207), although Youngblood also mentions that the film suffered from poor distribution, 'limited runs and rental "politics"' (ibid.: 208). Ultimately, however, it is difficult to deny the complexity of *The Man with the Movie Camera* and the demands that it places on 'ordinary' audiences. Vlada Petrić (1993) in his exhaustive shot-by-shot analysis of the film uncovers the highly complex chains of signification woven into *The Man with the Movie Camera* via the editing process. Petrić's study supports Noel Burch's assertion that: 'This film is not made to be viewed only once. It is impossible for anyone to assimilate this work in a single viewing' (cited in Petrić 1993: 78).

Key films
The Fall of the Romanov Dynasty (1927)
The Great Road (1927)
The Russia of Nicholas II and Lev Tolstoy (1928)

Esfir Shub (1894–1959)

Esfir Shub is an interesting female figure in a period of filmmaking dominated by men. She was initially employed by the Soviet government to re-edit foreign films to make them conform to the ideology of communism. Shub also re-edited old Tsarist newsreels

• **Plate 15.16**
The Man with the Movie Camera (VUFKU–British Film Institute)

to show the corrupt nature of the old order. Shub's practice of reassembling parts of existing films culminated in the adoption of the montage technique.

☐ CASE STUDY 6: ESFIR SHUB, *THE FALL OF THE ROMANOV DYNASTY* (1927)

Shub's first feature-length film, *The Fall of the Romanov Dynasty*, constructed entirely from old newsreels, was made to celebrate the Tenth Anniversary of the October Revolution, and it is claimed that 60,000 metres of film had to be examined in order to finish the project.[33] Shub provides new commentary on existing material by inserting intertitles between shots. By juxtaposing sequences of shots from different newsreels she also makes the audience draw new conclusions about the material. For example, she contrasts shots of an aristocratic gathering with shots of workers digging ditches. The intertitle reads 'by the sweat of your brow'. The intertitles and the juxtaposition of the images encourage the audience to assign an aberrant decoding to the original shots. In other words, the audience can deliberately 'misread' the images. Shub uses images which emphasise the pomp and splendour of Tsarist Russia, which in the context of the film look absurd and out of place; the audience is forced to be critical of this obvious display of wealth.

Although the film in principle uses montage in a way similar to that of Eisenstein or Pudovkin (in particular the way in which the audience are made active participants in the text), Shub does not make use of its rhythmic possibilities. The pace of the film is on the whole sedate, although it does put its political messages across in a powerful and convincing way. Recently, there has been a call by Graham Roberts for a re-evaluation of Esfir Shub; Roberts claims that Shub's contribution to the Soviet cinema has been undervalued (see Roberts 1991).

AUDIENCE RESPONSE

Viewers in the West may possibly already have an idea of the nature of the Soviet cinema after seeing extracts from films discussed previously such as Sergei Eisenstein's *Battleship Potemkin* or *October*. They may have wondered how many films such as these were made and how they were received by Soviet audiences that had only a few years previously gone through the upheaval of civil war. They may have pitied or even envied the Soviet cinema-goer – were these the only films that people could see on a Friday night? How could a largely uneducated population have coped with sophisticated material such as this?

Recent research into the Soviet cinema of the 1920s has encouraged new ideas. In the past, attention has focused on a number of key directors such as Pudovkin, Eisenstein and Vertov, whose films in the Soviet Union and later in the West were received with critical acclaim. We must, however, examine new evidence which points to the fact that Russian audiences were far more likely to be watching the Soviet 1920s equivalent of *Harry Potter and the Goblet of Fire* than the likes of *Battleship Potemkin*, *Strike* and *October*.

Richard Stites, in *Russian Popular Culture: Entertainment and Society since 1900*, reveals that the majority of Soviet directors were making mainstream films that were conventional in form and content. The montage film was the exception rather than the rule:

The most popular movie genres of the revolutionary period were the same as the foreign and pre-revolutionary Russian ones: costume drama, action and adventure, literary works adapted for the screen, melodramas, and comedy. Those who patronized them were not merely the *nepmanskaya auditoriya*, that is the bourgeoisie, alleged to be addicted to lurid sex films. Working-class clubs sponsored by the Communist Party also had to show some entertainment films or risk losing their audience.

(Stites 1992: 56)

Soviet audiences also favoured foreign films which were imported in large numbers throughout the 1920s.

But why were the Soviet propaganda films relatively less successful? Why would audiences rather see foreign and conventional Soviet genre films? Were foreign films perceived as being more exciting or exotic? Denise Youngblood, in *Movies for the Masses*, cites an interview conducted in 1929 with a Soviet cinema manager who recorded audience response:

He noted that 'the public watched [Dovzhenko's *Arsenal*] with great difficulty', and that attendance dropped to 50 percent of normal when his theatre screened *New Babylon*, Kozintsev and Trauberg's famous picture about the Paris Commune. Asked about the reaction to Vertov's *The Man with the Movie Camera*, he replied sarcastically, 'One hardly need say that if *New Babylon* didn't satisfy the spectator's requirements and "lost" him, then *The Man with the Movie Camera* didn't satisfy him either'.

(Youngblood 1992: 18–19)

The problem is clear. The Soviet propaganda films that were intended for the masses, from the illiterate peasant upward, simply were not being understood by Soviet audiences, whereas the clear, hero-led narrative structure of the foreign and Soviet genre films were far more straightforward and appealing. It is well documented that the American version of *Robin Hood* proved more successful in Soviet cinemas on all counts. The filmmakers involved in Soviet propaganda production, although committed to the ideals of communism, were also committed to experimenting with film form. The experimentation in this case clearly did not culminate in a popular cinema that appealed to the masses.

THEORETICAL DEBATES: MONTAGE VERSUS REALISM

For further discussion of realism and documentary film, see Chapter 8.

The montage technique has been widely acknowledged as a powerful means of expression, and to many cinema theorists montage is the essence of cinema. The technique, however, does have its opponents, among them the French film critic and theorist André Bazin.[34] Bazin was concerned with the cinema's ability to record 'reality'. He saw in cinema a means of capturing a record of events before the camera with minimum mediation. Bazin regarded the montage cinema of the Soviets (among others) as essentially non-realist because scenes could be manipulated and altered in many different ways. He claimed that the audience of montage cinema was essentially passive,[35] as the director forced the audience towards certain meanings.

For further discussion of Bazin and the French New Wave see Chapter 16, pp. 400–5.

Bazin saw montage cinema as being in direct opposition to a style of filmmaking associated with realism. Realism is a term often associated with the Hollywood cinema, but Bazin used it to refer to a style of filmmaking adopted by certain filmmakers such as Jean Renoir, a French director who felt that the power of cinema came not from editing but from mise-en-scène. The realists, unlike the montage filmmakers, took great pains to hide the artificial constructed nature of film. The long take, for example, was used frequently, as it made editing unnecessary. The use of the long take supported the claim that what was being watched was unmediated and therefore more 'realistic'. Bazin cited further devices that could enhance the 'reality' of a scene, for example, the use of deep-focus, wide-angle lenses, the long shot and a highly mobile camera, all of which meant that the filmmaker could preserve real time and space in individual scenes.

POSTSCRIPT TO THE 1920s

The 1930s and after: the decline of experimentation in the Soviet cinema

In the 1930s the Soviet authorities, under the guidance of Stalin, reacted to the unpopularity of many Soviet films by issuing strict guidelines on how films should be made. This set of 'rules', essentially demanding hero-led narratives and concerned with realistic subject matter, was termed 'Socialist Realism'. The head of the Soviet film industry outlined in 1933 why such a policy was necessary: 'A film and its success are directly linked to the degree of entertainment in the plot ... that is why we are obliged to require our masters [the filmmakers] to produce works that have strong plots and are organised around a story-line' (cited in Taylor 1986: 43).[36]

The policy of 'Socialist Realism' was combined with a complete ban on imported foreign films. By removing these positive representations of capitalism Stalin had also effectively made the Soviet film industry a monopoly; audiences could either see Soviet films or see no films at all.

The direct interest that the Soviet state took in the film industry reveals its perceived importance, but also had drastic consequences for many of the directors. It was noted by the authorities, for example, that several of these directors were not actually Communist Party members. (This may perhaps explain why they were more interested in form or technique than in making positive films about communism that were easy to comprehend.) The filmmakers of the 1920s discussed in this chapter were mostly not successful in the 1930s and 1940s. Eisenstein, for example, continued to make films, but the majority were either suppressed or had their funding withdrawn.

However, the decline of montage cinema could possibly be the consequence of another factor: technology. In October 1929 the first Soviet sound films were released, and with this advance in cinema technology came the almost immediate downfall of filmmaking practices that relied on either complex camera movement or rapid editing, as sound cinema initially required non-movable cameras and fixed microphones in order to record dialogue.

The legacy of the Soviet cinema: its influence on modern cinema[37]

The impact of Soviet films of the 1920s on the analysis of film and filmmaking itself was immediate and continues up until this day. The films, however, have not so much provided a model for successive filmmakers as been an inspiration for their work. The British Documentary Movement of the 1930s, for example, was influenced by Soviet montage as well as impressed by the idea that films could be a force for education. The filmmakers in this movement, however, did not conceive of films having a revolutionary role or even the role of questioning contemporary inequalities. Other filmmakers have been inspired by the Soviet cinema due to its rejection of the forms and conventions of the dominant Hollywood entertainment cinema. Jean-Luc Godard, for example, demanded that audiences participate in the construction of meaning in his films and so engage directly with social and political questions. The achievements of Eisenstein continue to impress film editors as well as contemporary film directors. The editor, Ralph Rosenblum, for example, states in his discussion of *Battleship Potemkin* that '[a]lthough the movie is filled with stunning moments, the massacre on the Odessa steps outweighs them all; it remains for editors everywhere the single most intimidating piece of film ever assembled' (Rosenblum and Karen 1979).

Direct references to Eisenstein's films are numerous, ranging from Bernardo Bertolucci's subtle allusions to *Strike* in his *Tragedy of a Ridiculous Man* (1981), through Brian de Palma's opportunistic reworking of the Odessa Steps sequence in *The Untouchables* (1987)[38] to Zbigniew Rybczynski's use of the same sequence in

Steps (1987)[39] in order to satirise cultural attitudes including the veneration of *Battleship Potemkin* as a work of art.[40] Dovzhenko's influence has not been directly political, but the films of Andrei Tarkovsky, a one-time pupil of Dovzhenko, and a film such as *My Childhood* (1972) by the Scottish filmmaker Bill Douglas, exhibit a similar emotional intensity.

NOTES

1 The term 'peasants' is used to describe those who worked on the land in the country, and the term 'workers' to describe those who worked within cities. This became a source of dispute in the 1920s when there was greater concern with efficiency and a more elaborate division of labour.

2 This was a planned attack by a relatively small force, not a mass uprising as chronicled by Eisenstein in his 1927 film *October*.

3 An unusual account of this period told from the point of view of the White side may be found in Mikhail Bulgakov's 1926 novel, *The White Guard* (available in the UK as a Flamingo paperback).

4 The British Film Institute has released a number of early Russian films on video (in ten volumes).

5 Protazanov was not in the Soviet Union for the full duration of this period; he emigrated briefly to Paris in 1920–23.

6 For more information on Protazanov, see Christie and Graffy (1993). For more information on the Russian cinema, see Leyda (1983); and Usai *et al.* (1989).

7 The first Russian studio was set up by Drankov in 1907.

8 The first half of this section is by Danny Rivers (film studies lecturer, West Kent College).

9 The context of this remark may be found in Leyda (1983: 161).

10 The civil war also resulted in trade barriers being set up which prevented the importation of film stock and cinema equipment into the Soviet Union. This had a dramatic effect on the film industry as the Soviet Union initially had no means of producing its own film stock and lenses.

11 Vladimir Vladimirovich Mayakovsky (1893–1930).

12 The team effort involved in the production of a feature film would clearly cost a great deal more than an individual artist producing a painting. The Russian film industry, although economically successful, needed to produce films that would appeal to a wide audience. The desire to experiment with film form, when the existing genres were popular, was therefore limited.

13 The mansion was in fact the White House.

14 Adapted from Kawin (1987: 99–101).

15 Bordwell, in *The Cinema of Eisenstein* (1993: 85), claims that the peacock could be seen as a diegetic image as it forms part of the treasures contained within the Winter Palace. Yuri Tsivian, in 'Eisenstein's *October* and Russian Symbolist Culture' (see Christie and Taylor 1993), puts forward the view that 'Eisenstein was hoping to attain the effect of Kerensky entering the peacock's asshole'.

16 Bordwell uses a technique pioneered by Barry Salt in his article 'Statistical Style Analysis of Motion Pictures', *Film Quarterly*, Vol. 28, No. 2, 1974–75.

17 Cited by Pudovkin at a lecture given at the London Film School in 1929.

18 The Moscow Arts Theatre under the direction of Konstantin Stanislavski developed a method of acting which required the actor to attempt to 'become' the character.

19 This may be inferred from the fact that Goskino made thirty-two prints of the film.

20 A well-known Russian playwright (1823–86).

21 The other seven films were never made.

22 Eisenstein bends historical fact in the film as the sailors on board the *Potemkin*, instead of persuading the Russian Fleet to join the struggle, were captured and the mutiny suppressed.

23 The scene has been much copied by recent filmmakers: see the section on the 'Legacy of the Soviet cinema: its influence on modern cinema' on pp. 393–4.

24 See Bordwell (1993: 74) for an excellent analysis of the sequence.

25 Leyda also points out that the same sequence caused 'an anxious debate in the German Reichstag on the size of the Soviet Navy'.

26 Pudovkin's films, like those of Eisenstein, were based on a body of theoretical writing.

27 Lecture given by Pudovkin at the London Film Society, 1929.

28 The theatre was founded in 1898 by Konstantin Stanislavski and Vladimir Nemirovich-Danchenko.

29 Published in the UK by Penguin (London, 1983).

30 The manifesto was reprinted in 1992 in a limited edition of 500 copies by Aldgate Press, London.

31 Section on Dovzhenko written by Danny Rivers (West Kent College).

32 Vertov in Russian from the Russian word for 'rotation' and was thus a reflection of his approach to the arts.

33 Soviet montage cinema tended to place stress on the importance of the director (auteur) and work in post-production, rather than scriptwriting and the screen.

34 Bazin was also editor of the French film journal *Cahiers du cinéma*.

35 Eisenstein rigorously opposed this view, claiming that the audience for his films played an active part in the text.

36 The head of Sovkino at this time was Boris Shumyatsky.

37 This section was written by Danny Rivers (West Kent College).

38 A statistical analysis of both scenes in terms of shot length/shot type reveals that they are also very similar in form.

39 A co-production of KTCA-TV Minneapolis and ZBIG Vision Ltd in association with Channel 4, London.

40 Woody Allen in *Love and Death* (1975) also makes reference to this sequence.

FURTHER READING

Aumont, J. (1987) *Montage Eisenstein*, London: British Film Institute.

Barna. Y. (1973) *Eisenstein*, London: Secker & Warburg.

Barron, S. and Tuchmann, M. (eds) (1980) *The Avant-Garde in Russia, 1910–1930: New Perspectives*, Los Angeles: Los Angeles County Museum of Art.

Bordwell, D. (1993) *The Cinema of Eisenstein*, Cambridge, MA: Harvard University Press.

Christie, I. and Gillett, J. (eds) (1978) *Futurism/Formalism/FEKS: 'Eccentrism' and Soviet Cinema 1918–1936*, London: BFI.

Christie, I. and Graffy, J. (eds) (1993) *Yakov Protazanov and the Continuity of Russian Cinema*, London: BFI/NFT.

Christie, I. and Taylor, R. (eds) (1993) *Eisenstein Rediscovered*, London: Routledge.

Dickinson, T. and de la Roche, C. (1948) *Soviet Cinema*, London: Falcon Press.

Eisenstein, S. (1970) *Notes of a Film Director*, New York: Dover Publications.

Eisenstein, S. (1986) *The Film Sense*, London: Faber and Faber.

Eisenstein, S. (1973) Film scripts of *The Mother, Earth* and *Battleship Potemkin* have been published by Simon & Schuster, New York.

Gillespie, D. (2003) *Russian Cinema*, Harlow: Longman.

Goodwin, J. (1993) *Eisenstein, Cinema and History*, Urbana: University of Illinois Press.

Kenez, P. (1992) *Cinema and Soviet Society 1917–1953*, Cambridge: Cambridge University Press.

Kepley, V., Jr (1986) *In the Service of the State: The Cinema of Alexander Dovzhenko*, Madison: University of Wisconsin Press.

La Valley, A. and Scherr, B. (eds) (2001) *Eisenstein at 100: A Reconsideration*, New Brunswick: Rutgers University Press.

Lawton, A. (ed.) (1992) *The Red Screen: Politics, Society, Art in Soviet Cinema*, London: Routledge.

Leyda, J. (1983) *Kino: A History of the Russian and Soviet Film* (3rd edn), London: George Allen & Unwin.

Marshall, H. (1983) *Masters of the Soviet Cinema*, London: Routledge & Kegan Paul.

Michelson, A. (ed.) (1984) *Kino Eye: The Writings of Dziga Vertov*, Berkeley: University of California Press.

Petrić, V. (1993) *Constructivism in Film: The Man with the Movie Camera – A Cinematic Analysis*, Cambridge: Cambridge University Press; first published 1987.

Roberts, G. (1999) *Forward Soviet: History and Non-fiction Film in the USSR*, London: I.B. Tauris.

Sargeant, A. (2000) *Vsevolod Pudovkin: Classic Films of the Soviet Avant-Garde*, London: I.B. Tauris.

Schnitzer, J., Schnitzer, L. and Martin, M. (eds) (1973) *Cinema in Revolution*, trans. D. Robinson, London: Secker & Warburg; reprinted by Da Capo Press, New York, 1987.

Stites, R. (1992) *Russian Popular Culture: Entertainment and Society Since 1900*, Cambridge: Cambridge University Press.

Taylor, R. (1979) *The Politics of the Soviet Cinema, 1917–1929*, Cambridge: Cambridge University Press.

Taylor, R. (ed.) (1988) *S.M. Eisenstein: Writings 1922–1934 – Selected Works Vol. 1*, London: BFI.

Taylor, R. (ed.) (1995) *Beyond the Stars: The Memoirs of Sergei Eisenstein – Selected Works Vol. 4*, London: BFI.

Taylor, R. (1998a) *Film Propaganda: Soviet Russia and Nazi Germany* (2nd edn), London: I.B. Tauris.

Taylor, R. (ed.) (1998b) *The Eisenstein Reader*, London: BFI.

Taylor, R. and Christie, I. (eds) (1991) *Inside the Film Factory: New Approaches to Russian and Soviet Cinema*, London: Routledge.

Taylor, R. and Spring, D. (eds) (1993) *Stalinism and Soviet Cinema*, London: Routledge.

Taylor, R. and Christie, I. (eds) (1994) *The Film Factory: Russian and Soviet Cinema in Documents, 1896–1939*, London: Routledge; first published 1988 by Routledge & Kegan Paul.

Taylor, R. and Glenny, M. (eds) (1994) *S.M. Eisenstein: Towards a Theory of Montage – Selected Works Vol. 2*, London: BFI.

Tsivian, Y. (1994) *Early Cinema in Russia and its Cultural Reception*, London: Routledge.

Usai, P., Codelli, L., Montanaro, C. and Robinson, D. (eds) (1989) *Silent Witnesses: Russian Films 1908–1919*, London: BFI.

Youngblood, D. (1991) *Soviet Cinema in the Silent Era: 1918–1935*, Austin: University of Texas Press.

Youngblood, D. (1992) *Movies for the Masses: Popular Cinema and Soviet Society in the 1920s*, Cambridge: Cambridge University Press.

Zorkaya, N. (1989) *The Illustrated History of Soviet Cinema*, New York: Hippocrene Books.

FURTHER VIEWING

VHS = available on video
DVD = available on DVD
16mm = available to hire on 16mm
Where neither symbol is listed, the film is not available to buy or rent

Selected Russian films of the 1910s

1908   *Sten'ka Razin*, Vladimir Romashkov–Drankov Studio (VHS)
1909   *A Sixteenth-century Russian Wedding*, Vasili Goncharov (VHS)
1910   *The Queen of Spades*, Petr Chardynin (VHS)
         Rusalka/The Mermaid, Vasili Goncharov (VHS)
1912   *The Brigand Brothers*, Vasili Goncharov (VHS)
         The Peasants' Lot, Vasili Goncharov (VHS)
1913   *The House in Kolomna*, Petr Chardynin (VHS)
         Merchant Bashkirov's Daughter, Nikolai Larin (VHS)
         Twilight of a Woman's Soul, Evgeny Bauer
1914   *The Child of the Big City*, Evgeny Bauer (VHS)
         Silent Witnesses, Evgeny Bauer (VHS)
1915   *After Death*, Evgeny Bauer
         Children of the Age, Evgeny Bauer
         Daydreams, Evgeny Bauer (VHS)
         Happiness of Eternal Night, Evgeny Bauer
1916   *Antosha Ruined by a Corset*, Eduard Puchal'ski (VHS)
         A Life for a Life, Evgeny Bauer (VHS)
         The 1002nd Ruse, Evgeny Bauer (VHS)
         The Queen of Spades, Yakov Protazanov (VHS)
1917   *For Luck*, Evgeny Bauer (VHS)
         Grandmother of the Revolution, Boris Svetlov
         The King of Paris, Evgeny Bauer
         The Revolutionary, Evgeny Bauer
         Satan Triumphant, Yakov Protazanov
1918   *Jenny the Maid*, Yakov Protazanov
         Little Ellie, Yakov Protazanov
         Still, Sadness, Still, Petr Chardynin

Selected Soviet films of the 1920s–40s

1922–25   *Film-Truth*, Dziga Vertov (a series of newsreels)
1924   *Aelita*, Yakov Protazanov (DVD/16mm)
         Cigarette-Girl from Mosselprom, Yuri Zhelyabuzhsky
         The Extraordinary Adventures of Mr West in the Land of the Bolsheviks, Lev Kuleshov (16mm)
         Kino-Eye, Dziga Vertov
         Strike, Sergei Eisenstein (DVD/16mm)
1925   *Battleship Potemkin*, Sergei Eisenstein (DVD, 16mm)
         The Death Ray, Lev Kuleshov
1926   *The Mother*, Vsevolod Pudovkin (V, 16mm)
         A Sixth of the World, Dziga Vertov (16mm)
1927   *The End of St Petersburg*, Vsevolod Pudovkin (DVD/16mm)
         The Fall of the Romanov Dynasty, Esfir Shub (DVD/16mm)
         The Great Road, Esfir Shub
         October, Sergei Eisenstein (DVD/16mm)
1928   *The Russia of Nicholas II and Lev Tolstoy*, Esfir Shub
         Storm Over Asia, Vsevolod Pudovkin (DVD/16mm)
1929   *Arsenal*, Alexander Dovzhenko (DVD/16mm)
         The Man with a Movie Camera, Dziga Vertov (DVD/16mm)
         The New Babylon, Grigori Kozintsev and Leonid Trauberg
         Old and New or The General Line, Sergei Eisenstein (16mm)
         Ranks and People, Yakov Protazanov
         Turksib, Victor Turin
1930   *Earth*, Alexander Dovzhenko (16mm)
1931   *Enthusiasm*, Dziga Vertov (16mm)

1934	*Chapayev*, Sergei and Georgy Vasiliev
1935	*Aerograd*, Alexander Dovzhenko
	The Youth of Maxim, Grigori Kozintsev and Leonid Trauberg (16mm)
1936	*Alexander Nevsky*, Sergei Eisenstein (DVD/16mm)
	We from Krondstadt, Yefim Dzigan (VHS)
1945	*Ivan the Terrible: Part I*, Sergei Eisenstein (DVD/16mm)
1946	*Ivan the Terrible: Part II*, Sergei Eisenstein (DVD/16mm)

Additional videos
The Secret Life of Sergei Eisenstein, British Film Institute Publishing, London, 1987 (VHS)

RESOURCE CENTRES

http://us.imdb.com/Sections/Countries/ SovietUnion
This is the Internet Movie Data Base (US) with a listing of 6175 Russian/Soviet films including details of producers, distributors, directors, casts, writers, composers of music, and other titles by which the film is known.

http://www.ssees.ac.uk/russcin.htm#films
A directory of internet sources on Russian cinema.

Chapter 16

The French New Wave

Chris Darke

■ The French New Wave

INTRODUCTION

The 'New Wave' (*la nouvelle vague*) refers to a group of filmmakers who, between the end of the 1950s and early to mid-1960s in France, momentarily transformed French cinema and had a great impact on filmmakers throughout the world. Those directors who came to prominence through the New Wave and who have remained major names in the pantheon of European 'auteur' directors include Jean-Luc Godard, François Truffaut, Eric Rohmer, Jacques Rivette, Claude Chabrol, Alain Resnais, Chris Marker and Agnès Varda.

For further discussion of auteur theory, see Chapter 4.

French critic Michel Marie lists a series of key factors that dictated the aesthetics of New Wave films:

1   the auteur–director also writes the screenplay;
2   a strictly broken-down **découpage** is not used and a significant place is left to improvisation in the conception of the sequences, the dialogue and the performances;
3   natural decor and locations are privileged over studio sets;
4   a minimal crew of a few people is used;
5   'direct sound' recorded at the moment of shooting is preferred to postsynchronisation;
6   traditional lighting set-ups, deemed to be cumbersome, are dispensed with so the director of photography tends to work with fast, ultra-sensitive film;
7   non-professional actors are used to interpret the characters;
8   if professional actors are chosen, they tend to be 'new faces' who are directed in a loose and free fashion.

(Marie 1998: 63)

découpage
A term that means the 'shot breakdown' of a scene.

While it has become identified in film history with the early work of the directors named above, the term 'New Wave' was not invented by them. It was coined by a journalist named Françoise Giroud who, in late 1957, wrote a series of articles on French youth for the weekly news magazine *L'Express*. Cinema, in the shape of this new generation of filmmakers, thus became associated with a 'youth' phenomenon. The association of 'youth' with New Wave cinema was sealed by the triumph at the 1958 Cannes Film Festival of *Les Quatre cents coups* (*The 400 Blows*), the debut feature film by the 27-year-old former film critic François Truffaut. A number of successful films by other directors followed, all of which enhanced the identity of New Wave cinema as 'youthful' and 'modern'; these included *A bout de souffle* (*Breathless*, Jean-Luc Godard, 1960), *Hiroshima, mon amour* (Alain Resnais, 1959) and *Les Cousins* (Claude Chabrol, 1959).

However, these new filmmakers had not emerged from out of the blue. They had all been involved in filmmaking for the best part of the 1950s, writing film criticism, making short films and documentaries. In fact, one of the most marked characteristics of the New Wave is its association with film criticism. Many of its main directors had a long relationship with the important monthly film magazine *Les Cahiers du cinéma et de la télévision* (literally meaning 'Cinema and television notebooks' and referred to as *Cahiers* hereafter) which had been founded by André Bazin and Jacques Doniol-Valcroze in 1951. Truffaut, Godard, Rivette, Chabrol and Rohmer had all written for the magazine throughout the 1950s. Thus the New Wave was in part characterised by the unusual phenomenon of film critics becoming successful filmmakers after having been influential and polemical writers. Before outlining some of the chief ideas that these filmmakers advanced in their work as critics, it is worthwhile describing the film culture that existed in France after the Second World War and on which the New Wave would have a profound impact.

• **Plate 16.1**
Young French directors at the 1959 Cannes Film Festival, including François Truffaut (front row, first left), Claude Chabrol (back row, first left) and Jean-Luc Godard (back row, third right)

POSTWAR FRENCH FILM CULTURE

While France was under Nazi occupation between 1940 and 1945, the importing of American films was banned by the collaborationist government of the Vichy regime. Shortly after the liberation of France in 1945 this backlog of American cinema started to hit the country's screens to the enthusiasm of French film-goers. This exposure to Hollywood films was a formative influence on the young critics who would become the directors of the New Wave in the late 1950s. For them, American cinema was more vital, more varied and considerably more exciting than the postwar productions of the French film industry which they derided as 'le cinéma de papa' ('Daddy's cinema'). Film culture in postwar France was bolstered by the growth in the number of magazines devoted to cinema (including *Positif*, the long-standing rival of *Cahiers*, founded in 1952) and the revitalisation of a network of 'ciné-clubs', where film screenings would be accompanied by public debates and lectures by critics. Between 1948 and 1949, an important ciné-club was established, 'Objectif 49', whose organisers included Jean Cocteau, Robert Bresson, Roger Leenhardt, René Clément, Alexandre Astruc, Pierre Kast and Raymond Queneau. As Doniol-Valcroze stressed, this ciné-club would 'constitute the first link in the chain which is resulting today in what has been called the nouvelle vague, the first jolt against a cinema which has become too traditional … [and] … brought together all those – critics, film-makers and future film-makers – who dreamed of a cinéma d'auteurs' (cited in Hillier 1985: 3). One of the founders of *Cahiers*, the highly influential film critic André Bazin, was instrumental in the 'ciné-club' movement and several future members of the New Wave were already writing film criticism for publications associated with 'ciné-clubs'. In addition, the work of the curator and film archivist Henri Langlois, along with his colleague Mary Meerson, was to be of great importance to a generation of film-goers who attended screenings at the Cinémathèque Française in Paris where they could see an eclectic range of films from around the world and from different periods of cinema history. All of these components of postwar French film culture contributed to a lively cinéphile community of viewers. The word '**cinéphile**' does not translate easily

cinéphile
A term describing someone with a developed intellectual interest in cinema. Cinéphilia was part of the cultural climate in which the New Wave emerged.

into English. It does not exactly denote a 'film buff', a 'film fan' or a 'cinema enthusiast' but someone who is intimately involved in the cultural condition of 'cinéphilia', a uniquely French approach to cinema that has traditionally argued for it as 'the seventh art'. Before they became influential critics on *Cahiers* and were internationally recognised as film directors, the chief figures in the New Wave were enthusiastic cinéphiles.

An example of the intellectual interest that was developing as regards cinema came in an essay published in 1948 by the critic, novelist and film-maker Alexandre Astruc. The essay, entitled 'The Birth of a New Avant-Garde: La caméra–stylo', argued that:

> Cinema is quite simply becoming a means of expression, just as all the other arts have been before it, and in particular painting and the novel. After having been successively a fairground attraction, an amusement analogous to boulevard theatre, or a means of preserving the images of an era, it is gradually becoming a language. By a language, I mean a form in which and by which an artist can express his thoughts, however abstract they may be, or translate his obsessions exactly as he does in the contemporary essay or novel. That is why I would like to call this new age of cinema the age of **'caméra–stylo'** (camera–pen) ... (by this) I mean that the cinema will gradually break free from the tyranny of what is visual, from the image for its own sake, from the immediate and concrete demands of the narrative, to become a means of writing just as flexible and subtle as written language.
>
> (cited in Graham 1968: 17–18)

Part of the legacy of the French New Wave lies in how it may be seen to have developed – both in terms of film criticism and filmmaking – some of Astruc's claims for what cinema could be.

FILM CRITICISM

Cahiers du cinéma, 'la politique des auteurs' and 'mise-en-scène'

Throughout the 1950s, the critics on *Cahiers* argued and polemicised for cinema as an art form. That is to say, they approached cinema from the point of view of the filmmaker who, they argued, could be seen as the 'author' – the 'auteur' – of the work. This idea of 'authorship' was to prove highly influential in film criticism and has remained, though not without controversy, a key approach in the study of cinema. Initially, the major influence in this approach was the work of André Bazin. A humanist, left-leaning Catholic, Bazin had been deeply involved in film education and criticism following the end of the Second World War and had founded a magazine called *La Révue du cinéma* which, in 1951, was relaunched as *Les Cahiers du cinéma et de la Télévision*. It was on this magazine that the future directors of the New Wave cut their teeth as critics throughout the 1950s.

The critical agenda that was developed in the magazine throughout the 1950s claimed for certain directors the status of artist, an approach that was known as **'la politique des auteurs'** ('author politics' or 'the auteur policy'). What was unusual about such an approach was that it was developed around the work of filmmakers who were working in the highly standardised and controlled industrial environment of Hollywood cinema. Those directors chiefly favoured included, among others, Alfred Hitchcock, John Ford, Howard Hawks, Fritz Lang and Otto Preminger. Hitchcock was a major reference for many of the critics who would later became filmmakers. For example, François Truffaut went on to publish a famous series of interviews with Hitchcock while Claude Chabrol and Eric Rohmer co-wrote a study of his films (Chabrol and Rohmer 1979; Truffaut 1983).

The *Cahiers* critics went looking for 'art' in popular cinema. They did so because they were concentrating predominantly on the formal qualities of films to see how these might reveal a set of themes and preoccupations that could be associated with the name of the director, be it Hitchcock, Lang or Ford. The critical approach that the *Cahiers* writers

For further discussion of art cinema and the avant-garde see Chapter 3, pp. 62–3 and 66–7.

caméra–stylo
A term coined by French writer Alexandre Astruc meaning 'camera–pen' and used to condense his argument for a 'personal' and self-expressive form of cinema.

politique des auteurs, la
Literally meaning 'auteur policy' or 'auteur politics' (although later translated by the American film critic Andrew Sarris as 'auteur theory'). It describes the position of *Cahiers du cinéma* as one which argued for the work of favoured directors as that of film artists or 'auteurs'.

• **Plate 16.2**
Alfred Hitchcock
receiving an award from
the New Wave actress
Jeanne Moreau in 1969

mise-en-scène
Literally meaning 'putting
in the scene' and
deriving from theatre.
A film's mise-en-scène
is taken to describe all
the elements visible in
a shot – actors, objects,
landscapes, and so
on. In terms of classic
auteur criticism, a
director's style may be
identified only through
the arrangement and
orchestration of such
elements, of the film's
mise-en-scène in other
words.

*For further discussion
of mise-en scène, see
Chapter 3, pp. 67–73.*

used to analyse films has become known as **mise-en-scène** criticism. The term 'mise-en-scène' derives from the theatre, where it refers to the practice of stage direction in which things are 'put into the scene', or, arranged on the stage. One of the most straightforward and concise expressions of the importance of the idea of mise-en-scène to auteur criticism comes from one of the *Cahiers* critics Fereydoun Hoveyda, who wrote in 1960:

The originality of the 'auteur' lies not in the subject matter he chooses but in the technique he employs, ie: the 'mise en scène', through which everything on the screen is expressed...the thought of a cinéaste appears through his 'mise en scène'.

(cited in Hillier 1985: 8–9)

Hoveyda goes on to explain:

What matters in a film is the desire for order, composition, harmony, the placing of actors and objects, the movements within the frame, the capturing of a movement or a look; in short, the intellectual operation which has put an initial emotion and a general idea to work. Mise-en-scène is nothing other than the technique invented by each director to express the idea and establish the specific quality of his work.

(ibid.)

It is useful to remember that the film criticism undertaken by writers on *Cahiers* throughout the 1950s was both highly influential and, at least initially, controversial. This controversy concerned the idea of 'art' being applied to the products of commercial American cinema. When systematically used to explore the *œuvre* (or 'body of work') of a director such as Alfred Hitchcock, John Ford or Fritz Lang, an 'auteurist' approach can discover the ways in which a director has consistently developed certain themes and how the style of that director has been developed and refined over time. However, the idea of the 'auteur' served another purpose apart from championing American cinema. It was part of a polemic against the state of French cinema which was actively developed in the pages of *Cahiers*. The most infamous expression of the journal's attitude towards postwar French cinema came in François Truffaut's article 'Une certaine tendence du cinéma français' ('A certain tendency of the French cinema') which was published in *Cahiers* No. 31 in January 1954. It was in this essay (which was largely devoted to examining the role of the scriptwriter in French cinema of the 1940s and 1950s) that Truffaut made a distinction between an auteur director and what he called a 'metteur-en-scène' (or, a director deemed to lack the 'personal vision' attributed to an auteur). For Truffaut, the metteur-en-scène was a filmmaker whose conception of cinema extends only as far as 'illustrating' a screenplay and being faithful to the written word: 'when they [the screenwriters] hand in their scenario, the film is done: the metteur-en-scène, in their eyes, is the gentleman who adds pictures to it' (cited in Nichols 1976: 233). It was the preponderance of films made either as literary adaptations or based on scripts by established screenwriters that Truffaut saw as evidence that French cinema was beholden primarily to literary criteria, rather than searching for specifically cinematic qualities. It is useful to remember here how critics such as Bazin and Astruc were arguing for a vision of cinema that did not wholly depend on validation by reference to the other established art forms. When Astruc wrote of the 'camera–pen' ('la caméra–stylo') he was not thinking of the screenplay as a means of cinematic expression, but of filmmaking itself as a form of artistic creation that could be as fluent, expressive and rich as written language, rather than its merely being in the service of adapting classic literary works.

Truffaut described the screenwriters and metteurs-en-scène as representing French cinema's '**Tradition of Quality**': 'they force, by their ambitiousness, the admiration of the foreign press, defend the French flag twice a year at Cannes and at Venice where, since 1946, they regularly carry off medals, golden lions and *grands prix*' (ibid.: 225). In other words, the Tradition of Quality represented the mainstream of French cinema of the day – internationally recognised, nationally dominant and, for Truffaut and many of his colleagues on *Cahiers*, the enemy. In the same article Truffaut set the names of metteurs-en-scènes associated with the Tradition of Quality – for example, Yves Allegret, Claude Autant-Lara and Jean Delannoy – against the names of other French directors such as Jean Renoir, Robert Bresson, Jacques Tati and Jean Cocteau, whom he held to be 'auteurs: who often write their dialogue and some of them themselves invent the stories they direct' (ibid.: 233). Truffaut argued for an idea of the auteur within the French context that is subtly different from the idea as it was applied to Hollywood cinema. It was taken for granted that in Hollywood the director worked within a large, powerful and regimented production system and collaborated with a host of other skilled people, from actors to camera operators, screenwriters to producers, and that the opportunity to exercise artistic control and to make creative decisions was concentrated in the act of directing. The mise-en-scène of the film was where the evidence of such decisions was seen to reside. However, in the French context, Truffaut uses the term 'auteur' for those directors whose control over their films extended to writing the dialogue and the stories, directors who were their own screenwriters; a degree of control that was impossible to conceive of in the classical Hollywood studio system. Thus Truffaut's polemic against the so-called Tradition of Quality was also a polemic against the mainstream establishment of the French film industry as well as being an assertion that it was possible to make films in another way, as is clear from his words: 'I do not believe in the peaceful coexistence of "The Tradition of Quality" and an "auteur's" cinema' (ibid.: 234). So, on the one hand, the development of auteur criticism with its emphasis on mise-en-scène (finding the 'personality' of the style, one might say) was a way of arguing for the artistic worth of

Tradition of Quality
A frequently derogatory term used by the critics on Cahiers du cinéma and referring to postwar, pre-New Wave French cinema characterised by its reliance on screenwriters and adaptations from literary classics.

• **Plate 16.3**
Roberto Rossellini,
the Italian neo-realist
director who greatly
influenced the New
Wave

popular cinema. On the other hand, it was also developed as a polemical assault on what was seen as the moribund state of French cinema.

Jacques Doniol-Valcroze, who co-founded *Cahiers* with André Bazin, believed that Truffaut's article was highly significant:

A leap had been made, a trial begun with which we were all in solidarity, something bound us together. From then on, it was known that we were *for* Renoir, Rossellini, Hitchcock, Cocteau, Bresson … and against X, Y and Z. From then on there was a doctrine, the 'politique des auteurs', even if it lacked flexibility.

(cited in Hillier 1985: 4)

Doniol-Valcroze made this statement in 1959 and the 'inflexibility' he identified in the 'politique des auteurs' had been examined by Bazin himself in an article published in *Cahiers* in April 1957 entitled 'On the politique des auteurs'. In this article Bazin examined the intellectual assumptions behind 'auteur' criticism and addressed its perceived 'inflexibility'. He also placed the idea within the editorial culture of the magazine itself:

Our readers must have noticed that this critical standpoint – whether implicit or explicit – has not been adopted with equal enthusiasm by all the regular contributors to *Cahiers*, and that there might exist serious differences in our admiration, or rather in the degree of our admiration. And yet the truth is that the most enthusiastic among us nearly always win the day. Eric Rohmer put his finger on the reason in his reply to a reader in *Cahiers* no. 64: 'When opinions differ on an important film, we generally prefer to let the person who likes it most write about it.' It follows that the strictest adherents of the 'politique des auteurs' get the best of it in the end, for, rightly or wrongly, they always see in their favourite directors the manifestation of the same specific qualities. So it is that Hitchcock, Renoir, Rossellini, Lang, Hawks or Nicholas Ray, to judge from the pages of *Cahiers*, appear as almost infallible directors who could not make a bad film.

(cited in Graham 1968: 137–8)

☐ CASE STUDY 1: *A BOUT DE SOUFFLE (BREATHLESS, JEAN-LUC GODARD, 1960)*

Jean-Luc Godard's debut feature was one of the films that marked the advent of the French New Wave, both in France and abroad. Its story is that of a young criminal, Michel Poiccard (Jean-Paul Belmondo), who, having casually murdered a policeman, returns to Paris to collect money he is owed and to persuade his American girlfriend, Patricia Franchini (Jean Seberg), to leave the country with him.

Patricia, who sells the *New York Herald Tribune* on the streets of Paris while attempting to establish herself as a journalist, betrays Michel to the police who shoot him dead when he tries to flee.

A bout de souffle is highly characteristic of the filmmaking style associated with the New Wave. The neo-documentary 'look' of the film was achieved partly through the use of a lightweight, handheld model of film camera called the Eclair which allowed for mobility and flexibility in shooting. In addition, the film marked the first of Godard's collaboration with the cinematographer Raoul Coutard, which would continue for fifteen films between 1960 and 1968. Coutard had been a photojournalist and documentary cameraman, and was accustomed to a style of shooting that was far removed from the more conventional and poised style of studio-based shooting that characterised the so-called Tradition of Quality. *A bout de souffle* was shot on black and white film stock normally used for still photography to further enhance the 'reportage' look. This 'realism' was part of the film's perceived modernity, in that it was filmed on the streets of contemporary Paris, a decision that was in part dictated by necessity – this was a low-budget film, after all, shot rapidly in only four weeks – but that emphasised the distance between the New Wave approach to filmmaking and that of the largely studio-bound Tradition of Quality.

A bout de souffle is heavily intertextual, a feature that was to remain a constant in Godard's work. The film is scattered with allusions to painting, literature and, above all, cinema. From the opening dedication to the small American B-movie studio Monogram Pictures, through Michel's adoration and imitation of Hollywood 'tough guy' Humphrey

• **Plate 16.4**
Jean-Paul Belmondo
and Jean Seberg in
A bout de souffle
(*Breathless*, Jean-Luc
Godard, 1960)

Bogart, Godard plays the cinéphile game of homage and quotation that would be characteristic of his own films and of the New Wave generally. In addition, the casting of the young American actress Jean Seberg as Patricia may be read in a variety of referential ways – as an incarnation of 'America' and, more specifically, as a nod to the émigré European director Otto Preminger who, while working in Hollywood, cast Seberg in the title role of *Saint Joan* (1957). *A bout de souffle* was seen to be 'revolutionary' in the way that it directly challenged the accepted rules of cinematic language. For example, in the sequence near the opening of the film where Michel drives towards a police speed-trap, he addresses the camera – and hence, the audience – directly, breaking the 'fourth wall' that is seen to be necessary for the spectator's identification with the film's fictional world. Famously, the film's use of jerky and discontinuous editing rhythms established the 'jump cut' as a (quickly clichéd) hallmark of New Wave style. But elements such as these should be set against the film's frequent use of long-take, mobile camera shots and the lengthy mid-film sequence in which Michel and Patricia canoodle in a bedroom.

In many ways, the film may be seen as the first of Godard's (increasingly ambiguous) love letters to Hollywood cinema. But it is a relationship marked by mutual incomprehension – as the love affair between Michel and Patricia becomes fraught with mistrust, linguistic misunderstanding and, ultimately, betrayal. Like many of the early New Wave shorts and debut features, *A bout de souffle* was the product of a collaboration between former *Cahiers* critics: the script was based on an idea by Truffaut, and Chabrol was the 'technical adviser' on the film. It was remade in America in 1983 by Jim McBride, starring Richard Gere and Valérie Kaprisky in the Belmondo and Seberg roles.

THE PRODUCTION CONTEXT OF THE NEW WAVE

One of the reasons for the worldwide influence of the French New Wave during the 1960s was its demonstration that it was possible to make exciting, dynamic and innovative films outside of an established production system. The situation that obtained within French cinema prior to the advent of the New Wave was one in which the industry was far from accessible to ambitious young filmmakers. The industry was largely studio-bound and heavily regimented. The way to become a director was to serve long years of apprenticeship as an assistant director before having the possibility oneself to direct. It was this institution of production that the New Wave was seen to have changed.

As films made within a certain production context, those of the New Wave can be examined from two complementary perspectives that are at the heart of any consideration of filmmaking: the production circumstances and the role of filmmaking technology.

Production circumstances

Two of the most common descriptions of New Wave films are that they were 'low-budget' productions that were made 'outside' the conventional system that obtained in France in the 1950s and 1960s. These features have held an abiding appeal for many filmmakers wishing to make films of an 'independent' and 'personal' nature. One can find echoes of the New Wave's example in the Brazilian '**cinema novo**' of the 1960s, in the '**movie brat' generation** of American independent cinema of the 1960s and 1970s, in the **New German Cinema** of the late 1960s and 1970s, as well as in the **Dogme 95** movement that emerged in Denmark in the mid- to late 1990s.

In a recent study of the New Wave, the French film historian Michel Marie examined what 'low budget' meant in terms of the production circumstances in French cinema between 1955 and 1959. Marie found that the average budget of a film in 1955 was 109 million old francs and in 1959, 149 million old francs (the conversion rate following the devaluation of the currency in 1960 saw 1 million francs being worth 10,000 francs). In 1959, of 133 films produced, 74 films cost more than 100 million old francs and 33 cost more than 200 million old francs. So, in 1959, there were 26 films made with a budget of

cinema novo
Or, 'New Cinema'. A movement of filmmakers that came to prominence in Brazil in the 1960s, the leading figure of which was Glauber Rocha. Influenced by the New Wave in France and the intellectual examples of Frantz Fanon and Che Guevara, 'cinema novo' called for filmmaking that emphasised 'the aesthetics of hunger' directed against a cinema of imperialism.

'movie brat' generation
A term that refers to the generation of American filmmakers who, following the decline of the Hollywood studio system in the 1950s, began to make films independently and were heavily influenced by the French New Wave and European 'art cinema' of the 1960s. Such directors include Martin Scorsese and Francis Ford Coppola.

less than 100 milllion old francs. But, as Marie stresses, the sole criterion of a 'low budget' did not qualify a film as being a New Wave production. Marie associates the relatively low budgets on which the New Wave films were made with a backlash among the *Cahiers* critics against films made on exceedingly high budgets, particularly *Notre Dame de Paris* (Jean Delannoy, 1956), a spectacular film made explicitly to compete with Hollywood films within the domestic market. Writing in *Cahiers* No. 71 (April 1957), Jacques Rivette claimed that what was missing in French cinema was 'the spirit of poverty … French cinema only stands a chance now in as much as other directors will take the risk of making films for 20 or 30 million francs, or even less' (cited in Marie 1998: 51).

It was generally agreed that, while French cinema was in a state of good financial health in the mid- to late 1950s, it was deemed to be less healthy in creative terms. However, there were filmmakers who had already set an example of the kind of production that would become characteristic of the New Wave. One of these was Jean-Pierre Melville who, in an interview in 1960, delivered the most concise definition of the characteristic features of New Wave films as being '**an artisanal system of production**, shot on location, without stars, with a minimal crew and on ultra-fast stock, without necessarily having a distributor lined up, without authorisation or servitude of any kind' (ibid.: 45). Melville was the pseudonym of Jean-Pierre Grumbach, the director of such films as *Le Silence de la mer* (1947), *Bob le Flambeur* (1955) and *Le Samourai* (1967), whose influence as a predecessor of the New Wave was explicitly acknowledged by Jean-Luc Godard who cast him in a cameo role in his debut feature *A bout de souffle*.

State subsidy

Marie attributes the relative 'health' of the French film industry to a number of factors. The cinema attendance figures between 1947 and 1957 averaged out at a robust yearly figure of 390 million; the domestic market was still largely dominated by French films (it would be in the 1960s that American films began to bite into their market share) and French films were proving highly exportable; in 1956 40 per cent of receipts were generated by sales of French films abroad. However, Marie identifies another crucial aspect of the production context in the 1950s: the role of state subsidy for filmmaking. Drawing on a revealing interview between Bazin, Doniol-Valcroze and the director of the **CNC** (Centre Nationale de la Cinématographie), written by Jacques Flaud and published in *Cahiers* No. 71 (1957) entitled 'The Situation of French Cinema', Marie examines the importance, as well as some of the ambiguous effects of such state aid to filmmakers. Marie cites a report by Flaud that questioned the consequences of state aid on the quality of French filmmaking: namely, that it tended to produce films 'treating relatively easy subjects, with international stars, taken from works by well-known writers, in other words, subjects that have already been tested in other art forms, thus creating films that are adaptations or remakes' (Marie 1998: 49). The paradox Marie identifies is that the CNC's criticisms are surprisingly close in their analysis, if not their tone, to the 'anti-Establishment' polemics of Truffaut and others on *Cahiers*:

This thesis was the institutional version of the more personal and polemical thesis put forward by François Truffaut. Jacques Flaud goes as far as to encourage producers to take risks, to try out new actors and to envisage artistic renewal…. This official programme was announced at the beginning of 1957 and one understands why the CNC would go on to do everything to support the first productions by Chabrol and Truffaut in granting their production companies the necessary dispensations, to the anger of the cinema technicians unions.

(ibid.: 49)

What emerges from Marie's close attention both to the well-documented polemics originating in the pages of *Cahiers* as well as to the institutional discourses on the state of French cinema is an unexpected overlap between the two. According to Marie, the 1957

New German Cinema
A movement in German cinema in the late 1960s and 1970s that called for a personal and auteur cinema in Germany to counteract the cultural imperialism of Hollywood. Notable directors who emerged included Wim Wenders, Rainer Werner Fassbinder, Alexander Kluge and Margerethe von Trotta.

Dogme 95
The name given to a collective of Danish filmmakers united around the figures of directors Lars Von Trier, Thomas Winterberg and Kristian Levering. Dogme 95 was the name of a manifesto that committed filmmakers to observing a cinematic 'vow of chastity' involving an ultra-realist approach to filmmaking using only digital video cameras.

artisanal system of production
A way of making films outside of an established 'industrial' means of production which emphasises a more craft-like and personal process hence allowing greater control of the filmmaking process.

CNC
Centre Nationale de la Cinématographie, the chief body of the French state that oversees policy

statement by the CNC may be seen to have played 'a decisive role in the emergence of the New Wave in the following year. This fact confirms that there was nothing "spontaneous" about the New Wave generation' (ibid.: 50).

The various types of state funding for filmmakers that became effective during the 1950s support Marie's assertion. Among these was the 'prime à la qualité' ('quality subsidy') which dated from 1953 and was intended to support films whose criteria was seen to be one of 'quality', films which would 'serve the cause of French cinema or ... open up new perspectives in the art of cinema' (ibid.: 48–9). Although it took until 1955 for certain films to benefit from this particular subsidy, the irony was that while the New Wave directors set themselves against what they saw as the Tradition of Quality in French cinema, they themselves would be the beneficiaries of a state subsidy promoting an idea of 'quality' in French film production.

It should be remembered that the state support of French cinema was set against the wider backdrop of policies put in place to aid French reconstruction. Principally the Blum–Byrnes agreement, signed in 1946 and amended in 1948, that, among other trade agreements, fixed a minimum quota of French films to be shown on French screens against non-French (predominantly American) films. So, state subsidy for French filmmaking may be seen as having been a way of preserving and encouraging domestic production in the face of international competition. In 1953, financial assistance became available for the production of short films and was instrumental in helping directors such as Chris Marker, Alain Resnais and Agnès Varda to make their first shorts. In addition, in 1959 a system of 'avances sur recettes' ('advances against earnings') was introduced, enabling producers to part-finance feature films by borrowing from a 'fonds de soutien' ('support fund') against their eventual profits. Many of the funding elements of state support remain in place to this day, although now modified by the close co-production ties established between the French film and television industries, and they account in part for the vitality of film production in France relative to other European countries which have largely capitulated to American hegemony.

□ CASE STUDY 2: *LES QUATRE CENTS COUPS* (*THE FOUR HUNDRED BLOWS*, FRANÇOIS TRUFFAUT, 1959)

Having earned himself a reputation as an 'enfant terrible' with his polemical critical writing in *Cahiers*, and having been barred from the Cannes Film Festival of 1958, in the following year, François Truffaut won Best Director at the festival for his debut feature *Les Quatre cents coups.*

The film was the first to feature the character of Antoine Doinel, played by Jean-Pierre Léaud, to whom Truffaut would return in a further five films, always using the same actor. Léaud plays Doinel as Truffaut's alter ego and *Les Quatre cents coups* was more than a little autobiographically derived. The young Antoine's unhappy home life, his troubles at school and his subsequent incarceration at a correctional centre for delinquent minors were based on Truffaut's own errant youth which saw him locked up for deserting from the army. In fact, it was the intercession of the film critic André Bazin that saved Truffaut from further punishment.

Like Godard's debut *A bout de souffle, Les Quatre cents coups* (The 'four hundred blows' refers to the administering of corporal punishment) was set in the apartments and on the streets of contemporary Paris. The film's lyrical, long-take, mobile camera style owed much to the influence of the filmmakers Jean Renoir, Robert Rossellini and Jean Vigo. The Italian neo-realist director Rossellini was to be an important adviser and champion of many of the young New Wave directors. Truffaut's own cinéphilia is evident throughout the film, although one might argue that it is more fully integrated into the plot and action than in Godard's debut. Whether at the level of the influence of those older directors admired by Truffaut, or simply in the scene in which Antoine steals a still from

• **Plate 16.5**
One of the emblematic
faces of the New Wave,
actor Jean-Pierre Léaud
as the young Antoine
Doinel in *Les Quatre
cents coups* (*The
400 Blows*, François
Truffaut, 1959)

a cinema of the sultry Harriet Andersson in Ingmar Bergman's *Summer with Monika* (1952) (Bergman was an important director for both Truffaut and Godard), the cinéphilic impulse to quote from and pay homage to other films informs *Les Quatre cents coups*. Although less formally audacious than Godard's debut, *Les Quatre cents coups* ends with an arresting freeze-frame image of Antoine on a beach and at the water's edge: the sense of narrative 'closure' is uncertain and suggests an ambiguous future for the young man. It is an image that implicitly contradicts the title caption that reads 'Fin' ('End') with its suggestion that Antoine's story is 'to be continued'. As indeed it was.

NEW DIRECTORS, NEW PRODUCERS

While certain young filmmakers such as Agnès Varda and Claude Chabrol established their own independent production companies to assist in the making of their first feature films (in Varda's case *La Pointe courte* [1954], in Chabrol's *Les Cousins* [1959]), there were other figures who were crucial to the production of films by New Wave directors, notably Pierre Braunberger, Anatole Dauman and Georges de Beauregard.

Pierre Braunberger began producing films in 1926 with works by Alberto Cavalcanti and Jean Renoir. The portfolio of his production company Les Films de la Pléiade was extensive, ranging from avant-garde films to commercial productions as well as works by precursors to the New Wave such as Jean-Pierre Melville (whom Braunberger supported in his adaptation of the novel *Le Silence de la mer* between 1947 and 1948) and the influential ethnographic documentarist Jean Rouch. Braunberger's involvement in producing documentaries and short fictions – both of which were genres of work important to the development of the New Wave – saw him working with figures who would become key directors in French cinema, including Alain Resnais whose films on artists, *Van Gogh*, *Guernica* and *Gauguin*, he produced between 1947 and 1948. Other directors' short films produced by Braunberger included *O Saisons, o châteaux* (Agnès Varda, 1957), *Le Coup du berger* (Jacques Rivette, 1956) and *Tous les garçons s'appellent Patrick, Une Histoire d'eau* and *Charlotte et son Jules* (Jean-Luc Godard, 1957, 1958 and 1959). He would continue to produce features by New Wave directors after their initial successes such as Truffaut's second film *Tirez sur le pianiste* (1960) and Godard's fourth film *Vivre sa vie* (1962).

Anatole Dauman founded Argos Films (with Phillipe Lifchitz) in 1951 as a company specialising in films about art and was responsible for producing important early works by two of the major 'Left Bank' New Wave filmmakers Alain Resnais and Chris Marker. Dauman produced Resnais' *Nuit et brouillard* (*Night and Fog*, 1955), a seminal documentary about the memory of the mass extermination of Jews, communists, gypsies and homosexuals in the Nazi 'death camps' of the Second World War. Dauman also produced the director's first ground-breaking feature film *Hiroshima, mon amour* (1959) and its follow-up *L'Année dernière à Marienbad* (1961). As regards Marker, Argos Films produced the director's early documentary-essay films *Dimanche à Pékin* (*Sunday in Peking*, 1956) and *Lettre de Sibérie* (*Letter from Siberia*, 1958). The relationship between Argos Films and Marker also includes the production of the filmmaker's singular black and white science fiction short *La Jetée* (1963). Other important and influential films produced by Argos included the ethnographic cinéma vérité exploration of Parisian life Chronique d'un été (1960) by Jean Rouch, as well as later works by Resnais (*Muriel, ou le temps d'un retour*, 1963), Godard (*Deux ou trois choses que je sais d'elle*, 1966, *Masculin Feminin*, 1966) and Robert Bresson (*Au Hasard, Balthazar*, 1966 and *Mouchette*, 1967).

The producer who was perhaps the principal supporter of New Wave filmmakers was Georges de Beauregard. Having produced Godard's highly succesful debut *A bout de souffle*, Beauregard went on to produce six other films by the director: *Le Petit soldat* (1960), *Une Femme est une femme* (1961), *Les Carabiniers* (1963), *Le Mépris* (1963), *Made in USA* (1966) and then, years later, *Numéro Deux* (1975). Beauregard also produced films by other New Wave directors including Jacques Demy (*Lola*, 1960), Jacques Rozier (*Adieu Philippine*, 1962), Claude Chabrol (*L'Oeil du malin*, 1962), Agnès Varda (*Cléo de 5 à 7*, 1961), Jacques Rivette (*Suzanne Simonin, la réligieuse de Diderot*, 1965) and Eric Rohmer (*La Collectioneuse*, 1966).

It is hard to conceive of New Wave cinema without the support of adventurous producers such as Dauman, Braunberger and de Beauregard who were able to support the ambitions of new filmmakers on relatively low budgets, as well as to maintain the momentum of production after the first flush of New Wave successes had passed.

☐ CASE STUDY 3: *LA JETÉE* (*THE PIER*, CHRIS MARKER, 1962)

La Jetée is a twenty-eight-minute, black-and-white film made entirely from a montage of still images (with the exception of a moment when the image moves in a conventionally 'cinematic' fashion). It tells the story of a soldier who, having survived the nuclear blast of 'the third world war', finds himself the subject of time-travel experiments in post-apocalypse Paris. It was the work of the filmmaker Chris Marker (real name: Christian-François Bouche-Villeneuve) who was associated with the 'Left Bank' grouping of the New Wave which was also seen to include Alain Resnais and Agnès Varda. Having been a writer and photographer, Marker collaborated with Resnais (he co-directed *Les Statues meurent aussi* (*Statues Also Die*, 1950) and wrote the narration for Resnais' 1957 short *Le Mystère de l'atelier quinze*) and distinguished himself with a series of highly individual documentary films including *Dimanche à Pékin* (1956) and *Lettre de Sibérie* (1958). Notable for the sophistication of their editing and their allusive, poetic commentaries, Marker's documentaries are often seen as defining a genre known as 'essay films'.

La Jetée is Marker's only foray into fiction and was the basis for Terry Gilliam's big-budget Hollywood 'remake' *Twelve Monkeys* (1995). But science fiction in *La Jetée* provides Marker with a narrative alibi – time-travel – by which to explore, with affecting poetry, the ideas of memory and history which are the key themes of all his work. Much

• **Plate 16.6**
La Jetée (*The Pier*,
Chris Marker, 1962)

has been written about this haunting film, acknowledged as one of the masterpieces of cinematic 'modernism'. Marker was a politically committed filmmaker, closely allied to the French left and active in the collective filmmaking groups that arose as a result of 'the events' of May 1968. Some of the themes that *La Jetée* touches on include the aftermath of war and atomic devastation; themes that Resnais also treated in *Nuit et brouillard* (1955) and *Hiroshima, mon amour* (1959). It has also been argued that, with its protracted scenes in which the 'time-traveller' is submitted to torture, *La Jetée* uses the science fiction narrative form as a way of commenting on the theme of political violence which was a major issue at the time. France was involved in a colonial war against Algeria, one of its former dependencies, and direct treatment of the subject could lead to censorship (as was the case with Godard's second film *Le Petit soldat* (1960, but banned until 1963)).

La Jetée alludes to a film that Marker has returned to several times in his career and which he sees as an exploration of the theme of 'impossible memory': Alfred Hitchcock's *Vertigo* (1958). When the time-traveller is sent back in time to pre-apocalypse Paris he meets a young woman and they walk together in the parks of Paris. Pausing at the stump

• **Plate 16.7**
Agnès Varda directing
actress Corinne
Marchand for *Cléo de 5
à 7* (Agnès Varda, 1961)

of an ancient tree, he indicates on the rings of the tree where, in time, 'he comes from'. It is a moment that directly quotes a sequence in *Vertigo* where Madeleine (Kim Novak) shows Scottie (James Stewart) when she lived and when she died by pointing at the rings on a sequoia tree. Marker has referred to *La Jetée*, only half in jest, as a 'remake' of *Vertigo*. If there is a body of work that best exemplifies Alexandre Astruc's idea of the *caméra–stylo*, it is that of Chris Marker.

☐ CASE STUDY 4: *CLÉO DE 5 À 7 (CLÉO FROM 5 TO 7, AGNÈS VARDA, 1961)*

Cléo de 5 à 7 was Agnès Varda's second feature film after her co-operatively produced and undistributed debut *La Pointe Courte* (1954) and, in characteristic New Wave style, the film is set squarely in and around contemporary Paris. In ninety minutes of film, it recounts ninety minutes in the life of Cléo Victoire (Corinne Marchand), a successful pop singer who wanders through Paris, attends a rehearsal, and meets friends and new acquaintances while she awaits the results of a medical test for cancer. The 'realism' so often associated with the New Wave's approach to filmmaking is here taken to a particular extreme, extended beyond close attention to the street-level life of Paris to a 'real-time' approach to the film's duration and the action of the plot. The running time of the film corresponds, almost exactly, to the length and space of Cléo's journey round Paris between 17:00 and 18:30 on 21 June 1961 and uses the radio news for that day.

The film is divided into a prologue (the only sequence in colour) and thirteen sections, each with their exact time and the name of a character whose presence inflects the scene. In its attempt to develop and explore a cinematic language by which to convey a woman's subjective point of view, *Cléo de 5 à 7* relates to Varda's earlier short film *L'Opéra-Mouffe* (1958) which depicted a local Parisian neighbourhood through the mind of a pregnant woman (Varda herself) who is preoccupied by thoughts of the

• **Plate 16.8**
Jean Renoir, the great French director who was much admired by the New Wave, with François Truffaut

forthcoming birth. In its contrast between Cléo's outwardly glamorous appearance and her fear of death, *Cléo de 5 à 7* consistently probes the boundaries between the singer's appearance and her internal world which are explored through an attention to the world around her and the ways in which she sees and registers that world.

Cléo's progress through the film develops from an almost narcissistic preoccupation with her own image – the first part of the film is full of mirrors and reflections, the outside world being, for her, less of a direct experience than an 'image' – through a more direct encounter with that world and its inhabitants. In particular, there is Cléo's encounter with a gentle young man in a park who has been conscripted and is on the point of leaving to fight in Algeria. Across the film, Cléo changes from a creature whose sole function, as a beautiful woman, is to be 'looked at' to a woman who herself looks, sees and encounters the world and the people around her; a transformation from being an 'object' to a 'subject'.

CHARACTERISTICS OF NEW WAVE CINEMA

Technology and aesthetics

One of the most important aspects of the New Wave relates to the changes in filmmaking technology that occurred after the Second World War. These changes had an impact both on how films were made and how they looked. Particularly significant as regards the New Wave was the availability of relatively cheap and lightweight cameras (the Eclair, Arriflex and Cameflex being the dominant new models of lightweight cameras) and sound-recording equipment (the portable Nagra tape-recorder, for example). Not only did the advent of such technology allow filmmakers to shoot with smaller, less cumbersome crews, it also allowed the New Wave directors to work outside the established system of French filmmaking. This conventional style of filmmaking (the so-called Tradition of Quality) privileged a studio-based method of production in which directors and cinematographers worked alongside a team of other personnel such as set designers, lighting designers and art directors. Being opposed to many of the films produced by such a system, New Wave directors were able to convert their polemical antagonism to such filmmaking into practice. Influenced by the examples of **cinéma vérité** documentarists such as Jean Rouch and neo-realist filmmakers such as Roberto Rossellini, both of whom made films based on direct encounters with the world around them, the New Wave directors used the new cameras and sound equipment to extend this approach in the context of fiction filmmaking.

In his recent historical study of the New Wave, Jean Douchet (who had been a critic on *Cahiers* at the same time as Godard and Truffaut) states that '[the] hand-held camera became one of the distinctive features of the New Wave'. It is important to remember two things here. First, that television was still in the process of establishing itself as the dominant entertainment medium in France in the 1960s, so the street-level, documentary look and feel of the New Wave films would have appeared very 'new' and 'modern' at the time, coming as something of a stylistic shock in comparison to the output of much of French cinema. Second, that the New Wave directors used this equipment in order to show the world of Parisian everyday life with greater 'authenticity' and 'directness' than had been hitherto possible in French cinema, but also to push at the limits of what was deemed 'acceptable' both in terms of cinematic conventions and subject matter. Douchet describes the significance of the new camera technology on the New Wave thus:

Carried around on the operator's shoulder, it (the lightweight camera) could closely follow the actor's every movement. A new intimacy developed between the camera and its subjects. The act of filming became a close physical encounter.... In terms of craft, the camera enabled filmmakers to abandon the use of heavy equipment (and its operators) and provided rapidity of movement and

cinéma vérité
A term for one of the strands in the flourishing of new forms of documentary that took place in Europe and America from the 1950s onwards. Partly aided by lightweight camera and sound equipment, cinéma vérité saw the film-maker operating as a participant–observer relative to the reality being filmed. Another tendency in this new form of documentary was known as 'Direct Cinema'.

execution (with less time required during filming). It gave them the ability to film from a variety of vehicles (the camera operator could work in anything from a car to a baby carriage) which allowed the use of camera movements that were not only unthinkable but impossible with dolly tracks. And it introduced the camera into actual spaces whose cramped quarters reinforced the impression of real life. Aesthetically, a new and unexpected style exploded across the screen and added a sense of buoyancy to otherwise serious issues.

(Douchet 1999: 204–5)

The freewheeling style of filmmaking that marked the New Wave cinema was highly influential around the world. Not only would many other directors be influenced by the 'look' of the New Wave films but documentary cinema found a new lease of life with the advent of cinéma vérité and 'Direct Cinema'. In addition, with the recent use of digital video cameras by independent filmmakers it is hardly surprising that references to the stylistic example of New Wave directors such as Godard and Varda should have become commonplace (see e.g. Kelly 2000).

There are, of course, exceptions to prove the very 'rules' that Michel Marie outlines at the beginning of this chapter. The soundtrack for *A bout de souffle*, for example, was entirely **post-synchronised** and neither of its lead performers, Jean-Paul Belmondo and Jean Seberg, were non-professionals. Belmondo was a relatively 'new face', however, and would soon become one of the leading actors associated with the New Wave generation.

Influences and precursors

In the December 1962 issue of *Cahiers*, the magazine published a 'Dictionary of 162 New Filmmakers'. By this time, the New Wave was no longer deemed to be the 'phenomenon' it had been in 1958–1959 but the sheer number of directors who had made one or two

For further discussion of documentary cinema, cinéma vérité and direct cinema, see Chapter 8.

post-synchronised
Referring to the process of adding and modifying some or all of a film's sound in a studio after the film has been shot and synchronising these sounds to the image track (also known as 'post-synching').

• **Plate 16.9**
Bridget Bardot and Jeanne Moreau in *Viva Maria!* (Louis Malle, 1965)

films in the intervening years indicated that a veritable explosion of filmmaking had taken place in France which, in part, contributed to this idea of the 'phenomenon' of the New Wave. Most of these films and filmmakers are now forgotten, and the New Wave is reduced to a handful of illustrious names and admittedly important, ground-breaking works. It is worth pointing out, however, a few of the figures who influenced this phenomenon and who could be said to have been its precursors.

One can divide such figures into the following categories: 'elders', 'early contem-poraries' and 'fellow travellers'. Of the elders, Jean-Pierre Melville has already been mentioned and his importance is undeniable, both in terms of the independence with which he produced his films but also in his abiding love of American cinema. Alexandre Astruc should also be mentioned as an example of a critic who also became a filmmaker prior to *Cahiers* writers making the same transition, although Michel Marie argues that Astruc's films *Les Mauvaises rencontres* (1955) and *Une Vie* (1958) cannot be considered as truly New Wave films because of their production circumstances and because the latter film featured the international star Maria Schell.

Two names are worth including in the 'early contemporaries' category: Louis Malle and Roger Vadim. Malle had been an assistant director on Robert Bresson's *Un Condamné à mort s'est échappé* (*A Man Escaped*, 1956), and his debut feature film *Ascenseur pour l'échafaud* (*Lift to the Scaffold*, 1957) had many elements that one might identify with the New Wave – a 'film noir' atmosphere and provenance (it was adapted from a thriller), a jazz score especially composed by the legendary musician Miles Davis, cinematography by Henri Decaë who would go on to shoot Truffaut's *Les Quatre cents coups*, and a lead actress in the shape of Jeanne Moreau who was to become one of the key performers associated with the New Wave. Vadim's debut feature *Et Dieu créa la femme* (1956) was admired by Godard and Truffaut for its 'modernity' largely because Vadim brought to the screen a new image of youthful, devil-may-care femininity in the shape of Brigitte Bardot, who was to become the major sex symbol of French cinema and an important signifier of many of those qualities – 'youth', 'modernity' and 'subversive' sexual freedom – that would be associated with the New Wave as an image of modern, postwar France both at home and internationally.

As regards 'fellow travellers', this category is more fluid depending on whom one includes. For example, Roberto Rossellini may be seen as an illustrious 'elder' relative to the generation of the New Wave. The influence of his 'neo-realist' films on the critical ideas of André Bazin is well documented, but his significance extends beyond this. His 1953 film *Viaggio in Italia* (*Voyage to Italy*) was a commercial and critical failure, except with *Cahiers* critics such as Rivette, Rohmer and Godard, who regarded it as an extremely 'modern' work that 'opened a breach' in the history of cinema. It would be through this very breach that they would propel their first films and Rossellini was an adviser to the young directors, even co-writing the screenplay for Godard's *Les Carabiniers* (*The Riflemen*, 1963). Jean Rouch was a documentary filmmaker who came from a background in ethnology and anthropology, and his creative studies of life and rituals in 'primitive' societies as well as in European society – *Les Maîtres fous* (1955), *Moi, un noir* (1958), *La Pyramide humaine* (1959) and *Chronique d'un été* (1960) were particularly influential works – presented the New Wave filmmakers with an example of how documentary and fiction could intermingle and inform each other. The work of Agnès Varda and Alain Resnais, as part of the so-called 'Left Bank' group of filmmakers who were contemporaries of the *Cahiers* critics, also demonstrated a lively interest in documentary filmmaking that would lead to full-length fiction films.

Actors and stars

If one of the defining features of the New Wave was its wholesale rejection of the cinematic values of the Tradition of Quality, this is particularly marked as regards actors and actresses. The New Wave rejection of the French 'star system' may be ascribed to

• **Plate 16.10**
Jean-Luc Godard and
Anna Karina share an
intimate moment

*Compare to the
Hollywood star system
discussed in Chapter 6,
pp. 129–37.*

*Compare the ideas
outlined here with the
conventions of classical
Hollywood cinema
discussed in Chapter 3,
pp. 61–82.*

a number of factors: New Wave directors could not afford to employ 'stars', did not wish to be beholden to the power that a 'star' could exercise over creative decisions deemed to be in the hands of the auteur and, put plainly, 'stars' did not correspond with the New Wave 'project' which was in search of 'youthfulness', 'modernity' and 'spontaneity'. Instead, the New Wave cast relatively unknown performers, or outright newcomers, and, in so doing, discovered a new generation of actors and, in some cases, created bona fide stars.

One such star was Brigitte Bardot. While Bardot was by no means an archetypal New Wave actress like Anna Karina or Jeanne Moreau, she came to represent a new image of femininity that was to differentiate her and her contemporaries from the actresses who preceded them. The impact of her role in *Et Dieu créa la femme* (Vadim, 1956) was important for the New Wave for a variety of reasons. The film conformed to a certain number of the key characteristics of New Wave filmmaking. It was shot with a relatively small crew on location (in the then relatively 'unspoiled' fishing town of St Tropez in the South of France). While it featured a 'star' in the shape of Curt Jurgens, it was Bardot's youthful insolence and her unruffled sexual freedom that led François Truffaut to write: 'It is a film typical of our generation … despite the vast audience that *Et Dieu créa la femme* will certainly find, only young spectators will be on Vadim's side, because he shares their vision' (cited in Vincendeau 2000: 85). Bardot's association with the New Wave was actually quite limited in terms of the films she made. With the exception of *Et Dieu créa la femme*, Bardot made only two other films with directors associated with the 'young generation' of filmmakers: *Vie privée* (*A Very Private Affair*, Louis Malle, 1961) and *Le Mépris* (*Contempt*, Godard, 1963). But there can be little doubt that her 'sex kitten' image and its connotations of a sophisticated yet earthy sexuality was important in opening up foreign markets for European art cinema abroad, particularly in the USA. As Vincendeau notes:

On the international film scene, the mid- to late 1950s saw both the break-up of the Hollywood studio system and concurrently, the rise of European art cinema: the films of Fellini, Antonioni, Resnais, Bergman, etc. As part of its drive to compete with Hollywood, European art cinema proposed a new kind of social and psychological realism which included a bid for explicit sexuality, made possible because of less stringent censorship codes. The different censorship laws and the more realistic genres of European films of the 1950s combined to produce a more 'natural' type of sexuality than Hollywood, best epitomized by Gina Lollobrigida, Sophia Loren and Silvana Mangano in Italian cinema. Women in peasant dresses, with bare feet paddling in rice fields, contrasted with the high glamour of Monroe and Lana Turner. Bardot was closer to the Italian model and *Et Dieu créa la femme* frequently features scenes of bathing, sea and beaches. European eroticism was bankable. Vadim said: 'Of course, some of [*Et Dieu créa la femme*'s] success came from its sexual frankness, and that's why so many of the first New Wave films, like Malle's *Les Amants* (1957) and Godard's *A bout de souffle* are equally casual about nudity. It's what distributors, especially American ones, were asking for.'

(ibid.: 92–3)

For male and female performers alike, the New Wave filmmakers 'concentrated on behaviour, looks and gestures rather than psychology' (ibid.: 117). Vincendeau elaborates on these features of New Wave acting styles as follows:

Its authenticity was grounded in a discourse of anti-professionalism. It was important that actors and actresses were seen not to act, especially in contrast to the Tradition of Quality cinema, which foregrounded polished performances, careful lighting and framing, experienced mastery of space, well-modulated delivery of dialogue. New Wave films foregrounded improvisation through filming on location, using available light and vernacular language. Performances matched this. Casual elocution and underplaying made performances appear 'modern' and blurred the distinction between fiction and document (reference to New Wave films as 'documentaries' on the actors are frequent). Lines are fluffed and movements are charmingly gauche.

(ibid.)

What the New Wave auteurs required of their actors and actresses was 'male doubles or female muses' (ibid.: 115). In terms of the 'male doubles', it is particularly striking when one considers Truffaut's casting of Jean-Pierre Léaud as his alter ego Antoine Doinel in the suite of films beginning with *Les Quatre cent coups*. Equally, Godard's 'discovery' of the relatively unknown Jean-Paul Belmondo (who was to become one of the most popular and enduring French male leading men for several decades) often saw him playing a surrogate for the director and his cinéphilic obsessions: consider Belmondo's 'caricature' of Bogart in *A bout de souffle*, for example. But whether the actresses were *gamine* types such as Anna Karina or Chantal Goya, or sophisticated and liberated 'modern' women such as Jeanne Moreau or Emmanuelle Riva, as Ginette Vincendeau stresses: 'The close relationship between actresses and filmmakers in the New Wave meant that while they played the traditional role of female object of desire, they, and not just the male alter-egos, also functioned as relayers of the film-maker's worldview' (ibid.: 116–17). Such 'close relationships' between directors and their leading actresses are often contextualised in cinéphilic terms with reference to other cinematic partnerships, such as those between Joseph von Sternberg and Marlene Dietrich or Ingmar Bergman and several of his actresses. Godard's relationship with Karina yielded seven films between 1961 and 1966, and Moreau was the partner of the directors of several of her major films in the 1960s, such as Truffaut and Malle. In fact, these 'cinéphile–svengali' partnerships may be said to be one of the characteristic features of European art cinema in the 1960s, from Federico Fellini's films with Giullieta Masina to Michelangelo Antonioni's films with Monica Vitti.

Society and politics

The social background against which the New Wave emerged was one of postwar reconstruction and modernisation which saw France enter an economic boom period known as the 'trente glorieuses', or the 'thirty glorious years' of prosperity and techno-logical advances. Presiding over this period was the figure of Charles De Gaulle, the *résistant* war hero who, from the establishment of the Fifth Republic in 1958, was the President of France until 1969. However, during the same period, France was involved in bloody, drawn-out conflicts with countries struggling to free themselves from their former colonial masters. The involvement of the French armed forces in Indo-China saw them endure a humiliating defeat at Dien Bien Phu in May 1954, but the increasing involvement of American troops in the region set the scene for the war in Vietnam which would be one of the defining political events of the 1960s. While France negotiated the independence of two of its colonies, Morocco and Tunisia, the situation in France's oldest colony, Algeria, proved to be more intractable, and fatally damaged the last five administra-tions of the French presidential structure known as the Fourth Republic. The colonial war between Algeria and France would last for eight years and claim the lives of 18,000 French soldiers and 250,000 Muslims, while allowing De Gaulle to recast the presi-dential structure of power – the Fifth Republic – in order to resolve the crisis. Massacres and atrocities in Algeria were committed by both the Nationalist pro-independence movement, the FLN (Front de Libération Nationale), and the shadowy, colonialist 'secret army' of the French, OAS (Organisation de l'armée secrète), with the conflict spreading to the French mainland both in the shape of the attacks on civilians but also in mobil-isation against the war by intellectuals, artists and those on the left-wing of the political spectrum. One such demonstration of opposition to the war in Algeria was the text supporting 'le droit à l'insoumission' (the right of soldiers to absent themselves without leave rather than serve in the war) signed by 121 prominent French intellectuals and artists including, among others, Jean-Paul Sartre, Simone de Beauvoir, Alain Resnais, Jacques Doniol-Valcroze, Pierre Kast and François Truffaut. It was immediately banned from publication and became known as the 'Manifeste des 121' ('The Manifesto of the 121'). The Evian Agreements of March 1962 finally led to full Algerian independence, despite a last-ditch campaign of terror launched by the OAS.

Compare with the rise of Soviet montage cinema as a result of the 1917 revolution. See Chapter 15.

The major political event of the 1960s in France occurred in May 1968 during which widespread demonstrations and strikes took place, disrupting public transport, closing banks, decimating industrial production and bringing the country to a virtual standstill. The two major forces of 'les évènements de mai' ('the events of May') were students and workers whose discontent with the French economic and social system was palliated by government action. The threat of a full-scale insurrection was thus soon snuffed out. The country's filmmakers were heavily involved in the 'events' of May 1968 but the politicisation of the New Wave (often accused of having been apolitical, if not right-wing) began a little earlier. One of the main causes of such radicalisation was the perceived heavy-handedness of the state and its willingness to exercise censorship. This was an important issue during the 1960s, extending to all areas of media and culture and effecting coverage of the Algerian war just as it did the mainstream media coverage of the 'events of May'. The former writers of *Cahiers* who had avoided direct political engagement during the Algerian war came to political consciousness through a variety of confrontations with the French state in the mid- to late 1960s.

The censorship of filmmakers' work, often resulting in the forbidding of public projection, had already alerted directors to the heavy-handedness of the state when it came to matters military – for example, Godard's *Le Petit soldat*, shot in 1960 but banned until 1963 – or clerical – Rivette's adaptation of Denis Diderot's play *La Réligieuse* was banned after protests by Catholic groups. But it was the decision of the Gaullist state in February 1968 to replace Henri Langlois as the head of the Cinémathèque Française that crystallised these misgivings and resulted in mobilisations and demonstrations that pre-dated the events of May by several months. The concerted campaigning efforts of many filmmakers protesting this decision was organised by *Cahiers* and resulted in Langlois' eventual reinstatement. Such activism generated a renewed confidence in the linking of culture and politics that would have profound repercussions throughout the milieux of filmmaking and criticism as well as further afield.

□ CASE STUDY 5: JEAN-LUC GODARD

Jean-Luc Godard has endowed cinema with a vast and inexhaustibly rich body of work. Since his debut in 1990 with *A bout de souffle*, Godard has made over forty feature films, numerous short films and many hours of video, not to mention his film criticism which, throughout the 1950s, preceded and overlapped with his career as a filmmaker.

In fact, Godard has frequently stated that he considers his filmmaking as much an exercise in criticism as his writing, an assertion that allows a way into his body of work. Godard's career is conventionally seen as divided into three phases. First, the New Wave period that begins with *A bout de souffle* and for which his writing on *Cahiers* and his short filmmaking throughout the 1950s may be seen as preparation. When the New Wave period is seen to end is a matter of historical debate. Some argue that the New Wave as a 'phenomenon' was over by 1962. Others argue that it can be extended up to the political events of May 1968. With Godard's increasing politicisation around that time, the 'second phase' of his work is seen to begin when the director jettisoned his auteur celebrity status and became involved in collective, explicitly ideologically motivated filmmaking; this period continues until 1972. Godard's 'third phase' occurs in the early to mid-1970s when the director returned to relatively mainstream filmmaking with films such as *Tout va bien* (1972) and *Sauve qui peut* (la vie) (1979). One of the most important developments in this period, and which continues to the present day, has been Godard's long-standing use and exploration of video technology.

During the New Wave years (1958–62) and in the immediate post-New Wave period (1962–68) Godard sustained a steady output of work, sometimes shooting two films simultaneously. During this period he made seventeen features and eleven

• **Plate 16.11**
Anna Karina and Eddie Constantine in *Alphaville* (Jean-Luc Godard, 1965)

shorts (including those made prior to *A bout de souffle*) and the time was marked by two consistent collaborations (excluding that with the producer Georges de Beauregard); first, with the cinematographer Raoul Coutard on fifteen features and, second, with the actress Anna Karina who was married to Godard for a period in the 1960s and with whom he made seven films and co-founded a production company, Anoushka Films.

In the films that Godard made up to 1968 a keen awareness of the history of cinema co-exists alongside a critical analysis of cinematic language and the possibilities of extending cinematic forms. As early as *A bout de souffle*, it is evident that Godard is both glorying in the generic possibilities of the Hollywood B-movie but also taking advantage of their use within a specifically French context by employing them against the backdrop of everyday Parisian life. Here, genre meets documentary. This is a crucial aspect of Godard's filmmaking: the desire to explore the fictional aspect of a documentary context and vice versa. He was deeply influenced in this by the work of the ethnographical documentarist Jean Rouch (Godard had studied ethnography at the Sorbonne in Paris in the late 1940s). Equally important in this regard was the example of the great Italian director Roberto Rossellini, whose 'neo-realist' films such as *Rome, Open City* (1945), *Paisan* (1946) and *Germany, Year Zero* (1947), as well as later films made with his wife Ingrid Bergman such as *Voyage to Italy* (1953), were highly influential for many New Wave filmmakers in their extremely 'modern' use of documentary modes to treat fictional storylines.

Throughout the 1960s, Godard used generic forms to analyse French society, politics and consumerism. *Alphaville* (1965), for example, employs science fiction and the spy thriller forms in a generic hybrid, as well as quoting liberally from German Expressionist cinema (the sequence printed in negative is a direct quotation from *Nosferatu, Eine Symphonie des Grauens* (F.W. Murnau, 1922), and sets these to work to produce a dystopian vision of an inhuman, technocratic society using only the existing modernist architectural forms of Paris as it was in 1965. Across a number of his films made in this period, such as *Vivre sa vie* (*My Life to Live*, 1962), *Une Femme mariée* (*A Married Woman*, 1964) and *Deux ou trois choses que je sais d'elle* (*Two or Three Things I Know about Her*, 1966), it became clear that Godard was as much a social critic with a camera as a film critic. This element of social criticism was to increase in significance in the late 1960s as Godard became more explicitly political in his analysis of consumer society (which he often likened to a form of 'prostitution' in advanced capitalist countries) and his increasing hostility towards American imperialism (this being the period of America's war in Vietnam) and what he saw as its propaganda vehicle, Hollywood cinema. By the time of *La Chinoise* (1967) and *Weekend* (1967), Godard had become fully radicalised by 'l'affaire Langlois' (see above). The political uprising of the 'events' of May 1968 – as a response to which Godard and others shut down the Cannes Film Festival in solidarity with workers' and students' protests – were to transform his career, as they would many others.

☐ CASE STUDY 6: AGNÈS VARDA

Agnès Varda's debut feature film *La Pointe courte* (1954) was dubbed by the French film historian Georges Sadoul as 'the first film of the New Wave' and Varda has frequently been described as 'the grandmother' of the New Wave. A former art student and professional photographer, Varda made her first film with no previous experience of filmmaking. *La Pointe Courte* told the story of a relationship set against the location of a fishing village. It was co-operatively produced by a company which Varda established specifically in order to make the film. Ciné-Tamaris has remained Varda's production company ever since and through it she has made sixteen feature films, as well as many documentaries and shorts.

Varda is often bracketed as part of the so-called 'Left Bank' grouping of the New Wave. This term, coined by the American film critic and former director of the New York Film Festival Richard Roud, was intended to distinguish the work of Varda, Alain Resnais and Chris Marker from that of the filmmakers who emerged from *Cahiers*. The 'Left Bank' filmmakers were frequent collaborators with each other: Resnais was the editor of *La Pointe courte* and Varda accompanied Marker to China to assist on the production of his 1956 documentary essay-film *Dimanche à Pekin* (*Sunday in Peking*). The 'Left Bank' filmmakers were distinguished by a number of characteristics: a practical relationship with documentary filmmaking, their literary affinities, close contact and interest in fine arts, and a more pronounced degree of left-leaning political commitment than the *Cahiers* directors.

That is not to say that these two groupings were mutually exclusive. *Cahiers* championed the work by the Left Bank group, and Godard, Doniol-Valcroze and Anna Karina appear in cameo roles in a short silent film inserted into Varda's second film *Cléo de 5 à 7* (1961).

For a more detailed discussion of Cléo de 5 à 7, see Case study 4.

As the only woman filmmaker associated with the New Wave, Varda's work is fascinating for a variety of reasons. From an early stage she practised what she called 'cinécriture' (a compound word made up of two French words, 'ciné' – cinema – and 'écriture' – writing; hence, 'cinematic writing'). One might say that all her films are examples of Alexandre Astruc's notion of 'le caméra–stylo' ('the camera–pen') in a woman's hands. Many of her films are explicitly about women's experiences and explore cinematic means of conveying female subjectivity. Varda was married for many years to another director who came to prominence during the New Wave period, Jacques Demy, who made a number of important and successful films including *Lola* (1960) and *Les Parapluies de Cherbourg* (*The Umbrellas of Cherbourg*, 1964), and who died in 1990.

The range of subjects covered by Varda's films include radical politics (*Black Panthers*, shot in the US in 1968) and the chronicle of the lives of two female friends coming to political consciousness through the 1960s and 1970s. *L'une chante l'autre pas* (*One Sings the Other Doesn't*, 1977). Many of her films are marked by her abiding interest in and love for the arts of painting, sculpture and photography. In 1985 Varda made a film about the short life and death of a young female drifter in the south of France, *Sans toit ni loi* (*Vagabond*), starring Sandrine Bonnaire, which was critically praised and reached international audiences.

More recently, Varda again claimed international attention and acclaim with her elegant and humane portrait of those living at the margins of French consumer society, *Les Glaneurs et la glaneuse* (*The Gleaners and I*, 2000), which won the European Film Academy Award for Best Documentary in 2000 as well as several prestigious American Film Critics awards. Shot on digital video, the film marked a kind of full-circle return to Varda's New Wave roots, the documentary-essay form updated with the new technology of digital video.

THE LEGACY OF THE NEW WAVE

In January 1999 *Cahiers* published a special supplement entitled 'The New Wave: A Legend in Question' which included seventeen articles reassessing the 'legend' of the French New Wave. The issue also featured a questionnaire in which a number of filmmakers from around the world were asked to respond to a series of questions, including: 'What did the phenomenon of the New Wave represent in your life?'; 'Was its influence positive or negative?'; 'Did the New Wave help you in making films?' The directors who responded included a combination of older and contemporary French filmmakers as well as illustrious international names such as Abbas Kiarostami and Martin Scorsese. It is instructive to listen to these two filmmakers, each from a very different culture and industry, the one Iranian, the other American, in what they had to say about the New Wave's impact. First, Scorsese:

Whether they're aware of it or not, all the filmmakers who have come since have been influenced by the New Wave ... the first films of Godard, Truffaut, Chabrol, Rivette, Rohmer and others gave you the feeling that you could make a film yourself, anyhow, with anyone, no matter what the story was and that you didn't need expensive materials, famous names or powerful lights. It was enough to go out into the streets and make a film and that it would work if you had the courage of your convictions.

(*Cahiers*, January 1999: 97)

And Kiarostami:

Perhaps you won't believe me if I tell you that the movement started in French cinema by the New Wave was followed day-by-day in Iran ... under the influence of New Wave filmmakers my way of imagining or envisaging cinema changed. Before, I believed that cinema belonged to superstars, to studios and spectacular sets. With the New Wave, I saw myself and my neighbours in films.

(ibid.: 96)

Before examining the considerable long-term influence of the New Wave, as attested to by Scorsese and Kiarostami, it is worthwhile considering the lifetime of the phenomenon in France. I have already explored some of the factors that encouraged the explosion of film production from 1958 onwards that became known as New Wave cinema, but it should be acknowledged how relatively short-lived this cinema was as a 'phenomenon'. That is not to say that the examples and possibilities for filmmakers represented by the New Wave expired along with its sure-fire commercial prospects, but to delineate a scale of time in which this 'phenomenon' may be seen to have existed. The standard film-historical time scale in which the New Wave is seen to have been born, flourished and expired was between 1958 and 1962, between the prize-winning success of Truffaut's *Les Quatre cents coups* at Cannes in 1958 and the second films by Godard, Truffaut and Chabrol that were released between 1961 and 1962. With Godard's *Une Femme est une femme* (1961), Truffaut's *Tirez sur le pianiste* (1960) and Chabrol's *Les Godelureaux* (1960) and *L'Oeil du malin* (1962), the novelty of the New Wave was seen to have worn off, with the public staying away and the critics unenthusiastic. This strict chronology serves to delimit the New Wave as a short-term, high-profile event in French cinema that quickly fell out of favour; a caricature of these films became current as being little more than a compendium of images of 'Saint Tropez, casual relationships, whisky and ennui' (de Baecque 1991: 138). In his recent study of the period, *A Portrait of Youth* (1998), the French cultural historian Antoine de Baecque points out also that there were larger transformations underway that should be considered when examining the immediate New Wave period. The backdrop to the New Wave was 'a long-term cultural evolution', one which saw the numbers of cinema spectators gradually decline throughout the 1950s and 1960s as television became the dominant form of mass entertainment and communication. In these terms, the New Wave may be seen as the momentary phenomenon of a national cinema revitalising the domestic scene while also soliciting considerable international attention.

The New Wave certainly modified some of the conditions of film production in France, for example, the tendency to move away from studio-based production to an increased emphasis on location-based filming. It also had an effect on distribution, particularly in the importance accorded to the state-supported circuit of specialised *cinémas d'art et d'essai,* which might be seen as a precursor of the 'art cinemas' that became a feature of international film distribution from the 1960s onwards. It is in these terms that the New Wave may be seen to have had a profound and continuing influence on cinema, both in France and internationally. It may be argued that, since the New Wave period, the idea of 'auteur' cinema has become virtually institutionalised in France. During the Socialist presidency of François Mitterand in the 1980s, the Minister of Culture Jack Lang instituted a series of policies that sought to defend French film production against American domination of the domestic film scene while paying particular attention to auteur production. Many of Lang's policies remain more or less in place to this day, and

Compare with the UK film industry in Chapter 13, pp. 322–7.

it has arguably been the French state's willingness to intervene, regulate and subsidise its national cinema that has contributed to its being the only European country with an active and vital national cinema.

The term 'national cinema' is increasingly questionable in a period of globalised capital and media, and it is useful to consider the extent to which the New Wave was an international phenomenon as much as it was national. Auteur filmmaking has been a significant part of the national industry since the 1960s and it is this form of filmmaking that tends to represent French cinema abroad, exporting more successfully than other, more populist, national genres such as comedies and thrillers. Thus it may be argued that the French films which successfully export abroad claim the mantle of 'art cinema' while losing some of their national specificity. Consider, for example, how the film *Amélie* (Jean-Pierre Jeunet, 2001), a huge popular success in France, was marketed as a reassuringly 'French art cinema' product in the UK.

As many critics have argued, one of the features of 'art cinema' is its simultaneously national and international character. During the 1960s, this sector of international cinema was the institutionalised space in which national cinemas competed for attention as the Hollywood studio system declined and American cinema turned to independent production. The international aspect of the New Wave legacy is complex and made up of many different strands. It should be remembered that the phenomenon of a 'new wave' of filmmaking was not restricted to France. In fact, 'la nouvelle vague' could be seen to have been one 'wave' (admittedly the first and perhaps most influential) following on from the international impact of Italian neo-realism, that would widen out as part of a tremendous renaissance in European national cinemas during the 1960s and 1970s and that would take in the strength of the Italian, Czech and German films of the period. The international appeal of European cinema throughout the 1960s depended on a combination of structural factors: a willingness to support domestic production, especially the work of new filmmakers, and a thriving international film culture able to circulate and promote such work. It might be said that one of the major legacies of the 'French New Wave' was that it was responsible for circulating not just films, but critical ideas as well. This was certainly the case with *Cahiers du cinéma*, which must rank as the most influential film magazine in the history of this field. As the directors of the New Wave became international celebrities, the ideas they had explored in their writing became international critical currency, particularly the notion of the auteur, which would become a cornerstone of early academic film studies. For a while in the 1960s, the magazine was published in English, a venture inaugurated by the American critic Andrew Sarris, who translated the term 'politique des auteurs' as 'auteur theory' and would go on to apply it to American filmmakers in his book *The American Cinema: Directors and Directions 1929–1968* (1996). Thus a 'politique', as a politics and a policy, became, through mistranslation, a 'theory'.

Both as a corpus of films and as a filmmaking example, the New Wave has continued to influence successive generations of French filmmakers. One way of considering how the memory and the myth of the New Wave still exerts a profound pull on auteur cinema – both in France and abroad – is by examining the persona of the actor Jean-Pierre Léaud. From his 1958 role as a child actor in *Les Quatre cents coups* and through his numerous reprisals of the character Antoine Doinel, Léaud has become an iconic figure in French cinema. Throughout the 1960s and 1970s he worked with a number of major auteurs, including Godard, Pier Paolo Pasolini and Bernardo Bertolucci, who cast him as a thinly disguised New Wave cinéaste in *Last Tango in Paris* (1972). It is in Bertolucci's film and in Jean Eustache's *La Maman et la putain* (*The Mother and the Whore*, 1973) that one can detect the iconic associations of Léaud's persona being modified and exploited by other directors who had been influenced by the New Wave but who were aware, sometimes uncomfortably, of coming after it. Eustache's film, a harrowing anatomisation of the emotional fall-out of the post-1968 period, put Léaud's persona as a petit-bourgeois Parisian solipsist to work in a particularly exacting fashion. Over the past decade or so,

Léaud's persona – one of madcap melancholy – has featured in a number of films as a way of looking back to the past of the New Wave and considering its legacy. Having been born into a cinema of film-fixated allusions, Léaud has literally 'grown up' on screen and now finds himself frequently cast as a kind of 'quotation' of himself, as an icon in inverted commas.

Recent films that have used Léaud in this self-reflexive manner include *I Hired a Contract Killer* (Aki Kaurismaki, 1990), *Le Pornographe* (*The Pornographer*, Bertrand Bonello, 2000) and *What Time Is it There?* (Tsai Ming-Liang, 2001). In France, Léaud has frequently taken roles in films by young French auteur directors who deliberately work with the self-referential register that his presence affords. Perhaps the most dizzyingly self-referential of such films is Irma Vep (Olivier Assayas, 1996), in which Léaud plays a washed-up, semi-demented French auteur unwillingly directing a TV remake of an episode from the silent serial films *Les Vampires* (Louis Feuillade, 1915–16). Léaud's character has chosen the Hong Kong martial-arts movie actress Maggie Cheung to play the silent cinema actress Musidora, who originally acted as *Irma Vep*, one of the film's eponymous gang of criminals. Irma Vep is an interesting and important film that proved to be something of an international cult success. It works with layers of cinematic allusions: to early cinema and the New Wave, to international genre films and contemporary French cinema. In the density of its allusions it is very much influenced by the New Wave and, in that sense, it is a film about cinema, about its numerous pasts, lost possibilities and possible futures, and a number of critics have examined the film's self-referentiality and its association with the movement (see e.g. Wilson 1999). One of the aspects that reinforces the conjunction between *Irma Vep* and the legacy of the New Wave is the fact that Assayas was once a critic on *Cahiers*, and he is not alone in having made the now time-honoured move from criticism to filmmaking that was a characteristic of the New Wave; other former writers on the magazine have followed the same path and established themselves as directors, including André Téchiné, Leos Carax, Pascal Bonitzer and Danièlle Dubroux.

THE FRENCH NEW WAVE IN THE TWENTY-FIRST CENTURY

Surely the filmmakers associated with the French New Wave of the early 1960s are now figures of mainly historical interest, their principal cinematic achievements firmly in the past? Far from it. With the exception of Francois Truffaut, who died in 1984 at age 52, Godard, Chabrol, Rohmer and Rivette from the original 'Cahiers du cinéma' gang, as well as Marker, Varda and Resnais from the so-called 'Left Bank' group, have all continued to make films. Now in their seventies and eighties, all have recently produced work that is as enduringly alive to the possibilities and challenges of cinema as the films of their youth. While Chabrol, Rivette and Rohmer have remained faithful to traditional forms of narrative cinema, Godard, Marker and Varda have continued to be open to new ways of working. To assess them collectively, as 'twenty-first-century filmmakers', is to take stock of a set of remarkable achievements. It is also worth noting that a new generation of British and American critics have recently begun to work on these directors, as witnessed by publications such as Catherine Lupton's study of Chris Marker (the first career-length survey in English), Emma Wilson's recent work on Alain Resnais and Douglas Morrey's book on Godard, the latter two as part of the excellent 'French Directors' series published by Manchester University Press, as well as the extremely useful work that appears in the pages of the journal *Studies in French Cinema*.

Having made four films since 2000, Claude Chabrol (born 1930) has so refined his glacially controlled examinations of French bourgeois *mores* that he might be considered now as a kind of French Hitchcock, making work for a mainstream audience while using his favoured genre of the thriller to explore cinematic questions of point of view and working with first-rate actresses like Isabelle Huppert, as in *Merci pour le chocolat* (2000) and *L'ivresse du pouvoir* (2006). Jacques Rivette (born 1928), too, becomes more 'Rivettian' as the years pass, combining the ludic and the spooky in his recent films *Va savoir* (2001) and the Emmanuelle Béart-led ghost story *L'Histoire de Marie et Julien* (2003). Having made two features and a short since the turn of the millennium, Eric Rohmer (born 1920) surprised many accustomed to his defiantly realist, low-budget style of filmmaking when, for his 2001 feature *L'Anglaise et le duc*, he opted to use CGI (computer-generated imagery) – with a twist, of course. Rather than employing such hi-tech means to render the eighteenth-century locations of the film's French Revolution setting, Rohmer re-created the period styles of paintings and artworks within whose digitally animated *tableaux* his characters circulate.

How useful is it still to consider these filmmakers in terms of their New Wave heritage? I suggest that it remains useful for three reasons that have to do with issues of production, technology and film culture. One of the enduring characteristics of these filmmakers is that they have remained steadfastly independent both in terms of their commitment to personal styles of 'auteur' filmmaking but also as regards their approach to how their films are made. Whether it has been through a long-term affiliation with a production company, such as Rohmer's with Les Films de Losange, or a more artisanal, 'cottage industry' mode of production such as Godard's company Periphéria based in his Swiss home town of Rolle, or Varda's Ciné-Tamaris based in her home on the rue Daguerre in the 14th arrondissement of Paris, they have remained defiantly independent. With such independence comes the liberty to experiment with new filmmaking technologies and new methods of exhibition and distribution. One of the most interesting aspects of recent work by Varda, Marker and Godard is its responsiveness to these aspects of what might be called 'twenty-first-century cinema'.

Since the multiple award-winning success of her digital video essay-cum-travelogue *Les Glaneurs et la glaneuse* (2000), Agnès Varda (born 1928) has produced a follow-up film ... *deux ans après* in which she caught up with some of the participants of the original film. Both films feature on the Ciné-Tamaris-produced DVD, along with a host of what Varda calls 'boni' (the plural of 'bonus'). Through her company, Varda has taken full advantage of the new medium of DVD, releasing restored versions of her own films, such as her New Wave classic *Cléo de 5 à 7* (1961), and those of her former husband Jacques Demy, such as *Les Parapluies de Cherbourg* (1964) and *Peau d'Ane* (1970). Among its lavish cornucopia of 'boni', the DVD of *Cléo* features rare and early works by Varda, including *L'Opéra Mouffe* (1958) and *Daguerréotypes* (1978). Varda has recently declared that she no longer intends to make feature films, opting instead to concentrate on making film installation works for galleries and museums. Coming from a more traditional fine-art background than the other New Wave directors, she has adapted with ease to this new form, making three installations since 2003 – *Patatutopia*, *Les Veuves de Noirmoutier* and *Le Triptyque de Noirmoutier* – and at the time of writing (April 2006), she has recently been commissioned to produce new work for the Fondation Cartier in Paris. Chris Marker (born 1921) perhaps best epitomises the spirit of multiple-media adventurousness characteristic of the most forward-looking New Wave directors and he, too, has been far from inactive in recent years, producing an essay film for French television (*Chats Perchés* (2004)), an installation work for the Museum of Modern Art in New York (*Owls at Noon: The Hollow Men* (2005)) which will form part of the much anticipated sequel to his 1999 CD-ROM *Immemory*, as well as releasing several DVD version of earlier works, including *La Jetée* (1962), *Sans soleil* (1982) and *Le Tombeau d'Alexandre* (1993). One of the most valuable aspects of the DVD format is that it can provide real research and reference value. For example, the recent Arte DVD releases of classic films by Marker's former colleague Alain Resnais (born 1922), *Hiroshima, mon amour* (1960) and *Muriel, ou le temps d'un retour* (1963), feature a host of rarely seen early works that would otherwise be inaccessible. The DVD of *Hiroshima* includes his magnificent collaborative essay films made with Marker, *Toute la mémoire du monde*

(1956) and *Les Statues meurent aussi* (1953), while the DVD of *Muriel* contains four early short films by Resnais on artists (*Gauguin* (1950), *Van Gogh* (1948), *Guernica* (1950–51) and *Le Chant de Styrène* (1958)).

Last, but by no means least, there is the continuing case of Jean-Luc Godard (born 1930). As well as having recently made several shorts, his last two feature films, *Eloge de l'amour* (2001) and *Notre musique* (2004), were more warmly received by international audience and critics than anything he has made for decades. And, to celebrate his fifty years of his filmmaking, the Centre Pompidou in Paris hosted a complete retrospective of his work between April and August 2006, as well as a new exhibition created by Godard, entitled *Voyages in Utopia*, and screening two new films, *Vrai faux passeport* (2006) and *Deux prières pour cinq refuzeniks* (2006). It is perhaps fitting that Godard's generation, which emerged from and was formed in Henri Langlois's cinema museum in years following the Second World War, now appears to have gone full circle (with cinema itself) *back* to the museum. Clearly, it is still too soon to give a definitive account of the significance of this generation's work for the simple reason that most of them are still working, but it is surely no exaggeration to say that they have been as revolutionary in terms of cinema in the twentieth and twenty-first centuries as the Impressionists were for painting in the nineteenth century.

CONCLUSION

Let us remind ourselves of some of the chief components of the 'legend' of the New Wave: a group of rebel filmmakers take on the established order of things and momentarily triumph. Apart from the insistently Oedipal tone of the war waged upon what they called 'Daddy's cinema' ('le cinéma de papa'), the example of the New Wave has been a constant inspiration to many independent filmmakers and, in France, has become institutionalised in a system of subsidy, support and education. The place of technology in the New Wave is crucial, and it would not be overly deterministic to argue that the equipment which the filmmakers used informed the filmmaking styles they achieved. But there were influences other than the role of lightweight cameras and sound equipment. There was the culture of intellectual enquiry into the nature of the cinematic medium that has been an enduring feature of French filmmaking since its earliest days. As I have outlined above, this tendency found its postwar expression in the cinéphilia of clubs, critics and filmmakers.

Writing in 1984, the influential French film critic Serge Daney offered an extremely interesting diagnosis of the legacy of the New Wave in which he argued that the 'worldwide public of cinéphiles' constituted – alongside the international audiences for American, Indian and Hong Kong cinemas – 'the last *universal* public'. Illustrating his contention with a series of provocative thoughts – on the actor Jean-Paul Belmondo, for example: 'Belmondo is an immense star here (in France) but on the global stage he's provincial' – Daney sums up with the following question: 'What does this mean, ultimately? That "national" cinema is almost finished?' (*Cahiers*, January 1999: 65). Almost twenty years later, it is possible to confirm that Daney didn't get it wrong and that what gets produced for this 'worldwide cinéphile public' is a kind of 'festival film' that might, with the right kind of cinéphilic promotion, still find wider circulation and hence a larger public. The ever-expanding network of film festivals that were crucial to forming the international image of the New Wave in the 1960s has, if anything, become even more important as the traditional distribution system of independent and art cinemas becomes increasingly overwhelmed by multiplex cinemas controlled by multinational media conglomerates. Examples of how 'national cinemas' may still, slowly and with much effort, emerge onto the world stage from festival circulation may be found during the 1990s in the examples of cinema from Hong Kong (the films of Wong Kar-Wai, for example), from Taiwan (e.g. Edward Yang's work) and from Iran (the prime example being Abbas Kiarostami's international success). In the era of globalisation, this begs the question whether it is any longer useful to talk of 'national' and 'international' cinemas rather than 'local' and 'global' cinemas. And if, as critics have argued, the New Wave emerged on the cusp of a 'crisis' in cinema marked by the decline of the Hollywood studio system, the advent of television and the decline in cinema attendance, then it opened up a minority 'breach' in this fragmentation of cinema audiences and contributed to precisely that 'worldwide cinéphile public' which still exists. Daney concludes by paraphrasing a statement made by Jean-Luc Godard: that he and his New Wave colleagues had succeeded in adding another country to the map of the world, and that country was called 'Cinema'.

FURTHER READING

Two useful surveys of the state of French cinema (in French):

Cahiers du cinéma Situation du cinéma français, May 1957, no.71.

Nouvelle vague: une légende en question, January 1999, hors séries.

Caughie, J., *Theories of Authorship*, Routledge and British Film Institute, London, 1981.

Cowie, P., *Revolution: The Explosion of World Cinema in the Sixties*, Faber, London, 2005.

Darke, C., 'Rupture, Continuity and Diversification: *Cahiers du cinéma* in the 1980s', *Screen*, Vol. 34, No. 4, winter 1993, pp. 362–80. An account of the major theoretical developments in *Cahiers* during the 1980s, much neglected by Anglo-Saxon critics.

—— *Alphaville* (Cine-Files French Film Guides), I.B. Tauris, London, 2005.

de Baecque, A. and Toubiana, S., *Truffaut: A Biography*, University of California Press, 2000.

de Baecque, A., *Les Cahiers du cinéma: Histoire d'une revue*, Tome 2: *Cinéma, tours détours 1959–1981*, Editions Cahiers du cinéma, Paris, 1991. An expansive French-language history of 'Cahiers' and a valuable history of postwar French film culture.

—— *La Nouvelle vague: Portrait d'une jeunesse*, Flammarion, Paris, 1998. A sociologically informed monograph on the background to the phenomenon of the New Wave.

Douchet, J., *French New Wave*, Distributed Art Publishers Inc.–Editions Hazan–Cinémathèque Française, Paris, 1999. A sumptuously illustrated and vividly written English-language history of the New Wave by a French critic who was active at the time.

Durgnat, R., *Nouvelle Vague: The First Decade*, Motion Publications, Loughton, 1963.

Esquenazi, J.-P., *Godard et la société, francaise des années 1960*, A. Colin, Paris, 2004.

'Film Comment': Dossier: 'Around the World with Chris Marker', May-June and June-July 2003

Frey, H., *Louis Malle*, University of Manchester Press, Manchester, 2004.

Graham, P. (ed.), *The New Wave: Critical Landmarks*, British Film Institute–Secker & Warburg, London, 1968. A valuable collection of texts by and about the New Wave.

Hayward, S., *French National Cinema*, Routledge, London, 1993. An extensive study of French cinema from the perspective of how a nation's self-image is informed by its cinematic representation.

Hayward, S. and Vincendeau, G. (eds), *French Film: Texts and Contexts*, Routledge, London, 1990. A crucial collection of essays on French cinema by major French and Anglo-Saxon critics; covers more than the New Wave period.

Hillier, J. (ed.), *Cahiers du cinéma 1: The 1950s, Neo-realism, Hollywood, The New Wave*, British Film Institute–Routledge & Kegan Paul, London, 1985. The first of four anthologies collecting translations of key *Cahiers* texts; this volume covers the New Wave period.

—— (ed.), *Cahiers du cinéma 2: 1960–1968*, British Film Institute–Routledge and Kegan Paul, London, 1986.

Lupton, C., *Chris Marker: Memories of the Future*, Reaktion Books, London, 2005.

MacCabe, C., *Godard: A Portrait of the Artist at Seventy*, Bloomsbury, London, 2003.

Marie, M., *La Nouvelle vague: Une école artistique*, Nathan, Paris, 1998. A highly detailed and scrupulously researched analysis of the context of the New Wave (in French).

—— *The French New Wave: An Artistic School*, trans. Richard Neupert, Blackwell, Oxford, 2002.

Morrey, D., *Jean-Luc Godard*, Manchester University Press, Manchester, 2005.

Neale, S., 'Art Cinema as Institution', *Screen*, Vol. 22, No. 1, 1981, pp. 11–41. A key essay on European art cinema as idea and institution.

Neupert, R., *A History of the French New Wave Cinema*, University of Wisconsin, Madison, 2002.

Nichols, B. (ed.), *Movies and Methods*, Vol. 1, University of California Press, Berkeley, 1976.

Smith, A., *Agnès Varda*, Manchester University Press, Manchester, 1998. The only English-language study of Varda's work; pays particular attention to Varda's interest in the 'female gaze' and fine art.

Vincendeau, G., 'France 1945–65 and Hollywood: The *Policier* as Inter-national Text', *Screen*, Vol. 33, No. 1, spring 1992, pp. 50–63. An intertextual analysis of Godard's *Alphaville* as a film that mediates French fascination/repulsion with America and its culture.

—— *Stars and Stardom in French Cinema*, Continuum, London, 2000. A study of the major stars of French film, examining personas and acting styles; includes material on Bardot, Karina, Belmondo and Delon.

Wilson, E., *Personal Histories: French Cinema since 1950*, Duckworth, London, 1999. A contemporary, post-New Wave reading of the theme of 'first-person filmmaking' in French cinema. An interesting critique of auteur cinema.

Wilson, E., *Alain Resnais*, University of Manchester Press, Manchester, 2006.

FURTHER VIEWING

1957	*Les Mistons* (*The Brats*, short, F. Truffaut)
1958	*Le Beau Serge* (C. Chabrol)
1959	*Charlotte et sons Jules* (short, J.-L. Godard)
	Les Cousins (*The Cousins*, C. Chabrol)
	Le Signe du lion (E. Rohmer)
1960	*Paris nous appartient* (*Paris Belongs to Us*, J. Rivette)
	Le Petit soldat (*The Little Soldier*, J.-L. Godard)
	Tirez sur le pianiste (*Shoot the Pianist*, F. Truffaut).
1961	*Une Femme est une femme* (*A Woman is a Woman*, J.-L. Godard)
	Jules et Jim (F. Truffaut)
1962	*Vivre sa vie* (*My Life to Live*, J.-L. Godard)
1963	*Le Mépris* (*Contempt*, J.-L. Godard)
1964	*Bande à part* (*Band of Outsiders*, J.-L. Godard, 1964)

	Paris vu par.. (J. Rouch, J.-L. Godard, E. Rohmer and others)
1965	*Alphaville* (J.-L. Godard)
	Pierrot le fou (*Crazy Pete*, J.-L. Godard)
1966	*Deux ou trois choses que je sais d'elle* (*Two or Three Things I Know About Her*, J.-L. Godard)
1967	*La Chinoise* (J.-L. Godard)
	Week-End (J.-L. Godard)
1968	*Ma nuit chez Maude* (*My Night at Maud's*, E. Rohmer)
1970	*Le Genou de Claire* (*Claire's Knee*, E. Rohmer)
1985	*Sans toit ni loi* (*Vagabond*, A. Varda)
1989–2000	*Histoire(s) du cinéma* (J.-L. Godard)
1996	*Irma Vep* (O. Assayas)
2000	*Les Glaneurs et la glaneuse* (*The Gleaners and I*, A. Varda)
2001	*Eloge de l'amour* (*In Praise of Love*, J.-L. Godard)

RESOURCE CENTRES

BiFi, Bibliothèque du film, 51 rue de Bercy, 75012 Paris (http://www.bifi.fr)
In the same building as the recently opened Cinémathèque Francaise, the BiFi is an excellent resource for French-language film-related materials; it includes a stock of DVDs and VHS tapes in its vidéothèque as well as a library of books and magazines and a resource for stills and posters.

http://www.ncl.ac.uk/crif/sfc/home.htm
Association for Studies in French Cinema publishes the journal *Studies in French Cinema* three times a year and organises an annual conference.

www.cahiersducinema.com
The monthly French film magazine *Cahiers du cinéma* has an excellent website with a selection of articles published in English and Spanish.

British Film Institute Library, 21 Stephen Street, London W1T 1LN
Institut Français, 17 Queensbury Place, London SW7 2DT
The Institut's library and médiathèque holds a large selection of French-language books, journals and periodicals as well as videos and CDs.

Glossary

30° A change in camera angle at the minimum of 30° is usual for each new shot at the same scene, thus ensuring the cut will edit smoothly. That is, there will not be a *jump cut*.

180° rule, the The 180° rule involves an imaginary line along the action of the scene, between actors involved in a conversation or the direction of a chase. The 'rule' dictates that this line should be clearly established and that the consecutive shots should not be taken from opposite sides of the line.

35mm film The measurement of film in millimetres (16mm, 35mm, 70mm) describes the length of the individual film negative frames which are exposed in order to capture an image; the larger the negative, the higher the resolution of the projected image. Larger format film such as 70mm, while superior in quality, is cumbersome to use and comparatively expensive to work with. There are also fewer cinemas able to screen formats other than the now standard 35mm print.

actualities The French term given to the short non-fictional films made in the early period (1895–1906 or so). These films often consisted simply of people going about their everyday business, or of particular events (sporting contests, visiting dignataries).

alternative Alternative cinema is defined with reference to **dominant**: it is an alternative (both economically and formally) to the dominant form. In any study concerning an 'alternative' cinema, the films would not only have to be examined in their own right, but also compared to contemporary dominant **Hollywood cinema**. A number of questions might have to be posed when analysing these alternative films: In what ways is this group of films different to the dominant cinema of the time? What are the possible reasons for the difference: cultural? economic? social? political? Could this 'alternative' way of making films, given the right conditions, have itself turned into the dominant cinema? The **Soviet cinema** of the 1920s, when compared to the Hollywood cinema of the same era, certainly may be regarded as alternative. In other words, alternative cinema offered a style of filmmaking that was radically different to the mass of films that was being produced in America.

animation The creation of artificial movement through a variety of techniques. Usually recorded one frame at a time, animation replicates naturalistic movement and creates the illusion of life in objects and images.

anthropomorphism The tendency in **animation** to endow creatures with human attributes, abilities and qualities. This can redefine or merely draw attention to characteristics which are taken for granted in live-action representations of human beings.

aperture The opening within a lens controlling the amount of light that passes through the lens to the film; the smaller the aperture, the less light will hit the film.

archetypes Embodiments of a range of ideas and identities.

art cinema   A term usually applied to films where the director has clearly exercised a high degree of control over the filmmaking process and thus the films may be viewed as a form of personal expression. This kind of filmmaking became common in Europe (hence the term 'European art cinema'), especially from the 1950s onwards, due to the funding structures and nature of the European film industries, which allowed directors greater artistic freedom than was to be found within the US system. In terms of style and content, art cinema is usually characterised by the way it differs from its commercial counterpart, **Hollywood cinema**: for instance, a drifting, episodic and open-ended narrative versus the tight cause-and-effect narrative of American cinema with its characteristic closure.

art-house   A crude shorthand way of referring to films in which artistic ambition and intellectual challenge are more important than the simple motive to provide entertainment. 'Great' art-house directors such as Bergman and Godard are unquestionably considered to be **auteurs**.

artisanal mode of production   A way of making films outside of an established 'industrial' means of production by using small budgets and minimal production teams. The term emphasises a more craft-like and personal process, hence allowing greater control of the filmmaking process.

associative mode   Approach to **documentary** which attempts to use footage in such a way as to provide the maximum degree of symbolic or metaphorical meaning on top of the literal information available in the image.

audience   Collectives of people responding to a film.

auteur   A French term that originated in the pages of the film journal *Cahiers du cinéma* in the 1950s to refer to directors who infuse their films with their distinctive personal vision through the salient manipulation of film technique. Auteurs, seen as genuine artists, were contrasted with metteurs-en-scène who were held to be technically competent directors who merely executed the processes of filmmaking without consistently stamping their 'personality' on the material from one film to the next. To study film as if it were the creative expression of a single individual, usually held to be the director, is often called **auteurism**.

auteurism   A critical approach to the study of film which identifies the director as responsible for whatever the viewer finds of thematic, stylistic or structural interest in a single film or across a body of work by one director.

avant-garde   Essentially non-narrative in structure and often intellectual in content, working in opposition to mainstream cinema. Literally the 'advanced guard' of experimental filmmakers who reject the dominant forms of mainstream cinema in favour of innovation and experiment in filmmaking, often producing non-narrative, non-illusionistic, sometimes abstract films. Avant-garde film is often self-conscious and frequently makes use of devices such as cuts to the camera crew, talking to the camera and scratching on film.

binary analysis   An approach which derives from cultural anthropology and particularly the work of Claude Lévi-Strauss. The study of binary opposites is a useful means of identifying structures at work in, for instance, the genre of a film.

biopic   A film which dramatises the biography of a real or imaginary person. It is usually characterised by a linear narrative. Examples of musical biopics range from *The Glenn Miller Story* (Anthony Mann, 1954) to *The Doors* (Oliver Stone, 1991).

blackface   Use of burnt cork or greasepaint to paint the face literally black. Originated in nineteenth-century minstrel theatre; used by both white and black performers.

blaxploitation   Movie studios' exploitation of what they believed were black urban audiences' tastes in film; beginning with Melvin Van Peebles's *Sweet Sweetback's Baadasssss Song*; concerned the years 1970 to 1974 in the USA; usually black-cast action films.

blue screen A process that involves the subject being filmed in front of a blue screen. Optical manipulation of this footage creates imagery of the actor against a black background. In addition, the actor's silhouette is set against a clear background. Using these two elements as **mattes** it is possible to place the action into any scene required.

Bollywood Bombay, the film capital of India.

bricolage The putting together of features from different genres and styles, self-consciously and usually playfully. This is one of the principal characteristics of **postmodernism**.

butch Description of behaviour patterns – such as aggression and sexual dominance – traditionally associated with masculinity.

camp A critical attitude which involves looking at texts less as reflections of reality and more as constructed sets of words, images and sounds at a distance from reality. The attitude often involves irony or detachment when considering this distance.

caméra–stylo A term coined by French writer Alexandre Astruc meaning 'camera–pen' and used to condense his argument for a 'personal' and self-expressive form of cinema.

canted framing A framing where the camera is not level, causing the mise-en-scène to appear slanted within the frame.

carnivalesque A term which refers to an atmosphere or attitude, found at carnivals and similar events, characterised by laughter, excess and vulgarity. Seen as a lower class resistance to the refined tastes of the dominant (upper and middle) classes.

CGI An acronym for 'computer-generated imagery', meaning the use of digital software to create, change or enhance aspects of mise-en-scène.

character/personality animation Many cartoons and more sophisticated adult animated films, for example, Japanese anime, are still dominated by 'character' or 'personality' animation, which prioritises exaggerated and sometimes caricatured expressions of human traits in order to direct attention to the detail of gesture and the range of human emotion and experience. This kind of animation is related to identifiable aspects of the real world and does not readily correspond with more abstract uses of the animated medium.

cinema apparatus The power of cinema as a system of communication, controlling and holding the spectator in place.

cinematograph Early term for cinema. Initially it referred to the camera/projector, but soon came to be used to refer to the practice and exhibition space.

cinema novo 'New cinema'. A movement of filmmakers that came to prominence in Brazil in the 1960s, the leading figure of which was Glauber Rocha. Influenced by the New Wave in France and the intellectual examples of Frantz Fanon and Che Guevara, 'cinema novo' called for filmmaking that emphasised 'the aesthetics of hunger' directed against a cinema of imperialism.

cinéma vérité A French term, literally meaning 'cinema truth'. Cinéma vérité emerged out of the filmmaking practices of Jean Rouch in France. Based on Vertov's approach, it acknowledged the impact of the filmmaking process upon the recording of 'actuality', and more readily recognised the subjectivity of the filmmaker in securing filmic evidence of what took place. Rouch essentially suggests that the documentary form must be defined through the integrity and purpose of its author. The value and purpose of 'actuality' footage in regard to its delineation of documentary 'truth' is therefore in direct relationship to the intention of those who produce it. The term is sometimes confused with a US kind of filmmaking which is actually closer to **direct cinema**. The confusion stems from the common 'immediacy 'that the films have – filming people with handheld cameras and portable sound-recording equipment – but cinéma vérité properly has a foundation of interaction between filmmaker and filmed, rather than the detachment seen in direct cinema films. Nevertheless, it is common to see a range of different films referred to as 'cinéma vérité (or sometimes just 'vérité'), and it is important to distinguish between them.

cinephilia   The notion of cinephilia refers to an intense love of, even obsession with, cinema. It implies both a way of watching and a way of speaking about film beyond the standard relationship between cinema and its spectator. Cinephiles are people who, in Andrew Sarris' phrase, 'love cinema beyond all reason', and who engage with film in highly specific ways.

classical Hollywood cinema   A particular narrative form which was exemplified by the films at the height of the studio system (1930–49). Although most Hollywood films still contain elements of classical narrative form, such as a central protagonist and a clear cause–effect relationship, film narratives, particularly since the success of movies such as *Pulp Fiction* (Tarantino, 1994), now play with plot and character with much greater flexibility.

close-up   Normally defined as a shot of the head from the neck up.

CNC   Centre Nationale de la Cinématographie, the chief body of the French state that oversees policy affecting filmmaking, including the subsidies accorded to cinema.

cognitivist processing   The process by which ideas that might be considered dangerous or anti-hegemonic are pulled in or incorporated into structures of order.

condensation   The compression of a set of narrative or aesthetic agendas within a minimal structural framework. Essentially, achieving the maximum amount of suggested information and implication from the minimum amount of imagery used.

consent decree   A court order made with the consent of both parties – the defendant and the plaintiff – which puts to rest the lawsuit brought against the former by the latter.

constructed   The fact of not being natural or inevitable; having been assembled or otherwise created to appear natural or inevitable.

conventions   Conventions are established procedures within a particular form which are identifiable by both the producer and the reader. The implication of the idea of conventions is that a form does not naturally mean anything, but it is an agreement between producer and user.

crane shot   A camera movement in which the camera moves above the ground in any direction (for which it is mounted on the arm of a special 'camera crane').

cross-cutting   Editing that alternates shots occurring in different story locations to imply that the events shown are occurring simultaneously.

cultural capital   First originating in the work of Pierre Bourdieu to describe the unequal distribution of cultural competencies and values principally across different social classes, the term has since been appropriated more generally to refer to the specific competencies and 'knowledges' of various social groupings, as well as the 'symbolic power' attained precisely from 'affiliation' to that group.

cultural studies   The cultural studies approach has gained academic respectability, partly due to the pioneering work of theorists such as Raymond Williams and Stuart Hall. Popular culture is now seen as a complex and worthy area of study, as being revealing about our society. Cultural studies has been influenced by Marxist theory, especially the theories of Antonio Gramsci, who used the term **hegemony** to describe the consensus that keeps the status quo in existence in society; capitalism keeps control by agreement of the people, yet there are still struggles for power which allow for change and adjustment in society. Cultural studies has, in more recent years, been a major influence on film studies, particularly in the study of popular film.

cut   The joining of two strips of film in the editing room, and the resulting immediate change from one image to another on-screen.

deconstruction   All media 'texts' are constructed. To understand all the components within each construction it is necessary to deconstruct the text and analyse all its elements. For example, the cartoon is made up of a number of specific aspects which define it as a unique cinematic practice, i.e. its frame-by-frame construction, its modes of representation and so on.

découpage   A term that means the 'shot breakdown' of a scene.

depth cues   These are provided by the arrangement of setting, lighting and props within the frame, which determines the degree to which the space depicted in the cinematic image appears to recede backwards and to take on three-dimensionality. Converging lines, size diminution, and the suggestion of different 'planes' in the fore-, middle- and background of the shot all accentuate the sense that there is a lot of space between the camera and the farthest visible object in the frame.

developmental animation   If *orthodox animation* emerges from Disney's 2D cel-animated tradition, developmental animation operates as the range of responses and oppositions to it. This might include the more overtly 'cartoonal' work by Warner Bros and MGM, or the range of approaches and styles from stop–motion animation, to clay animation, to cut-out animation and so on, which may still possess 'mimetic' references, but are nevertheless seeking to be more non-linear and non-objective in their approaches.

dialectical   A difficult term to define, as it has many different meanings. The *Collins English Dictionary* (2nd edn, 1986), for example, defines it as a 'disputation or debate, esp. intended to resolve differences between two views rather than to establish one of them as true'. The crucial factor to grasp in the context of Eisenstein's thinking, however, is the notion of change and the creation of a new order. Eisenstein would have defined dialectic with reference to **Marxist** philosophy, which believed that society was contradictory and in need of change.

diaspora   Meaning dispersal in the African American studies context, this term refers to populations of African descent around the world. Conceptually makes possible comparative studies of black people across national borders, while still accounting for significant cultural differences.

diegesis   The fictional world in which we presume the story takes place.

diegetic   The elements of a film that originate from directly within the film's **narrative**. For example, a popular song that is being played on the soundtrack would be diegetic if it were clear that it was coming from a source within the world of the film such as a car radio. See also **non-diegetic**.

dilution and amplication   The simultaneous capacity for **animation**, by virtue of its intrinsic artifice, to be viewed either as a language which dilutes its outcomes and effects, rendering them 'innocent' and 'dismissable', or as a language which inherently amplifies its literal, aesthetic and ideological perspectives, rendering them sometimes unacceptably challenging in their representational aspects.

direct cinema   American documentarists of the 1960s and 1970s believed that the advent of light, portable, technically sophisticated camera equipment enabled a breakthrough in the ways that documentary filmmaking could reveal personal and social 'truth'. The fact that the documentarist could literally film anywhere under any conditions meant that a greater intimacy could be achieved with the subject, heightening the sense that 'reality' was being directly observed, and that the viewer was party to the seemingly unmediated immediacy of the experience. Less controlled, unscripted, apparently spontaneous, the look and feel of 'direct cinema' arguably demonstrated a less deliberately authored approach.

discourse systems   A discourse is a mode of speech which has evolved to express the shared human activities of a community of people. Film studies has, like other academic disciplines, developed its own language – its own discourse system – to make possible the identification and 'mapping' of that area of human activity and experience with which it is concerned.

Disney dust   The term given to the glitter and sparkle that usually accompanies any form of magic or unearthly effect such as the glowing dust trail left by the flying Tinkerbell in Disney's *Peter Pan* (1953) and again in *Hook* (1991).

dissolve   Transition between shots with the first shot fading out to be simultaneously replaced by the second shot fading in. Often used to indicate an **ellipse**.

distribution   Division of the film industry concentrating on the marketing of film, connecting the producer with the exhibitor by leasing films from the former and renting them to the latter.

documentary   A non-fiction text using 'actuality' footage, which may include the live recording of events and relevant research material (i.e. interviews, statistics). This kind of text is usually informed by a particular point of view, and seeks to address a particular social issue which is related to and potentially affects the audience.

Dogme 95   The name given to a collective of Danish filmmakers united around the figures of directors Lars Von Trier, Thomas Winterberg and Kristian Levering. Dogme 95 was the name of a manifesto that committed filmmakers to observing a cinematic 'vow of chastity' involving an ultra-realist approach to filmmaking using only digital video cameras.

dominant   Refers to both economic strength and also to the dominant form or convention: dominant cinema in film studies is assumed to be **Hollywood**.

drama–documentary   Any format which attempts to re-create historical or typical events using performers, whether actors or not.

dystopia   A world of the future where everything has gone wrong.

eclecticism   An aesthetic style in which a new composition is composed wholly or in part from elements selected from a range of previous styles, forms, texts, genres, drawn from different periods and from both high and popular culture. This is one of the principal strategies of postmodern art. See also **intertextuality, palimpsest, recombinacy, self-reflexivity**.

economic presentation   All the components are designed to help us read the **narrative**. An examination of the first few minutes of almost any mainstream fictional film will reveal a considerable amount of information about characters, their social situation and their motivation.

editing   Sometimes also referred to as 'montage' (from the French 'monter', meaning 'to assemble'), this refers to the joining together of different pieces of film stock in post-production.

ellipse A gap in the continuity of time and space of the narrative – usually indicated in editing by means of a **dissolve** or **wipe**.

emblematic A typical representation, in this case symbolic of England.

essentialism A term describing the idea of a single, firmly fixed identity as regards **gender**, **sexuality** and other social elements. The opposite attitude is often described as social constructionism, implying that such identities are a product of one's society, attitudes and upbringing, and can vary or be changed.

establishing shot A shot using distant framing, allowing the viewer to see the spatial relations between characters and the set.

ethics Concerning morality, or codes of conduct. There is a strong ethical discourse running through the history of documentary, and debates to be had about the ethical dimension of things like reconstruction, filming people without their consent, informing the viewer of the extent of filmmaker intervention, and so on.

exclusive run Where a film is screened in only one movie theatre.

exhibition Division of the film industry concentrating on the public screening of film.

experimental animation Experimental animation is the avant-garde of the animation field, seeking to innovate with new styles and techniques, and often in purely abstract terms of expression. It should be stressed though that all forms of **animation** have 'experimental' aspects, and this both makes the form 'modern' and 'popular'.

exposition The use of voiceover or direct-to-camera address by a figure who is essentially directing the viewer in the reception of information and argument.

extreme close-up A framing in which the object shown takes up virtually the whole screen (as in a shot of a body part, such as a leg or an eye).

extreme long shot A framing in which the object shown (typically a human body shown from head to toe) fills a small fraction of the screen.

extra-textual In a broad sense, designates the 'outside' of the film/text, the range of cultural texts which relate in some way to the film/text; in a narrower sense refers to the non-filmic intertexts which in varying degrees relate to the film/text (such as marketing and promotional materials, film reviews, and so on).

eye-line match The 'eye-line' match is another convention of Hollywood editing that encourages identification with the protagonist(s), as the shots from their eye-line suggest a sense of **realism**.

fade An editing technique in which one of the juxtaposed images is a black screen. With a 'fade-out' the image slowly darkens; with a 'fade-in' the image slowly emerges out of darkness.

fade and mixes Where one image fades from view to be replaced by a separate image. When this is done with two images simultaneously the effect is known as a 'mix' or a **dissolve**.

faster speed film speed/speed of film stock Sensitivity of the photographic emulsion of the film to light; a higher speed of film will require less light (i.e. a smaller aperture may be used) in order to produce a properly exposed image; faster speed film stock tends to provide greater contrast in tone than a slower film stock.

feminism This is based on the belief that we live in a society where women are still unequal to men; that women have lower status than men and have less power, particularly economic power. Feminists argue that the media reinforces the status quo by representing a narrow range of images of women; for instance, woman as carer, as passive object, as an object of desire. Many feminists now argue that the range of representations for both male and female is limited and slow to change. In recent years feminism has become fragmented and it is difficult to argue that feminism is a complete area of study; but the relationship between **gender** and power relations in society may be seen as central to feminist thinking. For an interesting discussion on this area see Liesbet Van Zoonen (1994).

femme   Description of behaviour patterns – such as gentleness, sexual passivity, concern with dress and appearance – traditionally associated with femininity.

femme fatale   A term which originated in critical discourses on film noir; it refers to dangerous, seductive female characters who are normally literally 'fatal', in that they cause the death of the hero.

fetishism   Freudian theorists argue that fetishism is linked to the castration complex and is a form of male denial of the threat and fear of castration by the female. The female is made less threatening, more reassuring, by substituting her lack of a phallus with a fetish object such as high heels, long hair or turning her into a fetish object by exaggerating or fragmenting parts of the body such as lips or breasts.

film noir   A term developed by French film critics in the postwar period to describe a number of films produced in the 1940s. It has subsequently become a marketing device used to describe films with some of the lighting and **narrative** conventions of the period.

first-run   Important cinemas would show films immediately upon their theatrical release (or their 'first-run'). Smaller, local cinemas would show films on subsequent runs, hence the terms second-run, third-run and so on.

fly-on-the-wall   A term associated with a style of documentary filmmaking which attempts to present events as though the presence of the camera and film crew had not influenced them in any way.

focal length   This refers to the ability of a lens to bend the incoming light on to the film plane; a shorter focal length will provide a wider angle of view (which dictates what appears within the frame); a longer focal length will provide a narrower field of view but greater magnification of what is shown; for any given set of conditions a shorter focal length will provide a larger depth of field.

foley stage   Named after the sound editor Jack Foley, the foley stage is a sound-recording room equipped with a screen and the necessary items for the creation of sound effects.

formation   Each of us comes to a film with our own personal 'formation' – the result of all our life experiences. These will predispose us to certain interpretations of character, certain attitudes towards moral and political issues and certain emotional responses to events.

framing   The choices made about what to include within the frame and what to exclude.

free publicity   Free coverage of subjects that the media feel are newsworthy.

gay   A description of strong, positive sexual love and attraction between members of the same sex, used by extension to describe cultural products, such as film and video, concerned with similar themes. Mainly referring to males, it can also be used for any person.

gender   A name for the social and cultural construction of a person's sex and **sexuality**. Gender, sex and sexuality can overlap but are by no means an exact match. It is this 'mismatch' which has generated a fascinating body of film production and criticism.

hegemony   A set of ideas, attitudes or practices becomes so **dominant** that we forget they are rooted in choice and the exercise of power. They appear to be 'common sense' because they are so ingrained, and any alternative seems 'odd' or potentially threatening by comparison. Hegemony is the **ideological** made invisible. In relation to the development of cinema, it can be seen how **Hollywood** developed hegemonic status and power. The Hollywood form of genre-based **narrative** realist film is considered a 'common-sense' use of the medium. Other forms of cinema, by comparison, are more or less 'odd'. In looking at the early history of cinema we can begin to understand how and why Hollywood assumed this position.

heterosexual   A word used to name and describe a person whose main sexual feelings are for people of the opposite sex.

high-angle shot   A framing where the camera looks down from above on to the objects or scene filmed.

high-key lighting   This term refers to a lighting design (normally using a three-point system) where there is little contrast between the light and shadowed areas of the frame.

historiography   The study of how history is written – or constructed. This has become acutely important as we become more aware of how **narratives** are the result of processes of selection and construction. Film history, like other kinds of history, needs to be reflected upon, not just in relation to its content, but also in relation to the processes by which it has been written.

Hollywood cinema   In classical Hollywood cinema, the editing is designed to be 'invisible'. It is intended to allow the audience closer views and to see the point of view of different characters. The editing is used essentially to clarify what is taking place in the **narrative**. This type of editing had become **dominant** in Hollywood filmmaking by approximately 1920.

hommage   The French word for an act of paying homage, sincere respect.

homoerotic   A description of a text – prose, poem, film, painting, photograph – conveying an enjoyable sense of same-sex attraction.

homophobia   Irrational prejudice and hatred against a person because of their **homosexuality**.

homosexual   A word used to name and describe a person whose main sexual feelings are for people of the same sex. Mainly, but not exclusively, used in reference to males.

hypermediated culture   This describes the current state of post-media-saturated culture in which forms of work, leisure and entertainment, as well as many of the taken-for-granted activities that structure daily life, are predicted on, and determined by, the all-pervasive presence of highly integrated media forms and technologies. The notion of hypermediation, therefore, refers to the way that our experience of the world is channelled through an endless network of media texts.

iconic   The iconic is defined by the **dominant** signs that signify a particular person or object – Chaplin, for example, would be defined by a bowler hat, a moustache, a cane and some old boots; Hitler would be defined by a short, parted hairstyle and a small 'postage stamp' moustache.

iconoclasts   Filmmakers and documentarists committed to challenging the received construction and meanings of images, partially through the critique of those images, and mainly through the reconfiguration of imagery in a subjective style.

iconography   The visual codes of setting, props and clothing which enable us to recognise a film as belonging to a certain genre or type. It shares similarities with **mise-en-scène**.

identification   The process of identification allows us to place ourselves in the position of particular characters, either throughout or at specific moments in a movie. The devices involved include subjectivity of viewpoint (we see the world through their eyes, a shared knowledge, we know what and only what they know), and a sharing in their moral world, largely through **narrative** construction.

ideological effects   Effects of political significance, manipulating the spectator into an acceptance of specific ways of thinking about and relating to the world.

ideological function   Ideology is the system of ideas, values and beliefs held by individuals or groups within society. Ideological function refers to the way in which **ideology** is disseminated through films or other cultural forms. Audiences may of course refuse to accept the **dominant** ideological meaning in a film.

ideology   Although a complex issue, ideology may be seen as the dominant set of ideas and values which inform any one society or culture, but which are imbued in its social behaviour and representative texts at a level that is not necessarily obvious or conscious. There are two key definitions of this term, one provided by the nineteenth-century German philosopher Karl Marx, the other by the twentieth-century French Marxist philosopher Louis Althusser, drawing on Marx's original ideas. For Marx, ideology was the dominant set of beliefs and values existent within society, which sustained power relations. For Althusser, ideology consisted of the representations and images which reflect society's view of 'reality'. Ideology thus refers to 'the myths that a society lives by'. An ideological stance is normally politicised and historically determined.

illustrative mode   An approach to **documentary** which attempts to illustrate directly what the commentary/voiceover is saying.

impact editing   Editing that produces violent contrast between images, most often by switching between close- and long-shot scales.

impresario   Organiser of public entertainments; a manager of, especially, an operatic or concert company.

incoherent cinema   Influenced by the 'Incoherents', artists working between 1883 and 1891, a movement principally led by Cohl. This kind of **animation** was often surreal, anarchistic and playful, relating seemingly unrelated forms and events in an often irrational and spontaneous fashion. Lines tumble into shapes and figures in temporary scenarios before evolving into other images.

independent   This is a highly problematic term meaning different things in different situations. In the contemporary film industry it implies a production realised outside one of the Majors. It may be usefully divided into two areas. First, independent mainstream production, which aims to compete with the big studios but without any large financial backing, and thus finds it difficult to survive. Palace Films was one such casualty; the success of *The Crying Game* came too late to save its demise. Second, the term is used to describe filmmaking outside the mainstream sector, for instance, film workshops, **avant-garde** film, **feminist** film. The boundaries between these two areas are not always clear and may overlap.

inexportable   Critical term used to denote films of modest budget and ambition, only intended for distribution to their home markets. Adapted from Jean-Pierre Jeanncolas' use of the term with regard to certain French comedies.

Institutional Mode of Representation/IMR   The IMR is a broad categorisation of systems of **film form** and **narrative** characterising mainstream cinema from around 1915 onwards. It was perceived as replacing the Primitive Mode of Representation (a set of conventions used in early cinema between 1895 and 1905) as a gradual process in the first twenty years of cinema.

intentional fallacy A phrase coined by Monroe Beardsley to describe the difference between a text's meaning(s) and what its author intended. As such, criticism dependent on, or directed towards, uncovering the intentions of the author/artist falls foul of 'intentional fallacy' insofar as the meaning of a text is not fixed within it, but created in the historically situated act of reading.

intermedia The relations that exist between cinema, the film industry and other media at the levels of both capitalist business practices and textual forms.

internet A system of interlinking computers in a worldwide network (www/world-wide web). Since the internet was privatised in April 1995 the rise in monthly traffic on the net has been such that it represents a hundredfold increase in less than three years.

interpellation The process whereby the spectator of a film is drawn inside the psychic and physical life of the fictional world depicted by the film.

intertextuality This term, strongly linked with **postmodernism**, designates, in its narrow sense, the ways in which a film either explicitly or implicitly refers to other films (through allusion, imitation, parody or pastiche, for example), thereby triggering ideas and associations which might enrich our response, or in its broader sense, the various relationships one (film) text may have with other texts. See also **palimpsest**, **self-reflexivity**.

iris-in/iris-out Editing techniques in which the transition from one image to another is marked by the closing and reopening of an 'iris' or circular hole in the centre of the frame.

low-angle shot A framing where the camera looks up from below at the objects or scene filmed.

jump-cut An explicit and self-conscious editing decision to demonstrate a 'jump' in time, and to disrupt normal models of continuity editing.

juxtaposition In film studies, this usually refers to two different shots that have been joined together to make a contrast.

Kinematoscope Edison's first movie camera was relatively sophisticated and employed a series of sequential photographs mounted on a wheel and rotated.

lesbian A word used to name and describe a woman whose main sexual feelings are for other women. Coined as a medical term in the late nineteenth century, the word has been invested post-Stonewall with new ideas of openness and liberation. It may also be used to describe cultural products, such as film and video, dealing with lesbian themes.

liberal humanist A political perspective in which emphasis is placed upon an openness of democratic discourse and a multiplicity of perspectives which directly relate to the actual experiences of people and the fundamental principles relating to what it is to be 'human'.

'look', the Also, **gaze.** The 'look' and the 'gaze' developed as central concepts in relation to the control of the spectator. Cinematic looking has also been associated with theories of desire and pleasure, theories often founded in psychoanalysis.

long shot A framing in which the object shown (typically a human body shown from head to toe) fills around three-quarters of the height of the screen.

low-key image Light from a single source producing light and shade.

low-key lighting This term refers to a lighting design where there is a stark contrast between the light and shadowed areas of the frame. Frequently it is produced using only one light source.

magic lantern   A projection system comprising a light source and a lens used to project an image. Usually oil-lamp-fired, though many were later converted to electricity. Earliest known use was by Athanasius Kircher, recorded in a work published in 1646.

mainstream   Feature-length narrative films created for entertainment and profit. Mainstream is usually associated with **Hollywood cinema**, regardless of where the film is made.

Marxist theory   Argues that those who have the means of production have control in a capitalist society. The dominant class have control of the means of production and have an interest in perpetuating the dominant ideology. More recently, exponents of Althusserian Marxism, particularly post-1968, have argued that **mainstream narrative cinema** reinforces the capitalist system and that a revolutionary cinema is needed to challenge the dominant ideology.

masala movie   Spicy Indian movie overloaded with emotion.

match on action   A cut which joins two spaces together by virtue of the fact that an action shown in the first shot is then completed in the second.

match-move   Shots that have separate elements within them that need to be accurately matched, frame by frame. Usually involves live-action elements being coupled to **animation** or effects elements.

mattes   Opaque images that mask-out certain areas of the film negative. Subsequent passes through the camera allow the initial matted-out space to be exposed with another image.

matte shot   A type of shot in which aspects of mise-en-scène are photographed separately and then combined into one image in post-production. Opaque images mask out certain areas of the film negative, and subsequent passes through the camera allow the initially matted-out space to be exposed with another image. Nowadays, matting is often achieved using 'blue screen', a process where action is filmed in front of a blue screen; this footage is then used to create an image of the performers in front of a dark background, and a silhouette of the performer against a clear background, which is used to 'cut out' space for the performer in the scene on to which the action is to be matted.

mediation   A key concept in film and media theory, it implies that there are always structures, whether human or technological, between an object and the viewer, involving inevitably a partial and selective view.

medium long shot   Also known as the 'plan Américain' because of its frequency in classical Hollywood, this is a framing in which the human body is shown from mid-calf or knees upwards.

medium shot   A framing in which the human body is shown from the waist upwards.

merchandising   Where manufacturers pay a film company to use a film title or image on their products.

metamorphosis   The ability of a figure, object, shape or form to relinquish its seemingly fixed properties and mutate into an alternative model. This transformation is literally enacted within the animated film, and acts as a model by which the process of change becomes part of the narrative of the film. A form starts as one thing and ends up as something different.

metanarrative   Refers to an overarching account of some area of human experience – that attempts to make complete sense of that area. Meta-theory is, similarly, an overarching, all-embracing system for explaining some area of human experience. In film studies there has been a move away from metanarratives in historical studies and away from meta-theory in theoretical studies.

mise-en-scène Refers to both what is filmed (setting, props, costumes, etc.) and to how it is filmed (cinematographic properties of the shot, such as depth of field, focus, lighting, and camera movement). In an attempt to counter the imprecision of the term, this latter aspect is sometimes called mise-en-shot. Mise-en-scène is one way of producing meaning in films which can be both straightforward and extremely complex, depending upon the intentions and skill of the director (the metteur-en-scène: see **auteur**).

Modernism This refers to a dramatically experimental trend within the arts (painting, sculpture, architecture, literature, music and film) which grew up at the start of the twentieth century, encompassing a wide array of movements (Expressionism, Vorticism, Symbolism, Imagism, Surrealism) along with the innovations of individual artists not directly affiliated with a particular movement. Modernism involved a rejection of nineteenth-century styles, traditions and ideas, and a self-conscious (or 'self-reflexive') approach to aesthetic forms, in which artistic expression was itself explored, questioned and reinvented.

modernist A term used to describe early twentieth-century developments in art, literature, music, film and theatre which rejected **realism** as the dominant tradition in the arts. Modernist art is characterised by experiment and innovation, and modernist artists, because of their **avant-garde** practices, inevitably constitute a cultural élite.

modernist device Any device which undercuts the invisible telling of the story. A modernist device draws attention to itself and makes us aware of the construction of the narrative. It would be unclear in this instance whether the device is a consciously modernist one or a primitive one which unconsciously draws attention to itself.

montage From the French word meaning 'to edit', montage means the assembling of pieces of footage to form a whole. In film studies it usually refers to the style of fast editing adopted by the **Soviet** filmmakers of the 1920s.

movement image A term coined by Gilles Deleuze to refer to a cinema in which the image is at the service of the **narrative**, and in which the **audience** experience is of the 'movement' of the film towards the closure of narrative resolution.

'movie brat' generation A term that refers to the generation of American filmmakers who, after the decline of the Hollywood studio system in the 1950s, began to make films independently and were heavily influenced by the French New Wave and European **art cinema** of the 1960s. Such directors include Martin Scorsese and Francis Ford Coppola.

multiple exposures A number of exposures being made on a single frame of film. This usually entails the film being rewound in the camera for subsequent passes and further exposures. Multiple exposures are normally made with the assistance of **mattes**.

multiple run Where a film is shown simultaneously at a number of screens.

music hall Place for singing and dancing, variety and other entertainments.

myth A key term within media and cultural studies, a myth is something which is not true but which is repeated so frequently that it becomes part of the 'reality' of the people who share it. In some instances it can become part of a culture's 'common sense'. Myth is a means by which the **ideology** of a culture takes form.

narrative The idea that films have a primary function of telling a story.

narrative economy The efficiency with which a film tells its story. **Classical Hollywood** films have often been described as having a high degree of narrative economy, with few scenes or shots which do not contribute in some way to the telling of the story. Some genres, such as musicals or epics, where spectacle is an important element of the film's pleasures, may be said to have a lesser degree of narrative economy.

national cinema   A term commonly used to describe the filmic output of a particular country and to distinguish it from **Hollywood** filmmaking. It has also developed as an approach within film studies to explore how films are shaped by nationally prevailing socio-political and economic conditions. This approach to the study of cinema leads to an understanding of film as expressing or articulating a sense of national identity. However, defining a national cinema and adopting this approach can be problematic. For instance, rapidly changing national geographies, the increasing trend for pan-European funding for film projects and European co-productions make it increasingly difficult to clearly delineate a single country of origin.

negotiated reading   A negotiated reading of a media text is one that involves a certain give-and-take between our own views and experiences and those presented in the film text by its creator.

newsreels   Films consisting of six or seven short topical news stories released to cinemas twice a week and shown as part of the full supporting programme. Newsreels were produced from the 1910s to the early 1970s by which time they had largely been overtaken by television news. They were also shown in specialist news cinemas, often located in or near big railway stations.

noise   In the film industry, 'noise' refers to any barrier to successful communication.

non-diegetic   Refers to any element that remains outside the world of the film, such as voiceovers, credits and mood-setting music, that does not originate from the world of the film.

NRA (National Recovery Administration) programme   Government programme of the 1930s designed to rescue the US economy from the Great Depression (commonly known as the 'New Deal').

obscene   A work, or part thereof, may be found 'obscene' if it has a tendency to deprave and corrupt (i.e. make morally bad) a significant proportion of those people likely to see it.

oligopoly   A state of limited competition between a small group of producers or sellers.

oppositional reading   A reading of a media text which rejects the intentions of the creator of the text. It is most often associated with dis- or unpleasure. See also **preferred reading** and **negotiated reading**.

orthodox animation   Orthodox animation emerges from Disney's cel-animated tradition of work, augmented in the contemporary era by 2D and 3D computer-generated applica-tions. This kind of **animation** has a correspondence to a mimetic model of work – the use of configuration, classical narrative models, consistent aesthetic conditions – and echoes live-action practices, and 'real-world' conventions, while embracing the more 'fantastic' possibilities of the open language of animation.

overheard exchange   The recording of seemingly spontaneous dialogue between two or more participants engaged in conversation/observation.

overlapping editing   Editing where shots repeat part or all of the action shown in the previous shot.

paid advertising   Promotion on TV, radio, billboards, printed media and the **internet**.

palimpsest   Defined literally, a palimpsest is a manuscript written over a previous text that has been entirely or partially erased. In a figurative sense, however, the term is often used to describe a film or text with multiple levels of meaning created through dense layers of **intertextuality**. In this way, the term has become associated with **postmodern** aesthetics.

pan/whip-pan A 'pan' is a camera movement in which the camera itself remains in the same place but swivels round horizontally; a 'whip-pan' is a very fast pan.

participant observation A social science methodology where the researchers immerse themselves in the social context/group they are going to be studying, often for years at a time. In documentary terms, such an approach arguably leads to more 'natural' responses, as the subjects have become used to the filmmakers and cameras.

pastiche From the Italian verb 'to paste', this refers to a patchwork of references from, or imitations of, other works of art.

patent pool An association of companies, operating collectively in the marketplace by pooling the patents held by each individual company.

patriarchal society A society in which men have power and control. Women are generally disadvantaged and have lower status. It could be argued that we no longer live in a patriarchal society, but in a society in which men and women have equal opportunities. For instance, in the US, Sherry Lansing is head of Paramount Pictures and in the UK a number of women now have key roles in the media, particularly the BBC, where there are now women heads of channel programming. But many **feminists** would still argue that we have a long way to go in terms of politics, philosophy and economics before we live in a society in which men and women can be considered equal.

performative A person or object's capacity to produce an effect beyond the literal or stated intent or meaning.

performativity A concept derived from **cultural studies** whereby social groups develop self-awareness through shared actions that develop tastes, habits and attitudes in common. When applied to **gender**, you may wish to consider the popular conflation of masculinity and football, or femininity and shopping.

persistence of vision The phenomenon of persistence of vision is due to the momentary retention of an image on the eye's retina. This retention was found to be approximately one-tenth of a second by Chevalier d'Arcy in 1765 when he successfully carried out one of the first systematic scientific studies and presented his findings to the French Académie des Sciences.

Phenakistoscope Invented by the Belgian physicist Joseph Plateau in 1832, this is an optical device consisting of a disk with slots cut into its edge. When rotated, images on one side can be viewed with the aid of a mirror. The resulting stroboscopic images give the illusion of movement.

pink triangle A symbol originally worn by **homosexual** prisoners in Nazi concentration camps which was later taken up by **lesbian** and **gay** people as a reminder of past oppression and an icon of liberation.

pitch The height or depth of a musical sound as it is determined by its frequency relative to other notes.

pixillation The frame-by-frame recording of deliberately staged live-action movement to create the illusion of movement impossible to achieve by naturalistic means, i.e. figures spinning in mid-air or skating across grass. This can also be achieved by particular ways of editing material.

play-back Pre-recording of songs using good singers but with non-singing actors lip-synchronising on screen.

pluralistic multiple Refers in this instance to the fragmentation of society into different ethnic, social and cultural groups.

poetics of presence This may be used to describe moments of stillness in a film, such as a close-up of a face or a landscape shot. A complex range of ideas and emotions are contained within images that are not driven, as they are so often, by movement and action. We may become more aware of time, the relationship between past time and present time, and so more aware of the historical moment of the image. Whole films may be developed on the basis of creating this complex sense of 'presence'. (Compare Deleuze's opposition between the movement image and the time image.)

politique des auteurs   A term evolved from the *Cahiers du cinéma* approach to the study of French and **Hollywood cinema** in the 1950s, which attempted to identify directors who brought something personal to their films. It is used to describe particular bodies of filmmaking which are deemed to be characterised by the distinctive styles and visions of their directors. *See also* **auteurism**.

polysemic   Having many meanings; a polysemic text is likely to be less stable, more hotly contested by different sections of an audience.

postfeminism   The notion of postfeminism is a contested term used by different people in different ways to mean different things. It is used here to indicate a version of the popularised, and to some extent individualised, **feminism** that is different from (mainly in the sense that it comes after) the highly politicised feminism of the 1970s.

postmodern   Used by critics in a number of different ways, it can refer to the contemporary historical moment (the period after modernity); an artistic or aesthetic style which privileges surface appearances over 'deep meaning' or 'truth'. It is characterised by strategies of irony, **intertextuality**, pastiche, **bricolage**, eclecticism, **self-reflexivity**, and a theoretical position which adopts a sceptical attitude towards totalising notions of truth, reality, and progress. Postmodernism argues that theories such as psychoanalysis and **Marxism** are no longer viable because they attempt to give an all-encompassing view or understanding of society and culture. Postmodernism emphasises the fragmentation of viewpoints within our culture and the notion that there is no one philosophical truth.

post-structuralism   The critical movement away from an emphasis on the film text and the 'machinery' of cinema to an emphasis on the spectator's decoding of the text in order to create meaning. This represents a rejection of some aspects of the deterministic **Marxist**/Freudian theories at the heart of structuralism while still recognising that the spectator is himself or herself 'determined' by a range of factors (compare with **structuralism**).

post-synchronised   Referring to the process of adding and modifying some or all of a film's sound in a studio after the film has been shot and synchronising these sounds to the image track (also known as 'post-synching').

Praxinoscope   Invented by the Frenchman Emile Raynaud in 1878, this device was a more advanced and sophisticated version of the **Zoetrope**. Utilising mirrors and its own discrete light source, this was the forerunner of Raynaud's spectacular and charming, though ultimately short-lived, Theatre Optique.

preferred reading   A preferred reading of a media text is one in which the spectator takes the intended meaning, finding it relatively easy to align with the messages and attitudes of those who have created the text. See also **oppositional reading** and **negotiated reading**.

proactive observationalism   Documentary filmmaking in which specific choices are made about what material is to be recorded in relation to the previous observation of the camera operator/director.

 production   Division of the film industry concentrating on the making of film.

propaganda   The systematic construction of a text in which the **ideological** principles of a political stance are promoted, endorsed and made attractive to the viewer in order to influence the viewer's beliefs and preferences. Such a text may often include critical and exploitative ideas and imagery about oppositional stances. 'Point of view' in these texts is wholly informed by political bias and a specificity of intention to persuade the viewer of the intrinsic 'rightness' of the authorial position.

proto-animation Early live-action cinema demonstrated certain techniques which preceded their conscious use as a method in creating **animation**. This is largely with regard to stop-motion, mixed media and the use of **dissolves** to create the illusion of metamorphosis in early **trick films**.

psychoanalytic theory Based on the theories of Freud and, more recently, Lacan. Feminists argue that aspects of psychoanalysis are questionable because they are based on patriarchal assumptions that woman is inferior to man. Freud found female **sexuality** difficult and disturbing. Lacan argues that the mother is seen as lacking by the child because she has no phallus. Uncertainty about the role of the female in psychoanalytic theory has been picked up on by a number of feminists such as Mulvey, De Lauretis and Modleski, who question the inevitability of Freud and Lacan's theories which emphasise the importance of the phallus, penis envy and patriarchal supremacy.

queer Originally a negative term for (mainly male) **homosexuals**, this word has recently been reappropriated by critics, artists and audiences to describe a challenging range of critical work and cultural production among **lesbians** and **gays**, with an emphasis on diversity of race, nationality and cultural experience. The term is deliberately used to embrace a wider range of sexualities: lesbian, gay, bisexual and transgendered people and issues.

racist iconography Images that accompany racist rhetoric or racist contexts.

reactive observationalism Documentary filmmaking in which the material recorded is filmed as spontaneously as possible subject to the immediacy of observation by the camera operator/director.

reading a film Although films are viewed and heard, the concept of 'reading' a film implies an active process of making sense of what we are experiencing.

realism/reality The concept of the 'real' is problematic in cinema, and is generally used in two different ways. First, the extent to which a film attempts to mimic reality so that a fictional film can appear indistinguishable from documentary. Second, the film can establish its own world and can, by consistently using the same conventions, establish the credibility of this world. In this later sense a sciencefiction film such as *RoboCop* can be as realistic as a film set in a contemporary and recognisable world, such as *Sleepless in Seattle*.

With regard to **animation**, the animated form in itself most readily accommodates 'the fantastic', but Disney preferred to create a hyperrealism which located his characters in plausibly 'real' worlds which also included fantasy elements in the **narrative**.

reality TV A relatively recent development in television, and a form of highly structured programme using observational material of ordinary people. The programmes have a 'documentary' basis in the sense that they use acuality footage, but they are often shaped to fit specific formats (neighbours from hell, the rise of a successful business, a game show involving weekly tasks). In this respect, reality TV is a good example of how documentary can be taken and recontextualised by contemporary television to suit its schedules.

reappropriation The process whereby a previously oppressed group takes a negative term and turns it around to invest it with new meanings of power and liberation. Examples include 'black', 'virago' and '**queer**'.

recombinacy The aesthetic process of combining of elements drawn from a range of genres, styles, forms and periods in a new text/film. This is one of the principal aesthetic strategies of **postmodern** art. See also **intertextuality, palimpsest, self-reflexivity**.

reduced animation   Animation may be literally the movement of one line which, in operating through time and space, may take on characteristics which an audience may perceive as expressive and symbolic. This form of minimalism constitutes reduced animation, which takes as its premise 'less is more'. Literally an eye movement or the shift of a body posture becomes enough to connote a particular feeling or meaning. This enables the films to work in a mode which has an intensity of suggestion.

reflexive/performative documentary   Documentary which is much more subjective and **self-reflexive** in its construction, foregrounding the arbitrariness and relativity of 'objectivity', '**reality**' and 'truth'.

representation   The media *re*-presents information to its audience, who are encouraged by the mainstream media to see its output as a 'window on the world', as reflecting reality. Yet the process of representing information is highly complex and highly selective. Many **feminists** argue that the way notions of **gender** are represented by the media perpetuates and reinforces the values of a **patriarchal society**; for instance, men tend to take on strong, active roles, while women are shown as passive and relying on their attractiveness. There are exceptions to such narrow stereotyping: the 'strong' woman shown by Ripley in the *Alien* series and the two heroines in *Thelma and Louise* could be seen as positive, although rather more cynically they could be seen merely as 'role-reversal' films and thus as having purely novelty value. Representations often make use of **stereotypes** because they are a shorthand, quick and easy way of using information. It could be argued that the media production process encourages the use of stereotypes due to the pressure of time and budget. Many feminists point out that because so few women hold key positions in the media hierarchies, representations of women are bound to be from a male perspective.

rhetorical   Designed to persuade. Rhetorical strategies in **documentary** are those that relate to the film or programme's argument. This could be explicit (e.g. a voiceover or presenter actually stating what the argued points are), or it could be less immediately obvious (e.g. a filmmaker might cut from an image of a political leader to a library shot of a firing squad; this could be seen as an argument against the politician.

ripple-dissolve   A dissolve is an editing technique using superimposition, which produces a gradual transition between one image and the next, during which the two shots for a time occupy the frame simultaneously, appearing merged together; a ripple-dissolve emphasises this transition through the introduction of ripples, or waves, within the image.

Russian cinema   The body of films made in Tsarist Russia between 1907 and 1919.

Russian formalism   A literary theory which developed in Russia in the early 1920s, which sought to establish a scientific basis for the study of literature and literary effects.

saturation run   Where a film is shown simultaneously at an enormous number of screens (usually a minimum of 1,000 in the US–Canadian market), accompanied by heavy media promotion.

schema   A concept used in studies of the human thinking process. When we are confronted by a new experience, we look for familiar patterns that allow us to orient ourselves and make sense of what is in front of us.

scopophilia   Freudian term meaning the 'pleasure in looking', introduced to film analysis by Laura Mulvey, who pointed out that women are usually depicted in a passive role and are looked at, while men take on an active role, they look.

self-reflexivity   Used to describe films or texts which selfconsciously acknowledge or reflect upon their own status as fictional artefacts and/or the processes involved in their creation. This is one of the principal aesthetic strategies of **postmodern** art. See also **intertextuality, palimpsest, recombinacy.**

semiotics   The use of semiotics in film analysis has developed out of the theories of Ferdinand de Saussure, who argued that the meanings of words are not natural but are learned and socially constructed. Therefore, the meaning of a word, or in the case of film an image or sound, may be complex and layered.

sensory motor mechanism   Refers to the mental processing of audio-visual information in ways that allow us to 'place' and 'manage' the film experience. There is an implication that the automatic nature of this processing is part of the relatively passive pleasure of **mainstream** commercial cinema. Other kinds of cinema may disrupt the sensory motor mechanism.

sex   A word used to denote and describe a person's physical type according to his or her genital make-up. In academic discourse, this is primarily a scientific term.

sexuality   A name for the sexual feelings and behaviour of a person. When applied to groups of people (e.g. **heterosexuals**), ideas of social attitude and organisation are implied.

shot–reverse shot   Editing technique whereby conversations are filmed by cutting alternately between the faces of the interlocutors who are facing each other.

shot/take   One uninterrupted (uncut) image onscreen whether it is shot with a mobile or a stationary camera. During shooting, a 'take' refers to a single, uninterrupted recording of the camera before the director calls 'cut'.

shot scale   This refers to the range of shots which suggest the apparent distance of an object from the camera; it is conventionally defined according to the framing of the human form.

social realism   A form of **realism** which tries to capture in a 'truthful' way the lives of industrial working-class communities. Also known as 'working-class realism' and often used in relation to the 'new wave' films of late 1950s–early 1960s British cinema.

sophisticated hyperconsciousness   A term used by Jim Collins to describe the extreme 'knowingness' and high degree of media literacy evinced by both contemporary cinema and its audience.

sound-bridge   An audio connection between scenes, where sound from one scene continues into the beginning of the scene which follows, or where sound belonging to the opening of a scene begins during the close of the scene which precedes it.

Soviet cinema   Films made in the Soviet Union between October 1920 and 1991.

spectator   The individual responding to a film, as distinct from the collective response of an **audience**. Spectator study concentrates on the consumption of films that are 'popular' and are geared towards providing typical forms of cinematic pleasure – spectacle, emotion, plot, resolution – with conventional narrative and generic forms.

squash and stretch   Many cartoon characters are constructed in a way that resembles a set of malleable and attached circles which may be elongated or compressed to achieve an effect of dynamic movement. When animators 'squash and stretch' these circles they effectively create the physical space of the character and a particular design structure within the overall pattern of the film. Interestingly, early Disney shorts had characters based on 'ropes' rather than circles and this significantly changes the look of the films.

star system   The industrial apparatus which enables the building up of stars and their centrality to the advertising and promotion of films. This includes star contracts, ancillary advertising deals, fan magazines and so forth.

steadicam A technical development from the late 1970s that permits the use of a camera held by hand which walks with the action, but with the steadiness of a camera moving on rails.

stereotype Limiting perceptions about a group of people to just one aspect of them which is exaggerated.

stereotyping A quick and easy way of labelling or categorising the world around us and making it understandable. Stereotypes are learned but are by no means fixed, yet are often resistant to change. They tend to restrict our understanding of the world and perpetuate beliefs that are often untrue or narrow. For instance, the concept that only thin women are attractive is a stereotype promoted by much of the media in the late twentieth century (though there are some exceptions, for example, comediennes Dawn French and Roseanne); in other eras the opposite has been true. Stereotyping is not always negative, but tends to be very much concerned with preserving and perpetuating power relations in society. It is in the interests of those in power to continue to stereotype those with lower status in a negative light, thus preserving the status quo.

stop motion An animation technique whereby a 3D model is filmed a single frame at a time, the model being moved by the animator between exposures.

straight-on shot A framing where the camera is at the same level as the objects or scene filmed.

structuralism Founded on the belief that the study of society could be scientifically based and that there are structures in society that follow certain patterns or rules. Initially, most interest was centred on the use of language; Saussure, the founder of linguistics, argued that language was essential in communicating the **ideology**, the beliefs, of a culture.

Structuralists have applied these theories to film, which uses both visual and verbal communication, and pointed out that the text conveys an illusion of reality, so conveying the ideology of a society even more effectively.

studio system Usually seen to have developed from about 1920 and lasting until about 1950, the studio system indicated that period of Hollywood history in which the major studios controlled all aspects of the production, distribution and exhibition of their products.

substitution technique An early **trick film** technique used by George Méliès. It involved one object being filmed, the camera being stopped during filming and the object being replaced by a second object before filming recommenced. This was the basis of his famous vanishing-lady effect, used in many of his films.

superimposition The process by which more than one image is exposed on the same frames of the film stock.

surplus of meaning Meaning in excess of what is required to fulfil the functional requirements of the **narrative**; a 'surplus' will include ambiguity, complexity rather than clarity and simplicity.

suspending disbelief This refers to the ability a person has when engaging with a constructed object – film, play, novel – to repress his or her knowledge that the object is in fact just a 'construct', and respond to it as though it is real.

symbolism The means by which a filmmaker can assign additional meanings to objects/characters in a film. For example, in Dovzhenko's *Earth* and Eisenstein's *Old and New*, the tractor is a symbol of progress.

symmetry   Direct balance of imagery in the composition of the frame using parallel or mirrored forms.

synecdoche   The idea that a 'part' of a person, an object, a machine, may be used to represent the 'whole', and work as an emotive or suggestive shorthand for the viewer, who invests the 'part' with **symbolic** associations.

synergy strategy   Combined or related action by a group of individuals or corporations towards a common goal, the combined effect of which exceeds the sum of the individual efforts.

synthespians   A term which describes 'virtual' or non-human actors. The term relates to digitally scanned or motion-captured versions of 'real' actors, as well as entirely computer-generated characters.

taxonomy   The practice of classification. In this sense, the practice of classifying films into groups based on similarities of form and/or content.

testimony   The recording of solicited observation, opinion or information by witnesses, experts or other relevant participants in relation to the **documentary** subject; the primary purpose of the interview.

THX   A designation of sound reproduction quality in cinemas. The standards established necessitate the installation and maintenance of sound equipment to the specifications and according to the guidelines laid down by Lucasfilm Ltd.

tie-ins   Mutually beneficial promotional liaisons between films and other consumer products and/or personalities.

tilt   A camera movement in which the camera remains in one place but swivels up or down.

timbre   The tonal quality of a musical sound; timbre is what makes a saxophone sound different from a clarinet, for example.

time image   A development from the movement image. It suggests a cinema in which the narrative priorities of **mainstream** commercial cinema are replaced by ones which are more reflective. In particular, our understanding and experience of time becomes central.

topicals   The name given to non-fictional 'news' items in the early period of **documentary**. A royal visit, the opening of a factory, a sports event – anything that could be of interest to a local audience – could be labelled a 'topical'. As documentary developed as a form, topicals were subsumed into **newsreels** and other forms of film reporting.

track/tracking shot/dolly shot   A camera movement in which the camera moves horizontally by travelling along the ground (originally on 'tracks' on which a wheeled support – or 'dolly' – for the camera could be mounted).

Tradition of Quality   A frequently derogatory term used by the critics on *Cahiers du cinéma* and referring to postwar, pre-New Wave French cinema characterised by its reliance on screenwriters and adaptations from literary classics.

trick film   The generic term for the development of cinematic special effects using such techniques as **mattes**, **multiple exposures**, **proto-animation** and **substitution techniques**. Generally attributed to the pioneering French filmmaker George Méliès.

trust   A group of companies operating together to control the market for a commodity. This is illegal practice in the US.

two-shot   A medium-scale shot including two characters normally taken from the waist up. A variant is the cut between the two characters assuming the same eyelevel, body position and exchange.

uses and gratifications   A specific approach to the study of **audiences**. It considers how individuals and groups may consume a film or some other media product to satisfy their particular needs.

vertical integration   Where a company is organised so that it oversees a product from the planning/development stage, through production, through market distribution, through to the end-user – the retail consumer. In the case of the film industry, this translates to a company controlling production, distribution and exhibition of its films.

voyeurism   The sexual pleasure gained from looking at others.

wipe   Transition between shots where a vertical line sweeps across the screen taking us from one scene to the next.

wire frame   Three-dimensional shapes, with neither surface colour nor texture, illustrated through a pattern of interconnecting lines, literally a framework of 'wires' on a two-dimensional surface – the computer screen.

wire removal   The process of digitally removing any unwanted elements within a shot, such as a support for an animated object, puppet or prop. Used in the flying motorbike shot in *Terminator 2*.

Zoetrope   The forerunner of the **Praxinoscope**, this consists of a drum with vertical slots cut into the top edge. As the drum is rotated, the images on the inner surfaces, when viewed through the slots, achieve the same illusion of movement as with the **Phenakistoscope**.

zoom   A technique whereby the image appears to advance towards or recedes away from the viewer.

Bibliography

Aaron, M. (ed.), *New Queer Cinema: A Critical Reader*, Edinburgh University Press, Edinburgh, 2004.

Abramowitz, Rachel, *Is That a Gun in Your Pocket?* Women's Experience of Power in Hollywood, Random House, New York, 2000.

Adams, T.R., *Tom and Jerry*, Crescent Books, New York, 1991.

Adamson, J., *Tex Avery: King of Cartoons*, Da Capo, New York, 1975.

Agosterios, V., 'An Interview with Sally Potter', *Framework*, No. 14, 1979.

Alderson, David and Anderson, Linda (eds), *Territories of Desire in Queer Culture*, Manchester University Press, Manchester, 2000.

Aldgate, A. and Richards, J., *Britain Can Take It*, Basil Blackwell, London, 1986.

Allan, R., *Walt Disney and Europe*, John Libbey, London, 1999.

Allen, R. and Gomery, D., *Film History: Theory and Practice*, Newbery Award Records, New York, 1985.

Allinson, M., *A Spanish Labyrinth: The Films of Pedro Almodovar*, I.B. Tauris, London, 2001.

Allon, Yoram *et al.* (eds), *Critical Guide to North American Directors*, Wallflower Press, London, 2002.

Altenloh, Emile, 'A Sociology of the Cinema: Audiences', reprinted in *Screen*, Vol. 42, No. 3, autumn 2001.

Altman, Rick (ed.), *Genre: The Musical*, BFI–Routledge & Kegan Paul, London, 1981.

—— 'A Semantic/Syntactic Approach to Film Genre', *Cinema Journal*, Vol. 23, No. 3, 1984.

—— *Film/Genre*, BFI, London, 1999.

Andrew, D., *Concepts in Film Theory*, Oxford University Press, Oxford, 1984.

Angelini, S., 'The DVD Story', *Viewfinder*, No. 44, October 2001.

Ansen, David, 'The Accused', *Newsweek*, 24 October 2002.

—— 'All the Way to the Bank', *Newsweek*, 3 April 2006, online at http://www.msnbc.msn.com/id/12015263/site/newsweek (10 April 2006).

Armes, R., *The Ambiguous Image: Narrative Style in Modern European Cinema*, Secker & Warburg, London, 1976.

Arrington, Carl Wayne, 'Film's Avant-Guardian', *Rolling Stone*, 22 March, 1990.

Arthur, J., 'Technology and Gender', *Screen*, Vol. 30, 1989, pp. 40–59.

Ashby, J., 'Betty Box, "the Lady in Charge": Negotiating a Space for a Female Producer in Postwar Cinema', in J. Ashby and A. Higson (eds), *British Cinema: Past and Present*, Routledge, London, 2000.

Ashby, J. and Higson, A. (eds) (2000) *British Cinema: Past and Present*, Routledge, London.

Aumont, J., *Montage Eisenstein*, BFI, London, 1987.

Austin, B., *Immediate Seating: A Look at Movie Audiences*, Wadsworth Publishing Company, Belmont, CA, 1989.

Auty, M. and Roddick, N. (eds), *British Cinema Now*, BFI, London, 1985.

Babington, B. (ed.), *British Stars and Stardom: From Alma Taylor to Sean Connery*, Manchester University Press, 2001.

Babuscio, J., 'Camp and Gay Sensibility', in Richard Dyer (ed.), *Gays and Film*, BFI, London, 1977.

—— 'Camp and Gay Sensibility', in H. Benshoff and S. Griffin (eds), *Queer Cinema: The Film Reader*, Routledge, London, 2004.

Bad Object Choices (ed.), *How Do I Look? Queer Film and Video*, Bay Press, Seattle, 1991.

Balazs, B. 'Filming Death', in K. Macdonald and M. Cousins (eds), *Imagining Reality: The Faber Book of Documentary*, Faber & Faber, London and Boston, 1996, pp. 29–31.

Balcon, M., *Michael Balcon Presents . . . a Lifetime of Films*, Hutchinson, London, 1969.

Balio, T. (ed.), *The American Film Industry*, University of Wisconsin Press, Madison, 1976.

—— *Hollywood in the Age of Television*, Unwin Hyman, Boston, 1990.

Banner, L., *Women in Modern America*, Harcourt Brace Jovanovich, New York, 1984.

Barbas, Samantha, 'The Political Spectator: Censorship, Protest and the Moviegoing Experience, 1912–1922', *Film History*, Vol. 11, pp. 217–29.

Barker, Martin and Petley, Julian (eds), *Ill Effects – the Media Violence Debate*, Routledge, London, 1997.

Barker, Martin, Arthurs, Jane and Ramawani, Haridranath, *The Crash Controversy*, Wallflower Press, London, 2001.

Barna, Y., *Eisenstein*, Secker & Warburg, London, 1973.

Barnes, J., *The Beginnings of Cinema in England*, David & Charles, London, 1976.

—— 'Flightplan', *Sight and Sound*, Vol. 15, No. 11, 2005.

Barnouw, Erik and Krishnaswamy, S., *Indian Film*, 2nd edn, Oxford University Press, New York, 1980.

Barr, C. (ed.), *All Our Yesterdays: Ninety Years of British Cinema*, BFI, London, 1986.

—— *Ealing Studios*, Cameron & Hollis, Moffat, 1999.

—— 'Before *Blackmail*: Silent British Cinema', in R. Murphy (ed.), *The British Cinema Book*, BFI, London, 2003.

—— 'The Good Companions', in B. McFarlane (ed.), *The Cinema of Britain and Ireland*, Wallflower Press, London, 2005.

Barrier, M., *Hollywood Cartoons: American Animation in the Golden Age*, Oxford University Press, New York and Oxford, 1999.

Barrios, R., *Screened Out: Playing Gay in Hollywood from Edison to Stonewall*, Routledge, New York, 2002.

Barron, S. and Tuchman, M. (eds), *The Avant-Garde in Russia, 1910–1930: New Perspectives*, Los Angeles County Museum of Art, Los Angeles, 1980.

Barsam, R., *The Non-Fiction Film: A Critical History*, Indiana University Press, Bloomington and Indianapolis, 1992.

Barthes, Roland, *Image–Music–Text*, Fontana, London, 1977.

Baskaran, Theodore, *The Message Bearers: The Nationalist Politics and the Entertainment Media in South India, 1880–1945*, Cre-A, Madras, 1981.

—— 'Songs in Tamil Cinema', *The Eye of the Serpent*, East–West Books, Madras, 1996, pp. 38–61.

Basinger, Jeanine, *A Woman's View: How Hollywood Spoke to Women 1930-1960*, Chatto & Windus, London, 1993.

Bazin, A., *What is Cinema?*, Vol. 1, *Ontology and Language*, Editions du Cerf, Paris, 1958.

—— 'On the *Politique des auteurs*' (1957), trans. Peter Graham, in Jim Hillier (ed.) *Cahiers du Cinema*, Vol. 1: *The 1950s*, Routledge, London, 1996.

BBFC, online at http://www.bbfc.co.uk.

Beck, J., *Animation Art*, Flame Tree Publishing, London, 2004.

Beck, J. and Friedwald, W., *Looney Tunes and Merrie Melodies*, Henry Holt & Co., New York, 1989.

Begleiter, M., *From Word to Image*, Michael Wiese Productions, Los Angeles, 2001.

Bell, E., Haas, L. and Sells, L. (eds), *From Mouse to Mermaid: The Politics of Film, Gender and Culture*, Indiana University Press, Bloomington and Indianapolis, 1995.

Belton, John, 'Authorship and Film', *Film Quarterly*, Vol. 58, No. 3.

Benshoff, H., *Monsters in the Closet: Homosexuality and the Horror Film*, Manchester University Press, Manchester, 1997.

Benshoff, H. and Griffin, S. (eds), *Queer Cinema: The Film Reader*, Routledge, London, 2004.

Benson, Sheila, 'The Accused', *Los Angeles Times*, 14 October 1988.

Bergan, R., *Eisenstein: A Life in Conflict*, London, Time Warner Paperbacks, 1999.

Berger, John, *Ways of Seeing*, Penguin, London, 1972.

Berry, C., 'Happy Alone? Sad Young Men in East Asian Gay Cinema', in A. Grossman (ed.), *Queer Asian Cinema*, Harrington Park Press, New York, 2001.

Bergstrom, J., 'Rereading the Work of Claire Johnston', in C. Penley (ed.), *Feminism and Film Theory*, Routledge–BFI, London, 1988.

Bernstein, I., *Hollywood at the Crossroads: An Economic Study of the Motion Picture Industry*, Hollywood Film Council, Los Angeles, 1957.

Berry, D., *Wales and Cinema: The First Hundred Years*, University of Wales Press, Cardiff, 1994.

Bersani, L. and Dutoit, U., *Caravaggio*, BFI, London, 1999.

Betterton, R., *Looking On: Images of Femininity in the Visual Arts and the Media*, Pandora, London, 1987.

Billington, Michael, 'Proof', *Guardian*, 17 May 2002, p. 16.

Bilton, T., Bonnett, K., Jones, P., Lawsom, T., Skinner, D., Stanworth, M. and Webster, A., *Introductory Sociology*, Palgrave Macmillan, Basingstoke, 2002.

Birkos, A., *Soviet Cinema: Directors and Films*, Archon, Hamden, CT, 1976.

Bishop, L. 'Documentary Evidence', *Television*, August–September, Vol. 38, No. 7, 2001, p. 24.

Biskind, P., 'Going for Broke', *Sight and Sound*, October 1991.

Bobo, Jacquelyne, 'The Color Purple: Black Women as Cultural Readers', in E.D. Pribram (ed.), *Female Spectator: Looking at Film and Television*, Verso, London and New York, 1988.

Bogdanovich, Peter, 'New Kid on the Block', *Guardian*, 22 February 2002.

Boral, R.C. in Ashish Rajadhyaksha and Paul Willemen (eds), *Encyclopaedia of Indian Cinema*, 2nd edn, BFI, London, 1999.

Bordwell, David 'The Idea of Montage in Soviet Art and Film', *Cinema Journal*, Vol. 11, No. 2, 1972.

—— *Ozu and the Poetics of Cinema*, Princeton University Press, Princeton, NJ, 1988.

—— *Making Meaning: Inference and Rhetoric in the Interpretation of Cinema*, Harvard University Press, Cambridge, MA, 1989.

—— *Narration in the Fiction Film*, Routledge & Kegan Paul, London, 1986; repr. Routledge, London, 1990.

—— *The Cinema of Eisenstein*, Harvard University Press, Cambridge, MA, 1993.

Bordwell, David and Carroll, Noel, *Post-Theory: Reconstructing Film Studies*, University of Wisconsin, Madison, 1996.

Bordwell, David and Thompson, Kristin, *Film Art*, 4th edn, McGraw-Hill, London, 1994; repr. Knopf, New York, 1995.

Bordwell, D., Staiger, J. and Thompson, Kristin, *The Classical Hollywood Cinema*, Routledge & Kegan Paul, London, 1985; repr. 1994.

Bourne, S., *Brief Encounters: Lesbians and Gays in British Cinema 1930–1971*, Cassell, London, 1996.

Bowser, Eileen, *The Transformation of Cinema 1907–1915*, University of California, Berkeley, 1994.

Braddock, Jeremy and Hock, Stephen (eds), *Directed by Allen Smithee*, University of Minnesota Press, Minneapolis, 2001.

Brion, P., *Tom and Jerry*, Crown Publishers, New York, 1990.

Britton, A., 'The Invisible Eye', *Sight and Sound*, February, 1992, p. 29.

Brooks, Xan, 'Directing Masochism', *Guardian*, G2, 24 April 2002.

Brown, Georgia, 'Little Man Tate', *Village Voice*, 15 October 1991.

Brown, M., 'The Old Ones Are the Best', *Guardian*, 26 March 2001, pp. 16–17.

Bruzzi, S., 'Tempestuous Petticoats: Costume and Desire in *The Piano*', *Screen*, Vol. 36 No. 3, autumn 1995, pp. 257–66.

—— *Undressing Cinema*, Routledge, London, 1997.

—— *New Documentary: A Critical Introduction*, Routledge, London and New York, 2000.

Brundsen, C. (ed.), *Films for Women*, BFI, London, 1986.

Buckland, Warren, 'A Close Encounter with *Raiders of the Lost Ark*', in Steven Neale and Murray Smith (eds), *Contemporary Hollywood Cinema*, Routledge, London, 1998.

Bukatman, S., *Blade Runner*, BFI, London, 1997.

Buncombe, A., 'Coming Soon – City Centre Cinema Boom', *Independent*, 17 September 1998.

Burch, Noel, *Theory of Film Practice*, Secker & Warburg, London, 1973.

—— *Correction Please – or How We Got Into Movies*, Arts Council, London, 1979.

Burns, M., 'Women in Focus', *In Camera*, Spring 1992, pp. 3–5, 17–19.

Burrows, J., '"Our English Mary Pickford": Alma Taylor and Ambivalent British Stardom in the 1910s', in B. Babington (ed.), *British Stars and Stardom: From Alma Taylor to Sean Connery*, Manchester University Press, Manchester, 2001.

—— 'Big Studio Production in the Pre-quota Years', in R. Murphy (ed.), *The British Cinema Book,* 2nd edn, BFI, London, 2003.

Burston, P. and Richardson, C. (eds), *A Queer Romance*: *Gay Men, Lesbians and Popular Culture*, Routledge, London, 1995.

Burton-Carvajal, J., 'Surprise Package: Looking Southward with Disney', in E. Smoodin (ed.), *Disney Discourse*, Routledge, London and New York, 1994, pp. 131–47.

Buscombe, E., 'Sound and Colour', *Jump Cut*, No. 17, 1977.

Buscombe, E. and Pearson, R. (eds), *Back in the Saddle Again: New Essays on the Western*, BFI, London, 1998.

Butler, J., *Gender Trouble: Feminism and the Subversion of Identity*, Routledge, New York and London, 1990.

—— *Bodies that Matter*, Routlege, London, 1993.

Byars, J., *All that Heaven Allows: Re-reading Gender in 1950s Melodrama*, Chapel Hill, University of North Carolina Press, 1991.

Byron, S., 'Letter to Editor', *Film Comment*, Vol. 22, No. 5, October 1986, p. 76.

Cabarga, L., *The Fleischer Story*, Da Capo, New York, 1988.

Cahiers du cinéma: Situation du cinéma français, May 1957, No.71.

Calder-Marshall, A., *The Innocent Eye: The Life of Robert J. Flaherty*, New York: Harcourt Brace Jovanovich, 1966.

Campbell, D., 'Catholics Vilify *Dogma*', *Guardian* 13 November, 1999.

Campbell, R., 'Warner Bros in the 1930s: Some Tentative Notes', *The Velvet Light Trap*, No. 1, June 1971.

Canemaker, J. (ed.), *Storytelling in Animation*, American Film Institute, Los Angeles, 1988.

Cardullo, B. (ed.), *Bazin at Work*, Routledge, London, 1997.

Carroll, Noel, *Engaging the Moving Image*, Yale University Press, New Haven and London, 2003.

Caughie, John, 'Preface', in *Theories of Authorship: A Reader*, Routledge, London, 1981.

—— *Theories of Authorship: A Reader*, Routledge and BFI, London, 1988.

Cerisuelo, M., *Jean-Luc Godard*, Editions des Quatre-Vents, Paris, 1989.

Chabrol, Claude and Rohmer, Eric, *Hitchcock: The First Forty-Four Films*, Frederick Ungar, New York, 1979.

Chakravarty, Sumita S., *National Identity in Indian Popular Cinema, 1947–1987*, University of Texas Press, Austin, 1993.

Cham, M.B., *Ex-Iles: Essays on Caribbean Cinema*, Africa World Press, Trenton, NJ, 1992.

Champlin, C., 'What Will H. Hays Begat', *American Film*, Vol. 6, No. 1, October 1980.

Chandravarkar, Bhaskar, 'The Tradition of Music in Indian Cinema', *Cinema in India*, Vol. 1, No. 2, April 1987 to Vol. 3, No. 3, July–September 1989.

—— 'Growth of the Film Song', *Cinema in India*, Vol. 1, No. 3, pp. 16–20.

Chapman, J., *The British at War*, I.B. Tauris, London, 1997.

—— *Licensed to Thrill*, I.B. Tauris, London, 1999.

Chatman, S., *Story and Discourse: Narrative Structure in Fiction and Film*, Cornell University Press, Ithaca, NY, 1980.

Chatterji, G., *Mother India*, BFI Classics, London, 2002.

Chatterji, S., *Parama and Other Outsiders: The Cinema of Aparna Sen*, Parumita Publications, Calcutta, 2002.

Chibnal, S., 'Travels in Ladland: The British Gangster Film Cycle 1998–2001', in R. Murphy (ed.), *The British Cinema Book*, 2nd edn, BFI, London, 2003.

Chibnall, S. and Murphy, R., *The British Crime Film*, Routledge, London and New York, 1999.

Cholodenko, A. (ed.), *The Illusion of Life*, Power Publishers, Sydney, 1991.

Chopra, Anupama, 'Southern Invasion', *India Today*, 13 October 1997, pp. 38–40.

—— *Sholay: The Making of a Classic*, Penguin, New Delhi, 2000.

—— *Dilwalw Dulhania Le Jayenge*, BFI Modern Classics, London, 2002.

Christie, I. (ed.), *Powell Pressburger and Others*, BFI, London, 1978.

—— 'From the Kingdom of Shadows', in the catalogue to *Twilight of the Tsars*, Hayward Gallery, London, 1991.

Christie, I. and Gillett, J. (eds), *Futurism/Formalism/FEKS: 'Eccentrism' and Soviet Cinema 1918–1936*, BFI, Film Availability Services, London, 1978.

Christie, I. and Graffy, J. (eds), *Yakov Protazanov and the Continuity of Russian Cinema*, BFI–NFT, London, 1993.

Christie, I. and Taylor, R. (eds), *Eisenstein Rediscovered*, Routledge, London, 1993.

Chute, David, Review of *Lagaan: Once Upon a Time in India*, *Film Comment*, March–April, 2002.

Clover, Carol, *Men, Women and Chainsaws: Gender in the Modern Horror Film*, BFI, London, 1992.

—— 'White Noise', *Sight and Sound*, Vol. 3, No. 5, May 1993.

Cohan., S. and Hark, I. (eds), *Screening the Male*, Routledge, London, 1993.

Cohen, Scott, 'Strangers in Paradise', *Spin*, March 1990; online at http://www.sfgoth.com/~kali/onsite8. html (26/09/2001).

Colebroke, Claire, *Giles Deleuze*, London, Routledge, 2002.

Collins, C., 'British Film: The Next Generation', *Guardian*, 16 November, 2001.

Collins, Jim, *Architectures of Excess: Cultural Life in the Information Age*, Routledge, London, 1995.

Collins, J., Radner, H., Preacher Collins, A. (eds) *Film Theory Goes to the Movies*, American Film Institute and Routledge, London, 1993.

Cook, P., 'The Gold Diggers', *Framework*, Vol. 24, 1981.

—— (ed.), *The Cinema Book*, BFI, London, 1985.

—— *Fashioning the Nation: Costume and Identity in British Cinema*, BFI, London 1996.

—— 'No Fixed Address: The Women's Picture from *Outrage* to *Blue Steel*', in S. Neale and M. Smith (eds), *Contemporary Hollywood Cinema*, Routledge, London, 1998.

Cook, Pam and Dodd, Philip (eds), *Women and Film: A Sight and Sound Reader*, BFI and Scarlet Press, London, 1993.

—— (ed.), *Gainsborough Studios*, BFI, London, 1996.

Cooper, C., 'Slackness Hiding from Culture: Erotic Play in the Dancehall', in *Noises in the Blood: Orality, Gender, and the 'Vulgar' Body of Jamaican Popular Culture*, Duke University Press, Durham, NC, 1995.

Corner, J. (ed.), *Documentary and the Mass Media*, Edward Arnold, London, 1986.

—— *The Art of Record: A Critical Introduction to Documentary*, Manchester University Press, Manchester and New York, 1996.

Corrigan, Timothy, 'The Commerce of Auteurism', in *A Cinema without Walls: Movies and Culture After Vietnam*, Routledge, London, 1991.

—— *A Cinema without Walls: Movies and Culture After Vietnam*, Routledge, London, 1991.

Cotta Vaz, Mark et al., *Industrial Light and Magic: Into the Digital Realm*, Virgin Books, London, 1996.

Cowie, P., *Revolution: The Explosion of World Cinema in the Sixties*, Faber, London, 2005.

Cox, Alex, 'Is DVD Worth It?', *Guardian*, Friday Review, 23 February 2001.

Crafton, D., *Before Mickey: The Animated Film 1898–1928*, University of Chicago Press, Chicago and London, 1993.

Creed, B., 'From Here to Modernity: Feminism and Postmodernism', *Screen*, Vol. 28, No. 2, 1987, pp. 47–67.

—— 'Dark Desires: Male Masochism in the Horror Film', in S. Cohan and I. Hark (eds), *Screening the Male*, Routledge, London, 1993.

Creekmur, Corey K. and Doty, Alexander (eds), *Out in Culture: Gay, Lesbian and Queer Essays on Popular Culture*, Duke University Press, Durham, NC, 1995.

Cripps, T., *Black Film as Genre*, Indiana University Press, Bloomington, 1978.

—— *Slow Fade to Black: The Negro in American Film, 1900-1942*, 2nd edn, Oxford University Press, New York, 1993a.

—— *Making Movies Black: The Hollywood Message Movie from World War II to the Civil Rights Era*, Oxford University Press, New York, 1993b.

Cubitt, Sean, *The Cinema Effect*, MIT Press, Cambridge, MA, 2004.

Culler, Jonathan, *Structuralist Poetics*, Routledge, London, 1975.

Curtis D., *Len Lye: Exhibition Catalogue,* Watershed, 24 October 1987–29 November 1987, Arts Council, London, 1987.

Dale, A., *Comedy Is a Man In Trouble*, University of Minnesota Press, Minneapolis, 2000.

Dale, Martin, *The Movie Game: The Film Business in Britain, Europe and America*, Cassell, London, 1997.

Daniel, L. and Jackson, C. (eds), *The Bent Lens: A World Guide to Gay and Lesbian Film*, Roundhouse Publishing, Northam, 2003.

Darke, Chris, 'Rupture, Continuity and Diversification: *Cahiers du cinéma* in the 1980s', *Screen*, Vol. 34, No .4, winter 1993, pp. 362–80.

—— *Alphaville* (Cine-Files French Film Guides), I.B. Tauris, London, 2005.

Darley, Andrew, *Visual Digital Culture: Surface Play and Spectacle in New Media Genres*, Routledge, London, 2000.

Das, Veena, 'Introduction', in *Mirrors of Violence: Communities and Survivors in South Asia*, Oxford University Press, New Delhi, 1992.

Datta, Sangeeta, *Shyam Benegal*, World Directors, BFI, London, 2002.

Davies, J., 'Gender, Ethnicity and Cultural Crisis in *Falling Down* and *Groundhog Day*', *Screen*, Vol. 36, No. 3, autumn 1995, pp. 214–32.

Davies, J. and Smith, C.R., *Gender, Ethnicity and Sexuality in Contemporary American Film*, 2nd edn, Edinburgh, Keele University Press, 2001.

Davies, P. and Wells, P. (eds), *American Film and Politics: Reagan to Bush Jr*, Manchester University Press, Manchester, 2002.

DeAngelis, M., *Gay Fandom and Crossover Stardom: James Dean, Mel Gibson and Keanu Reeves*, Duke University Press, Durham, NC, 2001.

De Baecque, A., *Les Cahiers du cinéma Histoire d'une revue: Tome 2 Cinéma, tours détours 1959–1981*, Editions Cahiers du cinéma, Paris, 1991.

—— *La nouvelle vague: Portrait d'une jeunesse*, Flammarion, Paris, 1998.

De Baecque, A. and Toubiana, S., *Truffaut: A Biography*, University of California Press, Berkeley, 2000.

De Lauretis, T., 'Guerilla in the Midst – Women's Cinema in the 1980s', *Screen*, Vol. 31, No. 1, 1990.

De Nitto, D, *Film: Form and Feeling*, New York: Harper & Row, 1985.

Deleuze, Gilles, *Cinema 2: The Time-Image*, Athlone Press, London, 1989.

Denzin, N., *The Cinematic Society*, Sage, London, 1995.

Derne, Steve, *Movies, Masculinity and Modernity: An Ethnography of Men's Filmgoing in India*, Greenwood Press, Westport, CN, 2000.

Desai, J., *Beyond Bollywood: The Cultural Politics of South Asian Diasporic Film*, Routledge, New York and London, 2004.

Deschner, D., 'Anton Grot: Warner's Art Director 1927–1948', *The Velvet Light Trap*, Vol. 15, 1975.

Deuber-Mankowsky, A., *Lara Croft – Cyber Heroine*, University of Minnesota Press, Minneapolis, 2005.

Dhareshwar, Vivek and Niranjana, Tejaswini '*Kaadalan* and the Politics of Resignification: Fashion, Violence and the Body', *Journal of Arts and Ideas*, Vol. 29, January 1996.

Dhondy, Farrukh, *Bombay Duck*, Cape, London, 1990.

Diawara, M. (ed.), *Black American Cinema*, Routledge, New York, 1993.

Dickey, Sara, *Cinema and the Urban Poor in South India*, Cambridge University Press, Cambridge, 1993.

Dickinson, M. and Street, S., *Cinema and State: The Film Industry and the Government 1927–1984*, BFI, London, 1985.

Dickinson, T. and de la Roche, C., *Soviet Cinema*, Falcon Press, London, 1948.

Dillon, S., *Derek Jarman and the Lyric Film*, University of Texas Press, Houston, 2004.

Docherty, D., Morrison, D. and Tracey, M., *The Last Picture Show?*, BFI, London, 1987.

Donald, James, 'Stars', in Pam Cook and M. Bernink (eds), *The Cinema Book*, 2nd edn, BFI, London, 1999.

Donald, L. and Scanlon, S., 'Hollywood Feminism? Get Real!!', *Trouble and Strife*, Vol. 25, winter 1992, pp. 11–16.

Donnelly, K., *Pop Music in British Cinema*, BFI, London, 2001.

Doriaswamy, Rashmi, 'Hindi Commercial Cinema: Changing Narrative Strategies', in Aruna Vasudev (ed.), *Frames of Mind: Reflections on Indian Cinema*, UBS Publishers, New Delhi, 1995.

Doty, Alexander, *Making Things Perfectly Queer*, University of Minnesota Press, Minneapolis, 1993.

—— *Flaming Classics: Queering the Film Canon*, Routledge, New York and London, 2000.

Douchet, J., *French New Wave*, Distributed Art Publishers Inc.–Editions Hazan–Cinémathèque Française, Paris, 1999.

Dove, L., 'Feminist and Left Independent Filmmaking in England', *Jump Cut*, Vol. 10, No. 11, 1976.

Dovey, J., *Freakshow: First Person Media and Factual Television*, Pluto Press, London and Sterling, 2000.

Drabinsky, G., *Motion Pictures and the Arts in Canada: The Business and the Law*, Mcgraw-Hill Ryerson, Toronto, 1976.

Du Bois, W.E.B., *The Souls of Black Folk: Essays and Sketches*, Signet, New York, 1995.

Duclos, Denis, *The Werewolf Complex: America's Fascination with Violence*, Oxford University Press, New York, 1998.

Dudley, A., *The Major Film Theories: An Introduction*, Oxford University Press, Oxford, 1976.

Durgnat, R., *Nouvelle Vague: The First Decade*, Motion Publications, Loughton, 1963.

—— *A Mirror for England*, Faber & Faber, London, 1970.

Dwyer, Rachel, *All You Want Is Money, All You Need Is Love: Sexuality and Romance in Modern India*, Cassell, London, 2000.

—— *100 Bollywood Films*, BFI Screen Guides, London, 2005.

Dyer, Richard, 'Pasolini and Homosexuality', in P. Willemen (ed.), *Pier Paolo Pasolini*, BFI, London, 1977.

—— 'Resistance Through Charisma: Rita Hayworth and *Gilda*', in A.E. Kaplan (ed.), *Women in Film Noir*, BFI, London, 1978.

—— 'Don't Look Now', *Screen*, Vol. 23, Nos 3–4, 1982, pp. 66–7.

—— *Heavenly Bodies: Film Stars and Society*, Macmillan, Basingstoke, 1987.

—— 'Judy Garland and Gay Men', in *Heavenly Bodies: Film Stars and Society*, Macmillan, Basingstoke, 1987.

—— *Brief Encounter*, BFI, London, 1993.

—— *The Matter of Images: Essays on Representation*, Routledge, London, 1993.

—— *White*, Routledge, London, 1997.

—— 'Introduction to film studies', in John Hill and Pamela Church Gibson (eds), *The Oxford Guide to Film Studies*, Oxford University Press, Oxford, 1998.

—— *Stars* (1979), BFI, London, 1998.

—— *Now You See It: Studies on Lesbian and Gay Film*, Routledge, London and New York, 2002.

—— *The Culture of Queers*, Routledge, New York and London, 2002.

Dyer, R. and Vincendeau, G., *Popular European Cinema*, Routledge, London, 1992.

Dyson, L., 'The Return of the Repressed? Whiteness, Femininity and Colonialism in *The Piano*', *Screen*, Vol. 36, No. 3, autumn 1995, pp. 269–76.

Easthope, A., *What a Man's Gotta Do: The Masculine Myth in Popular Culture*, Unwin Hyman, Winchester, 1990.

Ebert, Roger, 'Dead Man Walking', *Chicago Sun–Times*, 1 December 1996; online at http://www.suntimes. com/ ebert/ebert_reviews/1996/01/1015392.html (10 May 2002).

—— 'The Accused', *Chicago Sun–Times*, 14 October 1998; online at http://www.suntimes.com/ebert/ ebert_reviews/1988/10/318971.html (10 May 2002).

—— 'Anna and the King', *Chicago Sun–Times*; online at http://www.suntimes.com/ebert/ebert_ reviews/1999/12/121701.html (10 May 2002).

—— 'The Matrix', *Chicago Sun–Times*, 23 April 2002; online at http://www.suntimes.com/ebert/ebert_ reviews/1999/03/033101.html.

—— 'Inside Man', *Chicago Sun-Times*, 24 March 2006; online at http://rogerebert.suntimes.com/aoos/pbcs. dll/article?AID=/20060323/REVIEWS/6031/4002/10 23 (10 April 2006).

Ehrenstein, D., 'Out of the Wilderness', *Film Quarterly*, Vol. 47, No. 1, 1993, pp. 2–7.

Eisenstein, Sergei M., *Notes of a Film Director*, Dover Publications, New York, 1970.

—— *The Film Sense*, Faber & Faber, London, 1986.

—— 'The Montage of Film Attractions', in Peter Lehman (ed.), *Defining Cinema*, Rutgers University Press, New Brunswick, NJ, 1997.

Ellis, John, *Visible Fictions: Cinema, Television and Video*, Routledge & Kegan Paul, London, 1982; repr. 1992.

Ellison, R., *Shadow and Act*, Vintage International, New York, 1964.

Elsaesser, Thomas, 'Vincente Minnelli', in Rick Altman (ed.), *Genre: The Musical*, Routledge & Kegan Paul–BFI, London, 1981.

—— (ed.), *Early Cinema*, BFI, London, 1990.

—— 'The Quality Film Adventure: British Critics and Cinema 1942-48', in A. Higson (ed.), *Dissolving Views: Key Writings on British Cinema*, Cassell, London, 1996.

—— 'The Blockbuster: Everything Connects, But Not Everything Goes', in Jon Lewis (ed.), *The End of Cinema as We Know It*, Pluto Press, London, 2001.

Enns, A., 'The Spectacle of Disabled Masculinity in John Woo's "Heroic Bloodshed" Films', *The Quarterly Review of Film and Video*, Vol. 17, No. 2, June 2000, pp. 137–45.

Epstein, E.J., *The Big Picture*, Random House, New York, 2005.

Erens, Patricia (ed.), *Issues in Feminist Film Criticism*, Indiana University Press, Bloomington, 1990.

Esquenazi, J.-P., *Godard et la société française des années 1960*, Paris, 2004.

Eyles, A., 'Exhibition and the Cinema-going Experience', in R. Murphy (ed.), *The British Cinema Book*, BFI Publishing, London, 2003.

Faber, L. and Walters, H., *Animation Unlimited: Innovative Short Films Since 1940*, Laurence King, London, 2004.

Falcon, R., *Classified! A Teacher's Guide to Film and Video Censorship and Classification*, BFI, London, 1994.

Farmer, Brett, *Spectacular Passions: Cinema, Fantasy, Gay Male Spectatorships*, Duke University Press, Durham, NC, 2000.

Farrow, B., 'Hollywood Runs Scared', *The Times*, 8 October, 1999.

Ferguson, M. and Wicke, J. (eds), *Feminism and Postmodernism*, Duke University Press, North Carolina, 1994.

Finney, A., *The Egos Have Landed*, Mandarin, London, 1997.

Fitzgerald, T., 'Now About These Women', *Sight and Sound*, Summer 1989.

Fleming, M. and Klady, L., '"Crying" All the Way to the Bank', *Variety*, 22 March, 1993.

Florence, P., 'A Conversation with Sally Potter', *Screen*, Vol. 34, No. 3, Autumn 1993, pp. 275–84.

Forbes, J. and Kelly, M. (eds), *French Cultural Studies: An Introduction*, Oxford University Press, Oxford, 1995.

Francke, L., *Script Girls*, BFI, London, 1994.

Frayling, C., *Spaghetti Westerns*, I.B. Tauris, London, 1998.

Frazer, J, *Artificially Arranged Scenes*, G. Hall, Boston, 1979.

Frey, H., *Louis Malle*, University of Manchester Press, Manchester, 2004.

Friedan, B., *The Feminine Mystique*, Penguin, London, 1963.

Friedmann, L. (ed.), *British Cinema and Thatcherism: Fires Were Started*, UCL Press, London, 1993.

Frith, S., *Music for Pleasure*, Routledge, London, 1988.

Fuller, Graham, 'Strictly Red', *Sight and Sound*, Vol. 11, No. 6, 2001.

Furniss, M., *Art in Motion: Animation Aesthetics*, John Libbey, London and Montrouge, 1998.

—— *Chuck Jones: Conversations*, University of Mississippi Press, Jackson, 2005.

Fuss, D. (ed.), *Inside/Out: Lesbian Theories, Gay Theories*, Routledge, New York and London, 1991.

Gabilondo, Joseba, 'Morphing Saint Sebastian', in Vivian Sobchack (ed.), *Meta Morphing and the Culture of Quick-Change*, University of Minnesota Press, Minneapolis, 2000.

Gaines, J., 'White Privilege and Looking Relations: Race and Gender in Feminist Film Theory', in S. Thornham (ed.), *Feminist Film Theory: A Reader*, New York University Press, New York, 1988.

Gallagher, Tag, 'Reading Culture, and Auteurs', *Screening The Past*, No. 12, http://www.latrobe.edu.au/screeningthepast/editorials/amed12a.htm (20 April 2006).

Ganti, T., *Bollywood: A Guidebook to Popular Hindi Cinema*, Routledge, New York and London, 2004.

Gates, H.L. Jr., 'New Negroes, Migration, and Cultural Exchange', in E. Hutton Turner (ed.), *Jacob Lawrence: The Migration Series*, Rappahannock, Washington, DC, 1993.

Gatiss, M., *James Whale*, Cassell, London, 1995.

Gaut, Berys, 'Film Authorship and Collaboration', in Richard Allen and Murray Smith (eds), *Film Theory and Philosophy*, Oxford University Press, Oxford, 1997.

Genette, G., *Narrative Discourse*, Cornell University Press, Ithaca, NY, 1980.

Geraghty, Christine, *British Cinema in the Fifties*, London, Routledge, 2000.

—— 'Re-examining Stardom: Questions of Texts, Bodies and Performance', in Christine Gledhill, and Linda Williams (eds), *Reinventing Film Studies*, Arnold, London, 2000.

Gerstner, David A., 'The Practices of Authorship', in David A. Gerstner and Janet Staiger (eds), *Authorship and Film*, Routledge, London, 2003.

Gever, M., Greyson, J. and Parmar, P. (eds), *Queer Looks: Perspectives on Lesbian and Gay Video*, Between the Lines–Routledge, Toronto, 1993.

Giannetti, L., *Understanding Movies*, 6th edn, Prentice-Hall, Englewood Cliffs, NJ, 1993.

Giannetti, L. and Eyman, S., *Flashback: A Brief History of Film*, 2nd edn, Prentice-Hall, Englewood Cliffs, NJ, 1991.

Gibbons, Fiachra, 'Meet Me in Margate', *Guardian*, 09 March 2001, online at http://film.guardian.co.uk/features/featurepages/0,4120,448694,00.html.

Gibbons, Fiachra, 'Actor Lays into "Trash Ethos" of US Films', *Guardian*, 24 August 2001; online at http://film.guardian.co.uk/News_Story/Guardian/0, 4029, 541765, 00.html (10 May 2002).

Gibbs, J., *Mise-en Scène: Film Style and Interpretation*, Wallflower Press, London, 2001.

Giles, J., *The Cinema of Jean Genet: Un chant d'amour*, BFI, London, 1991.

—— *The Crying Game*, BFI, London, 1997.

—— *Criminal Desires: Jean Genet and Cinema*, Creation Books, London, 2002.

Gillespie, D., *Russian Cinema*, Longman, Harlow, 2003.

Giroux, H., 'Brutalised Bodies and Emasculated Politics', *Third Text*, No. 53, winter 2000/1, pp. 31–41.

Gledhill, C., 'Some Recent Developments in Feminist Criticism', in S. Mast and M. Cohen (eds), *Film Theory and Criticism*, Oxford University Press, Oxford, 1985.

—— 'Pleasurable Negotiations', in D. Pribram (ed.), *Female Spectators: Looking at Film and Television*, Verso, London and New York, 1988.

—— 'Introduction', in *Stardom: Industry of Desire*, Routledge, London, 1991.

—— (ed.), *Stardom: Industry of Desire*, Routledge, London, 1991.

—— 'The History of Genre Criticism', in Pam Cook and Mieke Bernink (eds), *The Cinema Book*, 2nd edn, BFI, London, 1999.

—— 'Rethinking Genre', in Christine Gledhill and Linda Williams (eds), *Reinventing Film Studies*, Arnold, London, 2000.

—— *Reframing British Cinema, 1918–1928*, London, BFI, 2003.

Gledhill, Christine and Williams, Linda (eds), *Reinventing Film Studies*, London, Arnold, 2001.

Gomery, D., *The Hollywood Studio System*, Macmillan, London, 1986.

—— *Movie History: A Survey*, Wadsworth, Belmont, CA, 1991.

—— *Shared Pleasures*, BFI, London, 1992.

Goodwin, J., *Eisenstein, Cinema and History*, University of Illinois Press, Urbana and Chicago, 1993.

Gopalan, Lalitha, 'Avenging Women in Indian Cinema', *Screen*, Vol. 38, No. 1, 1997a, pp. 42–59.

—— 'Coitus Interruptus and Love Story in Indian Cinema', in Vidya Dehejia (ed.), *Representing the Body: Gender Issues in Indian Art*, Kali for Women, New Delhi, 1997b, pp. 124–39.

—— *Cinema of Interruptions: Action Genres in Indian Cinema*, BFI, London, 2002.

Gopinath, G., 'Queering Bollywood: Alternative Sexualities in Popular Indian Cinema', in A. Grossman (ed.), *Queer Asian Cinema*, Harrington Park Press, New York, 2001.

Gough-Yates, K., *Somewhere in England: British Cinema and Exile*, I.B. Tauris, London.

Graham, P. (ed.), *The New Wave: Critical Landmarks*, BFI–Secker & Warburg, London, 1968.

Grant, Barry Keith (ed.), *Film Genre Reader*, University of Texas, Austin, 1986.

—— (ed.), *Film Genre Reader II*, University of Texas, Austin, 1995.

Grant, Catherine, 'www.auteur.com?', *Screen*, Vol. 41, No. 1, 2000.

Grant, J., *Masters of Animation*, Batsford, London, 2001.

Greene, G., *The Pleasure Dome*, Secker & Warburg, London, 1972.

Greer, G., *The Female Eunuch*, Flamingo, London, 1971.

Grierson, J. 'The Documentary Producer', *Cinema Quarterly*, Vol. 2, No. 1, 1932.

—— *Grierson on Documentary*, edited and compiled by Forsyth Hardy, University of California Press, Berkeley and Los Angeles, 1966.

Griffiths, R. (ed.), *Queer Cinema in Europe*, Intellect Books, London, 2003.

—— *British Queer Cinema*, Routledge, London, 2005.

Grimes, C., 'Harry Potter and the Sales Team', *Financial Times*, 16 November, 2001.

Grossman, A. (ed.), *Queer Asian Cinema: Shadows in the Shade*, Harrington Park Press, New York, 2001.

Guerrero, E., *Framing Blackness: The African American Image in Film*, Temple University Press, Philadelphia, PA, 1993.

Guinness, A., *My Name Escapes Me*, Penguin, Harmondsworth, 1997.

Gunning, T., 'The Cinema of Attractions: Early Film, its Spectators and the Avant Garde', in Thomas Elsaesser (ed.), *Early Cinema: Space, Frame, Narrative*, BFI, London, 1990.

Hadleigh, B., *The Lavender Screen: The Gay and Lesbian Films*, Citadel Press, New York, 1993.

Halas, V. and Wells, P., *Halas & Batchelor Cartoons: An Animated History*, Southbank Books, London, 2006.

Hall, Stuart, 'Encoding/Decoding', in S. Hall, D. Hobson, A. Lowe and P. Willis (eds), *Culture, Media, Language*, Hutchinson, London, 1980.

—— 'When Was "Post-Colonial"? Thinking at the Limit', in Iain Chambers and Lidia Curti (eds), *The Post-Colonial Question: Common Skies, Divided Horizons*, Routledge, London, 1996.

Halle, R. and McCarthy, M. (eds), *Light Motives: German Popular Cinema in Perspective*, Wayne State University Press, Detroit, MI, 2003.

Hamer, D. and Budge, B., *The Good, the Bad and the Gorgeous: Popular Culture's Romance with Lesbianism*, Pandora, London, 1994.

Handel, L., *Hollywood Looks at its Audience*, University of Illinois Press, Urbana, 1950.

Hanson, E., *Out Takes: Essays on Queer Theory and Film*, Duke University Press, Durham, NC, 1999.

Hardy, F. (ed.), *Grierson on Documentary*, Faber & Faber, London, 1979.

Hardy, P. (ed.), *Raoul Walsh*, Edinburgh Film Festival Pamphlet, Colchester, 1974.

Haring, B., 'Digital Films Getting Serious', *USA Today*, 31 January, 2000.

Harper, S., *Picturing the Past: The Rise and Fall of the British Costume Film*, BFI, London, 1994.

Harper, S. and Porter, V., *British Cinema of the 1950s: The Decline of Deference*, Oxford University Press, Oxford, 2003l.

Harvey, S., *May '68 and Film Culture*, BFI, London, 1981.

Haskell, M., *From Reverence to Rape*, New English Library, London, 1973.

Hayward, S., *French National Cinema*, Routledge, London, 1993.

—— *Cinema Studies: The Key Concepts*, 2nd edn, Routledge, London, 2000.

Hayward, S. and Vincendeau, G. (eds), *French Film: Texts and Contexts*, Routledge, London, 1990.

Heck-Rabi, L., *Women Filmmakers – A Critical Reception*, Scarecrow Press, London, 1984.

Henderson, B. 'Toward a Non-Bourgeois Camera Style', in B. Nichols (ed.), *Movies and Methods*, University of California Press, Berkeley, 1976.

Hendrickson, N., 'What Happened to All the Women?', *Creative Screenwriter*, Vol. 10, No. 4, pp. 64–8.

Higson, A., *Waving the Flag: Constructing a National Cinema in Britain*, Oxford University Press, Oxford, 1985.

—— 'The Concept of National Cinema', *Screen*, Vol. 30, No. 4, 1989.

—— (ed.), *Dissolving Views: Key Writings on British Cinema*, Cassell, London, 1996.

—— 'Britain's Finest Contribution to the Screen', in Bruce Babington (ed.), *British Stars and Stardom*, Manchester University Press, Manchester, 2001.

—— (ed.), *Young and Innocent?*, Exeter University Press, Exeter, 2002.

—— *English Heritage, English Cinema*, Oxford University Press, Oxford, 2003.

Higson, A. and Ashby, J. (eds), *British Cinema: Past and Present*, Routledge, London, 1996.

Higson, A. and Maltby, R. (eds), *Film Europe, Film America*, Exeter University Press, Exeter, 2000.

Hill, Annette, *Shocking Entertainment*, John Libby, Luton, 1997.

Hill, J., *Sex, Class and Realism: British Cinema 1956–1963*, BFI, London, 1986.

—— *British Cinema in the 1980s*, Clarendon Press, Oxford, 1999.

Hillier, J. (ed.), *Cahiers du cinéma 1: The 1950s, Neo-Realism, Hollywood, The New Wave*, Routledge, London, 1996a.

—— (ed.), *Cahiers du cinéma 2: 1960–1968*, Routledge, London, 1996b.

Historical Journal of Film, Radio and Television, Vol. 5, No. 2, 1985.

Historical Journal of Film, Radio and Television, Vol. 11, No. 2, 1991.

Hoffer, T., *Animation: A Reference Guide*, Greenwood Press, Westport, CT, 1981.

Holcomb, Mark, 'The Lady Vanquishes: Red-Eyed Thriller Runs Out of Gas', *Village Voice*, 27 September 2005, online at http://www.villagevoice.com/film/0539,holcomb,68233,20.html (20 March 2005).

Hollis, R. and Sibley, B., *The Disney Studio Story*, Crown Publishers, New York, 1988.

Holloway, R., *Z is for Zagreb*, Tantivy Press, Cranberry, NJ, 1972.

Holmes, Tim, 'Too Cool for Words', *Rolling Stone*, 6 November 1986; online at, http://www.sfgoth.com/~kali/onsite3.html.

Holmlund, Chris, 'Impossible Bodies', in P. Kirkham and J. Thumin (eds), *You Tarzan: Masculinity, Movies and Men*, Lawrence & Wishart, London, 1993.

—— 'Masculinity as Multiple Masquerade', in S. Cohan and I. Hark (eds), *Screening the Male*, Routledge, London, 1993.

Holmlund, Chris and Fuchs, Cynthia (eds), *Between the Sheets, in the Streets: Queer, Lesbian and Gay Documentary*, University of Minnesota Press, Minneapolis, 1997.

Hood, John W., *The Essential Mystery*, Orient Longman, New Delhi, 2000.

Hoogland, R.C., *Lesbian Configurations*, University of Columbia Press, New York, 1997.

hooks, bell, *Black Looks: Race and Representation*, Turnaround, London, 1992.

—— 'The Oppositional Gaze: Black Female Spectators', in Manthia Diawara (ed.), *Black American Cinema: Aesthetics and Spectatorship*, Routledge–American Film Institute, London, 1993.

—— *Reel to Real; Race, Class and Sex in the Movies*, Routledge, New York, 1996.

Horrocks, R., *Male Myths and Icons: Masculinity in Popular Culture*, Macmillan, London, 1995.

Hunter, J. (ed.), *Moonchild: The Films of Kenneth Anger*, Creation Books, London, 2002.

Hunter, L., *Screenwriting*, Robert Hale, London, 1994.

Hurston, Z.N., 'What White Publishers Won't Print', in A. Walker (ed.), *I Love Myself When I'm Laughing*, Feminist Press, New York, 1979, pp. 169–73.

Hutchings, P., *Hammer and Beyond: The British Horror Film*, Manchester University Press, Manchester, 1993.

—— 'Genre Theory and Criticism', in Mark Jancovich and Joanne Hollows (eds), *Approaches to Popular Film*, Manchester University Press, Manchester, 1995.

—— 'The Matrix', *Scope*, posted, 1 November 1999; http://www.nottingham.ac.uk/film/journal/filmrev/the_matrix.htm, (23 April 2002).

Iampolski, Mikhail, *The Memory of Tiresias: Intertextuality and Film*, trans. Harsha Ram, University of California Press, Berkeley, 1998.

The Indian Cinematograph Code, Cinematograph Laws Research Institute, Hyderabad, A.P., 1982.

Innes, S., *Tough Girls, Women Warriors and Wonder Women in Popular Culture*, University of Pennsylvania Press, Philadelphia, 1999.

Iyer, Pico, *Video Night in Kathmandu: Reports From the Not-So-Far East*, Knopf, New York, 1988.

Izod, J., *Reading the Screen: An Introduction to Film Studies*, Longman, Harlow and York Press, Beirut, 1984.

James, Nick, 'Ballad of a Thinning Man', *Sight and Sound*, Vol. 10, No. 11 (November), 2000.

Jarman, D., *Dancing Ledge*, Quartet, London, 1984.

Jeffords, S., 'Can Masculinity Be Terminated?', in S. Cohan and I. Hark (eds), *Screening the Male*, Routledge, London, 1993.

—— *Hard Bodies: Hollywood Masculinity in the Reagan Era*, Rutgers University Press, New Brunswick, NJ, 1994.

Jenkins, Keith (ed.), *The Postmodern History Reader*, Routledge, London, 1997.

Jennings, M.L., *Humphrey Jennings: Film-Maker, Painter, Poet*, BFI, London, 1982.

Johnston, C., 'Women's Cinema as Counter Cinema', *Screen Pamphlet*, No. 2, 1973.

—— 'The Subject of Feminist Film Theory/Practice', *Screen*, Vol. 21, No. 2, 1980.

Jones, C., *Chuck Amuck*, Simon & Schuster, London, 1990.

Jones, T. and Ford, R., 'Porn Laws to Tighten as Censor Defeated', *The Times*, 17 May, 2000.

Jowett, G. and Linton, J., *Movies as Mass Communication*, Sage, Newbury Park, CA, 1989.

Julien, I., 'Black Is, Black Ain't: Notes on De-essentializing Black Identities', in G. Dent (ed.), *Black Popular Culture*, Bay Press, Seattle, 1992.

Julien, I. and McCabe, C., *Diary of a Young Soul Rebel*, BFI, London, 1991.

Kabir, N.M., *Bollywood: The Indian Cinema Story*, Channel 4 Books, 2001.

Kabir, S., *Lesbian Representations in Film*, Cassell, London and Washington, 1998.

Kaplan, E.A., *Women and Film: Both Sides of the Camera*, Methuen, London, 1983.

—— (ed.), *Psychoanalysis and Cinema*, American Film Institute–Routledge, London, 1990.

—— *Feminism and Film*, Oxford University Press, Oxford, 2000.

Kaplan, James, 'Give it Up for Sean Penn', *Observer*, 6 May 2001; online at http://www.guardian.co.uk/Archive/Article/0, 4273, 4181719, 00.html (10 May 2002).

Kapur, Geeta, 'Mythic Material in Indian Cinema', *Journal of Arts and Ideas*, Nos 14–15, July–December, 1987.

Kawin, B., *How Movies Work*, Collier Macmillan, London, 1987.

Kelly, Richard, *The Name of this Book Is Dogme 95*, Faber & Faber, London, 2000.

Kenez, P., *The Birth of the Propaganda State: Soviet Methods of Mass Mobilization 1917–1929*, Cambridge University Press, Cambridge, 1985.

—— *Cinema and Soviet Society, 1917–1953*, Cambridge University Press, Cambridge, 1992.

Kent, N., *Naked Hollywood*, BBC Books, London, 1991.

Keogh, Peter, 'Home and Away', in Jim Hillier (ed.), *American Independent Movies*, BFI, London, 2001.

Kepley, V., Jr, 'The Origins of Soviet Cinema: A Study in Industry Development', *Quarterly Review of Film Studies*, Vol. 10, No. 1, 1985.

—— *In the Service of the State: The Cinema of Alexander Dovzhenko*, University of Wisconsin Press, Madison, 1986.

Kepley, V., Jr and Kepley, B., 'Foreign Films on Soviet Screens 1922–1931', *Quarterly Review of Film Studies*, fall 1979.

Keysaar, H., 'The Toil of Thought: On Several Non-Fiction Films by Women', in C. Warren (ed.), *Beyond Document: Essays on Non-Fiction Film*, Wesleyan University Press, Hanover and London, 1996, pp. 101–37.

Khoklova, E., *Lev Shulov: Fifty Years in Film*, 2nd edn, Raduga Publishers, USSR, 1987.

King, G., *Film Comedy*, Wallflower Press, London, 2002.

Kirkham, P. and Thumin, J. (eds), *You Tarzan: Masculinity, Movies and Men*, Lawrence & Wishart, London, 1993.

—— *Me Jane: Masculinity, Movies and Women*, Lawrence & Wishart, London, 1995.

Kitses, J., *Horizons West*, Thames & Hudson, London, 1969.

Klein, N., *7 Minutes*, Verso, London, 1993.

Kofosky Sedgwick, Eve, *Between Men: English Literature and Male Homosocial Desire*, Columbia University Press, New York, 1985.

Koszarski, Richard, *An Evening's Entertainment*, University of California Press, Berkeley, 1994, Chapter 2.

Kramer, Peter, '"A Woman in a Male-dominated World": Jodie Foster, Stardom and 90s Hollywood', in Thomas Austin and Martin Barker (eds), *Contemporary Hollywood Stardom*, Arnold, London, 2003.

Kuhn, A., *Women's Pictures*, BFI–Routledge & Kegan Paul, London, 1982.

Kuzniar, A.E., *The Queer German Cinema*, Stanford University Press, Santa Barbara, CA, 2000.

La Franco, R., 'E-Cinema', *Red Herring*, 13 February, 2001.

La Valley, A. and Scherr, B. (eds), *Eisenstein at 100*, Rutgers University Press, New Brunswick, NJ, 2001.

Lacey, Nick, *Narrative and Genre*, Macmillan, London, 2000.

Landau, D. (ed.), *Gladiator: The Making of the Ridley Scott Epic*, Boxtree, London, 2000.

Lanier-Seward, A., 'A Film Portrait of Black Ritual Express: The Blood of Jesus', in G. Gay and W.L. Baber (eds), *Expressively Black: The Cultural Basis of Ethnic Identity*, Praeger, New York, 1987.

Lang, Robert (ed.), *D.W. Griffith – Birth of a Nation*, Rutgers University Press, New Brunswick, NJ, 1994.

—— *Masculine Interests: Homoerotics in Hollywood Film*, Columbia University Press, New York, 2002.

Langdale, Alan (ed.), *Hugo Münsterberg on Film. The Photoplay. A Psychological Study and Other Writings*, Routledge, London and New York, 2002.

Langdon, Matt, 'The Way of the Indie God', *If Magazine*, Vol. 13, No. 2, 2000; online at http://ifmagazine.com /common/article.asp?articleID=570.

Lant, A., *Blackout: Reinventing Women for Wartime British Cinema*, Princeton University Press, Princeton, NJ, 1991.

Lapsley, R. and Westlake, M., *Film Theory: An Introduction*, Manchester University Press, Manchester, 1988.

Larkin, Brian, 'Indian Films and Nigerian Lovers: Media and the Creation of Parallel Modernities', *Africa*, Vol. 67, No. 3, pp. 406–40.

Lawton, A., *The Red Screen: Politics, Society, Art in Soviet Cinema*, Routledge, London, 1992.

Lee, S., *Spike Lee's Gotta Have It: Inside Guerrilla Filmmaking*, Fireside, New York, 1987.

Lee, S. and Jones, L., *Do The Right Thing*, Fireside, New York, 1989.

Leff, L. and Simmons, J., *The Dame in the Kimono*, Grove Weidenfeld, New York, 1990.

Lehman, P., 'Don't Blame This on a Girl: Female Rape-Revenge Films', in S. Cohan and I. Hark (eds), *Screening the Male*, Routledge, London, 1993.

—— (ed.), *Masculinity, Bodies, Movies, Culture*, American Film Institute–Routledge, New York, 2000.

Lehman, P. and Maynes, J., 'An Interview with Susan Clayton', *Wide Angle*, Vol. 6, No. 3, 1981, p. 72.

Leigh, J., *The Cinema of Ken Loach: Art in the Service of the People*, Wallflower Press, London, 2002.

Lenin, V.I., in *Pravda*, No. 250, 7 November 1919; repr. in *Lenin: Economics and Politics in the Era of the Dictatorship of the Proletariat*, Progress Publishers, Moscow, 1978.

Leslie, E., *Hollywood Flatlands: Animation, Critical Theory and the Avant Garde*, Verso, London, 2002.

Levy, Emanuel, *Cinema of Outsiders: The Rise of American Independent Film*, New York University Press, New York, 1999.

Levy, Shawn, 'Postcards from Mars', in Jim Hillier (ed.), *American Independent Movies*, BFI, London, 2001.

Lewis, J., *The End of Cinema*, Pluto Press, London, 2001.

Leyda, J., *Kino: A History of the Russian and Soviet Film*, 3rd edn, George Allen & Unwin, London, 1983.

Lippard, C. (ed.) *By Angels Driven: The Films of Derek Jarman*, Flick Books, Trowbridge, 1996.

Lippard, C. and Johnson, G., 'Private Practice, Public Health: The Politics of Sickness and the Films of Derek Jarman', in L. Friedman (ed.), *British Cinema and Thatcherism*, UCL Press, London, 1993.

Livingston, Paisley, 'Cinematic Authorship', in Richard Allen and Murray Smith (eds), *Film Theory and Philosophy*, Oxford: Oxford University Press, 1997.

Lovell, Alan, '"I Went in Search of Deborah Kerr, Jodie Foster and Julianne Moore But Got Waylaid ..."', in Thomas Austin and Martin Barker (eds), *Contemporary Hollywood Stardom*, Arnold, London, 2003.

—— 'British Cinema: The Known Cinema?', in R. Murphy (ed.), *The British Cinema Book*, 2nd edn, BFI, London, 2003.

Lovell, T., *Pictures of Reality: Aesthetics, Politics and Pleasure*, BFI, London, 1983.

—— 'That Was the Workshop that Was', *Screen*, Vol. 31, No. 1, 1990a, pp. 102–8.

—— 'Landscapes and Stories in 1960s British Realism', *Screen*, Vol. 31, No. 4, 1990b, pp. 357–76.

Low, R., *Film Making in 1930s Britain*, George Allen & Unwin, London, 1985.

—— *The History of the British Film*, Routledge, London, 1997.

Lupton, C., *Chris Marker: Memories of the Future*, Reaktion Books, London, 2005.

MacCabe, Colin, 'Defining Popular Culture', in Colin MacCabe (ed.), *High Theory/Low Culture: Analyzing Popular Television and Film*, St. Martin's Press, New York, 1986.

—— *Godard: A Portrait of the Artist at Seventy*, Bloomsbury, London, 2003.

McCarthy, Todd, 'Inside Man', *Variety*, 20 March 2006, online at http://www.variety.com/review/VE111792 9955?categoryid=31&cs=1 (10 April 2006).

McCloud, S., *Understanding Comics*, Harper Collins, New York, 1993.

Macdonald, K. and Cousins, M. (eds), *Imagining Reality: The Faber Book of Documentary*, Faber & Faber, London and Boston, 1996.

McDonald, Paul, 'Star Studies', in Joanne Hollows and Mark Jancovich (eds), *Approaches to Popular Film*, Manchester University Press, Manchester, 1995.

—— *The Star System: Hollywood's Production of Popular Identities*, Wallflower Press, London, 2000.

Macdonald, Scott, *Avant Garde Cinema*, Cambridge University Press, Cambridge, 1993.

McFarlane, B. (ed.) (2005) *The Cinema of Britain and Ireland*, Wallflower Press, London, 2005.

MacKinnon, K., *Representing Man*, Arnold, London, 2003.

MacNab, G., *J. Arthur Rank and the British Cinema*, Routledge, London, 1993.

Malkovich, John, 'Captured by the Terrorist', *Guardian*, Friday Review, 27 April 2001.

Maltby, Richard, *Hollywood Cinema*, 2nd edn, Blackwell, Oxford, 2003.

Maltby, R. and Craven, I., *Hollywood Cinema*, Blackwell, Oxford, 1995.

Maltin, L., *Of Mice and Magic*, NAL, New York, 1987.

Man, W.J., *Behind the Screen: How Gays and Lesbians Shaped Hollywood*, Penguin Books, New York, 2002.

Manovich, L., *The Language of New Media*, MIT Press, Boston, MA, 2002.

Mapplebeck, V., 'Voyeurs and Victim TV', *Guardian*, Media Supplement, 1 December 1997, pp. 4–5.

Marie, M., *La Nouvelle vague: Une école artistique*, Nathan, Paris, 1998.

—— *The French New Wave: An Artistic School*, trans. Richard Neupert, Blackwell, London, 2002.

Marshall, H., *Masters of the Soviet Cinema*, Routledge & Kegan Paul, London, 1983.

Martin, Adrian, 'Sign Your Name Across My Heart, or "I Want to Write about Delbert Mann"', *Screening the Past*, Issue 12, 2001; online at http://www.latrobe.edu.au/screeningthepast/editorials/amed12a.htm (20 April 2006).

Martin, M. (ed.), *Cinemas of the Black Diaspora: Diversity, Dependence and Oppositionality*, Wayne State University Press, Detroit, 1995.

Massood, P.J., *Black City Cinema: African American Urban Experiences in Film*, Temple University Press, Philadelphia, PA, 2003.

Mast, S. and Cohen, M. (eds), *Film Theory and Criticism*, Oxford University Press, Oxford, 1985.

May, Larry, *Screening Out the Past: The Birth of Mass Culture and the Motion Picture Industry*, Chicago University Press, Chicago, 1980.

Mayer, K., 'Inside Man', *Sight and Sound*, Vol. 16, No. 5, p. 57.

Maynard, M., 'Current Trends in Feminist Theory', *Social Studies Review*, Vol. 2, No. 3, 1987.

Mayne, Judith, 'Lesbian Looks: Dorothy Azner and Female Authorship', in Bad Object Choices (ed.), *How Do I Look?*, Bay Press, Seattle, 1991.

—— *Cinema and Spectatorship*, Routledge, London, 1993.

—— *Directed by Dorothy Arzner*, University of Indiana Press, Bloomington, 1994.

—— 'The Critical Audience', in *Cinema and Spectatorship*, Routledge, London and New York, 1993.

Media Advocacy Group for the National Commission for Women, *A Gender Perspective for the Electronic Media*, New Delhi, March 1993.

—— *People's Perception: Obscenity and Violence on the Screen*, n.d.

Mellen, J., *Big Bad Wolves: Masculinity in the American Film*, Elmtree, London, 1970.

Memmi, A., *Dominated Man*, Beacon Press, Boston, MA, 1968.

Merck, M., '"Lianna" and the Lesbians of Art Cinema', in Charlotte Brunsdon (ed.), *Films for Women*, BFI, London, 1986.

—— 'On *Desert Hearts*', in M. Gever, J. Greyson and P. Parmar (eds), *Queer Looks: Perspectives on Lesbian and Gay Video*, Between The Lines–Routledge, Toronto, 1993.

Merritt, G., *Celluloid Mavericks*, Thunder's Mouth Press, New York, 2000.

Metz, C., *Psychoanalysis and the Cinema*, Macmillan, London, 1983.

Meyer, M. (ed.), *The Politics and Poetics of Camp*, Routledge, London, 1994.

Michelson, A. (ed.), *Kino Eye: The Writings of Dziga Vertov*, University of California Press, Berkeley, 1984.

Millet, K., *Sexual Politics*, Virago, London, 1977.

Milne, T. and Narboni, J., *Godard on Godard*, Da Capo, New York, 1986.

Mishra, V., *Bollywood Cinema: Temples of Desire*, Routledge, New York and London, 2002.

Modleski, T., *The Women Who Knew Too Much*, Methuen, London, 1988.

—— 'Three Men and Baby M', in E.A. Kaplan (ed.), *Feminism and Film*, Oxford University Press, Oxford, 2000.

Monaco, J., *The New Wave: Truffaut, Godard, Chabrol, Rohmer, Rivette*, Oxford University Press, Oxford, 1976.

Monk, C. and Sargeant, A. (eds), *British Historical Cinema*, Routledge, London, 2002.

Mora, G. and Brannan, Beverly, *FSA: The American Vision*, Harry N. Abrams, New York, 2006.

Morrey, D., *Jean-Luc Godard*, University of Manchester Press, Manchester, 2005.

Morrison, T., *Playing in the Dark: Whiteness and the Literary Imagination*, Harvard University Press, Cambridge, MA, 1992.

Moseley, Rachel, *Growing Up with Audrey Hepburn: Text, Audience, Resonance*, Manchester: Manchester University Press.

Movie Magazine, *The Films of Jean-Luc Godard*, Studio Vista, London, 1967.

Muir, A.R., 'The Status of Women Working in Film and Television', in L. Gammon (ed.), *The Female Gaze*, Women's Press, London, 1988.

Mulvey, L., 'Visual Pleasure and Narrative Cinema', *Screen*, Vol. 16, No. 3, 1975.

—— *Framework*, Vol. 10, Nos 6–7, 1977, p. 7.

—— 'Film, Feminism and the Avant-Garde', 1979.

—— 'Afterthoughts on Visual Pleasure and Narrative Cinema', *Framework*, Vol. 6, Nos 15–17, 1981.

—— *Visual and Other Pleasures*, Macmillan, London, 1989.

—— 'Visual Pleasure and Narrative Cinema', in *The Sexual Subject: A Screen Reader in Sexualtity*, Routledge, London and New York, 1995.

—— *Death 24x a Second*, Reaktion, London, 2006.

Murphy, J., 'A Question of Silence', in C. Brundsen (ed.), *Films for Women*, BFI, London, 1986.

Murphy, R., *Sixties British Cinema*, BFI, London, 1992.

—— (ed.), *British Cinema of the 90s*, BFI, London, 1999.

—— (ed.), *The British Cinema Book*, BFI, London, 2003.

Murray, Raymond, *Images in the Dark: An Encyclopedia of Gay and Lesbian Film and Video*, TLA Publications, Philadelphia, 1998.

Musser, Charles, 'The Travel Genre in 1903–1904: Moving Towards Fictional Narrative', in Thomas Elsaesser with Adam Barker (eds), *Early Cinema: Space, Frame, Narrative*, BFI, London, 1990.

—— *The Emergence of Cinema: The American Screen to 1907*, University of California, Berkeley, 1994.

Napper, L., 'A Despicable Tradition? Quota Quickies in the 1930s', in R. Murphy (ed.), *The British Cinema Book*, 2nd edn, BFI Publishing, London, 2003.

Napper, L. and Williams, M., 'The Curious Appeal of Ivor Novello', in B. Babington (ed.), *British Stars and Stardom: From Alma Taylor to Sean Connery*, Manchester University Press, Manchester, 2001.

Nathan, I., 'Blame-Spotting', *The Times*, 11 July, 2002.

Neale, Steven, 'Art Cinema as Institution', *Screen*, Vol. 22, No. 1, 1981, pp. 11–41.

—— *Genre*, BFI, London, 1990.

—— 'Questions of Genre', *Screen*, Vol. 31, No. 1, 1990, pp. 45–67.

—— *Genre* (1980), BFI, London, 1992.

—— 'Masculinity as Spectacle', in S. Cohan and I. Hark (eds), *Screening the Male*, Routledge, London, 1993.

—— *Genre and Hollywood*, Routledge, London and New York, 2000.

—— *Genre and Contemporary Hollywood*, BFI, London, 2002.

Neale, S. and Smith, M. (eds), *Contemporary Hollywod Cinema*, Routledge, London, 1998.

Newsweek International, 10 May, 1999.

Neupert, R., *A History of the French New Wave Cinema*, University of Wisconsin, 2002.

Nichols, B. (ed.), *Movies and Methods*, Vol. 1, University of California Press, Los Angeles, 1976.

—— 'Performing Documentary', in *Blurred Boundaries*, Indiana University Press, Bloomington and Indianapolis, 1994, pp. 92–107.

—— 'Film Theory and the Revolt Against Master Narratives', in Christine Gledhill and Linda Williams (eds), *Reinventing Film Studies*, Arnold, London, 2000.

—— *Introduction to Documentary*, Indiana University Press, Bloomington and Indianapolis, 2001.

Nielsen, Lars, 'Girl Power Got Me Through My Divorce', *Now*, 8 May 2002.

Niranjana, Tejaswini, 'Whose Nation? Tourists and Terrorists in *Roja*?', *Economic and Political Weekly*, Vol. 24, No. 3, 15 January, 1994.

Nouvelle Vague: une légende en question, January 1999, hors séries.

Nussinova, T., 'The Soviet Union and the Russian Émigrés', in G. Nowell-Smith (ed.), *The Oxford History of World Cinema*, Oxford University Press, Oxford, 1996.

Oakley, C.A., *Where We Came In*, George Allen & Unwin, London, 1964.

Ondaatje, M., *The Conversations: Walter Murch and the Art of Editing Film*, Alfred A. Knopf, New York, 2002.

Orr, J., *Cinema and Modernity*, Polity Press, London, 1993.

Paget, Derek, *No Other Way to Tell It*, Manchester University Press, Manchester, 1998.

Palmer, J. and Riley, M., *The Films of Joseph Losey*, Cambridge University Press, Cambridge, 1993.

Pandian, M.S.S., *The Image Trap*, Sage, New Delhi, 1992.

Parker, Deborah and Parker, Mark, 'DVDs and the Director's Intentions', in Thomas E. Wartenberg and Angela Curran (eds), *The Philosophy of Film*, Blackwell, Oxford, 2005.

Parkes, C., 'Everyone Goes to Hollywood', *Financial Times*, 13 March, 2001.

Parliamentary Debates, HMSO, London.

Patten, F., *Watching Anime, Reading Manga*, Stone Bridge Press, Berkeley, CA, 2004.

Peary, D. and Peary, G. (eds), *The American Animated Cartoon*, Dutton, New York, 1980.

Pencak, W., *The Films of Derek Jarman*, McFarland & Co, London, 2002.

Pendakur, Manjunath, 'Dynamics of Cultural Policy Making: The U.S. Film Industry in India', *Journal of Communication*, Autumn 1985, pp. 52–72.

—— 'India', in John A. Lent (ed.), *The Asian Film Industry*, Texas University Press, Austin, 1990.

—— *Indian Popular Cinema: Industry, Ideology and Consciousness*, Hampton Press, Crosshill, NJ, 2003.

Penley, C. (ed.), *Feminism and Film Theory*, Routledge–BFI, London, 1988.

Perez, Gilberto, *The Material Ghost*, Johns Hopkins University Press, Baltimore, MD, 1998.

Perkins, V., *Film as Film*, Penguin, London, 1972a.

—— 'The Cinema of Nicholas Ray', in I.F. Cameron (ed.), *Movie Reader*, November Books, London, 1972b.

Perry, G., *Forever Ealing*, Pavilion, London, 1981.

Perry, N., 'Will Sony Make it in Hollywood', *Fortune*, 9 September, 1991.

Person, Per, *Understanding Cinema: A Psychological Theory of Moving Imagery*, Cambridge: Cambridge University Press, 2003.

Petley, J., 'The Lost Continent', in C. Barr (ed.), *All Our Yesterdays: 90 Years of British Cinema*, BFI, London, 1986.

Petric, V., 'Dziga Vertov as Theorist', *Cinema Journal*, Vol. 1, autumn 1978, pp. 41–2.

—— *Constructivism in Film: The Man with the Movie Camera – A Cinematic Analysis*, Cambridge University Press, Cambridge, 1987.

Petrie, D., *Screening Scotland*, BFI, London, 2000.

Petrie, Ruth (ed.), *Film and Censorship – The Index Reader*, Cassell, London, 1997.

Phelan, Rev. J.J., 'Motion Pictures as a Phase of Commercialised Amusement in Toldeo, Ohio', reprinted in *Film History*, Vol. 13, No. 3, 2001.

Phillips, Patrick, *Understanding Film Texts*, BFI, London, 2000.

Pierson, J., *Spike, Mike, Slackers and Dykes: A Guided Tour Across a Decade of Independent American Cinema*, Faber & Faber, London, 1996.

Pilcher, J., 'I'm Not a Feminist, But ...', *Sociology Review*, November 1993, p. 4.

Pilling, J. (ed.), *Women and Animation, A Compendium*, BFI, London, 1992.

—— (ed.), *A Reader in Animation Studies*, John Libbey, London, 1997.

Pilling, J. and O'Pray, M. (eds), *Into the Pleasure Dome: The Films of Kenneth Anger*, BFI, London, 1989.

Pines, J., 'British Cinema and Black Representation', in R. Murphy (ed.), *The British Cinema Book*, 2nd edn, BFI Publishing, London, 2003.

Pines, J. and Willemen, P. (eds), *Questions of Third Cinema*, BFI, London, 1989.

Pirie, D., *A Heritage of Horror*, Gordon Fraser, London, 1973.

Plantinga, Carl and Smith, Greg M. (eds), *Passionate Views: Film, Cognition and Emotion*, Johns Hopkins University Press, Baltimore, 1999.

Polan, Dana, *Pulp Fiction*, BFI, London, 2001a.

—— 'Auteur Desire', *Screening the Past*, Issue 12, 2001b, http://www.latrobe.edu.au/screeningthepast?firstrelease/fr0301/dpfr12a.htm.

Pollock, G., *Vision and Difference*, Routledge, London, 1988.

Pollock, G. and Parker, R., *Old Mistresses*, Routledge & Kegan Paul, London, 1981.

Popple, S. and Toulmin, V., *Visual Delights*, Flicks Books, Trowbridge, 2000.

Porter, L. and Burton, A. (eds), *Pimple, Pranks and Pratfalls*, Flicks Books, Trowbridge, 2000.

—— (eds), *Crossing the Pond*, Flicks Books, Trowbridge, 2002.

Potter, S., www.yesthemovie.com, p. 104.

Powell, D., *Films since 1939*, British Council, London, 1947.

Powell, M., *A Life in Movies*, Heinemann, London, 1986.

Prasad, M. Madhava, *Ideology of the Hindi Film: A Historical Construction*, Oxford University Press, New Delhi, 1998, pp. 138–59.

Pribram, E. (ed.), *Female Spectators: Looking at Film and Television*, Verso, London and New York, 1988.

Propp, Vladimir, *Theory and History of Folklore*, Manchester University Press, Manchester, 1984.

Pudovkin, V. *Film Technique and Film Acting*, Gollancz, London, 1929.

Pulver, Andrew, 'The Revolution Starts Here', *Guardian*, 28 August 2001; online at http://www.guardian.co.uk/ Archive/Article/0, 4273, 4246163, 00.html (10 May 2002).

Radner, H., 'New Hollywood's New Women: Murder in Mind – Sarah and Margie', in S. Neale and M. Smith (eds), *Contemporary Hollywood Cinema*, Routledge, London, 1998.

Radway, J., *Reading the Romance*, Verso, London, 1987.

Rajadhyaksha, Ashish, 'The Phalke Era: Conflict of Traditional Form and Modern Technology', *Journal of Arts and Ideas*, Nos 25–6, 1993.

Rajadhyaksha, Ashish and Willemen, Paul (eds), *Encyclopaedia of Indian Cinema*, BFI–Oxford University Press, London, 1999.

Rajagopal, Arvind, *Politics After Television: Religious Nationalism and the Reshaping of the Indian Public*, Cambridge University Press, Cambridge, 2001.

Ranade, Ashok, 'The Extraordinary Importance of the Indian Film Song', *Cinema Vision India*, Vol. 1, No. 4, 1981, pp. 4–11.

Rangoonwala, Firoze, 'The Age of Violence', *The Illustrated Weekly of India*, 4–10 September, 1993, pp. 27–9.

Rancière, Jacques, *Film Fables*, Berg, Oxford, 2006.

Rao, Maithili, 'Victims in Vigilante Clothing', *Cinema in India*, October–December 1998, pp. 24–6.

Rawsthorn, A., 'Small Budget Movie with Big Ambitions', *Financial Times*, Weekend section, 27 January, 1996.

Razdan, C.K. (ed.), *Bare Breasts and Bare Bottoms*, Jaico, Bombay, 1975.

Read, Jacinda, 'Popular Film/Popular Feminism', *Scope*, January 2000; online at http://www.nottingham.ac.uk /film/journal/articles/popular_feminism.htm (14 February 2000).

Rees, A. L., *A History of Experimental Film and Video*, BFI, London, 1999.

Reeves, N., *Official British Film Propaganda*, IWM–Croom Helm, Kent, 1986.

Reid, M., *Redefining Black Film*, University of California Press, Berkeley, 1993.

Reid, T. and Peek, L., 'Potter Playtime ...', *The Times*, 6 November, 2001.

Reisz, K. and Millar, G., *The Technique of Film Editing*, Focal Press, London, 1953.

Renov, Alan, 'Introduction: The Truth About Non-Fiction', in *Theorising Documentary*, Routledge, New York and London, 1993.

Renov, Michael (ed.), *Theorising Documentary*, Routledge, London and New York, 1993.

Rhines, J., *Black Film/White Money*, Rutgers University Press, New Brunswick, NJ, 1996.

Richards, J., *The Age of the Dream Palace*, Routledge, London, 1984.

—— *Films and National Identity*, Manchester University Press, Manchester, 1997.

—— (ed.), *The Unknown 1930s*, I.B. Tauris, London, 1998.

Ringler, Kimberly, 'A Reading of *Dil Chahta Hai*', unpublished term paper submitted to Lalitha Gopalan for a tutorial on Indian cinema, Spring 2002.

Robbins, H.W., 'More Human Than I Alone', in S. Cohan and I. Hark (eds), *Screening the Male*, Routledge, London, 1993.

Roberts, G., 'Esfir Shub: A Suitable Case For Treatment', *Historical Journal of Film, Radio and Television*, Vol. 11, No. 2, 1991.

—— *Forward Soviet: History and Non-Fiction Film in the USSR*, I.B. Tauris, London, 1999.

Robertson, J., *The British Board of Film Censors: Film Censorship in Britain, 1896–1950*, Croom Helm, Kent, 1985.

Robinson, D., *World Cinema 1895–1980*, Methuen, London, 1981.

Robinson, David, *From Peep Show to Palace – the Birth of American Film*, Columbia University Press, New York, 1996.

Roddick, N., *A New Deal in Entertainment*, BFI, London, 1983.

Rony, F.T., *The Third Eye: Race, Cinema and Ethnographic Spectacle*, Duke University Press, Durham, NC, 1996.

Rosenbaum, Jonathan, *Dead Man*, BFI, London, 2000.

Rosenblum, R. and Karen, R., *When the Shooting Stops … the Cutting Begins: A Film Editor's Story*, Da Capo Press, New York, 1979.

Rosenthal, A., *The New Documentary in Action*, University of California Press, Los Angeles, 1972.

—— *The Documentary Conscience*, University of California Press, Los Angeles, 1980.

Rotha, P., *Celluloid: The Film Today*, Longmans, Green & Co., London, 1933.

—— *The Film till Now*, Vision, London, 1949.

Routt, William D. (1990), 'L'Evidence', *Continuum*, Vol. 5, No. 2; online at http://wwwmcc.murdoch.edu.au/ReadingRoom/5.2/Routt.html (8 January 2002).

Rowe, K., 'Melodrama and Men in Post-Classical Romantic Comedy', in P. Kirkham and J. Thumin (eds), *You Jane: Masculinity, Movies and Women*, Lawrence & Wishart, London, 1995.

—— *The Unruly Woman*, University of Texas Press, Austin, 1995.

Roy Levin, G., *Documentary Explorations*, Doubleday, New York, 1971.

Ruby, Jay, 'The Ethics of Image Making', in Alan Rosenthal and John Corner (eds), *New Challenges for Documentary*, 2nd edn, Manchester University Press, Manchester, 2005.

Rushdie, Salman, *The Satanic Verses*, Viking, London; New York, 1988.

Russett, R. and Starr, C., *Experimental Animation*, Da Capo, New York, 1976.

Russo, V., *The Celluloid Closet: Homosexuality in the Movies*, Harper & Row, New York and London, 1987.

Ryall, Tom, 'Teaching through Genre', *Screen Education*, No. 17, 1975–76, pp. 27–33.

—— *Alfred Hitchcock and the British Cinema*, Athlone Press, London, 1996.

—— 'Genre and Hollywood', in John Hill and Pamela Church Gibson (eds), *The Oxford Guide to Film Studies*, Oxford University Press, Oxford, 1998.

—— 'A British Studio System: The Associated British Picture Corporation and the Gaumont-British Picture Corporation in the 1930s', in R. Murphy (ed.), *The British Cinema Book*, 2nd edn, BFI Publishing, London, 2003.

Salt, B., 'Statistical Style Analysis of Motion Pictures', *Film Quarterly*, Vol. 28, No. 2, 1975.

Sampson, H.T., *Blacks in Black and White,* Scarecrow; 2nd edn, Metuchen, NJ, 1995.

Sanghera, S., 'E-Movies are Ready to Roll', *Financial Times*, 7 September, 2000.

Sargeant, A., *Vsevolod Pudovkin: Classic Films of the Soviet Avant-Garde*, I.B. Tauris, London, 2000.

Sarkar, Kobita, *You Can't Please Everyone: Film Censorship, the Inside Story*, IBH Publishing Company, Bombay, 1982.

Sarris, Andrew, 'Notes on the Auteur Theory in 1962', *Film Comment*, No. 27, 1963.

—— *The American Cinema: Directors and Directions 1929–1968*, Da Capo, New York, 1996.

Saunders, J., *The Western Genre: From Lordsburg to Big Whiskey*, Wallflower Press, London, 2001.

Schatz, Thomas, 'The New Hollywood', in Jim Collins, Hilary Radner and Ava Preacher Collins (eds), *Film Theory Goes to the Movies*, Routledge, London, 1993.

Schnitzer, J., Schnitzer, L. and Martin, M. (eds), *Cinema in Revolution*, trans. D. Robinson, Secker & Warburg, London, 1973; repr. Da Capo Press, New York, 1987.

Screen, Vol. 12, No. 4, Winter 1971–2. A special issue centred on Soviet film of the 1920s including translations from: LEF, Novy LEF, Brik, Kuleshov, Shkiovsky, Vertov, Mayakovsky Film Scenarios.

Sealy, Allan, *Hero*, Viking India Ltd, New Delhi, 1990.

Segal, M., *Slow Motion: Changing Masculinities, Changing Men*, Virago, London, 1997.

Sellars, Peter and Walsh, John (eds), *Bill Viola: The Passions*, Getty Trust Publications, Los Angeles, CA, 2003.

Sen, Mala, *India's Bandit Queen: The True Story of Phoolan Devi*, Harper Collins and Pandora, London, 1991.

Shaviro, Steven, *The Cinematic Body*, University of Minnesota Press, Minneapolis, 1993.

Sheinfeld, L., 'The Big Chill', *Film Comment*, Vol. 22, No. 3, May–June, 1986.

Shetty, Manmohan, 'Trends in Film Processing', *Lensight*, Vol. 3, No. 4, October, 1994.

Shohat, E. and Stam, R., *Unthinking Eurocentrism: Multiculturalism and the Media*, Routledge, New York, 1994.

Shusterman, Richard, *Pragmatist Aesthetics*, Rowman & Littlefield, Oxford, 2000.

Silents Majority, The, *On-line Journal of Silent Film*; online at http://www.silentsmajority.com.

Singh, Madan Gopal, 'Technique as an Ideological Weapon', in Aruna Vasudev and Phillipe Lenglet (eds), *Indian Cinema Superbazaar*, Vikas Publishing House, New Delhi, 1983.

Sinyard, N. and MacKillop, I., *British Cinema of the 50s: A Celebration*, Manchester University Press, Manchester, 2003.

Skillman, Terri, 'The Bombay Hindi Film Song Genre: A Historical Survey', *Yearbook for Tradition Music*, Vol. 18, 1986, pp. 133–44.

Sklar, R., 'The Making of Cultural Myths – Walt Disney', in D. Peary and G. Peary (eds), *The American Animated Cartoon*, Dutton, New York, 1980, pp. 58–65.

Slide, A., *Early Women Directors*, A.S. Barnes, New York, 1977.

Smith, Alison, *Agnès Varda*, Manchester University Press, Manchester, 1998.

Smith, M., *Contemporary Hollywood Cinema*, Routledge, London, 1998.

Smith, Murray, *Engaging Characters – Fiction, Emotion and the Cinema*, Oxford University Press, Oxford, 1995.

Smith, Paul, *Clint Eastwood: A Cultural Production*, University of Minnesota Press, Minneapolis, 1993.

Smith, P.J., *Laws of Desire*, Clarendon Press, Oxford, 1992.

—— *Desire Unlimited: The Cinema of Pedro Almodovar*, Verso, London and New York, 2000.

Smith, S., *Women Who Make Movies*, Hopkinson & Blake, New York, 1975.

—— 'Byte me …'; online at www.atomfilms.com (24 January, 2001).

Smith, Sean M., 'Jodie's Choice', *Premiere*, March 2002, pp. 44–9.

—— *Photography on the Color Line: W.E.B. Du Bois, Race and Visual Culture*, Duke University Press, Durham, NC, 2004.

Smith, V. (ed.), *Representing Blackness: Issues in Film and Video*, Rutgers University Press, New Brunswick, NJ, 1997.

Smith, Valerie, *Not Just Race, Not Just Gender*, Routledge, New York and London, 1998.

Smoodin, E. (ed.), *Disney Discourse* Routledge, London and New York, 1994.

Snead, J., *White Screens, Black Images: Hollywood from the Dark Side*, ed. C. McCabe and C. West, Routledge, New York, 1994.

Sobchack, Vivian (ed.), *The Persistence of History: Cinema, Television and the Modern Event*, Routledge, London and New York, 1996.

—— (ed.), *Metamorphing: Visual Transformation and the Culture of Quick-Change*, University of Minnesota Press, Minneapolis, 2000.

—— 'What Is Film History?, or, the Riddle of the Sphinxes', in Christine Gledhill and Linda Williams (eds), *Reinventing Film Studies*, Arnold, London, 2000.

—— *Carmel Thoughts: Embodiment and Moving Image Culture*, University of California Press, Berkeley, 2004.

Solomon, C. (ed.), *The Art of the Animated Image*, American Film Institute, Los Angeles, 1987.

Sontag, S., 'Fascinating Fascism', in B. Nichols (ed.), *Movies and Methods*, University of California Press, Los Angeles, 1976, pp. 32–48.

—— 'Notes on Camp', in *Against Interpretation*, Vintage, London, 2001.

Spicer, A., *Typical Men*, I.B. Taurus, London, 2001.

Squire, J. (ed.), *The Movie Business Book*, Columbus, London, 1986.

Srinivas, S.V., 'Devotion and Defiance in Fan Activity', in Ravi Vasudevan (ed.), *Making Meaning in Indian Cinema*, Oxford University Press, New Delhi, 2000.

Staiger, Janet, 'Authorship Approaches', in David A. Gerstner and Janet Staiger (eds), *Authorship and Film*, Routledge, London, 2003.

Stacey, Jackie, 'Desperately Seeking Difference', in *The Sexual Subject: A Screen Reader in Sexuality*, London and New York, 1992.

—— *Star Gazing: Hollywood Cinema and Female Spectatorship*, Routledge, London, 1994.

Stam, Robert, *Film Theory: An Introduction*, Blackwell, Oxford, 2000a.

—— 'The Author: Introduction', in Toby Miller and Robert Stam (eds), *Film and Theory: An Anthology*, Blackwell, Oxford, 2000b.

Starr, C., *Discovering the Movies*, Van Nostrand Reinhold Co., New York, 1972.

Stephenson, R., *Animation in the Cinema*, Zwemmer Ltd, London, 1969.

Steven, P. (ed.), *Jump Cut: Hollywood, Politics and Counter Cinema*, Between The Lines, Toronto, 1985.

Stevenson, W., 'Film Jackpot Solves Nothing', *Daily Telegraph*, 15 May, 1997.

Stewart, G., *Between Film and Screen – Modernism's Photo Synthesis*, University of Chicago Press, Chicago, IL, 2004.

Stewart, J.N., *Migrating to the Movies: Cinema and Black Urban Modernity*, University of California Press, Berkeley, 2005.

Stites, R. 'Soviet Movies for the Masses and Historians', *Historical Journal of Film, Radio and Television*, Vol. 11, No. 3, 1991.

—— *Russian Popular Culture: Entertainment and Society Since 1900*, Cambridge University Press, Cambridge, 1992.

Straayer, Chris, 'The Hypothetical Lesbian Heroine in Narrative Feature Film', in Corey K. Creekmur and Alexander Doty (eds), *Out in Culture: Gay, Lesbian and Queer Essays on Popular Culture*, Duke University Press, Durham, NC, 1995.

—— *Deviant Eyes, Deviant Bodies*, Columbia University Press, New York, 1996.

Street, S., *British National Cinema*, Routledge, London, 1997.

—— *Transatlantic Crossings: British Feature Films in the USA*, Continuum, London, 2002.

—— 'British Film and the National Interest, 1927–39', in R. Murphy (ed.), *The British Cinema Book*, 2nd edn, BFI Publishing, London, 2003.

Street, S. and Fitzsimmons, L. (eds), *Moving Performance*, Flicks Books, Trowbridge, 2000.

Subramanyam, Radha, 'Class, Caste and Performance in "Subaltern" Feminist Film Theory and Praxis: An Analysis of *Rudaali*', *Cinema Journal*, 35, No. 3, spring 1996, pp. 34–51.

Sweeney, G., 'The Man in the Pink Shirt: Hugh Grant and the Dilemma of British Masculinity', *Cineaction*, No. 55, July 2001, pp. 57–67.

Tarantino, Quentin, *Pulp Fiction – The Screenplay*, Faber & Faber, London, 1994.

Tasker, Yvonne, 'Dumb Movies for Dumb People', in S. Cohan and I. Hark (eds), *Screening the Male*, Routledge, London, 1993.

—— *Spectacular Bodies: Gender, Genre and the Action Movie*, Routledge, London, 1993.

—— *Working Girls*, Routledge, London, 1998.

—— (ed.), *Fifty Contemporary Film-Makers*, Routledge, London, 2002.

Taylor, R., *Film Propaganda: Soviet Russia and Nazi Germany*, Croom Helm, London, 1979.

—— *The Politics of the Soviet Cinema, 1917–1929*, Cambridge University Press, Cambridge, 1979.

—— 'Boris Shumyatsky and the Soviet Cinema in the 1930s: Ideology as Mass Entertainment', *Historical Journal of Film, Radio and Television*, Vol. 6, No. 1, 1986.

—— (ed.), *S.M. Eisenstein: Writings 1922–1934 – Selected Works*, Vol. 1, BFI, London, 1988.

—— (ed.), *Beyond the Stars: The Memoirs of Sergei Eisenstein – Selected Works*, Vol. 4, BFI, London, 1995.

—— (ed.), *S.M. Eisenstein: Selected Works – Writings 1934–1947*, Vol. 3, BFI, London, 1996.

—— (ed.), *The Eisenstein Reader*, BFI, London, 1998.

—— *Sergei Eisenstein Biography*, Cape, 1999.

—— *October*, BFI, London, 2002.

Taylor, R. and Christie, I. (eds), *Inside the Film Factory: New Approaches to Russian and Soviet Cinema*, Routledge, London, 1991.

—— *The Film Factory: Russian and Soviet Cinema in Documents, 1896–1939*, Routledge, London, 1994; first published 1988 by Routledge & Kegan Paul.

Taylor, R. and Glenny, M. (eds), *S.M. Eisenstein: Towards a Theory of Montage – Selected Works*, Vol. 2, BFI, London, 1994.

Taylor, R., Wood, N., Graffy, J. and Iordanova, D. (eds), *The British Film Institute Companion to Eastern European and Russian Cinema*, Vol. 2, BFI, London, 2001.

Thomas, Rosie, 'Indian Cinema: Pleasures and Popularity', *Screen*, Vol. 26, Nos 3–4, 1985.

Thompson, K. 'Early Alternatives to the Hollywood Mode of Production', *Film History: An International Journal*, Vol. 5, No. 4, December, 1993.

Thompson, K. and Bordwell, D., *Film Art: An Introduction*, 4th edn, McGraw-Hill, New York, 1993.

—— *Film History: An Introduction*, McGraw-Hill, New York, 1994.

Thompson, R., 'Pronoun Trouble', in D. Peary and G. Peary (eds), *The American Animated Cartoon*, Dutton, New York, 1980, pp. 226–35.

Thomson, H., 'Why Did the BBC Hide Away My BAFTA-Winning Series?', *Daily Telegraph*, 22 November 2001, p. 18.

Thoraval, Yves, *The Cinemas of India*, Macmillan India, New Delhi, 2000.

Thornham, S., *Passionate Detachments*, Arnold, London, 1997.

Tincknell, E. and Chambers, D., 'Performing the Crisis, Fathering, Gender and Representation in Two 1990s' Films', *Journal of Popular Film and TV*, Vol. 29. No 4, winter 2002, pp. 146–55.

Tinkcom, Matthew and Villarejo, Amy (eds), *Keyframes: Popular Cinema and Cultural Studies*, Routledge, London, 2001.

Toulmin, V., Russell, P. and Popple, S. (eds), *The Lost World of Mitchell & Kenyon*, BFI Publishing, London, 2004.

Truffaut, François, *Hitchcock*, Secker & Warburg, London, 1967.

—— 'A Certain Tendency of the French Cinema', in Bill Nichols (ed.), *Movies and Methods Vol. 1*, University of California Press, Berkeley, 1976.

—— *Hitchcock/Truffaut*, Editions Ramsay, Paris, 1983.

Tsivian, Y., *Early Cinema in Russia and its Cultural Reception*, Routledge, London, 1994.

Tudor, A., *Theories of Film*, Secker & Warburg for the BFI, London, 1974.

Turan, Kenneth, 'Contact', *Los Angeles Times*, 11 July 1997; online at http://www.calendarlive.com/top/1,1419,L-LATimes-Movies-X!ArticleDetail-4490,00.html (10 May 2002).

—— 'Inside Man', *Los Angeles Times* (11/07/1997), online at http://www.calendarlive.com/top/1,1419,L-LATimes-Movies-X!ArticleDetail-4490,00.html (10 May 2002).

Turner, Graeme, *Film as Social Practice*, Routledge, London, 1988; repr. London, Routledge, 1993.

—— (ed.), *The Film Cultures Reader*, Routledge, London, 2001, pp. 444–68.

Tyler, C., 'Porn Wars', *Financial Times*, Weekend section, 24 October, 1998.

Tyler, P., *Screening the Sexes: Homosexuality in the Movies*, De Capo, New York, 1993.

Uberoi, Patricia, 'The Diaspora Comes Home: Disciplining Desire in *DDLJ*', *Contributions to Indian Sociology*, Vol. 32, No. 2, 1998.

Usai, P., Codelli, L., Montanaro, C. and Robinson, D. (eds), *Silent Witnesses: Russian Films 1908–1919*, BFI, London, 1989.

Van Zoonen, L., *Feminist Media Studies*, Sage, London, 1994.

Vanaik, Achin, *The Painful Transition*, Verso, New York, 1991.

Vasudev, Aruna, *Liberty and License in Indian Cinema*, Vikas Publishing House, New Delhi, 1978.

Vasudevan, Ravi, 'Addressing the Spectator of a "Third-World" National Cinema: The Bombay Social Film of the 1940s and 1950s', *Screen*, Vol. 36, No. 4., 1995.

—— '*Bombay* and its Public', *Journal of Arts and Ideas*, Vol. 29, January, 1996, pp. 44–65.

Vaughan, Dai, *For Documentary: Twelve Essays*, University of California Press, 1999.

Vincendeau, G., 'France 1945–65 and Hollywood: The *Policier* as Inter-National Text', *Screen*, Vol. 33, No. 1, spring 1992, pp. 50–63.

—— *Stars and Stardom in French Cinema*, Continuum, London, 2000.

Vineberg, Steve, *Method Actors: Three Generations of an American Acting Style*, Macmillan, London, 1991.

Virdi, Jyotika, 'Reverence, Rape and Then Revenge: Popular Hindi Cinema's Woman's Film', *Screen*, Vol. 40, No. 1, 1999, pp. 17–37.

—— *The Cinematic Imagination: Indian Popular Films as Social History*, Rutgers University Press, New Brunswick, NJ, 2003.

Virilio, Paul, *War and Cinema: The Logistics of Perception*, Verso: London and New York, 1989.

Walker, A., *National Heroes: British Film in the Seventies and Eighties*, Harrap, London, 1985.

—— *Hollywood, England: The British Film Industry in the Sixties*, Harrap, London, 1974; repr. 1986.

—— 'The Scandal of Gambling', *Evening Standard*, 2 May, 2000.

Wallace, M., *Dark Designs and Visual Culture*, Duke University Press, Durham, NC, 2004.

Walters, S., *Material Girls*, University of California Press, Berkeley, 1995.

Ward, Paul, *Documentary: The Margins of Reality*, Wallflower Press, London, 2005.

Warner, K., *On Location: Cinema and Film in the Anglophone Caribbean*, Macmillan Education, London, 2000.

Warren, C. (ed.), *Beyond Document: Essays on Non-Fiction Film*, Wesleyan University Press, Hanover and London, 1996.

Wasko, Janet, *Hollywood in the Entertainment Age*, University of Texas Press, Austin, 1994.

—— *Understanding Disney*, Polity Press, Cambridge and Malden, 2001.

Watson, Paul, 'There's No Accounting for Taste: Exploitation Cinema and the Limits of Film Theory', in D. Cartmell *et al.* (eds), *Trash Aesthetics*, Pluto Press, London, 1997.

Waugh, T., *The Fruit Machine*, Duke University Press, Durham, NC, 2000.

Weiss, Andrea, 'A Queer Feeling When I Look at You: Hollywood Stars and Lesbian Spectatorship in the 1930s', in Christine Gledhill (ed.), *Stardom: Industry of Desire*, Routledge, London and New York, 1991.

—— *Vampires and Violets – Lesbians In Film*, Penguin, London, 1993.

Wells, P., *Art and Animation*, Academy Group–John Wiley, London, 1997.

—— (ed.), 'A Consideration of Animation and the Documentary Aesthetic', in *Art and Animation*, Academy Group–John Wiley, London, 1997, pp. 40–6.

—— *Understanding Animation*, Routledge, London and New York 1998.

—— '*Roughnecks*, Reality, Recombancy and Radical Aesthetics, *Point 11*, spring–summer 2001a, pp. 48–55.

—— 'Art of the Impossible', in G. Andrew (ed.), *Film: The Critic's Choice*, Ivy Press, Lewes, 2001b, pp. 308–39.

—— *Animation: Genre and Authorship*, Wallflower Press, London, 2002a.

—— *Animation and America*, EUP–Rutgers, Edinburgh and New Jersey, 2002b.

—— 'Where the Mild Things Are', *Sight and Sound*, Vol. 12, No. 2 (NS), February 2002c, pp. 27–8.

—— *Fundamentals of Animation*, AVA, Lausanne, 2006.

Whatling, C., *Screen Dreams: Fantasising Lesbians in Film*, Manchester University Press, Manchester, 1997.

White, P., 'Girls Still Cry', *Screen*, Vol. 42, No. 2, 2001, pp. 217–21.

Wiegman, R., 'Feminism, "The Boyz", and Other Matters Regarding the Male', in S. Cohan and I. Hark (eds), *Screening the Male*, Routledge, London, 1993.

Willemen, Paul, 'Anthony Mann: Looking at the Male', *Framework*, Nos 15–17, 1981.

Williams, Alan, 'Is a Radical Genre Criticism Possible?', *Quarterly Review of Film Studies*, Vol. 9, No. 2, 1984.

Williams, H., 'History in the Unmaking', *Guardian*, 16 April 2001, pp. 16–17.

Williams, Linda Ruth, 'Mother Courage', *Sight and Sound*, Vol. 12, No. 5, May 2002, pp. 12–14.

Willis, J., 'What's Up, Docs?', *Guardian*, 6 October 1997, p. 9.

Willis, D.S., *High Contrast: Race and Gender in Contemporary Hollywood Film*, Duke University Press, Durham, NC, and London, 1997.

Wilson, E., *Personal Histories: French Cinema since 1950*, Duckworth, London, 1999.

Wilton, T., *Immortal Invisible: Lesbians and the Moving Image*, Routledge, London, 1995.

Winston, B., 'The Tradition of the Victim in Griersonian Documentary', in Alan Rosenthal (ed.), *New Challenges for Documentary*, University of California Press, Berkeley, 1988.

Winston, B., *Claiming the Real: The Documentary Film Re-Visited*, BFI, London, 1996.

Winston Dixon, Wheeler, 'Introduction', in Winston Dixon (ed.), *Film Genre 2000*, State University Press of New York, Albany, 2000.

Wlaschin, Ken, 'Birth of the "Curry" Western: Bombay 1976', *Film and Filming*, Vol. 22, No. 7, April 1976, pp. 20–3.

Wollen, Peter, *Signs and Meaning in the Cinema*, rev.edn, Secker & Warburg–BFI, London, 1972.

—— 'Ideas of Authorship', *Screen*, Vol. 14, No. 3, 1973.

—— 'North by North-West: A Morphological Analysis', *Film Form*, Vol. 1, No. 2, 1976.

—— 'Godard and Counter Cinema', *Vent d'Est*', *Readings and Writings: Semiotic Counter-Strategies*, Verso, London, 1982.

Wollheim, Richard, *The Thread of Life*, Yale University Press, New Haven, CT, 1999.

Wood, R., *Hitchcock Revisited*, Faber & Faber, London, 1989.

—— 'Responsibilities of a Gay Film Critic', in Corey K. Creekmur and Alexander Doty (eds), *Out in Culture: Gay, Lesbian and Queer Essays on Popular Culture*, Duke University Press, Durham, NC, 1995.

Woolley, S., 'Last Palace Picture Show', *Guardian*, 30 October 1992.

Wright Wexman, Virginia (ed.), *Film and Authorship*, Rutgers University Press, New Brunswick, NJ, 2003.

Yearwood, G., *Black Film as a Signifying Practice: Cinema, Narration and the African Soviet Cinema in the Silent Era, 1918–1935*, UMI Research Press, Ann Arbor, MI, 1985.

American Aesthetic Tradition, Africa World Press, Trenton, 2000.

Youngblood, D., *Soviet Cinema in the Silent Era, 1918–1935*, University of Texas Press, Austin, 1991.

—— *Movies for the Masses: Popular Cinema and Soviet Society in the 1920s*, Cambridge University Press, Cambridge, 1992.

Zorkaya, N., *The Illustrated History of Soviet Cinema*, Hippocrene Books, New York, 1989.

Index

Italicised page numbers refer to illustrations or to information in accompanying captions

Related titles from Routledge

The Film Cultures Reader
Edited by Graeme Turner

This companion reader to *Film as Social Practice* brings together key writings on contemporary cinema, exploring film as a social and cultural phenomenon.
Key features of the reader include:

■ thematic sections, each with an introduction by the editor
■ a general introduction by Graeme Turner
■ sections: understanding film, film technology, film industries, meanings and pleasures, identities, audiences and consumption

Contributors include: Tino Balio, Sabrina Barton, Tony Bennett, Jacqueline Bobo, Edward Buscombe, Stella Bruzzi, Jim Collins, Barbara Creed, Richard Dyer, Jane Feuer, Miriam Hansen, John Hill, Marc Jancovich, Susan Jeffords, Isaac Julien, Annette Kuhn, P. David Marshall, Judith Mayne, Kobena Mercer, Tania Modleski, Steve Neale, Tom O'Regan, Stephen Prince, Thomas Schatz, Gianluca Sergi, Ella Shohat, Jackie Stacey, Janet Staiger, Robert Stam, Chris Straayer, Yvonne Tasker, Stephen Teo, Janet Wollacott, Justin Wyatt.

ISBN 10: 0-415-25281-4 (hbk)
ISBN 10: 0-415-25282-2 (pbk)

ISBN 13: 9-78-0-415-25281-2 (hbk)
ISBN 13: 9-78-0-415-25282-9 (pbk)

Available at all good bookshops
For ordering and further information please visit:
www.routledge.com

Related titles from Routledge

Film as Social Practice
Fourth Edition
Graeme Turner

This is the fourth edition of a classic student textbook which introduces film studies from a cultural studies perspective.

Film as Social Practice is distinctive in that it approaches the study of film as a social and cultural practice that does not end with the text. Rather than being examined as a set of canonical texts, film is examined as entertainment, as narrative and as cultural event. The focus is upon the cultural function of film.

This latest edition is fully revised and updated throughout, incorporating recent theoretical directions as well as updating the films referred to as examples or sites of analysis to include more recent and contemporary films.

This new fourth edition includes:

- New sections dealing with debates about spectacle versus narrative and with special effects among the 'languages' of cinema.
- An extended treatment of sound and its contribution to cinema
- A new section dealing with the consumption of cinema and cultural identities
- A revised and updated account of the structure and condition of the global popular feature film industry
- An increased number of updated illustrations

ISBN 13: 9-78-0-415-37513-9 (hbk)
ISBN 13: 9-78-0-415-37514-5 (pbk)

Available at all good bookshops
For ordering and further information please visit:
www.routledge.com

Related titles from Routledge

Film Studies: The Essential Resource
Peter Bennett, Andrew Hickman, Peter Wall

Film Studies: The Essential Resource is a collection of resource material for all those studying film at university and pre-university level. The Resource brings together a wide variety of material ranging from academic articles; advertisements; websites; interviews with directors and actors; magazines and newspapers.

Individual sections address:

- Codes – examines the language of film, production, narrative and canon.
- Concepts – considers genre, the auteur, stars and realism.
- Contexts – covers themes of textual analysis, theoretical perspectives, industry and audience.
- Cinemas – investigates Hollywood, British cinema, national cinemas and alternative takes.

With each extract introduced and contextualized by the editors, and suggestions for further activities and further reading included, *Film Studies: The Essential Resource* is the perfect resource to kick-start students' autonomy.

ISBN13: 978-0-415-36567-3 (hbk)
ISBN13: 978-0-415-36568-0 (pbk)

Available at all good bookshops
For ordering and further information please visit:
www.routledge.com

Related titles from Routledge

Cinema Studies: The Key Concepts
Second Edition
Susan Hayward

This is the essential guide for anyone interested in film. Now in its second edition, the text has been completely revised and expanded to meet the needs of today's students and film enthusiasts. Some 150 key genres, movements, theories and production terms are explained and analyzed with depth and clarity. Entries include:

- Auteur Theory
- Blaxploitation
- British New Wave
- Feminist Film Theory
- Intertextuality
- Method Acting
- Pornography
- Third World Cinema
- Vampire movies

A bibliography of essential writings in cinema studies completes an authoritative yet accessible guide to what is at once a fascinating area of study and arguably the greatest art form of modern times.

ISBN10: 0-415-227399 (hbk)
ISBN10: 0-415-227402 (pbk)

ISBN13: 9-78-0-415-227391 (hbk)
ISBN13: 9-78-0-415-227407 (pbk)

Available at all good bookshops
For ordering and further information please visit:
www.routledge.com

Related titles from Routledge

The Media Student's Book
Fourth Edition
Gill Branston and Roy Stafford

The Media Student's Book is a comprehensive introduction for students of media studies. It covers all the key topics and provides a detailed, lively and accessible guide to concepts and debates. This fourth edition, newly in colour, has been thoroughly revised, re-ordered and updated, with many very recent examples and expanded coverage of the most important issues currently facing media studies. It is structured in four main parts, addressing key concepts, media practices, media debates, and the resources available for individual research.

Individual chapters include: Interpreting media * Narratives * Genres and other classifications * Institutions * Questions of representation * Ideologies and power * Industries * Audiences * Advertising and branding * Research * Production organisation * Production techniques * Distribution * Documentary and 'reality TV' * Whose globalisation? * 'Free choices' in a 'free market'?

Chapters are supported by case studies which include: Ways of interpreting * *CSI: Miami* and crime fiction * J-horror and the *Ring* cycle * Television as institution * Images of migration * News * The media majors * The music industry, technology and synergy * Selling audiences * Celebrity, stardom and marketing * Researching mobile phone technologies * Contemporary British cinema.

The authors are experienced in writing, researching and teaching across different levels of pre-undergraduate and undergraduate study, with an awareness of the needs of those students. The book is specially designed to be easy and stimulating to use with:

* marginal terms, definitions, references (and even jokes), allied to a comprehensive glossary

* follow-up activities, suggestions for further reading, useful websites and resources plus a companion website to supporting the book at www.routledge.com/textbooks/0415371430/

* references and examples from a rich range of media forms, including advertising, television, films, radio, newspapers, magazines, photography and the internet.

ISBN 13: 978-0-415-37142-1 (hbk)
ISBN 13: 978-0-415-37143-8 (pbk)

Available at all good bookshops
For ordering and further information please visit: www.routledge.com

Related titles from Routledge

Introduction to Television Studies
Jonathan Bignell

'A wonderfully ambitious and clear introduction to television studies for the undergraduate reader.'
Gill Branston, University of Cardiff and co-author of *The Media Student's Book*

In this comprehensive textbook, Jonathan Bignell provides students with a framework for understanding the key concepts and main approaches to television studies, including audience research, television history and broadcasting policy, and the analytical study of individual programmes.

Features include a glossary of key terms, key terms defined in margins, suggestions for further reading at the end of each chapter, activities for use in class or as assignments, and case studies discussing advertisements such as the Guinness 'surfer' ad, approaches to news reporting, and programmes such as *Big Brother, The West Wing, America's Most Wanted* and *The Cosby Show*.

Individual chapters address:

*Studying Television
*Television histories
*Television cultures
*Television texts and narratives
*Television and genre
*Television production
*Postmodern television
*Television realities
*Television representation
*Television you can't see
*Shaping audiences
*Television in everyday life

ISBN 13: 978-0-415-26112-8 (hbk)
ISBN 13: 978-0-415-26113-5 (pbk)

Available at all good bookshops
For ordering and further information please visit:
www.routledge.com

Related titles from Routledge

The Television Studies Reader
Edited by Robert C Allen and Annette Hill

'A wonderfully ambitious and clear introduction to television studies for the undergraduate reader.'
Gill Branston, University of Cardiff and co-author of *The Media Student's Book*

The Television Studies Reader offers a roadmap to contemporary issues in the expanding and dynamic field of television studies. 38 cutting-edge essays lay out a wide array of approaches to the study of the changing phenomenon that is 'television' around the world.

The Reader pushes television studies well beyond the traditional equation of 'television' with terrestrial broadcasting, showcasing exciting new work on the wide variety of ways that television is experienced around the world and addressing issues of technology, industry, genre, representation, circulation, reception and audiences, production and ownership. It brings together contributions from leading international scholars to provide a range of perspectives on current television forms and practices, acknowledging both the status of television as a global medium, and the many and varied local contexts of its production and reception. A general introduction situates these important scholarly contributions to our understanding of contemporary television within the history of the academic study of television.

ISBN 13: 978-0-415-28323-6 (hbk)
ISBN 13: 978-0-415-28324-3 (pbk)

Available at all good bookshops
For ordering and further information please visit:
www.routledge.com